POLICE MISCONDUCT
A READER FOR THE 21ST CENTURY

MICHAEL J. PALMIOTTO
WICHITA STATE UNIVERSITY

Prentice
Hall

Prentice Hall, Upper Saddle River, New Jersey 07458

Library of Congress Cataloging-in-Publication

Police misconduct : a reader for the 21st century / Michael J. Palmiotto, editor.
   p. cm.
  Includes bibliographical references (p.).
  ISBN 0-13-025604-8
  1. Police misconduct—United States. 2. Police brutality—United States. 3. Police
    corruption—United States. 4. Police administration—United States. I. Palmiotto, Michael J.

HV8141 .P583 2001
363.2'3—dc21

00-059843

Publisher: Dave Garza
Senior Acquisitions Editor: Kim Davies
Production Editor: Megan Hill
Production Liaison: Barbara Marttine Cappuccio
Director of Manufacturing
  and Production: Bruce Johnson
Managing Editor: Mary Carnis
Manufacturing Manager: Cathleen Petersen
Art Director: Marianne Frasco
Cover Design Coordinator: Miguel Ortiz
Cover Designer: Bruce Kenselaar
Cover Image: Lars Topelmann / graphistock.images.com
Marketing Manager: Chris Ruel
Editorial Assistant: Sarah Holle
Interior Design, and Composition: Lithokraft II
Printing and Binding: R. R. Donnelley & Sons

Prentice-Hall International (UK) Limited, *London*
Prentice-Hall of Australia Pty. Limited, *Sydney*
Prentice-Hall Canada Inc., *Toronto*
Prentice-Hall Hispanoamericana, S.A., *Mexico*
Prentice-Hall of India Private Limited, *New Delhi*
Prentice-Hall of Japan, Inc., *Tokyo*
Prentice-Hall Singapore Pte. Ltd.
Editoria Prentice-Hall do Brasil, Ltda., *Rio de Janeiro*

10 9 8 7 6 5 4 3 2 1
ISBN 0-13-025604-8

CONTENTS

3   PHYSICAL ABUSE BY POLICE OFFICERS   183

PREFACE

In an era when police administrators are advocating closer ties with citizens in their communities, scandals such as corruption, brutality, illicit drug use, as well as other criminal activities committed by police officers do little to portray the positive image the agencies are striving to attain. For the past several decades, police misconduct has made news headlines all too frequently. The tragedy of these primetime police scandals is that they give a black eye to the police officer who has integrity and who refrains from committing even a minor act that could be construed as misconduct. A greater tragedy occurs when citizens of the community and the nation lose their confidence in the police. The reputation of a police agency transcends its immediate community and more often than not, affects surrounding communities and police departments. Not only does misconduct committed by an officer personally affect that officer, it also affects the community, the police department that employs the officer and every police department and police officer in America. Frequently, negative police actions caused by inappropriate police behavior reaches every corner of the nation, and at times, the world.

Police misconduct cannot be tolerated. Due to the nature of police work, law enforcement officers need to be held to higher standards than the average citizen. A tarnished image of policing cuts deep into the moral fabric of our nation's character. Throughout the world, people watch police officers to determine whether they are living up to the standards expected of those in a position of law enforcement and public trust. Police officers are expected to be protectors, not abusers of society. The primary responsibility of police in our society is to protect the human rights of all citizens regardless of socio-economic status, ethnic make-up, race, gender, or religious beliefs. When police officers abuse those same citizens they have sworn to protect, they are ethically and morally violating the oath they committed to the first day they joined the police force.

The collection of articles contained within this book has been divided into four sections. The first section, "Introduction to Police Misconduct," discusses legal issues pertaining to police authority and defines police misconduct. The second section, "Crimes Committed by Police Officers," discusses police corruption and reviews specific crimes that have been committed by law enforcement officers. The third section, "Physical Abuse by Police Officers," discusses police brutality, deadly force, and high-speed pursuits. The final section of the book, "Police Accountability," discusses the various techniques and strategies to control police misconduct. These techniques and strategies include police officer selection, investigation of police misconduct, civilian review, and civil litigation.

ABOUT THE EDITOR

Michael J. Palmiotto, Ph.D., is a Professor of Criminal Justice in the School of Community Affairs at Wichita State University. He has worked as a police officer in Westchester County, New York, and is the past Director of Criminal Justice and Police Training at the Community College of Beaver County, Monaca, Pennsylvania. He holds a masters degree from John Jay College of Criminal Justice (CUNY) and a doctorate from the University of Pittsburgh. He has published six books and numerous articles on policing and criminal justice issues.

PART 1

INTRODUCTION TO POLICE MISCONDUCT

Police misconduct in the United States has been a controversial issue since the inception of policing. Even as we enter the twenty-first century, police misconduct continues to be a major issue that may never be solved. Due to the nature of police work, police officers must project an image of authority and power. This authority often leads to confrontations with citizens who challenge, or appear to challenge, police decisions regarding law enforcement duties. The police, as a representative of society, must carefully guard their behavior while protecting the human dignity of those who have vested in them the power and authority to enforce the laws of society.

The first article written by Vincent J. Palmiotto, "Legal Authority of Police," traces the history of how the police obtained their legal authority. The author discusses United States Constitutional authority, landmark court decisions, legislative acts, and police practices that have occurred since the American colonial period. Restrictions on the power of municipalities that define the scope of police legal authority are also reviewed. This article provides an excellent foundation on the subject of police legal authority.

Article two, "Police as Symbols of Government and Justice" written by Alison McKenney Brown, provides an overview of strategies used to control unjust police behavior. Both internal controls, which originate within the police agency and external controls, which arise from outside the police agency, are discussed. Since the public expects its police officers to provide effective law enforcement within the limitations mandated by the United States Constitution, police agencies and officers who follow these guidelines are seen as positive symbols of government and justice. The police agencies and officers who fail to meet constitutional procedures create grounds for the public to distrust the police. Public distrust leads to an unwillingness to cooperate with police authority. This article also reviews due process within the context of policing and examines the effects of unjust policing.

In the third article, Michael J. Palmiotto describes why police misconduct continues to be a major issue even as we enter the twenty-first century. This article outlines and describes various types of police misconduct and wrongdoing. Acts of wrongdoing may or may not be performed for monetary gain. Perjury, sleeping on duty, drug use, police brutality, deadly force, and corruption are some examples of misconduct that are defined and explained.

Richard Kania, author of "Should We Tell the Police to Say 'Yes' to Gratuities?" advocates that it may be acceptable for police officers to accept gratuities. He provides an argument counter to those who believe that the acceptance of gratuities leads to corruption. Kania argues, based on his observations, that the acceptance of gratuities does not necessarily lead to corruption. The author of this article provides an excellent delineation on the various perceptions of the giver of gratuities and the police recipient of gratuities. In conclusion, Kania holds that the police officers should be trusted to make the ethical decision as to whether or not gratuities should be accepted.

In article five, Kim Michelle Lersch examines key issues that pertain to police misconduct toward minority citizens. She discusses this improper behavior and some of the problems associated with defining it, indicating that misconduct is difficult to delimit in some cases. This creates problems when trying to determine the level of misconduct; since it is hard to define misconduct, it is even more challenging to figure out to what extent the aberrant behavior has penetrated a given agency. The final section centers on minority citizens and the reasons why they can be easy targets for police misconduct.

ARTICLE 1

LEGAL AUTHORITY OF POLICE

Vincent J. Palmiotto
Church and Houff Law Firm,
Baltimore, Maryland

INTRODUCTION

In today's world, we see police everywhere. Whether we are driving, or walking in a city or town, we are bound to see someone who is a member of the law enforcement team. We see police walking on the street, cruising in their patrol cars, saddled on horseback and riding on bikes. We see city police, county police, state police, sheriffs and deputies. We see and read about federal law enforcement such as the Drug Enforcement Agency, the Federal Bureau of Investigation, and the Alcohol, Tobacco, and Firearms Agency. We watch television shows and movies that depict life as a cop. The presence of police and their function as law enforcement officers has become accepted as a necessary and integral part of our society. We are not startled, or even give a second thought to the presence and function of the police.

Have you ever stopped to think who the first police officers were or why there are so many different types of police officers, i.e.: federal, state, county, and city? Have you ever wondered where the police derive their legal authority from or what gives the federal, state, county, and local governments the right to form police departments and define the duties of police officers? Have you ever wondered what legal rights give police officers the authority to arrest citizens?

This article will address where states, counties, and city governments derive their power to enact police as well as discuss where police receive the power to enforce the laws passed by the state and local governments. Unfortunately, there is no simple answer that can explain how police are given legal authority. This is because the legal authority of the police comes from a variety of sources which include the U.S. Constitution, individual state constitutions, municipal charters, and state and municipal laws. Similarly, there is no simple or clear cut answer as to the scope of police authority. This is because the legal authority of police is constantly changing through the passing of new laws, the repealing of old laws, the courts interpretation of those laws, and society's perception of police and their function. As a result, landmarks such as the search and seizure and *Mapp v. Ohio,* 367 U.S. 643 (1961) and the stop and frisk case of *Terry v. Ohio,* 392 U.S. 1 (1968) have received considerable attention in the classroom, courtroom and law review articles. These landmark cases are just two examples in which the courts have defined the scope of the legal authority of police.

In order to fully understand the role of police within our society, we must first familiarize ourselves with the definition of police. The word *police* has been defined as a "branch of the government which is charged with the preservation of public order and tranquility, the promotion of the public, health, safety, and morals, and the prevention, detection's, and punishment of crimes" (Blacks 1979, 1156). Additionally, a police officer has been defined as "one of the staff of persons employed in cities and towns to enforce the municipal laws and ordinances for preserving the peace, safety, and good order of the community" (Blacks 1979, 1156). In sum, these definitions state that a police officer is the product of various governments, who employ them to ensure the tranquility and peace of the city by enforcing the laws of those governments. In order to get a clearer understanding of the role of police in society and how police duties have been defined, it is important to provide a brief history of the police.

HISTORY

The concept that a select group (i.e. police) could provide protection for its people through law and order has been around for thousands of years. Policing can be traced back to early tribal customs to the Code of Hammurabi (1947–1905 B.C.), ancient Greek city-states and the early Romans (Bopp and Shultz 1972). As you can see, the idea of laws and the enforcement of those laws is not something unique to the United States.

Colonial America

When the first settlers arrived in the New World, they passed laws based on systems they were familiar with in Europe. Due to this, the development and enforcement of laws varied from colony to colony.

Maryland, for example, was considered a military outpost in the 1600's and therefore employed a sheriff. This sheriff, called the "Chesapeake Sheriff," resembled an English sheriff. The duties of this position included making arrests, serving warrants, and collecting taxes, ministers' dues, and fees owed the governor. The sheriff had an incentive to be diligent in his duties as he was compensated by receiving ten percent of the monies he took in. The Chesapeake sheriff at first was chosen by the county court but later, in 1645, was picked from among eight members (Bopp and Shultz 1972).

Other colonies used military force to "police" civilians. Fort Pontchartrain in Detroit Michigan, was under martial law for its first hundred years, and New Orleans, Lousiana, was under martial law for its first eighty-five years before a constable system was instituted (Bopp and Shultz 1972).

In seventeenth century colonial America, the local sheriff was in charge of law enforcement in small towns. However, in bigger towns,[1] constables[2] were in charge of making arrests, and night watchman patrolled the streets (Friedman 1993).

The constables, who were daytime law enforcement officials, were responsible to the civil and criminal courts (Friedman 1993). A constable was not paid a salary, but rather received payment through fees which came from serving warrants and civil papers and from arresting offenders. Interestingly, the victim of an offense had the option to either seek out the constable and pay him for his services or to go directly to the local alderman's courts (Monkkonen 1992).

The night watchman's duties were to sound the alarm in case of an offense or fire. Early night watchmen were criticized for sleeping on duty, using noisy rattles to warn off potential offenders, and running from any real danger (Monkkonen 1992).

Since most of the first organized law enforcement systems began in large cities such as Boston and New York (Arm 1969), our discussion will focus mainly on these geographical areas.

Boston   The first night watch in Boston was founded on April 12, 1631 by the Boston Court. However, it was not until 1634 that the position of constable was created. In 1637, the city created a town watch which was staffed by its citizens. This town watch was unique because it was comprised of townspeople, not soldiers, who were appointed by the Boston government. In 1712, members of the town watch began to receive financial compensation for their services (Bopp and Shultz 1972). Constables, on the other hand, arrested drunks in order to sustain a continuous income (Monkkonen 1992). This system of law enforcement remained in effect until after the American Revolution (Bopp and Shultz 1972).

New York   From the time New York was founded by the Dutch, it was considered a necessity to have law enforcement. The first Director-General of New Netherlands (as it was called at the time) appointed a "schout fiscal" (sheriff-attorney) who doubled both as the policeman and prosecutor (Arm 1969). In 1643, the Dutch established a burgher watch to assist the schout fiscal in upholding the few laws that had been passed (Bopp and Shultz 1972). Additionally, in 1652 a rattle wacht (rattle watch) was formed. The rattle watch consisted of citizens who were equipped with rattles to summon assistance (Arm 1969) and were assigned to fixed posts. In 1658, New York established its first paid watch, which consisted of eight paid watchmen. When the British assumed control of New York from the Dutch, the position of high constable, whose main job was to oversee the police, was established. In 1693, the Mayor appointed the first uniformed officer, and a twelve man watch was

---

[1] These include the bigger cities we know today as Boston, New York and Philadelphia.

[2] It is interesting to note that there were various systems in place throughout the colonies establishing how a constable was chosen. For example, in Georgia, under a law enacted in 1759, constables were recruited under a draft system. (Friedman, p. 28).

selected to secure the city. In 1731, the first precinct house was constructed (Bopp and Shultz 1972).

In addition to the constable and night watchman, larger cities and towns employed sheriffs who were appointed by the governor for each county. The main responsibilities of sheriff were to enforce the law and act as the chief agent of the government for that colony. Specific duties included overseeing jury selection and being in charge of the jails and prisoners (Friedman 1993).

Post Revolution

These various systems of law enforcement were in place until the end of the Revolutionary War when the American colonies won their independence from England. Following the war, the Constitution of the United States was written and adopted as the supreme law of the Federal government. However, the legal authority of the police remained undefined. Even early city charters do not mention the police. The reason, perhaps, is that police as we know them today were not a known concept. Rather, as previously discussed, the law enforcement officials of cities and towns were constables, night watchmen, and sheriffs (Monkkonen 1992).

TENTH AMENDMENT

Although the U.S. Constitution does not provide for the founding of a police force, the Tenth Amendment does. The Tenth Amendment of the Constitution states: "The powers not delegated to the United States by the Constitution, nor prohibited by it to the States, are reserved to the States respectively, or to the people." In other words, "the powers not delegated to the United States by the Constitution, nor prohibited by it to the states, are reserved to the states respectfully or to the people." *New York v. United States,* 505 U.S. 144, 155 (1992).

To better understand where the power of the states comes from, we must first understand a little more about the Tenth Amendment. The Tenth Amendment has been scrutinized and interpreted by the Supreme Court. "If a power is delegated to Congress in the Constitution, the Tenth Amendment expressly disclaims any reservation of that power to the States; if a power is an attribute of state sovereignty reserved by the Tenth Amendment, it is necessarily a power the Constitution has not conferred on Congress." *New York v. United States,* 505 U.S. 144, 156 (1992); See *United States v. Oregon,* 366 U.S. 643 (1961); *Case v. Bowles,* 327 U.S. 92, 102 (1946); *Oklahoma ex rel. Phillips v. Guy F. Atkinson Co.,* 313 U.S. 508, 534 (1941). In other words, the Tenth Amendment "'states but a truism that all is retained which has not been surrendered.'" Id. (citing *United States v. Darby,* 312 U.S. 100, 124 (1941). "The States unquestionably do retai[n] a significant measure of sovereign authority . . . to the extent that the Constitution has not divested them of their original powers and transferred those powers to the Federal Government." Id. (citing *Garcia v. San Antonio Metropolitan Transit Authority,* 469 U.S. 528, 549 (1985)). In simpler terms, if the U.S. Constitution does not confer power to the Federal Government in a certain area, then the power to act resides within the states.

As mentioned earlier, the U.S. Constitution does not provide for the forming of a system of law enforcement. However, the Tenth Amendment gives states the power to enact laws and set up a police force. This power is then transferred to municipalities within the states. "To justify the State in . . . interposing its authority on behalf of the public, it must appear, first, that the interests of the public . . . require such interference; and, second, that the means are reasonably necessary for the accomplishment of the purpose, and not unduly oppressive upon individuals." Id. at 594–95, (citing *Lawton v. Steele*, 152 U.S. 133, 137 (1894)).

Although there is no clear definition of police power, it is this vague concept which gives the states their power to enact laws to protect the welfare of its communities and of its citizens. As a result, states have passed legislation to enact the formations of police departments in order to protect it citizens through its police power. As one court held, the police power is the exercise of the sovereign right of a government to promote order, safety, security, health, morals and general welfare within constitutional limits and is an essential attribute of government. *Marshall v. Kansas City, Mo.*, 355 S.W.2d 877, 883 (1962).

MUNICIPALITIES

If police power is held by the states, then how do the various municipalities within the states receive their power to enact legislation to set up police departments and define police duties and authority? The answer is that states have enacted legislation that provides for a police force in their large cities and defines the force's duties. Also, many states, through their constitutions and by legislation, have conferred upon its municipalities the power to form police departments and define the duties of the police employed within those departments.

For example, Title 62, Section 654, Code of Alabama 1940, extended police power to the City of Alabama in order to "provide for the safety, preserve the health, promote the prosperity, improve the morals, orders, comforts and convenience of the inhabitants of the City, and prevent and punish injuries and offenses to the public therein." *Yarbrough v. City of Birmingham*, 353 So.2d 75, 78 (Ala.Cr.App. 1977), (citing *Jefferson County v. City of Birmingham*, 256 Ala. 436, 55 A.2d 196; *Cavu Club v. City of Birmingham*, 269 Ala. 46, 110 So.2d 307; *Holloway v. City of Birmingham*, 55 Ala.App. 568, 317 So.2d 535). It is this statute that gives the city of Birmingham the power to confer upon its police the authority to act in order to prevent crime.

In Missouri, acts passed by the general assembly in 1861, created a board of police commissioners and expressly defined the police powers for the City of St. Louis (Sess. Acts 1860–61, p. 446 and Section 5, p. 448). These acts provided that "the police board should at all times of the day and night, within the boundaries of the City of St. Louis, preserve the public peace, etc., . . ." Additionally, Act 1867, Section 3, provided that "the board of police commissioners of the city should appoint and equip a certain number of policemen for the duty in the outskirts and open portions of the city, and elsewhere of the city."

The Supreme Court of the United States in 1883 declared that "Municipal corporations are instrumentalities of the State for the convenient administration of government within their limits. They are invested with authority to establish a police to guard against disturbance; and it is their duty to exercise their authority so as to prevent violence from any cause, and particularly from mobs and riotous assemblages." *Louisiana v. Mayor of New Orleans,* 109 U.S. 285, 287 (1883).

In Pennsylvania, the Borough of Wilson's Section 1121 of the Borough Code, Act of February 1, 1966, P.L. (1965); No. 581, 53 P.S. Section 46121 gave the Borough power to create a police department and the officers within the department.[3] The Pennsylvania court in *Slifer v. Dodge* addressed this statute and how the duties of the police chief and the police department are determined. "Neither the Legislature nor case law has satisfactorily defined the duties of a chief of police although the term itself indicates that he is to be the head of a department and exercise supervision over it." Id. (citing *Stitt v. Madigan,* 52 York L.Reg. 35 (1937)). However, ordinance may set out the duties. Id. (citing *Salopek v. Alberts,* 417 Pa. 592, 209 A.2d 295 (1965)). Since the statute did not set out the duties of the police chief or the police, but gave the power to the mayor to set out such duties, the court held that in the absence of a statute specifically setting out the duties of the police, "the officers of a police department have no more authority than that designated by the Mayor." Id. This is a clear example that a municipality does have the power to create a police department and to set out the duties and the authority of the police. Additionally, it is also an example of how are judicial system works. Although the states and municipalities have the power to pass the laws, they can and will be interpreted by the courts. As a result, the courts are instrumental in defining and interpreting the legal authority of the police.

The ordinance passed in the Borough of Wilson, Pennsylvania (No. 581, 53 P.S. Section 46 121, 1965), is an example of a municipality giving the power to the mayor to regulate and define the duties and authority of the police. However, the granting of this power is not confined to the Mayor of a municipality. In the City of Glasgow, Missouri, a law was passed in the nineteenth century which gave the city council the power to regulate the police force.

Until a statute has been passed by a state or municipality, there is no specific legal authority for the enactment of a police force. This is because police were not recognized at common law, which is a modern phenomena. "The rule well settled in this state is that before one acting in the capacity of a policeman can be said to be an officer of the city, there must have been adopted an ordinance of that city or village creating the office of policeman. The office of policeman, police patrolman, or assistant chief of police was unknown at

---

[3]The Code provides: "The borough council may designate one of said policeman as chief of police. The mayor of the borough shall have full charge and control of the chief of police and the police force, and he shall direct the time during which, the place where and the manner in which, the chief of police and the police force shall perform their duties, except that council shall fix and determine the total weekly hours of employment that shall apply to the policeman." This is an example of one code which has been enacted authorizing the creation of a police force and setting forth how the duties of the police shall be determined.

common law, and such office can be created only by statute or municipal ordinance" *Murphy v. Industrial Commission,* 189 N.E. 302, 303 (1934). "If no office is
created as required by the statute then there can be no such officer either de jure
or de facto, for there is no office to occupy." Id. at 304. (citing *City of Metropolis v.
Industrial Comm.,* 339 Ill. 141, 171 N.E. 167; *Bullis v. City of Chicago,* 235 Ill. 472, 85
N.E. 614; *Howard v. Burke,* 248 Ill. 224, 93 N.E. 775, 140 Am.St.Rep. 159.) As
a result, unless a statute enacting the office of police has been passed by the
legislature either at the level of the state or a municipality, there can be no police either in reality or by action.

In addition, due to the nature of police work, it is not possible to forsee
every situation a police officer will face. As a result, legislation cannot clearly
define every duty of a police officer.

The term "officer" implies "an authority to exercise some portion of the
sovereign power of the state, either in making, executing, or administrat-
ing the laws." *Olmstead v. New York,* 42 N.Y.Super. Ct. 481. In *Norton v. Shelby
County,* 118 U.S., 425, 65, Ct. 1121 (1886), the Supreme Court addressing this
issue held,

> An officer de facto is one whose acts, though not those of a lawful officer, the law,
> upon principles of policy and justice, will hold valid, so far as they involve the
> interests of the public and third persons, where the duties of the office are
> exercised—without a known appointment or election but under * * *
> circumstances of reputation or acquiescence as were calculated to induce people,
> without inquiry, to submit to or invoke his action, supposing him to possess the
> power and right claimed.

A California court looked to the Supreme Court's definition of a de facto
officer in attempting to define the duties of the police officer. The court held,
"When the police from time immemorial have exercised rights under circumstances of reputation or acquiescence as are calculated to induce people, without inquiry, to submit to or invoke their action, supposing them to possess the
power and right claimed, the exercise of those rights will become an integral
part of the duties incident to the office" *Noble v. City of Palo Alto,* 264 P. 529, 532,
89 Cal.App. 47 (1928). The Noble court used the following illustration to clarify its holding. A bicycle is found on the street and a police officer arrives on
the scene. The bicycle is claimed by more than one individual, therefore it is
the right of the police officer to take the bicycle and deliver it to city hall
where the rightful owner can claim possession of the bicycle. Id. As a result,
although a specific duty of the police has not been designated by statute or ordinance, if a duty or right of the police has been universally accepted, it will
become a part of the duty and authority of the police.

RESTRICTIONS PLACED ON THE POWER OF MUNICIPALITIES
TO DEFINE THE SCOPE OF POLICE LEGAL AUTHORITY

Although the state gives power to its municipalities to enact legislation to
form a police force and define the authority and duties of officers, these powers cannot conflict with or exceed the power given to them by the state.

A Missouri court in *State v. Stobie,* addressing the act passed by the general assembly which created a board of police commissioners in St. Louis, commented that such acts have withstood the test of constitutionality and judicial scrutiny. Further, they held:

> Laws like these, and those of other states providing a metropolitan police system for large cities, are based upon the elementary proposition that the protection of life, liberty, and property, and the preservation of the public peace and order in every part, division, and subdivision of the state, is a governmental duty which devolves upon the state, and not upon its municipalities any farther than the state in its sovereignty may see fit to impose upon or delegate it to the municipalities.

92 S.W. 191, 201 (Mo. 1906) (quoting *State ex rel. v. Mason,* 153 Mo. 23, 54 S.W. 524). The power of the municipalities to create a police force, however, must not exceed the power of the state's constitution or legislation. "It is not within the power of the framers of the scheme and charter,[4] contemplated by the Constitution, to vest such officers with powers inconsistent with, and not in harmony with, the general laws of the state creating such police system." Id.

Additionally, this issue was addressed by an Ohio court, which held, "The police power relates to the public peace, good order, and welfare, and to the public health. It is a power which is inherent in the sovereignty of the state, and it can be exercised only by the authority from the Legislature" *City of Cleveland v. Payne,* 74 N.E. 177, 178 (1905). "Municipal Corporations, in their public capacity, possess such powers and such only, as are expressly granted by statute, and such as may be implied as essential to carry into effect those which are expressly granted." Id. (quoting *Ravenna v. Pennsylvania Co.,* 45 Ohio St. 118, 12 N.E. 445). "It follows that, unless we can find in the statutes a distinct right to do so, a municipal corporation can neither enlarge nor restrict the duties of the police department as commonly understood. Id.

As a result, if a municipal statute provides for police authority which exceeds the authority given to the municipality by the state then it will be struck down by the courts.

THE COURTS EFFECT ON THE LEGAL AUTHORITY OF POLICE: THE FOURTH AMENDMENT

The case laws that have been cited within this article suggest that much of the police's legal authority is shaped by the courts. It is the nature of our system of government that where laws are enacted, they will be interpreted by the courts. As a result, how the courts interpret the U.S. and state constitutions, and legislation passed by the governments will either expand or restrict the police's legal authority.

---

[4]Sess. Acts 186-61, p446 and Section 5, p. 448, creating a police system for the city of St. Louis.

The courts interpret everything from the definition of a police officer to the authority of an officer to arrest a vagrant. "The title of policeman [may] be properly applied to one who performs services critical to public safety in the investigation and detection of serious crime—a person trained, equipped (with . . . gun, handcuffs, badge of the office and motor vehicles) and actually engaged in the detection of persons suspected of crime." *Commonwealth of Penn. Human Relations Comm. v. Beaver Falls City Council,* 366 A.2d 911, 914 1976), citing *Beaver Falls Council et al. v. Commonwealth of Pennsylvania Human Relations Commission,* 17 Pa.Cmwlth. 31, 330 A.2d 581, 583 (1975).

The Tenth Amendment is not the only amendment to the Constitution which defines the scope of a police officer's legal authority; the Fourth Amendment also helps delimit power.

This amendment, which prohibits unreasonable search and seizures, has been the subject of numerous books and law review articles. The courts have defined the legal authority of the police to arrest or stop and frisk an individual and to search a residence or automobile.

In order for the police to make an arrest, there must be probable cause. The Supreme Court has held that there is probable cause when the police officer has facts that are reliable and circumstances indicate that a suspect has committed or is committing a crime. *Beck v. Ohio,* 379 U.S. 89 (1964). If the police officer is without sufficient probable cause to make an arrest, he or she may still briefly detain a person for investigative purposes. However, the police officer must have reasonable suspicion, supported by reliable facts, that a criminal activity has occurred or that the person is involved in a crime. *Terry v. Ohio,* 392 U.S. 1 (1968). The police officer's reasonable suspicion may come from an informant or other form of information and need not come from personal knowledge. *United States v. Hensley,* 469 U.S. 221 (1985).

Additionally, a police officer does not have the legal authority to randomly stop a car. Rather, there must be a reasonable belief that the given vehicle violated a traffic law. *Delaware v. Prouse,* 440 U.S. 468 (1979). However, the Supreme Court has held that cars may be stopped at checkpoints, although there is not a reasonable justification to stop a vehicle if the vehicles are stopped according to a neutral standard (e.g. sobriety checkpoints, roadblocks near U.S. borders). *Michigan Department of State Police v. Stitze,* 496 U.S. 444 (1990); *United States. v. Martinez-Fuente,* 428 U.S. 543 (1976).

The courts have also addressed an officer's right to use deadly force, which is considered a Fourth Amendment seizure. The Supreme Court has held that unless a police officer has probable cause to believe that the suspect poses a significant threat of death or serious physical injury to the officer or others, it is unreasonable to use deadly force. *Tennessee v. Garner,* 471 U.S. 1 (1985).

Even though legislation passed by the state and its municipalities can define police duties and authority, there is virtually no area in which the courts have not played a major role in defining the legal authority of the police.

THE "MODERN" POLICE

The evolution of police from the early systems of law enforcement to the present has played a major role in defining the legal authority of police.

Four important innovations within the police system have helped define police authority as we know it today. First, the new "modern" police was organized with a command structure similar to that of the military. This created a communication system of orders and instructions that was far superior to that of the early constable and night watch systems (Monkkonen 1992). Secondly, city governments were restructured to allow the police to come under the mayor's office rather than the courts, as it had been in the past. This changed the focus of the officers' duties from court activities to the functions we recognize today (Monkkonen 1992). Thirdly, the cities instituted a requirement that their police wear uniforms. The uniform made the police more visible and more accessible to the public (Monkkonen 1992). Interestingly, the requirement to wear a uniform was met with resistance by both the public and the police officers when it was first instituted because the uniform was thought to be a sign of a lower caste (Walker 1977). Additionally, many questioned whether the police should walk around in "livery" provided at the citizen's expense (Friedman 1993). Finally, with the inception of the police patrol, the police became more visible to the public (Monkkonen 1992).

The police reform had the effect of making the police more organized and visible. This has been attributed, in part, to the public growing increasingly tired of the series of riots that occurred in major cities during the nineteenth century (Monkkonen 1992). Others have suggested that the increase in immigration, which led to higher crime rates, necessitated police organization (Hannon 1997). Still others have argued that the police reform was shaped by the same events that shaped early England (Hannon 1997). Regardless of the reason, the nineteenth century saw the police reform, which helped establish the role and authority of law enforcement.

Not only was the uniform not readily accepted by the public, but the authority of the police was not readily accepted either. The patrolman routinely encountered resistance to his authority even in a simple routine arrest. As a result, the early policeman's authority had to be established by using force (Walker 1977). Additionally, the early police did not have the authority to carry guns in the cities. For example, it was not until 1853 that the police in New York City were equipped with guns (Walker 1977). In Boston, it was not until 1884 that the police received the legal authority to carry guns (Friedman 1993).

CONCLUSION

The police today have the power to act in different situations. However, the legal authority of the police is not static. It has evolved over time and is constantly changing, even today. Every new legislation that is passed can have a possible effect on defining the scope of power of the police. Additionally, as society changes and these changes affect how our court system interprets laws, there will be constant changes in the nature of the police's legal authority. This seems appropriate, since the police, founded pursuant to the police power of the states, are here to protect the welfare of the citizens.

REFERENCES

Arm, W. *The Policeman, An Inside Look at his Role in a Modern Society.* New York, NY: E.P. Dutton & Co., Inc., 1969.

Beaver Falls Council et al. v. Commonwealth of Pennsylvania Human Relations Commission, 17 Pa.Cmwlth. 31, 330 A.2d 581, 583 (1975).

Beck v. Ohio, 379 U.S. 89 (1964).

Black's Law Dictionary, 6th ed. St. Paul, Minn. West Publishing Co., (1979).

Bopp, W.J., Shultz, D.O. *A Short History of American Law Enforcement.* Springfield, IL: Charles C. Thomas, 1972.

Borough of Wilson's Section 1121 of the Borough Code, Act of February 1, 1966, Public Law no. 581, 53 P.S. Section 46121 (1965).

Bullis v. City of Chicago, 235 Ill. 472, 85 N.E. 614 (1908).

Case v. Bowles, 327 U.S. 92, 102 (1946).

Cavu Club v. City of Birmingham, 269 Ala. 46, 110 So.2d 307 (1959).

City of Cleveland v. Payne, 74 N.E. 177, 178 (1905).

Commonwealth of Penn. Human Relations Comm. v. Beaver Falls City Council, 366 A.2d 911, 914 (1976).

Delaware v. Prouse, 440 U.S. 468 (1979).

Friedman, L.M. *Crime and Punishment in American History.* New York, NY: BasicBooks, 1993.

Garcia v. San Antonio Metropolitan Transit Authority, 469 U.S. 528, 549 (1985).

Goldblatt v. Hempstead, 369 U.S. 590, 594 (1962).

Gregory v. Ashcroft, 501 U.S. 452, 457 (1991).

Hannon, T. "The Division of Policing Labour: An Historical Background." *The Police Journal,* 70, no. 4, (1997): 325–330.

Holloway v. City of Birmingham, 55 Ala.App. 568, 317 So.2d 535 (1975).

Howard v. Burke, 248 Ill. 224, 93 N.E. 775 (1911).

Jefferson County v. City of Birmingham, 256 Ala. 436, 55 So.2d 196 (1951).

Louisiana v. Mayor of New Orleans, 109 U.S. 285, 287 (1883).

Mapp v. Ohio, 367 U.S. 643 (1961).

Marshall v. Kansas City, Mo., 355 S.W.2d 877, 883 (1962).

Michigan Department of State Police v. Stitze, 496 U.S. 444 (1990).

Monkkonen, E.H. *History of Urban Police,* "Crime and Punishment." Chicago: The University of Chicago Press, 1992.

Murphy v. Industrial Commission, 189 N.E. 302, 303 (1934).

New York v. United States, 505 U.S. 144, 155 (1992).

Noble v. City of Palo Alto, 264 P. 529, 532, 89 Cal.App. 47 (1928).

Norton v. Shelby County, 118 U.S. 425, 6 S.Ct. 1121 (1886).

Oklahoma ex rel. Phillips v. Guy F. Atkinson Co., 313 U.S. 508, 534 (1941).

Olmstead v. New York, 42 N.Y. Super. Ct. 481 (1967).

Ravenna v. Pennsylvania Co., 45 Ohio St. 118, 12 N.E. 445 (1887).

Salopek v. Alberts, 417 Pa. 592, 209 A.2d 295 (1965).

Slifer v. Dodge, 362 A.2d 471, 473 (Pa. Cmwlth. 1976).

State ex rel. v. Mason, 153 Mo. 23, 54 S.W. 524 (1899).

State v. Stobie, 144 Mo. 14, 92 S.W. 191, 201 (1906).

Stitt v. Madigan, 52 York L.Reg. 35 (1937).

Tennessee v. Garner, 471 U.S. 1 (1985).

Terry v. Ohio, 392 U.S. 1 (1968).

Title 62, Section 654, Code of Alabama (1940).

United States v. Darby, 312 U.S. 100, 124 (1941).

United States v. Hensley, 469 U.S. 221 (1985).

United States v. Martinez-Fuerte, 428 U.S. 543 (1976).

United States v. Oregon, 366 U.S. 643 (1961).

Walker, Samuel *A Critical History of Police Reform: The Emergence of Professionalism.* Lexintgon, MA: D.C. Health. 1977.

Yarbrough v. City of Birmingham, 353 So.2d 75, 78 (Ala.Cr.App. 1977).

POLICE AS SYMBOLS OF GOVERNMENT AND JUSTICE

Alison McKenney Brown
Wichita State University

INTRODUCTION

> We the People, in order to form a more perfect union, establish justice, insure domestic tranquility . . .

The beginning of the Preamble to the Constitution has served to remind the world of the purpose of the United States and the fundamental principles valued by its citizens. The establishment of justice, the second fundamental principle stated in the Preamble, did not end with the formation of the United States but has continued to serve as the basis for life-altering political, legal, and social decisions throughout this nation's history. But Americans have never perceived justice as a concept only applicable to actions requiring a national effort. Justice is a concept held dear at the individual level as well. Calling someone's actions "unjust" or "an injustice" is to insult that person's integrity and honor, and such an insult is rarely left unanswered. Without question, the concept of justice is as highly valued within this society today as it was at this nation's inception.

Although it is easy to see that the concept of justice is highly valued by society, the actual definition of justice is not so clear. "Justice" is understood to mean "just treatment." The dictionary defines the word "just" as "fair" or "morally right" (Oxford 1997). Defining the term "fair" is not especially helpful because it is defined as "just" (Oxford 1997). The problem with seeking a clear definition for these terms is that they are meant to convey broad societal concepts of morality, ethics, and fairness which change over time. For example, Americans of the last century would probably not define "justice" or "just treatment" in the same manner as society would generally understand those concepts today. At a time when the law permitted individuals to wear guns on a belt at their waist as a matter of course, justice may have had more to do with vengeance than with respecting the human rights of each individual. Today, however, society generally condemns any law enforcement officer who uses authority to exact vengeance for any crime, no matter how heinous. It is likely that one hundred years from now, society's understanding of justice will have changed from that of today.

The concept of justice within the context of policing is, in some situations, more readily definable due to the wording of the Fifth and Fourteenth Amendments to the U.S. Constitution. Those amendments guarantee each individual the right to expect a certain standard of treatment from the government. The Fifth Amendment makes this guarantee for the U.S. government when it prohibits depriving any person of "life, liberty, or property, without due process of law." The Fourteenth Amendment prohibits the same action by the states. Since many investigatory and protective actions by police are specifically intended to deprive people of life, liberty, or property, such actions may only occur within the constraints of due process. So, it can be inferred that due process has something to do with justice.

Due process is the foundation for determining the manner in which the government may exercise authority over those within its borders, both citizens and non-citizens. Although it has no fixed definition, due process is an understandable concept. The Supreme Court stated in 1952 that due process was the "least specific and most comprehensive protection of liberties . . ." (*Rochin v. California*, 342 U.S. 165, 72 S.Ct. 205, 96 L.Ed. 183 (1952)). Justice Frankfurter best explained the concept of due process when he stated that due process is a "respect enforced by law for that feeling of just treatment which has evolved through centuries of Anglo-American law" (*Joint Anti-Fascist Refugee Committee v. McGrath*, 341 U.S. 123, 162–63, 71 S.Ct. 624, 643–44, 95 L.Ed. 817, 849 (1951)). He also stated that due process represents "a profound attitude of fairness between man and man, and more particularly between the individual and government" (*Joint Anti-Fascist Refugee Committee v. McGrath* (1951)). Thus, while due process cannot be specifically defined, it is commonly understood to mean fairness and just treatment toward individuals by the government.

The concept of due process has been changed dramatically over the last fifty years by the United States Supreme Court. Whereas due process used to mean fundamental fair treatment, it now requires police to conform their actions to applicable laws and procedures. Some common examples of due process include the requirement that an officer have probable cause before arresting a suspect and that the suspect have the right to an attorney, the right to an impartial trial, and the right to be designated innocent of a crime until proven guilty beyond a reasonable doubt. While these changes have generated much public controversy, they have also served to educate the public. As a consequence of the changing legal concepts of due process, "public expectations about the quality of justice" have risen dramatically (Walker 1998). The public expects those who have the authority associated with being a police officer to strive to provide effective law enforcement within the limitations of both societal expectations and Constitutional requirements. Police who achieve this standard bring respect and honor to their profession and are seen as symbols of both good government and justice.

UNDERSTANDING THE RELATIONSHIP BETWEEN POLICING AND SOCIETY PERCEPTIONS OF JUSTICE

Any officer unwilling to make the connection between a free and open society and public trust in the police need only look to other societies where police are feared. In those societies, the police have fewer actual limitations upon their behavior and so are free to make individual rights secondary to effective enforcement of the law. These officers use their additional freedoms in law enforcement to improve their social and economic status. Sometimes this has included acting outside the law they are employed to enforce. The public quickly grows to distrust police they view as unjust and corrupt. When police lose their status as symbols of justice in society, the government which created the policing system is held accountable because the police, as agents of the government, continue to symbolize the government in the eyes of the people. A government unable to provide just law enforcement through its police force becomes vulnerable to other types of social problems. Too many social issues can lead to governmental instability. Thus the concept of police as symbols of both government and justice is more than an ideal, it is a critical part of a stable society.[1]

Examples of societies dealing with unjust and corrupt police are Brazil, China and Russia. Although these nations are attempting to rectify their policing problems, the following news reports illustrate how harmful unjust policing is upon a society.

Brazil

Human rights groups have described police forces in Sao Paulo and Rio de Janeiro as among the most violent in the world. "The police are badly trained and badly paid, and they're not respected," said Emir Sader of the Sao Paulo Center for the Study of Violence. "Instead of enforcing the law, they're raising the level of violence in this society."[2]

China

The Procuratorate (State Prosecutor) has the power to approve arrests made by the police either before or after the arrest has taken place. The Security Administration Punishment Act authorizes police to detain or arrest individuals who may not have breached the criminal law but nevertheless may be subjected to interrogation. The accused has no right to remain silent. The act also empowers the police to impose fifteen days of administrative detention. Moreover, there is a provision for extending the detention of someone in custody for months at a time during the investigative process, although the 1996 Law of Criminal Procedure now generally requires "special circumstances." Therefore the police power to detain a suspect at the pre-trial stage has been substantially increased.[3]

Post-Soviet Russia

Torture and ill-treatment of detainees at the time of and immediately after arrest is rampant in Russia today. In the first hours after detention, police regularly beat their captives, nearly asphyxiate them, or subject them to electroshock in the pursuit of confessions or testimony incriminating others. With the exception of a few particularly grave cases in which public exposure led to prosecutions, police carry out torture with complete impunity as the provincial and federal procuracies close their eyes to evidence of abuse. The courts commonly accept forced confessions at face value and use them as a basis for convictions.[4]

The impact that this type of policing has on Russian society can be demonstrated by data collected in recent polls of the Russian public.

Opinion polls conducted in recent years have shown that Russia's police force is in a deep crisis of legitimacy: Russian citizens do not trust their own police. One poll found that in 1998 more than 50 percent of respondents assessed police performance as bad or very bad . . . According to data from the Scientific Research Institute of the Ministry of Internal Affairs, around 60 percent of crime victims do not want to report crimes to the police as they see them not as a protector but as a source of increased danger. A television opinion poll carried out by the daily program *Segodniachko* on NTV (Russia's independent television channel) on December 10, 1998, found that the vast majority of Russians believe the police beat detainees . . . In June 1998, the daily newspaper *Segodnia [Today]* reported that an opinion poll in Moscow found that 43 percent of Muscovites would not contact the police under any circumstances, including opening the door to their apartment to police officers, and 37 percent feared police as much as criminals.[5]

Police injustice is not limited to other nations. The American public has witnessed police injustice with increasing frequency over the last decade. Low-cost video equipment combined with the unparalleled increase in television programs willing to air real-life moments caught on tape has brought about the mass dissemination of an incredible number of truly extraordinary visual images. One of those images is of a man lying prone on the street surrounded by a dozen police officers watching another officer repeatedly strike him with a nightstick. This video captured a moment in time in which a police officer did not act justly and the government failed to control its police.

Unfortunately for police officers, due to the very nature of their jobs, pictures of shocking, even brutal, moments will be captured on film more often than moments of heroism. Obviously the most interesting photographs of police at work are not of an officer explaining, discussing, or even warning someone that they are in violation of a law. An interesting photograph is one in which force is used to carry out the duties of law enforcement. Of course, the facts explaining what caused the situation to occur will not preface the photograph or videotape. Only that moment in which force was used to control a member of the public will be seen, and the public will be unforgiving.

The consequences of police forgetting to act justly may be found in the form of brutality or instances of low-level police misconduct such as rudeness or bullying.[6] In either form, the unjust behavior is shocking. The public's shock over acts of injustice arises out of more than the horrifying details of the stories, the graphic pictures, or even their own personal experiences with an unjust police officer. The shock comes from the basic feeling of betrayal of trust. Every person in the United States believes they have the constitutional right to trust that the police, as representatives of the government, will act justly. When the public is shown proof, time and again, that police act unjustly, they lose their ability to trust and question whether they and those they care about will be safe when dealing with the police.

The horrific riots that occurred at the conclusion of the state criminal trials of the officers who participated in the beating of Rodney King serve as a frightening warning that maintaining public trust cannot be a secondary concern for law enforcement. The public must be able to trust the police to always act in a manner which best serves the public interest as it is defined by law. Unfortunately developing and maintaining public trust is becoming increasingly difficult when powerful images, such as the Rodney King beating, show police acting in a manner that the average person would describe as violent and unreasonable.

A result of the public's distrust of police is a growing lack of willingness to submit to police authority.[7] Unfortunately for police, it is this very unwillingness to submit to authority that often causes officers to use force against those people whom they are hired to protect and serve.[8] All violence, whether necessary or unnecessary, adds to the public's distrust of police. This distrust leads to the unwillingness of some to submit to police authority, creating an increase in situations that escalate into violence, making the job of law enforcement more difficult and dangerous.

Consequently, while some police officers may wish to emphasize "effectiveness" over individual rights and expectations of justice, the long-term negative impact on public trust in police and government will eventually outweigh the short term gains in subduing criminals. To insure that all officers remember that they are government officials charged with protecting the public in a just manner, regardless of personal feelings or attitudes, methods for controlling police conduct have been developed. Some controls upon police behavior originate within the police agency and therefore are called *internal controls*. Other controls arise from authority outside the police agency and so are referred to as *external controls*. These controls, both internal and external to police agencies, reassure the public that the government holds police to the same high standard of behavior that the public expects from its police officers.

INTERNAL CONTROLS

Internal controls are those methods that a police agency uses to control officer behavior. Internal controls have existed within police departments in one form or another since the development of organized law enforcement. Most internal controls are embodied in policies and procedures developed by the police department, enforced by police supervisors, and adhered to by each police officer. The specific types of internal controls may vary slightly from police agency to police agency because of variances in culture found throughout American society, but the most common will be addressed below.

One of the most widespread means of internal control is supervision. Police agencies typically model their organizational structure on military agencies.

Usually, a chief of police is the highest police official and the officer is at the lowest level in the organizational hierarchy. The additional supervisory ranks are dependent upon the size of the police agency and the type of area being served. Very large agencies may have deputy chiefs, colonels, majors, captains, lieutenants, sergeants, detectives, and corporals. Very small agencies may have none of the additional supervisory levels.

There is not enough space in a chapter to analyze those characteristics which make a supervisor an effective means of internal control. It should be noted, however, that an exceptional leader is adept at controlling his subordinates as well as guiding them to be effective and just police officers. Because law enforcement often requires individuals to work alone and unsupervised as well as utilize a high degree of discretion, strong leadership is especially critical in policing agencies.[9] One of the most critical requirements of an effective supervisor, is the ability to teach and re-teach that in a democratic society which seriously respects civil rights and liberties "policing unavoidably includes a significant level of failure."[10]

Another form of internal control utilized by most policing organizations is commonly called *internal affairs*. This term is applied to a group of officers within the agency who are authorized to review, investigate, and decide the outcome of issues relating to police performance. Sometimes the internal affairs unit incorporates civilians, but usually it is composed entirely of officers. Citizen complaints of police injustice are usually forwarded to the internal affairs division for investigation. "No information about this decision making process is usually revealed to any member of the public other than the final decision."[11] Citizens are rarely told what evidence an internal affairs department relied upon in making their decision, nor are they given information about any other decision-making standard utilized in determining the outcome of a citizen complaint against a police officer. The lack of transparency in this process makes it an especially difficult system for the public to trust.

One of the strongest forms of internal controls is organizational culture. Peer pressure is used to force others to conform to the organizational culture which insures that all members behave in a commonly accepted manner. In police agencies, the organizational culture has evolved to such a specific set of standards it has been given its own name: the thin blue line (Glaser and Parker 2000). Unfortunately the "thin blue line" has evolved into an attitude that places organizational well-being before the needs of the public. This culture encourages tight bonds of friendship and loyalty between officers but discourages non-officer friendships. Equally as disturbing is the encouragement of an anti-management attitude as well as fierce resistance to any change in policing practices.[12]

To combat the effects of the thin blue line, most police agencies have adopted a code of ethics. A good example of a code of ethics has been promulgated by the International Association of Chiefs of Police.[13] It is a list of ethical mandates intended to serve as guidelines for police officers in the performance of their duties. The effectiveness of a code of ethics, however, is directly related to how seriously it is incorporated into training, supervision, and daily departmental decision making. Only by keeping it constantly within the thoughts and vision of each officer will it be eventually incorporated into their actions.

Although these and other internal controls have been utilized in most police agencies for many years, police injustice has not been eliminated. Thus external controls are also utilized to encourage the police to perform their duties justly.

EXTERNAL CONTROLS

To supplement internal controls of police conduct, several governmental entities outside police departments have used their own authority to control the conduct of police officers. External controls act as incentives for police to perform their duties in a just manner and impose penalties for failing to do so. External controls differ from internal controls in that they provide public penalties for failure to conform, while internal controls tend to be private actions kept confidential between the department and the offending officer. They also contrast with internal controls in that they act on all levels of police departments from the officer up through the police organization and may even impact a municipality or government that appears to bear some level of responsibility for the offense.

The courts, state prosecutors, and the federal government have all instituted methods for controlling the conduct of police officers. Additionally the public has some ability to seek compensation when police fail to perform their duties in a just manner.

Criminal Prosecution

The state imposes a measure of external control over law enforcement through their authority to criminally prosecute police officers for violations of the criminal law. If the state prosecutor believes that evidence shows a police officer to have acted willfully in causing harm, the prosecutor may file criminal charges against that officer. These cases are relatively rare.[14] "As of mid-June [1998] there were 548 local, state and federal law enforcement officers in federal prisons—up from 107 in 1994."[15] The number of ex-officers in state detention facilities is unknown.[16]

It is difficult to prosecute a police officer for acts occurring while on duty.[17] Witnesses to illegal police behavior may be afraid to testify. Those who do agree to testify may make poor witnesses due to credibility problems associated with being the type of person most likely to be victimized by police: the poor, the homeless, minorities, youth, or those with criminal histories.[18] The evidentiary problem is further compounded when the only other witnesses in the case are other members of the police department who feel compelled to abide by the informal police code of silence.[19]

In those cases which actually go to trial, a further hurdle is that juries are reluctant to convict police officers for acts arising out of their efforts to enforce the law.[20] A recent example of this tendency was seen during the state trial of the Los Angeles police officer who beat Rodney King. Even with a videotape showing the brutality, the state jury failed to find the officers at fault.

An additional difficulty in prosecuting police officers involves situations which create a conflict of interest involving the prosecutor. This arises when the prosecutor is in the position of prosecuting both the officer and the complainant. The police officer is being prosecuted for an illegal act committed against a complainant, but the complainant is also being prosecuted for the illegal act which originally brought him to the attention of the officer. Each is the witness against the other. The prosecutor may not be able to objectively deal with this type of intertwined case. In these situations it is often easier to encourage both parties to drop their charges against each other than to prosecute. If the charges are dropped, however, the police officer's criminal behavior is never addressed.

Tort Claims

Citizens may file civil suits against police officers, their supervisors, police agencies, and local governments when they believe any of those parties have caused them harm. These civil actions, called tort claims, are what the average citizen thinks of as suing another person. Tort claims against police officers, their superiors, and employers are brought in a civil court by the injured party and are based on either a theory of negligent behavior or allege actual intent to cause the harm.[21] The goal of a tort claim is to be financially compensated by the individual or entity who caused the harm.

A tort claim is not easy to pursue. First, the person alleging the harm must be able to afford the expenses connected to filing this type of case and following it through to completion. The expense involved in this type of lawsuit is often cost prohibitive to the people most likely to be victimized by police: the poor, the young, the homeless, the addict, and the criminal.[22] These people are also less likely to be believed when the only evidence is their word against that of a police officer. If the individual actually overcomes all the hurdles and wins a monetary judgment, it then becomes that individual's responsibility to force the other party to pay it, which can mean further legal battles.

Section 1983 Lawsuits

Federal civil law may be a more powerful tool than state civil law in the effort to externally control the behavior of police. The provision of what is now codified as 42 U.S.C. §1983, enacted as part of the Civil Rights Act of 1871, allows U.S. citizens to seek legal redress in Federal Court from public officials who abuse or misuse their authority. As public officials, police officers have often found themselves the targets of §1983 lawsuits. To file a §1983 suit, a citizen must allege that a public official has deprived them or caused others to deprive them of some rights, privileges or immunities secured by the Constitution and laws of the United States by an act that "would not have occurred but for the fact that the person committing them was an official then and there exercising his official powers outside the bounds of lawful authority."[23]

The U.S. Supreme Court explained the application and purpose of §1983 in *Mitchum v. Foster*. In that case the Court stated:

> The purpose of the federal civil rights statute (42 USCS 1983) authorizing an action at law, a suit in equity, or other proper proceedings for redress of a deprivation, under color of state law, of rights secured by the Federal Constitution and federal laws, is to interpose the federal courts between the states and the

people, as guardians of the people's federal rights, and thus to protect the people from unconstitutional action under color of state law, whether that action be executive, legislative, or judicial; in carrying out this purpose, Congress, by expressly authorizing a suit in equity as one of the means of redress, has plainly authorized the federal courts to issue injunctions in 1983 actions.[24]

A §1983 claim may also be brought against a local government if the injured party can show that the municipality had a policy or custom which caused one of its employees to deprive the plaintiff of his rights. Since 1989, municipal governments have also been held liable due to the theory that inadequate training leads some employees to act in such a way as to deprive the injured party of his constitutional rights.[25] This liability translates into millions of dollars in judgments to injured parties each year.

A supervisor is also liable under §1983 for his subordinates' actions. A supervisor may be held liable if he either directed the wrongful conduct or had actual knowledge of the wrongdoing.[26] A supervisor may also be found liable if he acquiesces in behavior which is prohibited by §1983. Acquiescence may be inferred from a "history of episodes indicating the supervisory official had actual knowledge of the wrongdoings."[27] Finally, failing to prevent a recurrence of an incident may also be the basis for supervisory liability under §1983.[28]

Section 1983 has never been an easy way for an individual to find relief for reasons analogous to the problems associated with tort claims. Most victims and witnesses lack both credibility and financial resources, making it difficult for jury members to identify and sympathize with them. Because of these problems, a victim of police injustice will have trouble finding an attorney willing to take the case.[29] Since few plaintiff-victims can afford counsel and most suits are taken on a contingency basis, an attorney undertakes an enormous financial risk when filing a §1983 lawsuit. Thus, attorneys have little incentive to accept the average case involving police injustice. Only cases involving powerful evidence which could result in a significant award of damages will merit the enormous investment of an attorney's time and resources.[30]

Winning the case is even more difficult than finding an attorney to pursue the claim. Juries who cannot identify or sympathize with the plaintiff-victim are not apt to rule in his or her favor. Additionally juries do not like to punish police officers for using their discretion even when they have used that discretion in a manner that does not meet the approval of jury members. The result is that most of these cases are lost.[31]

Finally, it should be noted that the courts are acting to limit the scope of §1983. Although this theory of liability is becoming more restrictive it remains a tool for reminding officers, supervisors, and others that the public expects them to act within the boundaries of justice.[32]

Section 14141 Actions

In 1994, the Federal Government promulgated a law authorizing the Attorney General to take any action necessary to stop patterns or practices of police injustice. This law is found at §14141 of Title 42, of the Violent Crime Control and Law Enforcement Act of 1994.[33] Section 14141 was initially overshadowed by other provisions of the Crime Control Act, but §14141 may prove to be the most significant provision of the Act.[34] Under this law, the U.S. Attorney General is authorized to bring civil actions against any police department or criminal justice agency engaged in a "pattern or practice" of depriving people of their constitutional or statutory rights and privileges.[35] Section 14141 creates an authority in the U.S. Justice Department to "intervene in police agencies in ways similar to involvement brought about by voting rights laws and the Fair Housing Act.[36] This means that the Attorney General is authorized to sue a police department in federal court in an effort to gain legal authority to intercede directly within the operation of a police agency.

The scope of this authority is best illustrated by the impact a §14141 investigation had upon the City of Columbus, Ohio. Columbus, while denying the allegations of the Justice Department, entered into a consent agreement with the Justice Department in late 1999.[37] The consent decree is a legal document detailing the changes which will occur within the City's police department and the time frame in which those changes must occur. For example, the police training program was given only a few weeks to obtain an internal program auditor. Although the City bears the responsibility of paying the auditor's salary, the internal auditor must submit reports about the training program to both the City and the Justice Department. The internal auditor is also authorized to suggest additional modifications to the training program beyond those stated in the consent decrees.[38] In this way, the Justice Department has oversight of the day-to-day operations of the training program to insure that the City is training its officers in accordance with federal law.

The City also agreed to changes in policies involving the use of force, incident reporting, internal affairs investigations, and to the development of "supervisory measures to promote civil rights integrity and reduce police misconduct."[39] Additionally, to ensure compliance with the agreement for a minimum of five years, an independent monitor was utilized. The monitor was given free access to all information within the department and will instruct department administration on how to fulfill the terms of the agreement.

Finally, the department must make reports to the Federal District Court every six months detailing its efforts to comply with the agreement. In short, the federal government has severely limited local control of the police function in Columbus until such time as the Attorney General determines that the municipality is willing and able to ensure that police will carry out their duties in a just manner.

Criminal Procedure

The courts in the United States have attempted to protect individual constitutional rights through the development of the rules of criminal procedure. Criminal procedure as it currently exists, "is a very recent American invention."[40] Generally, criminal procedure is a set of judicially created rules arising out of the Fourth, Fifth, and Sixth Amendments to the U.S. Constitution. These rules cover the procedures utilized by police, prosecutors, and the courts throughout the adversary system. For example, to ensure that an individual's Fifth Amendment privilege against self-incrimination is respected, police must read Miranda warnings to a suspect prior to conducting custodial interrogation. To protect the Fourth Amendment privilege against unreasonable searches and seizures, police must establish "probable cause to believe" that evidence of criminal activity will be found prior to conducting a search of an individual's home, property, or person. The penalty for a police officer's failure to comply with these and other applicable rules of criminal procedure is generally the exclusion or suppression at trial of any evidence which resulted from such omission.

The purpose of penalizing the state by forcing them to prove their case without using the illegally obtained evidence is to deter future illegal actions of police.[41] Excluding relevant evidence, such as a gun or a confession, makes it much more difficult for the state to prove its case against the accused. In some cases the exclusion of relevant evidence has ruined the state's case. In choosing to impose this penalty upon illegal police actions, the U.S. Supreme Court is clearly saying that two wrongs do not make a right. A criminal is not constrained in his actions by the due process clause of the U.S. Constitution, but a police officer is. An average citizen is not required to exercise due process in the performance of his daily responsibilities, but a police officer is. A police officer accepts this additional burden when he chooses to become a representative of the government and wield the authority inherent in the job of policing.

The rules of criminal procedure are limited, however, in their ability to control the behavior of police. The most significant limitation is that much of police work does not relate to gathering evidence so the threat of the exclusionary rule does not apply. [42] The Supreme Court recognized this limitation when it stated in *Terry v. Ohio* that the exclusionary rule is "powerless to deter invasions of constitutionally guaranteed rights where the police either have no interest in prosecuting or are willing to waive successful prosecution in the interest of serving some other goal."[43] The second significant limitation of the exclusionary rule is that the judge, in suppressing evidence, does not actually penalize the officer who collected it but penalizes the case against the accused. Unless a supervisor or supervisory policy within the police department penalizes an officer whose action has been deemed illegal by the court, there is nothing preventing the officer "'from doing as he pleases while forwarding cases on [to the courts on] a take it or leave it basis.'"[44] Thus, the courts do not have the ability to stop police injustice, only the ability to stop police injustice from coming into the courts.

CONCLUSION

Despite all of the efforts to control police behavior in the United States "the excessive use of force by police officers, including unjustified shootings, severe beatings, fatal chokings, and rough treatment, persists."[45] Reasons why this behavior continues to occur into the twenty-first century have been sought for years, but knowing "why" does little to ease the anger caused by unjust police action. Acts of police injustice toward the public, the very people whom each officer has sworn to protect and serve, continues to be a divisive and troubling issue in the United States.[46]

The frequent news stories about police officers who not only violate community standards of justice and morality but often are shown violating the law have worked to erode public trust in law enforcement.[47] The public's shock over acts of injustice arises out of more than the horrifying details of the stories, the graphic pictures, or even personal experiences with an unjust police officer. The shock comes from the basic feeling of betrayal of trust. When the public is shown proof, time and again, that they can no longer believe that the police are "just," their willingness to submit to the authority of government is reduced and the job of being a police officer becomes more dangerous.

Apart from §14141, which is too new to evaluate at this point, existing internal and external controls have all approached the issue of police injustice and dealt with the problem in specific ways. Internal controls try to guide and pressure police officers into conforming to agency standards, while external controls impose sanctions such as criminal and civil penalties. None of these controls, however, has managed to eliminate police injustice.

The answer is not in eliminating controls on police behavior, either. Although some law and order advocates may suggest that the controls serve no purpose, such a suggestion only shows a lack of understanding of the relationship between government, the police, and the public, as well as a desire to separate the police from this interrelationship. The implications of such short-sighted thinking are far reaching and serious. By advocating the reduction in controls upon police, one is essentially saying that the very foundations of liberty and justice upon which this nation was founded are secondary to the interests of law enforcement.

Existing methods of controlling police behavior have been successful at improving policing techniques. No longer do police enforce the laws like the police forces of the early twentieth century. Instead, they have evolved into polished, professional agencies. But, it appears that any further steps toward ensuring that police conform to standards of justice as set forth by government and the people must come from within each officer. The key to significantly reducing police injustice seems to lie in developing the character of police officers. As Michael Campion writes in his book *Character and Cops*:

> The habit of good character is "acquired by initiation and instruction from others—in the telling of stories; the explanation of decent behavior; the introduction to heroes, heroines, and villains; the exposure to the meaning of fundamental ideals, and the discussion questions." A person who is uncontrolled in some aspects of his character may behave like a person of bad character, if his passion for gain overrides his regard for the law." A police officer's fitness to wear the badge depends on the acquisition of habits of just behavior."[48] Officers who respect justice will have nothing to do with racial prejudices, will not exceed their authority in the exercise of discretion, abuse the powers of their office, falsify reports, or give perjured testimony."[49]

As the enforcement arm of government, maintaining an image of trustworthiness, intelligence, and fairness has always been an important aspect of policing. It is becoming even more important as society evolves into a progressively more informed and interconnected body. Neither law enforcement agencies nor officers may forget that the police are the most visible symbols of government and justice in this society. Consequently, they must hold themselves to a higher standard of morality and behavior than is required of the average citizen. In short, an officer of good character will understand and accept the fact that in this society he and his actions are seen as symbols of both government and justice.

REFERENCES

Avery, M. and Rudovsky, D. *Police Misconduct: Law and Litigation.* (1995).
Bandes, S. Symposium: Section 1983 Municipal Liability in Civil Rights Litigation. Introduction: "The Emperor's New Clothes." 48 DePaul Law Review 619 (Spring, 1999).
Black's Law Dictionary, 5th Ed. St. Paul, Minn. West Publishing Co., 241 (1979).
Bracey v. Grenoble, 494 F.2d 566, 3d Cir. (1974).
City of Columbus/U.S. Department of Justice proposed agreement, 8/16/99. In the United States District Court for the southern district of Ohio, eastern division.
Cohen, D. "Official Oppression: A Historical Analysis of Low-Level Police Abuse and a Modern Attempt at Reform." 28 *Columbia Human Rights Law Review* 165 (1996).
del Carmen, Rolando V. *Criminal Procedure: Law and Practice.* New York, NY: Wadsworth Publishing, 1998.
Delattre, Edwin J. *Character and Cops.* American Enterprise Institute for Public Policy Research, Washington, D.C. 1989.
Fu, Hualing. "A Bird in the Cage: Police and Political Leadership in Post-Mao China." *Policing and Society* 4, no. 4 (1994): 133, 138, 142–144.
Glaser, Mark A. and Lee E. Parker. *The Thin Blue Line Meets the Bottom Line of Community Policing.*
Hall, Dennis. "Report on Police Corruption Should Concern Every Officer." *Police,* (August 1998b): p 6.
Human Rights Watch. *Shielded From Justice: Police Brutality and Accountability in the United States.* New York (June 1998).
Human Rights Watch. *Confessions at Any Cost: Police Torture in Russia,* November 1999.
Joint Anti-Fascist Refugee Committee v. McGrath, 341 U.S. 123, 162–63, 71 S. Ct. 624, 643–44, 95 L. Ed, 817, 849 (1951).
Livingston, Debra, "Police Reform and the Department of Justice: An Essay on Accountability," 2 *Buffalo Criminal Law Review* 815, (1999).
Marvasi v. Shorty, 70 F.R.D. 14 E.D.Pa.1976.
Miller, M. "Police Brutality." 17 *Yale Law and Policy Review* 149 (1998).
Mirabella, M., "Brazilians Outraged By Police Brutality Cases," *CNN News Watch,* April 11, 1997, Rio De Janeiro, Brazil http://cnn.com/WORLD/9704/11/brazil.brutality
Mitchum v. Foster, 407 U.S. 225, 92 S.Ct. 2151, 32 L.Ed.2d 705 (1972).
Oxford Desk Dictionary and Thesaurus, American Edition. Berkeley Books, New York. 1997. p. 432–433.
Ohio v. Harris et al., 489 U.S. 378; 109 S. Ct. 1197; 103 L. Ed. 2d 412 (1989).
Patterson, Thomas E. Symposium: Panel Discussion: "Changes in American Life." 62 *Alabama Law Review* 1471 (1999).
Patton, A. "The Endless Cycle of Abuse: Why 42 U.S.C. § 1983 is Ineffective in Deterring Police Brutality." 44 *Hastings Law Journal* 753 March, 1993.
"Police Code of Conduct." *The Police Chief,* January 1992, p. 17.
Rochin v. California, 342 U.S. 165, 72 S. Ct. 205, 96 L.Ed. 183 (1952).
Senkel, Tara L. "Civilians Often Need Protection From the Police: Let's Handcuff Police Brutality." 15 *New York Law School Journal of Human Rights* 385 (Winter, 1999).
Terry v. Ohio, 392 U.S. 1, 88 S.Ct. 1868, 20 L.Ed.2d 889 (1968).
Tifft, Larry L. "Social Bases of Power and Power Exercise in Police Organizations" *Policing: A View from the Street.* Goodyear Publishing, Santa Monica, CA, p. 90 1978.
Via v. Cliff, 470 F.2d 271, 276 (3d Cir. 1972).

Walker, Samuel (1998) *Popular Justice: A History of American Criminal Justice,* 2nd Edition, New York; NY: Oxford University Press.

Weisberg, Robert, A New Agenda for Criminal Procedure. 2 *Buffalo Criminal Law Review* 367, (1999).

42 U.S.C. §1983 of the Civil Rights Act of 1871.

Pub. L. No. 103-322, 108 Stat. 2071 (1994) (codified at 42 U.S.C. 14141 (1994 & Supp. 1997)). 42 U.S.C. 210401 (1999).

NOTES

1. Patterson, Thomas E. Symposium: Panel Discussion: "Changes in American Life." 62 *Alabama Law Review* 1471 (1999).

2. Brazilians Outraged By Police Brutality Cases, *CNN News Watch,* April 11, 1997, from correspondent Marina Mirabella, Rio de Janeiro, Brazil. http://cnn.com/WORLD/9704/11/brazil.brutality/

3. Fu, Hualing. "A Bird in the Cage: Police and Political Leadership in Post-Mao China." *Policing and Society* 4, no. 4 (1994): 133, 138, 142–144.

4. "Confessions at Any Cost: Police Torture in Russia," *Human Rights Watch,* November 1999. ISBN 1-56432-244-0 Library of Congress Catalog Card Number:99-068011.

5. "Confessions at Any Cost: Police Torture in Russia," *Human Rights Watch,* November 1999. ISBN 1-56432-244-0 Library of Congress Catalog Card Number:99-068011.

6. Senkel, Tara L. "Civilians Often Need Protection From the Police: Let's Handcuff Police Brutality." 15 *New York Law School Journal on Human Rights* 385 (Winter, 1999).

7. Senkel, Tara L. p. 397.

8. Cohen, David S. "Official Oppression: a Historical Analysis of Low-level Police Abuse and a Modern Attempt at Reform." 28 *Columbia Human Rights Law Review* 165 (1996).

9. Tifft, Larry L. "Social Bases of Power and Power Exercise in Police Organizations" *Policing: A View from the Street.* Goodyear Publishing, Santa Monica, CA, p. 90 1978.

10. Delattre. p. 100.

11. Alison L. Patton, "The Endless Cycle of Abuse: Why 42 U.S.C. § 1983 is Ineffective in Deterring Police Brutality." 44 *Hastings Law Journal* 753 March, 1993.

12. Glaser, Mark A. and Lee E. Parker *The Thin Blue Line Meets the Bottom Line of Community Policing.*

13. "Police Code of Conduct." *The Police Chief,* January 1992, p. 17.

14. Miller, Marshall.

> Analysts point to a number of reasons to account for the paucity of prosecutions. First, evidentiary factors substantially reduce the probability of obtaining a conviction. Victims of police misconduct—frequently convicted felons, criminal suspects, or other marginalized members of society—often lack credibility before a jury. If the complainant has corroborating witnesses, they often suffer from the same credibility problems as the complainant. In many cases, the only witnesses to the incident are other police officers; the phenomenon of police officers covering for their colleagues through silence or prevarication is well documented and apparently widespread. Coupled with the heavy burden of proof in a criminal case and likely juror identification with the law enforcement officer, these evidentiary problems render prosecutions of police officers difficult to win and thus are infrequently brought.

15. Hall, Dennis. "Report on Police Corruption Should Concern Every Officer." *Police,* August 1998b, p. 6.

16. Hall, Dennis. "Report on Police Corruption Should Concern Every Officer." *Police,* August 1998b, p. 6.

17. Senkel, Tara L. p. 401.

18. Senkel, Tara L. p. 404.; Johnson, Richard R. "Citizen Complaints: What the Police Should Know." *The FBI Law Enforcement Bulletin,* Dec. 1998, v. 67 I 12 pl (5). Patton, Alison L. "The Endless Cycle of Abuse: Why 42 U.S.C. § 1983 is Ineffective in Deterring Police Brutality," 44 *Hastings Law Journal* 753, 763 (1993).

19. Patton, Alison L. "The Endless Cycle of Abuse: Why 42 U.S.C. § 1983 is Ineffective in Deterring Police Brutality," 44 *Hastings Law Journal* 753, 763 (1993); and Warren Christopher et al., Report of the Independent Commission on the Los Angeles Police Department p. 170 (1991).

20. Miller, Marshall. 154.

21. Michael Avery and David Rudovsky, *Police Misconduct: Law and Litigation,* 1–5 (1995).

22. Senkel, Tara L. p 404.; Johnson, Richard R. "Citizen Complaints: What the Police Should Know." *The FBI Law Enforcement Bulletin,* Dec. 1998, v. 67 I 12 pl (5). Patton, Alison L. "The Endless Cycle of Abuse: Why 42 U.S.C. § 1983 is Ineffective in Deterring Police Brutality," 44 *Hastings Law Journal* 753, 763 (1993).

23. 42 U.S.C. §1983 of the Civil Rights Act of 1871.

> Every person who, under color of any statute, ordinance, regulation, custom or usage, of any state or territory or the District of Columbia, subjects, or causes to be subjected, any citizen of the United States or other person within the jurisdiction thereof to the deprivation of any rights, privileges or immunities secured by the constitution and laws, shall be liable to the party injured in an action at law, suit in equity, or other proper proceeding for redress. For the purposes of this section, any act of congress applicable exclusively to the District of Columbia shall be considered to be a statute of the District of Columbia.

and *Black's Law Dictionary,* 5th Ed. St. Paul, Minn. West Publishing Co., 241 (1979).

24. *Mitchum v. Foster,* 407 U.S. 225, 92 S.Ct. 2151, 32 L.Ed.2d 705 (1972).

25. *City of Canton, Ohio v. Harris et al.,* 489 U.S. 378; 109 S. Ct. 1197; 103 L. Ed. 2d 412 (1989).

> Municipalities held subject to liability under 42 USCS 1983 for constitutional violations resulting from failure to train employees if such failure reflects deliberate indifference to constitutional rights.

26. *Via v. Cliff,* 470 F.2d 271, 276 (3d Cir. 1972).

27. *Bracey v. Grenoble,* 494 F.2d 566 (3d Cir. 1974).

28. *Marvasi v. Shorty,* 70 F.R.D. 14 (E.D.Pa.1976).

29. Patton, Alison L. "The Endless Cycle of Abuse: Why 42 U.S.C. § 1983 is Ineffective in Deterring Police Brutality," 44 *Hastings Law Journal* 753, 755 (1993).

30. Patton, Alison L. "The Endless Cycle of Abuse: Why 42 U.S.C. § 1983 is Ineffective in Deterring Police Brutality," 44 *Hastings Law Journal* 753, 755 (1993).

31. Patton, Alison L. 757 citing (Telephone Interview with Karol Heppe, Director of Police Watch, an organization in Los Angeles that provides initial counseling and referrals to victims of police abuse (Feb. 7, 1992); *see* Telephone Interview with Richard "Terry" Koch, attorney in Berkeley, California (Jan. 10, 1992) ("These suits are very tough to win."); Telephone Interview with Dan Stormer, attorney in Los Angeles, California (Jan. 27, 1992) ("Today, it is even more difficult to prevail in section 1983 suits because the courts are cutting back."); *see also* Irving Joyner, "Litigating Police Misconduct Claims in North Carolina," 19 *North Carolina Central Law Journal* 113, 143–44 (1991), at 114 ("[It is] extremely difficult to convince a jury of twelve citizens that police officers have violated the rights of others.").

32. Bandes, Susan. Symposium: Section 1983 Municipal Liability in Civil Rights Litigation. Introduction: "The Emperor's New Clothes" 48 *DePaul Law Review* 619 (Spring, 1999).

33. Pub. L. No. 103-322, 10 8 Stat. 2071 (1994) (codified at 42 U.S.C. 14141 (1994 & Supp. 1997)). 42 U.S.C. 210401 (1999).

> 14141. Cause of action

(a) Unlawful conduct. It shall be unlawful for any governmental authority, or any agent thereof, or any person acting on behalf of a governmental authority, to engage in a pattern or practice of conduct by law enforcement officers or by officials or employees of any governmental agency with responsibility for the administration of juvenile justice or the incarceration of juveniles that deprives persons of rights, privileges, or immunities secured or protected by the Constitution or laws of the United States.

(b) Civil action by Attorney General. Whenever the Attorney General has reasonable cause to believe that a violation of paragraph (1) [subsection (a) of this section] has occurred, the Attorney General, for or in the name of the United States, may in a civil action obtain appropriate equitable and declaratory relief to eliminate the pattern or practice.

34. Livingston, Debra, "Police Reform and the Department of Justice: An Essay on Accountability," 2 *Buffalo Criminal Law Review* 815, (1999).
35. Miller, Marshall. "Police Brutality." 17 *Yale Law and Policy Review* 149 (1998).
36. Livingston, Debra, "Police Reform and the Department of Justice: An Essay on Accountability," 2 *Buffalo Criminal Law Review* 815, (1999).

The Special Litigation Section of the Justice Department's Civil Rights Division has brought two civil suits pursuant to Section 14141—suits that have resulted in consent decrees with the police departments of Pittsburgh, Pennsylvania and Steubenville, Ohio. The Department, moreover, is reported to be investigating or monitoring at least nine other police agencies—in Los Angeles, California; Orange County, Florida; New Orleans, Louisiana; East Point, Michigan; Buffalo, New York; New York, New York; Washington, D.C.; Charleston, West Virginia; and Columbus, Ohio—in order to decide "whether to seek judicial orders on respect for governing law."

37. City of Columbus/U.S. Department of Justice proposed agreement, 8/16/99. In the United States District Court for the southern district of Ohio, eastern division:

2. In its Complaint, the United States alleges that officers of the Columbus, Ohio Division of Police ("CDP") have engaged and continue to engage in a pattern or practice of conduct that deprives persons of rights, privileges, or immunities secured or protected by the Constitution or laws of the United States, and that the City of Columbus has tolerated this conduct by failing adequately to train, supervise, and monitor police officers, and by failing to adequately receive citizen complaints of misconduct, investigate alleged misconduct, and discipline officers who are guilty of misconduct. In making these allegations, the United States recognizes that the majority of Columbus police officers perform their difficult jobs in a lawful manner.

38. City of Columbus/U.S. Department of Justice proposed agreement, 8/16/99. In the United States District Court for the southern district of Ohio, eastern division:

2. In its Complaint, the United States alleges that officers of the Columbus, Ohio Division of Police ("CDP") have engaged and continue to engage in a pattern or practice of conduct that deprives persons of rights, privileges, or immunities secured or protected by the Constitution or laws of the United States, and that the City of Columbus has tolerated this conduct by failing adequately to train, supervise, and monitor police officers, and by failing to adequately receive citizen complaints of misconduct, investigate alleged misconduct, and discipline officers who are guilty of misconduct. In making these allegations, the United States recognizes that the majority of Columbus police officers perform their difficult jobs in a lawful manner.

39. City of Columbus/U.S. Department of Justice proposed agreement, 8/16/99. In the United States District Court for the southern district of Ohio, eastern division:

2. In its Complaint, the United States alleges that officers of the Columbus, Ohio Division of Police ("CDP") have engaged and continue to engage in a pattern or practice of conduct that deprives persons of rights, privileges, or immunities

secured or protected by the Constitution or laws of the United States, and that the City of Columbus has tolerated this conduct by failing adequately to train, supervise, and monitor police officers, and by failing to adequately receive citizen complaints of misconduct, investigate alleged misconduct, and discipline officers who are guilty of misconduct. In making these allegations, the United States recognizes that the majority of Columbus police officers perform their difficult jobs in a lawful manner.

40. Weisberg, Robert, "A New Agenda for Criminal Procedure." 2 *Buffalo Criminal Law Review* 367, (1999).

41. del Carmen, Rolando V. *Criminal Procedure: Law and Practice* 4th Ed. Wadsworth Publishing, New York, 1998. at p. 82.

42. Livingston, Debra, "Police Reform and the Department of Justice: An Essay on Accountability," 2 *Buffalo Criminal Law Review* 815, (1999), from *Terry v. Ohio*, 392 U.S. 1, 13–14 (1968).

43. *Terry v. Ohio*, 392 U.S. 1, 88 S.Ct. 1868, 20 L.Ed.2d 889 (1968).

44. Livingston, Debra, "Police Reform and the Department of Justice: An Essay on Accountability," 2 *Buffalo Criminal Law Review* 815, (1999), quoting Weisberg, Robert, "Criminal Law, Criminology, and the Small World of Legal Scholars," 63 *University of Colorado Law Review* 521, 532–33 (1992).

45. "Shielded From Justice: Police Brutality and Accountability in the United States." Human Rights Watch. Washington June 1998 by Human Rights Watch. ISBN 1-56432-183-5; Library of Congress Catalog Card Number: 98-86155. http://www.hrw.org/hrw/reports98/police/uspo02.htm

46. "Shielded From Justice: Police Brutality and Accountability in the United States." Human Rights Watch. Washington June 1998 by Human Rights Watch. ISBN 1-56432-183-5; Library of Congress Catalog Card Number: 98-86155. http://www.hrw.org/hrw/reports98/police/uspo02.htm

47. Senkel, Tara L. "Civilians Often Need Protection From the Police: Let's Handcuff Police Brutality." 15 *New York Law School Journal of Human Rights* 385 (Winter, 1999).

48. Delattre, p. 10.

49. Delattre, p. 10.

ARTICLE 3

POLICE MISCONDUCT: WHAT IS IT?

Michael J. Palmiotto
Wichita State University

Since the inception of policing in the United States, police misconduct has plagued law enforcement agencies. As we enter the twenty-first century, we are no closer to eliminating this problem mainly because of the nature of police work, itself. The police in our society have a position of authority and power. This authority often leads to confrontations with those who challenge, or appear to challenge, police rulings. These confrontations create the illusion that the police often overstep their boundaries as a means to enforce law and order. It is often believed that the police have denied these citizens their human rights. In actuality, American police officers have the responsibility to protect the constitutional rights of all citizens. Unfortunately police officers are often accused of not fulfilling this role.

The police have a responsibility of legal authority that requires them to maintain the trust of the public. Reports of misconduct by police officers often cause citizens to lose their confidence in the police. Even the appearance of wrong-doing can justify a loss of respect. It is extremely important for the police to maintain the respect and trust of the people for whom they provide police service. This is because it is often through the help of the community, witnesses, and victims that the successful arrest and prosecution of offenders is achieved.

Police misconduct can be defined as a wrongdoing committed by a police officer. This wrongdoing can be a criminal act or a violation of departmental policies and procedures. Misconduct can be unethical or amoral and yet not be considered criminal. Police history indicates that a wide variety of police misconduct has occurred since the initiation of policing in our country. Such incidents include violation of civil rights, corruption, the commission of crimes, and excessive use of force. Police misconduct can reflect either individual, group, or organizational behavior. Regardless of the specific situation, police misconduct has taken place throughout U.S. policing, and it still occurs in our police agencies in the twenty-first century.

Academicians who are students of organizations advocate that most occupations provide their members with the opportunity for behavior misconduct. Police departments are no exception. There are three elements of occupational misconduct: "(1) opportunity structure and its accompanying techniques of rule violations, (2) socialization through occupational experiences, and (3) reinforcement and encouragement from the occupational peer group, i.e., group support for certain rule violations" (Barker 1977, 356). There are five conditions that must be met before individual misconduct can be attributed to faults within the police department itself:

1. For an action to be organizationally deviant, it must be contrary to the norms and/or rules maintained by others external to the police department;
2. For police misconduct to be organizational rather than individualistic in origin, the deviant action must be supported by internal norms which conflict with the police organization's formal goals and rules;
3. Compliance with the internal operating norms supportive of police misconduct must be ensured through recruitment and socialization;
4. There must be peer support of the misbehavior of colleagues;
5. For improper behavior to be organizationally deviant, it must be supported by the dominant administrative coalition of the police organization (Ludman 1980, 140–141).

If police officers do not gain financially because of their positions (i.e. accepting discounts, etc.) then informal rules often take precedence over formal department rules. Although police departments may have a policy forbidding officers from accepting free meals, the informal peer support acceptance process may allow the officer to violate the department policy without thinking he did anything wrong. Even recruits are socialized into the informal misconduct process often without recognizing that their behavior violates departmental regulations and/or criminal laws. The code of silence which has been integrated into most police departments provides a passive acceptance of police misconduct by officers refusing to be a party to departmental rule violations. Misconduct often occurs in police departments because police administrators refuse to recognize the existence of misconduct by their officers and do not take constructive action to stop inappropriate police behavior. Consequently, police misconduct can be defined as "actions (that) violate external expectations for what the department should do. Simultaneously, the actions must be in conformity with internal operating norms, and supported by socialization, peers, and the administrative personnel of the department" (Ludman 1980, 140).

POLICE WRONGDOING

Most types of police wrongdoings do not necessarily result in monetary rewards or material gain. Police officers who commit wrongful acts usually violate departmental policies, and often, criminal laws. According to Thomas Barker (1986), these forms of police misconduct include perjury, sex on duty, sleeping on duty, drinking on duty, and police brutality. Other types of misconduct may involve activities such as drug use while on duty. An explanation of each of these wrongdoings is as follows:

Perjury

When a police officer intentionally lies or falsifies the truth under oath, he or she commits the crime of perjury. Perjury is sometimes committed by officers in order to cover up their own illegal or inappropriate behavior, such as when an officer has planted evidence on a suspect or has questioned the suspect without informing him of his constitutional rights.

Sleeping on Duty

Most police departments have policies that forbid police officers from sleeping on duty. When police officers sleep on duty, it generally takes place on the midnight to 8 a.m. tour. Usually the hours between 2:00 a.m. and 6:00 a.m. are quiet times when police officers are rarely assigned a call. It is during these hours that officers tend to take naps. Traditionally, many police officers have second jobs to supplement their income. Working a second job makes it difficult for those working the midnight tour to stay awake.

Sex on Duty

The police officers often come into contact with a variety of people, and there are cases in which police officers have had sex on duty with a prostitute or with other individuals. For some police officers this may be an occasional act, while for others it can become a common occurrence. The author is aware of one police officer who roamed lover's lane during the late evening or early morning hours searching for young couples. He would chase the male away and intimidate the female into having sex with him. This came to the attention of the police chief when the mother of one young girl informed him of the situation. To catch the deviant officer, the police chief used a female and a male officer from another department, wired the female officer with an eavesdropping gadget, and instructed them to park in lover's lane. When the police officer approached the two undercover officers, he chased the male officer away and made sexual advances toward the female. His conversation with the undercover police officer was recorded and used as evidence. The police officer was then given the opportunity to resign or be prosecuted. The officer chose to resign.

Drinking on Duty

Most police departments have a percentage of police officers who enjoy alcoholic beverages. But some of these officers become addicted to drinking and will consume alcohol even while on duty. Since many communities have bars and liquor stores, it is easy for these police officers to obtain alcoholic beverages while on duty. Although most police officers sneak their drinking and make an attempt to hide it from their comrades, others officer are fairly open about their drinking situation.

Drugs on Duty

With the wide acceptance of drug use in our society, it should be no surprise that there are police officers who are using drugs. Police officers have access to drugs through the contacts they make with drug dealers and users. There are cases on record where police officers have confiscated drugs from dealers and users and then used the drugs themselves.

Police Brutality

The term, police brutality, is vague and tends to mean different things to different people. Some people consider verbal abuse to be a form of police brutality, while others limit it to physical abuse. Thomas Barker claims that when citizens accuse police of brutality, they are referring to a number of police actions. These include the use of:

1. Profane and abusive language,
2. Commands to move or get home,
3. Field stops and searches,
4. Threats,
5. Prodding with a nightstick or approaching with a pistol, and
6. The actual use of "Physical Force" (Barker 1986, 71)

Should profanity and abusive language by a police officer be considered brutality? Obviously, it is inappropriate for an officer to use profane and abusive language with a citizen because this behavior does not endear the citizen to the police officer or the department he represents. Additionally, the officer who conducts himself in an abusive manner toward citizens violates departmental policies.

Depending upon the circumstances and the situation, it is often appropriate for an officer to command a citizen to move along or head for home. For example, if a city has a curfew for teenagers, and a youngster is violating that curfew, the officer has a responsibility to tell the youngster to go home. As another example, if a group of citizens, regardless of their age, is blocking a roadway or an entrance of a store, the officer has an obligation to keep the passageway open and ask the group to move. At other times, however, an officer's demands for a group or an individual to move are nothing more than harassment.

The police have the legal right to make field stops in order to question citizens about their behaviors. For example, if a citizen is walking at 3:00 a.m. in a middle class neighborhood, an officer has the right to question that citizen about what he or she is doing in order to establish whether that citizen lives in the neighborhood or has a legitimate reason for being there. So when an officer stops a citizen under these circumstances, the officer is simply following police guidelines. There may be times when an officer stops an individual simply because he or she looks out of place, is dressed shabbily, or looks unkempt. This is perfectly acceptable. However, police officers do have the right to search someone they arrest or consider to be a danger to themselves or others.

Police officers have no legal right to prod any person with a nightstick. This is considered abusive behavior and is not condoned by the police agency. Officers who exhibit this type of behavior should be reprimanded. At times, for safety's sake, an officer may have to approach a citizen with his firearm drawn. If, for example, the person being stopped meets the description of a suspect who robbed a convenience store a few minutes ago. But when a police officer cannot provide a valid reason for having his weapon drawn on a citizen, the police department is responsible for taking disciplinary action.

Although there are certain situations in which police officers have the right to use physical force upon a citizen, excessive physical force is unnecessary and not legally justified.

Deadly Force

Deadly force can best be described as a force capable of causing serious bodily injury or death. Generally, the police have the authority to use deadly force to save their own lives or the lives of others. The use of deadly force by those responsible for policing can be traced back to the common law of England. In today's society, however, a police officer's legal authority to use deadly force is not only set forth in common law, but in statutory law and case law as well. Under common law an officer may, when necessary, use deadly force to apprehend someone who is believed to have committed a felony but not to merely prevent the escape of a misdemeanant. The rationale behind this action is that until the nineteenth century, virtually all felonies were punishable by death. If an officer killed an individual committing a felony, he was in a sense, doing the state a favor since the individual convicted of a felony would have received the death penalty, anyway.

In contemporary society, few crimes are punishable by death. In order to receive the death penalty, an individual must be convicted of murder in the first degree, however, this ruling is not uniform throughout the United States. There are some states that do not utilize capital punishment. Under these circumstances, police officers who use deadly force while apprehending an individual may, in effect, have recourse to exercise more authority and power than a judge or jury. After all, the most severe punishment an individual can receive is the loss of his or her life.

There are a variety of ways in which the physical actions of a police officer can result in deadly force. The most common of these is the use of firearms. Neck holds can cut off air circulation and/or blood flow, thus causing death. In Philadelphia in 1985, an incendiary bomb dropped from a police helicopter onto a house resulted in the deaths of eleven members of a militant group.

Appellate court decisions, statutory law, and departmental policies all provide guidelines that police officers must follow if deadly force is to be legally justifiable. In 1986, the U.S. Supreme Court struck down a "fleeing felon rule" which allowed police officers to use deadly force while trying to apprehend a suspect escaping from the scene of a crime. In *Tennessee v. Garner* the court stated:

> The use of deadly force to prevent the escape of all felony suspects, whatever the circumstances is unconstitutionally unreasonable. It is not better that all felony suspects die than they escape. Where the suspect poses no immediate threat and

no threat to others, the harm resulting from failing to apprehend him does not justify the use of deadly force to do so.

WRONGDOING FOR MATERIAL GAIN

Police officers who engage in corrupt acts gain economically by providing services they should already be performing, or by failing to perform services that are required by their position. Acts of corruption are characterized in three ways: "(1) They are forbidden by some norm, regulation, or law, (2) They involve the misuse of the officer's position and (3) They involve a material gain no matter how significant" (Barker and Wells 1981, 4). Police corruption is divided into ten types:

1. Corruption of Authority: Officers receive unauthorized free meals, services, or discounts and liquor;
2. Kickbacks: Officers receive money, goods, or services for referring business to towing companies, ambulances, garages, etc.;
3. Opportunistic Thefts: Opportunistic thefts from arrestees, victims, burglary scenes, and unprotected property;
4. Shakedowns: Officers take money or other valuables from traffic offenders or criminals caught in the commission of an offense;
5. Protection of Illegal Activities: Protection money accepted by police officers from vice operations or legitimate businesses operating illegally;
6. Traffic Fix: "Taking up" or disposal of traffic citations for money or other forms of material reward;
7. Misdemeanor Fix: Quashing of misdemeanor court proceedings for some form of material reward;
8. Felon Fix: "Fixing" of felon cases for money or other forms of material gain;
9. Direct Criminal Activities: Officers engage in serious felonies such as burglary, robbery, and larcenies;
10. Internal Payoffs: The sale of days off, holidays, work assignments etc. from one officer to another (Barker and Wells 1981, 4–5).

In a study of police corruption, Ellwyn Stoddard (1995) discovered that an informal code of behavior exists in police departments which either supports or condones police misconduct. According to Stoddard, certain forms of police misconduct, such as corruption, are socially prescribed within the organization. When recruits are indoctrinated into the police subculture, they soon recognize that the support of their fellow officers is important to ensure their personal safety and success as police officers. Furthermore, recruits are generally unfamiliar with police procedures and practices and are dependent upon the guidance of veteran officers. Like other members of our society, police officers want to be accepted by their fellow officers. If a recruit observes a senior officer involved in misconduct, the recruit faces the option of either looking the other way or reporting the misconduct. By reporting it, the recruit risks creating a difficult relationship (loss of trust, for example), not only with her fellow officers, but also with superiors. Ultimately, new police officers learn that it is best to keep quiet if misconduct by fellow officers is observed.

Many states have laws prohibiting police officers from accepting gratuities. In addition, there are police agencies that have adopted policies that forbid officers from accepting free meals, cigarettes, groceries, and other contributions. However, since tokens of appreciation are an integral part of our society, there are those individuals who do not consider it corruption for police officers to accept gifts.

Although there are degrees of corruption, some forms of corruption are much more serious than others. New York City police officers have used the term "grass-eaters" or "meat-eaters" in describing different forms of corruption. "Grass-eaters" are officers who accept gratuities from construction contractors, tow-truck operators, and gamblers who are not actively seeking illicit payments. "Meat-eaters" are officers who aggressively seek out financial gain that can yield a substantial amount of money, including gains from gambling, narcotics, and other offenses (Knapp Commission Report 1973, 65). Generally, some illegal activities such as gambling, narcotics, and prostitution cannot exist for very long without police protection or without an arrangement in which the police agree to look the other way.

In large cities like New York, there are many different types of gambling, e.g. the numbers game (similar to the lottery); betting on horses, dogs, or sporting events; card and dice games; and informal wagering. Police officers have been known to shakedown gambling operations on a systematic basis. This is because officers feel that society sees nothing wrong with gambling, and even when gamblers are arrested and convicted, they usually get nothing more than a slap on the wrist.

The prevalence of illicit drugs in our society creates opportunities for the police to engage in corrupt behavior. Although, police involvement in drug corruption may not be a common occurrence, it does account for the largest percentage of cases in which police corruption occurs. In some areas of the South, sheriffs have been known to run interference for drug dealers, and one sergeant in the Savannah, Georgia, police department operated his own drug gang. In another case, an officer provided information to a teenage drug dealer. If we search our newspapers and news magazines, we will find police officers in rural, suburban, and urban police departments who have succumbed to the temptation of easy drug money.

One New York City police officer, "Officer Otto," described police corruption to the Mollen Commission in the following manner: "Police officers view the community as a candy store. I know of officers stealing drug money from drug dealers, police officers stealing drugs from drug dealers. I know of police officers stealing guns and keeping them. I know cops committing perjury to conceal their crimes. I know of the use of excessive force (Pooley 1994, 17).

The Mollen Commission was created by Mayor David Dinkin following the discovery of a police drug ring in Brooklyn. One police officer was known to snort cocaine from the dashboard of his police cruiser. That same officer made $8,000 per week selling drugs and protection. Another group of rogue cops from Brooklyn, known as the "Morgue Boys" because they liked to do their drinking in an abandoned coffin factory, rampaged though black and Latino neighborhoods, snorting cocaine, stealing, dealing, and selling protection to drug dealers. They would knock doors down to gain entrance into apartments and then lie about their activities (Pooley 1994, 19).

The New York City Police Commissioner reported that 25 percent of the 191 officers assigned to a Harlem precinct were rogue officers, and most of the other officers were aware of the corruption. These corrupt cops were selling drugs, protecting drug dealers, and brutalizing citizens (Krauss 1994, 1). In one reported incident, an officer struck a drug dealer in the head, grabbed a bag of cocaine from him, and then shot him in the midsection. Over a three-year period, another officer made $60,000 stealing cash from drug dealers and selling drugs. Other officers accepted payoffs from neighborhood drug dealers who were trying to monopolize the area. Two officers divided $100,000 in cash they had taken from an apartment that they broke into illegally (Krauss 1994, 24). During the same period of time, sixteen police officers from a Bronx precinct, including two sergeants, were charged with graft. The officers were charged with robbery, burglary, larceny, filing false police reports, and insurance fraud (Krauss 1994, A1). A nine-year veteran of the Brooklyn police force was arrested on charges of burglary and larceny for taking money from an open safe while responding to a burglary call. He also was charged with insurance and mail fraud, stemming from an automobile insurance scheme (James 1995, B5).

Police officers around the United States have been charged with rape, robbery, domestic violence, child abuse, and murder. Police officers in Miami have been charged with murder, racketeering, robbery, cocaine trafficking, and aggravated battery (*Time* 1986, 72). In Detroit, four police officers were charged with the murder of a black motorist who was beaten to death. While robbing a Vietnamese restaurant, a New Orleans police officer put a bullet in the head of a security guard who happened to be her partner on the police force. The officer then killed all of the witnesses who could identify her. She was finally apprehended when a child of the owner, who had been hiding during the robbery, was able to identify her as the murderer (Gwynne 1995, 45). In Savannah, Georgia, a police officer placed his own child in scalding hot water. In Wichita, Kansas, an officer was charged with child molestation. In Galesburg, Illinois, a police officer was charged with bank robbery, and in Chatham County, Georgia, a law enforcement officer was caught robbing convenience stores, including one that was on his beat.

No one can say with certainty how serious or widespread police corruption is in our nation's police departments. In some instances, acts of police corruption are committed by single officers, in other instances they are committed by groups of police officers, and in some situations entire departments and city governments have been involved in corrupt behavior. Often, good officers refuse to come forward with evidence, and supervisors frequently refuse to take part in stopping corruption.

CONCLUSIONS

Police misconduct has occurred since the inception of policing in the United States. Acts of misconduct by police officers leave the public with a negative impression of the police. The legal authority possessed by the police requires that they maintain the trust of the citizens in their community. Any activity of misconduct demonstrated by police officers will cause citizens to lose confidence in and respect for the police. Even the mere appearance of police misconduct can create a loss of respect for the police.

This article reviewed and discussed various forms of police misconduct, which may or may not involve material gain. Material gain is not a requirement for an action to be considered misconduct; there are also acts of wrongdoing such as perjury, sex/drinking on duty, use of drugs, and police brutality. Police officers who take an oath to uphold the U.S. Constitution and their state constitution, as well as to enforce federal and state laws, should be expected to obey the same laws they have sworn to uphold and enforce. Citizens have the right to expect that police officers will be people of character who possess qualities of integrity and honesty. All police officers need to be models of decency and civility in our modern-day society, not law violators. Police brutality, drinking on duty, the use of drugs, or sleeping on duty is not acceptable behavior and cannot be condoned by other police officers or by society. The police have to be accountable for their actions, just like the people they arrest.

Even more damaging to the community, police department, and police officers are acts of police corruption and the unnecessary use of deadly force. Corruption is a horrendous crime that brings shame not only to those involved in this behavior but also to the police organization. Officers involved in corruption can never undo the harm they have done to the police department that employed them.

The taking of a life unnecessarily when deadly force has been used wrongly must be considered a serious breach of misconduct. There can be no greater offense than taking a life when it is unnecessary to do so.

Police conduct in the twenty-first century must change if officers are to achieve the recognition of professionalism they have been striving toward for over a century. Police officers can eliminate police misconduct by making their peers feel uncomfortable whenever they are involved in wrongdoing, no matter how trivial it may appear. It is up to the police themselves to control and keep misconduct to a minimum. It is only through this proactive approach that the elimination of police misconduct can be achieved.

REFERENCES

Baker, T. (1977). "Peer Group Support for Police Occupational Deviance." *Criminology,* Volume 15, No. 2 (November).

Baker, T. and Wells, R. (1981). "Police Administrator's Attitudes Toward the Definition and Control of Police Deviance." Unpublished paper presented at the Academy of Criminal Justice Sciences, Philadelphia, Pennsylvania.

Baker, T. (1986). "An Empirical Study of Police Deviance Other Than Corruption," in Thomas Baker and David Carter, *Police Deviance,* Cincinnati, OH: Anderson.

Gwynne, S.C. (1995). "Cops and Robbers." *Time,* Volume 145 (March 20).

Krauss, C. (1994). "Bratton Says Corruption Involves Dozens More Officers." *The New York Times,* (April 17).

James, G. (1995). "Police Officers Charged in Drug Corruption Sweep: Bratton Sees More Arrests." *The New York Times,* (September 7).

Ludman, R.J. (1980). *Police and Policing: An Introduction,* New York, NY: Holt, Rinehart, and Winston.

Pooley, E. (1994). "The Extraordinary Story of How an Underfunded and Unloved Team of Mollen Commission Investigators Unearthed the Dirtiest Corruption of them All: Untouchable." *New York,* Volume 27 (July 11).

"Slice of Vice." (1986). *Time,* Volume 127 (January 6).

Smothers, R. (1995). "Atlanta Holds Six Policemen in Crackdown." *The New York Times,* (September 7).

Stoddard, E.R. (1995). "The Informal 'Code' of Police Deviance: A Group Approach to 'Blue-coat crime.'" Victor E. Kappeler, ed., In *The Police and Society: Touchstone Readings,* Prospect Heights, IL: Waveland Press.

Tennessee v. Gardner (1986) 105 Supreme Court Reporter, 470 U.S. 901, 1701.

The Knapp Commission Report on Police Corruption (1973) New York, NY: George Brazillier.

SHOULD WE TELL THE POLICE TO SAY "YES" TO GRATUITIES?

Richard R. E. Kania
Pembrook State University

Most criminal justice educators are strongly opposed to public officials accepting minor gratuities. Arthur Aubry, Jr., for example, includes "[e]nforcement of the law courteously and appropriately at all times without fear or favor, never employing unnecessary force, and *never accepting gratuities of any sort*"[1] among his seventeen ethical principles for police officers. McMullan states that "a public official is *corrupt* if he accepts money or money's worth for doing something that he is under a duty to do anyway, that he is under a duty not to do, or to exercise a legitimate discretion for improper reasons."[2] And the International Association of Chiefs of Police has promulgated a widely reprinted "Law Enforcement Code of Ethics"[3] advocating the absolute prohibition of the acceptance of gratuities. Many leading government and criminal justice reformers advance similar views, arguing that even the most trivial gratuity is a temptation that can only lead our public officials into further unethical conduct.[4]

Voices occasionally argue that minor gratuities do not necessarily result in adverse consequences.[5] Others have claimed that such gratuities may have some positive effects for the social system.[6] The criticism directed at U.S. Attorney General Edwin Meese III during his Senate confirmation hearings—for having accepted gifts from Korean officials—recently revived this debate in the media: supporters of the Reagan Administration scoffed at the idea that minor gifts corrupt their recipients while critics of the Administration and of Mr. Meese argued otherwise.

Richard R.E. Kania, "Should We Tell the Police to Say 'Yes' to Gratuities?" (as appeared in *Criminal Justice Ethics*, Volume 7, Number 2, [Summer/Fall 1988] pp. 37–49). Reprinted by permission of the Institute for Criminal Justice Ethics, 555 W. 57th Street, New York, NY, 10019-1029.

For the criminal justice community, especially those interested in police practices, this ethical question has been a perennial topic of discussion. But however much the issue has been discussed, it seems never to have been subjected to an in-depth analysis. The ethical impropriety of accepting minor gratuities has been treated as though it were established fact, with only the degree of impropriety being in question.[7] What debate there has been has focused on the relative seriousness of the ethical violation, the response the criminal justice system should make in dealing with this pattern of misconduct, and the consequences that acceptance of such gratuities will have for the more serious corruption of police officers or other justice officials.[8]

It is my view that this discussion has gone on too long without a reconsideration of the initial assumptions that accepting minor gratuities is inherently wrong, or improperly obligates the police recipients to the givers, or inevitably leads recipients into genuine corruption. In contrast to the prevailing view, I take the position that *the police* especially, and, under certain circumstances, other justice officials *should be encouraged to accept freely offered minor gratuities and that such gratuities should be perceived as the building blocks of positive social relationships between our police and the public,* and not as incipient corruptors. Such a change in our perception of gratuities can be justified by a fuller understanding of the motives of their givers. Some, if not most, minor gratuities are offered to repay or reward the police *for services already rendered.* It is true that these services are the legal due of the givers, having been paid for by their taxes. But the givers need not see it this way, and may indeed feel they still owe a debt to the police. Thus the police need not assume that the gifts they receive are intended to generate subsequent indebtedness to the givers. This "heretical" viewpoint should be evaluated as objectively as the other issues related to the corruption problem, and if the evaluation indicates that there is merit in this alternative view, then criminal justice educators and police trainers should approach the topic of acceptance of gratuities more open-mindedly than in the past. Perhaps trainers and educators should even promote the acceptance of minor gratuities within certain carefully qualified contexts, under carefully crafted guidelines and standards.

SLIPPERY SLOPES, CAMELS' NOSES, AND UNJUSTIFIED ENRICHMENT

Certainly many will disagree with this heretical position. Their objections dominate the literature on gratuities. Several arguments have been marshalled against the practice of accepting gratuities, generally falling into two basic lines of ethical reasoning: the "slippery slope" and the unjustified enrichment strategies.

The slippery slope analogies are far more common. Generally stated, the argument claims that although taking minor gratuities may not be a serious ethical problem, it begins a process of gradual subversion of the recipient's integrity. Eventually the acceptance of petty gratuities leads to more serious unethical conduct. This line of reasoning is essentially teleological. The acceptance of gratuities is not seen as wrong in itself, but the associated consequences of bias, favoritism, and bribery are evil. The relatively innocent gratuity, the free cup of coffee, is, to introduce another popular metaphor, the nose of the camel of corruption, trying to find a way inside the tent of law enforcement.[9]

Consequentialist theorists argue that the police officer who accepts minor gratuities becomes obligated to provide preferential treatment to the gift givers, and is thus no longer capable of providing equal and unbiased police services. This favoritism is a serious unethical consequence of gratuity giving, whether accepting minor gratuities is also ethically wrong in and of itself.[10]

A second school of thought takes the even more uncompromising position that any gratuity is in and of itself wrong because it is an unjustified enrichment for doing services already fully compensated and, in fact, paid for by the public. Advocates of this position assert that public employees are entitled to nothing beyond their basic compensation for doing their duty. This is a deontological ethical position, which stands apart from any particular consequences of the act. Accepting gratuities is wrong even if no subsequent bribery, bias, or favoritism ever results.

ON BECOMING A HERETIC

My "heretical" position on this matter arises from the ethical deliberations I had within myself while serving as a police officer. I was faced with having to accept or decline unsolicited minor gratuities from merchants on my foot patrol beat. Like most police officers who have completed a modern, progressive police academy program, I knew that the conventional ethical standard obliged me to forego taking any gratuities and that it was even more unethical to solicit such gifts. At the academy the "why" was explained in terms of the probability of progressing to more serious, more unacceptable graft, as if the taking of a single gratuity were infectious.

When I arrived on the street, paired with a veteran officer, I was quickly shown that the supposedly unethical behavior was the social norm for the police and the merchants alike. Were all these police corrupt? By the literal application of the ethical standard which I had learned in the police course, they indeed were. But were they really? Their behavior generally suggested otherwise. Although the officers whom I observed took minor gratuities without much hesitation, they provided no inappropriate or illegal favors in return.

The memory of police academy training was there to explain: the merchants were potential favor seekers who eventually would call in their chits. It recalled George C. Homan's observation: "Persons that give much to others try to get much from them, and persons that get much from others are under pressure to give much to them."[11] The police were seen as selling their souls bit by bit, against a future act of overt favoritism or corruption which the merchant or restaurateur would demand of them.

But this did not seem to be a frequent outcome, for these chits were not being called in. The merchants and restaurateurs occasionally did ask the police to perform special services for them, but none of the requests were out of line with what might normally be expected from any police officer, corrupted or pure. This failure of verification did not mean that I was witnessing a failure of the police academy faith, but it did make me suspect that there was more to the issue than had been explained at the academy. Perhaps the temptations of the merchants had been carried out in some other spirit.

Perhaps there was no intention of calling in those chits for illegal favoritism or overtly corrupt police action. If these possibilities were to be accorded validity, then alternative explanations of the merchants' behavior were required. What other motivation might they have if not the future corruption of police officers?

I found a possible answer in the writings of a social anthropologist and in the offhand remarks of a short-order cook on the midnight shift in a restaurant on my beat. The social anthropologist was Edmund Leach, who wrote, "If I give you a present you will feel morally bound to give something back. In economic terms you are in debt to me, but in communicative terms the sense of reciprocal obligation is an expression of a mutual feeling that we both belong to the same social system."[12] Of course, I could have supposed that it was the police officer who was accruing the debt. That is how the short-order cook provided the missing analytical link. I tried to argue the cook out of giving me a free meal on a night-watch. The cook would have none of it and refused payment. I even reminded the cook that the owner gave only a percentage discount. In response, the cook replied that the owner did not work the midnight crowd, and had a lot less to be grateful to the police for. The short-order cook was grateful to the police; he felt that he was in a state of indebtedness to the police. The gratuities were not gifts given in expectation of future rewards, but, as Leach had explained, in repayment of the debt already owed by the late night cook.

WHO OWES WHOM?
THE COHESIVE VALUE OF GIFT EXCHANGE

My rationale for suggesting that police accept minor gratuities rests on the assumption that merchants and restauranteurs feel a genuine sense of debt toward the police who visit them. Offering these police minor gratuities helps settle the imbalance which merchants perceive. It is the giver who is indebted, not the police recipient.

What are the police doing that generates this debt? In the foregoing example they were visiting the establishment frequently on their rounds, providing the security that the short-order cook sought. Was this not a service that every police officer routinely was obliged to provide? Yes, most certainly it was. Did that fact in any way reduce the perception of the cook that he owed this officer and others in the police department a personal debt? No, it did not. I, true to my training, felt no debt was owed me, and so felt uncomfortable in accepting the free meals.[13]

An analogy can be drawn between gratuities given to police and "tips" given to salaried workers who provide personal services to which a consumer has a basic right as a consequence of doing business with the workers' employer. Tip-giving consumers feel socially obligated to tip when excellent service is rendered. Tip recipients accept the gifts in the recognition that they have performed to the satisfaction of the tipper. Neither need feel that the other has any subsequent claim on him/her after the transaction is concluded. Opponents of this analogy argue that it does not hold because the police are paid their wages to provide everyone with equally good public service. However, direct police service is not distributed evenly in society. There are heavy

consumers of police service, just as there are citizens who rarely, if ever, require direct police assistance. Equality in the actual provision of police service never occurs and is an unrealistic expectation, even if, in the abstract,
police protection is extended equally. The real imbalance in the consumption
of direct police service underlies the sense of debt felt by some heavy consumers of police service, and provides an ethical rationale for the giving and
accepting of gratuities.

To refuse a gift genuinely offered in gratitude would be to refuse the giver
the opportunity to satisfy his sense of obligation. As the French social anthropologist Marcel Mauss explained, "A gift not yet repaid debases the man who
accepted it, particularly if he did so without thought of return."[14] It would be
a rejection of that "expression of a mutual feeling that we both belong to the
same social system" of which Leach writes.

Police officers may indeed have both an ethical and pragmatic obligation
to accept such gifts. They are morally obligated to maintain good relations
with law-abiding members of the community. To decline the gifts is to insult
the givers, alienating them from the police. Alienation must be avoided for
practical, pragmatic reasons. If citizens feel alienated, the police are less able
to perform their duties. Of course, other means could be provided to enable
citizens feeling a sense of indebtedness to repay police assistance. Gifts to
police-sponsored benefits, rather than to police officers individually, and
non-material recognition in the form of letters of appreciation have been suggested in lieu of personal gratuities.[15] But the former fails to fulfill the giver's
need precisely because it is impersonal, while the debt is quite personal. The
letter of appreciation is entirely appropriate, but it is an option that is not
open to everyone. Effective letter-writing is not a uniformly distributed talent.
The free cup of coffee, meal discount, or small gift is personal, immediate, and
easily provided from resources at hand. Thus they are the most efficient means
of achieving and maintaining social cohesion and avoiding alienation.

The point I am making about social cohesion is far from original. Many
others beside Mauss and Leach have made the point that gift exchange has a
cohesive value. Yet this social cohesion has been identified in corrupt transactions as well as legal ones. Dorothy Bracey shows an awareness of it in her
examination of police corruption. Following the rules of value-neutrality in
functional analysis, she does not dwell on the propriety or impropriety of
these small scale "corruptors." Instead she identifies both harmful and useful
aspects of the practice and finds increased social cohesion as one of several
possible positive attributes of these exchanges.[16] Charles Kaut, studying institutionalized official "gift" exchange practices in the Phillippines, comes to
similar conclusions. Gratuities do increase social cohesion independently of
their alleged corrupting influences.[17]

Many who have studied the problem with an open mind have been able
to play devil's advocate, citing the positive features of gratuity acceptance,
without necessarily encouraging police to accept them.[18] If positive features in
the giving and receiving of gratuities do exist, then a broader teleological approach in ethical reasoning might be more appropriate, one more utilitarian in
nature, that looks to the balance between advantages and disadvantages in accepting gratuities.[19]

This broader utilitarian reasoning which I am now encouraging has generally been discounted or ignored amid the claims about the probabilities of

slippery slopes and camels' noses. This is especially disconcerting because there is evidence to show that the slippery slope argument is a fallacy.[20] The New York City Police investigated by the Knapp Commission felt that the slope was not irresistible: they made a sharp distinction between the unacceptably corrupt "meat eaters" and the acceptably corrupt "grass eaters."[21] Subsequent research on police attitudes and opinions confirms that police make and adhere to distinctions between acceptable and unacceptable practices, even though these distinctions do not conform to the statutory distinctions between legal and corrupt practices.[22] Michael Banton found that some police clearly reject the notion that a gratuity obligates them to the donors.[23] The knowledge that police officers can draw and stay within the lines between grass-eating and meat-eating corrupt practices may mean nothing to those who argue that both meat- and grass-eating are intolerably corrupt. But if we are evaluating the consequentialist arguments, ought we not to examine *all* the consequences of the rule? Its violation may carry some police down slippery slopes to favoritism and bribery. But its violation can also produce worthwhile social cohesion and provide indebted citizens an opportunity to express their genuine appreciation. True, its nonviolation may protect some police from temptation and corruption. And the loss of social cohesion could be remedied in other ways. But is this justification enough? Does its faithful observance produce only favorable consequences?

Empirical studies of the consequences of faithfully following the rules against taking gratuities are very rare; there may be none.[24] There do not appear to be many police who never violate the rule against taking gratuities. One study of sworn officers in three small police departments found no one who would "report a fellow officer for" free coffee, free movie access, a discounted or free meal.[25] So common were "free meals, discounts, small favors such as cigarettes or free drinks or similar" in the multi-cities, participation observation studies of Donald Black[26] and Albert Reiss[27] on actual police practices, that the final reports made no effort to record them in the results of police misconduct. Yet several probable negative consequences of following the rule can be suggested.

CONSEQUENCES OF FOLLOWING THE PUBLISHED FORMAL NORMS

What might occur if a police officer declined to accept a minor gratuity offered by a merchant or restaurateur? Ideally, the police ought to be protected from more serious vice. Realistically and empirically, however, this is not likely to be the only result, even if it were to be one result of such rule-abiding behavior. At best, experience demonstrates that an awkward situation might develop. The merchant might become politely insistent, and if the officer persisted in resisting the offer, ill will might result. The police officer might bargain away the gift, by disclaiming an interest in it, or by throwing up departmental policy as a barrier to its acceptance, perhaps to find the gift-giver offering clever ways to avoid the restrictions. The officer might stall by deferring acceptance or otherwise declining to take possession of the gift, while not actually refusing it. If the officer remained adamant about refusing the gift, however, harm might be inflicted on the social relationship between officer and merchant.

I have had personal experience of some of these techniques and have witnessed others. In one case, I was offered a Christmas gift from the manager of a small, privately owned department store, a $10.00 gift certificate made out in my name. I declined to accept it, citing departmental policy, only to discover the same certificate in my mail at home a few days later, modified to have "Mrs." inserted before my name. That same Christmas I was offered a bottle of Scotch at a tavern-restaurant, declined by saying that I did not drink Scotch, and then was confronted with questions about my drinking preferences. My only escape was a lie about not drinking alcohol, which made the tavern manager uneasy in my presence thereafter. Perhaps my most effective escape was to defer acceptance of the gift until I was out of uniform or off duty, and then fail to collect it. This technique usually was successful, but it did not represent an actual refusal of the gift or denial of its acceptability. I had accepted these gifts in principle, as it were, and delayed only in taking delivery.

What if an officer does not employ such games to avoid the unauthorized gifts? What if he completely refuses, flatly spurning the offer? I had a junior officer assigned to me for training, an officer of unquestionably strong moral character who accepted the academy creed at face value. He steadfastly refused even the most minor discounts from restaurateurs, and twice became embroiled in arguments over the matter in my presence. On the second occasion, the argument actually became heated, and the inflexible officer accused the restaurant owner of trying to corrupt the police force. At that point, the officer was verbally evicted from the establishment and told not to return. The argumentative officer was called an "ass-hole" to his face and, in my opinion, had earned the label for his rigid refusal to accept an inconsequential discount. In the few months left of that inflexible but ethical officer's appropriately short, difficult, but uncorrupted, police career, he found it necessary to bring a bag lunch and eat in the car while his "corrupted" partners ate at discount in neighborhood eateries. This deviation from the "unethical" behavior of his peers served to provide the businesses of his patrol sector less on-site protection than was provided by the "corrupt" police who continued to accept meal discounts in the spirit in which they were offered. Although an isolated case does not an empirical proof make, it does illustrate one of the possible consequences of rejecting a minor gratuity, originally offered in a spirit of genuine gratitude.

ARE ALL PROFFERED GRATUITIES EXPRESSIONS OF GRATITUDE?

The position I am proposing here does not assume that all gratuities are offered in a spirit of genuine gratitude. Certainly it seems unlikely that they would be. Some givers give with ulterior motives, just as the police academy warnings have suggested. An equally serious concern is that the gifts are offered out of a sense of obligation, habit, or worse still, necessity.

In some cities the practice of gathering in gifts is undertaken with the zeal of tax collecting on a 100 percent commission basis. The merchants likewise view the visiting police officers as free-lance tax collectors.[28] In such cases, the practice of gift giving and acceptance has become so institutionalized that both parties see it as a compulsory social requirement rather than a gift freely given.[29] The police can—and occasionally do—carry self-solicitous activities too far, and merchants sometimes make official complaints.[30] Obviously such abuse of merchants is totally indefensible, and does not fall within the scope of what could properly be called a gift or gratuity.

If the motives of the giver are improper and the police officer accepts the benefit with knowledge and acceptance of those motives, then the exchange is unethical, as the police academy instructs. If the police officer solicits "freebies" and is a "moocher" then his conduct is, as Banton observed, a form of extortion.[31] That too is totally unethical, as all will recognize. But these two unethical scenarios do not exhaust all the possibilities of motives and interpretations in an exchange situation.

The ethical quality of an exchange is a relative matter, requiring some understanding of the intentions and perceptions of both the giver and the recipient. A giver can perceive his/her offer as expressing a gift in a genuine sense of appreciation, as expressing a gift from a sense of social obligation, as making an investment to secure future good will from the recipient, as placing a deposit on future services or favors, as paying off the recipient to gain an illegal advantage, or as surrendering something of value under pressure from an official who might otherwise cause the giver harm. The recipient, too, may view the object or service offered in one of several ways. He/she may accept the gift as an expression of gratitude, as a ritual offering to achieve or maintain positive social ties, as a credit against future services to be provided, or as an inducement to overlook law violations. Or, the gift can be extorted from the giver as protection from harassment or arrest, be it justified or falsely arranged. Moreover, there can be situations when the perceptions of one of the parties do not match the perceptions of the other. Some of the potential combinations may be completely innocent and fully ethical, merely innocuous, or completely improper and therefore unethical. To decide which of these combinations should be criticized and which should be condoned or even encouraged, we need to understand the motivations of both actors in the exchange and, furthermore, to decide whose perception should determine the moral character of the exchange.

The Perception of the Giver

1 *Reward Given:*   The giver is acknowledging that a significant legal and ethical service has been rendered to him/her by the police recipient. The reward is a token which serves to honor and repay that positive service.

2 *Gift Given:*   The giver is acknowledging that an ongoing social, legal, and ethical relationship exists between him/herself and the police recipient. The gift is a token that expresses appreciation for this continuing pattern of valued, reliable service rendered by the police recipient. From the point of view of the giver, it helps settle a social debt owed to the police officer.

3 *Gratuity Given:*   The giver is acknowledging that an ongoing legal and ethical relationship exists between him/herself and the law enforcement agency

of which the recipient is a member. The gratuity is a token that serves to foster and maintain that positive relationship with the recipient and other police officers. Thus the token is given to continue a pattern of reliable service rendered by the department over an extended period of time.

4 *Investment Made:* The giver is offering a token to indicate that he/she is interested in establishing a special relationship between him/herself and the law enforcement agency of which the recipient is a member and that the investment is a token which serves to initiate that preferred relationship with the recipient and other police officers. The giver hopes to place the police recipient into social debt. The benefits the giver envisions receiving in return need not be illegal or unethical but exceed normal standards of or entitlements to police services.

5 *Bribe Offered:* The giver is making a payment to acquire a specific illegal or unethical police service or to preclude the lawful exercise of a proper police function. No positive, integrative social relationship derives from the exchange. The bribe is the purchase price of the service actively sought. It is understood to conclude the immediate interaction without any further obligation by either party, although additional transactions may follow. The transaction clearly is unethical.

6 *Arrangement Initiated:* The giver is making a payment to acquire or continue ongoing illegal or unethical police services or to preclude the future lawful exercises of police functions. The payment is an installment on the purchase price of the services actively and repetitively sought. It is understood to be one in a series of illegal transactions. An integrative (although illicit) social relationship will derive from the exchange. The transactions clearly are unethical.

7 *Shakedown Paid:* The giver is coerced into offering a payment to the law enforcement official to avoid the threat of the lawful exercise of a proper police function or an unlawful abuse of police authority. No positive, integrative social relationship derives from the exchange. Future payoffs may be solicited from the giver, but the transaction is intended to conclude the immediate interaction. The transaction clearly is unethical.

The Perception of the Police Recipient

A *Reward Received:* The recipient is aware that a legal and ethical service has been rendered to the giver and that the reward is a token that serves to honor and repay that positive service. The token is accepted in a shared recognition of the significance to the giver of the service, even if that service is only part of the legal and professional expectations associated with the recipient's office.

B *Gift Received:* The recipient is aware that an ongoing social, legal, and ethical relationship exists between him/herself and the giver and that the gift is a token that serves to repay the debt that the giver feels exists and to maintain that positive social relationship. The token is accepted in a shared recognition of a pattern of reliable service over an extended period of time, even if that service is only part of the legal and professional expectations associated with the recipient's office.

C *Gratuity Received:*   The recipient is aware that an ongoing legal and ethical relationship exists between the police department and the giver and that the gratuity is a token which serves to maintain that positive social relationship. The token is accepted in a shared recognition of a pattern of reliable service over an extended period of time, even if that service is only part of the legal and professional expectations associated with the department's mission.

D *Understanding Reached:*   The police recipient accepts the token as an investment made by the giver to establish a special relationship between the giver and the law enforcement agency of which the recipient is a member. The police recipient acknowledges that he/she has been placed in social debt. The relationship he/she envisions may or may not be fully legal or ethical, but the act of acceptance is unethical because the relationship agreed to place the giver in a special, preferred status vis-a-vis access to valued police services.

E *Bribe Accepted:*   The recipient is accepting a payment to provide a specific illegal or unethical police service or to preclude the lawful exercise of a proper police function. No positive, integrative social relationship derives from the exchange. The bribe is accepted as the purchase price of the service provided. It concludes the immediate interaction without any further obligation by the recipient, although additional transactions may follow. The transaction clearly is unethical and illegal.

F *Installment Collected:*   The recipient is collecting a payment "on the pad" for ongoing illegal or unethical police services or to preclude the future lawful exercises of police functions. The payment is an installment on the purchase price of the services being provided. It is understood to initiate or continue an ongoing series of illegal transactions. An integrative (although illicit) social relationship will derive from the exchange. The transaction clearly is unethical and also is illegal.

G *Bribe Extorted:*   The recipient is seeking out a payment to provide a specific illegal or unethical police service or to preclude the lawful exercise of a proper police function under the officer's control. The officer is compelling the recipient to enter into the bargain. No positive, integrative social relationship derives from the exchange. The payment is demanded as the purchase price of the service offered. It is understood to conclude the immediate interaction without any ongoing commitment to provide the same service again, although additional transactions may follow and a coercive pad arrangement may be compelled. The transaction clearly is unethical and also is illegal.

WHOSE VIEW DETERMINES ETHICAL QUALITY?

These perceptions give rise to a dual scale of exchange-based relationships, some of which, in my view, are clearly ethical, some questionable, and some indisputably unethical. They may be appropriately reciprocal, that is, the giver and the recipient may have the same interpretation of the exchange, or they may be mismatched, which introduces an ambiguity into the exchange. Some of the more likely combinations are presented in the table opposite (Table 1).

If both police officers and gift-givers see the gift the same way, as an ethical repayment of a debt owed the police, no problems arise and no ethical violation exists. However, as Table 1 demonstrates, mismatches in perceptions will occur. I believe that the perception of the recipient toward the exchange is more critical than that of the giver in the categorization of an exchange as ethical or unethical.[32] However, the perception of the giver also is quite relevant, for it can be the source of ambiguity and future friction between the giver and recipient. That is a significant concern with which both giver and recipient must be prepared to deal if the exchange is not to generate conflict at a later time.

Although it is my opinion that the intent and perceptions of the giver are not as important to the characterization of the exchange as those of the recipient, the officer must act in a manner that emphasizes his, not the giver's, perspective. Otherwise, it is the giver's perception that will govern the exchange. The acceptance is ethical for the police officer so long as he/she takes the gift either as a ritual offering to seal a social relationship or as a true reciprocal gift for police services properly provided. If the gift is accepted as a payment for future legal or quasi-legal services, then the officer is committing him/herself to an unspecified obligation that he/she owes to no other citizen. This is a violation of the special trust that exists between the police officer and the general public. If the officer enters into the exchange with the perception that he/she does owe a special obligation to a single citizen, then that sense of exclusive obligation is what makes the acceptance unethical.

When the perceptions of the giver and the recipient do not coincide, ambiguity exists and problems arise, as actual experiences reveal. When I was still a police officer, frequently I was offered small tokens from merchants on my foot beat. Initially I interpreted these as gratuities but occasionally found it necessary to reject some offers that seemed to be investments. One lounge in particular routinely offered me free liquor, which I always declined. After I had put aside the blue uniform for other employment, I returned there only to have the offer repeated. Even after making it clear that I no longer served as a police officer, the "gift" offer stood. This suggested that the previous offers had not been intended as "investments" after all. I had been inappropriately suspicious of the owner's motives. In the case of another officer, the reverse was true. Having become accustomed to free meals at one restaurant, an officer returned there some time after being assigned to another beat. The bill for the full price was presented, and the officer did not have sufficient cash to pay. He had to summon another officer there to help him out with the payment. What he had been taking as a "gratuity" or "gift" had been an "investment" that the manager no longer had to keep up.

Another example from my own experience is especially enlightening. At one cafeteria where officers were treated to substantial discounts and occasional free meals, two officers were approached by the evening manager who was holding a city parking ticket. The evening manager asked the officers if either had written the ticket. One had. The officer concerned commented that he had not recognized the manager's car. He added that he would have given

TABLE 1

RELATIONSHIPS OF GIVER'S PERCEPTIONS TO POLICE'S PERCEPTIONS

Nominal Category	The Giver's Perception	The Police Perception
The True Reward 1-A (fully ethical)	A Reward Given: Offered in gratitude for a major contribution or heroic act by the police.	A Reward Received: Accepted in acknowledgement of the significance of the act to the giver.
The True Gift 2-B (fully ethical)	A Gift Given: Offered to express genuine gratitude for a pattern of valued, legitimate police services previously rendered to the giver.	A Gift Received: Accepted without further obligation, a debt thus having been repaid to the recipient police officer by the giver.
The Ambiguous Gift 2-C (fully ethical)	A Gift Given: Offered to express genuine gratitude for a pattern of valued, legitimate police services previously rendered to the giver.	A Gratuity Received: Accepted in a spirit of continuing reciprocal social obligation meant to maintain legal ties.
The True Gratuity 3-C (fully ethical)	A Gratuity Given: Offered to express a wish that legitimate police services provided to the giver be continued.	A Gratuity Received: Accepted in a spirit of continuing reciprocal social obligation meant to maintain legal ties.
The Uncalled Debt 3-D (unethical only for the police)	A Gratuity Given: Offered to express a wish that legitimate police services provided to the giver be continued.	An Understanding Reached: Accepted in credit for unspecified future legal, quasi-legal, or illegal favors or advantages.
The Bad Investment 4-C (ethical only for police)	An Investment Made: Offered to promote future legal advantages, secure favors, or otherwise gain the giver special status.	A Gratuity Received: Accepted in a spirit of continuing reciprocal social obligation meant to maintain legal ties.
The Understanding 4-D (unethical)	An Investment Made: Offered to promote future legal advantages, secure favors, or otherwise gain the giver special status.	An Understanding Reached: Accepted in credit for unspecified future legal, quasi-legal, or illegal favors and advantages.
The Bribe 5-E (unethical and illegal)	A Bribe Offered: Offered to exempt present illegal actions or omissions from police investigation, arrest, or interference.	A Bribe Accepted: Accepted to overlook or ignore present illegal activities or omissions of the gift-giver.
An Arrangement 6-F (unethical and illegal)	An Arrangement Made: Offered to exempt present ongoing illegal actions or omissions from police investigation, arrest, or interference.	An Installment Collected: Accepted to overlook or ignore ongoing illegal activities or omissions of the gift-giver.
The Shakedown 7-G (unethical and illegal)	A Shakedown Paid: Paid unwillingly to secure protection from police enforcement activities or threats of harassment.	A Bribe Extorted: Demanded to overlook or ignore present or future illegal activities or to avoid overt harassment.

him the opportunity to take corrective action if he had recognized it, allowing him to feed the elapsed meter. This was a common police courtesy of that department, although one easily criticized for its potential for biased application and abuse. When the manager asked if the officer "could do something about the ticket," the officer sought to reject the suggestion of after-the-fact ticket fixing. He responded by saying that, if the man would put the fine into the ticket envelope and seal it, the officer would take it to the police station when he ended his duty tour, thus saving the man postage or a special trip. The evening manager appeared annoyed, but did precisely what the officer suggested. The officer and his companion officer both left the cafeteria suspecting that their free and discounted meals there were a thing of the past. To the officers' surprise, that was not the case. After eating elsewhere for a few days, trying to avoid an anticipated unpleasant scene, one of the officers returned to the establishment while making routine rounds. The evening manager made a point of apologizing to the officer, and commented that he was concerned that his behavior had upset the police so that they were avoiding eating at his place of business. (This was an accurate perception).[33]

Initially the evening manager had viewed the exchange as an "investment." The officers' behavior had challenged that perception, making it clear that they had accepted the meals only as a "gratuity." This episode worked to the advantage of the police not only by correcting the manager's misconception but also by establishing the ethical viewpoint of the officers.

Of course, another set of circumstances might have arisen had the officers not been resolute in their perception of the intent of the earlier exchanges. Had the officers yielded to the expectations of the manager, the exchange would have been converted from a problematically ethical to an unethical one. For this reason I contend that the police officer should be responsible for determining and asserting the character and the ethical quality of any such exchange.

The police officer who allows the giver to set the ethical terms of the exchange relationship has abrogated his responsibilities. Yet as we currently educate our police officers in police academies and college classrooms, we teach them to do precisely that. The academics and trainers who assert that the expectations of the givers determines the relationship deny the individual police officer control over the character of that relationship. Worse yet, the closed-minded position that any and every gratuity is corrupting creates a psychological stigma that virtually all police officers must bear. If one free cup of coffee makes a public official corrupt, then nearly all police are corrupt. Because I refused to accept the logic of this label, I now challenge this inference. But what of the many police who accept the label and continue to violate the rule? Might we not anticipate a "self-fulfilling prophecy," an application of labeling theory to law enforcers? To return this decision to the police officers who wish to be viewed and wish to view themselves as uncorrupted, teachers and trainers need to take into account the police officers' points of view, not to eliminate them from consideration.

How is the recipient to manage the difficult situations that he or she will daily face? I contend that the police recipient first must be shown that the simple acceptance of gifts and gratuities does not ipso facto make him or her corrupt. To continue advancing that old, uncritical line of reasoning is to compel the officer to make the wrong choice in such cases. We know that most will accept the gifts and gratuities, making them, in this uncompromisingly rigid view, "corrupt." The situation parallels that described by labeling theorists. If the taker of minor gifts is defined as corrupt, the recipient who takes a gift in good faith is thereby categorized as fallen. A further decline from grace would be a small step to take, as the slippery slope analogy implies.

CONCLUSION

Can we rely upon our police to make distinctions between legitimate gratuities and unethical offers on their own or without close ethical monitoring? An argument could be made on either side of the question. Police officers are compelled to make critical ethical distinctions daily—decisions about the use of intentional violence or deadly force, discretionary decisions about arrests, searches, and seizures, decisions about intervention in domestic and personal conflicts at the fringes of the criminal law, and a hundred other matters.

To trust them with another ethical decision should not overburden their abilities to make such decisions. However, just as we do not send our police onto the streets of our communities unschooled in the prevailing public attitudes about these other ethical questions, we should not ignore the matter of minor gratuities. Those whose duty is to train, teach, and educate our criminal justice practitioners have an obligation to do so wisely, with a full understanding of the consequences of their instructions for those who are required to carry them out. It seems reasonable that the expectations we have of them and the guidance we give them be as real and realistic as the situations into which we thrust them when they are called upon to make these ethical distinctions.

The basic assumption of critics of gratuities is that the gratuity is offered to create a sense of obligation in the police officer. But it can be argued with equal plausibility that the donor gives in order to satisfy his/her own sense of obligation to the police officer. The recipient of the "tip" knows that this small bonus is a reward for services previously provided, not a payment for future services as yet unspecified. The merchants or restaurateurs offering police officers gratuities may be seen, and usually will see themselves, as expressing appreciation, not engaging in subtle corruption. Why should ethical theorists seek to portray the practice otherwise?

The current ethical instructions concerning gifts and gratuities are neither realistic nor advantageous to sincere police officers seeking to make hard ethical choices. However, if one were to educate the officer to another point of view, such as that proposed in this paper, that taking gifts with an ethical intent does not automatically corrupt, then the officer who wishes to remain untainted by corruption would be fortified in his or her own self-esteem. To generate unnecessary guilt in police faced with offers of trivial gifts and gratuities is folly. No advantage for the criminal justice system can be demonstrated in such procedural restrictions. New corruption is invited simply because corruption already is inferred from situations where no corrupting influence was intended.

NOTES

An earlier version of this paper was presented to the Academy of Criminal Justice Sciences in Orlando, Florida, in 1986. The author wishes to acknowledge and thank Drs. Charles Kaut, Dorothy Bracey, Thomas Barker, and Reed Adams for their helpful ideas but accepts personal responsibility for the heresy offered herein.

1. Aubry, Jr., *The Value of Ethics in the Police Service*, 12 POLICE 41 (1967).
2. McMullan, *A Theory of Corruption*, 9 SOC. REV. 183-84.
3. Reprinted in S. WALKER, THE POLICE IN AMERICA: AN INTRODUCTION 245 (1983).
4. Aubry, Jr., *supra* note 1, at 42.
5. Feldberg, *Gratuities, Corruption, and the Democratic Ethos of Policing: The Case of the Free Cup of Coffee*, in MORAL ISSUES IN POLICE WORK 267-76 (F. Elliston & M. Feldberg eds. 1985).
6. *See, e.g.*, Bracey, *A Functional Approach to Police Corruption* JOHN JAY COLLEGE CRIMINAL JUSTICE CENTER MONOGRAPHS No. 1 (1976); *Police Corruption in Britain and America: A Functional Approach* 1 POLICE STUD. 16-23 (1978); Corruption as a Response to Legal Innovation, paper presented at the annual meeting of the American Anthropological Association, Washington, D.C. (Dec. 5, 1980) *See also* Kaut, *Utang Na Loob: A System of Contractual Obligation Among Tagalos*, 17 SW. J. OF ANTHROPOLOGY 256 (1961), and E. LEACH, CULTURE AND COMMUNICATION: THE LOGIC BY WHICH SYMBOLS ARE CONNECTED (1976).
7. *See, e.g.*, Stoddard, *The "Informal Code" of Police Deviancy: A Group Approach to Blue-Coat Crime*, 59 J. OF CRIM. L., CRIMINOLOGY, & POLICE SCI. 203, 205 (1968), AND T. BARKER & J. ROEBUCK, AN EMPIRICAL TYPOLOGY OF POLICE CORRUPTION 21-24 (1973).
8. Cohen, *Exploiting Police Authority*, 5 CRIM. JUSTICE ETHICS, Summer/Fall 1986, at 23.
9. J. Kleinig, The Slippery Slope Problem, lecture 23, at 1-3 (1987) unpublished lecture notes, John Jay College of Criminal Justice, The City University of New York.
10. *Id.* at 1.
11. Homan, *Social Behavior As Exchange*, 63 AM. J. SOC. 606 (1958).
12. E. LEACH, *supra* note 6, at 6.
13. A legitimate and compelling argument can still be raised against the practice if the police ignore non-givers and frequent only those commercial establishments that offer gratuities. Proper discipline and supervision can overcome the tendency to gravitate toward donors. For example, some police departments have policies that require police officers to select different eating places each day, that prohibit loitering at any single place of business, or that require officers to visit each open business during his/her rounds.
14. M. MAUSS, THE GIFT: FORMS AND FUNCTIONS OF EXCHANGE IN ARCHAIC SOCIETIES 63 (I. Cunnison trans. 1967).
15. Both John Kleinig in a personal letter (Oct. 5, 1987) and an anonymous reviewer of an earlier version of this paper have made these suggestions.
16. Bracey, *supra* note 6, *A Functional Approach to Police Corruption*.
17. Kaut, *supra* note 6.
18. J. Kleinig, *supra* note 9.
19. Proponents of the more restrictive deontological ethical posture occasionally associated with the criticism of gratuity acceptance are unlikely to be mollified. Even if the acceptance of gratuities had only socially positive consequences, the fact that they constituted unauthorized enrichment would nonetheless make their acceptance wrong.
20. Feldberg, *supra* note 5, at 268-70.
21. THE KNAPP COMMISSION, THE KNAPP COMMISSION REPORT ON POLICE CORRUPTION 65-66 (1972).
22. *See, e.g.*, Fishman, *Measuring Police Corruption*, JOHN JAY COLLEGE CRIMINAL JUSTICE CENTER MONOGRAPHS No. 10, (1978), and R. Kania, Discipline in Small Police Forces: An Ethnographic Examination of Bureaucratic Social Control (1982) (Ph.D. diss., U. Va).

23. M. Banton, The Policeman in the Community 58, 223 (1964).

24. I am unable to find any.

25. R. Kania, *supra* note 22, at 63.

26. D. Black, Police Encounters and Social Organization: An Observation Study (1968) (Ph.D diss., U. Mich.).

27. A. Reiss, Jr., The Police and the Public, 159ff. (1971).

28. The motion picture *Freebie and the Bean* (1974) (edited and produced by Richard Rush, screenplay by Robert Kaufman) illustrates most vividly a heavy-handed, mooching police officer's abuse of merchants.

29. Cohen, *supra* note 8, at 30.

30. Meyer, Jr., *A Descriptive Study of Police Corruption,* 40 Police Chief, Aug. 1973, at 38-41.

31. M. Banton, *supra* note 23, at 221.

32. An anonymous reviewer of an earlier version of this paper remarked in opposing my arguments, "A policy of no gratuities is the only workable policy because it requires a reform only of the police and not of society." Turning this line of reasoning to my advantage, police policy makers have some control over the indoctrination of the police and virtually none over the indoctrination of the public at large. This being so, it makes more sense to view the gift as the honest giver offers it, and to train our police accordingly.

33. Michael Banton reports a similar scenario in which "a man . . . because he had given the police free meals, thought he could ignore the parking regulations; he was promptly disabused by this idea, and officers stopped visiting his premises." *See supra* note 23, at 58.

POLICE MISCONDUCT AND MINORITY CITIZENS: EXPLORING KEY ISSUES

Kim Michelle Lersch
University of South Florida, Florida

This manuscript provides a review of the literature concerning key issues associated with acts of police misconduct and minority citizens in the United States. First, the issue of what types of behaviors are defined as 'police misconduct' is explored. Second, the level of police misconduct is discussed. Finally, the question of whether or not minority citizens are targeted for harassment and abuse is addressed.

Keywords: Police misconduct; minority citizens; police performance; excessive force

Because of the extensive world-wide press coverage, the very mention of the name 'Rodney King' elicits images of the worst in police-minority citizen relations: A group of white officers savagely beating an unarmed black male citizen. In the aftermath of the Rodney King incident, virtually every police agency in the country came under both internal and external scrutiny in how its officers interacted with minority citizens. The Christopher Commission, in its review of the practices of the Los Angeles Police Department, uncovered a number of disturbing trends. The Commission concluded that local policing was not applied in a fair and non-discriminatory way for all citizens of Los Angeles. Furthermore, while African Americans were found to be the primary targets of abuse in contacts with police officers, Latinos, Asians, and homosexuals were also victims (Independent Commission on the Los Angeles Police Department, 1991).

Kim Michelle Lersch, "Police Misconduct and Minority Citizens: Exploring Key Issues" (as appeared in *The Justice Professional,* Vol. 12, No. 1, 1999, pp. 65–82). Reprinted with permission.

The highly publicized statements of officer Mark Furman, a former detective with the Los Angeles Police Department, added fuel to the police/ minority citizen controversy. Coming just a few short years after the Rodney King incident and the civil unrest that followed in Los Angeles and other major cities in the United States, Furman, in a taped interview, admitted to assaulting and using racial slurs against African Americans and Latino citizens. While officials of the Los Angeles Police Department dismissed Furman's comments, stating his actions and attitudes were unrepresentative of the majority of officers affiliated with the Los Angeles department, others have disagreed. As stated by Hatchett, (1996: 17), "for every highly publicized case of police brutality against blacks like Fuhrman's, there are hundreds more which never get beyond the back pages of the newspaper or are not reported at all."

The relationship between the police and minorities, especially African Americans, has been marked by a long history of violence and mistrust. From 1920 through 1932, white police officers killed 54 percent of the 749 African Americans killed by white persons in the south and 68 percent of those killed elsewhere (Myrdal, 1944). Further, in an analysis of 76 race riots occurring between 1913 and 1963, the immediate precipitating event in 20 percent of the uprisings was the killing of or interference with African American men by white police officers. This percentage increased dramatically in 1964 through 1967: Seven of the 14 major riots that occurred in that period could be traced directly to white policemen's misconduct against African American citizens (Feagin and Hahn, 1973). In an analysis of the civil unrest that marked the 1960s era, The National Advisory Commission on Civil Disorders (1968) concluded that the actions of urban police were a cause of the revolts occurring in major cities. The Kerner Commission report, as it is commonly know, further cited the widespread belief among African Americans in the occurrence of policy brutality and a separate system of justice, one for minorities and one for whites.

Over the past decade, civil disturbances sparked by a police–citizen encounter have continued to plague our urban areas. A riot broke out in Miami, Florida in 1989 after a police officer shot and killed an African American motorcyclist. In 1992, uprisings occurred in Los Angeles, Atlanta, and other major U.S. cities as a result of four white police officers' acquittal in the videotaped beating of Rodney King. Finally, in 1996, the city of Saint Petersburg, Florida experienced a disturbance after a white police officer fatally shot an African American male during a traffic stop.

These incidents and trends, while compelling, do not provide a clear answer to the research question explored here: Are minority citizens systematically targeted for harassment and abuse by law enforcement officials? Despite the efforts of police practitioners and scholarly evaluators to answer questions concerning police misconduct and minority citizens, it is surprising how little agreement exists in our basic knowledge in this area. There is little consensus of opinion as to what, exactly, police misconduct is. When does the use of force become excessive?

There are definitional differences, often along lines of race, as to what sorts of behaviors fall under the definitions of 'police misconduct' and 'excessive force.' For example, in a poll conducted by *Time* magazine in the wake of the Rodney King incident, while 92 percent of the African Americans surveyed felt that excessive force had been used against King, only 72 percent of the Caucasians voiced a similar belief (Lacayo, 1992). It is surprising that, in what many would consider as one of the most blatant examples of police use of excessive force, not all agree that the actions of the police were questionable.

The *Time* magazine poll illustrates a very important issue in the evaluation of police practices: We do not all agree on basic concepts associated with police behavior. One cannot have a meaningful discussion of the problem of police misconduct without a clear grasp of the relevant issues and basic definitions. Therefore, it is the purpose of this manuscript to explore key issues concerning police misconduct and minority citizens. Specifically, the following questions will be discussed:

1. What types of behaviors are defined as 'police misconduct?'
2. What is the level of police misconduct?
3. Are minority citizens targeted for harassment and abuse?

WHAT IS POLICE MISCONDUCT?

Before entering into a discussion of questionable police practices, one must first define what sort of behaviors constitute police misconduct. While this may seem to be a relatively elementary issue, no clear definition exists. At the most basic level, misconduct by law enforcement officials has been defined as 'improper and/or illegal action(s) and/or conduct by the officer (Hatchett, 1996). However, this broad definition is virtually useless. The police may have one definition of what sorts of behaviors are 'improper,' the courts another, and citizens' viewpoints may be shaped by race and/or social class (Adams, 1995). Further, what is 'improper conduct' in one situation may be judged as proper in another.

The Issue of Force

The ability to use force is central to the role of police officers. Some researchers have argued that it is the use of coercive force that distinguishes the field of policing from all other professions (Pate and Fridell, 1993). No other public service agency or group of professionals has the legal authority to use coercive force (Walker, 1992). As phrased by Klockars (1985: 9–10), "No police anywhere has ever existed, nor is it possible to conceive of a genuine police ever existing, that does not claim a right to compel other people forcibly to do something. If it did not claim such a right, it would not be a police."

Even in the area of the use of force, it is difficult to find definitions that are unambiguous. Almost 30 years ago, Bittner (1970) provided a strong critique concerning the lack of a clear definition as to what, exactly, excessive force is. Calling discussions of the lawful use of force 'meaningless,' Bittner further stated that "our expectation that policemen will use force, coupled by our refusals to state clearly what we mean by it (aside from sanctimonious homilies) smacks of more than a bit of perversity." Now almost three decades have passed, and we still do not know what excessive force is.

Legal Definitions of Excessive Force

While the ability to use force is intrinsic to an officers' role as a social control agent of the state, this authority is not granted without limitations. There are legal constraints on the ability to use force. According to the Supreme Court, the use of force at the time of arrest must be "objectively reasonable" in consideration of all the "facts and circumstances of each particular case, including the severity of the crime at issue, whether the suspect poses an immediate threat to the safety of the officers or others, and whether he is actively resisting arrest or attempting to evade arrest by flight *(Graham v. Connor*, 490 U.S. 386, 1989)." The Supreme Court went on to recognize the fact that the determination of reasonableness must account for the fact that officers are often forced to make split-second decisions—"in circumstances that are tense, uncertain, and rapidly evolving—about the amount of force that is necessary in a particular situation." This clarification adds ambiguity—one must determine the reasonableness of an officer's actions in light of the 'heat of the moment,' so to speak. An officer may be fearful for his or her life as a situation unfolds, and this emotional state will impact the determination of how much force, if any, is necessary to calm a tense situation.

While the courts may assert that this definition of excessive force is useful in evaluating the actions of officer, a problem arises when judging cases in which the facts are unclear (Adams, 1995). It is the extremely exceptional case that is caught on videotape as a situation unfolds; most determinations of whether or not an officer's actions constituted the use of excessive force are made based on the statements of witnesses, the complainant, and the officer, which may or may not agree. Further, as illustrated in the Rodney King incident, even when a situation is caught on videotape, evaluations concerning the appropriateness of an officers' actions may not be in agreement.

Departmental Rules and Regulations

If legal definitions of excessive force are somewhat ambiguous, what about departmental definitions? Departments may develop guidelines and directives designed to limit discretion and to let individual officers know what types of behaviors will not be tolerated. These policies may be met with varying levels of success. In a classic study of the effectiveness of restrictive departmental guidelines on the use of deadly force, Fyfe (1979) reported that after the New York City police department had established clear guidelines in the use of firearms in 1972, the mean number of firearm discharges declined by 29.1 percent. Further, the most significant decline occurred in the more controversial category of shootings that involved no direct threat to the life of the officer or other citizens.

While departmental rules and regulations may be successful in some situations, there are limits to their effectiveness. As discussed by Walker (1992), it is virtually impossible to write a rule that covers every situation that an officer may encounter. Even if this were possible, the overall effectiveness of the officer would suffer because he/she would become overwhelmed trying to comply with rules and regulations governing every action. As a result, policies are inherently vague, designed to cover a broad range of situations.

For example, Klockars (1995: 22) offers the following as a comprehensive policy on the police use of force: "Police officers shall work in ways that minimize the use of force." While this policy provides a seemingly clear departmental philosophy concerning the use of force, the directive would not be especially helpful in trying to decide whether or not an officer acted inappropriately in a specific situation. Just as legal definitions of excessive force are inherently ambiguous, departmental guidelines are also vague and unclear.

Even if an explicit rule is in place, compliance is another issue. In an environment of lax supervision, officers may not be held accountable for their behavior. The Christopher Commission recognized that the problem of the use of excessive force in the Los Angeles Police Department was a problem of leadership and supervision of the front line officers. A rule is useless if it is not enforced.

Citizen Perceptions and Definitions

Research has consistently demonstrated that, regardless of race, the majority of the general public views the police in a favorable light. However, as discussed by Flanagan and Vaughn (1995), these perceptions vary greatly based on the characteristics of both citizens and of neighborhoods, and the frequency and tone of citizen–police contacts. For example, African Americans and other minority citizens consistently provide lower evaluations of their local police than do Caucasians. Minority citizens have historically viewed the police as oppressors of rights and freedoms as opposed to guardians of liberties (Flanagan and Vaughn, 1995; Locke, 1995). Minorities are also less likely to voice support for the use of force by police (Blumenthal *et al.*, 1972; Williams, Thomas and Singh, 1983).

While research suggests that minorities are more critical of their local police than are Caucasians, racial differences also exist in the definition of what sort of behaviors constitute 'police misconduct,' especially with respect to the use of force. As phrased by Flanagan and Vaughn (1995: 125), "White residents in the suburbs have a different idea of police use of force than inner city African Americans." Locke (1995: 134) notes that "in some quarters, any unwarranted or unwelcome police conduct may constitute brutality." The use of racial slurs, profane or abusive language, and other forms of verbal abuse have also been defined as 'police brutality' by many citizens, especially among minority citizens (Adams, 1995 ; Locke, 1995; President's Commission on Law Enforcement and Administration of Justice, 1967; Worden, 1995).

Beyond Excessive Force: Non-violent Acts of Misconduct

While little uniformity exists between the courts, police agencies, and the general public in the definition of what sorts of behaviors constitute excessive force, there is even less consistency in the evaluations of non-violent acts of misconduct associated with harassment, surveillance, and overall demeanor. With respect to the relations between police and minority citizens, research addressing discriminatory practices in the areas of arrest and the use of deadly force are plentiful (see, for example, Black, 1980; Fyfe, 1982; Petersilia, 1983; Smith, Visher and Davidson, 1984). However, few studies have been conducted that focus on police/citizen interactions in which no criminal offense was committed, no arrest made, and no acts of violence recorded (Browning *et al.*, 1994). Again, part of the problem is the lack of a clear operationalization of what, exactly, police misconduct is. One citizen may perceive an officer's actions as totally acceptable, while another may view the same behaviors as threatening and obnoxious.

As an example, in a previous research study I analyzed the citizen allegations of misconduct that had been filed with the internal affairs office in large police agency. Complaints of non-violent harassment were the most common type of allegation, accounting for almost half of the citizen complaints (49.7 percent). In one of the complaints included in this category a citizen had alleged that, during the course of a routine traffic stop, an officer had rested his hand on his service revolver. The citizen filing the complaint of misconduct felt that this action was extremely intimidating and involved an unnecessary display of force. There was no indication that the officer had spoken in a threatening manner, nor had he been disrespectful to the citizen in any way. However, this behavior resulted in an official report of police misconduct against the officer, for which he received counseling. While in this case the particular citizen was very upset by the behavior of the officer, another citizen may not have even noticed the resting hand on the revolver.

WHAT IS THE LEVEL OF POLICE MISCONDUCT? THE COUNTING OF THE UNDEFINED

The lack of a clear operationalization of the terms 'police brutality' and 'police misconduct' clouds the interpretation of empirical studies of the phenomenon. No one knows exactly how many incidents of police misconduct occur. This issue is further complicated when researchers attempt to use various research methodologies to count incidents of police misconduct. A number of indicators, including the use of observational studies, analyses of citizen complaints, and citizen surveys have been used. While the use of multiple indicators is an advancement, each data source has its own unique measurement problems. Observers may differ on the definition of what behaviors constitute violent police conduct, citizens may file frivolous complaints, and survey results may be affected by recent highly publicized events.

Observational Studies

In this type of data collection technique, trained observers ride along with the officers, taking notes on their actions. These types of studies are very time consuming and expensive, and there is some debate whether or not the behavior of the officer is affected by the presence of the field observer.

Probably the most well known observational study of police misconduct was conducted by Albert J. Reiss Jr. (1968). In this analysis, trained individuals in three cities observed police–citizen encounters for seven days a week in a seven week period in the summer of 1966. Reiss tried to maintain a high level of reliability in the classification of the incidents as violent, providing clear conditions as to what actions by the officer constituted the improper or unnecessary use of force. A total of 36 different field observers were used, some of whom were former police officers (who may have a different perception of what use of force actions are improper or unnecessary). Even though Reiss tried to ensure consistency of classification, when a panel of experts reviewed the incidents, only 20 of the 37 incidents that Reiss' field observers judged to involve improper use of force were classified in a similar manner (President's Commission on Law Enforcement and Administration of Justice, 1967).

Citizen Complaints

Citizen complaints of misconduct have been labeled as "one of the most badly abused police-based statistics" (West, 1988: 113). Critics have pointed to both the underreporting and overreporting of allegations of misconduct. Individuals may choose not to report acts of misconduct for a number of reasons: lack of confidence with the abilities of the police to monitor their own; complaint procedures that are intimidating, complicated, or otherwise difficult to use; or possibly, if the citizen has a history of criminal activity, the citizen may not wish to draw any additional attention to him or her self. Walker and Bumphus (1992) reported that only one-third of the people who believe that they have been mistreated by police officers pursue the matter by filing an official complaint.

While some critics oppose the use of citizen complaints as a measure of police practices because of under reporting of incidents, over reporting may also be a problem. Citizens may define misconduct more broadly than the departmental definition of wrongdoing. Further, some complainants may be displeased with how an officer performed his or her duties, when in fact the actions of the officer were legally constrained (for example, "I wanted the officer to make an arrest and he refused"). While some citizens may be fearful of filing an official complaint of officer wrongdoing, others may file unfounded, frivolous complaints. Furthermore, some complaints may be made with the hope of securing an upper hand in the plea bargaining process (Adams, 1995).

Finally, citizen allegations of misconduct may be a reflection of confidence in the complaint process itself (Pate and Fridell, 1993). Departments with excellent community relations may have higher rates of citizen complaints because people feel more comfortable reporting acts of misconduct to the agency.

Citizen Surveys

Many of the problems associated with citizen surveys may be found in any basic undergraduate research methods text. A survey is only as good as its design, and responses may be influenced by the sequencing of questions, language that is unclear, or statements that are biased (Taylor, 1994). Further, the method by which the respondents were selected for inclusion may also influence the survey results.

In the special case of surveys soliciting opinions about police misconduct, opinions may be greatly influenced by highly publicized events, such as the beating of Rodney King, the assault of migrant workers after a high speed chase in California, or the death of a young black motorist at the hands of the police in a Pittsburgh suburb. For example, in the wake of the Rodney King incident, a Gallop Poll was conducted in which respondents were asked the following question: "Do you think there is any police brutality in your area or not?" Thirty five percent of the citizens surveyed answered the question 'yes,' which was an increase of nearly four times the number of similar responses when the question was posed in a 1965 survey (Maguire *et al.*, 1993, cited in Flanagan and Vaughn, 1995). It cannot be known whether the citizens were reacting to the highly publicized Rodney King incident or their perceptions of the level of police brutality had, in fact, increased fourfold independent of the King beating.

ARE MINORITY CITIZENS TARGETED FOR HARASSMENT AND ABUSE?

In many forms of police misconduct, officers are able to select their victim. Citizens who find themselves victims of police misconduct tend to be those who have limited credibility and/or are defined as marginal by the general public (Kappeler, Sluder and Alpert, 1994). Therefore, citizens with less power and fewer resources, such as minority group members, would be more likely to experience police misconduct. In the next section, this issue is explored. Recognizing the limitations of the various research methodologies used to explore police misconduct, the results of observational studies, analyses of citizen complaints, and survey findings are presented and discussed. While the results of observational studies provide mixed answers to the research question posed here, the findings from analyses of citizen complaints and surveys are quite clear. Minority citizens are more likely to file complaints of police misconduct and to provide lower overall evaluations of police practices.

Results of Observational Studies

In the previously discussed observational study conducted in the summer of 1966 by Reiss, a total of 3,826 encounters were observed with 37 of these encounters classified as violent. In the violent encounters, a total of 54 policemen were involved, 45 of whom were white. Reiss found that the rate for the use of excessive force against white citizens was twice the rate for blacks. Further, he concluded that police officers were more likely to use force against members of their own race (Reiss, 1968).

Friedrich (1980), in an analysis of Reiss' original data, reported that while rates of force against white and African American citizens were almost identical, African Americans were more often treated with reasonable force and less often treated with excessive force. The findings of the multiple regression analysis suggested that the characteristics of the citizen in terms of sex, age, socioeconomic class, and race had minimal influence. While Friedrich noted a slight tendency for white patrol officers described as more prejudiced in their attitudes toward blacks to use more force against African American citizens, he concluded that overall, citizen race did not have much of an impact on an officers' decision to use force.

Cruse and Rubin (1973) employed four trained observers who rated the behavior of twelve patrolmen in their contacts with 1,400 citizens in the city of Miami, Florida. The findings suggested that while officers may have voiced severe antiblack sentiments, no appreciable difference was detected in the behavior of the officer whether he or she was working in a predominantly African American or white zone. Further, the researchers reported that older, more experienced officers of either race were found to be more sympathetic and controlling when interacting with members of their own race. Cruse and Rubin noted that the number of citizens the officer encountered had a greater impact on the officer's reported level of stress than did the individual characteristics of the citizen (such as age, race, gender or demeanor).

Worden (1995), in an analysis of data collected for the Police Service Study during the summer of 1977, reported that the police were more likely to use force in their interactions with minority citizens. These results were based on reports from trained observers in 24 police departments in Rochester, New York, Saint Louis, Missouri and Tampa-Saint Petersburg, Florida. In a bivariate analysis of 5,688 police–citizen encounters, the use of both reasonable force and improper force was more likely if the citizen was black, male, and over the age of eighteen. Using multinomial logit analysis, Worden reported that even when controlling for demeanor and the presence of physical resistance, the effect of the race of the citizen was still a significant predictor. Worden suggested that officers may be, on average, more likely to use a coercive approach when dealing with African American suspects than when in their encounters with white citizens.

Results of Analyses of Citizen Complaints

The majority of law enforcement agencies have some type of procedure by which citizens may file complaints against officers (for a discussion of various complaint systems, see Perez and Muir, 1995). In a climate of favorable police-community relations, citizens should feel free to report questionable behavior and allegations of misconduct by officers to the appropriate authorities without fear of reprisal or retaliation (Cox, 1996). Unfortunately, this is not always the case, especially for minority citizens.

George Holliday was the man who videotaped the infamous Rodney King beating. Both Mr. Holliday and Paul King, brother of Rodney, attempted to report the incident to the Los Angeles Police Department. Neither one succeeded. When Paul King asked to file a complaint of excessive force, he was asked by a sergeant whether or not he had ever been in trouble. Mr. Holliday felt that the officer he spoke with was so uninterested in the videotape and his allegations of police misconduct that he turned to the media.

The Christopher Commission, in its review of the practices of the Los Angeles Police Department, reported that the complaint system was in fact skewed against complainants. Noting uncooperative intake officers, long waits, and inadequate investigations, the Commission called for a major overhaul of the disciplinary system. The Commission also observed that in many of the divisions heavily populated by Latino residents, there was often no Spanish speaking officer available to assist with citizens wishing to file a complaint (Report of the Independent Commission, 1991).

In spite of the fact that official complaints were discouraged, between 1987 and 1990 a total of 4,400 complaints of misconduct were filed against the Los Angeles Police Department. While black citizens in the city of Los Angeles comprise only 13 percent of the city population, 41 percent of these official complaints against officers were filed by blacks (Rohrlich and Merina, 1991).

The overrepresentation of minority complainants is not a phenomenon exclusive to the Los Angeles Police Department. Several studies of citizen allegations of misconduct have found that minority citizens, especially blacks, are more likely to file complaints against the police (Pate and Fridell, 1993; Kerstetter, Rasinski and Heiert, 1996; Wagner, 1980). In an analysis of the complaints filed against the a large police department located in the Southeastern United States, Lersch (1998) reported that while minority citizens accounted for 22.2 percent of the city population, 50.5 percent of the complaints against the agency were filed by minorities. Additionally, minority citizens were more likely to accuse officers of excessive force, and the complaints were more likely to stem from a proactive police initiated contact.

Results of Citizen Surveys

Since the advent of public opinion polls in the 1960s, minorities have consistently rated police performance lower than Caucasian Americans (Cox, 1996; Flanagan and Vaughn, 1995; Smith, Graham and Adams, 1991; Walker, 1992). In one of the early studies of citizen ratings of the police, Bayley and Mendelsohn (1969) reported that non-Caucasians rated the performance of the police at a lower level than did Caucasians, even when controlling for age, gender, and other background influences. According to a 1970 Harris poll, only a fifth of the African American respondents felt that local police officers applied the law equally; 62 percent felt cops were against African Americans; 73 percent felt their local law enforcement agents were dishonest; and 67 percent felt police officers were more concerned with injuring African Americans than in preventing criminal acts (Feagin and Hahn, 1973).

Other more recent polls suggest that African Americans were more likely than Caucasians to report harassment and to know someone who was a victim of police misconduct (Bessent and Tayler, 1991; Kappeler, Sluder and Alpert, 1994; for an excellent review of recent public opinion polls concerning the police, see Flanagan and Vaughn, 1995). A survey conducted by the Joint Center for Political and Economic Studies in April, 1996, reported that 43 percent of African Americans considered "police brutality and harassment of African-Americans a serious problem" in their own communities (Johnson, 1997). In a Gallup poll conducted in September, 1995, African American citizens were three times were likely to report that the police in their community treated blacks worse than whites (Johnson, 1997). Browning *et al.* (1994) reported that while 46.6 percent of the African Americans sampled reported being "personally hassled by the police," only 9.6 percent of the white citizens reported a similar experience. Further, 66 percent of blacks reported knowing someone who was watched by the police when he/she had done nothing wrong, compared to only 12.5 percent of whites.

African Americans are more likely to report suspicion and lack of confidence in the practices of the police than are white citizens. In a poll conducted by the Princeton Survey Research Associates in August of 1995, 53 percent of blacks felt that the "kind of improper behavior by police described on the Fuhrman tapes (racism and falsification of evidence)" was common among their local police. Only 15 percent of the white citizens surveyed reported a similar belief. Finally, in the area of confidence in the police, while only 8 percent of whites reported little or no confidence in the police, 35 percent of the African Americans reported a similar evaluation (Johnson, 1997).

DISCUSSION

It was the purpose of this manuscript to explore a number of issues concerning police misconduct, especially with respect to minority citizens. Unfortunately, few clear answers have emerged. If one considers the number of journal articles, books, reports, media accounts and coverage, there are literally thousands of written works that discuss police behavior. In spite of both the importance of the topic and the level of public interest, we still do not have a grasp on even the most basic of issues concerning police misconduct. What types of behaviors are defined as 'police misconduct?' That depends on whom you ask. What is the level of police misconduct? We truly do not know. Just as researchers do not have a clear and accurate count of the number of crimes committed in this country, we will probably never know how many acts of police misconduct against citizens truly occur.

With respect to the development of definitions that characterize exactly what behaviors constitute police misconduct, this is another task that is virtually impossible. Every situation is different, and actors will define and evaluate the behavior of the police based on their own personal status. The officers at the scene, the department as a whole, the community (which is not a homogeneous entity), the courts, and the media may all have different evaluations of the same behavior. Furthermore, the criteria of "I'll know it when I see it" is useless when trying to develop guidelines for patrol officers in their interactions with citizens. And, as illustrated in the case of Rodney King, many people did not 'know it when they saw it.'

In the exploration of whether or not minority citizens are targeted for harassment and abuse, one clear point emerges: Minority citizens *perceive* poor treatment at the hands of police, and when given the opportunity to voice their displeasure, minority citizens do. Minority citizens are consistently more likely to file complaints of misconduct against police officers and, since the advent of public opinion polls, have provided lower evaluations of police practices and services than have white citizens. Does this trend indicate that police treat minority citizens differently, or is this a reflection of definitional differences as to what sorts of behaviors constitute police misconduct? While it may be somewhat surprising (and frustrating) to some, the current state of the research does not provide conclusive evidence of systematic bias and abuse.

In a discussion of a possible correlation between the race of the officer, the race of the citizen, and incidents of abuse of authority, Ogletree *et al.* (1995) state that "The authors of this book concede that there is little hard data to support the extensive anecdotal evidence that the worst incidents of police abuse, and the majority of cases of police abuse, are committed by white officers on nonwhite citizens. Nonetheless, we stand by the assertion. Police abuse in America largely consists of white officers abusing minority citizens (1995: 71)." This statement asserts what many feel is common knowledge: Despite the lack of data, everyone knows that minorities experience differential treatment at the hands of law enforcement officers. However, in a discussion by Locke (1995) on the topic of persons of color and police abuse of force, the only indisputable evidence concerning the use of force and minority citizens is that minorities are disproportionately shot at by the police. As phrased by Locke (1995: 139), "Beyond this finding, there is little that researchers can assert empirically about the police use of appropriate and excessive force that is not in dispute."

In the discussion of various observational studies presented in this manuscript, the results concerning police misconduct and minorities were inconclusive. While Worden (1995) suggested that officers may be more likely to use force with African American suspects, Friedrich (1980) found a weak relationship at best. Reiss (1968) and Cruse and Rubin (1973) reported that officer behavior, whether sympathetic or coercive, was more of an intraracial phenomenon.

The purpose of this manuscript is not to dismiss police misconduct against minority citizens as a myth. Obviously, there are serious community relations problems between the police and minority communities. Walker (1992) argues that even the term "police–community relations" is a euphemism for police–race relations. The police have not had a proud history in their relations with racial minorities in this country. Although it is an arguable point, many would agree that when compared to officers employed in the 1960s, contemporary police are better trained, educated, and less likely to abuse their power (Brown, 1988). However, the legacy of the past remains.

It may be that the manner in which police interactions are socially constructed depends on an individuals' frame of reference, which may include personal experience, observations of the experiences of others, and anecdotes that have been passed down from one generation to the next. Middle-class whites may not only have a different definition of police use of force than inner-city African Americans, but their frame of reference by which to categorize interactions with the police may very well be different. Individuals who have been brought up with images of 'Officer Friendly' may be more likely to dismiss an officer's rudeness as someone having a bad day, while those who have been brought up to fear the actions of the police may classify an officer's terse actions as threatening, aggressive, and deliberate. The perceptions of misconduct are just as damaging as actual misdeeds, and it is clear that police agencies still have some work to do to correct their image.

REFERENCES

Adams, K. (1995). Measuring the prevalence of police abuse of force. In W.A. Geller and H. Toch (Eds.), *And justice for all: Understanding and controlling police abuse of force* (pp. 61–98). Washington, D.C.: Police Executive Research Forum.

Bayley, D.H. and Mendelsohn, H. (1969). *Minorities and the police: Confrontation in America.* New York, NY: Free Press.

Bessent, A.E. and Tayler, L. (1991, June 2). Police brutality—Is it no problem? *Newsday,* p. 5.

Bittner, E. (1970). *The functions of the police in modern society.* Chevy Chase, MD: National Institute of Mental Health.

Black, D. (1980). *The manners and customs of the police.* New York, NY: Academic Press.

Blumenthal, M.D., Kahn, R.L., Andrews, F.M. and Head, K.B. (1972). *Justifying violence: Attitudes of American men.* Ann Arbor, MI: University of Michigan.

Brown, M.K. (1988). *Working the street: Police discretion and the dilemmas of reform.* New York, NY: Russell Sage Foundation.

Browning, S.L., Cullen, F.T., Cao, L. Kapache, R. and Stevenson, T.J. (1994). Race and getting hassled by the police: A research note. *Police Studies,* 17, 1–12.

Cox, S.M. (1996). *Police: Practices, perspectives, problems.* Boston, MA: Allyn and Bacon.

Cruse, D. and Rubin, J. (1973). Police behavior. *Journal of Psychiatry and Law,* 1, 215–229.

Feagin, J.R. and Hahn, H. (1973). *Ghetto revolts: The politics of violence in American cities.* New York, NY: The MacMillan Company.

Flanagan, T.J. and Vaughn, M.S. (1995). Public opinion about police abuse of force. In W.A. Geller and H. Toch (Eds.) *And justice for all: Understanding and controlling police abuse of force* (pp. 113–132). Washington, D.C.: Police Executive Research Forum.

Friedrich, R.J. (1980). Police use of force: Individuals, situations, and organizations. *The Annals of the American Academy of Political and Social Science,* 452, 82–97.

Fyfe, J.J. (1981). Who shoots? A look at office race and police shooting. *Journal of Police Science and Administration,* 7, 309–323.

Fyfe, J.J. (1981). Blind justice: Police shootings in Memphis. *Journal of Criminal Law and Criminology,* 73, 707–722.

Graham v. Connor (1989). 490 U.S. 386; 109 S.Ct. 1865.

Hatchett, D. (1996, January). Bad attitudes, bad race relations, bad cops. *The Crisis,* 103, 17–23.

Independent Commission of the Los Angeles Police Department (1991). *Report of the Independent Commission on the Los Angeles Police Department.* Los Angeles, CA: International Creative Management.

Johnson, J. (1997, September). Americans' view on crime and law enforcement: Survey findings. *National Institute of Justice Journal,* 223, 9–14.

Kappeler, V.A., Sluder, R.D. and Alpert, G.P. (1994). *Forces of deviance: Understanding the dark side of policing.* Prospect Heights, IL: Waveland Press.

Kerstetter, W.A., Rasinski, K.A. and Heiert, C.L. (1996). The impact of race on the investigation of excessive force allegations against police. *Journal of Criminal Justice,* 24, 1–15.

Klockars, C. (1985). *The idea of police.* Beverly Hills, CA: Sage.

Lacayo, R. (1992, May). Anatomy of an acquittal. *Time,* 30–32.

Lersch, K.M. (1998). Predicting citizen race in allegations of misconduct against the police. *Journal of Criminal Justice,* 25, 1–11.

Locke, H.G. (1995). "The color of law and the issue of color: Race and the abuse of police power." In W.A. Geller and H. Toch, (Eds.) *And justice for all: Understanding and controlling police abuse of force* (pp. 133–150). Washington, D.C.: Police Executive Research Forum.

Maguire, K. Pastore, A.L. and Flanagan, T. J. (eds.) (1993). *Bureau of Justice statistics sourcebook of criminal justice statistics—1992.* Washington, D.C.: U.S. Government Printing Office.

Myrdal, G. (1944). *An American dilemma.* New York, NY: Harper and Brothers.

National Advisory Commission on Civil Disorders (1968). *Report of the National Advisory Commission on Civil Disorders.* New York, NY: Bantam Books.

Ogletree, C.J., Jr., Prosser, M., Smith, A. and Talley, W. Jr. (1995). *Beyond the Rodney King story: An investigation of police conduct in minority communities.* Boston, MA: Northeastern University Press.

Pate, A.M. and Fridell, L.A. (1993). *Police use of force: Official reports, citizen complaints, and legal consequences.* Washington, D.C.: Police Foundation.

Perez, D.W. and Muir, W.K. (1995). Administrative review of alleged police brutality. In W.A. Geller and H. Toch (Eds.) *And justice for all: Understanding and controlling police abuse of force* (pp. 205–222). Washington, D.C.: Police Executive Research Forum.

Petersilia, J. (1983). *Racial disparities in the criminal justice system.* Santa Monica, DA: Rand Corporation.

President's Commission on Law Enforcement and Administration of Justice (1967). *A national survey of police–community relations: Field surveys V.* Washington, D.C.: U.S. Government Printing Office.

Reiss, A.J., Jr. (1968). Police brutality—Answers to key questions. *Trans-action, 5,* 10–19.

Rohrlich, T. and Merina, V. (1991, May 19). Racial disparities seen in complaints to LAPD. *Los Angeles Times,* p. 1.

Smith, D.A., Graham, N. and Adams, B. (1991). Minorities and the police: Attitudinal and behavioral questions. In M.J. Lynch and E.B. Patterson (Eds.) *Race and Criminal Justice* (pp. 22–35). New York, NY: Harrow and Heston.

Smith, D.A., Visher, C.A. and Davidson, L.A. (1984). Equity and discretionary justice: The influence of race on police arrest decisions. *Journal of Criminal Law and Criminology, 75,* 234–249.

Taylor, R.B. (1994). *Research Methods in Criminal Justice.* New York, NY: McGraw-Hill, Inc.

Wagner, A.E. (1980). Citizen complaints against the police: The complainant. *Journal of Police Science and Administration, 8,* 247–252.

West, P. (1988). Investigation of complaints against the police: Summary report of a national survey. *American Journal of Police, 7.* 101–121.

Walker, S. (1992). *The police in America: An introduction* (2nd ed.). New York, NY: McGraw Hill.

Walker, S. and Bumphus, V.W. (1992). The effectiveness of civilian review: Observations on recent trends and new issues regarding the civilian review of police. *American Journal of Police, 11,* 1–26.

Williams, J.S., Thomas, C.W. and Singh, B.K. (1983). "Situational use of police force: Public reactions." *American Journal of Police, 3,* 37–50.

Worden, R.E. (1995). The 'causes' of police brutality: Theory and evidence on police use of force. In W.A. Geller and H. Toch (Eds.) *And justice for all: Understanding and controlling police abuse of force* (pp. 31–60). Washington, D.C.: Police Executive Research Forum.

PART 2

CRIMES COMMITTED BY POLICE OFFICERS

In the article, "Parameters of Police Misconduct," William Hyatt defines the many parameters of corruption. Since criminality depends on the intention of the actor, in many instances no definitive line exists between a corrupt and a non-corrupt act. This appears to be particularly true in the extraordinarily complex areas of deception and street justice practiced by many police officers. This article reviews how departmental policies and attitudes can promote a climate in which corruption can flourish. A periodic housecleaning of some bad apples will not eliminate the root cause of the potential for corruption within the department.

The article "Police Perceptions and the Norming of Institutional Corruption" by Robert McCormack examines the inclination for wide-scale corruption to be tolerated in large law enforcement agencies, especially those in major urban areas. These deviances often take the form of bribes, shakedowns, sex on duty, etc. McCormack presents a corruption model and discusses the factors that affect the levels of normed graft, as well as ways of controlling the problem.

David E. Sisk in "Police Corruption and Criminal Monopoly: Victimless Crimes" presents an interesting theory on bribery. Sisk indicates that victimless crimes will lead to police accepting bribes whenever victimless crimes are prohibited. According to David Sisk, the bribery system resembles a tax system that reduces the taxed activity the most if markets are structured monopolistically. The desirability of a bribe system is questionable since it promotes police corruption; it can encourage police to promote criminal activities and organizations that pay them.

Sean Grennan in "Historical Perspective of Police Corruption in New York City" traces corruption in the New York City Police Department from the end of the nineteenth century to the last decade of the twentieth century. Historically, law enforcement corruption comes into the public eye about every twenty years, and commissions are appointed to investigate the issue. Grennan posits, however, that the police corruption issue has never been resolved in New York City.

In "Drug Related Police Corruption: The Miami Experience," Kim Michelle Lersch reviews drug-related police corruption. During the 1980s, the City of Miami experienced substantial social unrest to racism, Cuban migration, poor police management, and lack of supervision of inexperienced officers. This article discusses the relaxed screening mechanisms in the recruiting and employing of novices. Also reviewed are the crimes of "The River Cops," the incompetence of the Internal Affairs Unit, and the Rotten Apple theory.

Peter Krasksa and Victor Kappeler in their article on "To Serve and Pursue: Exploring Police Sexual Violence Against Women" identify and explore police sexual violence, formerly an unaddressed criminological phenomenon. Using data from federal litigation cases and media sources, the authors examine the incidents, distribution, and nature of these crimes against women. Their analysis incorporates both feminist literature and police studies, providing for the development of a police sexual violence continuum and the exploration of theoretical, conceptual, and practical issues.

Michael Birzer, in the article "Crimes Committed by Police Officers," reviews the various types of crime committed by law enforcement officers. Police officers have been known to violate the law while both on and off duty. Professor Birzer provides an overview of these infractions, including murder, robbery, child molestation, and shoplifting.

A R T I C L E 6

PARAMETERS OF POLICE MISCONDUCT

William D. Hyatt
Western Carolina University
Criminal Justice Department

Although the police, or anyone else for that matter, can misbehave in any number of ways, in this article the misconduct considered will be restricted to bribery in its various forms: the use (or misuse) of street justice, lying while on the job, and the management and attitudes of patrol officers that foster and promote such conduct.

Bribery

1. free or discounted meals and services
2. acceptance of kickbacks
3. theft occurring during investigations
4. shakedowns
5. fixing cases
6. protection of illegal activities
7. internal bribery for favorable assignments

Lying While on the Job

8. use of street justice
9. lying

Management and Officer Attitudes that Foster Corruption

10. whistleblowing

Although items 2, 3, 4, 6, and 9 are typically labeled as corruption in the minds of both the public and law enforcement, items 1, 5, 7, 8, and 10 represent gray areas that may or may not be corrupt, depending on the circumstances. In an analogy to the concept posited in *Broken Windows,* (Wilson and

Kelling 1982) failure of a department to eliminate minor issues can lead to major violations.

Most of our major metropolitan police forces, as well as our federal, state, and small law enforcement agencies have experienced the shocking, devastating, highly publicized investigations of corruption that seem to occur all too often.

There seems to be a pattern to these scandals. First, there is the investigation and arrest of a single officer or a small group of officers who are acting together, usually beginning with suspicions of superiors, the complaint of an outraged citizen, or sometimes the tip of an informant to the media. The scandal quickly widens and grows as word leaks out and more citizens step forward to claim that they have also been victims of misconduct by these or other officers. The news media and other public officials soon start investigations of their own. Tips from paid informants abound, and those under indictment, particularly those charged with victimless crimes such as narcotics possession, prostitution, and gambling, begin a wailing chorus in the hope of trading their place in the dock for a police officer whom they accuse of some form of corruption.

The pace quickens again as some additional low-level and occasionally middle-management officers are also charged. Commissions are formed to review the activities of the department under question. These commissions typically consist of elected officials, well-known citizens and sometimes self-proclaimed outside experts, who examine in detail every facet of the organization.

Allegations fly in every direction. Officers making routine stops are regularly threatened that if they issue a citation to the person they have detained, they will be the next one reported for improper conduct. Every form of conduct from the most serious to the most trivial is examined, and the slightest missteps are publicized and reprimanded. Careers are ruined or at least seriously thrown off track. Justice grinds, into its lowest and slowest gear, if not to a halt.

Those who have been indicted are then dismissed from the force. Upper-level administrators are allowed to resign or accept early retirement. Administrators below the top are reassigned or dismissed, and havoc reigns. Then after a few months of hectic activity, the smoke begins to clear, and the new administrators announce that the bad apples have been excised and all is well again. And after a brief respite, the cycle begins again.

History has shown that the replacement of a few administrators and the prosecution or termination of a few rotten apples is seldom, if ever, a long-term solution to the problem of corruption. An examination must be made into the circumstances that allowed the corruption to occur in the first place, as opposed to merely reacting to the misdeed after the fact. Correcting situations that allow misconduct to occur will lead to agencies that are not readily susceptible to corruption.

In one of the most thorough investigations of corruption, the Knapp Commission (Knapp Commission 1972) demonstrated how corruption is able to seed itself and grow. Named after its chairman, William Knapp, it made an extensive investigation not only into the New York City Police Department, but also into the root causes of the malfeasance. These findings, which have been widely published and studied, concluded that in order for corruption to flourish such a grand scale, there had to be support functions in place at every level of the department, and that these support systems had to be institution-alized within that department. The Commission found, among other things, that "group loyalty, . . . stubborness, hostility, and pride" (Knapp Commission 1972, 6), among officers had created a climate in which dishonesty was able to flourish. Many members of the force, aware of the misconduct, chose not to eliminate it and were indirectly responsible for the tainting of other officers. For example if officers are using recovered stolen property for personal use without a reprimand from within the department, this creates an atmosphere which encourages more general corruption. Such an atmosphere does not au-tomatically corrupt every officer, but it certainly does make it easier for some-one who might be susceptible to temptation to succumb without feeling guilty. If one form of corruption is acceptable, it becomes easier to justify other types as well.

The Knapp Commission also refuted the concept of "a few rotten apples." While all institutions, including law enforcement, find themselves with em-ployees at many levels who have a penchant for dishonesty, these employees are few and far between and for the most part can be screened out in the hiring process. If this is true, however, then it must be more than just law enforcement personnel with bad moral character who become involved in corruption.

It is important to distinguish between corruption and police misconduct as it is used in this text. Corruption denotes misuse in some form of the offi-cer's position in return for an actual or expected reward, whether material or intangible. Police misconduct, which can be used to include corruption, is any improper activity committed without the expectation of either material or in-tangible reward. General police misconduct will be excluded from this dis-cussion. Some activities can be classified as both misconduct and corruption, depending on the circumstances. For instance, engaging in sex on duty would be considered misconduct. But if the sexual activity was with a prostitute with the understanding that this favor would protect her from prosecution by that officer, it would also constitute corruption.

TYPES OF CORRUPTION

The types of corruption to be considered here can broadly be grouped as follows:

Free or Discounted Meals or Services

Free or discounted meals and services are often available to either uniformed law enforcement officers or all law enforcement officers upon showing their badge. In fact, one writer said, "Police corruption begins with the notion that policemen by some divine right are entitled to free meals, free movies and cut rate prices on virtually everything that they buy" (Inciardi, 1996). There are generally three reasons why free services or discounts are offered to law en-forcement officers and to an extent, these reasons determine whether corrup-tion is involved.

Many business owners think that maintaining police presence protects their business. These owners believe that potential crime can be averted because criminals will be reluctant to rob or cause trouble in a restaurant frequented by police. This line of reasoning supposes that the police will give extra attention to finding the person who caused trouble for their restaurant owner. If the officers accept the free or discounted items knowing this is the purpose for which they are offered, this is corruption, either because they intend to fulfill the owner's expectation, or because they are taking the items under false pretenses, knowing they will not do what the owner thinks they are agreeing to do.

Some businesses, such as hardware or clothing stores or markets, do not directly benefit from a perceived police presence. Nevertheless, these owners give free items and services to officers out of fear of getting on a police bad list. This bad list, whether real or imagined, includes a fear that police will not be attentive to their problems, such as the removal of a difficult customer or a juvenile gang blocking the entrance to the store. It also includes preventing unwanted attention to occurrences such as health and code violations, customers who double park in front of the store, or fail to put money in the parking meter. If the officers do not dispel this notion of the store owner, these practices would be categorized as corruption. If the officers clearly explain that the owner will receive the same treatment with or without the favored treatment, then the benefits would not be corruptly received.

Some business owners are concerned that the police are performing a difficult and dangerous service for them and the rest of the community for relatively low wages. These owners want to show their appreciation for the officers' efforts in the only manner available to them. They also believe that giving substantial discounts is good for business; the officer will recommend the store to his friends, and even at a discount, the store is still likely to make a profit. These acts cannot be considered corruption.

Kickbacks

Kickbacks are payments in the form of money, goods, or services that a law enforcement agent receives for directing people that he comes into contact with toward a particular service provider. Kickbacks are most commonly received from bail bondsmen for persons the policeman has arrested, ambulances and wrecker services that the officer calls to the scene of an accident, and legal referrals made to (usually) people he has arrested. Although this type of payment is usually small, some officers have been reported to make an actual business of this type of conduct. One such person was an officer in Tampa who is reported to have gone through the police department files to obtain the names of burglary victims and turn them over to a high pressure security system salesman (Inciardi 1996).

According to one survey of police chiefs in the southeast, only 48% of the departments had any regulation covering kickbacks from bondsmen, while 52% had regulations covering kickbacks by lawyers, and 60% had regulations covering such payments by wrecker services (Barker 1982; Annarino 1996). What is of even greater interest is that over half of the chiefs responding in this survey said that they would punish such conduct by either a reprimand or suspension, and only three indicated that they would press criminal charges even though the actions would have been criminal in their states.

If we accept the notion that a person is incapable of attaining a fully developed ethical and incorruptible approach to law enforcement without the assistance and support of his employing institution, then it is not surprising that kickbacks are common; this survey would seem to indicate that such conduct is either condoned or tolerated by the leaders who are expected to set the moral tone for any law enforcement agency.

Opportunistic Thefts

Opportunistic theft is the taking of money or property from arrestees, burglary scenes, and unprotected properties by the officer during the course of duty. The most common form of theft is referred to as "shopping." Officers, when called to the scene of a burglary, pocket items missed by the burglars. These officers theorize that the insurance company will pay for these items anyway, so there is no real harm done by their actions. Some officers even justify such actions by arguing that if they had not taken the item in question, the owner of the premises would have taken it himself and made a claim with the insurance company for the loss of that item. Thus, they have saved the owner from committing an illegal act.

In the survey referred to in the last section, (Barker 1982; Annarino 1996), less than 60% of the departments had any regulations covering opportunistic theft, and less than 35% of police chiefs would have brought criminal charges against an officer found to have engaged in this type of conduct even though it differs only in degree from the act being investigated.

Shakedowns

A shakedown is the taking of money or property from an arrestee caught with the fruits of a crime in his possession. Drug dealers are often victims of this crime, especially during arrests and the execution of search warrants. The shakedown entails taking drugs, property, or cash from the arrestee or the scene of the crime. The items may be resold or used unofficially in the department or by the officers involved.

Referring again to the previous survey, only 61% of the departments queried had any regulations pertaining to shakedowns, and only 37% of the chiefs said they would press criminal charges, even though this would clearly represent the commission of a felony (Barker 1982; Annarino 1996).

Bribes Related to Cases

This broad category covers anything from the acceptance of a cash payment for not writing a motorist a traffic ticket to an officer accepting money for shading his testimony in a felony trial in order to give the defendant an opportunity to be acquitted. Although the level of seriousness can be argued, in criminal terms, all of the actions are equivalent, since each represents the officer selling his or her service to allow someone to escape the consequences of improper conduct.

Less than 75% of the departments in the previously cited survey had regulations regarding bribes received by officers for any reason. Only 16% of the chiefs surveyed said that they would press criminal charges in anything short of a felony, and only 42% said they would press charges even if the bribe were paid with regard to a felony charge (Barker 1982; Annarino 1996).

Protection of Illegal Activities

Protection of illegal activities takes two forms. The most common type of protection is the acceptance of bribes in order to allow certain victimless crimes, such as illegal alcohol or narcotics sales, prostitution, and gambling to operate unmolested by law enforcement activity. More sinister are several cases prosecuted by the author; officers in Miami, Florida, were actually providing physical protection to narcotics dealers during the drug transactions and were even performing debt collection for them on occasion.

One of the more unusual variations on protection occurred more than once in Philadelphia, Pennsylvania, when raids were made on bookmakers and numbers operators by the Federal Bureau of Investigation and the Internal Revenue Service. In Philadelphia during the late sixties and early seventies, bets would not be cancelled if a bookie or numbers banker lost his records in a raid. As a result, customers could claim they had a winning bet and demand payment. Obviously, such a situation could bankrupt the gambler, and it was not uncommon for the gambler to offer the agents a substantial payment in return for a copy of the records. While bribery is illegal, a question arises regarding the bookmakers' rights as citizens. The law enforcement code of ethics talks about protection without fear or favor. The bookmaker should be entitled to some protection, i.e. a copy of his records, so that he will not be made a victim in an fashion unrelated to the confiscation of his records. This situation, a case prosecuted by the author, was ultimately resolved by a rule in Philadelphia that all bets were canceled in the event of the seizure of the bookmaker's records.

Of the departments surveyed in the study cited, less than 61% had regulations governing the taking of money for protection, and less than 30% of the chiefs said that they would press criminal charges if such conduct was brought to their attention (Barker 1982; Annarino 1996).

Internal Payoffs

This is a form of internal bribery in which officers pay one another to either acquire good assignments or avoid unpleasant ones. While such a payment would not be illegal under most criminal statutes, it does pose an interesting ethical problem. About 40% of the departments surveyed had regulations governing this conduct, and not surprisingly, less than 30% of the chiefs surveyed indicated that they considered this offense serious enough that they would fire the officers involved. However, none of the chiefs indicated that they would press criminal charges in this matter (Barker 1982; Annarino 1996). This violation is important because condoning bribes in this case encourages taking bribes in other areas.

Payments for Protection

Little complex thought is needed to determine that taking bribes to not enforce the law against people who are committing crimes is improper. Assume however, for purposes of examination, that a law enforcement officer is assigned to a high street-crime beat which contains gamblers and narcotics dealers, none of whom law enforcement has ever been able to successfully prosecute.

An executive decision is made at the highest level of the department that gambling laws will simply not be enforced, and law enforcement efforts will be focused elsewhere. If the gamblers, being unaware of this decision, continue to offer the officer payments to allow them to operate freely, is this protection considered illegal, or merely a form of the free or discounted services previously discussed? While the aforementioned survey did not specifically ask this question, it seems likely that few, if any, chiefs would take action under these circumstances.

Abuse of Authority or Street Justice

"Calling the cops" is usually not so much a request for enforcement of due process by law enforcement agents as it is a cry for someone with authority to forcefully intervene in a seemingly unresolvable situation. It is a request for an officer to use the power of the state to resolve a variety of problems, most of which fall outside the strict bureaucratic purview of the officer's authority and duty. It is from these requests, whether articulated or merely understood by the officers, that most street justice situations arise.

Historical Antecedents to Street Justice

The police function was originally one of peacekeeping, primarily because American society, particularly in its urban areas, did not have the mechanisms in place to handle the problems of an increasing heterogeneous society. The city governments in power during the 1800s and early 1900s, in order to achieve an inexpensive measure of order and tranquility in the poorer areas of their jurisdictions, chose instead to give the police unofficial street justice authority. In the lower-class areas, the police represented not only a law enforcement agency, but a social agency of last resort as well, because the political system had not otherwise provided for these people. As a result, within neighborhoods, particularly lower socioeconomic ones, individual policemen became institutionalized as the last resort for problems of all sorts, criminal and non-criminal, because the residents of these neighborhoods did not have financial access to the private problem-solving methods of the wealthier groups.

Defining Street Justice

Discussions of street justice often include all manner of violations by law enforcement up to and including extortion and protection rackets operated by the officers. For purposes of this article, these areas will be excluded, as will situations involving excessive force, except where the force is deliberately used as part of a punishment administered by the officer to accomplish what that officer perceives as a just result to the situation being dealt with.

As used here, street justice means that the officer acts in a given situation in an extralegal manner to accomplish a purpose that he or she perceives as just and appropriate under the circumstances. Although the term normally carries a negative connotation and is often applied to police brutality, it is used here simply as any action or inaction taken by the officer that is technically in contravention to his or her duty as defined by either state statute or departmental regulations as a police officer.

Street justice situations can be divided into three groups, and this grouping can substantially impact the acceptability of extralegal behavior within our society.

1. In some instances officers resort to extralegal conduct in an effort to correct a perceived wrong to a third person or to the community in general that, again in their perception, could not be adequately addressed by our criminal justice system.
2. Secondly, officers use street justice in order to accomplish some perceived social good for the community as a whole.
3. Finally, officers resort to extralegal conduct in order to correct a perceived slight to the officer, the department, or the societal concept that the officer represents.

Correcting Perceived Wrongs

There has been considerable debate about the effectiveness of incarceration in the last few years. The accepted theory had been that incarceration or the other legal sanctions available to the court, in addition to punishing the individual, also reformed, rehabilitated, and deterred that individual and others from committing crime. There has been much discussion in the relevant literature and studies in recent years disputing the reformation, rehabilitation, and deterrence arguments. Assuming that incarceration accomplishes none of these objectives, does this change the wrongfulness of either street justice or the propriety of making arrests?

Some of the impetus for street justice appears to come from the idea that retributive justice really doesn't accomplish very much. The fact that the state and not the victim is given vengeance, i.e. positive retributivism, by the punishment inflicted on the defendant demonstrates the validity of this argument. The victim is expected by law to avail himself or herself of the civil legal remedies provided in order to be made whole. The recovery of damages suffered by the actual victim is simply not part of the job of the police or the criminal justice system. Yet most police officers become law enforcement officers because they want to help people. With this motivation, the concept of street justice makes imminent sense, because it accomplishes what all parties to the action, except perhaps the alleged offender, really want. That is near-on-the-spot justice for the real, not the legal victim without the interminable wait for the civil process, which by no means assures justice.

Law enforcement officers, at the behest of the community in which they work, often express moral codes that are in conflict with the due process model mandated by the courts. The situations facing an officer often resolve themselves into the conflicting dilemmas of his or her duty as outlined by the due process model or of righting a wrong that has occurred. The following example may illustrate this problem. A situation that may arise might be the theft of $100 from a poor family by an equally poor neighbor. The due process model of justice calls for the police to arrest the offender and process him through the system. Yet this does not solve the problem for the family which has been robbed, particularly if the scenario concludes with the incarceration of the thief. While punishment in the form of incarceration would theoretically teach the offender a lesson, it could quite conceivably result in putting the offender's family on welfare due to the loss of the main breadwinner. This would harm both them and society, which is now supporting them. Further, it would prevent the victim from recovering his money. Under these circumstances, street justice, although illegal would better serve both parties. The officer could threaten the offender and his family with all manner of bad things to force them to either return the money or find a way to repay the theft in short order, then simply drop the matter, with perhaps a few additional threats to the offender until the money was repaid.

Correcting Perceived Social Injustice

It seems clear that law enforcement officers are routinely placed on the horns of a dilemma. The expectations of residents on a beat are that the officer assigned to that beat will solve all of the problems that arise in whatever way is necessary. At the same time, however, these same residents have been conditioned to view the officer as one who acts within the law. Thus the officer is expected to stay within the law to achieve justice when dealing with situations that would be handled more effectively using extralegal means. For instance, illegally rousting a drug dealer so often that he leaves the neighborhood would undoubtedly serve the interests of the residents of the officer's beat, but obviously not the interests of either the drug dealer or the concept of our civil or constitutional rights in general. The officer is faced with the difficult but not unusual choice of protecting more abstract and general rights or the concrete present needs of the community that he is assigned to serve and protect.

The officer's superiors will also expect that the officer handle the problem in the most efficient and least objectional manner available. The technical instructions to the officer are certainly to act in accordance with the law and the code of ethics that has been prescribed to govern his conduct. If the officer ignores the troublemaker because the conduct, although offensive, is technically not a violation of the law, both the officer and law enforcement, in general, will be berated by the community. If, on the other hand, the officer bends the rules or their application in order to make the troublemaker conform to acceptable norms, the officer will be cheered by the residents of the community. The officer's superiors are also likely, at least implicitly, to condone the officer's conduct, unless for some reason a public objection is raised to the action taken, at which time the cheering of the crowd will quiet, and the departmental command will sternly point to the rules and reprimand the officer for not staying within the mandate of the law.

Street Justice and the Attitude Test

The application of street justice discussed to this point has been of the type that is generally acceptable, at least to the community in which the officer operates. The type of situation where the action taken by the officer is to right a specific wrong to a member of the community or to accomplish some result that will be of positive benefit to the segment of society that the officer is assigned to serve and protect, as opposed to avenge a wrong directed specifically at the officer. Let us turn now to the third situational grouping suggested above, the situations in which the officer is acting out personal vengeance as opposed to achieve some goal that will benefit society or a particular victim.

The police, more than any other occupation or profession, with the possible exception of the military in a time of war, rely on their peers to protect and support them and share with them the violent aspect of their assignments, resulting in a high degree of comradeship or esprit de corps among persons in the police profession. This feeling transcends racial, ethnic, sexual, and departmental lines and encompasses all of those who share the common risks and pressures. This camaraderie appears to occur whether or not the others are known to the particular officer, or if known whether they are liked or disliked by that officer (Skolnick 1975).

The law enforcement officer, because his or her work requires him or her to be occupied continuously with potential violence, develops a perceptual shorthand to identify certain kinds of people as potential threats, that is, persons who use gesture, language, and attire the police officer has come to recognize as a possible prelude to violence. This does not mean that violence by the symbolic assailant is necessarily predictable. To the contrary, the policeman is merely responding to the vague indication of danger suggested by appearance.

The street officer's perception of constant danger, even though not normally a reality, is nevertheless quite real. This perception can cause the officer to overemphasize the danger of the job and overreact in nondangerous situations where the persons involved are perceived to fit the mold of the symbolic assailant. This, in turn, can result in self-fulfilling prophecies and violence where none need have occurred. This perception of constant danger, reinforced by academy training and the war stories of other officers and spectacularized by the media, particularly fictional television media, has caused officers to develop courses of action which redefine legal requirements and selectively interpret departmental regulations, laws of the legislature, and rulings of the courts in order to carry out their perceived mission in a relatively safe manner. Since much of what a policeman does, and particularly does not do, on the streets is largely invisible, these extralegal methods that become commonplace actions are seldom seriously questioned or evaluated. Thus street justice may potentially be reviewed, at least departmentally or judicially, less often than those acts of officer's whose mode of operation more formally adheres to the strict requirements of the law and applicable departmental regulations.

Adding to the problems are the training and socialization every officer receives, both at the academy and in the locker rooms. By their training and socialization, officers are conditioned to believe that they must win every verbal and physical encounter, or lose face and therefore authority in the community. Whether or not it is true that officers will actually lose some measure of authority in the community, it is unquestionably the perception that they must win every encounter. This belief escalates many situations into the use and abuse of street justice, particularly since approximately 80% of these use of force incidents involve misdemeanors and noncriminal violations or situations (Reiss 1971). In more than half of these situations, the citizen is not physically aggressive but is either verbally abusive or defiant of the officer's authority.

Seventy percent of the citizens involved in the situations in this study are reported to have either been drinking or were drunk (Wintersmith 1974).

In conjunction with the above, the macho theory also plays a substantial role and is by no means restricted to male officers. Most professional groups in our society have various ways of demonstrating competence in areas that the average person has not mastered. A police officer has only the ability to ride around in a car or dominate someone, verbally or physically, in order to prove his worth. Since riding in a car is unlikely to impress many people, some officers feel the need to demonstrate their professional competence by exercising verbal or physical dominance over those they come in contact with in the course of their duties.

One study concluded that in terms of the attitude test, 25% of recruits entering the academy felt that the use of force was necessary and justified for citizens who unjustly insulted or cursed an officer. This rose to 34% after one year on the force, demonstrating the socialization process in action (Klockars 1980).

Abuse of an officer is not only confined to cursing, it can include the refusal to identify oneself by other than a street name, non-obscene gestures or posture, the demand for an officer's badge number, or even a request for information regarding why a person is being searched or detained. Even failing to show the deference that a police officer believes appropriate under the circumstances can be a basis for street justice in the form of the use of force. Part of the attitude check is the idea that most people have something to hide, and if they are not properly deferential to the officer, they probably represent a danger to that officer. Even though the probability of unexpectedly happening upon a dangerous felon or someone in the act of committing a crime is quite low, officers are trained and socialized to believe that every person is a potential threat and thus must be treated in a manner that conveys to the person the foolhardiness of any action that the officer would resent.

Carl Klockars has referred to the reactions that go into the attitude test, although he did not relate them to the attitude test, as "the operative assumption of guilt," meaning that in order for the police to work safely and efficiently, the officer must assume that every citizen in question is guilty and virtually any action on the part of that citizen, whether talking too much or too little, being too calm or too excited or even the way the person stands, is confirmation of "the worst of all possible guilt" (Klockars 1980). This assumes that the person is not only guilty, but dangerously so, and furthermore the citizen may pose a danger to the officer if the officer does not take steps to neutralize the danger.

Another factor adding to the use of street justice and the requirement of passing the attitude check is, in Dr. Klockar's words, "The great guilty place assumption" (1980, 59). Because of the officer's constant exposure to what has been called the great seamy underside of our cities' personalities, the officer sees threats and crimes everywhere, with a park being variously a "muggers paradise" or a "weirdos' convention" or a bunch of "sickos" who represent as much danger to the officer as would the wilds of the jungle.

Officers will make the same judgments of citizens, not usually out of a sense of racism, but simply as an attempt to see the worst in everyone and everything in order to prepare for combat. The "not guilty (this time) assumption" assumes that everyone whom the officer stops is engaged in some illegal activity, and if an investigatory stop or even a street search of the person fails to uncover evidence of that activity, it is only due to that person's luck, as opposed to a miscalculation on the part of the officer.

Citizens who fit into the category of the symbolic assailant and do not show proper deference to the police, particularly if they are encountered at night or in what is perceived to be hostile territory, are approached and dealt with by the officers in a defensive manner which often includes harsh and rude behavior in an attempt to intimidate and therefore control the individual. This attitude toward the individual logically creates either a smoldering resentment in the individual or outright defiance toward the police officer's attitude, which in turn is interpreted as a challenge to police authority, and is one more step down the path toward a physical confrontation. This potential confrontation is important to the police officer because it is the danger of this person that he or she is trained for, and it is this person who legitimizes the police as protector of the public and often provides the excitement for which the officer joined the force.

Dangers of Street Justice

The complaint that officers use harmful street justice because they are bad people is usually not justified. But in many instances involving extralegal behavior to right a wrong against the officer's authority, officers act because they are tired, frustrated, or upset by something such as a high-speed chase, or just because they have been beaten down by all they have seen in the streets. This reaction cannot be used as an indictment of street justice per se, or necessarily of the officer, but rather is an indictment of the system which has allowed this situation to be created in the first place.

Various terms are used by officers to describe their condition after too many shift changes, bad diets, and long hours of inactivity in the patrol car. These epithets can also encompass the changes that occur in an officer who entered policing for the purpose of helping people and now feels thwarted and frustrated at every turn. The combination of the above can turn a good law enforcement officer into one who gradually begins to abuse the position of law enforcement by using street justice over a period of time. This attitude and the acts that follow from it are supported and reinforced by the attitudes of the department in classifying people and the prejustification that the officers engage in. It is suggested in this scenario that at first most officers become indifferent, then verbally aggressive, and later physically aggressive and, finally, physically abusive.

Two studies found that almost half of police-initiated assaults occurred when the civilian openly defied the police authority or failed to "pass the attitude test" (Barker 1982; Annarino 1996). The conclusion appears to be that if the officers would employ the "golden rule" in their approach to citizens, there would be less need for violence.

In some instances the concept of police abuse and violence can become so institutionalized within a department that a situation such as the one that occurred in Philadelphia happens. The United States Department of Justice filed a suit in 1979 alleging that the 8000-person Philadelphia police force had engaged in a systematic pattern of violence and abusive and degrading actions toward the inhabitants of that city (Croft 1986). The suit claimed that the actions of the department as a whole shocked the conscience. This case, which was ultimately settled prior to trial, raises the question of whether any person in the department could ethically claim to have acted in a proper manner with what were contended to be such obvious violations occurring all around them.

The argument often advanced to explain how such things could happen is the theory of a few rotten apples. This means that the department as a whole is pure, clean, and ethical, but that a few bad people, i.e. "rotten apples," are making everyone look bad. This theory becomes difficult to accept in situations such as were alleged to have occurred in Philadelphia. There must be another factor that causes men and women with psychological profiles similar to the average citizen to become part of conspiracies of silence, as happened in these situations. It seems that the police code of silence contributes to the problem by creating a self-imposed shroud of secrecy and seeming-protection over the only people empowered by the state to act against those who overstep the bounds of justice.

Lying

Lying in the course of enforcing the law can engender a positive result by use of an illegal action. A falsification can protect an officer from the consequences of a previous or anticipated action, as well as provide a simple but illegal solution to a short-term problem.

For example, a clearly guilty defendant is on trial and has lied under oath about the arrest. She has also bribed a witness to substantiate her story. When the arresting officer is put on the stand, he has two choices. He can repeat truthfully what happened during the arrest, in which case the jury may believe the perjured defendant and her witness. His other option is to testify truthfully to all the pertinent facts but falsely state that the witness was forty or fifty feet away and it was too dark to see, in which case the jury will most likely believe the testimony of the officer and convict the defendant.

Although the lie may accomplish justice in this case, two serious harms could come about. First, if every officer was able to lie whenever it appeared that a guilty defendant might be freed for some improper reason, our system of justice would be undermined. Likewise, if it became public that the officer had lied to gain the conviction, the department's credibility would be seriously damaged, both before the court and the community, thereby rendering it ineffective.

When a judge pronounces perjury to be wrong, he is viewing the lie from a moral law view, deeming such actions to be wrong because they will undermine the system of justice. A police officer, however, is not charged with the job of evaluating the effect on society as a whole. He or she is sent to a beat to perform an organizational function, namely to keep order. In many cases this role can be better fulfilled with some judicious deception of those people who deserve to be deceived. To the officer on the beat trying to keep some semblance of social order, doing whatever will best serve and protect the people at that time may seem to be the proper thing to do. Much like our discussion of long and short term views, a person's perspective on lying can also depend on the type of job they have to perform and the circumstances of the situation.

Lying as a Function of Circumstances

Many people enjoy playing poker. Most, if not all of these people, would agree that the game of poker would lose most of its allure if lying were not allowed. Imagine that you are playing in a stud poker game with several good friends. The best man at your wedding, who is sitting to your left, bets a quarter, and when it is your turn to bet, you call his quarter and raise a quarter. Your friend takes a long look at the ace, king, queen and ten of hearts that you have showing and asks, "Are you bluffing or do you really have a red jack under there?" You do not; you have a four of spades and are simply trying to bluff your friend, who has two pairs showing. Do you feel that in the name of ethics and honesty you should be required to advise him that you are, in fact, bluffing?

No poker player would ever support such a proposition. It is the expectation that bluffing (which is simply a nice name for lying) will be employed whenever there is a likelihood of it succeeding. The enjoyment of poker at the entertainment level is based on the element of deception and uncertainty. If you say that you do have the jack of hearts, your friend is not likely to believe you. He expects you to try to deceive him. Likewise, if you say that you have the four of spades, your friend would not put any faith in your answer. If your bluff succeeds, all the players will congratulate you on your nerve and cunning. No one will say that this was a dirty trick to play on the best man at your wedding. Deception is understood to be part of the game, and if you are deceived then it is a risk you assumed when you sat down to play in the game. However, if after the hand had finished, your friend expressed an interest in purchasing your four-year-old sports car for his wife to drive to work and asked you to give him an assessment of its mechanical condition, he and all of the others at the table would expect an honest answer from a friend and would be shocked and hurt if you used deception to convince your friend to buy a car that you knew to be a worthless pile of junk. This is true even though everyone had just excepted with perfect equanimity that you had tried to deceive him on the last poker hand.

In many ways, poker is analogous to law enforcement. There are certain aspects of law enforcement where the officer is expected to tell the unvarnished truth, be fair, and act in accordance with established rules. There are other areas however, where deception is accepted and even expected of the law enforcement officer, such as undercover work. Any crook with an ounce of street smarts knows there are undercover agents and informants lurking in the shadows and takes every precaution to avoid being deceived by them. If our criminal errs, however, and mistakenly takes an informant or undercover agent into confidence, the dealer will react much as the players in the poker game reacted. A cocaine dealer knows that there are undercover officers; most treat as a fact of life. Although they, like the loser in the poker bluff, are disappointed at the outcome, they do not feel that they have been treated unfairly, even though they have been lied to and deceived and will have to pay a substantial penalty for their gullibility. However, that same cocaine dealer would react with shock and fury if the agent, instead of trapping the dealer by deception, testifies in court that the dealer had tried to sell him cocaine, when in fact this was not true. Theoretically, there should be no difference. In both instances the dealer was guilty of being a dealer and in both instances should be punished as a result of the agent's investigation. But the difference is profound. Like the poker game, the dealer has assumed the risk that if he or she sells cocaine on several occasions, the chance of selling to an undercover agent increases. However, the dealer can not accept the fact that a law enforcement agent could go into court and commit perjury in order to convict the dealer, regardless of the dealer's obvious guilt.

Thus in situations where the rules permit the officer to use deception, then all involved accept the deception and do not consider it unethical. The act of deception is not inherently wrong. It is only wrong in situations where there is not a general understanding that the rules of the game permit deception on the part of one or more of the players. This is one of the reasons that we would be angered if a friend lied to us, but perhaps only disappointed in ourselves if a total stranger lied to us. We have different expectations in the two situations. We feel we have the right to expect honesty from our friend, while we have no such understanding with a stranger. With this stranger you are, or should be, on your guard. With your friend, you believe that there is no need to carefully scrutinize his or her every word because of the implied understanding of honesty.

Thus this section will not focus on undercover policing, where there is a clear understanding that the police or other law enforcement agents may employ deception, but will rather focus on the areas of enforcement where the officers find it useful to use deception and there is no understanding between the parties that deception will be permitted.

Lying and Deception

A lie is a statement which you do not believe to be true made with the intent to deceive. Even if you are mistaken, and the fact that you are relating is true, your statement is still a lie because you did not believe it to be true when it was spoken. A lie should be defined so that other than affirmative assertions are recognized as lies. For instance giving a nod of the head is an assent to a proposition even though there are no words spoken. Under these circumstances even silence can be construed as a statement. Deception, which has the same end as the lie, namely to deceive the hearer into believing some fact which the speaker does not believe to be true, may or may not involve an untruthful statement. If your spouse comes home with a dented left front fender that was not dented when he or she left in the morning and smells strongly of beer, you may suspect that your spouse has been drinking and driving. If you ask your spouse, "Were you drinking when you smashed up our car?" and your spouse says "No," it is likely that your spouse is trying to deceive you and unlikely that your spouse is lying since it is quite unlikely that there was drinking at the specific moment the accident occurred. In all likelihood the drinking was completed before he or she began to drive the car. If however, you ask "Have you been drinking?" and the answer is, "Absolutely not!" this would be a lie (if in fact he or she had been drinking).

The interesting thing about deception is that a person may tell the absolute truth with the clear intent to deceive. Then if the deception is discovered, the deceiver can honestly say, "What I told you was true; you just leaped to a conclusion." You, of course, would feel that you had not leaped to a conclusion, but that you had been pushed to that conclusion. Perhaps we can describe deception as a push to a conclusion by the speaker, rather than a leap by the hearer. The deception leads to make an unwarranted assumption, while the lie makes a direct assertion of fact.

Types of Deception

The following catagories were first outlined by Sissela Bok and remain perhaps the most effective catagorization of deception to date (Bok 1978).

1) The Noble Lie The noble lie has become the justifying cry of all public officials caught in a deliberate and undeniable misstatement of the truth. The Iran/Contra hearings before Congress in the summer of 1987, as well as the more recent zippergate investigations of President Clinton's actions were replete with justifications of lies told to Congress, the United States populace, and others for the noble purpose of protecting our country and way of life. Of more concern than the lies told is perhaps that the people who were explaining them (at least in the Iran Contra hearings) probably believed that they had acted in the best interests of their country. Colonel North's lies were presented as noble lies, not for personal gain or aggrandizement, but for the good of a worthy cause.

Sissela Bok adds further detail to the noble lie: in an imminent crisis, the public would not react properly if the truth were told; and the public, being relatively unsophisticated, simply cannot comprehend the complex and elaborate dealings that are required; thus a "certain amount of illusion is needed in order for public servants to be effective" (Bok 1978, 169). An illustration of this would be a case in which a vicious murderer is on the loose and the police chief is trying to calm fears so as to protect the community stability. The chief might say that the police force was making excellent progress on the case and there would soon be an arrest, so as to quell the community's fears. In reality, however, the investigation could be in complete disarray with no good leads. This lie could be considered justifiable from the chief's perspective, since it preserves the community's peace of mind. However, it can also be argued that these fabrications were intended to protect the chief from criticism and are therefore quite base. The difficulty with noble lies is that quite often they have base or selfish motives underlying them, and their noble qualities can often be a mere excuse for the popular bureaucratic activity described by the initials C.Y.A. Thus they are no less corrupt than a lie told to avoid being punished for some illegal action.

2) The Harmless Lie Telling a little white lie such as saying that someone looks nice when in fact they do not, seems harmless and even appropriate under some circumstances. A question can be raised, however, as to whether the motives behind the lie should be considered. If we say that a pure motive can justify the lie, then have we not justified the noble lie, which by definition is offered for a perceived *high purpose*? If, on the other hand, we say that motive does not matter, have we said in effect that the lie to protect the feelings of a friend is just as unethical as one told for purely selfish motives, and is this what we really believe? In the context of this discussion, this comes into play in the form of a slight twist of the truth in order cover a fellow officer's actions which are not perceived as deserving the punishment which will occur if the truth is known.

3) The Expected Lie   The expected lie is told when the other party knows, or at least should know, that you have moral authority to lie. An example of this would be the poker game and the undercover activity discussed in the last section. If the general understanding is that lies can be told in these circumstances, then it can certainly be argued that this type of lie is always ethical, at least so long as it is kept within the bounds of the agreed-upon rules.

4) The Necessary Lie   This is a lie that must be told to achieve a public good, at least a good in the mind of the speaker. Assume that in a police department that has had difficulty recruiting minorities, an extremely effective African American officer is correctly accused of using excessive force in an arrest. The departmental regulations call for the dismissal of any officer using excessive force, without exception. The chief decides that it best serves the interests of the public to keep the officer on the force since the officer's work has generally been outstanding and it would be difficult to hire a replacement. In order to do this the chief covers up the officer's involvement in this matter by using necessary lies and deception for the good of all concerned.

5) The No-Effect Lie   There are times when a lie can be used to accomplish a desired result while ultimately having no effect on the outcome of the event or decision. Your dentist's statement that you should "Hold still; this won't hurt a bit," is one such lie. In order for the dentist to properly drill out the cavity in your tooth, you must hold still. The lie that it won't hurt has no effect on the outcome, which, in this case, is the pain. The lie is told to facilitate something that will be accomplished one way or another, but with slightly less trouble if the lie is told. Consider the situation of an officer who operates a radar unit to catch speeders. The officer has made an arbitrary decision that noone going less than sixty-two miles per hour in a fifty-five zone will be arrested. Experience has shown the officer, however, that even allowing seven miles over the speed limit is not sufficient to avoid the sometimes violent arguments and even fights in court over the ticket. The officer, however, has devised a strategy for avoiding this problem. State law has a sliding fee scale for speeding; the faster you are going, the greater the monetary fine. When the officer clocks a car doing sixty-five miles per hour in a fifty-mile-per-hour zone, the driver is informed that radar indicated that the vehicle was traveling at sixty-nine miles per hour. The driver will then predictably object and argue, and the officer will allow the driver to beat him down to a charge of sixty-five miles per hour. Under these circumstances the driver is happy because there has been a reduction in the charge. The initial lie of the officer has had no effect whatsoever on the final outcome. If the driver had not objected, the officer would still have reduced the mileage with the statement, "at least this will reduce the punishment a little," and everyone would be happy, resulting in far fewer nasty arguments and angry motorists.

6) The Deserved Lie   The deserved lie is told in response to a request for information based on the theory that if the person requesting the information is foolish, unfeelingly mean, or obnoxious enough to ask the question, that person deserves to be lied to. Assume that two officers with both search and arrest warrants have just been dispatched to the house of a person alleged to sell illegal drugs from that address. Before the police arrive, the person in question calls your office and asks whether an arrest warrant has been issued.

If the caller is told the truth, it is likely that all of the drugs in the house will be disposed of before the arrival of the officers, thus thwarting the effect of the warrant. You ask for the caller's full name and then request that the caller hold the line while you check. You leave the phone to get a coke. Next, you verify the spelling of the name and tell the caller that you didn't find any warrants in that name. This is obviously an untrue but deserved answer. The same rationale is used to justify lies in support of a partner when being questioned by an internal affairs investigator concerning an allegation that your partner has, on occasion, had a beer while on duty. If internal affairs is ignorant enough to think you would give up your partner in such a minor matter, they deserve to be lied to.

7) The Self-Deception Lie   The most dangerous lie that can be told is the lie to one's self, yet it is probably the most common. No one likes to believe that he or she has acted in a deliberately bad manner. We all want to think that if something has happened, it is the fault of others, not ourselves. This is the basis of the strategy of blaming the victim when interrogating a suspect. The danger in this lie is that if it succeeds, we have deluded ourselves into losing our perspective of the situation, and without that, we are utterly incapable of evaluating or taking any effective action with regard to it.

Why Officers Lie

It is impossible to list all the reasons why law enforcement officers tell lies in certain situations and not in others, just as there can be no definitive list of the reasons that the rest of us tell lies on some occasions but not on others. The only thing that can be stated with any degree of certainty is that most of us lie, or at least attempt deception, on occasion. While the frequency may vary, it is impossible to travel through the complexities and conflicting demands of modern life without occasionally resorting to some form of deception. This is true even though most of us would not use deception to deliberately harm someone, and often the deception is for the purpose of avoiding hurting another's feelings. Having indicated that there cannot be a definitive list of reasons, consider the following as some of the more common rationalizations, which would justify deception.

Taking a Short-term Rather than Long-term Perspective   Consider the situation of the officer who overstates by five miles per hour the actual rate of speed of the motorist, fully intending to ultimately charge the person with the correct speed. Using a short-term perspective, it would be difficult to argue that this is inherently corrupt, since it will ultimately have no effect in the motorist's case and will not impact any other person. On the other hand, if word got out that the police patrolling the highways routinely overstated a motorist's speed, the public would quickly lose confidence in our law enforcement system. Even if an officer said that he or she was charging only our actual speed, why should we believe the officer since we know that officers have lied in the past? The danger here is that we are a society based on trust. If you doubt this, consider how often you would be willing to fly if you learned that the airlines had been lying to the public about the number of airline accidents each year in order to keep people from refusing to fly. Consider the trust we place in a physician when we allow him to place us, unconscious, on an operating table and cut into our bodies or our faith in the federal government when we pay taxes each year amounting to over a trillion dollars with the expectation that the money will be used for our benefit. In the short run, the officer's lie in this example is not likely to cause any harm or be bad in itself, but in the long run, if other officers routinely do this, all confidence will be lost in our law enforcement system, and it will cease to operate effectively.

When Lying is so Systemic that it is Perceived as Expected Using the above example, assume that motorists have now learned that a police agency by whom you are employed routinely overstates mileage by a certain amount. If you are honest about the motorist's speed, nobody is going to believe you, because the reputation is that everyone does it. Likewise, if everyone in the agency uses certain lies to their advantage on a regular basis, with no problems occurring, you will begin to believe that lying in that situation is not as bad as you first perceived it, and from there it is a very small step to beginning to lie in that situation yourself.

Procedure vs. Substance Some law enforcement officers feel that the only serious statutes are those which govern criminal conduct. They often view the rules of criminal procedure, which are judge-made as opposed to being created by a legislature with the approval of the chief executive, as less important than the criminal laws. Thus if a rule of criminal procedure has to be bent or broken by deception, this is acceptable in the view of some officers, so long as justice has been accomplished.

Lying as a Requirement of the Job It is not unusual in law enforcement investigations to have more to do than there is possibly time to accomplish, yet agencies often expect all of the assignments to be completed anyway. When these circumstances exist, shortcuts are periodically taken and then become the normal way of getting the job done. One shortcut is, of course, deception. If an officer is required to file a written report showing, as some agencies require, that he or she has done something on every investigation assigned to them, the officer will be virtually forced to resort to deception if the case load is more than can reasonably be handled. If the officers each have a total of 127 active investigations, then they might develop a habit of driving by the scenes of crimes or the suspects' houses each month on their way home, then writing a report asserting that the crime scene was again checked for clues or that surveillance was conducted. While these statements would not be outright lies, they would clearly be statements intended to deceive superiors into believing that something had been done on a case when that was not true. When it is departmental policy to condone such deception, it becomes a very short step to more objectionable deceptions.

When is a Lie Acceptable? As has been discussed, there are some instances when an officer is expected to use deception in performing the job assigned, such as undercover investigations or some aspects of interrogation. When lying is expected on some occasions and is judicially condoned under certain circumstances, it sometimes becomes difficult for officers to distinguish between when it is proper and when it is improper. Under these circumstances, lying may appear to be appropriate when it serves the officers' purposes, rather than when it is right.

Offensive vs. Defensive Lies   To determine the wrongfulness of a lie, should a distinction be made between those that are intended to benefit us in some affirmative way and those that protect us? In the old movies, it was only the villain who tried to distract the hero to make him fall into the alligator pit or be bitten by the giant spider so that the villain's nefarious schemes would succeed. When the villain pulled his dastardly deceptions, the audience would always boo and shout a warning to the hero. When the hero, faced with impossible odds shouted for the bad guys to look out behind them, we always cheered for the imaginative action. Was our reaction solely because it was our hero, or did we even then distinguish between the nature of the two deceptions; one being offensive, used for personal gain, and the other being defensive in nature, used for the self-preservation? It is clear that most people react more negatively to an offensive lie, where the person is trying to deceive for the purposes of gaining something, than a defensive lie uttered for the purpose of protecting oneself. Many officers would also seem to make this distinction, feeling that there is a vast gulf of difference between perjury on the witness stand in a criminal trial and a mere statement under oath to help a fellow officer out of a difficult situation.

Should a distinction be made between lies told to trick someone or secure a conviction and those told to protect an officer? Such an idea is seductive, but would not an internal affairs investigation into alleged thefts by an officer represent a threat to the officer? Under these circumstances, would we be willing to say that the officer is morally justified in attempting to deceive the investigators? Many questions, including who would make the distinction between offensive and defensive, make such a concept difficult in terms of its application.

Whistle-Blowing, Informing, Leaking, and Covering Up   In this section certain distinctions need to be made concerning terms that are often used interchangeably. The distinctions are important since the ethical considerations involved in each can vary considerably. Whistle-blowing is a term commonly used to refer to making information that should be kept secret available to the public. The motive of the whistle-blower is to protect the public, but often the act has heavy political or ideological overtones and sometimes also represents a desire for a moment in the limelight. The act of whistle-blowing is a public act (meaning that the whistle-blower makes no attempt to hide his or her identity) to correct a wrong that is not normally directed specifically at the whistle-blower.

Informing, unlike whistle-blowing, is usually a private delivering of information to another so the other person acts on it. The usual vision that springs to mind when we hear the term *informant* is a sleazy, cowardly, quasi-criminal individual whispering in the ear of a person who would never consider associating with the informer were it not for the information that the informant has. As used here, however, an informant is simply any person who tells another of the acts of a third person for the purpose of allowing the recipient of the information to act on the information if he or she so chooses. It is not restricted to those who inform for pay or immunity, nor to those who inform to "get back at" someone they dislike. A police officer who, on observing his or her partner commit an illegal act, immediately arrests the partner, is not an informer. The officer who includes the illegal act in a report of the incident is acting as an informant since the information, rather than being acted on directly, is being passed on to another for action. There is no ethical connotation, positive or negative, inherent in the act of either informing or whistle-blowing. Their moral value, like most situations posed here, depends on the circumstances surrounding the incident.

Leaking, as used here, is a combination of informing and whistle-blowing. The leaker is normally in possession of information that his or her position requires be kept confidential, much as the whistle-blower. In this case, however, in order not to be exposed to possible retribution the leaker whispers the information in the ear of another who is in a position to make the information public in such a way as to allow the leaker to remain anonymous, as was the case of Deep Throat in the Watergate scandal. A distinction for purposes here is that the leaker is normally supplying information for the purpose of embarrassing his or her employer into taking or refraining from taking some action, not particularly for the purpose of allowing the recipient to act appropriatly, other than to make the information public. In other words, the whistle-blower makes a public stand and accepts the possible consequences of the act, while the leaker wishes to achieve the success of the whistleblower without the risk of being identified. As in the case of whistle-blowing, strong policy or political overtones are normally present in the motive to act, as well as perhaps a desire for revenge against the person or entity being reported.

As an illustration, assume the chief of police is keeping a mistress and using agency funds to support her. A whistle-blower, as defined here, would take evidence of the chief's misconduct to the papers in an effort to have him ousted for his misdeeds. An informer, on the other hand, would pass the evidence onto either a member of the city council or the chief's wife for such action as they might deem appropriate. A leaker would pass the information to a reporter for the purpose of stopping the actions of the chief through embarrassment, while staying safely in the shadows in case things did not go as planned.

Covering Up   Covering up is the converse of the above actions and, as used here, is either the failure to report or act on the improper behavior of another for personal reasons. It also includes the affirmative actions of attempting to assist the guilty person in concealing his or her acts so as to avoid exposure and possible punishment. Covering up includes looking the other way when another is doing something improper. As defined here, deliberate avoidance of the facts so as to be able to assert, with technical truthfulness, that you do not know what happened is covering up from an ethical as opposed to legal standpoint, just as surely as is helping the guilty party dispose of evidence of guilt. A person who has knowledge of an unethical or illegal act on the part of another cannot claim not to have acted corruptly merely by inaction. Thus, it can be argued that not only is the officer taking the bribe acting corruptly, but all of those who have knowledge of the bribe are equally corrupt, even though they received no part of it.

Factors Contributing to Support of Subculture Activities

In addition to the above, other factors contribute to the support, or at least tolerance, of corrupt acts of fellow officers. The effect of these various considerations will be different from officer to officer, but will affect all to some extent.

Being a Snitch   To maintain their power, repressive governments throughout history have depended on informants within both the general public and organized opposition to their tyranny. An informant is perceived as a traitor who has violated the sanctity of a confidence entrusted to him. Even as children, most of us recall that one of the vilest names that we could be called was tattle-tale. Police and criminals alike view the informer with distaste. While the police find it necessary to cultivate informers in order to maintain order and solve crimes, they generally do not like or respect them. Police view informers as necessary evil, to be dealt with but not admired. While there is a difference between an informer trading information for money or other favors and an officer doing his sworn duty, the analogy will nevertheless be a factor in any officer's determination of whether to report the misdeeds of a colleague. Many officers view this as the conflict of two ethical values; the need to do one's duty and report the misdeed, and the need not to be a tattle tale.

Dependence   Dependence on other officers for safety and support increases an officer's need to be accepted by fellow officers. Since the other officers know of an officer's need to be accepted, they are less likely to be won over with ingratiating comments and small favors. In return for acceptance, they demand absolute and unquestioned loyalty to the group. Unquestioned loyalty and support between officers is important for both physical and emotional survival in law enforcement. It bolsters the officers' confidence and provides the moral support of which they have been deprived by the marks of office such as the uniform and the weapon. It allows the officer to deal with or at least tolerate the perceived hostility and indifference of the public he or she is supposed to be protecting. If an officer violates the prime rule of the subculture by informing on another officer, he or she will almost certainly lose his or her position in the group and with it, the peer support needed to survive the rigors of the job.

Public Overreaction   Because the media and the public traditionally overreact to any revelation of law enforcement corruption or misdoing, there is a natural reluctance on the part of most officers to take an action that could seriously damage the whole department and deprive it, at least for the short term, of community support and respect. In their view, this deprivation would also make it difficult to complete their protective function, thus also denying their service to the public and gratifying only the news media and critics of the police.

Code of Silence   The law enforcement code of silence, covering all of the things that an officer learns but cannot discuss, leads to a natural reticence to disclose any information about a fellow officer. It has been widely researched and determined that loyalty and conformity are major requirements of the subculture and because of these and the natural air of secrecy that is fostered by the nature of the job, a code of silence concerning the misdeeds of officers is inevitable. This code covers repeating only those things which someone else has a need to know. This code and the underlying requirement of loyalty to fellow officers allows an officer to justify a failure to report improper conduct by saying that the superior did not need to know, or if he or she did need to know, that it was the superior's duty to find out.

Promotional Policies   Generally speaking, it is nearly impossible for an officer to obtain a promotion if he or she is not accepted within the cadre of the agency. Since virtually all promotions are made from within the ranks, an officer needs the support of the other officers in order to be promoted. In many instances, the rite of passage for acceptance into the organization is the unspoken agreement either to participate, or at least ignore minor acts of corruption by other officers. Once an officer is promoted, he or she is now supervising basically the same group that the officer was recently supporting in their minor corruptions. Imagine the difficulty of a new sergeant disciplining a former partner for sleeping while on duty when he had condoned (or participated in) the same activity only a short while ago. Thus the system of agency advancement can contribute to the difficulty of acting against many corrupt acts of fellow officers.

The Total Role

The role of a law enforcement officer is a total one, meaning that because of the isolation from the rest of the public and the requirement that he or she be on duty twenty-four hours a day, an officer is immersed in the role of law enforcement with little opportunity to evaluate his or her actions in light of personal ethical beliefs. This immersion allows small steps to be taken which are corrupt as a whole but individually do not seem wrong. Several Watergate participants expressed this view indicating that no single step that they took in the cover-up seemed improper. It was only when they stepped back and examined what they had done in its totality that the immorality of the acts became clear.

Acceptability of Deception   The fact that deception is permitted and even encouraged in many aspects of law enforcement makes the law at times appear to be merely a game rather than a rational system for maintaining order and achieving justice. When something is viewed as merely a game, strict adherence to the rules can seem less important than if the acts concerned real matters.

Discretion to Act   Officers are unofficially given discretion to charge or not charge citizens as they deem appropriate, after having considered all of the circumstances of the particular incident. This approach has also been judicially approved in other situations but can present problems for an officer who is deciding whether or not to inform. This discretion can help justify taking into account extraneous factors such as damage to the agency from adverse publicity, damage to the career of the officer, punishment which may not be proportionate to the offense, probability of damage to the informer's own career, and what seems just under the circumstances. This discretion, while not unreasonable, contributes to corruption in many agencies by allowing the corrupt officers' associates to exercise their discretion not to act.

Clean vs. Dirty Bribes

A clean bribe is ordinarily thought of as a payment for services which are not directly related to the police officer's duty. Payments by lawyers, bail bondsmen, and towing services for referrals of people in need of their services would fall in this category. If a person asks the police officer for the name of a wrecker to tow their damaged car, the argument goes, the officer can, not corruptly, suggest a particular service. If the service compensates the officer, there has been no harm to the citizen as long as the standard fee for towing is charged. The harm, if any, would be to the other towing companies to whom the officer owes no duty. Therefore such actions, whether forbidden by regulation or not, are not generally considered corrupt.

It can be argued that there is a distinction between violations of the law, such as theft or bribery, and violations of rules, such as sleeping on duty or violating regulations and citizens' rights by applying street justice to a situation. The feeling expressed in justifying this is that the first are laws for everyone to follow, while the latter apply only to the police and therefore are not as important, particularly since a citizen doing the same thing would not be punished in any meaningful way. The attitude of most police executives reinforces this view by showing a remarkable lack of interest in punishing such misconduct.

Since law enforcement officers are considered to be on duty twenty-four hours a day, should the activities they participate in during personal time be subject to the same scrutiny that we attempt to require while they are on duty, or should they be subject to the same rules as other citizens? For instance, is a police officer required to report his or her partner when it is discovered that the partner is cheating on his or her electric bill by rigging the meter? It would seem that rules, in order to be fair, must be fairly and equally applied. If this is not a matter that would otherwise be prosecuted, it would not seem that informing is required, although the agency would undoubtedly be harmed if it became public knowledge that an officer was stealing electricity. In this case, the final distinction also comes into play. Is an officer required to act against another on strong suspicion or only when actual knowledge is obtained? More simply, can an officer ethically ignore a confirmed or suspected dishonest deed to justify not reporting an incident?

SUMMARY

This article has not only attempted to define some of the parameters of corruption, but also tried to illustrate why in many instances no clear line can be drawn between a corrupt and a non-corrupt act. In many cases, the criminality depends on the intention of the actor, particularly in the extraordinarily complex areas of deception and street justice. An attempt has also been made to demonstrate how departmental policies and attitudes can promote a climate in which corruption can flourish and that a periodic housecleaning of some bad apples will not eliminate the root cause of the potential for corruption within the department.

REFERENCES

Annarino, W. (May, 1996). Unpublished survey of police attitudes.

Barker, T. (March, 1982). "Police Administrators' Attitudes Toward the Definition and Control of Police Deviance." *FBI Law Enforcement Bulletin,* Washington, D.C.: Federal Bureau of Investigation.

Bok, Sissela. (1978). *Lying: Moral Choice in Public and Private Life.* New York: Pantheon Books.

Brenner, R. and Kravitz, M., eds. (1979). *A Community Concern: Police Use of Deadly Force,* Washington, D.C.: United States Department of Justice.

Brown, M. (1981). *Working the Street: Police Discretion and the Dilemmas of Reform,* New York: Russell Sage Foundation.

Charles, M. (1986). *Policing the Streets,* Springfield, Illinois: Charles C. Thomas.

Croft, Elizabeth. (1986). "Police Use of Force: a Twenty-Year Perspective." Paper presented at the annual meeting of the Academy of Criminal Justice Sciences.

Inciardi, J. (1996). *Criminal Justice,* Fort Worth: Harcourt Brace.

Klockars, C. (1980). "The Dirty Harry Problem." In *The Police and Violence,* edited by Sherman, L., Spec. Philadelphia: The American Academy of Political and Social Science.

Knapp Commission, (1972). *The Knapp Commission Report on Police Corruption,* New York: George Brazille.

Reiss, A., (1971). *The Police and the Public,* New Haven: Yale University Press.

Skolnick, J., (1975). *Justice Without Trial: Law Enforcement in a Democratic Society,* 2d ed., New York: John Wiley and Sons.

Wilson, J. Q. and Kelling, G. L. (March, 1982). "Broken Windows: The Police and Neighborhood Safety. " *Atlantic Monthly.*

Wintersmith, R., (1974). *Police and the Black Community.* Lexington, Mass.: D.C. Heath and Co.

ARTICLE 7

POLICE PERCEPTIONS AND THE NORMING OF INSTITUTIONAL CORRUPTION

Robert J. McCormack
Department of Law and Justice, The College of New Jersey,
Trenton, New Jersey USA
(Received 10 February 1996: in final form 26 July 1996)

This paper discusses the phenomenon of corruption in major urban police departments in the United States and explores the tendency in most to tolerate corruption at damaging levels. It presents a model of the "normed corruption" dynamic and posits that corruption much like other organizational problems such as police shootings, auto chases, abuse of sick time, etc., can be controlled administratively with strong leadership and consistent effort. The paper also discusses long and short term approaches to corruption management in police agencies.

Keywords: Police, police corruption, institutional corruption, corruption factors, corruption control, ethical awareness.

POLICE CORRUPTION: A BRIEF REVIEW

In Forces of Deviance: Understanding the Dark Side of Policing, Kappeler, Sluder and Alpert point out that corruption among police is not new or peculiar to the late 20th century. "To study the history of police is to study police deviance, corruption and misconduct" (Kappeler *et al.*, 1994: 30).

Policing in England in the pre-industrial revolution era was a civilian endeavor centered in small groups of families organized to assure public safety. Groups called tithings and hundreds were headed by constables and shire-reeves appointed to the offices. This system apparently worked well in rural areas. However, by the beginning of the 18th century, the office of the constable in the larger cities was notoriously corrupt. " . . . constables performed

Note: This paper is an expanded version of a paper, Police Perceptions and the Norming of Police Corruption, presented at the Annual Meeting of the American Society of Criminology in Miami, Florida on November 10, 1994.

'shakedowns' of citizens by accepting payment to keep criminal matters out of court . . . and were bribed to forego law enforcement so that gin shops could remain open . . . not only was the law enforcement system corrupt, but the political system and the government were also rife with corruption" (Kappeler *et al.*, 1994: 31–32).

Among the London Metropolitan police created by the British Parliament in 1829 to replace the watchman/constable system, dismissals and forced resignations for behavior that included drunkenness, receiving gambling payoffs, soliciting sexual favors and accepting gratuities were common.

In the United States the "British" model of policing was quickly adopted because of its remarkable impact on social disorder and crime. However, as opposed to its centrally organized structure, U.S. policing developed locally, mainly on a city by city basis. The police became subject to political control as officers were appointed and promoted by local political leaders and became "bag men" or collectors of graft. " . . . if there is a common theme that can be used to characterize the police in the 19th century, it is the large-scale corruption that occurred in most police departments across the United States" (Uchida, 1993).

> In many large cities the police virtually ignored laws against drinking, prostitution and gambling. Nonenforcement of the law, in many cases, was directly tied to systematic payoffs made to the police. Corruption in many departments was controlled at the precinct level but often involved officers throughout the department. St. Louis, for example, had repeated incidents of top-ranking police officials notifying operators of gambling operations that a police raid was about to take place. In New York City precinct captains often controlled systematic payoffs from illegal businesses . . . standard monthly payoffs were $100–$300 for poolrooms, $50–$150 for brothels, and $50–$300 from gambling houses . . . it is estimated that saloons in New York City paid $50,000–$60,000 each month to police and politicians (Kappeler *et al.*, 1994: 43,44).

Over the years reformers made efforts to clean up policing. The federal legislation creating civil service (the Pendleton Act of 1883) was designed to rescue policing from the politicians and was one of the most helpful initiatives. It established a merit-based system of selecting and promoting police personnel that was adopted by many city and state governments. It formed a foundation for subsequent efforts to "professionalize" the police in the early years of the 20th century. Despite these efforts there have been many police corruption scandals—followed by reforms—over the years that have involved officers in almost every major city police agency in the country.

In 1967, in the *Task Force Report: The Police, the President's Commission on Law Enforcement and the Administration of Justice* cautiously pointed out that "at least in some cities a significant number of officers engage in varying forms of criminal and unethical conduct." It indicated that the Commission's "limited studies affords no basis for general conclusions as to the exact extent of police dishonesty or the degree to which political corruption affects police service today" (Task Force Report, p. 473).

Since that time, however, police corruption has become an issue of major concern to community and governmental groups with the introduction of narcotics as an important variable in the corruption equation. The theft (from street dealers) and sale of narcotics by police officers has reached epidemic proportions in some police agencies. As a result, the dimensions and the impact of administrative efforts to control corruption have become the subject of closer examination and its nature has become better understood.

FOCUS ON NEW YORK CITY

Primarily as a response to a nationally publicized corruption scandal in New York City in the early 1970's, much research has been conducted and many articles and books written about police corruption. The extensively researched report of the New York City scandal, entitled "Commission to Investigate Allegations of Police Corruption and the City's Anti-Corruption Procedures," better known as the Knapp Commission Report, was the product of one of the most extensive investigations of the subject ever conducted and its anti-corruption recommendations have been widely implemented within police agencies.

The Commission found corruption to be wide-spread. It rejected the "rotten apple" theory and instead maintained that the problem was systemic; that it involved all sectors of the Department. Patrol officers "were not found to receive money on nearly so grand or organized a scale (as other sectors), but the large number of small payments they received presented an equally serious if less dramatic problem." The report indicated that corrupt policemen fell into two basic categories, meat-eaters and grass-eaters. "The meat-eaters are those patrolmen who . . . aggressively misuse their police powers for personal gain. The grass-eaters simply accept the payoffs that the happenstances of police work throw their way." It insisted that not all police officers were corrupt if petty mooching was excluded from the calculations, but that even they contributed to its systemic nature. In fact, according to the commission, *grass-eaters were the heart of the problem because their great numbers tend to make corruption 'respectable'*.

This later point regarding grass-eaters and meat-eaters is perhaps the most significant and universally applicable finding of the Commission. It applies not only to New York City but to policing where ever it is taking place and clearly indicates the point at which anticorruption efforts must start. Consistent and determined leadership following the New York City scandal showed that by controlling and reducing "respectable" or "normed" corruption to its lowest possible level ("taking anything besides your paycheck is corrupt," Patrick Murphy, NYC Police Commissioner), an ethical department ethos can begin to emerge. Initially, the developing ethos consists of the collective perceptions of officers as to the rightness or wrongness of their behavior as it is conditioned by sanctions. Over time these perceptions become reasonable expectations of management. Once an ethical ethos takes hold it must be supported until it becomes internalized and probity becomes not only a function of sanctions but of individual officer self discipline. In such departments engaging in serious or criminally defined corruption becomes exceedingly more difficult because the new ethos does not support it.

For a variety of reasons, the success in controlling corruption in the New York City Police Department after the scandal lasted only a little more than a decade. During that period, however, it was generally agreed by students of the Department that serious systemic corruption had been virtually eliminated. This was the result of sustained attention to the problem on the part of its executive staff, appropriate manpower allocations to deal with the problem, and determined effort and continuity of leadership within the internal affairs unit of the Department.

The level of corruption in the Department began to rise again in the early 1980s as the leadership, safeguards and priorities introduced following the scandal changed. A serious narcotics corruption conspiracy in the mid-1980s was followed and eclipsed by the revelations of the Mollen Commission (on police corruption) in the early 1990s. It was clear by then that the era of systemic corruption had returned. The Mollen Commission's report continually referenced the lack of leadership and commitment on the part of the Department's executives as the reasons for corruption's reappearance, duration and pervasiveness (Commission, 1993).

THE NORMED CORRUPTION MODEL

The normed corruption model is presented in illustration #1. It maintains that agency leadership and fair and consistent discipline shapes police officers' perceptions as to the probity of their job related behavior. Activities of officers that do not generally merit disciplinary action when discovered become normed (respectable, as the Knapp Commission suggests). Conversely, activities which, when observed, consistently result in disciplinary action (fines, suspensions or dismissals) become less frequent where the possibility of detection is real. To the degree that the leadership of a police agency specifically defines marginal activities it considers to be unethical (ex., accepting free or discounted meals, accepting gifts and gratuities, shopping in uniform, etc.), communicates this disapproval unequivocally, and fairly sanctions officers who transgress, normed corruption is reduced to its lowest common denominator. This process requires determined and persistent effort over a considerable period of time—several years, perhaps a decade as suggested by one reform chief (Law Enforcement News, 1976)—before significant and consistent behavioral change occurs. Eventually, what were once operating procedures largely ignored evolve into the actual day-to-day routine of the agency; what was acceptable under former leadership is no longer tolerated. As standards are enforced and internalized they come to represent a consensus among officers regarding appropriate behavior.

Such a multi-year struggle to impact corruption is not inconsistent with other managerial efforts to improve the quality of personnel and services delivered to the public by the police. Change in most bureaucracies comes slowly and involves shaping the perceptions of officers in the organization. In the final analysis, officers' perceptions are the factors that determine the outcome of most police incidents. James Q. Wilson concludes that policies within a police agency should reflect a general underlying principle that will guide the use of discretion in cases where no rules seem to apply. Controlling subordinates depends only partly on sanctions and inducements; it also requires instilling in them a shared outlook or ethos that provides for them a common definition of the situations they are likely to encounter (Wilson, 1969: 131).

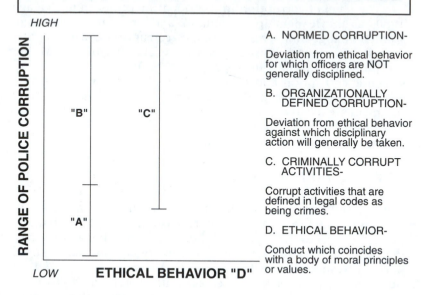

A POLICE CORRUPTION CONTROL MODEL

HIGH

RANGE OF POLICE CORRUPTION

"B"   "C"

"A"

LOW   ETHICAL BEHAVIOR "D"

A. NORMED CORRUPTION-

Deviation from ethical behavior for which officers are NOT generally disciplined.

B. ORGANIZATIONALLY DEFINED CORRUPTION-

Deviation from ethical behavior against which disciplinary action will generally be taken.

C. CRIMINALLY CORRUPT ACTIVITIES-

Corrupt activities that are defined in legal codes as being crimes.

D. ETHICAL BEHAVIOR-

Conduct which coincides with a body of moral principles or values.

This model proposes that administrative discipline shapes police officers' perceptions of the range of normed corruption in an agency. What one would not generally be disciplined for becomes custom. In agencies where the normed corruption level is high, some criminally corrupt activities become normed. Conversely, as the range of organizationally defined corruption is expanded, the range of normed corruption contracts.

ILLUSTRATION 1

FACTORS EFFECTING LEVELS OF NORMED CORRUPTION

The following are among the most important factors that impact on the levels of normed corruption in an agency:

The Political Environment

Efforts to reform police agencies in communities in which there is a high level of political corruption, and little community interest or effort to eradicate it, are almost always doomed to failure. Sherman points out that the best prospect for true police reform is after a major police corruption scandal

(Sherman, 1975a). A new police chief or commissioner with the support of local governmental officials and a clear mandate to do the job has perhaps the best chance of eliminating systemic corruption and reducing entrepreneurial corruption to a minimum.

Police Leadership

Ethical leadership over time is the most important factor in reducing improbity to its lowest level. Effective leadership is acknowledged as a vital resource for corruption control, and formerly corrupt departments have succeeded in re-establishing integrity under the guidance of effective and forceful leaders (Ward and McCormack, 1987: 114). Specific strategies regarding the leadership role of the chief of police are addressed in the latter part of this paper.

Recruitment/Retention Policies

Current police recruitment and retention policies in many major cities tend to bring to policing officers that in previous years would not have been hired and/or to retain officers who should have been screened out during the recruit training or probation periods. Police agencies that do not have at least a ten to fifteen percent dismissal rate during the training and probationary periods are probably not using these periods effectively. In many of the more selective police agencies that view the academy training as part of the selection process, dismissal rates can be as high as fifty percent.

Education Requirements

There is a growing body of literature on policing which indicates that college educated officers perform better than their high school educated peers (Lynch, 1976; Hoover, 1989; Cohen & Chaiken, 1972; Smith, Locke & Walker, 1968; Bowker, 1980). There has also been a dramatic increase in the number of college graduates attracted to policing as a career. Since college graduates tend to be older than many of the officers being recruited directly out of high school and have experienced the leavening nature of an undergraduate education one might expect that their moral maturity might be higher than that of traditional candidates. Allen Shealy's early research in this area should be expanded upon. He reports that " . . . preemployment variables exist that can be measured during preemployment screening and are predictive of judged moral conduct of policemen" (Shealy, 1978: 13). Given the growing complexities of police work and the ability of police salaries to keep pace with those in the private sector, it makes sense for police agencies to compete with the private sector for the most promising candidates each year.

Police Unions

The Knapp and Mollen Commissions previously referred to, pointed out that concern for the possible alienation of leaders of the police fraternal organization was a major factor that affected more aggressive investigation and prosecution of known criminal acts by groups of police officers. Efforts should be made to reduce the impact of police unions on the legitimate exercise of managerial prerogatives on the part of police executives.

CORRUPTION CONTROL RATHER THAN ELIMINATION

Most experts agree that police corruption cannot be entirely eliminated and that control is the only realistic approach to the problem. Formal control systems designed to shape the perceptions and expectations of officers and at the same time reduce discretionary action have the greatest potential for producing behavioral change (Simpson 1977: 129). While these initiatives are essential, any program that seeks to control corruption on a long term basis must consider the informal organization as the dominant force for change. The long term goal of corruption management, then, should be to develop an organizational environment that regulates itself through positive peer pressure (McCormack, 1987: 154).

In departments that have a serious corruption problem, corruption management programs must address both short and long-term remedies. Short term approaches are basically Hobbesian in nature. They involve (1) heightening the perceptions of agency personnel regarding the problem of corruption, (2) setting specific policy guidelines for police conduct, (3) enforcing the guidelines by means of a proactive system of internal supervision, and (4) having agency-wide dissemination of information concerning the nature of resultant disciplinary action. The long term objective is to develop a consistently shared outlook among officers supportive of the new ethical policies of the department. The secret to the success of a corruption-control program, then, is bridging the gap between coercion and cooperation.

Developing Ethical Perception Patterns

While initially one may view a beginning phase of corruption control program as a rather primitive attempt at behavioral change, the long-range effects of such a process should not be underestimated. If one assumes that most police officers are basically honest, hardworking people who wish to do a good job, a pervasive organizational effort to root out serious corruption provides officers with an opportunity to resist peer group pressure to act unethically. **A strong proactive internal affairs initiative coupled with an uncompromising and consistent implementation of sanctions provides an excuse for being honest that may be acceptable to many of the rank and file.** After all, every police officer recognizes the consequence of being caught in a corrupt act. Under intense supervision, reluctance to engage in unethical behavior may be viewed not only as acceptable but also perhaps as prudent by other officers. As a result, many officers who are seeking ethical guidance may secretly welcome such efforts if policies are realistic and fair.

This approach to corruption management requires accountability at every level of the agency. Control requires clear guidelines for subordinates, as this minimizes the use of discretion. Staff monitoring and inspection are essential. It should be pointed out that this sanction driven model is not purely theoretical. The reduction of police corruption through the implementation of more effective managerial control is well documented. Police scandal followed by organization change and reform has been reported by Sherman (1975a) in the police departments of New York City; Oakland, California; Newburg, New York; and "Central City." Williams (1973) cites similar examples in the cities of Seattle, Washington, and Louisville, Kentucky. Both the Knapp and Mollen Commission Reports include many recommendations for tightening administrative controls. In several of the above departments, the long-term result of strong managerial leadership was long term change.

A Multi-Disciplinary Approach

The short-term effect of strong internal controls will produce noticeable behavioral change as a result of the heightened risk of detection. Long-term change depends more upon internalizing new ethical standards. It is here that knowledge generated by social scientists may be applied. If, for example, corruption is viewed as a function of anomie, the administrator may opt for a program that would increase salaries and reduce opportunities for illegal gain. If subcultural differences are seen as the primary cause of corruption, activities designed to align police subcultural values more closely with those of the community (assuming an ethical community environment) may be effective on a long-term basis. Socio-psychological theories would suggest improved screening of recruits particularly in the area of moral maturity and more selective assignment.

The only effective approach to corruption management, therefore, is a multi-disciplinary one. While one does not need to understand fully the root causes of the problem to initiate a program to address it, long-term success depends upon resolving specific problems related to causality. It is in this area that the failure of many anti-corruption efforts can be found.

CONCLUSION

According to proponents of organizations theory, the key to effective managerial accountability is to have clear operational policy guidelines for subordinates, as this minimizes the use of discretion. Standards must also be set for all supervisors, and authority commensurate with responsibility delegated to each. Staff monitoring and inspection of administrative and operational units to insure disciplinary effectiveness of lower level supervisors is essential. The impact of improved managerial accountability will not only tend to improve the effectiveness and efficiency of the agency but will also, if applied with the same vigor to corruption management, go a long way in reducing systemic corruption.

Organizational theories have perhaps great pragmatic value in the initial stages of corruption control. There is a sufficient amount of literature in the field to indicate that control by means of positive and negative discipline will have a significant impact. It has been suggested, however, that tight managerial controls should be applied in combination with other techniques: "what maintains conformity to organizational policy is a good balance of pride and fear, deterrence and voluntary compliance" (Sherman, 1975b: 9). Simpson sagely points out that "the question of what constitutes a good balance" seems, however, to be what constitutes the problem in this discussion (1977: 136).

REFERENCES

Bokwer, L. (1980) "A theory of educational needs of law enforcement officers." *Journal of Contemporary Criminal Justice.* 1 (1), 17–24.

Cohen, B. and Cahiken J. (1972) *Police background characteristics and performance: Summary.* New York: Rand Institute.

——— (1993) Commission to Investigate Allegations of Police Corruption and the Anti-Corruption Procedures of the New York City Police Department: Interim Report and Principal Recommendations. New York: Mollen Commission.

Hoover, L. (1989) "Education." In *The encyclopedia of police science,* edited by W. G. Bailey 165–70. New York: Garland Publishing.

Kappeler, V. E., Sluder, R. D. and Alpert, G. P. (1984) *Forces of Deviance: Understanding the Dark Side of Policing.* Prospect Heights, Illinois: Waveland Press.

——— (1972). The Knapp Commission Report on Police Corruption, New York: George Barziller, Inc.

Lynch, G. (1976) "Contributions of higher education to ethical behavior in law enforcement." *Journal of Criminal Justice,* 4(4), 285–90.

McCormack, R. J. (1987) Update: Confronting Police Corruption: Organizational Initiatives for Internal Control. In R. H. Ward and R. J. McCormack, *Managing Police Corruption: International Perspectives.* Chicago, Illinois: Office of International Criminal Justice, The University of Illinois at Chicago.

——— (1973) National Advisory Commission on Criminal Justice Standards and Goals: Police. Washington, D.C.: U.S. Government Printing Office.

——— (1976) *Patrolling Corruption from the Top.* Interview of Charles Gain, Chief of the San Francisco Police Department by Robert McCormack. New York: Law Enforcement News: September 7:9.

Shealy, A. E. (1978) Police Integrity: *The Role of Psychological Screening of Applicants.* New York: Criminal Justice Center, John Jay College of Criminal Justice.

Sherman Lawrence (1975a) *Controlling police corruption: Final Report.* Washington D.C.: National Institute of Law Enforcement and Criminal Justice, Grant no. 75N-99-00-24-G.

——— (1975b) Controlling police corruption: What works? Paper presented at the American Society of Criminology. Toronto: 9.

Simpson, A. (1977) *The Literature of Police Corruption: A Guide to Bibliography to Theory, Vol. 1.* New York: John Jay Press.

Smith, A., Lock, B. and Walker, W. (1968) "Authoritarianism in police college students and non-police college students." *Journal of Criminal Law, Criminology & Police Science,* **50**, 440–43.

Uchida, C. D. (1993) "The Development of the American Police: An Historical Overview." In R. G. Durham and G. P. Alpert (eds) *Critical Issues in Policing: Contemporary Readings 2nd edition*. Prospect Heights, Illinois: Waveland Press.

Ward, Richard and McCormack, Robert (1979) *An anti-corruption manual for administrators in law enforcement 1st edition.* New York: John Jay Press.

Williams, R. (1973) *Vice Squad.* New York: Thomas Y. Crowell.

Wilson, J.Q. (1969) "What Makes a Better Policeman?" Atlantic, Vol. 223, No. 3, March: 131.

POLICE CORRUPTION AND CRIMINAL MONOPOLY: VICTIMLESS CRIMES

David E. Sisk*
San Francisco State University

In the absence of perfect price discrimination, monopoly will reduce output; thus Buchanan[1] has proposed that the public should encourage, or at least take a benign view of, the monopolization of criminal activity. In this note, I investigate Buchanan's proposal by taking account of the well-documented role of police as input suppliers to criminals specializing in victimless crimes. The input police supply is simply the right to operate in a given police jurisdiction, and the payment police receive may be formally prearranged with criminals. That such payments are labeled "bribes" and that police who collect bribes are labeled "corrupt" should not be allowed to obscure the analysis of the activity. Collection of bribes by police is, in principle, no different than any benefit to employees above their salary: the greater are such benefits, the less will be the salary necessary to call forth a given work force. In the case of police, the collection of bribes will reduce the price of police to the public. The bribe system is, thus, similar to a tax system in which revenues are earmarked for a particular expense item; bribes impose costs just as do taxes and are earmarked for the payment of police salaries. The public thus appears to have the moral satisfaction of prohibiting activities which, in fact, are only being taxed. Unfortunately, the bribe system is quite likely to turn police into accomplices in crime, not only in victimless crimes but in crimes

---

*Department of Economics, San Francisco State University.

[1]James Buchanan, A Defense of Organized Crime? in Economics of Crime and Punishment 119 (Simon Rottenberg ed. 1973).

with victims as well. The superior moral posture acquired by promoting laws against victimless crimes is, thus, very costly indeed.

I. BRIBES

From the viewpoint of law enforcement, there is an important distinction between victimless crimes, such as gambling and prostitution, and crimes with victims, such as robbery and murder. For victimless crimes there is no "victim" to monitor police performance in a specific case; therefore, the opportunity arises for a capturing officer to accept a bribe and let the offender go free. (The official reward structure should also favor arrests of dangerous criminals, and such criminals will tend to be those who perpetrate crimes on victims.) With a victim-monitor at hand, police are constrained to arrest a criminal who is captured. Of course, negative externalities or neighborhood effects of victimless crimes may be imposed on bystanders, inducing them to perform the role of victim-monitors; this would force police to forgo bribes and arrest offenders. In general, one would expect bystander monitoring to increase with the level of illicit activity. Bribes for victimless crimes appear to fall into two categories: collections or "scores" by individual policemen who happen in the course of their duties to come across a unique or unanticipated crime, such as a floating card game, and formally prearranged collections or "pads" by a particular police unit or units from an ongoing illicit operation established in a fixed location within the unit's jurisdiction, for example, numbers operations.

Of course, a simple tax on the illicit activity would serve to impose costs just as well, but apparently public mores simply do not permit the implicit condoning of certain activities. The difference between a tax and a bribe system is not, however, that the tax increases the government revenues while the bribe does not. Bribes are a reward for police employment and, therefore, will reduce the public payments required to attract labor into police employment. The effect of such bribes will tend to be larger if the bribes are widely shared among all police rather than being kept by a few police. Even in the latter case, the chance of being assigned to duties with high potential for collecting bribes should lower the supply price to the force; however, the variance of such returns will be reduced if bribes are generally shared throughout the force. And, indeed, sharing occurs through two routes. First, police who collect bribes directly will find that other police will demand a share. For instance, the Knapp Commission reported that police who scored would have to tip police clerks for typing services.[2] Second, if particular divisions within a police force receive more bribes than others, then the rate of promotions within those divisions may be reduced relative to others. Thus, police who do not collect bribes get promoted faster and receive higher legal salaries. Such a situation need not come about through an explicit decision process. Vice squads, for example, may be known to take bribes. Other police consider

---

[2]Knapp Commission, The Knapp Commission Report on Police Corruption (N.Y. City Commission to Investigate Allegations of Police Corruption, 1972).

them corrupt, and membership on the vice squad will constitute a prima facie case against promotion. Give the available promotions, more go to police on other duties. Slower promotions do not cause resignations or failure to attract replacements to the vice squad, for squad members are compensated with bribes.[3] In effect, the public salaries of police are held below equilibrium, and police collect the difference by catching and taxing offenders. This is analytically identical to the case of waiters who are paid low salaries and earn tips from customers contingent on performance. A policeman who shuns bribes is no different than a waiter who shuns tips. In both cases, the individuals would be working for a below equilibrium wage, and the hostility of co-workers would be expected.

II. BRIBES, MARKET STRUCTURE, AND CORRUPTION

The bribe system not only imposes costs on criminal activity, but may also promote police corruption, defined here as police actions which increase criminal activity. The impact of the bribe system on the level of criminal activity and police corruption will depend on the structure of the market for the illicit output and the market for the right to operate or sell such an activity in a police jurisdiction.

A. Competition in Input and Output Markets

To begin the analysis, assume that all markets are competitive. Among the inputs sold and purchased competitively is the right to operate or sell in a given police jurisdiction. This market structure will occur in the case where independent criminals each have the option of locating their activity in different police jurisdictions without loss of customers; thus, any police unit attempting to charge a bribe above the competitive rate would simply find criminals moving to other jurisdictions.

The demand by criminals for the police input is simply the marginal product of the input weighted by the price of the product, or the value of marginal product of the input. The bribe charged a captured offender depends on the costs to a policeman of forgoing an arrest. The cost to a policeman of forgoing an arrest in order to accept a bribe from a captured offender is the expected value of any reward he might receive for the arrest, for example, a commendation, which might assist in securing a promotion, plus the value of the expected

---

[3]An alternative system is to award bonuses to police who arrest offenders, rather than force the police to collect their rewards directly from offenders. This system has two serious drawbacks. First, an arrest may require the use of considerably more resources than does the taking of a bribe. Second, it would be more difficult to redistribute these bonuses away from the police who collect them: a policeman who received bonuses would also expect to be promoted more rapidly. Harold L. Votey has suggested that a workable, noncorrupting system would be to license victimless crimes and allow police to collect the fees for the city. Of course, the substitution of licensing for bribes should induce producers to come forth voluntarily to pay the fee rather than wait to be caught.

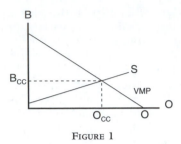

FIGURE 1

punishment for accepting a bribe.[4] Both reward and punishment will increase with the rate of output of the illicit activity due to complaints by third parties; therefore, the bribe per unit of police input will increase with the level of illicit activity.

In order to keep dimensions appropriate, the supply of police input, *S*, is in terms of the expected or average (assuming risk neutrality) bribe. Supply thus depends on the costs to police of forgoing an arrest and the costs of detecting and capturing offenders. If the costs of detection and capture were prohibitive, then the effective supply of police input to criminals would be perfectly elastic at a zero price or bribe. If all offenders were costlessly captured, then the supply price would equal the cost of forgoing an arrest. Since costs of capture are generally positive but not prohibitive, the supply price per crime committed will be less than the cost of forgoing an arrest. In Figure 1, equilibrium is determined by the equality of demand and supply, *VMP = S*, with sales 0_{CC} and average bribe B_{CC}. This bribe does not, however, reflect the maximum that a captured offender would be willing to pay. That maximum depends on the expected penalty,[5] while in competitive markets the bribe depends on the costs to the police of forgoing an arrest. This opens up the possibility that under a different market structure the bribe may be higher and illicit output lower.

In this strictly competitive environment, the possibility of police corruption does not appear to be overwhelming. Nonetheless, the possibility clearly exists that police may be the subjects of blackmail by criminals who have paid them bribes and the payoff required of police may be forbearance when the criminal commits a crime with a victim. More important, there are strong forces working to monopolize criminal activities, and with monopolization the possibility of police corruption grows.

---

[4]I ignore here the obvious possibility that the costs of arrest will be positive to the policeman since he forgoes the opportunity to collect bribes if he is employed in the time-consuming process of arresting an offender. This factor would tend to lower the equilibrium bribe.

[5]In fact, the capturing policeman may be able to increase the expected punishment to an offender who refuses to pay a bribe. The Knapp Commission, *supra* note 2, reports that a policeman would plant incriminating evidence in order to force a bribe from a known offender. The evidence could also incriminate the offender in a more serious crime than he had indeed committed, for example, planting heroin on a marijuana retailer.

B. Output Monopoly

First, consider the case suggested by Buchanan, with all markets competitive except for the monopolization of the final illicit output. This market structure would occur where a single producer of the illicit output has the option of locating in different police jurisdictions without losing customers. The criminal monopolist will now take account of the fall in product price as output increases. In the input market he will do this by valuing marginal product, not by price, but by marginal revenue which lies below price. In Figure 2, the new equilibrium occurs with marginal revenue product equal to supply, $MRP = S$, and with the average bribe reduced to B_{MC} and the use of police input reduced to O_{MC}. As Buchanan notes, the monopolist may also obtain a monopsony position in the purchase of inputs; if so, he would reduce still further his purchases of the police input as he takes account of the increase in the average bribe as his purchases increase.

From Buchanan's perspective, this market structure is superior to the competitive because output of the criminal activity is reduced. However, in this evaluation Buchanan ignored the bribe system and the possibility of police corruption. In particular, the criminal monopolist will not only bribe police to leave him alone, but may also bribe them to assist in the establishment and maintenance of his monopoly position. While the monopoly may actually reduce gross bribes to police, it will also vastly reduce the cost of bribe collection, possibly increasing net bribes, and so may be quite appealing to police. Additionally, police will then actually arrest would-be entrants into the monopolist's territory, and the arrest record will thus obscure the fact that they are indeed taking bribes. Clearly, since a single criminal organization now pays the portion of police salary which in competitive markets police would have to collect from many smaller competitors, a client relationship will develop. Police will have an incentive to maintain and promote the monopolist in order to insure bribes. This could include active assistance in promoting the monopoly, for example, forcing independent criminals to merge. It could also include a reluctance to enforce any laws against the monopoly, especially since with a continuing relationship police will become much more vulnerable to blackmail than in competitive markets where contacts are more random.

C. Input Monopoly

An alternative method to reduce the criminal activity to a monopoly level is via the establishment of an input monopoly. In particular, assume that only

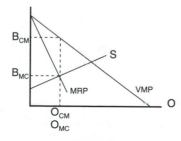

FIGURE 2

the police input is monopolized. This market structure would occur when a single police unit controls a jurisdiction and independent criminals will lose revenue if they move to other jurisdictions. The retailing of these illicit activities generally occurs in localized areas, and customers would be lost if the retail outlet were not convenient, so this case appears realistic. The police will now behave just as an output monopolist, taking account of the fall in product price as sales increase, and maximizing profits where the marginal revenue product curve equals the supply curve as in Figure 2, with $MRP = S$ and with output lowered to O_{CM} but the bribe raised to B_{CM}.

The reduction of illicit activity to monopoly levels may thus be obtained not only by promoting organized crime, as was suggested by Buchanan, but also by appropriately structuring jurisdictions to give police monopoly power over the right to sell the illicit activity. This may explain why police departments have special vice or narcotics squads which have city-wide jurisdiction. While retail markets for many of these activities may be quite localized, a boundary problem can exist where police jurisdictions abut; allowing offenders to move among jurisdictions may reduce police to offering rights to sell on a competitive basis.

Achieving monopoly levels of illicit activity via police input monopoly appears to be socially superior to doing so via criminal output monopoly. First, if police are input monopolists and criminals are competitors, all monopoly profits accrue to the police. Police profits will, I have argued, be captured as public revenues, for these profits reduce the cost to the public of a given-sized police force. The reduced cost may also result in an increase in the police force and in law enforcement. Concomitantly, the argument used by Backhaus[6] against Buchanan, that the profits of a criminal output monopolist would be used to finance further criminal activity, has no force in this case. Second, Backhaus argued that economies of scale will allow a criminal monopolist to produce at a lower cost, and thus produce more, than a competitive industry; however, in this case criminals remain independent of each other so no such economies occur. Third, as Tullock[7] has suggested, real resources must be devoted to the acquisition and maintenance of a monopoly position. In particular, a criminal monopoly will have to employ threat and force to exclude entrants from the market, and at least part of potential monopoly profits, the redistribution from customers, will be converted into social costs. These added social cost make the monopoly less attractive than was suggested by Buchanan. If, as seems likely, the cost of establishing a police input monopoly is less than that of establishing an illicit output monopoly, a smaller portion of the expected monopoly profits will be converted to social costs. Whether police corruption will be more or less extensive in this case is not clear. First, a client relation with a single criminal monopolist will not develop as in the case of output monopoly. But, second, explicit structuring of police units in order to maximize bribes will involve the whole police hierarchy in the search for income via bribes: condoning bribes may remove all ethical constraints on police corruption.

[6]Jurgen Backhaus, Defending Organized Crime? A Note, 3 J. Legal Stud. 623 (1979).

[7]Gordon Tullock, The Welfare Costs of Tariffs, Monopolies, and Theft, 5 W. Econ. J. 224 (1967).

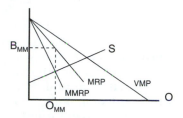

FIGURE 3

D. Input and Output Monopoly

Unfortunately, it is not likely that competition will persist in the output market; rather, one can expect to see monopoly on both sides of the market. Here I will assume that though illicit activities are monopolized, there is a different monopolist for different activities, for example, a heroin monopolist, a marijuana monopolist, and so forth, so the criminal monopolist does not have monopsony power over the police input.[8] This case clearly demonstrates how corruption is likely to nullify reductions in criminal activity due to bribes and monopoly. In this case, criminals and police independently take account of the fall in market price as output expands. The demand curve facing police is now the criminal's marginal revenue product curve, but the police as monopolists now equate the curve marginal to the marginal product curve to their supply curve in order to maximize profits. In Figure 3, optimization occurs where $MMRP = S$, with output reduced below the monopoly level to O_{MM} and the bribe B_{MM}. The price of the final output is thus greater, and quantity is lower than the monopoly level, as are profits. There is, thus, an incentive for police and criminals to reach an agreement to expand output to the monopoly level and share the increment in profits. The characteristic solution to this problem of "successive monopoly" as offered in the industrial organization literature is for the input monopolist to integrate vertically with the output monopolist, in this case making the criminal an employee and reducing the price of the output to the monopoly level. Clearly, in this case such integration would identify the police with the criminal monopoly and lead to corruption even beyond that of previously discussed cases. As an alternative to vertical integration, the input monopolist could charge the correct monopoly bribe and require of the output monopolist that he purchase a minimum amount of input, O_{CM}, or require that he sell his final output at the correct monopoly price. Either of these options would require that the police gain intimate knowledge of criminal operations as well as preserve the client relationship, so corruption would be almost as likely as if true vertical integration occurred.[9]

---

[8]If there were a single criminal organization which monopolized all illicit activities in a police jurisdiction, then such an organization would have monopsony power over the police input. This would result in a bilateral monopoly situation with a single seller, the police, and a single buyer, the criminal. The economic literature offers no definitive solution to this problem, but it appears that some form of vertical integration or an elaborate exchange of information will be necessary to maximize joint profits. The result, then, will have similar implications for police corruption as the case discussed in this section.

[9]See note 8 *supra*.

III. CONCLUSION

Given the costs of monitoring police performance in victimless crimes, it seems likely that a bribe system will develop whenever prohibitions against these types of activities exist. Clearly, the bribe system resembles a tax system that reduces the taxed activity and will reduce it the most under the condition that markets are structured monopolistically. Nonetheless, the social desirability of the bribe system is highly questionable because it promotes police corruption. In particular, the bribe system will induce police to promote the criminal organizations that pay them, and such promotion will include a reluctance to enforce laws against crimes with victims when committed by these same organizations. Indeed, under certain circumstances, police may be induced to play an active role in managing criminal organizations.

The bribe system and the corruption it causes can, incidentally, be removed by abolishing laws against victimless crimes. If the true consequence of such laws, police corruption, and the possibility of using taxes to impose costs on these activities were well publicized, supporters of such laws could no longer hide behind a shield of morality.

HISTORICAL PERSPECTIVE OF
POLICE CORRUPTION IN NEW YORK CITY

Sean Grennan
Long Island University–C.W. Post Campus

Since its inception in 1844, the New York City Police Department (NYPD) has continually had problems with corruption. Throughout the past 155 years, there have been six major police corruption scandals in the city. In 1894, the Lexow Commission was set up to investigate allegations of police brutality, corruption, and tampering with elections. Approximately 19 years later, after allegations that a police lieutenant had been involved in a murder, the Curran Commission was created to investigate police corruption. Then, in 1932, the Seabury Commission was instituted to investigate dishonesty in the Magistrate's Court, and it was discovered that members of the police department were involved in this corruption scandal as well. The Helfand Commission was set up in 1949 in response to information about gamblers preying on college students in Brooklyn. The commission found a gambler who was willing to squeal about police corruption. A little over 20 years later, after a police officer complained about corruption in the NYPD, the Knapp Commission was created by Mayor John V. Lindsey to investigate these allegations. Finally, in 1993, the Mollen Commission was created after Officer Michael Dowd and five other officers were arrested for drug trafficking by the Suffolk County police (Chin 1997).

In 1844, rising crime rates and an increase in public disorder brought about the creation of a police agency in New York City. During the first 54 years of its existence, members of the (NYPD) patrolled Manhattan. Then in 1898, the outer boroughs of the Bronx, Brooklyn, Queens and Staten Island became part of the City of New York. Up until the early part of the twentieth century, appointments, assignments and promotions within the NYPD were controlled by the corrupt politicians in Tammany Hall. Tammany Hall was the Democrats' political machine and members of the NYPD could not do anything without consulting and/or paying off these corrupt politicians.

According to McDonald (1999), appointment to the position of police officer in New York cost a new appointee about $300.00. A promotion to precinct detective cost $3,000; sergeant, $5,000; lieutenant, $10,000; and captain, $15,000. All money had to be paid to Tammany Hall prior to the elevation in rank.

One famous member of the NYPD who rose through the ranks quickly because of the corrupt system was Alexander "Clubber" Williams. He was appointed to the NYPD in 1866 and was promoted to captain in 1872. In 1876, Williams was appointed the commanding officer of the 29th precinct. Williams nicknamed this area the Tenderloin because it contained as many legitimate entertainment centers as it did illegitimate amusement locations. Clubber Williams' notoriety as a corrupt and brutal cop was exposed by journalist Jacob Riis after a police officer working for Williams clubbed former president Ulysses S. Grant. Writer Augustine E. Costello was also beat up after Costello exposed Williams' corrupt activities in the police department. During his career in the NYPD, Williams was brought up on departmental charges 358 times and had to pay fines for his actions on 224 occasions. Yet in 1894 he stood in front of the Lexow Commission and admitted that he owned an estate in Connecticut, a steam yacht, and a bank account containing over $300,000 dollars (Chin 1997).

In the early 1890s, the New York Mail Express called the NYPD "a ghastly sinkhole of official impropriety," and the Brooklyn Daily Eagle deemed the NYPD "the most corrupt, brutal, incompetent organization in the world" (McDonald 1999, 47). The newspaper attacks on police impropriety and extortion were also echoed by the Reverend Charles Parkhurst from the pulpit of his Madison Square Presbyterian Church starting in 1892 (Chin 1997).

Another very powerful and corrupt member of the NYPD was William Devery, who rose to the rank of chief of police in the NYPD. Devery came under the scrutiny of the Lexow Commission in 1894. This commission was formed in March of that year in response to the allegations of police corruption by both business and reform organizations. Clarence Lexow, a state senator from Rockland County, headed this commission which was funded by private organizations because of the lack of support from the state government. The investigation by the Lexow Commission discovered systematic extortion from houses of prostitution, gambling establishments, con-men, bars, stores, construction sites, and any other type of business or person from whom profit could be gained by corrupt members of the NYPD. Once the findings of the Lexow Commission were released, a number of high-ranking members of the NYPD, including Chief Devery, were removed from their positions. Devery, after appeal, was reinstated in 1896 to his position as police chief and was appointed police commissioner of the NYPD in 1897. The Lexow Commission did an excellent job in exposing corruption within the NYPD but accomplished very little in its attempt to eliminate it. In 1898 the Reverend Parkhurst was once again preaching against police corruption from his pulpit at the Madison Square Presbyterian Church. Parkhurst was aghast over the appointment of Devery as the police commissioner of the newly consolidated NYPD (Chin 1997).

Seventeen years later, the Curran Commission was created after allegations were made that a police lieutenant had been involved in the murder of a gambler. The alleged murderer, Lieutenant Charles Becker, was the commanding officer of the strong arm squad a vice unit directly under the command of the police commissioner. A small-time gambler named Herman Rosenthal was paying Becker not to raid his gambling location. Becker did raid the location, and a short time later Rosenthal went to the district attorney's office and volunteered to testify about police corruption. Several days after giving the district attorney a statement about Becker, Rosenthal was lured to a hotel in the midtown area of Manhattan where he was shot to death. As a result of the Rosenthal murder, the Curran Commission was created to investigate both the murder and the increase in police corruption within the NYPD (Chin 1997).

A subsequent investigation into the murder of Rosenthal revealed that Becker had allegedly forced several gamblers to assist him in committing this crime. These gamblers proceeded to hire four street thugs known as Gyp the Blood, Whitey Lewis, Lefty Louie, and Dago Frank, who were all arrested and indicted with Becker a short time later (Reppetto 1978, 84). Becker admitted to extorting money from gamblers but denied murdering Rosenthal. The first trial found all five men guilty of murder, but this decision was reversed by the New York Court of Appeals because of the trial judge's detrimental conduct towards the defendants. Within a short period of time, a second trial took place and all five defendants were found guilty of murder and sentenced to death. After a number of appeals, Becker was electrocuted on July 30, 1915, in Sing Sing prison. Becker had many supporters who claimed the gambling establishment in New York City set him up, because he double-crossed them by raiding their gambling operations after taking protection money from them (Reppetto 1978; Chin 1997).

As a result of the Curran Commission's investigation into police corruption, it was found that once again the department was full of corrupt cops. Money was extorted from a variety of arenas including gambling operations, houses of prostitution, businesses, hotels and for giving false testimony. A total of 18 officers were indicted by the Manhattan District Attorney's Office for extortion, including eight inspectors, one captain, one sergeant, and eight police officers (Chin 1997).

Recommendations were made by members of the Curran Commission to help remedy the corruption problem within the NYPD. These proposals included indepth background checks on new recruits as well as additional training for recruits, plainclothesmen and detectives. The commission also recommended the creation of new advancement practices to prevent corruption in the promotional process, the revision of detective duties so that they would be more responsible for their activities and the creation of a confidential unit within the department to insure the maintenance of honesty and integrity.

During this same time period, a citizens' committee reviewing corrupt practices in the NYPD noted that "corruption is so ingrained that the man of ordinary decent character entering the force and not possessed of extraordinary moral fiber may succumb" (Knapp Commission Report 1972, 62).

A number of the proposals suggested by the Curran Commission were enacted, including a confidential squad to expose corrupt police officials. Several years after the conclusion of the Curran Commission's investigation, two events took place that would have major effects on the NYPD. The first occurrence involved the growing influence of organized crime on the NYPD through the use of bribery, and the second event was the creation and enforcement of laws prohibiting the sale or possession of alcohol in the United States.

The ethnic Irish, who had ruled most of the organized crime in New York City for the past four decades, had moved on and became politicians involved in Tammany Hall or public office. Once elected to public office, they could make a lot more money by just collecting their salary and grabbing all the bribes that were made available to them. With the Irish moving into politics, a new ethnic/religious group stepped forward to run organized crime in New York City. A Jewish organized crime group led by Arnold Rothstein, took over the operation of gambling and prostitution in most major areas of New York City. Rothstein was the first member of organized crime to invest illegitimate money into legitimate businesses. He also set up "pads" (protection money) for uniform, plainclothes, and supervisory police personnel. In most cases, this money was paid on a monthly basis, usually with a senior officer in the unit picking up the money at the end of the month (Chin 1997).

Prohibition, on the other hand, provided the up-and-coming members of Italian organized crime with the funds needed to move into other illegal activities plus take over control of organized crime nationwide. Prohibition was also a valuable tool for corrupt cops who made a great deal of money shaking-down bootleggers and speakeasy owners. This was a time when police commanders, knowing that gang members were gaining too much power on the street, reinstituted the strong-arm squads of the Clubber Williams era. The members of the strong-arm squads were allowed to freely roam areas of the city that were frequented by members of organized crime. When gang members were located by these squad members, the members of the gang were harassed, beaten up, or shot. This gave members of the squad unit extraordinary power which led to numerous accusations of corruption. In many causes, however, their corrupt activities involved brutality, not money.

During the early 1900s and through the twenties, it was not only the police who were profiting from a corrupt justice system. It seems that magistrates, bailbond persons, court personnel, and attorneys were also extorting money from anyone who entered the magistrate's courts. Corruption within the magistrate's courts was brought to the attention of the governor, Franklin D. Roosevelt. He demanded that some action be taken to alleviate the corruption problem in the magistrate's courts (Chin 1997).

During August of 1930, Samuel Seabury, the former New York State Court of Appeals judge, was appointed to investigate the problem of corruption in magistrate's courts. A short time after his appointment, Judge Seabury's investigation discovered the involvement of the police in this scandal. What the investigation proved was that the police, court officials, judges, lawyers, bailbond persons, politicians, and members of organized crime had formed an alliance as a totally corrupt team (Chin 1997).

Almost every case presented in magistrate's courts was the result of arrests made by members of the NYPD. Ultimately the verdict in almost all of these cases was determined by the testimony of an arresting officer, who was usually a vice cop. In many cases, right after the arrests had been made, the arresting officer would propose to the defendant a possibility that the arrest would go no further providing the offender could come up with a specific amount of cash. So a person who was arrested and could immediately provide cash was set free once the officer was paid off. Offenders who could not or would not pay the fee set forth by the police at the arrest scene, were brought into the local police station for arraignment. Once the arrested person appeared at arraignment, a bailbonds person, who had already received high praise from the police officer, would be introduced to the arrested person. The defendant was then whisked off to the bailbond person's office where the arrestee's finances were examined. An offender would then have to produce some type of financial identification such as a bank book, checkbook, stocks, etc. The identification was then handed over and assigned to the bailbonds person. Subsequently, the bailbonds person accompanied the offender along with the financial documentation to the issuing institution where an excessive sum was withdrawn. An exorbitant amount of money was then charged for bail. Usually it was double or triple the normal amount. Added to this were additional charges amounting to a disproportionate sum of money for fixing the case with the police, paying lawyer fees, and paying off the prosecutor to go easy on the victim in case of a guilty verdict. In the majority of these cases, if the defendant had any type of assets, they would almost totally disappear during the prosecution of this case. If the bailbonds person ascertained that the offender had supplementary funds, the accused would be compelled by the bailbonds person to part with the rest of the assets (Chin 1997).

Once the offender was fleeced for as much money as he or she owned, the case was processed through the magistrate's court. If the defendant supplied the necessary amount of funding to be acquitted, the trial concluded with an acquittal. If the accused did not supply the necessary amount of assets, he or she was usually convicted, regardless of guilt. Vice squad members, in some cases, used informers to set up a target for what they called the doctor's racket. The informer would enter a doctor's office when the doctor was not present, claiming injury or sickness. U.S. currency was then placed in a set location in the doctor's office. The informer would start undressing in front of the nurse or secretary. A member of the vice squad would then break into the location and place the nurse or secretary under arrest for prostitution. An alternative to the doctor's racket was the landlady racket which was done in a similar manner with the same end result; the tenant was arrested for prostitution and the landlady for running a house of prostitution. This is called a double whammy; graft was collected from both defendants (Chin 1997).

In an attempt to determine the magnitude of the corruption by officers assigned to the vice unit, the Seabury Commission requested a check into the assets of some members of the vice squad. This investigation disclosed that Officer Quinlivan and his wife had over $88,000 in their bank accounts. Officer R. E. Morris had a total of $50,000 in two accounts, Lieutenant John Kenna had approximately $229,000 and Officer Brady had over $14,000 (Chin 1997). During the course of this asset investigation, not one of these officers could explain how they obtained any of the money in their bank accounts (Chin 1997).

This investigation resulted in every member of vice squad being reassigned to uniform. Thirteen of the officers were convicted of crimes committed while working in the vice squad. Some attorneys were disbarred for being involved in these corrupt acts. Four judges resigned, and two were removed from the bench (Chin 1997). The goal that Seabury had hoped to attain was reached when Mayor Jimmy Walker resigned from office. Yet the real culprit in making sure that Walker did not return to office was the Catholic Church. A recommendation was made by the Church that the mayor not run in the next election because his morals made him unfit to fill that position (Chin 1997).

The Seabury Commission's recommendations led to the elimination of magistrate's court, the children's court, and the court of special sessions. It helped rid the system of the corrupt and antiquated station house arraignments that were replaced by arraignments in front of a magistrate. There were many more recommendations made by the Seabury Commission, but few to correct the continuing corruption problem in the NYPD (Chin 1997).

It was less that 20 years later that the Helfand Commission undertook an investigation into a complaint that students from Brooklyn College were being preyed on by gamblers. What was revealed during this inquiry was that Harry Gross, a gambler who was arrested during this investigation, was paying over a million dollars a year to members of the NYPD to protect his gambling operations. Gross ran one of the largest gambling operations in New York City. After being apprehended for his gambling operations, Gross realized that he would be facing major time in prison and decided to discuss police corruption in an effort to lessen his sentence. Gross gave incriminating information on twenty-one officers who were ultimately indicted for conspiracy and extortion. A total of sixty other officers from the rank of police officer to assistant chief inspector were named but not indicted as co-conspirators to these charges (Chin 1997). Just before the trial began, Gross disappeared for a short period of time and then came back and refused to testify against the officers. The cases against these officers were dismissed and because of the double jeopardy clause; they could not be tried again on the same charges. Gross did testify at the NYPD departmental trials, and due to his testimony, many officers were dismissed from the police department.

Helfand's investigation discovered that in many cases the vice squad officers were arresting "stand-ins," people paid by the gambler to be taken into custody for gambling charges. Usually, the stand-in was arrested, booked, and then taken to court, where the case was dismissed within a short period of time. This prevented any breach in the gambling operations of the bookmaker. Naturally, this type of action by the gambler usually added a little more monetary incentive to the arresting officer, who then made sure there was not enough evidence in the case to constitute a crime (Chin 1997).

The Helfand Commission's investigation resulted in the arrest and conviction of twenty-two officer's and sixty-seven other officers were dismissed after being tried and convicted at a police department trial. It has been estimated that somewhere between 350 to 400 officers resigned from the department during and after this investigation. This investigation also resulted in every plainclothes officer in the city being transferred back to uniform. Another group of officers who were alleged to have taken money from gamblers were found guilty of either refusing to testify or lying about their bank accounts. One example is Captain Joseph Workman, who was found guilty of perjury for refusing to divulge where he had obtained $16,000 in U.S. currency (Chin 1997).

Another result of this commission was the submission of resignations by the chief inspector August Flath, the police commissioner William O'Brien, and Mayor William O'Dwyer. Helfand also had the city council put in place a new law that prevented police officers from retiring when they were petitioned to appear before the grand jury (Chin 1997). After a series of articles in the *New York Times* related to corruption in the NYPD, Mayor John V. Lindsey created a commission headed by Whitman Knapp to investigate the alleged corrupt activities of members of the NYPD. Just prior to the creation of the Knapp Commission, ex-plainclothes officer Frank Serpico's testimony in court and department trials led to charges being filed against nineteen officers. Serpico testified that each member of this plainclothes unit received $800 a month, referred to as a nut. The nut was the amount of money given to each officer in the unit on a monthly basis. The money came from the "pad," total amount of money gathered from gambling locations in that division each month. Other disclosures that were exposed by the Knapp Commission were that some plainclothes units were paid as much as $3500 a month by gambling establishments within their division or jurisdiction. Plainclothes officers in midtown Manhattan had a nut of $300 to $500 a month, while plainclothes officers in Harlem received a nut of $1500 a month. Supervisors in these plainclothes units received anywhere from a share and a half to three shares from the pad. If a plainclothes officer received $1000, a supervising sergeant would receive a share and a half, which amounted to $1500, and a lieutenant would receive $3000 or three shares from the pad (The City of New York 1972).

Knapp Commission investigators discovered that the plainclothes officers were not the only police officers extorting and stealing money. Investigators found that members of the narcotics squad were also corrupt. Payments called scores were prevalent throughout the narcotics division. The amount of the score could range anywhere from a several hundred to a million dollars. In reality, there is a great deal more money involved in narcotics trade than there ever could be in gambling or almost any other type of police corruption.

Corruption within the detective division was based on the same principles as the plainclothes units. Each month a specific amount of money came in from gambling, juice joints (locations that sold alcohol after liquor stores were closed), after-hour clubs, defendants wanting their cases to disappear at the stationhouse, and other illegal dealings. At the end of every month, each detective received one share, each sergeant received three shares, and the lieutenant was rewarded with five shares of the pad. Any other money made by detectives was known as a score, and this could be done individually or with other members of the detective unit. It was up to the detective or group of detectives that made the score to decide whether or not to share the money with the squad supervisors, but it was certainly a good idea to give the bosses a piece of the action.

During the Knapp Commission investigation, I was assigned to a Manhattan detective squad. Early one morning we hit a shooting gallery, a location where drug addicts live and inject heroin into themselves, looking for a suspect in one of my homicide investigations. When we entered the apartment there were about eleven junkies sleeping. A search of the location turned up about a dozen glassine envelopes containing heroin, needles and eyedropper used to inject heroin, and $1500 in U.S. currency in the top drawer of an end table. I asked if the cash belonged to any of the junkies, and no one acknowledged ownership. Upon return to the precinct, I was approached by another officer who suggested that we keep the money and split it up evenly among the three detectives and a supervisor. I informed the officer that he knew that was not my style, and I would voucher the money. As I was typing up the voucher, a supervisor came into the room and suggested that I voucher $500 and we each take $250. Once again, I said no and continued to voucher the money. All the money was vouchered and given to the desk lieutenant to be placed in a safe before being shipped to headquarters for safekeeping. As the prisoners were being removed from the stationhouse to go to court for booking, one of the prisoners asked me if I had his $500. I knew at that moment we had walked into a setup. The next day the same junkie returned to the precinct and specifically asked for his $1500. I happened to be down by the desk when this same person came into the station. He said that the cops in this precinct were lucky that I was honest. If any of the cops had taken the money, Knapp Commission investigators would have been all over this place. He further stated that he knew some of the other cops would have taken the money, but they should thank the Lord that the cop who found the money was honest. I never had any regrets being, and staying, an honest cop.

Uniformed patrol officers, on the other hand, picked money from gambling locations, juice joints, and bars on a weekly basis. Usually radio car partners would stop by a specific location, and one of the bosses of the illegal operation would come out and drop anywhere from a twenty to a hundred dollar bill into the police vehicle. This money was split by the partners in the radio car. Some partners would make scores by shaking down motorists, drug dealers, prostitutes, tow truck drivers, after hour clubs, or whoever else they thought they could shakedown for a couple of dollars. Sergeants on patrol picked up their own graft by going to the location on a weekly basis and picking up the money. In some cases, the sergeant picked up the money for the lieutenants and captain while in other cases, the money was delivered to the stationhouse to be split up by the supervisors.

I will never forget some of my first experiences in policing. After graduating from the police academy, I was assigned to a Manhattan precinct, but before going there, I was sent for training to be one of the first scooter cops in the NYPD. After training I was sent to the old 22nd Precinct now known as the Central Park Precinct. Upon my arrival at the 22nd Precinct, I asked for a locker and was told there were no lockers available. An old-time officer told me that if I dropped a "pound," a five dollar bill, in the clerical man's desk drawer, I would get a locker. I did as I was told, and I was immediately assigned a locker. It was common knowledge that to get assigned to a specific post or radio car sector, an officer had to grease the palm of the clerical man in the precinct. It is incredible but true; no matter what you did in a precinct, you had to pay for the right to do it. The only area where an officer, as far as my experience and knowledge shows, did not have to pay was in the case of promotion to third grade detective or any supervisory rank. Although to gain promotion in grade as a detective, money sometimes played a part as to whether or not a person got promoted within the detective division.

The Knapp Commission investigation discovered that corruption was widespread within the NYPD. Corrupt officers were categorized into two groups. First, there were grasseaters who took whatever money came their way. They were radio car partners who would stop by each week to pickup their money. This was the same money that police officers had been stopping by to pick-up for over a hundred years. Then, there were meateaters who would go out each day looking to shake people down whether they be motorists, pimps, gamblers, or drug dealers. Grasseaters took money because it was a way of life. With a salary of only $7000 a year, sometimes grass money helped these officers stay home with their kids rather than take a second or third job. As I said, grasseaters were picking up the same money that cops were picking up during the Lexow Commission investigation. It was wrong, but it was a common practice. This was the way the older officers trained younger officers, a way of life that, in many cases, involved some type of corruption.

Another instance comes to mind when I think of police corruption. While a member of the Tactical Patrol Force (TPF), I was assigned one night to drive a fill-in supervisor. The fill-in supervisor was a sergeant from the 24th precinct who was scheduled to work until midnight. At approximately 10:30 p.m., the sergeant stopped at three different pizza places in the 24th precinct and then wordlessly got back in the car. At 11:15 p.m., he told me to go back and stop at the same restaurants. He came out of each one with a pizza, and after finishing them, we went to the sergeant's car, and he put the empty boxes in the trunk.

Four years later, while assigned to a Manhattan squad, I was called to the internal affairs unit on false allegations that my partner and I had gained $500 from a shakedown. When I was taken in for questioning, much to my surprise the officer in the room was the man I had driven four years ago, who had been promoted to lieutenant. I was amazed at the irony: I had done nothing wrong but was about to be questioned by a corrupt cop.

When he started interrogating me, I asked him about the night we drove around the 24th precinct. He immediately turned off the tape recorder and left the room. About fifteen minutes later a captain, with whom I had worked in the Central Park precinct came into the room. He informed me that he had told all the other internal affairs supervisors that I was one of the most honest cops he had ever met. He told me to do a special report about the case and it would disappear. It did disappear because the last thing internal affairs ever wanted to do was to upset an honest cop.

There are so many stories associated with being honest in the 1960s and early 1970s that sometimes it can be considered funny to be an honest cop. On two occasions it came to the point of having my life threatened because of the fear among the other officers that I was from the Internal Affairs Division. These threats were due to my refusal to participate in any type of corrupt activities. Yet I never put myself in a place where I had to give up another cop. When I look back at my police career with the NYPD, I sometimes think that in some ways I was just as corrupt as other officers. I knew what was going on, and I did nothing to correct the problem. I had succumbed to peer pressure from the mighty blue wall.

During the early days of the Knapp Commission, attempts were made to locate officers who would describe corrupt activities within the department. The first officer consulted was Frank Serpico, who had originally come forward with corruption allegations against officers in the 7th plainclothes division in the Bronx. Serpico was assigned to the 7th division and after a short period of time realized that the whole office was corrupt. He then approached a friend, Inspector Cornelius Behan, with the information. Behan relayed the allegations to the division administrator Deputy Inspector Philip Sheridan, who told Behan that as far as he knew, there was no corruption in the 7th division. Behan recommended that Serpico discuss his evidence with 1st Deputy Commissioner John Walsh, but Walsh never contacted Serpico as he promised Behan he would do. Meetings were held with Mayorial Assistant Jay Kriegel and Commissioner of Investigations Arnold Fraiman without any further results. Finally in October of 1967, Serpico went to see the division commander Philip Sheridan. Inspector Sheridan informed his supervisors, and finally the NYPD started the long-awaited corruption investigation. This investigation resulted in nineteen officers receiving departmental charges and ten of those officers being indicted by either state or federal grand jury for various crimes related to their corrupt activities (The City of New York 1972).

Frank Serpico was able to come up with a viable source to aid the Knapp Commission in the person of detective Bob Leuci, later to be know as Prince of the City. Leuci had been assigned to the Special Investigation Unit (SIU) of the NYPD Narcotics Division prior to meeting Serpico. At first Leuci refused to cooperate with the Knapp Commission. It wasn't until March 1971 that Leuci finally agreed to work for the Knapp Commission. He was then reassigned to the SIU as an undercover cop to catch corrupt officers. Knapp's claim on Leuci was that he was an honest cop who had come forth due to his own volition. This was the same Bob Leuci who was nicknamed Baby Face by prostitutes throughout the City of New York. It wasn't until later that Leuci admitted that he had taken money from drug dealers and lied while giving testimony in drug cases (*New York Times* 1986). There was one specific case involving this same Knapp Commission agent/informer/undercover cop. Leuci arrested a Drug Enforcement Agency informer and snitch, Santiago Valdes, for possession of three ounces of heroin, which was the total amount of heroin that Valdes had in his possession at that time. When Valdes arrived in court, he discovered that he had been charged with possession of two kilos. This is only one example of Leuci's illegal activities as a member of the NYPD. Another is the case of a police suicide during the Knapp Commission that never seemed right to a lot of people. Detective Joe Nunziata, a member of the same SIU unit as Leuci, was found dead in his own vehicle. Investigators came to the conclusion that Nunziata had killed himself by shooting himself in the chest. During my police career in the NYPD, I had spent a good deal of time investigating homicides and suicides. I do not ever recall anyone committing suicide in the same way as Nunziata had. My years of police experience seem to indicate that Nunziata, who was set up by Leuci during the Knapp Commission investigation, may not have killed himself. This, however, is just one of the mysteries left unanswered by the NYPD and the Knapp Commission.

Another officer used by the Knapp Commission to catch corrupt cops was Bill Phillips, who had been caught by Commission investigators extorting money from a madam who ran a house of prostitution in midtown Manhattan. Phillips built a number of cases against other police officers. Ultimately, Phillips was identified as the person who murdered a loanshark in Manhattan several years prior to the creation of the Commission. He was convicted of this crime and is presently serving a life sentence in a New York State Correctional Facility.

One last person who testified and was used to gain information by the Knapp Commission was Waverly Logan. Logan was assigned to the Preventive Enforcement Patrol (PEP) squad that worked in uniform and plainclothes in Manhattan's sixth division, an area that covers East and Central Harlem. The PEP squad was made up of about forty minority officers who were assigned to this unit so that the minority community in this area would feel closer to the police. Well, it did not work out the way the NYPD planned. Before long, the PEP squad gained the reputation of being Sinbad and the Forty Thieves. It seems that everybody in Harlem was complaining about the corrupt activities of the PEP squad, including gamblers, drug dealers, prostitutes, restaurant owners, etc. On several occasions, members of this elite unit used their guns to force prostitutes to commit oral sex on them. On another occasion, several members of this unit were vouchering $24,000 they recovered on a vehicle stop of a major drug courier. One can only wonder how much money was really there if these cops vouchered $24,000. Waverly Logan is another example of someone whose background is questionable but who testified before the Knapp Commission.

The use of these types of agents was very helpful to the success of the Knapp Commission, although in just about every case, the crediblity of these turn-around cops is questionable. I know that all of these undercover officers were not as pure as the Knapp Commission would like us to believe. Yet, in reality, the best way to catch crook is to use another crook. This is especially true if the first crook is a police officer; then the second crook must be a police officer as well.

The Knapp Commission findings demonstrate the ineptness of the NYPD Internal Affairs Unit to fight corruption in the NYPD. This is especially true when we consider that since the inception of the NYPD, no Commission has ever been able to stop corruption in any plainclothes/vice unit that was part of the NYPD. One thing the Knapp Commission did discover was that police officers had finally realized that shaking down drug dealers was far more profitable than taking money for gambling or any other type of vice.

The Knapp Commission set out to uncover specific patterns of police corruption but instead discovered that many corrupt acts were committed by individual members of the NYPD acting in their own behalf. There were a number of cases where there was collusion among a group of officers, but not as many as were anticipated by the Commission. In fact, if one were to examine police corruption during this time, one would discover that grasseaters made up about fifty percent of the department. About twenty percent of all officers were considered meateaters, and the other thirty percent were honest but not informers. These officers realized that by taking the minuscule amount of money that was involved in most corrupt acts, they would ruin their careers.

Interestingly enough, a total of 310 cases involving a total of 627 police officers were given to a First Deputy Commissioner's Special Force, which was set up by the mayor to investigate all the cases initiated by the Knapp Commission (The City of New York 1972). This special unit was to be answerable to a special prosecutor's office that was created by New York State Governor Nelson Rockefeller.

In an effort to curb corruption in the NYPD, Maurice Nadjari was appointed by Nelson Rockefeller as the head of New York State's Office of Special Prosecutor. The main purpose of this office was to investigate corruption within the criminal justice system, but it was not long before that Nadjari started corruption cases against politicians. In 1976, not long after Nadjari started indicting and convicting judges and other politicians, the new governor of New York, Hugh Carey, had Nadjari removed from office. Most police officers disliked Nadjari because of his office's investigations into police corruption. Yet they have to admit that he was the only prosecutor hired to investigate police corruption that went out of his way to also investigate corruption within the political system, especially campaign contributions.

A little more than a decade later, the Buddy Boy case came to light in the 77th precinct in Brooklyn. It seems that a group of precinct cops, who became known as the Buddy Boys, set up their own corruption club. These officers were involved in a scheme that stole money, drugs, and guns from local narcotic dealers in the 77th precinct. The main suspect in this group, Henry Winter, was caught on video tape taking money from drug dealers. A total of thirteen officers were arrested in this case with seven being convicted of various charges. All thirteen officers were dismissed from the department.

One of the alleged ring leaders, Brian O'Regan, committed suicide after being indicted on drug charges by a Brooklyn grand jury. It seems strange that almost 10 years later Officer Henry Winter, the real ring leader of Buddy Boys who turned against his buddy Brian O'Regan, also committed suicide. The Buddy Boys case should have been an indication to the NYPD that drug-related corruption would not go away.

Then, in May of 1992, six members of the NYPD were arrested in Suffolk County for cocaine trafficking. A short time after these arrests, New York Police Commissioner Lee Brown called the NYPD Internal Affairs system for catching corrupt cops "a system police agencies across the country look to" (Wolff 1994, 3). About six weeks later, Mayor David Dinkins named Milton Mollen to head a special panel to investigate corruption in the NYPD.

Michael Dowd's drug arrest in Suffolk County opened up a Pandora's box. Once Dowd was taken into custody, he realized the only way to get out from under the weight of possible life imprisonment was to give up his partners in the drug business. It was not long before we found out that Dowd's gang had committed numerous crimes. They had robbed and beaten up drug dealers, burglarized drug locations, sold drugs, lied in court to get drug dealers' charges dismissed and many other crimes (The City of New York 1994). Michael Dowd devised and carried out a plan to create his own corrupt kingdom. He gathered his group of followers from both the 75th and the 73rd precincts in Brooklyn, and they proceeded to commit some of the most heinous crimes ever committed by police officers. The final result was a minimal amount of time in jail for some very serious crimes against the people and city they served. Dowd even admitted to snorting cocaine in a patrol car during his tour of duty.

The Cawley case in the 46th precinct was very similar, except Bernard Cawley and his police gang were far more violent, kicking down doors and beating up drug dealers and users until they would tell where the drugs or money were hidden. Like Dowd's gang, this group also did whatever was necessary to extort drugs and money from drug dealers (The City of New York 1994).

There were a number of other precinct corruption cases mentioned by the Mollen Commission, but very few facts are revealed in this report. It is apparent that this Commission had very little clout, because it did not produce any real criminal cases or indictments against corrupt members of the police department. This commission held televised hearings that made corrupt cops, who were allowed to openly misrepresent the truth, sound like heroes.

The most amazing part about the cases reviewed by the Mollen Commission is that they were very serious corruption cases involving the participation of members of the NYPD in the drug trade. Police drug gangs were uncovered in several precincts throughout the city. These cases were simply reviewed by the Mollen Commission, because the Mollen Commission accomplished absolutely nothing except building the ego of Milton Mollen. The joke of this whole investigation is that the criminal system along with the Mollen Commission allowed Michael Dowd, probably the most corrupt cop ever, to receive a sentence with parole after only eleven years in prison.

What we have seen in the NYPD throughout the years is patterned corruption that has, as yet, ceased to exist. There does not seem to be any clear answer for stopping police corruption in New York City. A good deal of possible solutions exist, but when an agency has 50,000 employees, as does the NYPD, personnel supervision is very difficult.

There are several possible solutions to this problem. First, creating more supervisory positions would give the supervisor fewer subordinates to manage and more of an opportunity to oversee the activities of their subordinates. A major responsibility of the supervisor is to assure the honesty of their subordinates, and they must be properly trained to perform this task.

The second possible solution involves the hiring practices of a police agency. An agency as large as the NYPD must make it a priority to seek the best candidates available to them. I recall that when an examination was given for the position of police officer in the NYPD, anywhere from thirty- to fifty-thousand candidates would apply and take the examination. As recently as October of 1999, 15,000 people applied, but only about 10,000 candidates took the examination. An agency as large as the NYPD should recruit candidates from throughout the United States. Requiring sixty college credits is a step in the right direction, but it does not necessarily guarantee that the agency is getting the best candidates. A thorough assessment must be done to determine the best type of candidate for the position of police officer.

One problem that must be corrected if the NYPD hopes to attract a better candidate is salary. Presently, the NYPD is one of the worst-paid police agencies in the metropolitan area. The average police officer with the Nassau or Suffolk County Police Departments receives top pay of about $75,000 a year. A typical officer in the NYPD receives top pay of about $52,000 a year. There is no doubt that a member of the NYPD has a far more hazardous job than either a Nassau or Suffolk County police officer. Yet whenever a test is given for the position of police officer in either Nassau or Suffolk county, anywhere from 50–60,000 people apply to take the exam.

A solution that has been recommended by every commission that has examined corruption in the NYPD has been internal and/or external monitoring of the police. It seems that since the mid 1990s, the NYPD has put in place a superb Internal Affairs Bureau (IAB) to monitor corruption within the NYPD. An external board to monitor the activities of an IAB is not a bad thing because there is always a chance that the IAB may mishandle an investigation. Most police agencies are opposed to a civilian agency overseeing department policy and/or activities. One must remember that the one thing the outside world has never been able to enter is the secretive world of policing. This is the blue wall of silence, or whatever else one might call it. Even as a retired member of this police agency, I would never be allowed to gain access to certain information or be trusted as a colleague again. I am an outsider who is even less trustworthy because I am also an academic. Until police agencies are able to alleviate that, outsiders are not allowed in, and the blue wall of silence will remain in place.

Throughout this article, we have reviewed the problems that the NYPD has had with corruption. It seems inevitable that at least once every twenty years a major corruption scandal takes place within the NYPD. Up until the 1970s corruption always involved some type of vice or extortion that involved payments to avoid being arrested or prosecuted for a violation or a crime. Then in the late 1960s and early 1970s, corruption involving narcotics came into view. Police officers realized that nickel-and-dime shakedowns were nothing compared to the hundreds or thousands of dollars available from narcotics shakedowns. This is something a police agency must realize in all of its anti-corruption efforts. The enemy is the large amounts of money made available from drug trafficking. The question that police agencies have to consider is how to get their officers to remain honest and avoid the enticement of drug money. As we enter the new millinium, the ever-present temptation that drug money presents to police officers may be the biggest challenge our law enforcement community will ever face. Let's hope that nowhere in the near future is there another corruption scandal in the NYPD.

REFERENCES

Chin, Gabriel J. (Ed.) (1997). *New York City Police Corruption Investigation Commissions, 1894–1994.* Buffalo, NY: William S. Hein & Co.

McDonald, Brian. (1999). *My Father's Gun.* New York: Penguin Putnam, Inc.

Pundam, Todd S. "Police Corruption: A Look at History." *New York Times.* September 24, 1986, section B, p.4.

Reppetto, Thomas. (1978). *The Blue Parade.* New York: The Free Press.

The City of New York. (1972). *The Knapp Commission Report Commission: Commission to Investigate Allegations of Police Corruption and the City's Anti-Corruption Procedures.* New York: City of New York.

The City of New York. (1994). *The Mollen Commission Report: Commission to Investigate Allegations of Police Corruption and the Anti-Corruption Procedures of the Police Department.* New York: City of New York.

Wolff, Craig. (1994) "Corruption in Uniform: Chronology–Tracking Police Corruption Over the Years." *The New York Times,* July 7, 1994, section B, p. 3.

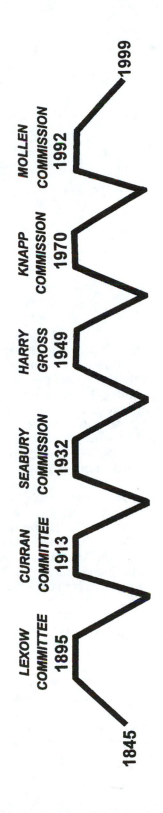

150 YEAR HISTORY

N.Y.P.D.

CORRUPTION SCANDALS

1845

LEXOW COMMITTEE 1895

CURRAN COMMITTEE 1913

SEABURY COMMISSION 1932

HARRY GROSS 1949

KNAPP COMMISSION 1970

MOLLEN COMMISSION 1992

1999

ARTICLE 10

DRUG RELATED POLICE CORRUPTION: THE MIAMI EXPERIENCE

Kim Michelle Lersch
University of South Florida

In the 1980s, drug-related police corruption took center stage in the public media following a number of highly publicized incidents of systematic criminal activities committed by sworn law enforcement officers. In the New York City Police Department, thirteen officers were indicted on a number of charges, including stealing and selling drugs. In Washington D.C. hundreds of drug cases had to be dropped because drugs were stolen while in police custody. Over 100 officers were suspected of having ties to the crack cocaine trade in Detroit, and even in rural Tennessee, sheriffs were charged with the distribution of drugs that had been seized in raids. In the late 1980s, nearly ten percent of the entire Miami Police Department was suspended or fired after a drug-related scandal.

In this article, the events leading up to the corruption scandal involving the Miami Police Department (MPD) will be explored. The Miami case is unique in some aspects because of the history of the city and the dramatic growth of the Miami Police Department prior to the problems of the mid 1980s. While the particulars of the Miami case may not be directly applicable to other agencies, there are still lessons to be learned from the Miami experience.

WHAT IS CORRUPTION?

There is a great deal of disagreement among scholars and policing experts as to what sort of behaviors are included under the term, corruption. Some definitions of police corruption are very broad and include a variety of behaviors, such as taking bribes or gratuities, verbal abuse on citizens, acts of brutality, and even homicide (Kappeler, et. al. 1994; United States General Accounting Office, 1998). In this analysis, I will use a more traditional definition of police corruption, which has two elements. Police corruption includes behaviors that involve the misuse of police power, authority, or position for the actual receipt or expected receipt of material rewards or personal gain.

Traditional police corruption was typically marked by a relationship that was mutually beneficial for both the officer and the citizen involved. A motorist may offer an officer a bribe in exchange for the officer ignoring his traffic violation, or a prostitute may trade cash for immunity from arrest. In the special cases of drug-related police corruption, these behaviors can become more serious. In his analysis of a number of law enforcement agencies, Carter (1990, 90–91) identified the following behaviors as typical of drug related corruption:

- Accepting bribes from drug dealers/traffickers in exchange for tip information regarding drug investigations, undercover officers, drug strategies, names of informants, etc.
- Accepting bribes from drug dealers/traffickers in exchange for interference in the justice process such as non-arrest, evidence tampering, perjury, etc.
- Theft of drugs by the officer from property rooms or laboratory for personal consumption of the drug or for sale of the drug
- Street seizure of drugs from users/traffickers without an accompanying arrest with the intent of converting the drug to personal use
- Robbing drug dealers of profits from drug sales and/or their drugs for resale
- Extorting drug traffickers for money (and sometimes property such as stereos, televisions, etc.) in exchange for non-arrest or non-seizure of drugs

In the case of the Miami Police Department, especially among the notorious River Cops, the criminal actions of the officers related to their corrupt drug activities included all of the above behaviors and even a few others including witness tampering, conspiracy to commit murder, and murder. In order to fully understand how such a scandal could happen among those sworn to protect and to serve, it is important to review some of the history of the city of Miami and the implications for the Miami Police Department.

MIAMI: A CITY OF CHANGE AND UNREST

The city of Miami is located on the eastern coast of the state of Florida. Measuring 34 square miles in area, Miami is the largest of the 26 municipalities located within Dade County. In the mid 1980s the population of the greater Miami area totaled more than 1.7 million people, the majority of whom were foreign born. As is the case with most major Southern cities, the city of Miami has had its share of racial turmoil. Many of these incidents could be traced to questionable confrontations between the police and minority citizens.

In May, 1980, the city of Miami experienced a serious social uprising as a result of the death of motorcyclist Arthur McDuffie at the hands of Metro-Dade police officers. At approximately 1:15 a.m. on December 17, 1979, McDuffie, a 33-year-old black insurance agent, was seen heading north along

North Miami Avenue by a sergeant with the Dade County Public Safety Department. McDuffie popped a wheelie, gave an obscene gesture to the sergeant, and raced away. After being pursued by over a dozen patrol vehicles, McDuffie finally stopped his motorcycle. McDuffie was beaten by at least six of the responding officers, and he died a few days later.

After an unsuccessful attempt to cover up the incident, five Metro-Dade officers were charged with manslaughter and/or tampering with evidence, and a sixth was later charged with second-degree murder. The trial was moved to the city of Tampa, where an all-white jury returned verdicts of not guilty (Porter and Dunn 1984; Sechrest and Burns 1992). The verdict set off almost of week of rioting in the streets of Miami, which resulted in 18 deaths, hundreds of people hospitalized, and over $100 million dollars in property damage (U.S. Department of Justice 1980).

The 1980 riot was not the first incident of social unrest in the Miami area. In August, 1968, racial tensions culminated in several days of rioting. As was the case with the majority of the riots that occurred during the era of civil unrest in the 1960s, the police came under fire for allegations of discrimination and differential treatment, especially with respect to the black community. In June, 1970, the Rotten Meat riot took place. This unrest began with blacks picketing a white owned store whose owners were accused of selling spoiled meats and other products to poor African Americans residing in the area. In the period from July, 1970 to July, 1979, twelve other disturbances occurred in the greater Miami area. All of these violent episodes could be traced to actions of the police against minority residents (Porter and Dunn 1984).

While the seeds for a major uprising had already been sown, in the fifteen month period prior to the 1980 rioting there were a number of highly publicized incidents that further frustrated the black community. First, five white Metro Dade County Officers who were looking for drugs raided the home of Nathaniel Lafleur, a black junior high school teacher. Both Lafleur and his son were beaten in the search, in which the police had raided the wrong house. Four of the officers were suspended without pay for their participation in the incident.

Second, Randy Heath, a 22-year-old black male was fatally shot by a white off-duty police officer from the city of Hialeah Police Department. The grand jury found no evidence of criminal wrongdoing in the case, although the officer was cited for negligence in the mishandling of his weapon.

Third, a Florida Highway Patrol Officer sexually molested an 11-year-old black female in the city of Homestead. The officer, who was white, pleaded *nolo contendere* to the charges and was given three years probation. The black community felt that the patrolman had received lenient treatment because of his race.

The fourth incident involved Dr. Johnny Jones, Miami's first black public school superintendent, who was accused of attempting to steal nearly $9,000 in plumbing fixtures for a home he was having built. An all-white jury heard the case against Jones, a prominent and popular black leader. Jones was found guilty and sentenced to three years in prison. While this case did not involve allegations against the local police, the black community felt that this decision reinforced their belief that the criminal justice system was biased against blacks.

Finally, the incident involving motorcyclist Arthur McDuffie occurred. The black community was outraged that Janet Reno, the State Attorney, did not charge the officers involved with murder. The verdict of not guilty triggered the 1980 riots.

Unfortunately, the racial unrest did not stop with the major riot of 1980. In the three-year period that followed, four other cases involving white officers accused of killing blacks were heard by all white juries. The fourth of these cases, involved an officer who was acquitted of all charges following the death of a black Overtown youth. This resulted in another riot that took place in December of 1982.

THE CUBAN MIGRATION TO MIAMI

While there was a great deal of tension and mistrust between the black community and the police during this time, there was another source of anger and frustration for the black community: Cuban immigrants. The arrival of Cubans to Miami began in December, 1965, with the Freedom Flights from Varadero, Cuba. These twice-daily flights resulted in more than 100,000 Cuban refugees arriving in the city of Miami during the first year alone.

When the refugees arrived, they often competed with blacks for jobs, especially in the service and clerical-type occupations. The newly arriving Cubans set up businesses in their own ethnic communities, often with the assistance of the United States Government, which provided loans and other assistance to minority group members trying to establish small businesses. In just a few short years, the average gross earnings for a Hispanic-owned and operated business was nearly double that for the average black-owned business (Porter and Nunn 1984).

Tensions between the black and Hispanic communities living in the Miami area were further heightened with the mass migration of nearly 125,000 Cubans over a six month period in 1980. The Mariel Boatlift, as it became known, began on April 4, 1980 when Fidel Castro announced that he was withdrawing guards posted outside the Peruvian Embassy in Havana. In two days, more than 10,000 Cubans had asked for political asylum at the embassy. Then, on April 20, Castro announced that anyone who wished to move to the United States was free to do so through the port of Mariel (Aguirre, et. al. 1997). The month of May brought over 85,000 Cuban immigrants to the United States, and another 20,000 arrived in June. The port was finally closed for open migration on September 26, 1980.

Most of the Marielitos made the Miami area their new home. Upon their arrival, the Cuban refugees were housed in tents in the end zone of the Orange Bowl. However, when the exhibition season was about to begin for the Miami Dolphins, the immigrants were moved to Tent City, which was created in Little Havana under the Inerstate 95 overpass along the Miami River (Mancini 1996).

Since only twenty percent of the new arrivals had family members in the United States who could act as their sponsors, it was clear that someone had to take care of the basic needs of the new residents. Unfortunately, the bulk of the expense was to fall on local and state governments, which caused even further resentment and hostility towards the new arrivals (Unzueta 1981). Even among the Cuban community, there was not open acceptance of the Marielitos, who were viewed as being very different racially, socioeconomically, and in their values and beliefs than those who had migrated in years prior to the boatlift. As a result of these factors, the assimilation of these new arrivals into the fiber of American society was more difficult.

There was a great deal of fear and suspicion of the Marielitos. Anyone who voluntarily left Cuba was labeled by the Cuban government as a member of the lumpenproletariat, or social scum. The official policy of the Cuban government required that anyone leaving must publicly confess that they were criminals and/or social degenerates. In some cases, people wishing to hasten their flight from Cuba bribed officials from the Committees for the Defense of the Revolution in order to receive their *cartas de escoria,* or dreg's letters, which officially labeled them as social deviants and resulted in expedited immigration.

In addition to those who had assumed the label of a criminal only for immigration purposes, Castro also allowed a number of individuals who had been serving their prison sentences to leave the country. Along with those who had been serving their prison sentences, a number of ex-convicts were also included, as well as nearly 600 individuals suffering from various mental illnesses (Gordon 1982), although the number of persons with mental problems has been estimated to be as high as 6,000 (Sechrest and Burns 1992). Political prisoners, homosexuals, and members of certain religious groups, like Jehovah's Witnesses and Seventh-Day Adventists also found themselves classified as antisocials and were encouraged to migrate. Others found their way to the United States after they were rounded up by the Cuban police and Committees for the Defense of the Revolution and forced to leave the island country against their will (Garcia 1983).

No one knows exactly how many mentally ill persons, prisoners, and ex-convicts arrived in the Mariel boatlift. The Cuban government refused to provide the U.S. Immigration and Naturalization Services with official documents on those individuals arriving in the U.S., such as court records or medical documents. Based on the available information, Bach (1980) estimated that 84 percent of the Marielitos did not have prison records in Cuba, and Montgomery (1981) asserted that only 7 percent of the newly arriving immigrants had serious criminal histories.

No matter what the official numbers were regarding their criminality or mentally capacity, the Marielitos were viewed as dangerous people. Not long after the arrival of the Marielitos, the city of Miami received the dubious distinction of the Murder Capital of the United States. As a group, the Marielitos did engage in higher levels of criminal activities than the pre-Mariel Cuban population. In Dade County, where Mariel immigrants accounted for approximately 5 percent of the county's population, the new residents were responsible for 8.6 percent of the felony bookings, which was five times the rate for the pre-Mariel Cubans. The Marielitos also accounted for 22 percent of the misdemeanor offenses. Furthermore, while the felony arrest rate for the general population was 174 per 100,000 residents, the rate for the Marielitos was much higher: 258 per 100,000 (Sachs 1984; Sechrest and Burns 1992).

While it was easy to attribute the dramatic increase in the crime level to the Marielitos, the picture was only partially true. In the case of homicides, there was a 68 percent increase in the Dade County homicide rate from 1979 to 1980. Marielitos were responsible for only 25 percent of this increase, and the victims in most of these homicides involved other newly arriving Marielitos (Mancini 1996).

In addition to the rise in violent crime, the Miami area was also becoming a top port for the importation of illegal drugs. In 1982, the United States and Colombia seized a record 6.4 million pounds of marijuana, which only scratched the surface of the volume of marijuana arriving in the port city. Boats were arriving regularly, hauling several hundred kilograms of cocaine in hidden compartments. Violence and open drug dealing were becoming more and more common in Little Havana, so much so that the police had nicknamed the area, Little Vietnam.

CONSENT DECREES AND AFFIRMATIVE ACTION: SETTING THE STAGE

The Miami Police Department had not kept up with the demands placed on its services. First, there was a hiring freeze from 1975 to 1977. Then, as a result of the rioting, a high number of officers (mostly white) resigned from the Miami Police Department. While the attrition rate increased from 7 percent to 16 percent after 1979, these officers were not replaced. In 1974, the department numbered 777 sworn officers. Six years later, the size of the agency dropped to 654 officers. Given the sharp increase in the population of the Miami area coupled with the rising crime rate, these officers were sorely missed.

Historically, law enforcement agencies have not been viewed as attractive places of employment for blacks and other minorities, and the Miami Police Department was no exception. In the 1920s and 1930s, old photographs show hooded members of the Ku Klux Klan riding in the funeral processions of white officers killed by blacks in the Miami area. In 1944, the Miami Police Department hired its first black officers, and these individuals were assigned to a segregated unit. From 1975 to 1980, the number of black officers had remained virtually unchanged, even though there was an increase in the black population of the city. As late as 1982, the MPD had only 80 African American officers, and only 16 of these officers were employed above the level of patrol officer. In a city that was comprised of 25 percent African American residents, this under-representation of blacks was perceived by many minority residents as another indication of the discrimination of the police and the criminal justice system against minorities.

In the early 1970s, Leonard Cohen, an African American MPD officer, had filed suit against the city of Miami, charging that the agency was discriminating against blacks and other minorities in their promotional and hiring practices. The resulting Cohen Consent Decree, which was signed in October 1973, mandated that African American officers were to be hired in order to adequately reflect the composition of the city of Miami.

In 1975, a second suit filed by the U.S. Department of Justice alleged that the City of Miami was discriminating against minorities and women in its employment practices. This second consent decree required that 56 percent of individuals hired by the city had to be minorities and women. Because of the hiring freeze, these mandates were not put in place until 1980 when the MPD's budget was increased, thereby allowing for the hiring of a large number of police officers. The City Commission increased the hiring goals mandated by the Affirmative Action Consent Decree from 56 percent to 80 percent.

Furthermore, the City Commission restricted the pool of potential applicants first to residents of the city of Miami, and then, when these potential candidates were exhausted, the pool was extended to residents of Dade County.

From 1981 to 1982, there was a virtual hiring frenzy in the MPD. A total of 714 officers were hired, more than doubling the size of the agency in a very short time. Prior to the consent decrees the MPD had recruited applicants on a national level, and the majority of the applicants were not deemed acceptable for employment as police officers. In the early 1980s the emphasis had changed from screening out the less than desirable applicants to screening in and hiring those individuals who were minimally qualified based on relaxed screening standards.

The responsibility for screening applicants and the ultimate hiring decisions were removed from the control of the MPD and placed with the City Commission and the Department of Human Resources. An applicant's test results were not shared directly with the MPD; instead, the agency was given a list of qualified applicants from which the MPD was obliged to hire. As a result, individuals who previously would have been denied employment were now welcomed on the police department. Individuals with poor work histories, credit problems, poor driving records, and criminal records were now offered positions with the MPD. It was not uncommon for recruits to be called out of their academy classes only to be arrested for outstanding criminal warrants. In the case of the River Cops, the background investigations of several of the officers indicated that the officers had been terminated for on-the-job thefts, a violation of moral turpitude that in previous times would have eliminated them from employment consideration.

The relaxed screening mechanisms were especially troublesome in the area of drug use. A failed polygraph examination could no longer be used as a sole disqualifying factor. It is difficult to ask an applicant about his or her prior drug use without the use of a polygraph examination. However, if an applicant denied using drugs and the polygraph detected a falsehood, this incident could not automatically eliminate the candidate from consideration. Furthermore, while disclosure of any prior use of cocaine, heroin or other drug would have automatically eliminated a candidate from consideration prior to the hiring blitz, these standards were also relaxed. While any heroin use still would eliminate a candidate from consideration (assuming, of course, that this information was revealed without the use of a polygraph), cocaine use was dependent on the level of use. More than half of the River Cops had a history of prior drug use, and several had admitted having friends who were drug dealers. Again, given the pressure placed on the MPD to screen in, as opposed to screen out applicants, these individuals were permitted to join the force.

In addition to the lowered employment standards during this time, the standards for the promotion of supervisory personnel had been reduced as well. The consent decrees mandated increases in the level of minority supervisors, and the result was that less experienced officers were often promoted. Especially troublesome was the lack of seasoning among the field training officers. A field training officer assumes an important role in the socialization of a new recruit into the culture of the police department, guiding the inexperienced through their fragile first months of employment. Unfortunately, officers with less than a year's experience became field training officers, and were responsible for making recommendations as to whether or not a recruit should be retained beyond the probationary period (Delattre 1989). Poorly trained and inadequately supervised, these new recruits were soon on their own, unleashed in a volatile city.

THE RIVER COPS

Among the new officers recruited by the MPD during the hiring blitz under the lax standards was a group of 19 Hispanic officers who became known as the River Cops. These officers were accused of a variety of state and federal crimes, including using the MPD as a racketeering enterprise to commit acts of felony: murder, threats involving murder, civil rights violations, robbery, possession of narcotics, and various conspiracy charges. Ultimately, the officers were convicted of varying charges from murder to conspiracy, and were given prison sentences that averaged 23 years.

The criminal careers of the River Cops began by stealing drugs and cash from motorists stopped for traffic violations, and culminated in major drug rip-offs (Dombrink 1988). In one of the first River Cops heists which occurred in September, 1984, K-9 Officer Rodolfo 'Rudy' Arias, acting on a tip from a major drug trafficker named Luis Rodriguez, stopped and searched a vehicle. Inside, Arias found a small amount of cocaine and $16,000 in cash, which never made it to the MPD evidence lock-up. A month later, Arias and two other River Cops, Armando Lopez and Felix Beruvides, raided a poker game in Little Havana, where they seized $3,500 in cash. In April of 1985, Officers Coello and Garcia stopped motorist Menelao Estevez, who was carrying $11,000 in cash. The officers arrested Estevez for carrying an unregistered gun, and at booking Estevez was given a receipt for about half of the money. Estevez filed a formal complaint with internal affairs against the officers, but he later withdrew the allegation.

Then, in March, 1985, another officer was unintentionally drawn into the web of corruption. Officer Armando Estrada was stopped by Armondo Un, who was a drug runner for Luis Rodriguez. Estrada knew Un, who was very upset that another officer had just stolen $1,000 from him. Un had asked for Estrada's assistance in recovering the money. Estrada was able to recover the stolen money and, when unable to locate Un, returned to money to Rodriguez. Rodriguez gave officer Estrada half of the recovered funds for his trouble, and from then on, the officer was hooked. The relationship between Officer Estrada and Rodriguez further developed. Rodriguez offered to provide Estrada with information on other drug dealers under the agreement that Estrada would leave his customers alone. Estrada agreed, and eventually he and his partner, Roman Rodriguez, were regularly collecting several hundred dollars a week in payoff money.

Officer Estrada had another acquaintance who was a major drug dealer named Pedro Ramos. Ramos informed Estrada that a major load of cocaine was hidden in a vessel called the *Mitzi Ann*, which was docked at the Tamiami Marina. Ramos actually owned part of the load, but wished to stage the heist in order to keep a greater portion of the profits. Estrada invited his partner Roman Rodriguez and nine other current and former Miami Police officers, some of whom were on duty at the time of the rip-off, to assist with the heist.

The officers found several hundred kilograms of cocaine in secret compartments on the boat, as well as two men who were supposed to be guarding the load. The men were forced into the water, where they swam safely to the opposite bank.

About two weeks later on July 29, 1985, the River Cops staged a second major drug heist. Again, Ramos tipped off Officer Estrada about a major shipment of 400 kilograms of cocaine that would be arriving from Columbia aboard the *Mary C.* This time, Estrada, Rodriguez, and six other officers raided the Jones Boat Yard, where a crew of seven was unloading the contents of the vessel into a van. Again, the crew was forced into the water, but this time three of the men were unable to swim and drowned. The officers stole the van full of cocaine. While some of the cocaine was ultimately kept for personal consumption, most was sold. Ultimately, it was the testimony and cooperation of Un, Ramos, and Rodriguez that led to the convictions of the River Cops.

LIVING THE HIGH LIFE: WHERE WAS INTERNAL AFFAIRS?

At the time, the salary for a patrol officer in the city of Miami was approximately $27,000 annually. However, the take-home pay for the River Cops was obviously much higher. Officer Pedrera, who was present at both of the major heists, was able to purchase three Corvettes, a Cadillac, a new home worth a quarter of a million dollars, furnishings, and vacations in Europe. Oswald Coello bought two Corvettes—one for himself and one for his girlfriend, as well as a Lotus. Reggie Caprio bought a gas station ($271,000), a seafood business ($37,000), a Corvette, a Porsche, a boat, a Mercedes-Benz, leased a home in the Florida Keys and made lavish home improvements. Several other River Cops purchased expensive homes, automobiles, Rolex watches, jewelry, and other symbols of wealth. The officers did not try to hide their purchases from the MPD. Given the virtual non-existent supervision and oversight, these extravagances seemed to go unnoticed.

In fact, the police had stopped two of the River Cops after high speed chases in their sports cars. Two days after Oswald Coello had resigned from the MPD in August, 1985, he was stopped by a Florida Highway Patrol officer. Coello had been clocked at 120 miles per hour in his Lotus. When the FHP officer stopped Coello, he found $4,500 in cash and a small amount of cocaine in the car. In this highly publicized incident, a handcuffed Coello ingested the bag of drugs after the FHP officer had placed it on the roof of the Lotus. A few months later, Armando Lopez was fired as a result of being stopped while doing 90 m.p.h. in a residential area while driving his Porsche. The officer who initiated the traffic stop noticed a strong smell of marijuana, but Lopez refused to submit to a urinalysis and was ultimately fired for insubordination. Two months prior to this incident, Lopez had been stopped under similar questionable circumstances in the Keys, but was given only a reprimand for the incident.

The Internal Affairs office of the MPD had developed an early warning system in the 1980s, which was supposed to alert the agency to problem officers. If an officer had accumulated three or more citizen complaints in a calendar year or had a high frequency of use of force in their arrests, he or she was asked to meet with a city psychologist. At least two of the River Cops had been identified as problem officers, one being Officer Coello. In just three years with the MPD, Coello amassed 21 citizen complaints.

While a few of the River Cops had come to the attention of internal affairs for their acts of misconduct, others had been given awards and commendations for their work on the streets. Several were the top producers in terms of arrests. Roman Rodriguez had received positive performance evaluations, and Officer Estrada had often been commended for his efforts. Rodolfo Arias had been named Officer of the Month, and had been a serious contender for 1985's Officer of the Year Award. While clearly, the officers were engaging in serious acts of misconduct, some were also doing enough legitimate work to throw off their supervisors.

Furthermore, the Internal Affairs Unit had other problems to worry about other than just the River Cops. From January, 1985, to November, 1987, no less than 72 MPD officers were suspended, fired, or asked to resign due to acts of misconduct. By 1988, this number had risen to 100 officers. The majority of officers dismissed or suspended were from the group of recruits hired during the era of relaxed standards.

Interestingly, even with the advent of the Early Warning System and the obvious problems with the rank and file officers, the number of reprimands per 100 officers per year experienced a steady drop. In 1975–76, 32.9 officers per 100 were reprimanded. However, in 1985–86, this rate dropped to 15.0 officers per 100. This decrease should be viewed in light of the dramatic increase in the size of the force. Also, it should be noted that officers who had received punishment, such as loss-of-time or suspensions, dropped in the early 1980s, but rose again in 1985–86. As argued by Sechrest and Burns (1992), these figures were indicative of lax supervision and loosened internal controls, which "may have helped 'set the stage' for corruption to flourish" (1992, 309).

ROTTEN APPLES OR A CULTURE OF CORRUPTION?

The most popular explanation for police corruption and deviance is known as the rotten apple theory (Walker 1999). In this explanation, acts of misconduct are confined to a few unruly persons who, due to individual deficiencies, cloud the good name of the majority of police officers. Somehow these individuals slipped through the cracks, successfully avoiding the employment screening mechanisms designed to detect such problem officers and were able to join the force. Once identified, it is easy to eliminate the problem by simply firing the individuals involved. While this theory of official misconduct has proven to be popular among police administrators, many researchers and outside evaluators dismiss this explanation, classifying the simplistic theory as a myth (Barker 1994; Stark 1972) or as a mask for broader, system-wide problems (Geller and Toch, 1995).

The rotten apple theory has been applied to the Miami Police Department. However, this explanation alone is not adequate to explain the deviant acts that occurred. As argued by Delattre (1989) and Sechrest and Burns (1992), the problems experienced by the Miami Police Department were predicated by structural pressures as well as the presence of rotten apples. The sharp rise in crime, the relaxed employment standards, and even Affirmative Action have been blamed for the crisis experienced by the MPD. However, the structural influences on the behavior of the police could also be traced to the decline in moral standards in the city of Miami, thereby promoting a culture of corruption and greed.

The Miami of the early 1980s was marked by a number of highly publicized scandals involving questionable acts committed by individuals of power and influence. The Hot Suits Case involved allegations that several well-known local leaders, including the Metro-Dade County Manager and an Assistant State Attorney, had purchased stolen brand-name suits at heavily discounted prices. Miami Public School Superintendent Dr. Johnny Jones was convicted of grand theft. Officers from other local agencies within Dade County were arrested and charged with various crimes, such as racketeering, narcotics trafficking, sex crimes involving children, and theft from crime scenes. Even officers employed at the federal level were not immune from corruption; an FBI agent pled guilty to allegations of accepting bribes stemming from the protection of drug trafficking activities, and several customs agents were indicted on charges related to their alleged involvement in assisting in a marijuana smuggling operation.

Beyond the limits of the Dade County line, other cities were experiencing problems with the behavior of their officers. In the city of Philadelphia a total of 31 officers, including the deputy commissioner, were convicted of crimes stemming from their involvement in gambling-related misconduct. The New York City Police Department, plagued by numerous major corruption scandals throughout its history, found itself under scrutiny once again when 13 officers were indicted on charges related to the theft and sale of drugs. In the city of Boston, the behavior of top administrators as well as rank and file officers were examined after allegations of bribes and payoffs emerged (Dombrink 1988). The police chief of the City of Detroit was convicted of charges related to the embezzlement of $2.6 million. Clearly, the culture of corruption had extended far beyond the confines of South Florida.

The decade of the 1990s did not bring much relief in the area of drug related corruption. Police agencies from a number of large cities came under federal scrutiny, including Atlanta, Chicago, Cleveland, Los Angeles, New Orleans, Savannah, and Washington D.C. From fiscal years 1993–1997, a total of 640 officers were convicted as a result of corruption investigations led by the Federal Bureau of Investigation. Of those officers convicted, nearly half were involved in drug-related offenses (United States General Accounting Office 1998).

BEYOND MIAMI: WHAT CAN BE DONE?

Corruption has been defined as one of the oldest and most persistent problems facing American law enforcement agencies (Walker 1999). Given the nature of police work with low levels of supervision, persistent temptations, and constant exposure to deviant lifestyles and alternative definitions of right and wrong, the control and prevention of corruption will continue to be an issue facing police administrators well into the next millennium.

The United States General Accounting Office (1998), in its review of recent cases of drug-related corruption, identified a number of prevention techniques designed to reduce the prevalence of corruption. The following were included among the suggested means: making a commitment to integrity from the rank and file officers to top administrators; establishing and enforcing standards of accountability; raising employment standards; extending the probationary period, and establishing an independent body to oversee agency personnel and the internal affairs unit; and a strong commitment to community policing. The culture of policing needs to be modified to encourage a more positive work environment that is supportive of integrity. Furthermore, the effect of the culture of the city cannot be ignored. If a city is tolerant of corruption, officers and other public servants will be acculturated into a mindset in which deviant activities are accepted and rationalized.

The prevention techniques addressed several levels: modifying the individual characteristics of the officers who were selected for employment; establishing mechanisms to ensure that these higher standards were reinforced and maintained, and changing the social structure of the agency and the city to one that discourages corrupt activities from thriving. These prevention techniques appear to be a lesson learned from the problems experienced by the city of Miami in the 1980s. The incidents that occurred in Miami were brought about by both the structural pressures of the time as well as poor selection and screening standards, which resulted in a number of rotten apples serving as police officers. Other agencies can learn from the mistakes of Miami. Unless both the social structure and the individual deficiencies of the officers are addressed, behaviors such as what was found with the River Cops will be repeated.

REFERENCES

Aguirre, B.E., Saenz, R., and James, B.S. (1997). "Marielitos Ten Years Later: The Scarface Legacy." *Social Science Quarterly, 78,* 487–507.

Bach, R.I. (1980). "The New Cuban Immigrants: Their Background and Prospects." *Monthly Labor Review, 103,* 39–46.

Barker, T. (1994). "Peer Group Support for Police Occupational Deviance," in Barker T. and Carter, D.L. (Eds), *Police Deviance,* 3rd ed., Anderson Publishing Company, Cincinnati, OH: 45–58.

Carter, D.L. (1990). "Drug-Related Corruption of Police Officers: A Contemporary Typology." *Journal of Criminal Justice, 18,* 85–98.

Delattre, E.J. (1989). *Character and Cops: Ethics in Policing.* Washington, D.C.: American Enterprise Institute for Public Policy Research.

Dombrink, J. (1988). "The Touchables: Vice and Police Corruption in the 1980's." *Law and Contemporary Problems, 51,* 201–232.

Garcia, M. (1983). "The Last Days in Cuba: Personal Accounts of the Circumstances of the Exit." *Migration Today, 11,* 13–22.

Geller, W.A. and Toch, H. (1995). "Improving Our Understanding and Control of Police Abuse of Force: Recommendations for Research and Action," in Geller, W. and Toch, H. (Eds), *And Justice for All: Understanding and Controlling Police Abuse of Force,* Police Executive Research Forum, Washington, D.C.: 277–337.

Gordon, A.M. (1982). "Caribbean Basin Refugees: The Impact of Cubans and Haitians on Health in South Florida." *Journal of the Florida Medical Association, 69,* 523–527.

Kappeler, V.E., Sluder, R.D., and Alpert, G.P. (1994). *Forces of Deviance: Understanding the Dark Side of Policing.* Prospect Heights: Waveland Press, Inc.

Mancini, C. (1996). *Pirates in Blue: The True Story of the Miami River Cops.* Miami: National Association of Chiefs of Police.

Montgomery, P. (1981). "For Cuban Refugees, Promise of the United States Fades." *New York Times* (April 19).

Porter, B. and Dunn, M. (1984). *The Miami Riot of 1980: Crossing the Bounds.* Lexington: Lexington Books.

Sachs, S. (1984). "Many More Refugees Than Expected are Proving to be Repeat Offenders." *The Miami Herald* (December 23).

Sechrest, D.K. and Burns, P. (1992). "Police Corruption: The Miami Case." *Criminal Justice and Behavior, 19,* 294–313.

Stark, R. (1972). *Police Riots: Collective Violence and Law Enforcement.* Belmont: Wadsworth Publishing Company.

United States Department of Justice (1980). *Prevention and Control of Urban Disorders: Issues for the 1980s.* Washington, D.C.: University Research Group.

United States General Accounting Office (May, 1998). *Law Enforcement: Information on Drug-Related Police Corruption.* Washington, D.C.: United States General Accounting Office.

Unzueta, S.M. (1981). *The Mariel Exodus: A Year in Prospect.* Miami: Office of the County Manager.

Walker, S. (1999). *The Police in America.* Boston: McGraw-Hill.

ARTICLE 11

TO SERVE AND PURSUE: EXPLORING POLICE SEXUAL VIOLENCE AGAINST WOMEN*

Peter B. Kraska

Victor E. Kappeler
Eastern Kentucky University

This study identifies and examines an unexplored criminological phenomenon, termed here police sexual violence. Analysis and interpretation of quantitative data and case studies are used to explore the subject. Two data sets, one from federal litigation cases and the other from a media source, provide the material for examining the known incidence, distribution, and nature of this form of police crime and sexual violence against women. The data include 124 cases of police sexual violence; 37 of these are sexual assault and rape cases committed by on-duty police officers against female citizens. The analysis of case studies draws on and integrates feminist and police studies literature, allowing for the development of a police sexual violence continuum and the exploration of theoretical, conceptual, and practical issues. The conclusion explores the cultural and structural context within which police sexual violence against women occurs.

Criminologist's study of crime has yielded two critical realizations. First, crime crosses all economic, social, and occupational strata. The traditional criminological focus on lower-class, "predatory" street criminals is shifting to offenders within professions and institutions often held in high esteem by the public, such as religious leaders, physicians, corporate executives, government officials, and family members. One of the most persuasive examples of the ubiquitous nature of wrongdoing comes from the study of lawbreaking within the societal institution mandated with enforcing the criminal law. Interest in police crime has risen since the Rodney King episode and the Mollen Commission's rediscovery of corruption in the New York City Police Department.

*This is a revised version of a paper presented at the 1992 annual meetings of the American Society of Criminology, held in New Orleans.

Peter B. Kraska and Victor E. Kappeler, "To Serve and Pursue: Exploring Police Sexual Violence Against Women" (as appeared in *Justice Quarterly,* Vol. 12, No. 1, 1995, pp. 85–109). Reprinted with permission from The Academy of Criminal Justice Sciences.

Preoccupation with street crime has also, in the past, inhibited our attention to persons *victimized* by crime. This is especially true for those who suffer violence occurring in the family, in interpersonal relationships, and in the workplace. Years of research and scholarship have been required to reconceptualize these offenses as serious crime rather than private or personal matters. This reconceptualization has led to a second critical realization: these offenses are often committed against women not at random, but systematically, because of their status as women (Bart and Moran 1993; Caufield and Wonders 1994; Dobash and Dobash 1992; Kelly 1988; Russell 1982; Stanko 1985). Feminist scholarship is significantly affecting how the academic community views crime, particularly violence against women; yet the undertaking to legitimate the study of gender as a crucial component in the crime dynamic continues (Caufield and Wonders 1994; Daly and Chesney-Lind 1988; Simpson 1989).

Incorporating these realizations allows exploration of an important instance of neglecting the "female" component in police crime. From the research and literature on excessive use of force, one would assume that police commit unjustifiable acts of violence only against men, and that women suffer no *direct* and systematic mistreatment at the hands of police officers (Alpert and Fridell 1992; Friedrich 1980; Fyfe 1978; Geller and Karales 1981; Geller and Scott 1991). This neglect, a result of research orientation as well as oversight, is inconsistent with the international literature, in which police mistreatment of women (particularly sexual violence) is receiving widespread attention (Amnesty International 1991; Chapman 1991; Women's Rights Project 1992). Noting this omission, our research identifies and examines what we will call "police sexual violence" (PSV) against women. PSV not only identifies a unique and potentially important criminological phenomenon; in addition, it is significant because it theoretically informs both feminist and police studies. Balancing these two often incompatible sources of literature creates difficulties, even in appropriately labeling the phenomenon under study. Although we are examining males' behavior, we also recognize PSV as a form of women's victimization (Reinharz 1992).

WOMEN AND THE POLICE: REVIEWING THE LITERATURE

Historically the police have viewed women as marginal to the police role and function. Early in the twentieth century, women were first allowed to perform police functions associated with social work, but even as late as 1971, only 10 or 11 women in the entire United States were patrol officers (Garmire 1978). Although the number of women on patrol has increased (Carter, Sapp, and Stephens 1989; Reaves 1992a) and several studies affirm their competence (Hale and Wyland 1993), the integration of women into paramilitary police organizations still meets with opposition (Christopher Commission 1992; Hale and Wyland 1993; Martin 1990; Radford 1989). Public policing continues to be a predominantly male institution, not only in who it employs but also in the ideology and culture from which it operates (Hunt 1990; Radford 1989; Roberg and Kuykendall 1993; Young 1991).

Male exclusivity in policing often clashes with the interests of women as 1) victims of crime, 2) coworkers, and 3) law-breakers (Moyer 1992; Radford

1989; Stanko 1989). Our purpose here is to examine the literature from feminist and police studies that explores the relationship between women and police, especially as it pertains to PSV against women.

Police Deviance Literature

In the past three decades, research on police corruption, deviance, and misconduct has proliferated. This research has taken the form of government reports (Christopher Commission 1992; Knapp Commission 1972) as well as independent research (Barker 1977; Carter 1990; Sherman 1974; Stoddard 1968; Westley 1970). Historically, however, most of the literature focused on police corruption as opposed to police deviance. Only recently has deviance not associated with corruption received scholarly consideration (Barker 1978; Carter 1990; Hunt 1990; Kraska and Kappeler 1988; Sapp 1986). These studies reveal a consistent pattern of misconduct that contradicts traditional conceptualizations of police corruption.

The police literature that alludes to PSV addresses the phenomenon as "police sexual misconduct," emphasizing the on-duty "consensual sex" activities of a male officer with a female citizen (Barker 1978; Lagrange 1993). One study surveyed 43 officers in a southern city and found that the proportion of officers in that department perceived as having sex on duty was almost 32 percent (Barker 1978). That study makes clear why many researchers and most police organizations emphasize consensual sex rather than instances of PSV.

> The police officer comes into contact with a number of females during his routine patrol duties. These contacts occur under conditions which provide numerous opportunities for illicit sex. . . . The officer also has the opportunity to stop a number of women coming home after a night of drinking. An intoxicated female may decide that her *sexual favors* are a small price to pay in order to avoid arrest for driving while intoxicated. . . . The woman may also be coerced into the act by a "rogue" officer, but on numerous occasions the women is more than a willing partner. . . . There are also a number of women who are attracted to the uniform or the aura of the occupation (Barker 1978:266; emphasis added).

Similarly, an author of a recent police textbook writes that "police officers are subjected to incredible temptation to deviate. . . . the opportunities for easy money, drugs, and sex are seemingly endless. . . ." (Lagrange 1993:235).

The opportunity structure that facilitates police deviance is certainly an element in understanding police crime. Yet much of the policing literature assumes implicitly that police are a desired sexual commodity who are routinely tempted by women willing to trade "sexual favors" for leniency (see, for example, Sapp 1986). This "consensual sex" assumption inhibits alternative, more victim-based conceptualizations of police sexual violence. The view of this phenomenon as a problem of sexual favors assumes tacitly that deviant police are passive actors who are "corrupted," rather than active "corruptors." More important, it undermines the recognition of "police sexual deviance" as violent crime committed against women by relegating it to "sexual favors;" as a result, the coercive nature of these encounters is masked. This assumption of consensual sex also reinforces the untested notion that only the rogue, aberrant officer would use direct coercion, force, or the authority of the badge in such encounters. The "rogue" argument has been dispelled in the best of the police literature (Sherman 1974, 1978; Stoddard 1968; Westley 1953, 1970). Collectively, this thinking, promotes a lack of serious attention to the phenomenon, promotes a conceptualization of police sexual deviance that denies the violence associated with sexual victimization, and negates the possibility of a systematic or occupationally generated form of police victimization of women.

A close reading of Sapp's (1986) study raises questions about the assumption that PSV is an occasional act committed by rogue officers. This is perhaps the only research in either the policing literature or women's studies which directly addresses several types of PSV against women. Sapp collected interview data from "several hundred" (the actual number not specified) law enforcement officers in seven states. Although the study suffers from the usual limitations associated with informal interviewing, the findings reveal a clear pattern of what Sapp termed "police sexual harassment" of female citizens. One interviewee describes the phenomenon.

> You bet I get (sex) once in a while by some broad who I arrest. Lots of times you can just hint that if you are taken care of, you could forget about what they did. One of the department stores here doesn't like to prosecute. . . . If it's a decent looking woman, sometimes I'll offer to take her home and make my pitch. Some of the snooty, *high class broads turn on real quick* if they think their friends and the old man doesn't have to find out about their shoplifting (Sapp 1986:88; emphasis added).

Drawing from traditional policing literature, Sapp contends that the combination of unique opportunity, police power and authority, and the relative isolation of police-citizen encounters all facilitate sexual harassment of female citizens by police (Kappeler, Sluder, and Alpert 1994). Sapp traces the lack of recognition of this phenomenon, and the lack of institutional will to control it, to agency apathy, which he characterizes as a dangerously unenlightened "boys will be boys" attitude among police administrators and supervisors. His research, however, does not explore the possibility that within this environment of willing women ("high class broads turn on real quick"), male police officers may use even more overt forms of coercion through the use or threat of physical force, along with the authority of the uniform and the badge, to sexually harass, assault, or even rape female citizens. In addition, in some instances of sexual violation, the officer may not be pursuing a consensual sexual encounter, but may use police authority solely for sexual degradation or humiliation.

Feminist and Women's Studies Literature

The questionable assumptions found in the policing literature are not evident in the international human rights literature (Chapman 1991). Amnesty International and the division of Human Rights Watch have both recognized PSV against women as a serious human rights problem (Amnesty International 1991; Women's Rights Project 1992). The report by Human Rights Watch on the Pakistani police found that "more than 70 percent of women in police custody are subjected to physical and sexual abuse by law enforcement agents, yet not a single police official has been subjected to criminal penalties for such abuse" (Women's Rights Project, 1992:2). A 1991 Amnesty report notes the systematic police abuse of women in countries around the world, including acts such as rape, sexual humiliation through frequent and unnecessary strip-searches, the use of police power and privilege to gain sexual advantage, and degrading verbal abuse.

The human rights literature on violence against women constitutes the only definite examination of PSV against female citizens. Historically, feminist literature has focused on how legal institutions, specifically the police, have mistreated women as victims of men's violence (Daly and Chesney-Lind 1988; Lafree 1981; Radrod 1989; Simpson 1989). Although we will not review this expansive literature here, we will consider a more direct form of PSV—occupational sexual harassment—for two reasons. First, it provides a well-documented instance of male police officers sexually harassing women. Second, it furnishes an instructional theoretical account of sexual harassment in police agencies that might be applicable to the police harassment of female citizens not working in policing organizations.

Since women's entry into policing in the mid-1970s, researchers have examined the problem of sexual harassment of female police employees (Hale and Wyland 1993; Martin 1980, 1990). Sexual harassment constitutes the most conspicuous warning to women that they do not belong in any substantive way to this male-dominated occupation (Hale and Wyland 1993; Martin 1992). Susan Martin (1990:290) found that "most women officers have experienced both sex discrimination and sexual harassment." Her most recent research finds that of 70 female officers interviewed,

> two-thirds of the women identified at least one instance of sex discrimination and 75 percent reported instances of sexual harassment on the job. . . .
> Descriptions of the harassment faced by the first group on women on patrol indicated that frequently it was blatant, malicious, widespread, organized, and involved supervisors; occasionally it was life-threatening (Martin 1992:290).

Those who attempt to explain what underlies this harassment reach the same conclusion as those who scrutinize police-biased handling of violence against women in general: the cause is a sexist, highly masculine organizational ideology. Some observers have made note of the ideology (Christopher Commission 1992, Harris 1973), but researching this aspect of police culture is a relatively new undertaking. Probably the two most revealing works are those by Hunt (1990) and Young (1991). Using qualitative data collected from 18 months of fieldwork, Hunt (1990) examined the underlying logic of sexist ideology in a large urban police department. She excavates the components of a sexist police culture, highlighting (among other things) how the constructed image of the "moral woman" threatens the secret amoral world of male policing, and how policemen use degradation and humiliation to neutralize the perceived power that policewomen have or might obtain in the organization. Her conclusion has important implications for PSV against women:

> [I]t is important to acknowledge that sexism is not simply a product of sex role learning but it has a deep structure which is articulated in every aspect of the police world. As such, it is organizationally crucial to the practice of policing as well as the occupational identity of individual police (Hunt 1990:26).

Young (1991) reaches similar conclusions when examining anthropologically his 30 years of law enforcement experience in England. He likens police culture to that found in other all-male organizations, where shared values combine to form a "cult of masculinity" used as a legitimating ideology to denigrate and deny the value of women. His work exposes the consequences for women within the organizations: "My own observations suggest that policemen are overtly and consistently hostile towards women in 'the job,' and that the social control of these women is inevitably a burning issue" (Young 1991:193). Thus, the link between the institutionalized sexist ideology of the police and occupational sexual harassment is well established. Our research asks whether this cultural environment also operates outside the police organization, affecting some police officers' willingness to sexually harass, humiliate, and violate female citizens.

The policing literature assumes that "police sexual misconduct" most often involves "consensual sex," sexual favors, and rogue officers; the feminist literature makes clear that the traditional police culture, along with the occupational role and structural position of the police, may provide the appropriate organizational and cultural context for PSV against women. Thus instances of this phenomenon, if discovered, would be consistent with both the policing and the feminist literature reviewed here. In exploratory fashion, our research addresses two preliminary points. First, by using two incidence-based data sets, one from federal litigation cases and the other from media accounts, we inquire into the known scope and distribution of PSV. Second, to understand the nature of this phenomenon and how it informs and is informed by the existing feminist and policing literature, we develop a PSV continuum using illustrative case examples.

METHODOLOGY: THE DOUBLE BIND OF SECRECY

The difficulty of acquiring knowledge on this sensitive topic cannot be overstated. The wall of secrecy in policing, which conceals these crimes ("the blue wall of silence"), forms a difficult barrier for the researcher (Manning 1978; Skolnick 1966; Westley 1953). Even in the infrequent cases where some sort of wrongdoing becomes departmental knowledge, it is almost impossible to obtain information without a court order or a covert and perhaps ethically problematic research design. (Even the Christopher Commission could not access the personnel files of the officers involved in the Rodney King beating).

The secrecy bind only magnifies when one looks to the other potential source of data—those victimized by PSV. Victims of sexual violence in general have few incentives to pursue a formal complaint, as well as many disincentives including the fear of being blamed for the incident and the fear of not being believed. Not being believed and "the fear of depersonalizing and humiliating institutional procedures and interpersonal hassles to which victims of sexual violence are frequently subject" may be intensified when the offender is a police officer (Schneider 1993:57). In short, the "blue wall of silence" and the barriers to reporting combine to form a double bind of secrecy that makes data virtually unavailable to researchers.

Therefore we relied on cases in which victims overcame these obstacles and made public their victimization. Three avenues of public disclosure are possible: a formal complaint filed with the police department, the filing of a criminal complaint or a lawsuit against the officer and the department, and the disclosure of the incident to the press. We first collected data for this study using media accounts of PSV found in a national newspaper between 1991 and the first six months of 1993.[1] Second, we examined all published cases decided by the Federal District Courts between 1978 and 1992 in which the police were sued under 42 U.S.C. Section 1983, alleging some form of sexual violence.[2] These data are limited in that they include only reported incidents of PSV that reached the media, or cases pursued by a plaintiff in the federal courts. Thus our data provide only an indication of how often someone goes public with a complaint; they can tell us little about the *upper range* of the frequency of PSV. Finally, we use relevant comments derived from interviews with key criminal justice personnel, police officers, lawyers, and rape crisis workers to illuminate the nature of PSV against women.[3]

To establish a coding system for these cases, we examined the existing literature on violence against women and on police deviance, and made an initial coding of randomly selected cases. We coded the manifest content of each case in a stratified random sequence to distribute any coder bias. We developed a data classification system to enable the content analysis to determine the variety of PSV, geographic and demographic descriptors, political subdivision and employing agency, and the organizational position of the offending law enforcement officer.

We use illustrative cases in the second part of this study to examine the range of behaviors and the nature of PSV incidents. As Reinharz (1991) notes, case studies are an important tool for exploring relevant issues, examining relationships between factors, developing potential theories and concepts, and understanding the nuances of an unexplored, difficult-to-research phenomenon. This method highlights these dimensions inductively, following a longstanding epistemological tradition of developing "grounded theory" (Glaser and Strauss 1965).

We found a diverse range of incidents constituting "police sexual violence," which required a definition that could encompass different police behaviors. Drawing heavily on the work of Kelly (1988), our definition includes *those situations in which a female citizen experiences a sexually degrading, humiliating, violating, damaging, or threatening act committed by a police officer through the use of force or police authority.* As Kelley (1988:40) points out, this definition of sexual

---

[1]The newspaper source in the "Across the Nation" section of *USA Today*, supplemented, when practical, by the collection of local newspaper accounts of these incidents. We realize the limitations in using newspaper accounts, but, as Marx observes, "media accounts are too often ignored by academic analysts. I have found them an invaluable source of cases, ideas, and questions" (1988:xxi).

[2]These data were extracted from a larger data set of published cases decided by the Federal District Courts and associated with police liability. Only about 12 percent of civil rights cases decided by the courts are actually published (Olson 1992).

[3]We conducted formal and informal interviews during a two-year period. These included interviews with victims of PSV (n=5), members of the media reporting on PSV (n=3), police officials (n=15), police officers who have engaged or currently are engaging in PSV (n=6), and lawyers involved in litigating PSV (n=6). We conducted these interviews to educate ourselves about this phenomenon, not as the empirical foundation for this research.

violence makes no direct reference to the "imputed intentions of the violator." This point is important because an officer ordering a body-cavity search in the back of a patrol cruiser may not overtly intend sexual humiliation, but that may be the effect nonetheless.[4]

FINDINGS AND ANALYSIS

A Continuum of Police Sexual Violence

Instances of PSV examined ranged from invasions of privacy of a sexual nature to forcible rape. Consequently we conceptualized PSV on a continuum to avoid focusing only on extreme incidents. The continuum also allows us to explore the sociostructural links between these different forms of violence (Ahluwalia 1992; Kelly 1988). It is based on the "obtrusiveness" of the police behavior, and ranges from unobtrusive to obtrusive to criminal (see Table 1). "Unobtrusive" behavior includes behaviors such as voyeurism, viewing sexually explicit photographs or videos of crime victims, and other invasions of privacy. Obtrusive sexual behavior includes unnecessary, illegal, or punitive pat-down searches, strip searches, body-cavity searches, the provision of police services or leniency for sexual advantage, the use of deception to gain sexual advantage from citizens, and some instances of sexual harassment.[5] Criminal behavior involves certain instances of sexual harassment, sexual assault, and rape.

Known Incidence and Distribution

We found a total of 124 cases of police sexual violence (see Tables 2 and 3). Thirty-three of these came from a single national news source between January 1991 and June 1993; 91 came from the legal database mentioned above (there is no overlap between cases reported from each source). Although the federal litigation data begin in 1978, almost 51 percent of the cases have been filed since 1988. Among these federal cases, 10 percent (n=9) involved unobtrusive PSV incidents, 74 percent (n=67) obtrusive incidents, and 16.5 percent (n=15) criminal behavior. About 9 percent (n=8) were rapes, 9 percent (n=8) were sexual assaults, and 9 percent (n=8) were violations of privacy (n=8). The remaining cases, 74 percent (n=67), involved the use of strip or body-cavity searches by the police. Most cases involved only one officer; however, 11 percent of the incidents involved two or more officers. Eighty-seven percent of the violations were committed by line officers; administrative personnel were involved in 12 percent of the cases.

The 67 victims of strip and body-cavity searches had been charged with relatively minor legal infractions; in fact, 78 percent (n=45) had been charged

---

[4]One shortcoming of this definition is that it may not include those instances of PSV which were degrading and exploitative, but were not perceived as such by the victim. One such case occurred in Florida, where several deputy sheriffs exchanged sex for extra security with a mentally disturbed late-night clerk at a Circle K store ("Florida Deputies" 1990).

[5]See Marx (1992) for an excellent discussion of the police use of sex and deception in law enforcement.

TABLE 1

A Continuum of Police Sexual Violence

Continuum Category	Range of Behaviors	Institutional or Cultural Support	Operational Justification	Range of Legal Sanctions
Unobtrusive Behavior	Viewing, victims, photographs, and sexually explicit videos, invasion of privacy, secondary victimization	Possible institutional and cultural	Crime control investigation, examine evidence, review evidence for case preparation	Civil lawsuit
Obstrusive Behavior	Custodial strip searches, body cavity searches, warrant-basd searches, illegal detentions, deception to gain sexual favors, provision of services for sexual favors, sexual harassment	Possible institutional and cultural	Preservation of evidence, ensure security, control contraband, law enforcement, hampers enforcement efforts, necessary for covert investigations	Civil lawsuit to possibly criminal
Criminal Behavior	Sexual harassment, sexual contact, sexual assault, rape	Linked to institutionalized police characteristics	None	Civil lawsuit to criminal

with either misdemeanor crimes or mere traffic violations. Only 22 percent (n=13) of the women subjected to this police practice had been charged with a felony violation; most of these cases did not involve violations that would

TABLE 2

Frequencies of Police Sexual Violence, by Continuum Categories

Continuum Category	News Source		Federal Litigation Cases		Total	
	(f)	%	(f)	%	(f)	%
Unobtrusive	4	12.1	9	9.9	74	59.7
Obtrusive	7	21.2	67	73.6	13	10.5
Criminal	22	66.7	15	16.5	37	29.8
Total	33	100	91	100	124	100

TABLE 3

FREQUENCIES OF POLICE SEXUAL VIOLENCE, BY OFFENSE TYPE

Type of Offense	News Source (f)	News Source %	Federal Litigation Cases (f)	Federal Litigation Cases %	Total (f)	Total %
Violation of Privacy	10	30.3	8	8.8	18	14.6
Strip Search	2	6	67	73.6	69	55.6
Sexual Assault	12	36.4	8	8.8	20	16.1
Rape	9	27.3	8	8.8	17	13.7
Total	33	100	91	100	124	100

justify the use of an intrusive search. Police lost 69 percent of the claims brought against them, an extremely high percentage compared with all other areas of civil litigation: the police generally lose fewer than 10 percent of such actions (Kappeler 1993; Kappeler, Kappeler, and del Carmen 1993). A civil judgment against the police was not a sufficient deterrent: many of the cases were brought against recidivist police organizations that refused to change their practices. Indeed, the legal system provided little incentive to curb the unlawful use of strip and body-cavity searches—the average damage award against a police organization was only $27,182. This figure is more than $100,000 below the average damage award level against the police for the use of excessive force (Kappeler et al. 1993).

In the data from the national news source, only 2 cases, or 6 percent of all the cases, involved strip searches. The relative absence of reports of illegal strip searches probably reflects what the media deem newsworthy. The bulk of these cases were sexual assaults (n=12) and rape (n=9), constituting almost 64 percent of all the instances of PSV. In contrast to the federal cases, the media tended to focus on the extreme instances of PSV: 12 percent (n=4) of these cases involved PSV incidents that fell within the "unobtrusive" segment of the continuum, 21 percent (n=7) were obtrusive, and 67 percent (n=22) were criminal. About 16 percent of these cases involved two or more officers; 84 percent involved a single officer. Nearly 30 percent (n=10) of the violations were committed by administrative personnel (chief, captain, sergeant, and sheriff), and the remaining 70 percent by line officers.

When we combined the two data sets, we found 37 cases of either rape or sexual assault by a police officer, or 30 percent of the incidents. Administrative and supervisory personnel were involved in 16 percent (n=20) of all cases; 12 percent (n=15) involved two or more officers. Therefore the notion of the "rogue" line officer is challenged. Moreover, several cases involved law enforcement personnel from agencies in different political jurisdictions, acting in concert (see illustrative case below under "secondary victimization").

How were these incidents of PSV distributed geographically and by political jurisdiction? Both data sets revealed that defendants from municipal law enforcement were involved in 64.5 percent of the cases (n=80), officers from sheriff's departments in 21 percent (n=26), officers from different political jurisdictions in 6.5 percent (n=8), and state and federal officers in 8 percent (n=10) (see Table 4). The proportions of cases coming from different

TABLE 4

FREQUENCIES OF POLICE SEXUAL VIOLENCE, BY POLITICAL JURISDICTION

Political Jurisdiction	News Source		Federal Litigation Cases		Total	
	(f)	*%*	*(f)*	*%*	*(f)*	*%*
Municipal	24	72.8	59	64.8	83	66.9
County	6	18.2	21	23.1	17	21.8
State	1	3	0	0	1	.8
Federal	1	3	2	2.2	3	2.4
Multijurisdictional	1	3	8	8.8	9	7.3
Other	0	0	1	1.1	1	.8
Total	33	100	91	100	124	100

agency levels are similar to the proportions of officers employed at these lev-els (see Reaves 1992a, 1992b). Geographically, instances of PSV were reported in 31 of the 50 states and were dispersed throughout all regions.

Interpreting Exploratory Data

These data must be interpreted cautiously because of their exploratory nature and the double bind of secrecy. Either to reject their significance or to claim that PSV is a pervasive problem is to overstep the exploratory nature of this research. Because of the methodology employed, however, these 124 cases may represent only the tip of the iceberg. Two factors support our claim. First, the policing and feminist literature reviewed earlier identify not only a clear precedent for police sexual violence against women, but also an organiza-tional, structural, and cultural environment favoring this form of victimi-zation. Second, even if one considers only the most extreme form of PSV (rape), the research suggests a pattern in several geographical areas whereby the reporting of police rape by a single victim brought forth three to five ad-ditional victims, usually raped by different officers. This pattern was found in Dallas, in several areas in southern California, in Houston, and in Maryland (Boyer 1992; Ford 1992; Makeig 1993; O'Conner 1993; Platte 1991; Shen 1990). In 1992 alone, for example, four alleged victims of police rape surfaced in Dallas; each victim accused a different officer. The clinical supervisor of a Dallas rape crisis center subsequently reported that their organization assists two or three women a year who have been raped by on-duty Dallas police of-ficers. These women have not reported the incident to the police because "they're afraid of retaliation" (O'Conner 1993:274). Again, the data presented here include only those incidents in which victims overcame reporting obsta-cles and made a formal complaint; most likely, these constitute only a small percentage of the actual cases.

Illustrative Cases, Issues, and Interpretations

We identify an entire range of behaviors (unobtrusive to obtrusive to crimi-nal) as police sexual violence. A continuum counters the tendency to view the more extreme forms of sexual violence as aberrations, which severs them from their common structural and cultural bases. In examining actual cases of PSV along the continuum, the objective is to analyze, in exploratory fashion, the relevant theoretical, conceptual, and practical issues.[6] In this way the phenomenon can inform feminist and policing studies, while the literatures in those areas can aid in understanding this form of violence against women and police crime.

Unobtrusive: Secondary victimization.   The cases in this section include instances of PSV that fall on the least obtrusive end of the continuum. In these cases, the police violate a victim's privacy rights—a type of "secondary victimization." In *DiPalma v. Phelan* (1992), for instance, a 16-year-old female reported to the police that she had been sexually abused by her father. The police department assured her that if she signed a supporting deposition, her wish to remain anonymous to anyone unconnected with the criminal investigation would be honored. Her father pleaded guilty to the charges. Because he was employed by the municipality, the Town Board requested all documentation about the case. Despite the promise of confidentiality and the highly sensitive information in the police file, the police cooperated with the Town Board and released the information. The State Supreme Court dismissed the young woman's cause of action because "neither case law nor statute clearly establishes that a sex crime victim's constitutional right to privacy is violated by the disclosure of her identity."

Although this case does not involve violent physical contact, it demonstrates deception by police and a lack of sensitivity, which resulted in "official" victimization. The judiciary sanctioned this form of secondary police victimization, an indication of possible institutionalization of this practice. It is also significant that the violation occurred in the administrative setting of both the police institution and municipal government; it was not the act of a rogue officer.

James v. City of Douglas (1991) demonstrates a more direct form of police victimization in which deception was used to gain a crime victim's confidence and then to violate her privacy. Celeste James went to the police with allegations that her business partner was attempting to extort insurance money by threatening to show her family a videotape of herself and her business partner engaged in sexual activity. The tape was made without her knowledge or consent. She expressed her reluctance to cooperate with the investigation because of the embarrassing nature of the tape. The police assured James repeatedly that if she cooperated, they would handle the tape discreetly. The tape, once confiscated by the police, was handled otherwise: several police officers at the scene of the search viewed it in its entirety; no one ever logged it in as evidence; and copies were made and circulated throughout much of the department. During one of the "viewings," the chief of police, the assistant chief, the sheriff of the county, and a sheriff's deputy were all present. The court ruled that the showing of the videotape violated a "clearly established constitutional right to privacy."

---

[6]We selected cases that illustrated the upper and lower bounds of the continuum categories, and that provided detailed descriptions of the facts and circumstances in the cases. Several other cases in the litigation database would have served equally well.

This case, in which officers engaged collectively in a contemporary form of voyeurism, points to the cultural acceptance, throughout the rank structure of these particular agencies, of violating a female crime victim's trust. Sapp (1986) lists voyeurism as one way in which some "sexually deviant" officers entertain themselves while on duty. This case illustrates the unique access of the police to such private material, and how responsibly they handle female victims of sexual violence. Men's "sexual access" to women (Kelly 1988) and the police handling of male violence against women (Dobash and Dobash 1992) are both important issues in feminist scholarship.

Obtrusive: Strip and body-cavity searches.   In moving along the PSV continuum to the "obtrusive" category, it is important to note again that the human rights literature recognizes the police abuse of strip and body-cavity searches as a serious and prevalent form of PSV. Almost 74 percent of the federal litigation cases examined here involved the alleged illegal use of strip body-cavity searches; the police lost nearly 70 percent of these cases.

The police examination of a female's body and body cavities is extremely intrusive and violating. Because of "operational necessities," however, the police can engage legally in many behaviors that would be considered criminal if performed in a different context (Brodeur 1981). For the recipients of a body-cavity search, however, context and pretenses of operational justification mean little. The plaintiffs in the following cases likened the experience to "rape" and "being violated in the most extreme way." Technically, the legality of a search depends not on its effect on the recipient but on whether the police conducted the search out of "necessity," based it on reasonable suspicion, and conducted it within constitutional guidelines. The following cases illustrate how the police sometimes employ this tactic for their own pleasure or to sexually degrade, humiliate, or intimidate women.

In *Rodriquez v. Fuetado* (1991), the police were clearly more interested in degradation and intimidation than in collecting incriminating evidence. They suspected Rodriquez of trafficking in illegal drugs and sought a warrant, which a judge approved, to search her vagina for narcotics. The police appeared at her residence late at night, forced the door open, and found her and her husband sleeping in bed (an unlikely occasion for harboring drugs in a body cavity). The police told Rodriquez that they had a warrant to search her vagina, and repeatedly demanded that she reach in and "take out the stuff." When she refused to cooperate, the police drove her to the local hospital.

Rodriquez still protested the search; under duress and coercion, the physician on duty

> put on rubber gloves and proceeded to insert a probe into the plaintiff's vagina. He then removed the probe, placed one hand on the plaintiff's stomach, and inserted his fingers or some other instrument far into her vagina.

No drugs were found.

The courts ruled against the plaintiff, but did claim that they were "deeply troubled" by the search.

> The fact that the plaintiff was taken to the hospital by the police in the middle of the night to have her vagina searched raises, at the very least, the possibility that

the police were more interested in intimidating the plaintiff than they were in finding narcotics. It is difficult to imagine a more intrusive, humiliating, and demeaning search. . . .

Interestingly, the court did not mention the propriety of the judge's actions in issuing a warrant for this invasive search, or in failing to limit the fashion in which it was conducted.

More controversial are cases in which the police conduct "investigatory strip searches" in the field. The court ruled only partially against the police in *Timberlake v. Benton* (1992). In this case, two teenage females were driving a truck owned by a relative suspected of drug trafficking. Even though the police had no information linking the two women to the illegal distribution of drugs, the "drug task force" supervisor (a male) ordered a female officer to conduct a complete strip and body-cavity search in the back seat of a patrol cruiser. The females suspects stripped; they were ordered onto their hands and knees with their posteriors facing the open doorway and highway in *plain sight* of male officers at the scene. The drug enforcement officer hinted at his motive for the search when he threatened the women with future strip searches unless they provided information about their relative. The court ruled that the women were not entitled to punitive damages but that the police might be liable for injuries resulting from the search. The court also noted that this police department had a history of conducting illegal "non-custodial investigatory strip searches."

These cases raise several important issues. Illegal strip and body-cavity searches have remained civil rights violations rather than crimes, even though the law allows excessive force by police to be conceptualized as both a civil and a criminal act. One could argue that the differential treatment of these cases by the judiciary serves to condone these practices. One lawyer who specializes in suing the police sheds light on the difficulty of such cases: "We don't like strip search cases. . . . What you have to remember is that there are no damages when cops search suspects and the courts are unwilling to allow punitive awards in these situations . . . "

These police practices cannot be explained away as the rogue cop circumventing the law for personal gain. Brodeur's (1981:135) insight about other forms of police organizational deviance applies here: "It is a mistake to hold that it is for the most part informal practices that circumvent the law. These practices are to a significant extent grounded in the law." The judiciary in *Rodriquez* not only failed to rule against the police department, but also approved of the search by issuing the warrant. Because the police are in a unique position to conduct searches of a person's most private physical self, one would think that stringent constitutional constraints would be in place. In practice, however, our data suggest that police organizations routinely disregard the rule of law, opting to absorb the token damage awards that juries are likely to impose.

That component of the masculine belief system in policing which supports unnecessary strip and body-cavity searches may also exist in the judiciary and the bar. The legal and media cases used here demonstrate a sexist, culturally based belief held by some police, judges, and lawyers that women are capable of carrying drugs and weapons inside their body cavities, and do so regularly. As one Ohio Supreme Court justice wrote: "Even if Fricker had been concealing contraband . . . it would require a quantum leap in logic to conclude that such contraband would be routinely carried within a body cavity" *(Fricker v. Stokes,* 1986:206). Unlike forms of "deviance," therefore, this form of police wrongdoing leads us to ask to what degree this type of PSV is linked to legal, organizational, and cultural elements of the police and justice system.

Obtrusive /Criminal: Police Sexual Harassment.   Police sexual harassment falls into the gray area between the "obtrusive" and the "criminal" categories. Such harassment of female citizens in itself, unlike harassment in the workplace, is not directly proscribed by law; even in its most serious forms, it is rarely handled as "crime" by a police department or the criminal justice system. As evidenced by the cases cited below, however, certain behaviors involved in police sexual harassment could be defined as crime, such as false imprisonment, battery, or sexual abuse.

U.S. v. Langer (1992) illustrates a typical instance of police sexual harassment. A patrol sergeant employed by a municipal police department was convicted of stopping and detaining five female drivers, one of them on two occasions. Each stop was made at night on a deserted stretch of highway, under the pretense of enforcing drunk driving laws. The officer usually informed the women that they needed a ride home. One of his victims was a 19-year-old female, whom he falsely accused of driving while intoxicated. He insisted on taking her for a ride in his patrol car to "sober her up." After driving around for some time, the sergeant pulled his patrol car into a deserted spot overlooking a lake. He then told his detainee that she was very understanding and attractive, and that he wanted to take her out. After she declined, stating that she had a boyfriend, the officer persisted in questioning her about her relationship with her boyfriend. She asked to be taken back to her car; the officer refused, and instead drove her to a diner. He repeatedly refused her requests to be released, but eventually released her. In the woman's words, "He walked me to my car and I took my keys and I opened the lock, and he opened up my car door for me, and when I turned around to get into the car, he grabbed me by the shoulders and pushed me against the car with his body and kissed me." The sergeant subsequently called her several times and left messages on her answering machine.

With only slight changes, the same scenario would be standard fare in depicting interactions between police and female citizens in popular entertainment. A male police officer pulls over a female who attracts him and coyly threatens her with a traffic ticket, while they deliver sexual innuendoes to one another. In another common depiction, a male police officer assigned to protect a vulnerable woman exploits his position as an occasion for romance. These customary portrayals are important because they point to society's acceptance of male police officer's using state authority and power to pursue women sexually. Yet none of the cases examined here displays a female who reciprocated with sexual innuendo or banter, or seemed willing to offer "sexual favors." In a sexist organization, this broader cultural support may have real-world consequences. Sapp's (1986) research identified police sexual harassment as a pervasive and tolerated form of police misconduct.

The same behavior—exploiting a gender-based power difference to make sexually demeaning or suggestive remarks under the threat of a sanction—

certainly would constitute sexual harassment or extortion in the workplace (MacKinnon 1979). Feminist scholars are exploring contexts beyond the workplace in which sexual harassment takes place, such as doctor/patient or professor/student (Belknap and Erez forthcoming). The sexual harassment of women by male police officers is particularly significant: the often-discussed power differential exists not only because the harasser is male, but also because he has the state-sanctioned power to detain, arrest, and use physical force if the female does not cooperate. Unlike the college professor, the physician, or even the employer, the police officer can invoke operational necessity, sometimes with institutional support, to engage in a range of potentially abusive behaviors, most significantly the legitimate use of violence. This extreme difference in power helps us understand police rape, the most extreme form of PSV.

Criminal: Police Rape.   Rape falls at the extreme end of the PSV continuum. In several cities and states (discussed earlier), the discovery that police officers have raped female citizens while on duty causes outrage among some, disbelief among others, and shock among nearly all people. This type of crime raises many important theoretical and legal issues.

We found an obvious pattern when reviewing the rape cases cited here. The incidents resemble the sexual harassment case cited above, in that they involve a police officer who pulls over a female citizen for some traffic violation (generally driving under the influence), threatens her with arrest, and takes her to a secluded location for some outwardly legitimate reason. The difference here is that the police officer then rapes his victim.

A 33-year-old veteran officer in southern California, for example, used to lie in wait for women outside bars and restaurants, pull them over on false charges, convince them that they were about to be arrested, follow them to a secluded spot (a remote lake), and then rape them in the back seat of his patrol car. The police suspected that over the years, this may have happened to numerous women with no serious departmental inquiry. Only three women of the 30 interviewed eventually came forward with charges (Ford 1992).

In Houston in 1992, several women made claims against a Houston police officer; only one resulted in prosecution. This case involved a 23-year-old woman who worked for an attorney. Earlier on the evening of the arrest, she had been at a nightclub. The officer pulled her over, said he smelled alcohol on her breath, and took her driver's license and insurance card "[Officer] Potter told her to follow him to a nearby parking garage that he called his 'sleeping spot.'" In the victim's words, "I was real apprehensive and frightened, but he just started asking about my background and family. I thought he was just going to write out the ticket in the car and let me go." (Zuniga 1992:15A). Instead the officer made sexually degrading comments and ignored her pleas for freedom. He then ordered her out of the patrol car and told her: "You could go to jail and get raped by the (blacks) or would you rather bend over or lay down?" (Zuniga 1992:15A). The police officer then raped her over the hood of the patrol car. Afterward he apologized for having to leave because he was 30 minutes late to his last call. The woman returned home, called a rape crisis hotline, and then went to the hospital for a rape examination.

The real significance for this study is that these particular officers, as members of the select group of persons empowered to enforce the state's laws and protect the citizens, exploited their unique access to female citizens, and their power and authority as police, to engage in sexually violent behavior.

Also important is the pattern of raping women who are out late at night and suspected of being intoxicated. As one officer told the first author during the data collection stage, he and five other officers in his department routinely go out "bimbo-hunting": they wait outside the bars, pull over women who "should be home with their boyfriends," and sexually harass them. Part of the logic of sexism is that women are expected to abide by certain norms of feminine sexuality and to remain in their "proper place" (Hatty 1989; Scully 1990). A police officer told Hatty (1989:79), "I see a lot of women who are drunk all the time. They're just sluts. They should be looking after their kids." The predatory dynamic here might include the sexist belief among some police that women who go drinking and who frequent bars have a lower status, possibly so low as to be "police property," and therefore are subject to victimization and/or open to sexual extortion (Lee 1981).[7]

Another important concern here is that the difficulties faced by women in reporting sexual violence in general may only be intensified when the offender is a police officer. In 1991 the California Supreme Court awarded $150,000 to a woman raped by an on-duty police officer 10 years earlier. (The officer served 18 months in prison.) The woman hoped the ruling would encourage other victims of police rape to overcome their fear of reporting. As she stated, "I was afraid at the time that no one would believe me". Several cases demonstrate that this fear may not be unfounded.

In *Parrish* v. *Lukie* (1992), Officer Lukie drove a female detainee to an isolated portion of North Little Rock and forced her to perform oral sex. The police were aware of Lukie's history of sexually assaulting women on the job, but no action was ever taken. The court ruled:

> [W]e find overwhelming evidence to support the jury's finding that North Little Rock police officers operated in a system where reports of physical or sexual assault by officers were discouraged, ignored, or covered up.

As with sexual violence against women in general, the difficulty for several victims of police rape was presented by the courts, even when the police took the complaint seriously. In a period of only 11 months, four different Dallas police officers were accused of raping female citizens. Three of the cases went to the grand jury, with the Dallas police department asking for an indictment of rape; all of these cases were reduced to the misdemeanor offense of "official oppression." The jury, guided by the prosecutor, determined that the cases lacked the legal requirement of "use of force." In each case, police officers pulled over women on false traffic violations and sexually assaulted them. The juries did not find evidence of coercion because the women did not attempt to leave the scene of the incident, or did not "fight back."

---

[7]Although in this research we could not account for the race of the officers and the victims, the Dallas anecdote near the end of this section illustrates the possibility that the dynamic of lowering the victim's status may include the victim's race as well as "a female drinking late at night." See Sims (1976) for an instance of sexual abuse, by the justice system, of black females in a southern jail.

One victim's account reveals the reason. After an evening at a nightclub with her two daughters, she was pulled over by a Dallas police officer for driving while intoxicated.

> He said, "I want you to step out. . . ." He grabbed me by the elbow and led me between the two cars. . . . The whole time I was intimidated. I was really scared of this man; there was just something about him. He made me feel like I was going to comply no matter what. He had the authority. At that point, I lost it. I was in this man's control. For me to holler, to try to run away on foot, wouldn't have done any good. We were out in an empty parking lot at two in the morning. What was I going to do? Run to the police station? . . . He unzipped my pants and pulled them down to my hips. Then he grabbed me by my arm again and flung me around. I thought, "My God, this man is going to sodomize me." I've never been sexual that way. I'm Hispanic and we don't do this. . . . Nothing was being said by this man. Nothing was talked about. . . . (O'Conner 1993:231).

Some feminist scholars place the male ability to use force and coercion at the center of their analysis of crimes against women and their oppression (see Kelly 1988). The above account illustrates how the assaulting police officer's possession of state-sanctioned power, along with the power of being male, rendered overt force unnecessary. As Hannah Ardent states, "[F]orce is only used when power is in jeopardy" (Kelly 1988:22). Because the criminal and the civil law have failed to extend their conceptualization of coercion or force to women's victimization at the hands of the police, several women's groups are advocating a new law in Texas which would classify a police officer's uniform and badge as an instrument of force. As in the ruling in *Miranda v. Arizona* (1966), this law would assume that the authority of the police when detaining a suspect inherently creates the threat of force.

CONCLUSION: BUILDING LINKS ALONG THE CONTINUUM

The extreme power differential between policemen and female citizens comprises only one of several links connecting the various forms of PSV against women. Others are a sexist organizational ideology, judicial and legal support or tolerance for some types of PSV, and the structural position of the police.

In this paper we examine a unique form of police crime and violence against women. Two literatures—police studies and feminist studies—are most appropriate for contextualizing theoretically the range of behaviors defined here as PSV against women. The policing literature focuses mainly on on-duty consensual sex; feminist studies primarily examine "secondary victimization" of women by the police. The only direct examination of PSV is found in the descriptive international human rights literature. The feminist and the policing literature overlap in their examination of male police officers sexually harassing female police and citizens; they also expose a cultural and structural setting conducive to PSV. The policing literature allows for the conceptualization of power, authority, and opportunity, but generally masks the gender bias of the police occupation and the law with discussions of aberrant officers, sexual favors, and consenting females. The feminist literature illuminates the bias and the systemic differential treatment of citizens based on gender, but fails to fully recognize the nuances of police power, authority, and opportunity as they influence police crime.

The dual elements of police secrecy and reporting obstacles for victims inhibit the type of data available on this sensitive topic. Our research has provided an exploratory examination of the known incidence and nature of the many forms of PSV through a database of federal litigation, media cases, and interviews.

A critical element throughout the PSV continuum is the sexist nature of the conventional police culture. Feminist studies have discussed at length how a sexist organizational ideology in a police department can harm female victims of crime, coworkers, and lawbreakers. As Hunt (1990) found, sexism is a deep structure within policing, manifested in the "occupational identity of individual police." Other feminist studies have discovered that a sexist culture in any organization which has access to women can constitute a governing structural factor in sexual violence. Martin and Hummer (1989) examined the conditions and processes in college fraternities which facilitate sexual violence against women. Copenhaver and Grauerholz's statement about their research succinctly highlights the parallel between fraternities and police organizations:

> Martin and Hummer's research provides insight into how social institutions such as fraternities encourage sexual violence against women. Fraternities norms and practices, especially the preoccupation with loyalty, group protection and secrecy, use of alcohol, involvement in violence and physical force . . . create an atmosphere conducive to sexual violence against women (1991:31).

Our research exposes a darker consequence of this ideological environment. It supplements a growing realization in police studies, largely due to feminist scholarship, that police studies should involve another significant "ism"—beside racism, cynicism, and isolationism—necessary for an understanding of police crime and culture (Hunt 1991, Young 1991; Roberg and Kuykendall 1993). Police academics and some police agencies are beginning to recognize the importance of addressing this aspect of policing.

> Departments must attempt to accelerate change with respect to the traditional sexist police culture. Although some significant strides have been made with respect to de-emphasizing the highly militaristic/masculine approach to police organization and management over the past decade, such traditions are firmly entrenched and difficult to overcome (Roberg and Kuykendall 1993:405).

Another common element on the PSV continuum is the structural position and situational opportunity of the police to commit acts of PSV. The police possess exceptional access to women, often in situations with little or no direct accountability. Each form of PSV examined here—invasion of privacy, strip and body-cavity searches, sexual harassment, and rape—involves exploitation of this privileged position by both patrol officers and administrative personnel. Strip and body-cavity searches are especially relevant because they have organizational and institutional support.

The structural position of police in society includes their occupational role as trusted "citizen protectors." Because women's personal safety and their fear of sexual violence are fundamental issues in feminist studies (Ahluwalia 1992; Stanko 1991), PSV adds a critical dimension to the ambivalence in the literature about relying on the police and criminal justice system to "protect" women (Caufield and Wonders 1993; Edwards 1990; Klein and Kress 1976; Radford 1989; Thorton 1991). As several authors point out, violence against women is committed most often by those to whom women turn for protection (Stanko 1993). Each instance of PSV in this study adds credibility to this feminist insight.

These sociocultural links demonstrate the importance of conceptualizing PSV on a continuum. In this way we can avoid viewing police crime as simply an aberration committed by a rogue officer; we can place it within an entire range of less obtrusive behaviors, all of which have common structural and cultural roots. The concept of the continuum also allows for the recognition that PSV in some forms may be institutionally supported, and in other forms may be connected to institutionalized characteristics of the police (see Table 1). The intellectual environment in crime and justice studies is ripe for scrutinizing more closely the crime committed by the institution ostensibly designed to control it, and the critical role gender bias plays.

REFERENCES

Ahluwalia, S. (1992) "Counting What Counts: The Study of Women's Fear of Crime." In J. Lowman and B.D. MacLean (eds.) *Realist Criminology: Crime Control and Policing in the 1990s,* pp. 246-263. Toronto: University of Toronto Press.

Alpert, G. and L. Fridell (1992) *Police Vehicles and Firearms: Instruments of Deadly Force.* Prospect Heights, IL: Waveland.

Amnesty International (1991) *Women in the Front Line: Human Rights Violations against Women.* New York: Amnesty International Publications.

Barker, T. (1977) "Peer Group Support for Police Occupational Deviance." In T. Barker and D. Carter (eds.), *Police Deviance,* pp. 9-21. Cincinnati: Anderson.

——— (1978) "An Empirical Study of Police Deviance Other Than Corruption." *Journal of Police Science and Administration* -3:264-72.

Bart, P.B. and E.G. Moran, eds. (1993) *Violence against Women: The Bloody Footprints* Newbury Park, CA: Sage.

Belknap, J. and E. Erez (forthcoming) "Redefining Sexual Harassment: Confronting Sexism in the 21st Century." *The Justice Professional.*

Boyer, E.J. (1992) "Rape Claim Twisted, Officer Says." *Los Angeles Times,* February 13, pp. B3, B14.

Brodeur, J.P. (1981) "Legitimizing Police Deviance." In C.D. Shearing (ed.), *Organizational Police Deviance,* pp. 127-160. Boston: Butterworth.

Carter, D.L. (1990) "Typology of Drug Corruption." *Journal of Criminal Justice* 2:85-98.

Carter, D.L., A.D. Sapp, and D.M. Stephens (1989) *The State of Police Education: Policy Direction for the 21st Century.* Washington, DC: Police Executive Research Forum.

Caulfield, S.L. and N.A. Wonders "Personal AND Political: Violence against Woman and the Role of the State." In K.D. Tunnell (ed.), *Political Crime in Contemporary America: A Critical Approach,* pp. 79-100 New York: Garland.

——— (1994) "Gender and Justice: Feminist Contributions to Criminology." In G. Barak (eds.), *Varieties of Criminology: Readings from a Dynamic Discipline,* pp. 213-230. Westport, CT: Praeger.

Chapman, J.R. (1991) "Violence against Women as a Violation of Human Rights." *Social Justice* 2:54-70.

Christopher Commission (1992) *Report of the Independent Commission on the Los Angeles Police Department.* Los Angeles: Christopher Commission.

Copenhaver, A. and E. Grauerholz (1991) "Sexual Victimization among Sorority Women: Exploring the Link between Sexual Violence and Institutional Practices." *Sex Roles* ¹/₂:31-41.

Daly, K. and M. Chesney-Lind (1988)"Feminism and Criminology." *Justice Quarterly* 4:497-538.

Dobash, R.E. and R.P. Dobash (1992) *Women, Violence and Social Change.* New York: Routledge.

Edwards, S. (1990) "Violence against Women: Feminism and the Law." In A. Morris and L. Gelsthorpe (eds.), *Feminist Perspectives in Criminology,* pp. 71-101. Philadelphia: Open University Press.

"Florida Deputies Accused in Security for Sex Plot."(1990) *Crime Control Digest,* December 31, p. 5.

Ford, A. (1992) "Deputy Accused of Sex Assaults on Duty." *Los Angeles Times,* October 21, p. A25.

Friedrich, R.J. (1980) "Police Use of Force: Individuals, Situations, and Organizations." *Annals of the American Academy of Political and Social Sciences* 452:82-97.

Fyfe, J.J. (1978) "Shots Fired: Examination of New York City Police Firearms Discharges." Doctoral dissertation, State University New York, Albany.

Garmire, B.L. (1978) *Local Government, Police Management.* Washington, DC: International City Management Association.

Geller, W.A. and K.J. Karales (1981) "Split-Second Decisions: Shootings of and by Chicago Police." Chicago: Chicago Law Enforcement Study Group.

Geller, W.A. and A. Scott (1991) "Deadly Force: What We Know." Washington, DC: Police Executive Research Forum.

Glaser, B. and A. Strauss (1965) "The Discovery of Substantive Theory: A Basic Strategy Underlying Qualitative Research." *The American Behavioral Scientist* 6:5-12.

Hale, D.C. and S.M. Wyland (1993) "Dragons and Dinosaurs: The Plight of Patrol Women." *Police Forum* 3:1-8.

Harris R. (1974) *The Police Academy: An Insider's View.* New York: Wiley.

Hatty, S.E. (1989) "Policing and Male Violence in Australia." In J. Hanmer, J. Radford and S.A. Stanko (eds.), *Women, Policing, and Male Violence: International Perspectives,* pp. 70-89. New York: Routledge.

Hunt, J.C. (1990) "The Logic of Sexism among Police." *Women and Criminal Justice* 2:3-30.

Kappeler, V.E. (1993) *Critical Issues in Police Civil Liability.* Prospect Heights. IL: Waveland.

Kappeler, V.E., S.F. Kappeler, and R.V. del Carmen (1993) "A Content Analysis of Police Civil Liability Cases: Decisions of the Federal District Courts, 1978-1990." *Journal of Criminal Justice* 21:325-37.

Kappeler, V.E., R. Sluder, and G.P. Alpert (1994)*Forces of Deviance: Understanding the Dark Side of Policing.* Prospect Heights, IL: Waveland.

Kelly, L. (1988) *Surviving Sexual Violence.* Cambridge, UK: Polity.

Klein, D. and J. Kress (1976) "Any Woman's Blues: A Critical Overview of Women, Crime and the Criminal Justice System." *Crime and Social Justice* 5:34-49.

Knapp Commission (1972) *The Knapp Commission Report on Police Corruption.* New York: George Brasiller.

Kraska, P.B. and V.E. Kappeler (1988) "A Theoretical and Descriptive Examination of Police On-Duty Drug Use." *American Journal of Police* 1:1-36.

Lafree, G.D. (1981) "Official Reactions to Social Problems: Police Decisions in Sexual Assault Cases." *Social Problems* 5:582-94.

Lagrange, R.L. (1993) *Policing American Society.* Chicago: Nelson-Hall.

Lee, J.A. (1981) "Some Structural Aspects of Police Deviance in Relations with Minority Groups." In C.D. Shearing (ed.), *Organizational Police Deviance,* pp. 49-82, Boston: Butterworth.

MacKinnon, K. (1979) *Sexual Harassment of Working Women.* New Haven: Yale University Press.

Makeig, J. (1993) "Officer to Serve Time for '88 Rape." *Houston Chronicle,* February 26, p. A26.

Manning, P.K. (1978) "The Police: Mandate, Strategies and Appearances." In L.K. Gaines and T. Ricks (eds.), *Managing the Police Organization,* pp. 22-49. St. Paul: West.

Martin, S.E. (1980) *Breaking and Entering: Policewomen on Patrol.* Berkeley: University of California Press.

———— (1990) *On the Move: The Status of Women in Policing.* Washington, DC: Police Foundation.

———— (1992) "The Changing Status of Women Officers: Gender and Power in Police Work." In I.L. Moyer (ed.), *The Changing Role of Women in the Criminal Justice System,* pp. 281-305. Prospect Heights, IK: Waveland.

Marx, G.T. (1988) *Undercover: Police Surveillance in America.* Berkeley: University of California Press.

———— (1992) "Under-the-Covers Undercover Investigations: Some Reflections on the State's Use of Sex and Deception in Law Enforcement." *Criminal Justice Ethics* (Winter/Spring):13-24.

Moyer, I.L. (1992) "Police/Citizen Encounters: Issues of Chivalry, Gender and Race." In I.L. Moyer (ed.), *The Changing Role of Women in the Criminal Justice System,* pp. 60-80. Prospect Heights, IL: Waveland.

O'Conner, C. (1993) "Explosive Charges of Cops Who Rape." *Glamour,* March, pp. 231, 274-78.

Olson, S.M. (1992) "Studying Federal District Courts through Published Cases: A Research Note." *Justice System Journal* 3:782-99.

Platte, M. (1991) "Officer Suspected of Rape Probably Knew of Stakeouts." *Los Angeles Times.* August 17, pp. A26.

Radford, J. (1989) "Women and Policing: Contradictions Old and New." In J. Hanmer, J. Radford and E. A. Stanko (eds.), *Women, Policing, and Male Violence: International Perspectives,* pp. 13-45. New York: Routledge.

Reaves, B.A. (1992a) *State and Local Police Departments, 1990* Washington, DC: Bureau of Justice Statistics, U.S. Department of Justice.

———— (1992b) *Sheriff's Departments, 1990.* Washington, DC: Bureau of Justice Statistics, U.S. Department of Justice.

Reinharz, S. (1992) *Feminist Methods in Social Research.* New York: Oxford University Press.

Roberg, R.R. and J. Kuykendall (1993) *Police and Society.* Belmont, CA: Wadsworth.

Russell, D. (1982) *Rape in Marriage.* New York: Collier.

Sapp, A. (1986) "Sexual Misconduct by Police Officers." In T. Barker and D. Carter (eds.), *Police Deviance,* pp. 83-95. Cincinnati: Anderson.

Schneider, B.E. (1993) "Put Up and Shut Up: Workplace Sexual Assaults." In P.B. Bart and E.G. Moran (eds.), *Violence against Women: The Bloody Footprints,* pp. 57-72. Newbury Park, CA: Sage.

Scully, D. (1990) *Understanding Sexual Violence.* New York: Routledge.

Shen, F. (1990) "Veteran Arundel Officer Charged with Rape in Car." *Washington Post,* February 20, pp. 17A.

Sherman, L.W. (1974) *Police Corruption: A Sociological Perspective.* Garden City, NY: Doubleday.

———— (1978) *Scandal and Reform: Controlling Police Corruption.* Berkeley: University of California Press.

Simpson, S.S. (1989) "Feminist Theory, Crime, and Justice." *Criminology* 4:605-31.

Sims, P. (1976) "Women in Southern Jails." In L. Crites (ed.), *The Female Offender,* pp. 137-148. Lexington. MA: Heath.

Skolnick, J.H. (1966) *Justice without Trial: Law Enforcement in a Democratic Society.* New York: Wiley.

Stanko, E.A. (1985) *Intimate Intrusions.* London: Unwin Hyman.

——— (1991) "State Supreme Court Holds Los Angeles Liable for Rape by Officers." *Los Angeles Times,* September 8, p 17.

——— (1989) "Missing the Mark? Police Battering." In J. Hanmer, J. Radford, and E.A, Stanko (eds.), *Women, Policing, and Male Violence: International Perspectives,* pp. 46-69. New York: Routledge.

——— (1991) "When Precaution Is Normal: A Feminist Critique of Crime Prevention." In A. Morris and L. Gelsthorpe (eds.), *Feminist Perspectives in Criminology,* pp. 173-83. Philadelphia: Open University Press.

——— (1993) "Ordinary Fear Women, Violence and Personal Safety." In P.B. Bart and E.G. Moran (eds.), *Violence against Women: The Bloody Footprints,* pp. 155-64. Newbury Park, CA: Sage.

Stoddard, E.R. (1968) "The Informal Code of Police Deviancy: A Group Approach to Blue–Coat Crime." *Journal of Criminal Law, Criminology, and Police Science* 59:201-13.

Thorton, M. (1991) "Feminism and the Contradictions of Law Reform." *International Journal of the Sociology of Law* 19:453-74.

Westley, W.A. (1953) "Secrecy and the Police." *Social Forces* 34:254-57.

——— (1970) *Violence and the Police: A Sociological Study of Law, Custom and Morality.* Cambridge, MA: MIT Press.

Women's Rights Project (1992) *Double Jeopardy: Police Abuse of Women in Pakistan.* New York: Human Rights Watch.

Young, M. (1991) *An Inside Job: Policing and Police Culture in Britain.* Oxford: Clarendon.

Zuniga, J.A. (1992) "HPD Officer Is Indicted in Sex Attack." *Houston Chronicle,* December 19, pp. 29, 15A.

CASES CITED

DiPalma v. Phelan, 57 F. Supp. 948 E.D.N.Y. (1992)

Fricker v. Stokes, 22 St. 3d 202 (Ohio 1986)

James v. City of Douglas, GA, 941 F.2d 1539, 11th Cir. (1991)

Miranda v. Arizona, 384 U.S. 436 (1966)

Parrish v. Lukie, 963 F.2d, 8th Cir. (1992)

Rodriquez v. Fuetado, 575 F. Supp. 1439 Mass. (1991)

Timberlake by Timberlake v. Benton, 786 F. Supp. 676, M.D. Tenn. (1992)

U.S. v. Langer, 958 F.2d 522, 2nd Cir. (1992)

ARTICLE 12

CRIMES COMMITTED BY POLICE OFFICERS

Michael L. Birzer
Washburn University

Over the past several decades, the United States' society has witnessed a vast influx in crime. It appears that crime has not only increased but has steadfastly progressed to extraordinarily violent levels not previously experienced. One can not pick up a newspaper, read a magazine, or turn on the TV without the mention of crime. In his landmark text *Police Administration (1977),* O.W. Wilson wrote that next to war, crime is the greatest immediate threat to lives and property and the failure of society to diminish criminality imposes a tremendous hardship on people, not only in terms of loss of life and property, but also in terms of fear and suspicion which distract from our peace of mind and comfort. Wilson asserted this in 1977, and as we start the new millennium, these same concerns afflict American society.

Citizens depend on the police to prevent, control, and suppress criminal activity. In this sense the police have a very important mandate which is crucial to public safety. The police have a very perplexing and difficult job, and they represent peace of mind for many citizens given that they are a phone call away 24 hours a day. All too often citizens feel trapped in their own communities. As a result, they place a vast amount of trust and confidence in the police to keep them and their communities safe and secure. Skolnick and Bayley (1986, 1) eloquently summarized the sentiment that many in the United States possess when they stated, "The nation's chronic frustration with the criminal justice system is captured in headlines that scream at us daily from the front pages of newspapers."

The Problem

The police are charged with keeping the peace and enforcing the many criminal codes and statutes. The police represent a sense of orderliness in what can paradoxically be a rather chaotic society from time to time. The public place high expectations on the police to provide impartial, honest and democratic policing. Furthermore, the public entrusts the police to be the directors of community standards and to uphold democratic values. When the police become the lawbreakers themselves, it results in devastation to both the police profession and the community.

It has become all too familiar in the recent past to glance at the headlines of our local and national newspapers and read that individual and groups of police officers allegedly committed some gross misconduct or some heinous and deplorable crime. It is apparent that many citizens have lost faith in the ability of the criminal justice system to effectively create solutions to the complexities of crime and disorder. Unfortunately, when the media reports an act of police misconduct it only adds to the lack of faith that many maintain in regards to the criminal justice system. When the police commit crimes, it diminishes public trust and confidence and inhibits their ability to carry out instrumental functions.

A review of police history reveals that police crimes are nothing new. The United States may certainly be more exposed and aware of police misconduct today due to the influx of television news programs and commentary. The President's Commission on Law Enforcement and Administration of Justice in 1967 reported that police crime and misconduct had become a very significant problem and that stark measures were needed to uproot it. The Commission noted that acts of police misconduct vary widely in nature. The most common are improper political influence; acceptance of gratuities or bribes in exchange for non-enforcement of laws, particularly those relating to gambling, prostitution, and liquor offenses, which are often extensively interconnected with organized crime such as the fixing of traffic tickets, minor theft, and occasional burglaries. The Commission's report also revealed instances of police officers in high crime neighborhoods engaging in such practices as rolling drunks and shakedowns of money and merchandise in the very places where respect for the law is so badly needed. It should be noted that police misconduct includes a wide array of deviant acts. For example, Palmiotto (1997) asserted that police misconduct includes such violations as civil rights, corruption, the commission of crimes, and the excessive use of force.

The police are given an extraordinary amount of power by the states. The police can lawfully use force against a citizen when justified, including the use of deadly force. Furthermore, the police may detain a citizen and make an arrest resulting in a loss of individual freedoms for extended periods of time. The very powers granted to the police have steadfastly become the topic of debate and scrutiny. Many scholars have been very critical of the police in their use of authority to restrict freedoms. Alpert and Dunham (1988) asserted there has always been a concern about the powers given to the police by the states which allow the police to use force. Where power is given as in the case of policing, there is always a potential for its abuse.

A Brief Discussion of Police Misconduct and Corruption

Much of the literature on police misconduct centers on the issue of corruption. Police corruption has been defined in various ways, and some scholars have developed typologies and theoretical underpinnings of police corruption.

For example, Roebuck and Barker defined police corruption as, "any type of proscribed behavior engaged in by a law enforcement officer who receives or expects to receive by virtue of his official position, an actual or potential unauthorized material reward of gain" (1974, 428). Goldstein (1975) claimed that police corruption involves both misuse of a police officer's authority and some form of material gain.

According to Barker (1977) police misconduct differs in the respect that misconduct usually involves perjury, sex on duty, sleeping on duty, drinking on duty, or police brutality. However, not all cases of police wrongdoing constitute corruption. For example, the police officer that drives while under the influence of drugs or alcohol may not necessarily be corrupt even in light of the fact that he or she is in violation of the law. Likewise, an officer that smokes marijuana at a party is not necessarily corrupt. Each of these examples involves the police violating the law but does not necessarily indicate that the police are misusing their authority. Before discussing specific types of crimes committed by the police, it may be helpful to examine a few typologies of police corruption and misconduct that have been developed in the literature.

Barker and Wells (1981, 265) found police corruption characterized in three ways: "(1) They are forbidden, by some norm, regulation or law, (2) They involve the misuse of the officer's position and (3) They involve a material gain no matter how significant." Additionally Barker and Wells claim that there are 10 types of corrupt police behavior:

1. Corruption of Authority: Officers receive unauthorized free meals, services, or discounts and liquor;
2. Kickbacks: Officers receive money, goods or services for referring business to towing companies, ambulances, garages, etc.;
3. Opportunistic Theft: Opportunistic thefts from arrestees, victims, burglary scenes, and unprotected property;
4. Shakedowns: Officers take money or other valuables from traffic offenders or criminals caught in the commission of an offense;
5. Protection from Illegal Activities: Protection money accepted by police officers from vice operations or legitimate businesses operating illegally;
6. Traffic Fix: "Taking up" or disposal of traffic citations for money or other forms of material reward;
7. Misdemeanor Fix: Quashing of misdemeanor court proceedings for some material reward or gain;
8. Felon Fix: "Fixing" of felony cases for money or other forms of material gain;
9. Direct Criminal Activity: Officers engage in serious felonies such as burglary, robbery, and larcenies;
10. Internal Payoffs: The sale of days off, holidays, work assignments etc. from one officer to another (1981, 4).

There has been minimal attention in the literature devoted specifically to police officers who commit crimes. Most of the literature devote an enormous amount of attention to placing crimes committed by the police in certain typologies and rarely addresses police crimes as a separate deviance. In light of this void, the remainder of this article will focus solely on crimes committed by the police.

CRIMES COMMITTED BY THE POLICE

Historically, police officers have been involved in committing a myriad of both property crimes and crimes against persons. Crimes committed by police officers have included sexual assaults, robberies, domestic violence, child abuse, and even murder in some cases. Crimes committed by the police have been reported in all geographical areas of the United States. Drawing from Barker and Well's typology, the cases discussed throughout the remainder of this article fall within the categories of direct criminal activity, shakedowns and opportunistic theft.

Violent Crimes and Sexual Assaults Committed by Police

Violent crimes committed by police officers send a shocking and numbing effect throughout the community and the ranks of policing everywhere. This point can best be illustrated by an incident which occurred during the 1980s in Miami, Florida. It was during this time that seven Miami police officers, dubbed the Miami River Cops, were charged with dealing large amounts of drugs and robbing drug dealers of their money. Three of the officers were charged with murder and four were charged with the theft of $13 million of cocaine from a boat being guarded by drug smugglers. This investigation was believed to be the tip of the iceberg, and detectives involved in the investigation believed that the officers under investigation were part of an organized group engaged in large scale criminal conduct. According to Dorschner (1993) the 1980s left the Miami Police Department devastated. It was during this time that 75 officers were arrested for various criminal charges.

Many police scholars and practitioners alike have attempted to offer explanations for such wide spread violations of the law by officers in one department. Much of the analyses have centered on the massive hirings in the 1980s to integrate the department. Others have argued that the issue centers on an affirmative action agreement between Miami and the federal government to significantly increase the number of minority police officers (Gaines, Kappler, and Vaughn 1997). It has been argued that in many cases, background investigations on applicants were done in a rather expedient manner which may have resulted in the hiring of less-qualified or questionable candidates. Perhaps there were people hired that never should have been hired. This was the case with the Miami River Cops. Dorschner (1993) found that one of the Miami River Cops admitted to cocaine and marijuana use and also had been fired from a previous job at the Florida Power and Light Company for falsifying meter reports, a job that he held for less than three months.

Other cities in Florida have not been immune from problems of police breaking the law as exemplified by the case that occurred in 1996 in Fort Myers, Florida. Dantzker (2000) reported that in this case a police officer, while on duty, allegedly sexually assaulted a nineteen-year-old female. The victim had called the police to report drug activity in her neighborhood. The officer accused the victim of being a possible suspect and proceeded to search her. The victim then reported that she was forced to perform oral sex on the officer. The officer was fired and charged with sexual assault.

On August 17, 1999, a former Redford Township, Michigan, police officer was arraigned on charges that he forced five women to have sex with him while he was on duty. He was also charged with use of a firearm in the commission of a crime, because the uniformed officer was armed when the alleged sexual assaults occurred. The officer was fired after an internal investigation (*Law Enforcement News* 1999).

On October 21, 1999, four Indianapolis, Indiana, police officers were indicted by a grand jury for beating several men and women who were partying in a busy downtown entertainment district. The officers have since been terminated from the police department and this incident became known as the policemen's brawl (Sanders 1999).

In another case, it was reported that a nine-year veteran of the Indianapolis Police Department was forced to resign after two women complained that he had threatened to arrest them if they did not have sex with him. The officer had used his patrol car computer to get their names, addressees, and phone numbers after noting their license plates. The jury indicted the officer on nine felony charges of bribery, sexual battery and sexual misconduct.

On June 25, 1999, in Fort Worth, Texas, the chief of police fired five officers accused of hogtying a man who subsequently died in their custody. The district attorney and the Federal Bureau of Investigation investigated this incident to see if any crime or civil rights violation occurred. According to the report, the officers violated many departmental orders, used excessive force, lied, falsified documents, and orchestrated a cover-up about the hogtying. The term, hogtie, means to tie a person's bound feet and hands together behind his or her back. Many police departments have condemned the hogtying of suspects due to a large amount of in custody deaths that have been reported. In this particular incident, several witnesses reported seeing the police hogtying the victim, but the officers involved denied it.

An Associated Press wire report dated February 26, 1988, reported that five New York City police officers were indicted on federal civil rights charges in the case of Abner Louima, a Haitian immigrant. In this incident, the police officers allegedly beat and sodomized Abner Louima with a stick after he was arrested. Two of the police officers also attacked the victim in the bathroom of the precinct station. The officers reportedly kicked the victim and stuck a stick into his rectum. During this assault, the victims hands were cuffed behind his back. The Mayor of New York relieved the commander and the executive officer of the station where the incident took place of their duties. Furthermore, as a result of this incident, eight officers were relived of duty and one sergeant was suspended. The sergeant was present in the station when the incident occurred.

Four New York City police officers are currently being tried in a New York court for second degree murder. These charges stem from a February 4, 1999, incident in which the officers fired 41 rounds from their handguns at Amadou Diallo, an unarmed West African immigrant. Nineteen rounds from the officers handguns struck the victim, who subsequently died as a result of the gunshot wounds. The officers testified that they began shooting at the victim after they saw what they believed to be a gun in the victim's right hand. The electronic media reported that many in the African American community have been very critical of the police in New York. This incident further exacerbated the already strained relationship between the police and the African American community.

In Detroit, Michigan, four police officers were charged and subsequently convicted of murder. This case stemmed from the November 5, 1992, beating death of a black motorist named Malice Green. In this incident, two of the police officers were convicted of beating the victim to death with a flashlight. Conser and Russell (2000) reported that there were a total of seven officers present before the event ended. This raises perplexing questions as to why other officers allowed the beating to continue. These same questions were salient in the case where Rodney King was beaten by Los Angeles police officers in 1992. In the Malice Green incident, the City of Detroit was held civilly liable for his death and settled a lawsuit in which Green's family was compensated 5.1 million dollars.

The Los Angeles Police Department (LAPD), which once prided itself on being the most professional police agency in the United States has not been immune from its share of police involvement in rogue criminal activity. For example, the recent probe into allegations of misconduct in the LAPD has revealed alarming levels of police involvement in crimes. Lait and Glover (1999) reported that in the LAPD, police involvement in crime and misconduct is significantly larger than officials publicly acknowledge.

The allegations include police officers stealing drugs from drug dealers and using street prostitutes to sell narcotics. Furthermore, investigators believe that a sergeant assigned to the Rampart Station's Anti-Gang Unit instructed officers to plant guns on unarmed suspects. The sergeant has also been accused of condoning massive coverups and staging fictitious crime scenes such as the one in which a nineteen-year-old unarmed man was shot by police in October, 1996. In this incident, Javier Francisco Ovando was paralyzed as a result of the shooting, framed by the police and sentenced to prison for 23 years. Following the trial, one of the LAPD officers involved in this incident began cooperating with investigators and made a statement that he and his partner handcuffed Ovando, shot him, and planted a gun on him, then lied about the confrontation in court. In October of 1999, the victim was released from prison and has since then filed a lawsuit against the city of Los Angeles.

Many allegations of misconduct in the LAPD scandal have come from a former LAPD officer who is cooperating with investigators as part of a deal to cut time off his cocaine theft sentence. The former officer has furnished information to investigators that has characterized two police shootings as unjustified. The former officer told investigators that more than 30 current and former anti-gang officers at the Rampart Station were involved in routinely breaking the law by either committing crimes or covering them up. According to Lait and Glover (1999) of the *Los Angeles Times,* there have been five or six questionable shootings by LAPD officers. These authors reported that there may be more questionable shootings revealed in the near future.

To date, 20 officers have been relieved of duty, suspended, fired, or have voluntarily resigned. There have been 32 criminal cases reversed as a result of the investigation. Furthermore, according to Lait and Glover (1999), more than 70 officers are under investigation for either committing crimes or covering up criminal activity. This incident along with the 1992 beating of motorist

Rodney King at the hand of LAPD officers has left the department demoralized and searching for answers.

One other horrid case of a police officer turned killer took place on March 4, 1995, in New Orleans. Gwyne (1995) of *Time Magazine* reported the tragic story of a New Orleans police officer who entered a Vietnamese restaurant to commit robbery and murder. The police officer shot and killed the security guard stationed in the restaurant who was an off-duty police officer and also her partner. After shooting the security guard, she then executed the son and daughter of the restaurant's immigrant owners. The officer then fled the scene of the crime and returned a short time later in her patrol car in response to the emergency call on her radio. The owner's child who was hiding in a walk-in refrigerator watched the triple murder. This witness subsequently identified the police officer as the murderer. The police officer had moonlighted at the restaurant as a part-time security officer, where she apparently planned the robbery.

In 1996, a former New Orleans police officer was sentenced to death for arranging the murder of a women who had filed a brutality complaint against him. This same officer was one of several New Orleans officers charged in a 1994 FBI sting for transporting and guarding shipments of cocaine. New Orleans has experienced extraordinary levels of crimes committed by their police department. Lyman (1999) reported that in New Orleans, dozens of police officers have been arrested on charges that included rape, robbery, drug dealing, theft, and murder.

In 1990, a New Jersey police officer was attending a law enforcement conference in Cincinnati when he allegedly robbed a bank. The officer then attempted to elude Cincinnati Police in a lengthy car chase but was subsequently stopped and arrested. In his hotel room, investigators found and seized 346 packages of heroin. The officer was believed to be the Camouflage Bandit who had robbed seven banks in New Jersey (More 1998).

In 1996, a Wichita, Kansas, police officer was charged and convicted of indecent liberties with a child. The officer was fired from the department with close to 20 years of service. In the same year, a Seattle, Washington, police officer was charged with patronizing a prostitute. This charge stemmed from the officer giving the prostitute freedom in return for sex. Similarly, a Phoenix, Arizona, police officer was arrested for releasing a suspected prostitute in exchange for having sex with him.

On July 28, 1999, a Denver, Colorado, police lieutenant was arrested on suspicion of sexual assault on a child. Investigators reported that the police lieutenant had been on medical leave for about one month when he was accused of sexually assaulting a young girl. The accused police lieutenant had 25 years of service with the Denver Police Department (*Law Enforcement News* 1999b).

Drug Crimes Committed by the Police

Drug crimes committed by the police have become terribly more common. Narcotics trafficking allows the police to make a great deal of money. This may come in the form of officers turning their heads and allowing drug sales to take place in return for money. It may involve police officers actually selling, possessing, and using drugs. Drug crimes committed by the police are increasingly being given a vast amount of attention. Palmiotto (1997) found that drug corruption among police officers is not a common occurrence but that it does account for the largest percentage of cases in which police corruption occurs. Carter (1999) found that drug-related corruption of police officers is particularly problematic and that while overall incidents of police corruption have declined, the cases of drug related corruption have increased. A drug crime involving a sheriff's department occurred in Topeka, Kansas, on April 15, 1999, when the local newspaper, *The Capital Journal,* reported that a Shawnee County Deputy Sheriff was charged and arrested on six counts of perjury and one count of official misconduct (Fry 1999). Fry (1999) reported that the deputy, a former narcotics detective, was a central figure in a six day hearing in March of 1999 into allegations of misconduct within the Shawnee County Sheriff's Department. According to the report, the disappearance of drug evidence and allegations of corruption and cover–up of the deputy's cocaine abuse were topics during the evidence hearing linked to a minor drug case.

What makes this case so deplorable is that the sheriff allegedly had knowledge of the deputy's cocaine abuse problem and wanted to handle it as a workers compensation claim. Subsequently, the sheriff has been charged with two counts of felony perjury linked to his sworn testimony in February and March of 1999, when he indicated the he did not have knowledge that the deputy used illegal drugs. Recently, the Attorney General for the State of Kansas had initiated action to remove the sheriff from office.

Campbell and Gillis (1996) reported that seven officers serving with the Chicago Police Department's Tactical Unit were indicted by a federal grand jury for allegedly stealing and extorting $65,000 from undercover Federal Bureau of Investigation agents posing as drug dealers. The officers have been charged with 21 separate counts of conspiracy to commit robbery and extortion and the illegal use of firearms. Interestingly, according to the *Chicago Sun Times,* drugs were found in four of the indicted officers' police lockers. Cases that resulted from the work of the accused officers could be dismissed and some imprisoned defendants may be released.

In Atlanta, Georgia, seven police officers were arrested in 1995 on charges which included stealing money during drug searches and extorting money from citizens in exchange for police protection. This was also the case in New York City, where 16 police officers were implicated in a scandal that came to light in 1994 in Harlem. Several of these officers plead guilty to a myriad of charges which included stealing cash from drug dealers, extorting money from criminal suspects and falsifying arrest records.

Rosenzweig (1999) reported that a sheriff's deputy in Tucson, Arizona, was arrested while on duty in January 1999 and charged with conspiracy to distribute illegal drugs. The deputy was part of a rogue team of officers who plotted to break into homes in Malibu Canyon, North Hollywood, and Huntington Beach, California, to steal drugs and money. The investigation was initiated by California authorities and lead investigators to Arizona. Four officers were involved in this case, three of whom were from California including a California highway patrol trooper and a Bureau of Narcotic Enforcement officer. The latest arrest was the deputy from Tucson, Arizona. The officers armed and wearing bullet-resistant vests reportedly broke into homes where drugs were stored and, if someone was home, the officers pretended to be on a police raid. The first break-in occurred in Huntington Beach, California, and yielded nothing more than a television set. In one other rogue operation, the officers confronted two persons in a Malibu Canyon home and allegedly seized one pound of marijuana and about $12,000 in cash. The officers then had the couple sign official-looking papers acknowledging the seizure.

In 1989 at Muskogee, Oklahoma, the local sheriff was arrested and indicted on charges of racketeering and drug conspiracy. The sheriff was accused of taking bribes to protect marijuana growers and participating in an illegal gambling operation. The sheriff was convicted of soliciting tens of thousands of dollars in bribes from marijuana growers and a nightclub owner who operated a dice game and sold alcohol without a license. The club owner in the case testified that the sheriff charged $400 a week in return for protecting a craps game, then raised the rates when business was booming. Another witness testified that the sheriff asked him for $20,000 to protect his marijuana operation.

Sweeney (1999) reported that a Jacksonville, Florida, sheriff's deputy was arrested for cocaine conspiracy charges while he paid undercover officers $90,000 for 11 pounds of cocaine. The deputy was arrested while attempting to flee federal and state agents after they secretly videotaped a drug deal with the officer near an area where he was assigned to patrol.

In 1997, the Sedgwick County Sheriff's Department fired a detective after he had been accused of steeling drug evidence for his own personal use. Furthermore, the detective was accused of an improper relationship with a defendant in a drug case. This incident sparked an array of questions about protocol and leadership within the sheriff's department. Furthermore, the drug cases in which the detective was involved were subject to review by the department and the local district attorney's office.

In 1996, three Detroit police officers and one former officer were named in a federal indictment, which accused them of being key players in a major cocaine smuggling ring. The officers were apparently involved in a Texas-to-Michigan cocaine smuggling ring (*Law Enforcement News* 1996).

Dempsy (1999) reported that in New York in 1992, six police officers were arrested and charged with buying drugs in their inner-city precincts and selling them in the suburban communities in which they lived. The arrests led to allegations of murders committed by the same officers. Furthermore, it was alleged that internal affairs investigators knew of the corrupt acts by these officers for years prior to the arrests and had taken no action.

A former Bardstown, Kentucky, police officer was charged October 20, 1999, with removing or destroying over three kilograms of cocaine from the department's evidence room. The 29-year-old former officer was indicted on 52 counts of theft and other crimes relating to evidence that had not been recovered from drug arrests in 1997 and 1998. Drugs were found at the former officer's residence after evidence was reported missing in May 1998 (*Law Enforcement News* 1999c).

Other Miscellaneous Crimes Committed by Police

More (1997) reported that a San Jose, California, police officer admitted to committing three burglaries while in uniform. The property that the officer took in the burglaries was described as rings, bracelets, and computers. The officer committed the crime to support his gambling addiction. In the early

1980s the Sedgwick County Sheriff's Department in Wichita, Kansas fired and charged four deputies and their supervisor with an array of charges including burglary, theft, and arson. These officers eventually pleaded guilty to committing the crimes while on patrol during the midnight shift. Several other deputies were suspended for having knowledge of the activities and not reporting them.

A case involving the police intentionally fabricating evidence was reported by the Associated Press on December 8, 1995. The headline read, "Former Death Row Inmate Cleared of Murder in Illinois." The defendant in the case was tried three times and sent to death row for the slaying of a 10-year-old girl. The suspect was released from prison when it was discovered that police investigators involved in the case perjured themselves and fabricated evidence against the defendant during the trial. The case against the defendant hinged on incriminating statements authorities said he made; however, the Associated Press reported that the investigators testified that they did not take notes and that their notes were lost or destroyed. A court-appointed special counsel and the Federal Bureau of Investigation are investigating the way in which case was handled.

On January 15, 2000, the Associated Press reported that a Junction City, Kansas, police detective was indicted on perjury charges. Furthermore, it was reported that the Junction City, Chief of Police was fired over the incident. This incident stemmed from allegations that were made against a defendant who spent six months in jail awaiting trial for attempted arson, telephone harassment and violating an order for protection. The charges were eventually dropped.

In Hamilton County, Kansas, an investigation has been initiated into alleged misconduct inside of the Hamilton County Sheriff's Department. The county attorney is holding inquisition hearings in what the county attorney described as an ouster procedure for the sheriff. The charges were not specifically cited; however, according to Kansas law, the grounds for the ouster of a public official are: (1) willful neglect to perform a duty required by law or (2) violation of any statute involving moral turpitude.

Kelley (2000) reported that an Oklahoma highway patrol trooper was arrested for shoplifting in the Wal-Mart store in Ada, Oklahoma. The state trooper was taken into custody by Ada Police Department officers after he was reportedly seen by loss-prevention officers attempting to leave the Wal-Mart with merchandise he had not purchased. The trooper reportedly had a young child in his care at the time. The total amount of the merchandise the trooper was allegedly attempting to steal exceeded $100, and he was arrested for grand larceny.

Lyman (1999) reported that in Detroit, federal agents arrested three city police officers in 1997 who were planning a home invasion in the suburb of Southland, Michigan, with the intent to steal one million dollars in cash. Similarly, in March 1998, Starr County, Texas, Sheriff Eugenio Falcon resigned from office after pleading guilty to conspiracy to commit burglary. Furthermore, an investigation revealed that the sheriff along with other officers referred prisoners to a local bail bond business in exchange for kickback payments.

In March 1998, an on-duty Arkansas State trooper was assigned to investigate a fatality accident. When he arrived, he stole credit cards and $1,100 in cash from the wallet of the fatality victim. There was a subsequent internal investigation, and the trooper was fired and charged with theft. On September 8, 1999, the former trooper pleaded guilty to the crime (*Law Enforcement News* 1999).

In 1997, a twenty-five-year veteran of the F.B.I. was indicted on charges of stealing more than $400,000, including at least $104,000 that was mob money, according to F.B.I. investigators. Interestingly, the F.B.I. reported that the agent was the lead person in the arrest of Nicholas Sullivan, a leader of an organized crime family in south Florida. The agent was reported to have had a serious alcohol and gambling addiction (Raab 1997).

REFLECTIONS

When the police commit crimes, it not only undermines public confidence but it also creates a sense of uneasiness in the community. Unfortunately, the data reveals that police involvement in criminal activity illustrates that many of the problems that plagued policing in the past are alive and well. Johnson (1998) asserted that between 1994 and 1998, over 500 officers in 47 cities were convicted of various federal crimes. Local and state authorities in 32 other jurisdictions were also engaged in active investigations or prosecutions of police.

The United States law enforcement industry is extremely large and complex with over 18,000 federal, state and local agencies (Walker 1999). In light of this data, it is somewhat ensuring that the bad apples in policing truly represent the slightest percent. It is also important to note that the large percentage of police officers in this country are honest, hard-working women and men who report to work every day with the goal of making a difference in their community.

When one or a small group of officers engage in a violation of the law, the community develops a sense of mistrust in the police which may take many years to re-establish. Police involvement in criminal misconduct in one geographical area of the country will assuredly affect policing as a whole. In other words, if a group of police officers in Los Angeles are discovered to have committed a number of deplorable crimes, this not only effects Los Angeles but also has an impact in the midwest, the south, and the east. For example, the author, while serving as a law enforcement officer in Kansas, recalls many negative attitudes and comments directed toward law enforcement in general with the Rodney King case. Sometimes, a general lack of faith in law enforcement as a whole is experienced across the country as a result of incidents such as the Rodney King beating.

Paradoxically, and all too often, this lack of faith is found to be more prevalent in minority communities. Historically, minority communities have been at the receiving end of acts of police criminal misconduct. This has created a problematic environment which centers on the state of police-minority relations. Yates and Pillai (1993) asserted that there is widespread indifference and even outright resentment toward the police among African Americans, Hispanics, Native Americans, and other minority groups that stem from many years of police abuse toward minorities. Other scholars stress the point that the images held by many minority communities of the police are that they are corrupt and abuse their power (see President's Commission on Law Enforcement and Administration of Justice 1967; The Knapp Commission Report 1973; Carter and Radelet 1999; Alpert and Dunham 1988; Yates 1995).

The advances made in policing over the past few decades are grounds for extreme optimism in many respects. Unfortunately, police criminal misconduct thought of as a past concern for police administrators has once again reared its ugly head. The 1980s and 1990s have seen insurmountable cases of criminal misconduct on the part of the police. This complexity has been brought into the spotlight by committees such as the Mollen Commission, which during the 1990s spent over 22 months investigating the nature and extent of corruption in the New York City Police Department and found that the drug trade caused the most serious police corruption.

The Christopher Commission was another committee which spent a considerable amount of time studying the Los Angeles Police Department following the brutal beating of Rodney King at the hands of Los Angles police officers. More recently, a special task force investigating police corruption in the Los Angels Police Department has asked prosecutors to charge three officers with crimes ranging from assault to perjury. Unfortunately, acts of police corruption, criminal misconduct, racism on the part of the police and wrongdoing for whatever reason still exist as we enter into the new millennium.

Police leadership must engage police misconduct in all forms head on. This is an awesome and painstaking responsibility and police leadership should continually explore different options available in combating police corruption and wrongdoing. Options should include continually improving the quality of recruits entering into the police service, aggressively recruiting minorities into policing, strengthening supervision through effective training, placing greater emphasis on the service side of policing, continuing community based policing, and enhancing recruit training in the areas of police corruption and misconduct. Furthermore, police executives and commanders must work studiously to break the code of silence, which is prevalent in many police agencies. It is well known that even honest police officers, when made aware of police criminal misconduct or other forms of corruption, have a tendency to keep quiet. They simply do not want to get involved or snitch on another officer, since this may be perceived as an act of disloyalty to fellow officers.

CONCLUSION

The battle against all forms of police misconduct will require courageous action on the part of police leadership. Those holding leadership and command roles in U.S. police forces have a responsibility to the honest, hard-working women and men who wear the badge to eliminate all forms of police misconduct, corruption, racism, and wrongdoing that may exist within the ranks of policing. The conditions that promote police misconduct in all of its ugly forms must be destroyed. Equally important, police leadership has an awesome responsibility to the general citizenry to ensure that honest and competent police officers serve their communities.

REFERENCES

Around the Nation. *Law Enforcement News.*

Around the Nation. *Law Enforcement News,* 30 September 1999.

Around the Nation. *Law Enforcement News,* 15 September 1999b.

Around the Nation. *Law Enforcement News,* 30 November 1999c.

The Associated Press. "Former Death Row Inmate Cleared of Murder in Illinois."
    8 December 1995.

The Associated Press. "Death Row Prisoner Freed: Prosecutorial Misconduct."
    9 December 1995.

The Associated Press. "Muskogee, Oklahoma Sheriff—Racketeering."
    9 December 1995.

Alpert, G.P. and Dunham, R.G. (1988). *Policing Urban America.* Illinois: Waveland
    Press Inc.

Barker, T. (1977). "Peer Group Support for Police Occupational Deviance." *Criminology*
    15, No. 2, 356.

Barker, T. and Wells, R.O. (1981). "Police Administrator's Attitudes Toward the
    Definition and Control of Police Deviance." Paper presented at the Academy of
    Criminal Justice Sciences, Philadelphia, Pennsylvania.

Campbell, M. and Gillis M. "West Side Cops Held in Drug Sting." *Chicago Sun Times,*
    21 December 1996, p. 1.

Carter, D.L. and Radelet, L.A. (1999). *The Police and the Community.* New Jersey:
    Prentice Hall.

Coleman, J. (1985). *The Criminal Elite.* New York: St. Martin's Press.

Conser, J.A. and Russell, G.D. (2000). *Law Enforcement in the United States.* Gaithersburg,
    Maryland: Aspen Publishers.

Dantzker, M.L. (2000). *Understanding Today's Police.* Upper Saddle River, NJ:
    Prentice Hall.

Dempsy, J.S. (1999). *Introduction to Policing.* Boston: West/Wadsworth Publishing
    Company.

Dorschner, J. (1993). "The Dark Side of the Force." *Critical Issues in Policing:
    Critical Readings,* edited by Dunham, R.G. and Alpert, G.P. Prospect Heights, Ill.:
    Waveland Press.

Fry, S. Oblander Hearing Scheduled for June. *The Topeka Capital Journal.* 15 April 1999,
    p. 1.

Fry, S. "Sheriff Challenged." *The Topeka Capital Journal.* 12 January 2000, p. 1.

Fry, S. "Women to Plead Innocent in Case that Led to Firing of Police Chief." *The
    Topeka Capital Journal.* 15 January 2000, p. 2.

Fry, S. "Meneley Delay Denied." *The Topeka Capital Journal.* 15 January 2000, p. 1.

Gaines, L.K., Kappeler, V.E. and Vaughn, J.B. (1997). *Policing in America.* Cincinnati,
    OH: Anderson Publishing Co.

Goldstein, H. (1975). *Police Corruption: A Perspective on its Nature and Control.* Washington,
    DC: Police Foundation.

Gwyne, S.C. (1995). "Cops and Robbers." *Time* 145, 45.

Johnson, K. "44 Law Enforcement Officers Arrested in a Sting, Cleveland Area FBI
    Raids Hit Five Agencies." *USA Today.* 22 January, 1998, p. A3.

Kelley, A. "OHP Trooper Arrested at Ada Store for Shoplifting. " *The Ada Evening News,*
    No. 260, 11 January, 2000.

The Knapp Commission. (1973). *The Knapp Commission Report on Police Corruption.*
    New York: George Braziller.

Lait, M. and Glover, S. LAPD Corruption Probe Grows to 7 Shootings, New
    Allegations, *The Los Angeles Times.* 22 October 1999, p. 1.

Lyman, M.W. (1999). *The Police: An Introduction.* Upper Saddle River, NJ: Prentice Hall.

More, H.W. (1998). *Special Topics in Policing.* Cincinnati, OH: Anderson Publishing Co.

"On the Side of the Law?" Not Necessarily." *Law Enforcement News.* 31 December 1996.

Palmiotto, M.J. (1997). *Policing: Concepts, Strategies, and Current Issues in American Police Forces,* Durham, NC: Carolina Academic Press.

President's Commission on Law Enforcement and Administration of Justice. (1967). *The Challenge of Crime in a Free Society.* Washington, D.C: U.S. Government Printing Office.

President's Commission on Law Enforcement and the Administration of Justice. (1967). *Task Force Report: The Police.* Washington, DC: U.S. Government Printing Office.

Raab, S. "Arrest of Agent Threatens to Taint a Major Mob Case." *New York Times.* 14 June, 1997, p. A1, 26.

Roebuck, J.B. and Barker, T. (1974). "A Typology of Police Corruption." *Social Problems,* (21) 3, 422–437.

Rosenzweig, D. "4th Officer Arrested in Probe of Drug Theft." *The Los Angeles Times.* 22 December 1999.

Sanders, K. (1999). "Police Brutality in Indianapolis." *Pittsburgh Post-Gazette.* October.

Skolnick, J.H. and Bayley, D.H. (1996). *The New Blue Line: Police Innovation in Six American Cities.* New York: The Free Press.

Sweeney, K. "Police Officer Charged in Plot to Deal Cocaine." *Times Union Newspaper.* 10 February 1999, p. 1–2.

Wagner, A.E. and Decker, S.H. (1993). "Evaluating Citizen Complaints Against the Police." *Critical Issues in Policing: Critical Readings,* edited by Dunham, R.G. and Alpert, G.P., Prospect Heights, Ill.: Waveland Press.

Walker, S. (1999). *The Police in America: An Introduction.* Boston, MA: McGraw-Hill Book Co.

Wilson, O.W. and McLaren, R.C. (1977). *Police Administration.* New York: McGraw-Hill Book Co.

Yates, D.L. (1995). "Prejudice in the Criminal Justice System." *American Prejudice: With Liberty and Justice for Some,* edited by R.H. Ropers. New York: Plenum Press, 185–207.

Yates, D.L. and Pillai V.K. (1993). "Race and Police Commitment to Community Policing." *The Journal of Intergroup Relations, XIX,* (4), 15–23.

PART 3

PHYSICAL ABUSE
BY POLICE OFFICERS

"The Police Officer's Ethical Use of Force" by James D. Sewell examines the use of physical duress in the line of duty. He emphasizes the need to define ethical and unethical uses of force, which continually presents difficulties due to the uniqueness of each situation. For Sewell the answer lies in carefully selecting and training candidates to become officers. In addition, he also places the burden of ethical conduct with the leaders of the agency, who should be modeling correct behavior as well as punishing those actions which are not ethical.

The article written by Regina G. Lawrence, "Accidents, Icons, and Indexing: The Dynamics of News Coverage of Police Use of Force," studies media coverage of the use of force by police. The author, who did a six-year study of police use of force, writes that the incentive to do this study was initiated by the Rodney King incident. Lawrence concludes in this article that "Dramatic accidental events that suggest new attention to emerging problems can license news organizations both to devote more attention to emerging public problems and to develop challenging framings of those problems" (p. 327).

In the article "How Police Justify the Use of Deadly Force," William B. Waegel examines how police interpret, explain, and justify the use of force. Waegel reviews the police subculture which provides insight into how officers defend their actions. In this article Waegel provides insight on the investigation of police shootings by illustrating three shooting cases from his field research. He also explains the contradictions that exist on the use of deadly force by police officers.

Richard Frey, author of "The Abner Louima Case: Idiosyncratic Personal Crime or Symptomatic Police Brutality?" reviews the facts of the Abner Louima case in which a New York police officer physically abused and sodomized a Haitian immigrant. The author raises the question as to whether this is evidence of a deeply corrupt faction of the police force or an isolated, exceptional incident. Frey also revisits unanswered questions concerning the role of the police and the legal system.

"The Right to Run: Deadly Force and the Fleeing Felon" by Michael D. Greathouse reviews *Tennessee v. Garner*, which involved the death of a burglary suspect who was fleeing the scene of the crime. The U.S. Supreme Court ruled that using deadly force on a fleeing suspect is violation of the suspect's Fourth Amendment rights.

Sorensen, Marquart, and Brock focus on the use of deadly force by law enforcement officers in "Factors Related to Killings of Felons by Police Officer: A Test of the Community Violence and Conflict Hypotheses." The authors present the conflict hypothesis, which proposes that police-inflicted fatalities are not equally distributed in communities (i.e. there are tendencies for more people of certain races/economic groups to be killed), and the community hypothesis, which holds that police violence is in direct proportion to the community in question. These hypotheses were tested by examining data from the Supplemental Homicide Reports, which showed that there was a relationship between race and felons killed. However, the greatest correlation was between felons killed and the rate of economic inequality, which indicates that this factor should be taken into account when explaining police-caused homicides in general.

Robert Scott and Michael Copeland in "Technological Innovation and the Development of Less-than-Lethal Force Options" provide an up-to-date review of various forms of police technology that can be used to subdue individuals or groups of individuals without causing serious bodily harm to the offender. The authors specifically discuss several forms of less-than-lethal technology along with reviewing various miscellaneous technologies that fall into the less-than-lethal weapons category. In the last section of this article, Scott and Copeland outline lethal issues and constraints that the modern police officer will encounter.

"Police Pursuits and the Use of Force: Recognizing and Managing 'The Pucker Factor'—A Research Note" written by Geoffrey Alpert, Dennis Kenney, and Roger Dunham studies the issue of high-speed pursuit as a deadly force. The authors examine data from four metropolitan areas: Miami, FL; Omaha, NE; Mesa, AZ; and Aiken Country, SC. The authors queried suspects who ran from police about their experiences, asked officers about their attitudes, conducted public opinion polls, and collected pursuit forms. According to the study, problems often occur after a high-speed chase. The officers, whose adrenaline levels have risen in the course of the pursuit, can overreact in trying to apprehend a suspect, especially if the person continues to resist arrest. The article offers several suggestions for improving the officers' behavior in this area, including better training, supervision, and accountability.

In the next article, "The Most Deadly Force: Police Pursuits," authors Geoffrey Alpert and Patrick Anderson discuss the issue of high-speed pursuits as deadly force. The authors provide the reader with a general discussion on police and police cars, police pursuits, and high-speed pursuit policies. The question "Why Pursue?" is raised by Alpert and Anderson. The role of the social scientist and the use of research as they relate to police pursuits are also discussed by the authors.

The final article, "The Other Deadly Force: An Analysis of One State's High-Speed Pursuit Guidelines" by Donald R. Liddick, suggests that the police officer's patrol vehicle is often used as a weapon of deadly force. In this study Liddick examines pertinent court cases and academic research and recommends policies to aid departments in apprehending suspects while at the same time preserving the safety of both officers and civilians. Finally, he offers suggestions for forming written high-speed pursuit guidelines.

THE POLICE OFFICER'S ETHICAL USE OF FORCE

James D. Sewell, Ph.D
Florida Department of Law Enforcement

Significant academic and professional literature, especially in recent years, has focused on the use of force, particularly deadly force, by the police. Much of the literature has emphasized cases in which the use of force has been outside legal or policy guidelines. Media coverage of now-famous incidents of egregious police conduct, such as Arthur McDuffie in Miami, Rodney King in Los Angeles, and Abner Louima in New York City, has underscored the need for increased control over and review of police activity. For all the criticism which may be leveled at agencies and individual officers, particularly in specific incidents, one fact must be recognized: police officers in the United States have, by law and training, been vested with the authority to use force, up to and including deadly force, during the course of the performance of their official duties. Skolnick and Fyfe (1993) have already succinctly stated the heart of the issue:

> As long as some members of society do not comply with law and resist the police, force will remain an inevitable part of policing. Cops, especially, understand that. Indeed, anybody who fails to understand the centrality of force to police work has no business in a police uniform. (37)

Within our legal system, the fact that officers use force is not the issue. The use of force should be viewed as a tool which officers must employ from time to time in order to protect society and its citizens. The more definitive issue is the ethical use of such force. In any discussion regarding an officer's ethical right to use force, a number of questions must be addressed:

– How do we define the ethical use of force?
– What is the extent of police use of force?
– How do we continue to assure the ethical use of force by our police personnel?

THE ETHICS OF FORCE

To reflect that the issue of professional ethics and proper ethical behavior permeates American law enforcement appears a trite pronouncement. Yet it is an issue which cannot be overestimated and must underscore all law enforcement conduct. As Peak, Stitt, and Gleason (1998, 20) have explained:

> Ethics may be defined as the discipline "dealing with what is good and bad
> and with moral duty and obligation" (*Webster's New World Dictionary* 1981:389).
> Proper ethical behavior has always been the cornerstone of policing and is what
> communities expect of their public servants. Citizens give up the right to enforce
> or take the law into their own hands and vest substantial law enforcement
> authority with the police. The police, as representative agents of the government,
> must democratically respect citizens' rights, attempt to serve their best interests
> and take actions that positively affect or help people.

Law enforcement officers are, of course, charged with enforcing the law while simultaneously obeying its constraints on their own behavior. The actions of the individual officer within the legal framework reflect a subtle distinction which is important to discuss, the distinction between a legally correct use of force and an ethically correct one. This distinction is particularly clear in a discussion about the use of deadly force. In the parlance of a cop, a police shooting is classified as either good or bad. A *good shoot* meets applicable state law, fits within the policy guidelines of the department, and falls under the judicial constraints imposed by the United States Supreme Court case of *Tennessee v. Garner;* a *bad shoot* fails to meet at least one of these criteria. Yet for the practitioner, an ethical shooting is more basic. Was it the right thing to do? Was resorting to deadly force the only way to handle this situation? Did the officer have any other recourse? Can a shoot be legal and not ethical? Yes! Can a shoot be ethical but not legal? Probably not! Are such decisions easy? No!

The same issues arise in other applications of force. If, to a cop, the use of force is considered good, it meets legal guidelines and departmental policy. Yet questions centering around the ethical use of force go further: was it necessary for the circumstances, or did it become excessive? Was it applied to achieve compliance or custody rather than pain or punishment? Did the officer have sufficient skill or even patience to deal with a difficult person who verbally or physically resisted a lawful police request? Did the officer conduct him or herself in such a manner that force became inevitable? As a result of training, experience, and foresight, could the officer have exercised any other options? The issue of legal and ethical use of force frequently falls within what Peak and his co-authors have defined as ethical dilemmas:

> True ethical dilemmas are situations that are no-win in nature, where you are
> "damned if you do and damned if you don't." Klockars (1980:33) conceived of
> such situations in terms of means and ends, stating that a genuine moral dilemma
> is "a situation from which one cannot emerge innocent no matter what one does—
> employ a dirty means, employ an insufficiently dirty means, or walk away." An

example might be when a police officer stops a weaving vehicle and discovers that the driver is a close friend, relative or off-duty police officer. (1998, 21)

The dilemma in deciding to use force can be especially vexing. A motorist leads many police officers on a twenty-mile pursuit, then refuses to comply with their instructions. Does an officer have a right to determine that, at some point, the force necessary to effect an arrest should also include some punishment to add physical consequences (pain) to the motorist's actions so, perhaps, he will more quickly obey police instructions in the future? A mentally disturbed homeless person swinging a knife or a club is ten feet away from an officer. Is deadly force justified? As Bittner explained, the real dilemma

is connected with the dire nature of the circumstances in which it is relevant, raising concerns about officers' physical safety. The point is not to prevent the use of physical force, especially deadly force, but to relegate it to the status of the last and unavoidable resort. Contrary to the word "manhunt," humans may never be hunted, and while a dangerous animal may be killed on sight, a dangerous person must be afforded the opportunity to yield. No pressure of circumstances may obscure the fact that the target is a fellow human being.

However, the forbearance demanded of officers is often put into question because some of the people with whom they deal often behave in ways that appear to bely their own humanity. But even this does not alter what one fallible human being owes another fallible, even fallen, human being. For ultimately, the consideration extended to the seemingly undeserving person is not intended for his or her personal benefit, but expresses the moral integrity of the one who extends it. It enhances the dignity of human life, especially in situations where extending it appears to be hopelessly misspent. (1999, 2)

THE EXTENT OF POLICE USE OF FORCE

While comprehensive national data on police use of force are generally lacking, the National Institute of Justice, the Bureau of Justice Statistics, and the Bureau of the Census conducted a Police–Public Contact Survey in 1996. Based on that nationally representative sample, the researchers involved in this study were able to extrapolate to the national population and estimate (Greenfeld, Langan, and Smith 1995, iv–v):

- An estimated 44.6 million persons (21% of the population age 12 or older), most commonly men, whites, and persons in their 20's, had a face-to-face contact with a police officer during 1996.
- The most common reasons cited for contact with police among residents age 12 or older:
  - An estimated 33% of residents who had contact with police had asked for or provided the police with some type of assistance;
  - An estimated 32% of those who had contact with police had reported a crime, either as a victim or a witness; and
  - Receiving traffic tickets and being involved in traffic accidents

- For just under a third of those with contacts, the police initiated the contact; for most, nearly half of those with contacts, the citizen had initiated the contact.
- An estimated 1.2 million persons, or about 0.6% of the population age 12 or older, were handcuffed during 1996.
- An estimated 500,000 persons (0.2% of the population age 12 or older) were hit, held, pushed, choked, threatened with a flashlight, restrained by a police dog, threatened or actually sprayed with chemical or pepper spray, threatened with a gun, or experienced some other form of force. Of the 500,000, about 400,000 were also handcuffed.
- The total estimated number who were handcuffed or were hit, held, pushed, choked, threatened with a flashlight, restrained by a police dog, threatened or actually sprayed with chemical or pepper spray, threatened with a gun, or who experienced some other form of force was 1.3 million persons (0.6% of the population age 12 or older).

ASSURING ETHICAL CONDUCT

Regardless of the number of persons subjected to force by police, how do we reinforce the ethical use of force by U.S. law enforcement officers? How do we assure that our communities are protected by men and women who are willing to use force, as well as provide all police services, in only the most legal and ethical manner? How do we assure the development, promulgation, and sustainability of the highest organizational ethics, which an individual officer can embrace and use in carrying out his or her professional responsibilities? The creation and maintenance of an organizational environment which demands ethical and values-based conduct, especially in the use of deadly force needs to be established. There are ten specific, interrelated, and closely linked actions which are key to ensuring ethical conduct.

As Braunstein and Tyre (1999, 124) have noted:

> Organizational culture—an organization's past and present influences, beliefs, myths, and patterns of behavior—is powerful in shaping member behavior and is itself open to being shaped by its members and by its leaders . . . when police leaders and administrators tolerate an unethical organizational culture, they are derelict in their duties and responsible for the unethical actions of their troops.

To this end, it is critical that the organizational culture of a law enforcement agency support only the highest standards of ethical behavior, especially in situations in which force is applied. It is of the utmost importance that these values, enforced by the organization and accepted by the police subculture, respect both the role of police officers and the public they serve; acknowledge the use of force as appropriate but only under specified legal and ethical circumstances; and reinforce and perpetuate only the highest ethical conduct in both word and deed. The adoption of a clear values statement for a department is an essential first step. Tables 1 and 2 reflect examples of such statements. Police executives and administrators can realize such departmental standards through the regular exposure of decisions, actions, and personnel to these values and by the use of quality control mechanisms, such as a departmental ethics officer, with agency-wide authority for assuring compliance.

TABLE 1

MIAMI-DADE POLICE DEPARTMENT MISSION STATEMENT

The Miami-Dade Police Department will commit its resources in partnership with the community to:

- Promote a safe and secure environment, free from crime and the fear of crime
- Maintain order and provide for the safe and expeditious flow of traffic
- Practice our core values of integrity, respect, service, and fairness

INTEGRITY

Integrity is the hallmark of the Miami-Dade Police Department and we are committed to the highest performance standards, ethical conduct, and truthfulness in all relationships.

We hold ourselves accountable for our actions and take pride in a professional level of service to all.

RESPECT

We treat all persons in a dignified and courteous manner, and exhibit understanding of ethnic and cultural diversity, both in our professional and personal endeavors.

We guarantee to uphold the principles and values embodied in the Constitution of the United States and the State of Florida.

SERVICE

We provide quality service in a courteous, efficient, and accessible manner.

We foster community and employee involvement through problem-solving partnerships.

FAIRNESS

We treat all people impartially, with consideration and compassion.

We are equally responsive to our employees and the community we serve.

TABLE 2

LITTLETON, COLORADO, POLICE DEPARTMENT VALUES

In support of our mission, we are committed to upholding these values: we believe government should be a part of and not apart from the community.

WE VALUE:

Problem solving
Open communication
Development of community pride
Trust
Recognition of and respect for diversity within our community

We believe that everyone should feel safe and secure within our community.

WE VALUE:

Crime prevention
Fair enforcement of laws and ordinances
Compassionate treatment of victims of crimes
Progressive and proactive police methods
Identification and apprehension of criminal offenders
Safe movement of traffic through our community

We believe in enhancing the quality of life and reducing fear in our community.

WE VALUE:

Commitment to quality of service
Promoting a sense of trust and respect for each other
Creative risk taking and initiative
Sharing information through education and involvement

We believe in pursuing the highest professional standards in managerial, operational and personal performance.

WE VALUE:

Integrity and ethical behavior
Responsibility and accountability
Recruiting and hiring the best applicants
Training and developing our employees to their highest potential
A work environment that promotes personal and profesional growth
Reasonable discretion
Recognition for personal and community achievement

Proper Selection

While the organization's culture and values provide the framework of professional ethical standards and conduct, men and women are its foundation. For that reason, the selection of new personnel is the key to an organization's survival and future success. There are, of course, a number of accepted practices in any acceptable hiring process: written examination, oral board interview, psychological assessment, physical examination, physical agility test, polygraph examination, and drug screening. Most important, however, is the use of an extensive, comprehensive background or personal history investigation. Recognizing that the best predictor of future behavior is past history, it is critical to carefully examine a police candidate's employment and personal histories, especially as they reflect on his or her work ethic, maturity, people skills, and depending on the circumstances, propensity for aggressive behavior or violence. Our efforts must assure that only the most mature and intellectually and ethically well-prepared individuals begin a law enforcement career.

For all our effort at proper selection, however, we must recognize that preemployment screening tools are not the panacea to all our problems. The summary of the Report of the Independent Commission on the Los Angeles Police Department is telling in this regard:

> Improved screening of applicants is not enough. Police work modifies behavior. Many emotional and psychological problems may develop during an officer's tenure on the force. Officers may enter the force well suited psychologically for the job, but may suffer from burnout, alcohol-related problems, cynicism, or disenchantment, all of which can result in poor control over their behavior. A person's susceptibility to the behavior-modifying experiences of police work may not be revealed during even the most skilled and sophisticated psychological evaluation process . . . In addition, supervisors must understand their role to include training and counseling officers to cope with the problems policing can often entail, so that they may be dealt with before an officer loses control or requires disciplinary action. (1991, xvi)

While an emphasis on entry-level officers is important, it is only one part of a bigger selection picture. Selection of an agency's leadership—the promotion of personnel especially to first-line supervisory positions—is even more critical in defining and assuring an organizational culture which is ethical and values-driven. Promotional processes which successfully recognize and reward both existing and potential leadership ability and a demonstrated commitment to ethical performance of law enforcement duties form the foundation for all of an agency's efforts at proper and professional officer conduct.

Realistic and Values-Based Recruit Training

Training of police recruits in the appropriate use of force is, of course, critical. Especially with mandated minimum levels of recruit training adopted in most states, recruits have been exposed to and are evaluated on their knowledge of law and policy and their technical skills in the application of force. The tactics of force and proficiency in its application, especially in the use of deadly force, have been the focus of police training efforts for many years.

Yet two other areas related to the use of deadly force are equally vital. First, the education of an officer in decision-making on when to use force, rather than simply on proficiency or how to apply force, has expanded over the last several years, especially with the use of firearms simulation technology. The paper target can now be replaced with real-life scenarios, and our officers-in-training, whether during the academy or in-service, can experience far more believable use of force scenarios and ultimately better grasp the applicability of the organization's ethical standards to use of force situations. The utilization of the concept of the continuum of force as a training instrument has sought to foster the broader, interlocking possibilities of action in an officer's decision to use force and reflect the progression of events which most frequently lead to this decision.

Second, a key component to that training and education in decision-making is the ethics of the situation: when the use of force is not only legally justified but morally appropriate. The core values of an agency and its personnel are those placed on human life, on its relationship to and respect for all its citizens, including those on the receiving end of police action, and on the appropriate role of police in preserving the peace and protecting the community. These are especially important when the image of policing for many young recruits is based on real life television series depicting cops, and new hires appear to be younger with less real-world experience and exposure than their preceding generations. As Bittner emphasized, "The rule here is that whatever a situation may seem to demand and however it develops, police officers' actions are limited by respect for the humanity of the people involved" (1999, 2).

The importance of recruitment, selection, and training of officers as part of the ethical foundation of an organization and its individual members cannot be overemphasized. Throughout the entire process, the organization's message about its values and the expected conduct of its officers must be clear, consistent, and unambiguous. Within the academy itself, the same message, with learning incrementally built upon ethical standards and based on realistic applications to work on the street, is imperative for the organization and its personnel. Delattre (1992) has raised a caution about the use of ill-prepared officers, especially when they lack experience or are unsupervised:

> The effects are disheartening to watch. In one mid-Atlantic city, beset by a history of corruption in government and poor performance by some police, inexperienced officers sometimes jeopardize others and themselves by failing to take proper control in risky situations. They seem not to know how to use their legitimate authority to minimize danger, and their judgment is too lacking in foresight to prevent clever and assertive suspects from manipulating them.

> Such incompetent officers are normally vulnerable to panic, and therefore to brutality. When they feel a situation getting away from them, they tend to behave rashly and unpredictably. This makes them dangerous to suspects, bystanders, and each other. One distinguished senior officer, after we had observed this problem together, said to me, "They don't want to listen. We can't seem to teach them much." (3)

Proper Field Training

Yet no matter how realistic academy training may be, it pales in comparison to the lessons a young officer learns on the street. This application of weeks of training becomes another block upon which future ethical conduct is built and sustained. For that reason, it is critical that formalized field training maximize a structured program of learning. It must utilize only the best-prepared field training officers with both a firm grounding in agency values and professional ethics and the tact, skills, and patience necessary to be an effective teacher and recognize that its ultimate mission is not only to eliminate individuals ill-suited or ill-prepared for law enforcement but to assure the future success and most ethical performance of new officers.

In-Service Training

As is the case with recruit-level preparation, on-going training of in-service personnel should concentrate on continued proficiency, enhancement of decision-making abilities, and reinforcement of ethical and values-driven use of force. The nature of the police subculture, with its tendency to perpetuate macho actions and decision-making, requires that the latter be particularly strong and meaningful. Experienced officers must clearly understand the types of ethical conduct and professional judgment which will be tolerated and rewarded. Concurrently, they must recognize the means, techniques, and tactics available to them so that unethical and inappropriate use of force is not viewed as their only viable option.

Adequate Supervision

It is clear from both literature and case studies (e.g. Report of the Independent Commission on the Los Angeles Police Department 1991; Skolnick and Fyfe 1993) that officers often resort to unethical, inappropriate, or illegal use of force when supervision is lacking or is a party to the violations. In many cases, the supervisors themselves have been rewarded for force which is clearly out of line with professional policing tenets. Again, strong, unambiguously ethical organizational culture and forceful leadership within the agency are paramount.

As is the case for line officers, supervisors should be rewarded and promotions should occur only as a result of that conduct which is in keeping with the organization's and profession's values. As the agency's eyes and ears on officer misconduct and those most able to reward or sanction behavior on a timely basis, supervisors must clearly understand the agency's message and their role in expressing and enforcing it. At the same time, these critical personnel should sincerely believe that the agency and its administration will stand behind and clearly support them in those decisions and actions necessary to assure ethical conduct, actions which may at times conflict with the mores of the traditional police subculture.

Early Identification and Intervention

It is clear that a professional agency must develop a system by which officers who inappropriately use force early in their career are identified and appropriately addressed. Departments can no longer afford to ignore repeated incidents by a small group of officers. In placing early identification and intervention in a particularly contemporary framework, Scrivner (1994) noted:

> The need for early intervention parallels the "broken windows" argument (Wilson and Kelling 1982) that had significant impact on how police leadership came to reframe the crime control mission. The argument that early signs of community deterioration were forerunners of more serious criminal problems could be applied to the human behavior dimension of the police organization. Police managers would be well-advised to pay attention to the clear signals that suggest deterioration in officer behavior, the behavioral equivalent of "broken windows", *before* it results in excessive force complaints. If police treat abuse of force as they do serious crime in the community, by waiting until it happens, then their personnel practices, like incident-driven policing, constitute a reactive than a proactive response. An incident-driven frame of reference [on the other hand] can create institutional barriers to effective intervention. (9–10)

There are a variety of methods by which such early identification can occur, mostly based on the leadership within the agency, community needs and support, and professionalism of the officers. The Miami Dade Police Department in 1981, for instance, instituted a formalized tracking system to identify persistent patterns of behavior and determine an appropriate course of corrective action. Using a similar system of timely data gathering and analysis, the Kansas City, Missouri, Police Department "recognized that communication was the medium for change both in identifying at-risk officers and in enhancing their skills to reduce complaints against them" (Braunstein and Tyre 1999, 129). The New York Police Department, on the other hand, recently implemented force-related integrity testing, utilizing verbally confrontational *stings* to gauge officer conduct in stressful situations and following up with discipline, counseling, or other corrective action as necessary.

Timely Discipline

Appropriate discipline in its two forms, rewards and punishment, reinforces positive and deters negative behavior. To be most effective, such discipline must be sure, i.e. it will occur; it must be consistent, i.e. notwithstanding extenuating circumstances, it must be applied similarly to similar conduct; and it must be administered in a timely fashion. The latter becomes especially important in use of force situations; failure to act in a timely fashion encourages inconsistency, fosters an attitude that the consequences of and accountability for conduct are unimportant, and fails to clearly establish the cause-effect relationship necessary for discipline to work.

Strong Leadership

While supervision is an important ingredient to deterring police abuse of force on a daily basis and proper management of resources is a necessity, *leadership* at the highest levels is vital. To survive in today's communities, police agencies cannot afford executives who choose to ignore their responsibility to set the agency's tone and direction. These same leaders must accept their role and obligation as aggressive, assertive ethicists who can define and demand proper and acceptable officer conduct; mold the organization, its culture, and its values; and articulate and clarify the philosophy, role, and scope of policing in contemporary communities. Delattre's comments (1991) regarding the leader's role in organizational integrity are particularly applicable to the issue of ethical use of force:

> Today's police leaders must teach the young what policing is and what it stands for. It is not just personal integrity the newcomers will need to witness, but the integrity of police departments as such—that reciprocity of respect for decency without which individuals cannot depend on their institutions and institutions cannot depend on them. They will need to witness integrity in the *de facto* policies and practices of police departments and in the vitality of those policies as they are embodied in individual police. (26)

There is an interesting dilemma centering around leadership and organizational change. Frequently it is the misuse of force by officers which brings a change in departmental leadership. The new chief, as change agent, is expected to quickly turn around organizational culture, personnel attitudes, and individual performance. Yet the political pressure on this executive and at times, unrealistic expectations for the length of time true change requires, make it difficult to foster a completely changed culture which both institutionalizes and operationalizes a consistent theme of values. Such an issue is a major reason a number of authors (e.g Williams, Cheurprakobkit, and Kirchhoff, 1999) have argued for the need for chief executive contracts.

On-Going Research and Analysis of Police Use of Force Incidents

McEwen has already lamented that "the basic problem is the lack of routine, national systems for collecting data on incidents in which police use force during the normal course of duty and on the extent of excessive force" (1996, 2). While the Bureau of Justice Statistics and National Institute of Justice have expanded efforts at data collection at the national level, particularly assessing police–public contact, statistics and data analysis remain disjointed, incomplete, and, at best, a sketchy assessment of not only inappropriate, excessive, or unnecessary use of force but those millions of public contacts where police force was limited, ethical, and appropriate.

The need, then, is for the development of quality data at the local, state, and national levels. Such data, similarly reported and collected as the FBI's Uniform Crime Report, can and should adequately and accurately reflect incidents and circumstances of police use of force; successful and unsuccessful applications, techniques and tactics; and discipline and training efforts. Such information is necessary if we are to fully understand the nature of police–citizen encounters resulting in the application of some form of force and, ultimately, to assure the ethical conduct of our officers.

In summary, then, in our efforts to safeguard society, we have invested our protectors with the legal authority to use force. That force is restricted by specific laws, court decisions, agency policies, professional training, and circumstances of the particular incident. Most importantly, professional and personal ethics provide a standard against which any application of force can and must be weighed.

Those ethical standards of the profession are inculcated within the organization and the individual officer in a variety of ways. At its heart, however, are distinct values about the police role, proper authority, and ethical conduct which must be sustained within the organization and police subculture and embraced and brought to life by an agency's leadership and its individual members.

REFERENCES

Alpert, G. P. and L. A. Fridell. (1992). *Police Vehicles and Firearms: Instruments of Deadly Force.* Prospect Heights, IL: Waveland Press.

Bittner, E. (1999). "Ethical Dilemmas." *Subject to Debate,* 13(11), 2.

Braunstein, S. and M. L. Tyre. (1999). "Are Ethical Problems in Policing a Function of Poor Organizational Communications?" in Sewell, J. D. *Controversial Issues in Policing.* Boston, MA: Allyn and Bacon, pp. 123–138.

Charette, B. (1994). "Early Identification of Police Brutality and Misconduct: The Metro Dade Police Department Model." in *Human Resources in Criminal Justice.* Tallahassee, FL: Florida Criminal Justice Executive Institute, pp. 53–59.

Delattre, E. J. (1991). *Against Brutality and Corruption: Integrity, Wisdom, and Professionalism.* Tallahassee, FL: Florida Criminal Justice Executive Institute.

Delattre, E. J. (1989). *Character and Cops: Ethics in Policing.* Washington, DC: American Enterprise Institute.

Delattre, E. J. (1992). "Judgment in Police Work." *Perspectives on the Professions,* 11(2), 2–3.

Delattre, E. J. (1996). *Organizational Integrity and Executive Leadership.* Tallahassee, FL: Florida Criminal Justice Executive Institute.

Garner, J. H., T. Schade, J. Hepburn, and J. Buchanan. (1995). "Measuring the Continuum of Force Used By and Against the Police." *Criminal Justice Review,* 20(2), 146–168.

Greenfeld, L. A., P. A. Langan, and S. K. Smith. (1997). *Police Use of Force: Collection of National Data.* Washington, DC: U. S. Government Printing Office.

Independent Commission on the Los Angeles Police Department (1991*). Report of the Independent Commission on the Los Angeles Police Department.* Los Angeles, CA.

International Association of Chiefs of Police (IACP). (1997). *Ethics Resource Guidebook.* Alexandria, VA: IACP.

Klockars, C. B. (1980). "The Dirty Harry Problem." *The Annals of the American Academy of Political and Social Science,* 452:33–47.

McEwen, T. (1996). *National Data Collection on Police Use of Force.* Washington, DC: National Institute of Justice.

Peak, K. J., B. G. Stitt, and R. W. Gleasor. (1998). "Ethical Considerations in Community Policing and Problem Solving." *Police Quarterly,* 1(3), 19–34.

Endnote: The author would like to express his appreciation to Chief Darrel Stephens, Chief Mitchell Tyre, Dr. Gerald Williams, Colonel George Fox, and Sarah Poynter Owens for their invaluable assistance and suggestions in the preparation of this chapter.

Scrivner, E. M. (1994). *The Role of Police Psychology in Controlling Excessive Force.* Washington, DC: U. S. Government Printing Office.

Skolnick, J. H., and J. J. Fyfe. (1993). *Above the Law: Police and the Excessive Use of Force.* New York: The Free Press.

Strandberg, K. W. (1999). "To Shoot or Not to Shoot." *Law Enforcement Technology,* 26 (8), 32–36.

U. S. Department of Justice, National Institute of Justice (1993). *Community Policing for Safe Neighborhoods 2000: Partnerships for the 21st Century* (Conference Proceeding). Washington, DC: U. S. Government Printing Office.

U. S. Department of Justice, National Institute of Justice, Office of Community Oriented Policing Services (1997). *Police Integrity: Public Service With Honor.* Washington, DC: U. S. Government Printing Office.

Williams, G. L., S. Cheurprakobkit, and W. E. Kirchhoff. (1999). "Police Executive Contracts: Are They a Foundation for Successful Tenure?" in Sewell, J. D. *Controversial Issues in Policing.* Boston, MA: Allyn and Bacon, pp. 103–122.

Williams, G. T. (1999). "Reluctance to use Deadly Force: Causes, Consequences, and Cures." *FBI Law Enforcement Bulletin,* 68(10), 1–5.

ARTICLE 14

ACCIDENTS, ICONS, AND INDEXING: THE DYNAMICS OF NEWS COVERAGE OF POLICE USE OF FORCE

Regina G. Lawrence
University of Washington

This study explores the construction of news about police use of force in the *Los Angeles Times* over a six-year period culminating in the crisis generated by the Rodney King beating. The data presented here indicate that the "indexing" norm may not fully explain the pattern of inclusion of nonofficial voices and challenging views in the news. Dramatic news events apparently can license journalists to usher challenging views into the news in significant proportions, even in the absence of or prior to elite conflict. These findings are explained in part by the characteristics of police brutality news itself, and in part by news organizations' conversion of dramatic "accidental events" into "news icons." A comparison of media treatment of two dramatic cases of alleged police brutality, however, suggests that while dramatic events can bring challenging ideas into the news, both the characteristics of events and the presence of elite conflict are crucial to the ultimate effect of those events on the construction of public problems in the news.

Keywords   accidental events, indexing, journalistic norms, news icons, police brutality

A well-established and ever-growing body of research has explored how news organizations construct the news, with an eye toward understanding how they decide not only what events, but what sources and ideas journalists include in and exclude from the news. In this view, journalists act as managers of the national symbolic arena (Gans, 1979), and in that capacity as "selectors" of what voices and views are heard (Ericson et al., 1991).

The primary finding of this work has been the predominance of official sources and officially sanctioned ideas in the news. Established news beats

The author thanks Lance Bennett, Timothy Cook, Steve Livingston, and the anonymous reviewer for their many helpful comments, and the Goldsmith Awards Program of the Joan Shorenstein Center on the Press, Politics, and Public Policy for their support.

correspond with institutional boundaries, leading journalists to rely heavily on institutionally positioned officials (Bennett, 1996; Cook, 1994). These elites act as "authorized knowers," considered by journalists to be the most "legitimate" sources of news (Tuchman, 1978). Officials' interest in routinizing the daily business of governing and communicating with the public, combined with journalists' interest in routinizing news production, create a well-recognized symbiotic relationship between reporters and official sources (Cohen, 1963; Gans, 1979; Sigal, 1973).

Recent work on the "indexing hypothesis" captures this dynamic and extends it to account more fully for variations in the content of the news over time. The hypothesis contends that "mass media news professionals, from the boardroom to the beat, tend to 'index' the range of voices and viewpoints in both news and editorials according to the range of views expressed in mainstream government debate about a given topic" (Bennett, 1990, p. 106). Thus, when key decision makers are in serious conflict over a political issue, the news tends to reflect that debate; when elite consensus reigns, the range of debate in the news narrows to reflect that consensus. In the absence of elite conflict, journalists are unlikely independently to stir up debate by seeking out a broader range of voices and views to include in the news. Thus, the indexing norm serves as a decisional guide while reflecting a journalistic orientation toward power and politics that cedes to officials the responsibility for setting the political and news agendas. It reflects the fact that mainstream journalists often presume the legitimacy of officials, while meting out legitimacy more stingily to nonofficial actors.

NONROUTINE POLITICS AND THE LIMITS OF INDEXING

The indexing norm corresponds with routine politics: "normal" policy making in which political elites, within established institutional settings, formulate, propose, and argue over alternative approaches to public problems. In other words, indexing explains patterns in news coverage of issues that are already on the governmental agenda. But what happens in political contexts that are not characterized by such routine policy debates? Bennett (1990, p. 107) suggested that "the range of social voices in the news is likely to vary widely from one issue area to another," and that in some political contexts, the indexing norm may not be applicable. Some studies have suggested that other norms guide journalistic coverage of different political settings, such as elections (Zaller et al., 1994).

This study pursues this question by examining news coverage of police use of force and police brutality in the *Los Angeles Times* (LAT) from 1987 through 1992, a period culminating in the political crisis generated by the beating of black motorist Rodney King by officers of the Los Angeles Police Department (LAPD) in March 1991 and the uprisings following the acquittal of those officers in May 1992. The term "police use of force" will be used to refer to that broad set of police actions that involves physical coercion of citizens and suspects. "Police brutality" is a subset of police "use of force"— police coercion that is challenged or "problematized." Although some instances of police use of force come to be understood as instances of brutality, many do not. As outlined in the methodological discussion, the subject of this study is newspaper coverage of police use of force, not just of those actions that come to be described or defined as acts of brutality.

Police brutality is not an issue that is generally associated with the kind of "normal" politics described above, especially the national-level foreign policy debates in which the indexing norm has been most convincingly demonstrated. American policing policy is highly decentralized and rarely subject to national public debate. Rather, it is almost exclusively a "local" issue. It is also an issue that political elites and police officials at the local and national levels generally try to keep off of the political agenda. For them, allegations of brutality are politically vexing. In the increasingly diverse, conflicted, and economically hard-pressed environment of America's major urban centers, allegations of excessive force are a potential match in a tinderbox. Police and public officials thus often respond with assertive public relations strategies when a potentially explosive case of alleged brutality captures public and media attention. At all times, they practice institutionalized systems of information control.

Simmering tensions in Los Angeles during the late 1980s are indicated by Figure 1, which shows that mentions of police brutality in the LAT rose fairly steadily from 1987 through 1990, and increased dramatically in 1991 with the Rodney King beating.[1] Nonetheless, despite evidence that brutality was a serious problem in Los Angeles,[2] police officials, district attorneys, and political leaders were reluctant to call attention to it until images of the Rodney King beating filled television screens around the world (Chevigny, 1995; Davis, 1990; Domanick, 1994). That event set off serious political conflict in the city,

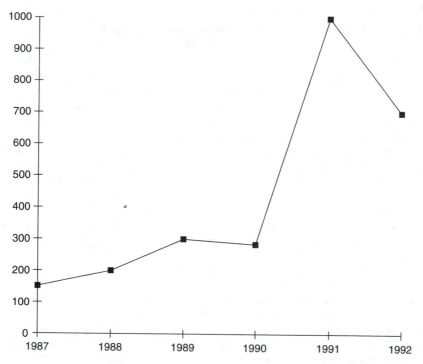

FIGURE 1.   Number of stories mentioning police brutality, *Los Angeles Times,* 1987–1992.

which culminated in a damning investigation of the LAPD by the Christopher Commission, and the ultimate resignation of LAPD Chief Daryl Gates. The impact of that event extended beyond Los Angeles, leading to congressional hearings and a Department of Justice investigation of brutality not only in Los Angeles, but across the country.

The indexing hypothesis leads us to expect certain patterns in the news about police use of force during this period. It suggests, first of all, that since police brutality was not on the political agenda—much less a matter of elite conflict—until 1991, few nonofficial voices would be heard until then. It also suggests that the presence of nonofficial voices and challenging views should have been comparatively greater in news about police use of force in 1991 and 1992, the only years during the time period studied in which police brutality generated serious political conflict at both the local and national levels.

The findings reported here, however, indicate that the indexing norm alone does not fully explain the inclusion of voices and views in the news about police use of force. The data do indicate a significant increase in the number of nonofficial voices and challenging views in 1991 and 1992. But they also show that as a *proportion* of all voices in the news about police use of force, nonofficial voices are rather prominent regardless of the presence of elite conflict over the issue. They also indicate that the inclusion of high proportions of critical nonofficial voices appears to be triggered as much by particularly dramatic cases of police brutality as by elite conflict. Such events appear to license journalists to grant more legitimacy to challenging framings of police use of force.

METHOD

This study rests on two measures of the range of debate in the news, one of which is the relative strength of nonofficial voices each year. Following the methodology employed by Bennett (1990) and by Bennett and Manheim (1993), all entries in the *Los Angeles Times* (LAT) Index pertaining to police use of force were examined. Given the brevity of Index entries, the data reported here are best regarded as indicative of the relative prominence of voices and views, rather than as measures of the absolute number of such voices and views in the news. All views about police brutality, or police use of force more generally, appearing in both news items and editorials were identified, and categorized according to whether they were made by officials or nonofficials.[3] A total of 593 Index entries were identified as containing views about police use of force, out of 1,189 Index entries on the subject of police use of force, and approximately 2,500 total entries regarding police.

Another measure of the range of debate represented in the news is the breadth of views available regarding the issue being covered. In previous indexing studies, the key indicator of breadth of views in the news has been their valence vis-á-vis White House policy (Bennett, 1990; Bennett & Manheim, 1993). In the present study, a rather different approach to coding views was required, for police brutality is rarely if ever official policy in the sense of being openly acknowledged and advocated. Rather, what acts constitute brutality is usually a highly controversial matter, and officials tend to deflect criticism of police behavior by explicit or implicit argumentation about what *causes* police to use force, as is discussed further below. Thus, an important indicator of breadth of views in the news about police use of force is the constellation of frames or "causal stories" being advanced by various sources in the news, and the degree to which commonly advanced official frames are challenged (Stone, 1989).

In order to measure the range of debate in police use of force news, then, statements in LAT Index entries were coded according to what causal stories about police use of force they offered. In particular, views were coded according to whether they offered what I have labeled individualizing or structural framings of police use of force.[4] The essential difference between these lies in whether the phenomenon of police brutality is understood as a problem of "bad apples" or bad systems. Individualizing frames tend to be advanced by officials or by their supporters, when compelling evidence of excessive force surfaces. One such argument is that police use force because suspects cause them to. On this view, suspects' threatening behavior causes police officers to respond with force to subdue them. According to this causal story, "police brutality" is an inappropriate label for what is actually necessary police behavior. A second common official explanation for police use of force is that police brutality is caused by "rogue cops," who, because of personal failings or inadequate attention to proper procedure, get out of hand. The problem, according to this frame, is essentially one of discrete, even random cases of excessive force. This is essentially the explanation Daryl Gates offered for the beating of Rodney King, when he maintained that the beating was "an aberration."

Structural causal theories of police brutality, on the other hand, tend to be advanced by those seeking to expand the scope of political conflict. These "challenging" frames, as they will be collectively referred to, are also of two main types, both of which rest on the assertion that brutality is patterned or systematic rather than random. One is often stated by would-be reformers: Brutality is caused by a lax or corrupt system within particular police departments or city governments. In this view, responsibility for the problem lies at the top of the local chain of command—beyond, if a remedy is not forthcoming—and police brutality can be solved by changing leadership, establishing civilian oversight of police, or establishing better political accountability of local officials. More radical structural frames argue that police brutality is an expression of a political and legal system committed to the continued oppression of certain groups—ethnic minorities, the poor, women, gays and lesbians—or a problem endemic to the nature of police work, which breeds an insular and aggressive subculture among officers. Some views of police brutality could not so easily be placed in either the individualizing or the structural category, and were coded as "mixed." These were included with structural views in the data that follow, because they do include structural, conflict-expanding argumentation.

Views that did not offer any particular framing of police use of force were coded as "descriptive" views. Typical descriptive views included statements about police policy, statements about the disposition of particular police brutality cases, statements of emotion, and unelaborated charges by alleged victims, their families, or witnesses claiming that police had on some occasion used excessive force. Unlike many official statements, most claims of brutality reported in the Indexes did not offer any causal explanation for police behavior, a fact that will become significant in the data analysis that follows.

Finally, some views simply were uncodable, either because they were too incomplete to be categorized, or because they did not fit easily into the coding scheme. Wherever possible, the full text of the news items was obtained via the Nexis database in order to clarify the views mentioned in the Index; otherwise, such views were coded "unknown."

FINDINGS: VOICES AND VIEWS IN POLICE USE OF FORCE NEWS

The data indicate that the prominence of nonofficial voices and challenging frames in the LAT, when measured in raw numerical terms, did increase dramatically in 1991 and 1992, as the indexing hypothesis would predict (see Figure 2). However, examining the data in a different way raises several interesting questions and suggests a different and more nuanced argument. That is, it makes sense to consider underlying patterns of representation by examining whether nonofficials win a greater *share* of the news hole and challenging views become not only numerically more prominent, but proportionally more prominent during periods of elite conflict.

Figure 3 shows nonofficial voices and structural views as *proportions* of all voices and views pertaining to police use of force reported in each newspaper. They reveal, first of all, that nonofficials constitute a fairly high proportion of voices, regardless of levels of elite conflict. Nonofficials consistently constituted over 40 percent of voices on the subject of police use of force—a rather surprising finding given the typical predominance of elites in other news domains. Nonofficial voices may be unexpectedly loud because only *voices expressing views* in the Index entries were coded—not mere reports of activities. Police news does not differ significantly from other news domains in that the bulk of news stories typically focus on the activities of officials and institutions. Yet citizens do appear to have a consistent and rather substantial voice in police use of force news. An examination of a random sample of the full

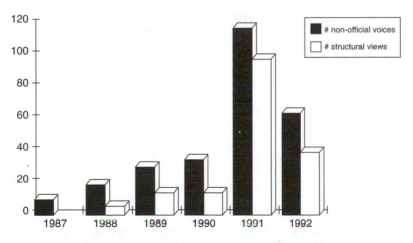

FIGURE 2. Number of nonofficial voices and structural views in police use of force items, *Los Angeles Times* index, 1987–1992

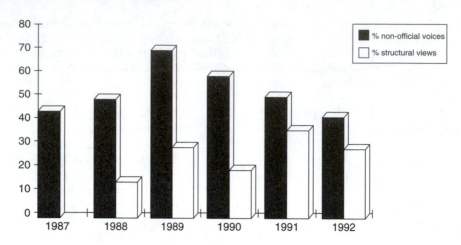

FIGURE 3.   Proportion of nonofficial voices and structural views in police use of force items, *Los Angeles Times* index, 1987–1992.

text of LAT police brutality stories confirms that official activities receive more attention than nonofficial activities in actual news stories, but also indicates that nonofficials expressed themselves in an average of 45 percent of police brutality stories from 1989 to 1991. Contrary to what the indexing hypothesis would seem to predict, the proportion of nonofficial voices in the LAT actually *decreased* in 1991 and 1992 over the two previous years.[5]

Moreover, the inclusion of challenging framings of police brutality, when measured proportionally, does not neatly coincide with periods of elite conflict. Figure 3 illustrates that, as the indexing hypothesis might lead us to expect, 1991 did see the highest proportion of such views across all years, with 1992 relatively high as well. But 1989, a year unmarked by official conflict over police brutality in the Los Angeles area, exhibited an equal proportion of challenging framings as well, and a higher proportion of nonofficial voices than 1991 or 1992.[6] Furthermore, a disjuncture is apparent between voices and views. Whereas the proportion of nonofficial voices remained relatively high over time, the proportion of structural framings fluctuates significantly. This disjuncture raises an intriguing question, for what may be more important than their obtaining a voice in the news is what nonofficial voices *say*.

In short, neither the proportion of nonofficial voices nor that of challenging views appears to have been indexed strictly to elite conflict. Explaining these patterns of reporting requires elaboration of dynamics other than indexing, some of which pertain to the issue of police brutality itself, and some of which pertain to news organizations' handling of dramatic news events.

Use of Force News: Straining the Limits of Presumed Legitimacy

Journalists face a particularly challenging task when meting out legitimacy to officials and nonofficials in news about police use of force, and how nonofficial voices and views will be treated is not always certain. On one hand, the presumed legitimacy of the police weighs heavily. Past research has demonstrated the typically symbiotic relationship between reporters and police that underlies the construction of news about policing and crime (Ericson et al., 1989, 1991; Fishman, 1980). Journalists undoubtedly develop routine ways of handling police use of force news—stock plots and stereotypes, standard sources—which protect their relationship with the institutions they cover. Not surprisingly, the police version of alleged acts of brutality often wins out in news portrayals.

Moreover, journalists are likely to scrutinize rather suspiciously those who press police brutality claims. Not only do such claims attack the departments and officials on whom journalists depend to do their jobs, they may directly challenge the legitimacy of entire political regimes. Such challenges are just the kinds of political discourse that are most thoroughly marginalized in the news. People claiming to be victims of police brutality, and people who act as their spokespersons (lawyers, activists), are in this sense much like antiwar protesters and other social movement participants, and can elicit the same kind of marginalizing news coverage noted by Gitlin (1980), Entman and Rojecki (1993), and others. Finally, people pressing brutality claims are often nonwhite and relatively poor, and often have criminal records. If nothing else, they often face a resisting-arrest charge resulting from their altercation with police. These are not the kinds of people who are typically accorded much legitimacy in the news.

On the other hand, instances of police use of force often become news through legal claims made by citizens against police or the government that employs them. Thus, news about police brutality exhibits a different "phase structure" than political news generated on executive and legislative beats (Fishman, 1980). In police brutality news, claims-making by alleged victims is often the initiating phase of a story, and the story is followed according to its progression through the legal system, from grand jury investigation to indictment and trial. Citizens pressing legal claims against officials may be perceived by journalists as legitimate political "players" in a way that citizens engaging in grassroots politics are not. Legal proceedings provide a story with "legs" and, perhaps, a stamp of legitimacy.

Furthermore, the kinds of claims that police brutality victims make are different from those made by antiwar protesters and other activists, for they claim specific, sometimes quite extensive corporeal harms inflicted directly and intentionally by persons empowered by the state with the means of deadly force. These are claims unlike those made by other alleged victims of mistreatment by the state, such as government employees who allege job discrimination or welfare recipients who allege arbitrary treatment by welfare officers, or, even more dissimilar, antiwar and other activists, because their claims call directly into question political legitimacy in its most fundamental sense. Reporting police brutality thus involves publicizing the most serious of citizen grievances against the state.

Finally, even if they do not take them seriously on grounds of morality or political philosophy, journalists are likely to see police brutality claims as making for good news. As media critic Howard Rosenberg (1991, p. F1) has put it, "violence by criminals against police is dog biting man. We expect this of criminals precisely because they are criminals. Police beating [someone] is man biting dog. It's a case of the good guys—the ones sworn to protect the public and whose integrity is crucial to civilized society—becoming the bad guys."

This is not to assert that alleged victims of police brutality have *carte blanche* access to the news, or enjoy the same presumed legitimacy granted to officials. However, the gravity of the issue, combined with the differently situated citizen and the dramatic value inherent in police brutality claims, strain the limits of the indexing norm by straining the limits of the presumed legitimacy of official actors—and presumed illegitimacy of nonofficial actors—on which the indexing norm rests. It is perhaps not surprising, then, that nonofficials constitute a fairly high proportion of voices in use of force news.

The fluctuation of structural views over time can be explained largely by analyzing the composition of nonofficial voices. Alleged victims, their families and attorneys, and witnesses to alleged acts of brutality constituted one of three major groups of nonofficial voices. This group outnumbered the two other major groups, one comprised of activists and community leaders and the other comprised of experts, in three of six years. Significantly, these were the three years—1987, 1988, and 1990—with the fewest structural views.

These facts help to explain the disjuncture between voices and views shown in Figure 3. Victims, their attorneys, families, and witnesses generally provide accounts of particular instances of alleged police brutality rather than structural framings of those events or of police violence more generally. The bulk of daily reporting on police use of force consists of such descriptions, usually defended by police claiming that force was necessary to counter a suspect's violent behavior. Thus, whereas officials routinely offer a compelling causal story to frame police use of force, the most commonly cited nonofficial sources often do not. As Table 1 shows, it is activists and community leaders,

TABLE 1

TYPES OF VIEWS EXPRESSED BY NONOFFICIALS, *LOS ANGELES TIMES,* 1987–1992[a]

	Victims, families, attorneys, and witnesses (N = 101)	Activists, community leaders (N = 74)	Experts (N = 23)
Percent expressing descriptive views	84	41	26
Percent expressing structural view[b]	14	57	61
Percent of nonofficial sources[c]	39	29	9

[a]Only nonjournalists are represented in this table; editors, columnists, and other professional news writers are excluded.

[b]Since voices could express views other than descriptive or structural, the percentages in the first two cells of each column do not necessarily total 100%.

[c]The other 33% of nonofficial voices was comprised of residents of various communities, members of juries, opinion-poll respondents, and miscellaneous others. None of these groups constituted more than 7% of the total.

along with experts, who more typically provide challenging frames. It is worth noting that nonofficials, especially those with challenging views, were more likely to enter the news via the editorial pages than the news pages. Whereas the voices appearing in the news pages were 56 percent official and 45 percent nonofficial, on the editorial pages 21 percent were officials, 35 percent were columnists or editors, and 44 percent were nonjournalist nonofficials. Sixty-one percent of nonofficial voices on the editorial pages expressed challenging views, and 49 percent of editorial-page voices were those of experts or activists. As mentioned above, the voices of activists, community leaders, and experts outnumbered the victim group in three of the six years examined here—the years when structural framings were most prominent. The entrance of these more critical nonofficials into the news arena thus becomes a key issue of interest. The periodic inclusion of challenging views appears to depend in part on the appearance of dramatic news events.

Accidents and Icons: Journalistic Uses of Dramatic Events

The indexing hypothesis directs our attention to the fact that at the heart of corporate journalism is a reluctance to flag particular issues for public and governmental attention independent of official cues. At the same time, the media jealously guard their agenda-setting potential, exhibiting a marked suspicion of citizens who might wish to step up to the media microphone to publicize issues of concern to them. Critical media research has demonstrated, for example, the difficulty that grassroots activists often have in using the media to set the public and governmental agendas (Entman & Rojecki, 1993; Gitlin, 1980).

Other journalistic norms, however, may encourage patterns of reporting in which the media more actively set the political agenda, while bringing marginalized views into the mainstream. That possibility is suggested by Bennett and Lawrence's (1995) examination of news coverage of the infamous garbage barge *Mobro*, which wandered the high seas in 1987 looking for a port that would accept its cargo. Journalists imbued the barge with an explicit and urgent meaning, casting it as an indicator of a looming garbage crisis and a symbol of a nation quickly burying itself in trash. In the same year as the barge sailed into the news, moreover, reporting on garbage problems and recycling increased dramatically. Meanwhile, officials played "catch up" with the barge/recycling story as it brought environmentalists' claims of impending environmental catastrophe into the news with new force.

The dynamics of icon-driven news reflect in part Molotch and Lester's (1974) insights regarding "routine" versus "accidental" news events. Most news events, Molotch and Lester observed, are events conceived and executed by officials as they carry out their daily duties and perennial attempts to manage their public images. Some news events, however, are "accidents." Not planned as news events by officials, accidental events are often problematic for officials, who must attempt to frame them in ways that contain their meaning and impact. Accidents can "have results which are the opposite of routine events. [They can foster] revelations which are otherwise deliberately obfuscated by those with the resources to create routine events" (p. 109). Accidents can bring to light ideas, values, and discourses which tend otherwise to be suppressed by the sheer weight of officially created news events.

Accident-driven news differs from the indexing of voices and views associated with routine politics/routine news. As journalists seek to contextualize and make sense of dramatic accidental events, the news gates may open to new voices and ideas. When official frames seem unable to contain the meaning of dramatic accidental events, the news and editorial pages may become places where other frames are explored more openly. Moreover, the characteristics of some accidental events suggest challenging framings of public problems. In such circumstances, journalistic suspicion of grassroots voices competes with a professional interest in crafting dramatic and competitive news stories that compellingly "make events mean" (Hall et al., 1978). Accidents may therefore represent an alternative way for citizen voices and challenging ideas to enter the news.

Certain conditions seem necessary, however, in order for journalists to use an accidental event in this fashion. First, the characteristics of the event itself must offer dramatic narrative possibilities and suggest challenging framings of public problems. Second, in order for marginalized discourse to appear in the news, journalists must have such discourse available to them through sources, either organized or loose-knit and ad hoc, that are actively advancing challenging ideas. Given the ideal of objectivity which guides their work, journalists are unlikely to construct such discourse on their own.[7]

A third condition brings us full circle to the indexing norm. Accidental events met with official conflict or disarray are more likely to become full-fledged news icons than events met with an official united front. Officials may respond to accidental events with a unified voice and thus successfully depress their effect on the political agenda. They may respond with classic "symbolic politics," co-opting media attention and public emotion (Edelman, 1964), or they may simply bow to the pressures generated by a widely publicized event and enact new policies designed to respond to whatever public problem the event is taken to indicate. The boost given to antiterrorism legislation by the July 1995 Oklahoma City bombing offers one example. But officials may not always manage the effects of icon-driven news effectively. In some circumstances, news icons may stimulate political dynamics that spin out of official control; in others, some officials attempt to exploit accidental events by pressing initiatives that generate conflict with other officials. When accidental events set off conflict or disarray among elites, they create the very political situations that trigger the indexing norm. Although accidental events create opportunities for challenging framings of problems to enter the news, such opportunities are more likely to be fully realized when accidental events trigger elite conflict.

ICONS AND NEAR-ICONS: RODNEY KING AND DON JACKSON

This tentative model of accidents-to-icons helps to explain the relative prominence of challenging views about police brutality not only in 1991 and 1992, but in 1989 in the absence of elite conflict. For 1989 witnessed a near-icon: the case of Don Jackson.

In January 1989, Don Jackson, an African American police officer on leave from the Long Beach Police Force, invited the local NBC affiliate to film him as he drove through Long Beach in an old rental car and shabby clothes.

Jackson believed that African Americans were systematically subject to brutal and arbitrary treatment by police throughout southern California and the nation, and he hoped to illustrate that argument with a filmed "sting." Jackson's car was stopped by police, and as hidden cameras whirred, an altercation ensued in which a white officer, spewing a string of obscenities, grabbed Jackson and pushed him into a plate-glass store front, shattering the glass. The image was replayed on local and national television, even appearing on *The Today Show*.

The Jackson event contributed significantly to the high proportion of challenging views found in 1989, displayed in Figure 3. The case so captured media attention that 24 percent of 1989 LAT police use of force stories were about Jackson's case, more than any other single case that year. Jackson and like-minded activists gained a voice in both news pieces and editorials, arguing passionately that his video demonstrated the racism not only at the root of police brutality, but at the root of American history. Indeed, Jackson's views constituted 60 percent of all causal views about police use of force expressed in 1989.

Don Jackson became a focal point for a simmering nationwide crisis in public confidence in the police, and a precursor of the storm soon to descend on Los Angeles. Despite their similar effects on the proportions of challenging views in the news, however, the Rodney King event had a much more significant effect on the amount of reporting about police brutality, as evidenced by Figure 1. It also had a more significant effect on the content of that reporting. A comparison of a random sample of LAT stories appearing from 1989 to 1991 (obtained through the Nexis database) reveals that in 20 percent of 1989 and 30 percent of 1990 stories, the most challenging view offered by nonofficials was that the victim of an incident of brutality had not provoked the brutality. In contrast, only 6 percent of 1991 stories contained that sort of view, which was replaced by more explicitly structural ideas about what causes police to use excessive force: department- or society-wide racism, permissive police management, and an ugly police subculture. Moreover, a comparison of headlines and story leads reveals that in 1991, 14 percent of story headlines contained challenging framings of brutality, compared with only 3 percent in 1989 and 5 percent in 1990. And 25 percent of story leads contained such framings, as compared with 6 percent in 1989 and 13 percent in 1990.[8] In 1991, then, it was much more common to encounter views in the news such as the following:

> The cops (in Los Angeles) are trained that they are soldiers in the war on crime, rather than members of the community who are there to arrest people and bring them to court. (Sociologist James Fyfe, in Tobar, 1991)

> The Los Angeles Police Department sanctions brutality by enforcing an implicit code of silence regarding misconduct by officers. The beating of Rodney Glenn King was an aberration only because a bystander made a video recording of the incident. (Activist Carol Watson, LAT Index, March 3, 1991)

> The beating of Rodney G. King is a case of "us versus them," typifying the tendency of tightly knit groups to divide the world into

opposing camps, to devalue and dehumanize outsiders and, under certain conditions, to commit terrible violence against them. In embattled groups such as the police or military, these tendencies are especially common, some psychologists say. (Scott, 1991)

THE DYNAMICS OF ICON MAKING

The differential effect of the Jackson and King events—both of which were dramatic videotaped news events that seemingly illustrated the claim that minorities are routinely subjected to arbitrary and violent treatment by police—raises the question of why the Rodney King beating changed the framing of police use of force in ways that Don Jackson's altercation with police did not. An obvious explanation lies in the different characteristics of the two events. Jackson's treatment was at the hands of a single officer from the suburban Long Beach Police Department. Although apparently brutal, that treatment paled in comparison to the specter of more than 20 police officers of the LAPD surrounding a prone man while four officers beat and kicked him repeatedly. These characteristics, however, do not offer a full explanation for the differential treatment accorded the two stories. The greater effects of the Rodney King event on the news are arguably due to two additional factors: the origins of the Don Jackson event, and the elite conflict that followed the Rodney King beating.

Limiting Conditions: The Origins of Events

Qualitative evidence suggests that even though the Don Jackson event boosted the proportion of challenging framings of police brutality in the news, it met with journalistic suspicion that limited its effect as a news icon. Journalistic discomfort with the Jackson video surfaced almost immediately, as the local station that participated in the "sting" was put on the defensive by accusations that it had overstepped the bounds of objective journalism. Indeed, four of the seven LAT editorials dealing with the Jackson event actually focused on criticizing or defending KNBC's role in the sting. And Jackson himself was the focus, especially in the LAT, of as much or more attention than were his claims of systematic police mistreatment of blacks. This is especially notable in a lengthy profile piece that appeared in the LAT on May 27, 1989, more than four months after Jackson's video first hit the airwaves (Pasternak, 1989). Describing Jackson's "heady days" in the limelight, the article claimed Jackson "has seized the moment by the throat. He has plans, major plans, for his crusade and for himself." The 2,400-word article raised questions about Jackson's motives, describing his financial difficulties prior to the taped altercation and his much-improved prospects as a new-found favorite son of civil rights organizations. This piece echoed the theme of an earlier LAT profile of Jackson, which introduced its subject by saying: "Jackson's tactics have been debated from the opinion pages of newspapers to the Los Angeles barber shop he uses. Some have questioned his actions, while others have asked: Who is Don Jackson and what is he trying to prove?" (Rainey, 1989).

Thus, while Jackson won a hearing for his views, he also was subjected to the same kinds of marginalizing techniques often used against activists and other grassroots citizens who attempt to stage "direct action" to capture media attention and put their concerns before the public. This suggests that the possibility of activists intentionally creating news icons is limited by news organizations' reluctance to be "used" by nonofficials to push particular problems and framings of problems onto the public agenda.

Just as important, Jackson's videotaped altercation did not suggest challenging framings of police use of force quite as clearly as Jackson asserted. In fact, the event could be explained in terms of the common, officially sanctioned framing of police use of force. As the president of the Long Beach Officers Association put it, "Mr. Jackson's motives are apparent to any human being. If you go looking for trouble, you find it." (Woodyard, 1989). In other words, the video suggested that the officer manhandled Jackson because Jackson prompted him to—a charge Jackson, for obvious reasons, had trouble defending himself against. The camera, after all, had captured him arguing with the officer, and the "sting" had been deliberately sought. The King video, in contrast, did not show the events leading up to King's beating, and thus invited viewers to project onto it a different—and more politically volatile—causal narrative.[9] Thus, Rodney King was perhaps deemed a more legitimate or authentic victim than Don Jackson, freeing journalists to use the Rodney King event more proactively and creatively.

Enabling Conditions: Elite Conflict

Jackson's "sting" boosted the proportion of nonofficial voices and challenging views in the news despite the fact that it did not engender significant elite conflict, but instead was met with a fairly low-key and unified official response. Some local city council members responded to Jackson's video by supporting the establishment of a civilian review board to oversee the police department, an initiative that had been resisted in the past. Moreover, the Long Beach police immediately got on board, supporting the creation of the board and providing a blueprint for its structure. The initiative passed the council in 1989 and was put before the city in a general election the following year. Meanwhile, the case triggered little if any official response outside Long Beach.

In contrast, elite reaction to the King beating, though initially muted at the local level, eventually became quite prolonged and divisive. In the immediate aftermath of the beating, the predominant official framing of the event was LAPD Chief Daryl Gates's adamant rejection of suggestions that the beating indicated any need for restructuring of the department, and his insistence that the beating was an "aberration." Within two weeks, however, city council member Michael Woo began to exploit the event to force changes in the LAPD. Mayor Tom Bradley refrained from calling publicly for Gates's resignation for nearly a month. Then, having carefully tested the waters, Bradley finally began an open effort to force his long-time nemesis from office by calling for Gates's resignation and announcing the formation of a commission, headed by Warren Christopher, charged with investigating allegations of systematic brutality, racism, and sexism in the LAPD.

These proved to be only the opening volleys in a prolonged elite battle. Because of a Progressive-era effort to professionalize the LAPD, the chief of police was insulated from direct political control, and thus Bradley could not fire Gates. When the Police Commission, prompted by Bradley, voted to suspend Gates, the suspension was overruled the next day by the City Council and lifted by an appeals court three days later. Thus, the crisis became not only a question of police personnel and policy, but a question of who was really in charge of local government. Meanwhile, Gates continued to balk at the prospect of resigning, even after the Christopher Commission, in July 1991, issued a highly critical report recommending thorough procedural and structural reforms of the department, and calling for Gates to resign. Some of the structural reforms suggested by the commission were implemented in a ballot measure passed in June 1992, shortly after which Gates finally left office.

Elite debate and action following the King beating was not confined to the local arena. Within days, the congressional Black Caucus demanded a federal investigation of what they called "systematic" police brutality across the nation. The Justice Department responded with an expanded investigation of the LAPD, taking evidence from more than 100 lawsuits filed against the department, and with an analysis of more than 15,000 brutality complaints from around the country filed with the FBI over the previous six years. And national political figures from Jesse Jackson to Joseph Biden to President George Bush weighed in on the beating, the LAPD, and the question of whether or not Gates should resign.

This protracted elite and interinstitutional conflict gave journalists an ongoing series of pegs on which to hang stories about police brutality. Elite conflict also engendered institutional forums such as the Christopher Commission hearings, in which complaints against the LAPD could be aired. Those forums legitimized police critics, as did the commission's report, which echoed many of those critics' charges against the LAPD. Thus, a variety of news stories appeared in 1991 exploring such subjects as the methods police employ to subdue suspects, the prevalence of racial prejudice among police officers, and the prospects for reform of the LAPD and other police departments across the country.

ICONS, INDEXING, AND THE DYNAMICS OF AGENDA-SETTING NEWS

The data examined here suggest that although elite conflict clearly is important to the amount of coverage an issue receives, it is not the only factor influencing the composition of voices and views in the news. Accidental events appear to have some independent influence as well. New organizations, rather than simply reacting to elite conflict, may be licensed by dramatic news events to expand the range of voices and views in the news, and indeed may thus precipitate and expand elite conflict, which then further encourages the expansion of debate in the news.

These dynamics are suggested by examining the LAT's use of public opinion polls in the aftermath of the Rodney King beating. As indicated in Table 2, only five news stories mentioning police in the time period examined here reported the results of opinion polls; all but one occurred in 1991. Significantly, the first of the 1991 stories was published long before conflict

TABLE 2

REPORTING OF OPINION POLLS ABOUT POLICE, *LOS ANGELES TIMES*, 1987–1992

Date reported	Subject
2/13/90	Most residents approve of police performance.[a]
3/10/91	Majority of Los Angeles residents say police brutality is common.
3/22/91	One-third agree Gates should resign immediately over Rodney King beating.
4/6/91	Majority thinks Bradley's call for Gates to resign was politically motivated, but supports Police Commission's placement of Gates on 60-day leave.
7/16/91	Majority agrees with Christopher Commission recommendations.

[a]This poll did find that nearly one-half of African Americans polled believed there was a "fair amount" of police brutality in Los Angeles.

broke out publicly among local officials. It appeared on March 10, and the poll itself was conducted on March 7 and 8—the first two days in which the Rodney King beating was reported in the LAT (Rohrlich, 1991). The poll asked Los Angeles residents whether they believed police brutality was commonplace; two-thirds averred that it was. The poll also "found widespread belief among Anglos, blacks and Latinos that King was beaten because he was black and that police generally are tougher on blacks and Latinos than they are on Anglos." It found that three-fourths of Angelenos favored the establishment of a civilian board to review alleged cases of misconduct. And it found that one in eight respondents thought that Chief Gates should step down immediately because of the King beating. What is more significant than the numbers supporting these various propositions is the fact that the LAT asked such leading questions, ushering the public into what had not yet become an elite debate.

Later LAT polling more closely indexed the public voice to official conflict, but also contributed to the expansion of that conflict. On March 20, Mayor Bradley, resisting public pressure to initiate open battle with Gates, told reporters that the only way for the LAPD and the city to resolve the crisis generated by the King beating would be for Gates to "remove himself" from office. Bradley, in a characteristic nonconfrontational style, cast his remark as a suggestion, not an official pronouncement. That same day, the LAT conducted a poll measuring support for the idea, and found that a third of Angelenos now thought Gates should resign immediately and a majority believed that Gates was substantially responsible for the beating. The paper also asked again if racist feelings were common among police officers; this time, two-thirds of respondents said they were. Thus, on March 22, one day before the first nonminority elected officials—three California congressmen, including Henry Waxman—would call openly for Gates' resignation, prompting Bradley's call one week later, the LAT reported that this option would have considerable public support.

CONCLUSION

The data presented here are somewhat limited in temporal scope. They also are limited by the absence of an independent register of elite debate against which to measure media behavior (Zaller et al., 1994; also Althaus et al., in this issue). However, they are suggestive both of the importance of the indexing norm and of its limits.

Put simply, in nonroutine political contexts involving issues that are generally kept off the political agenda, accidental events may become especially important factors determining how much and what kind of news coverage—and governmental attention—such issues receive. Dramatic accidental events that suggest new definitions of public problems can license news organizations both to devote more attention to emerging public problems and to develop challenging framings of those problems, while setting in motion political dynamics—elite debate, political struggle, scandal, reform—that engage further news media attention. The interaction of icons and indexing thus offers a promising area for future explorations of journalistic norms.

NOTES

1. Data for Figure 1 were obtained by searching the Nexis database for the words "police" and "brutality" in close proximity for each year from 1987 to 1993.
2. For example, the Christopher Commission found that the city of Los Angeles had paid at least $20 million to settle excessive force cases between 1986 and 1990 (Chevigny, 1995). These figures do not include payments for other forms of police misconduct, nor do they include payments made by the county to settle suits brought against the Sheriff's Department.
3. The coding reported here was done by the author. For 20 percent of the 1991 entries (the year representing the largest number of stories as well as the broadest range of views), utilizing a coder unfamiliar with the hypotheses of this study, intercoder reliability of 95 percent was established on the tasks of identifying which entries contained views about police use of force and whether voices should be categorized as official or nonofficial. Voices that were impossible to identify accurately from the Index entries were identified, if possible, by consulting the full text of the news item, obtained from the Nexis database.

The author also coded *New York Times* Index entries for the same time period, using the same coding scheme. Patterns very similar to those reported here were found, with differences being attributable largely to the timing of local police use of force events. Those data are further outlined in forthcoming work.
4. Intercoder agreement was 86 percent on the task of coding views in the Index entries as individualizing, structural, mixed, or unclear.
5. Analysis of the *New York Times* Index for the same time period reveals quite similar patterns: Over 40 percent of voices each year were nonofficial, with the proportion lower in 1991 than in the two previous years. The proportion was somewhat higher in 1992, reflecting not only coverage of the Los Angeles riots, but of a case of alleged brutality in Washington Heights in July 1992, which led to days of rioting and numerous charges of racism against the New York Police Department.
6. Again, *New York Times* coverage exhibited similar patterns, with 1989 showing the highest proportions of both nonofficial voices and challenging views across all years examined. As discussed further below, this seemingly anomalous finding is explained in part by the case of Don Jackson, and in part, in the *New York Times* data, by

subsequent cases in New York City that year, which echoed Jackson's claims about racist police violence.

7. Gamson and Modigliani (1989) provide an example of an accidental event that wasn't: a partial meltdown at the Enrico Fermi nuclear reactor outside Detroit in 1966. Despite its seriousness (the plant was shut down manually after the automatic operating system failed, followed by a six-month period in which officials tried to figure out ways to remove the damaged fuel from the plant), the accident was barely reported on, registering its first mention in the *New York Times,* where it was described as a "mishap," five weeks after it occurred. The authors contend that no oppositional spokespersons were available to journalists that would allow them to construct the story as anything other than a mishap.

8. Headlines and story leads from a random sample of 1989, 1990, and 1991 LAT stories mentioning police brutality were coded for the presence or absence of oppositional framings of police brutality. The figures reported are the results of single-factor analysis of variance among the three groups of data; tests of significance yield $p = .002$ for the differences in headlines and $p = .016$ for the story leads.

9. The defense in the criminal trial of the officers charged with beating King countered this fact by "deconstructing" the video, allowing them to make the official causal story—that King was responsible for his own brutalization—more compelling.

REFERENCES

Bennett, W. Lance. (1990). Toward a theory of press–state relations. *Journal of Communication, 40*(2), 103–125.

Bennett, W. Lance. (1996). *News: The politics of illusion.* New York: Longman.

Bennett, W. Lance, & Manheim, Jarol B. (1993). Taking the public by storm: Information, cuing, and the democratic process in the Gulf Conflict. *Political Communication, 10,* 331–351.

Bennett, W. Lance, & Lawrence, Regina G. (1995). News icons and the mainstreaming of social change. *Journal of Communication, 45*(3), 20–39.

Chevigny, Paul. (1995). *Edge of the knife: Police violence in the Americas.* New York: The New Press.

Cohen, Bernard C. (1963). *The press and foreign policy.* Princeton, NJ: Princeton University Press.

Cook, Timothy E. (1994). Domesticating a crisis: Washington newsbeats and network news after the Iraq invasion of Kuwait. In W. Lance Bennett & David L. Paletz (Eds.), *Taken by storm.* Chicago: University of Chicago Press.

Davis, Mike. (1990). *City of quartz.* New York: Verso.

Domanick, Joe. (1994). *To protect and to serve.* New York: Pocket Books.

Edelman, Murray. (1964). *The symbolic uses of politics.* Urbana, IL: University of Illinois Press.

Entman, Robert, & Rojecki, Andrew. (1993). Freezing out the public: Elite and media framing of the U.S. anti-nuclear movement. *Political Communication, 10,* 155–173.

Ericson, Richard V., Baranek, Patricia M., & Chan, Janet B. L. (1989). *Negotiating control: A study of news sources.* Toronto: University of Toronto Press.

Ericson, Richard V., Baranek, Patricia M., & Chan, Janet B. L. (1991). *Representing order: Crime, law, and justice in the news media.* Toronto: University of Toronto Press.

Fishman, Mark. (1980). *Manufacturing the news.* Austin, TX: University of Texas Press.

Gamson, William A., & Modigliani, Andre. (1989). Media discourse and public opinion on nuclear power: A constructionist approach. *American Journal of Sociology, 95*(l), 1–37.

Gans, Herbert J. (1979). *Deciding what's news.* New York: Vintage.

Gitlin, Todd. (1980). *The whole world is watching.* Berkeley, CA: University of California Press.

Hall, Stuart, Critcher, Chas, Jefferson, Tony, Clarke, J., & Roberts, B. (1978). *Policing the crisis*. New York: Holmes and Meier.

Molotch, Harvey, & Lester, Marilyn. (1974). News as purposive behavior: On the strategic use of routine events, accidents, and scandals. *American Sociological Review, 39*, 101–112.

Scott, Janny. (1991, March 28). Violence born of the group. *Los Angeles Times*, p. Al.

Sigal, Leon V. (1973). *Reporters and officials*. Lexington, MA: D.C. Heath.

Stone, Deborah A. (1989). Causal stories and the formation of policy agendas. *Political Science Quarterly, 104*(2), 281–300.

Pasternak, Judy. (1989, May 27). Ex-officer's crusade against discrimination; "Star" of police video seizes spotlight. *Los Angeles Times*, p. 1.

Rainey, James. (1989, January 20). Officer hits the prime time with video camera. *Los Angeles Times*, p. 1.

Rohrlich, Ted. (1991, March 10). The Times poll; Majority says police brutality is common. *Los Angeles Times*, p. Al.

Rosenberg, Howard. (1991, April 8). Media coverage of the King case: Guilty or Innocent? *Los Angeles Times*, p. Fl.

Tobar, Hector. (1991, March 18). Training; A casualty on the street. *Los Angeles Times*, p. Al.

Tuchman, Gaye. (1978). *Making news: A study in the construction of reality*. New York: The Free Press.

Woodyard, Chris. (1989, January 17). Citizen review of police urged after taped sting. *Los Angeles Times*, Section 2, p. 1.

Zaller, John, Chiu, Dennis, & Hunt, Mark. (1994). *Press rules and news content: Two contrasting case studies*. Paper presented at the 1994 Annual Meeting of the American Political Science Association, New York.

How Police Justify the Use of Deadly Force*

William B. Waegel
Villanova University

Police shoot people while performing their occupational activities. This paper examines how police interpret, explain, and justify the use of lethal force. Formal rules governing this area of police behavior are vague, produce uncertainty, and provide only weak guidance for officers. The occupational subculture of police contains a set of shared understandings as to when, why, and against whom shooting is justified. Subcultural understandings also constitute resources upon which members may draw to explain and account for shooting incidents after the fact. Official accounts produced for outside audiences are fashioned in line with publicly acceptable and legally justified reasons for shooting,

An average of 600 citizens are killed annually by police in the United States (Sherman, 1980:4). Fyfe (1981:381) estimates that in 1978 an additional 1,400 persons suffered serious injury from police shootings. The capacity to use force is the core of the police role and the unifying theme in police work (Bittner, 1970). Previous research in this area has directed relatively little attention to how police themselves view the use of lethal force against citizens.

Empirical studies have attempted to measure the extent of, and provide an explanation for, the use of lethal force by police. Sherman and Langworthy (1979:553) attributed 3.6 percent of all homicides to the police for the period 1971–1975. Kobler (1975:164) documents a consistent 5 to 1 ratio of police killing to police killed during the 1960s. More than half of those killed by police are members of minority groups (Sherman, 1980:11). A 1963 study of eight major cities found that the police homicide rate for blacks was nine times higher than for whites (Robin, 1963).

Police killings vary greatly between jurisdictions. For the period 1950–1960, the rates ranged from 1.4 deaths per 10,000 police officers in Boston to 63.4 deaths per 10,000 officers in Akron, Ohio (Robin, 1963). Kania and Mackey (1977) found that, for the years 1961–1970, police in Georgia had the highest rate of killing of 37.9 per one million residents, while police in

*The author thanks an anonymous *Social Problems* reviewer for suggestions. Correspondence to: Department of Sociology, Villanova University, Villanova, PA 19085.

William B. Waegel, "How Police Justify the Use of Deadly Force" (as appeared in *Social Problems*, Vol. 32, No. 2, [Dec. 1984], pp.144–155). Reprinted by permission of University of California Press ©1984 by *The Society for the Study of Social Problems*.

Hawaii, New Hampshire, and Wisconsin killed slightly under three persons per one million residents.

The patterns revealed in survey research have provided the basis for efforts to explain police violence. Kania and Mackey's (1977) ecological study found a significant relationship between the rate of police homicide and the level of violent crime in the community. They suggest that police are predisposed to use violence against citizens in response to the level of violence they encounter in their working environment. Jacobs and Britt (1979), using the same data, found that police homicides were highest in states with the greatest economic inequality. Their findings challenge previous interpretations of police violence simply as a response to levels of violence in the community.

Some researchers have suggested that occupational stress may also be a factor in police killings. Research has shown that police suffer disproportionately from stress-related health problems (including gastrointestinal disorders and heart disease), alcoholism, marital and family problems, emotional disorders and suicide (Duncan, 1979:v). Blackmore (1978) argues that police hostility and aggression may also be related to occupational stress.

Another explanation, rooted in the sociology of occupations, emphasizes the influence of the work environment on attitudes, values, and behavior. Westley (1953:216) was the first to apply this perspective to police violence:

> The policeman uses violence illegally because such usage is seen as just, acceptable, and, at times, expected by his colleague group and because it constitutes an effective means for solving problems in obtaining status and self-esteem which policemen as policemen have in common.

The occupational environment of the police generates a collective emphasis on secrecy, an attempt to coerce respect from the public, and a legitimation of almost any means to accomplish an important arrest. In the everyday activities of policing, these values take precedence over legal responsibilities. Thus, in certain areas of police work—for example, the apprehension of an armed felon or the handling of a sex offender—the police justify excessive physical force as good, proper, and useful.

This paper examines police use of lethal force from a different perspective—that of the police themselves. Police departments have formal procedures to investigate cases in which police officers fire their weapons and incidents in which citizens are wounded or killed by officers. These procedures determine, after the fact, whether the shootings were legal and warranted, or illegal and unwarranted. Similarly, police training manuals and administrative guidelines attempt to specify the circumstances under which officers may, or should, draw and fire their weapons. Thus, a formal, bureaucratic set of procedures exists to evaluate, document, and explain police violence.

At another level, the occupational subculture of the police involves a set of understandings, beliefs, practices, and a language for talking about all problematic aspects of their work, including the shooting and killing of citizens. This perspective includes both prospective beliefs that influence the decisions of officers to use their weapons, and retrospective interpretations of events that have already occurred. The prospective beliefs might be called "techniques of neutralization" because they permit officers to violate both the general cultural prohibition against taking life and sometimes also the specific regulations of the police department and the law about the circumstances under which the police may use their weapons. The retrospective elements may be called "vocabularies of motives" or "accounts" (Mills, 1940; Scott and Lyman, 1968); they reveal the specific ways people either excuse or justify their actions when required to do so.

Any explanation of police violence must take into account how the police themselves account for and explain their use of weapons. This paper concentrates on the informal beliefs that permeate the police occupational subculture. It focuses on how the police themselves interpret and account for incidents in which they fire their weapons and wound or kill someone.

First, I describe the methods and data for my analysis. Second, I discuss procedures that formally govern this area of police behavior. Third, I look at prospective elements of the police subculture that guide the police in their use of weapons. Finally, I examine retrospective accounts of "incidents of police killing" that occurred during my research.

DATA AND METHOD

The data for this paper come from two sources. First, I spent 10 months in 1976 and 1977 as a participant-observer in a police department in a city in the northeastern United States.[1] During my research, three police shootings occurred. The focus of my research was detective work. One of the citizens was shot by a detective, and I arranged to accompany that officer on his shift the day following the shooting. The other two shootings involved patrol officers. These incidents were widely discussed in the department at the time, and provided an opportunity to observe the police perspective on, and interpretation of, actual cases. In addition, I interviewed officers at length, discussing their use of firearms and past shooting incidents within the department. Quotations in this paper are taken from these interviews, unless otherwise attributed.

The second source of data is my analysis of 459 police shootings in Philadelphia between 1970 and 1978 (Waegel, 1984). This study employed accounts by police, witnesses, and surviving victims collected by the Philadelphia Public Interest Law Center (Jackson, 1979). The center's work is respected by legal scholars, as indicated by its citation in a major appellate court decision (*Matza v. Schnarr* 1976) on police use of lethal force.

LEGAL RULES, FORMAL PROCEDURES, AND SUBCULTURAL UNDERSTANDINGS

Police use of firearms is formally governed by state laws and the policies and guidelines of particular police departments. Legal standards have been in transition since the early 1970s. The traditional common-law standard, the "fleeing felon rule," permits the use of deadly force to arrest any felon suspect. Since 1970, many states have departed from the traditional standard and restricted

---

[1]For a discussion of the field role adopted by the author, the use of key informants, and other methodological issues involved in participant observation of the police, see Waegel (1979;1981).

the use of deadly force only to incidents involving specific forcible felonies or to situations involving defense of life. In both of the jurisdictions I studied, statutory change departing from the fleeing felon standard occurred during the 1970s. Typical of the departmental guidelines are those provided in the Philadelphia Policeman's Manual:

> There are three instances in which a police officer may fire his revolver at another human. They are:
> 1. To protect his own life, when it is in imminent danger.
> 2. To protect the life of another.
> 3. In an effort to prevent the commission of certain violent felonies or to prevent the escape of a violent felon, but *only after all* other means have been exhausted.

Police use of firearms is embedded in a background of shared understandings developed out of occupational experiences and collegial discussions of past shooting incidents and their consequences. Shootings have a special prominence in the police subculture. They are the stuff of "real" police work as opposed to routine peace-keeping activities. That police are given guns and required to carry them 24 hours a day is a feature of the police world which has an importance that cannot be underestimated. The gun is a symbol which sets off the police and their work from other persons and occupations. Every police intervention takes place against an awareness of the ultimate power that can be brought to bear. When that power is used, the significance of the event extends beyond the particular incident. To shoot with state sanction is an experience virtually unique to police. It strikes at the heart of the police role, and is one of the matters around which subcultural solidarity is built. Shootings activate personal emotions, anxieties, sentiments, and recollections; all officers know that they may face the decision to shoot at any time. Tales of past shootings occupy a prominent position in the folklore of policing, frequently recounted to instruct new members and to reinforce the messages and injunctions they carry.

Every shooting of a citizen is subject to formal review. At the very least, police departments conduct internal inquiries. The officer is required to explain the grounds for the shooting in a written report. Beyond this, there may be an external review, either by prosecutors in conjunction with the departmental investigation or in the form of separate investigations by the public prosecutor or the coroner's office.

Central among the understandings police hold about shooting are that the review process is generally "friendly" and that the legal standards are sufficiently vague so that nearly all shootings can be interpreted to fit the legal criteria for justifiable police homicide. These understandings are grounded in accumulated knowledge about the review process and its outcomes.

That these views have an empirical basis is suggested in the literature on police use of lethal force. Kobler's (1975) study of 1,500 fatal police shootings found only three cases in which criminal punishment resulted. Harding and Fahey (1973) examined 85 fatal shootings by Chicago police during 1969 and 1970; in 11 of these, available information revealed *prima facie* cases for murder or manslaughter, but only one officer was charged and tried. Both studies discuss features of the formal review process that operate to produce very low rates of prosecution. Moreover, the vague character of formal standards and guidelines for using lethal force (eg., "reasonable belief," "substantial risk," "only when all other means have been exhausted") has led Milton *et al* (1977:57) to observe that "their impact on the conduct of police officers is questionable."

PROSPECTIVE NEUTRALIZATIONS

The occupational subculture of the police contains special beliefs and understandings about using firearms against citizens. Legal norms formally governing the use of deadly force may be rendered situationally ineffective through reference to shared understandings about justifications for infractions. Sykes and Matza (1957) examine such justifications as "techniques of neutralization" which precede deviant behavior and release the actor from conventional rules and prohibitions.

In the neutralization framework, violations are exceptions to otherwise accept rules. Accordingly, the justification for violation is usually specific to certain kinds of persons and circumstances or to the achievement of certain ends. The police officers I interviewed related their justifications to circumstances ("it's not wrong because of the special circumstances involved"), the characteristics of the victim ("it's not wrong because the person deserves it"), or the higher purpose achieved ("it's right because of the ends served"). While analytically distinguishable, these beliefs blend together, form packages of meaning, and constitute working formulas for the officer on the street. Only certain types of persons deserve violent treatment and then only under certain kinds of circumstances.

A set of beliefs centering on the peculiar character and demands of police work generates a preparedness to "shoot first" in potentially dangerous situations. Many officers spoke of the uncertainty, anxiety, and danger they experience in their work—for example, while searching for an armed suspect and suddenly confronting a person in a dark alley. Such situations require split-second decisions which, if incorrect, can result in serious injury or death to the officer. One plainclothes officer, describing this type of circumstance in police work, remarked, "I'm not gonna get my ass shot by one of those scums while I'm trying to do my job."

Most police officers believed that mistakes are unavoidable due to the special nature of police work.[2] Past incidents in which an officer's hesitation resulted in injury or death to the officer or a colleague were prominent parts of the folklore of police work. A "war story" told to me on several different occasions involved a young officer who had hesitated in shooting and was killed at the scene of an armed robbery. The hesitation and fatal consequences were attributed to assumptions made by the officer because the first suspect to appear— and the one who shot the officer—was an attractive, white woman. Frequent recounting of such incidents and the lesson they carry crystallizes

---

[2]Reiss (1971:278) found that some officers "even carry pistols and knives that they have confiscated while searching citizens; they carry them so they may be placed at a scene should it be necessary to establish a case of self-defense."

and cements a subcultural injunction: when dealing with certain kinds of persons and situations, be ready to shoot if you think you have to and worry about the paper work later. The conventional wisdom embodied in the saying "I'd rather be judged by twelve than carried out by six" is familiar to every urban police officer.

Some police shootings involve circumstances in which officers are afraid for their personal safety; a person may be confronted who suddenly turns toward an officer or is seen holding an object, and the officer spontaneously shoots. The nature of police work involves managing situations where persons make sudden or unexpected body movements—what police call "suggestive moves." Under these circumstances, police view shooting first as self-defense. However, this orientation is specific to certain territories and categories of people, and if the person encountered does not fit a stereotype connoting danger, officers may hesitate to shoot.

Sykes and Matza (1957:668) describe the process by which members of certain groups are selected as deserving of abusive treatment:

> By a subtle alchemy the [actor] moves himself into the position of an avenger. . . . The moral indignation of self and others may be neutralized by an insistence that the injury is not wrong in light if the circumstances. . . . It is not really an injury; rather it is a form of rightful retaliation or punishment.

This neutralization technique, termed "denial of the victim," acts as a motivation. Regarding the other as a person who deserves victimization serves as a cue for action.

Police work commonly involves relying on minimal cues to assess the character and likely behavior of persons encountered. The police literature contains rich descriptions of the stereotyping schemes employed by officers and the differential treatment of citizens who fit the stereotypes (Bittner, 1967; Skolnick, 1967; Van Manaan, 1978). Stereotypes link different modes of police behavior to different categories of persons encountered (Waegel, 1981). Police commonly use negative stereotypes (e.g., "animals," "scrotes," "assholes") in dealing with persons displaying specific attitudes, behaviors, or characteristics such as race or type of dress. Persons so categorized are viewed as different in essential ways from respectable citizens; their imputed moral inferiority renders them deserving of harsh or abusive treatment. Police need only listen to sentiments frequently expressed within the wider culture to find support for their beliefs concerning rightful or deserved punishments. Public figures who call for the castration of rapists or the use of penal colonies or other repressive responses to crime may contribute to a moral climate favoring informal sanctions by police.

Blatant racism in the larger society also contributes to the moral climate. During the investigation of a particularly gruesome homicide involving minorities, a detective remarked to a colleague, "Maybe Hitler was right, he just had the wrong group." In urban areas where minorities are over-represented in serious crimes, many police interpret race as a major "cause" of crime. The general devaluation of minority groups by large segments of the wider culture nourishes beliefs about the propriety of harsh or abusive treatment.

Beliefs about minorities are reinforced by experiences which are unique to police, especially interaction with injured and angry crime victims. At crime scenes and during investigations, injured victims, friends, and by-standers sometimes advocated extra-legal treatment: "If you ever catch the guys who did this, you should kick their asses." Some victims urged the police to avenge their crimes. Out of their occupational experiences police develop working assumptions about categories of people. As one veteran, plainclothes officer said to me during a homicide investigation in which all the parties involved were lower-class blacks, "You've got to understand, these people are animals, and we're here to keep peace among the animals."

In another incident, both police officers accepted the idea that excessive force toward blacks fell within the zone of acceptable behavior. In the aftermath of a police shooting which I describe below, the shooter was approached by an officer from his former patrol platoon and asked what had happened. The officer described the circumstances, then concluded: "What was I supposed to do?" Without hesitation the patrol officer replied, "What's another dead nigger anyway?

The belief that some persons, under certain circumstances, "deserve to be shot"—though strongly held by some segments of the urban police—is not sufficiently potent to neutralize the general cultural prohibition against unwarranted killing. This belief prepares the officer to shoot, and weakens external controls, but does not in itself allow the officer to shoot. But it combines with other beliefs about the police role and the circumstances under which shooting is desirable to form a frame of reference for when to shoot.

Occupational experiences generate cynicism among police toward the rule of law (Skolnick, 1967). They believe that justice is frequently thwarted. They "know" people are guilty but often go unpunished. As a result, police see themselves as unavoidably caught between two wrongs: it's wrong that criminals don't get what they deserve, and it's wrong to take justice into one's own hands. The dilemma is addressed by a subcultural injunction: sometimes a cop has to break the law to enforce the law. Accordingly, unlawful police conduct such as perjury is rendered acceptable among large segments of the police subculture by reference to the positive ends which motivate the behavior. Illegal police methods are not simply the lesser of two evils; rather, they become the means which ensure that offenders get what they deserve. So long as police methods are directed toward the end of dispensing just deserts, they fall within the police definition of acceptable behavior.

How far this definition extends and whether it includes legally unwarranted shootings varies. It may be influenced, for example, by exposure to atrocious, violent crimes. Police see the consequences of criminal behavior in ways which other segments of society seldom experience: mutilated, dismembered, decaying bodies, and victims who are battered, bloodied, and permanently disfigured and disabled. Officers who have seen the worst of what some people do to others have strong feelings that the offenders should be punished one way or another.

Veteran plainclothes officers in particular have strong feelings toward the perpetrators of violent crime. A detective described an incident in which he shot and killed a person in a robbery stake-out. Information obtained from an informant, a heroin addict facing multiple felony charges, indicated that a corner store would be robbed that night. Officers concealed themselves in a back room. The suspect entered, grabbed money from the cash register, and turned to run out of the store. By prearranged plan, the clerk dropped to the floor as an officer came out of the back room with a sawed-off shotgun. The officer yelled, "Halt," in order to make the suspect turn toward him. The officer then fired both barrels at close range. "People ask me how I feel about shooting somebody," he said. "After what I've seen people do to one another, it doesn't bother me a bit to shoot one of these people." Interviews with officers assigned to areas or police functions not involving regular experience with violent crime generally did not reveal the same level of animosity toward offenders.

During focused interviews and informal discussions about police shootings, the following sentiments and beliefs were expressed:

> I no longer believe in the jury system after some of the cases I've seen. Twelve middle-class jurors judge an animal. We get a guy off the streets and within three or four days he's back committing more crimes. And those bastards in the federal courts, they sit back there in their robes on their benches and they don't understand the situation.

> You know, the public wants us to do this [shoot] when we catch one of these people.

> When we shoot somebody in one of these things [a robbery stake-out] we don't get any more of this type of robbery for a while.

The willingness to dispense justice on the streets was rooted in three widely shared beliefs: (1) Shooting a suspect dispenses a version of justice not commonly dispensed by the courts. (2) The public wants the police to shoot suspects when they are seen committing a crime. (3) Shooting suspects has a deterrent effect which benefits law-abiding citizens. When these beliefs converge with the perception of a suspect as the type of person who deserves to be shot, police are more likely to use their weapons. Popular sentiments about violent crime support such views. The return to the use of the death penalty, widely applauded by police, is taken as evidence of the true desires of the public for the harsh treatment of dangerous offenders. Influential politicians, appealing to law-and-order sentiments among their constituents, advocate get-tough, deterrence-based policies. The notion that the courts, through the exclusionary rule, the Miranda warning, and other rulings which limit police power, handcuff the police and thwart justice is not without considerable support in public opinion.

The media provide an important source of public images and understandings about the police and crime. Television super-cops such as Starsky and Hutch, and Kojak, and the movie character Dirty Harry routinely eliminate undesirables with their firearms. The continued popularity of such characters suggests a significant public appetite for this kind of police conduct.

RETROSPECTIVE ACCOUNTS

Investigations of police shootings call for the construction of an account (Scott and Lyman, 1968). Accounts are socially approved vocabularies for reducing or relieving responsibility, or for neutralizing an act or its consequences when conduct is called into question. Accounts may be offered to explain one's own behavior or that of others. In occupations where mistakes are likely occurrences, members develop a collective rationale and build up collective defenses against the lay world (Hughes, 1971:318).

A shooting is perhaps the most dramatic event in policing. To the officer, it is the ultimate clash of good against evil. Subcultural sentiments are mobilized as officers seek out information and discuss, interpret, and evaluate the incident. Van Maanen (1980:153) notes that this talk among colleagues "also 'normalizes' a shooting, since it is only through discourse that a sense of typicality can emerge." Colleagues interpret the event by locating it within a familiar vocabulary of motives (Mills, 1940). As information is collected, accounts are fashioned which explain the incident as an instance of understandable and warranted conduct. In the police view, shootings are almost always justified, even though outsiders might disagree. Outsiders, police believe, do not fully understand the context of police work. This view is reflected, for example, in the almost universal resistance by police to civilian review boards or other mechanisms for external review of police conduct (Lundman, 1980:173).

How police retrospectively account for and explain their use of firearms is illustrated in the following three cases from my field research.

1) The police obtained a warrant to search the home of a person believed to be trafficking in illegal weapons. The resident was a middle-aged black man with no prior criminal record. The information, obtained from a juvenile informant facing serious charges, was entirely erroneous. Probable cause was fabricated in the application for a search warrant. Under the "no-knock" law, the officers kicked open the door with no prior warning. The first two officers to enter wore flak jackets and carried shotguns and were responsible for meeting any resistance. The resident was in the kitchen with three children, slicing vegetables for dinner. When the noise and commotion occurred at the front door, the man moved toward the front room holding an onion in one hand and a knife in the other. A plainclothes officer, entering behind the first two, saw a man with a knife moving forward and shot him with his handgun. The man was seriously but not critically wounded. His first statement was, "Somebody is gonna get sued over this."

I had ridden with the officer who shot the man for three weeks earlier in the research period, and accompanied him on the shift following the shooting. He had already been interviewed by prosecutors and police investigators. Visibly upset by the incident and its potential consequences, the officer spent most of the shift simply driving around the city. On numerous occasions, he was approached by uniformed officers or stopped to talk with colleagues and was commended for the shooting. Twice he was told to "improve your aim next time." It was understood that the shooting was a mistake of a kind which had been made in the past and which any member might make in the future. The officer's account of the incident centered on placing it in an understandable context:

> What could I do? I thought it was either him or me. You know all cops make mistakes. There's not cop in here who hasn't made a mistake. I've got a split second to decide what a jury can take all week to decide.

A police department account of the incident that was made public assigned responsibility for the shooting to the juvenile informant, described both the resident and the officer as victims, and explained the finding of justifiable use of a firearm in terms of the rapid, unexpected, and confusing events at the scene.

2) Police were called to the residence of a 23-year-old Hispanic ex-Marine by reports that he was acting violently, breaking windows, and spraying family members with tear gas. Family members fled the house and the man locked himself inside, alone. The first two uniformed officers to arrive were told of the man's history of mental problems and of efforts to bring a relative to the scene who had been able to calm the man during previous outbursts. The officers agreed to wait. A white sergeant arrived minutes later and made a decision to enter the house. The door was broken in and the sergeant, gun drawn, entered the residence. He was followed at a distance by another officer, while the third remained outside arguing with and restraining family members. After several minutes of silence, a single shot was fired. The sergeant had climbed the stairs to the third floor, confronted the man who was holding a shotgun, and shot him once in the head.

Controversy surrounded the incident, and a minister and leader of the Hispanic community described the shooting as a "brutal assassination." Although some officers confided to me privately that the sergeant used poor judgment in entering the house and was attempting to "be a hero," the basic interpretation of the event was that the sergeant "had no choice" since he was confronted with a weapon. Colleague accounts placed responsibility on the victim for threatening the officer with a gun; regardless of other circumstances, when a suspect has a gun, shooting is seen as self-defense. Four separate investigations of the shooting were conducted: by the police department, the city prosecutor, the state attorney general, and the U.S. Attorney's office. Each produced a finding of justifiable homicide.

3) A young black man entered a fast-food restaurant and purchased a soda while holding a large knife in his hand. The man reportedly acted in a bizarre manner, although he paid for the soda did not threaten anyone. Police were notified and a young white officer, working alone, was first to respond to the "man with a knife" radio call. As the officer approached the scene, he saw the man standing on the sidewalk with the knife still in hand. The officer stopped his car directly in front of the man, drew his revolver, and positioned himself behind the open door of the car with his gun pointed at the man. He shouted at the man to drop the knife. The man stopped but did not drop the knife, and the two were frozen in this position for a brief time. Apparently, the man then made a sudden movement and the officer fired six times. This incident generated relatively little controversy. Police are required to respond to situations involving armed and potentially dangerous persons. This event was seen as an instance of that class of situations where offenders place an officer's life in danger, and shooting first is viewed as a natural, understandable, and warranted response. My inquiries about the propriety of the officer's response or alternative ways of handling the encounter met with replies of "What was he supposed to do?"

Vocabularies of accounts become routinized within groups and subcultures. Conduct becomes explainable by locating it within such a routine account. When an officer explains a shooting by saying, "It happened so fast" or "I didn't have any choice," further explanation may not be required. Colleagues can fill in and flesh out the account using background understandings about the nature of policing and the use of force. What Rubinstein (1973) has called "cop's rules"—informal, subcultural understandings about acceptable methods of handling persons and situations—provide a common context of interpretation.

Routine ways of accounting for a shooting centered on deflecting responsibility to the conduct of the person shot or to special circumstances at the scene. Grounds for a shooting were commonly expressed in terms of the theme, "It was him or me." This justification was applicable to a wide range of situations, and was explicit or implicit in accounts of incidents whenever the victim was armed. In each of the three cases described above, accounts were fashioned around a kill-or-be-killed theme.

An important variant of this deflection of responsibility to the conduct of the person shot involves what police call a "suggestive move."[3] A suspect is confronted; the suspect makes a quick movement into a pocket or unexpectedly turns toward an officer holding an object; the officer shoots spontaneously only to learn later that the suspect was unarmed. One of the Philadelphia shootings I studied involved a young black man in the vicinity of a robbery scene who was ordered to stop and was shot when he turned toward the officers holding a shoehorn in his hand. The anxiety associated with police functions such as area searches for armed felons and the sudden, unexpected movements persons sometimes make when confronted by police represents special circumstances which may generate a *belief* that shooting is in self-defense. Knowledge that accounts centering on suggestive moves have worked in the past suggests their applicability for explaining subsequent incidents.[4]

Most accounts, then, are fashioned to justify the conduct of the shooter; particular features of the situation permitted or required the officer to shoot. Ambiguities in the application of legal rules ("a reasonable belief that your life is in imminent danger") to particular situations provide fertile grounds for the construction of justifying accounts. The notorious reluctance of juries to convict police charged in shooting incidents (which, of course, police are well aware of) suggests a wider appreciation of this problematic quality of the rules governing the use of lethal force.

However, other shootings cannot reasonably be justified in terms of the kill-or-be-killed theme. Some shootings are mistakes. Here, accounts are fashioned as excuses, which acknowledge the error but mitigate or deny culpability. In the first case described above, the police department offered excuses

---

[3]That accounts centering on suggestive moves are not specific to the department I studied but are a common way police explain shootings is suggested by the statement of the project director of a deadly force study funded by the Justice Department. In a press interview, Arnold Binder recommended that "civilians should be advised of police training techniques so they do not inadvertently prompt a police shooting by acting in a way that a police officer would consider threatening. . . . [Citizens] must not behave in such easily misinterpreted ways as reaching rapidly into a pocket or into a glove compartment" (*Philadelphia Inquirer,* 1982).

[4]During my fieldwork, a veteran plainclothes officer described how an account centering on a "suggestive move" by a suspect generally led to a departmental review board finding of justified firearms use: "All you have to do is say he reached into his pocket and you saw something in his hand. Then you have a reasonable *belief* the guy is armed and they can't do anything about it."

based on the erroneous information provided by the juvenile informant. Had it not been for the juvenile's deceit, it was claimed, the shooting never would have occurred. Further, had the information been accurate and a large cache of weapons actually had been inside the residence, the police response probably would have been warranted. Such appeals to defeasibility (Scott and Lyman, 1968:48) are available as excuses because of general cultural understandings that incomplete or imperfect knowledge may diminish a person's responsibility for conduct.

The ultimate excuse, entailing a complete denial of responsibility, is the "accidental discharge." Probably only the shooter, and perhaps a partner or a few close colleagues, ever know whether this excuse is accurate or whether it is manufactured *post facto* because other reasonable grounds were not available. But accidental discharges do happen, generally in the context of a violent physical encounter where a suspect tries to take an officer's gun. The empirical frequency of this occurrence is not the issue. "War stories" about such incidents are part of the folklore of police work. An account centering on accidental discharge thus is available for situations where all else fails. It may be used for incidents where an officer lost control of his emotions, panicked, or for other reasons shot under legally unwarranted circumstances.

During an interview, a retired police officer described a case in which an accidental discharge account was fabricated to "cover up" an illegal shooting. An officer had shot and killed a man at point-blank range while the latter's hands were up. The exact motivation was unknown, but there had been a history of "bad blood" between the two. An account was contrived indicating that, as the officer was holding the man at gunpoint, the man lunged for the gun and grabbed the barrel pulling it toward him. This movement pulled the trigger against the officer's finger, causing the gun to discharge into the man's chest. The retired officer took a revolver, removed the bullets from it, and demonstrated to me the details around which the story was contrived. At the end of the demonstration, he rolled his eyes in an expression of disbelief. After a pause, he added "But, the guy was a bad job anyway."

Of the 459 shootings I studied in Philadelphia, 22 were accounted for as accidents. Eight involved bystanders hit by stray bullets or ricochets. The remaining 14 were explained as accidental discharges. Ten were attributed to a struggle or other physical contact with a suspect which caused the discharge, three were said to have occurred during chases, and one while a suspect was being frisked.[5] In the most publicized of these cases, a 19-year-old black man was arrested for a traffic violation and taken to the police station. While handcuffed at the station, the man pushed an officer and fled. He was pursued, caught, and shot by a white officer while lying on the ground. The officer was charged with manslaughter, tried, and acquitted.

People change their accounts for different audiences; explanations are fashioned in ways calculated to earn audience acceptance. The background understandings which make colleagues receptive to certain accounts are unlikely to be shared by other audiences. It should be expected, then, that accounts given

---

[5]Fyfe (1979) reports a similar use of accidental discharge accounts of New York City police. Following the implementation of an administrative order banning warning shots, there was "a great and unexpected increase in reported accidental 'shots in the air' fired by police who 'tripped on curbs' while pursuing fleeing suspects" (Fyfe, 1979:313).

to colleagues may be quite different from official accounts provided in press releases. Indeed, the concerns and purposes of administrators frame the fashioning of official accounts. Van Maanen's (1980:150) examination of official reconstructions of shooting incidents suggests that administrators attempt to demonstrate (1) that the police presence at the scene was warranted; and (2) that selected facts of the case fit the legal justifications for the use of deadly force. What is released for public consumption, then, is an account "that is documented in a politically, culturally, and legally viable fashion" (Van Maanen, 1980:151). In large police departments, the process becomes routinized: accounts become reinterpreted and refashioned to fit common public understandings of when and why police must shoot. The clearest illustration is seen in stakeout shootings where a familiar and standard script is trotted out: the suspect, armed with a handgun, turned and pointed the gun at an officer; the suspect had a long criminal record.

DISCUSSION

Formal rules, standards, and guidelines provide areas of uncertainty and therefore permit negotiation of the meaning of these formulations (Manning, 1978:78). Bittner (1970:4) argues that this defeasible quality of formal rules provides the essential structure to the police role:

> While there may be a core of clarity about [their] application, this core is always and necessarily surrounded by uncertainty. . . . No measure of effort will ever succeed in eliminating, or even in meaningfully curtailing, the area of discretionary freedom of the agent whose duty it is to fit rules to cases.

Formal prescriptions about the use of lethal force reflect political and cultural contradictions and accommodations regarding the sanctity of life and property and the protection and safety of citizens and enforcement agents. When police are sent out to do disagreeable and sometimes dangerous work, they carry with them latitude and flexibility in drawing the lines about acceptable methods. The law, as Matza (1964) has observed, contains the seeds of its own neutralization.

Police, then, operate within a wider context enabling them collectively to identify and negotiate particular instances in which the use of firearms are warranted as exceptions to the general rule. The police subculture contains interpretive schemes for addressing the practical problems of when to shoot first, who are the proper recipients of deadly force, and why and under what circumstances suspects deserve to be shot.

Against the background of general cultural and specific legal prohibitions against taking life, police assemble a sense of justification for their uses of lethal force. Particular incidents are accounted for by drawing on familiar subcultural understandings about "why these things happen." Common forms ("it was him or me," "the person made a suggestive move") locate responsibility outside the officer and within features of the event or the conduct of the suspect. In the retrospective interpretation of that frozen moment when the trigger was pulled, "it happened so fast" or "I was so scared I just started shooting" or even "the scum deserved it" may ultimately become an accidental discharge. The infrequency of sanction and the often-heard cries of cover-up which inflame the issue may be understood as products of the official accounting work performed.

Finally, the defeasible quality of the formal rules governing police use of lethal force has important implications for the legal and political debate over when such force is warranted. The volatility of the issue and the identification of police shootings as factors in urban riots (President's Commission, 1967) have brought calls for more effective controls over police use of firearms. A favored political response has been the enactment of statutory change formally restricting circumstances under which firearms may be used. The efficacy of this response appears problematic. This paper suggests that such control efforts operate against a background of entrenched subcultural beliefs and justifications that are organizationally and politically nourished. The relevance of the nourishment is suggested by research which shows that changes in an administrative climate of tolerance or in the friendly nature of internal review procedures result in reductions in the number of police shootings (Fyfe, 1979; Reiss, 1980).

REFERENCES

Bittner, Egon
    1967   "The police on skid row: A study of peace-keeping." American Sociological Review 32(5):699–715.
    1970   The Functions of the Police in Modern Society. Washington, DC: U.S. Government Printing Office.
Blackmore, John
    1978   "Are police allowed to have problems of their own?" Police Magazine 1(3):47–55.
Duncan, Skip
    1979   Police Stress. Washington, DC: U.S. Government Printing Office.
Fyfe, James J.
    1979   "Administrative interventions or police shooting discretion: An empirical examination." Journal of Criminal Justice 7(4):309–323.
Harding, Richard W. and Richard P. Fahey
    1973   "Killings by Chicago police, 1969–1970: An empirical study." Southern California Law Review 46:284–315.
Hughes, Everett C.
    1971   "Mistakes at work." Pp. 316–325 in Everett C. Hughes (ed.), The Sociological Eye. Chicago: Aldine Atherton, Inc.
Jackson, Anthony
    1979   Deadly Force Report. Monograph. Philadelphia: Philadelphia Public Interest Law Center.
Jacobs, David, and David Britt
    1979   "Inequality and police use of deadly force: An empirical assessment of a conflict hypothesis." Social Problems 26(4):403–412.
Kania, Richard, and Wade Mackey
    1977   "Police violence as a function of community characteristics." Criminology 15(1):27–48.
Kobler, Arthur
    1975   "Police homicide in a democracy." Journal of Social Issues 31(1):163–184.
Lundman, Richard J.
    1980   Police and Policing. New York: Holt, Rinehart and Winston.

Manning, Peter K.
  1978 "Rules, colleagues, and situationally justified actions." Pp. 71–90 in Peter K. Manning and John Van Maanen (eds.), Policing: A View From the Streets. Santa Monica, CA: Goodyear Press.
Matza, David
  1964 Delinquency and Drift. New York: John Wiley and Sons.
Mills, C. Wright
  1940 "Situated actions and vocabularies of motive." American Sociological Review 5:904–913.
Milton, Catherine H., Jeanne W. Halleck, James Lardner, and Garry L. Abrecht
  1977 Police Use of Deadly Force. Washington, DC: Police Foundation.
Philadelphia Inquirer
  1982 "Gun courses for police criticized." February 26:sec. A, p. 9.
         Philadelphia Police Department
  1978 Policeman's Manual. Philadelphia, PA.
President's Commission on Law Enforcement and the Administration of Justice
  1967 Task Force Report: The Police. Washington, DC: U.S. Government Printing Office.
Reiss, Albert
  1971 The Police and the Public. New Haven, CT: Yale University Press.
  1980 "Controlling police use of deadly force." Annals of the American Academy of Political and Social Science 552:122–134.
Robin, Gerald
  1963 "Justifiable homicide by police officers." Journal of Criminal Law, Criminology and Police Science 54(2):225–231.
Rubinstein, Johnathan
  1973 City Police. New York: Ballantine.
Scott, Marvin B., and Standord M. Lyman
  1968 "Accounts." American Sociological Review 33(l):46–62.
Sherman, Lawrence
  1980 "Perspectives on police and violence." Annals of the American Academy of Political and Social Science 452:1–12.
Sherman, Lawrence, and Robert Langworthy
  1979 "Measuring homicide by police officers." Journal of Criminal Law and Criminology 70(4):546–560.
Skolnick, Jerome
  1967 Justice Without Trial. New York: Wiley.
Sykes, Gresham, and David Matza
  1957 "Techniques of neutralization: A theory of delinquency." American Sociological Review 22 (6):664–670.
Van Maanen, John
  1978 "The asshole." Pp. 221–238 in Peter K. Manning and John Van Maanen (eds.), Policing: A View From the Street. Santa Monica, CA: Goodyear Press.
  1980 "Beyond account: The personal impact of police shootings." The Annals of the American Academy of Political and Social Science 452:145–156.
Waegel, William B.
  1979 "Routinization and typification in investigative police work." Unpublished Ph.D. dissertation, University of Delaware.
  1981 "Case Routinization in investigative police work." Social Problems 28(3):263–275.
  1984 "The use of lethal force by police: The effect of statutory change." Crime and Delinquency 30(1):121–140.
Westley, William A.
  1953 "Violence and the police." American Journal of Sociology 49(l):34–41.
Case Cited
Mattis v. Schnarr, 547 F. 2d 1007, 1976.

THE ABNER LOUIMA CASE: IDIOSYNCRATIC PERSONAL CRIME OR SYMPTOMATIC POLICE BRUTALITY?

Richard G. Frey
SUNY-Brockport

Incidents of police brutality are not new, nor is concern about what they mean. The media age brings news of such incidents not just to the attention of the locality involved, but to the world at large. In March, 1991, the video tape showing the Los Angeles police beating of Rodney King aired on news programs across the nation. In August, 1997, the Abner Louima brutality case proved that a video tape is not a prerequisite to garnering the public's attention and brought a perverse continental symmetry to police crime in the nation's two largest cities. Both cases raised the question of whether the spotlighted acts should be seen as aberrant criminal conduct or inevitable manifestations of a deviant police subculture. This article describes what happened and how the case reflects some of the unresolved debates about the police and legal system.

THE INCIDENT

On Monday, December 13, 1999, former New York Police Officer Justin Volpe was sentenced to 30 years in prison for his sodomizing assault of Abner Louima, a Haitian immigrant. As the central defendant in the trial of police officers on federal criminal civil rights charges growing out of their conduct towards Louima, Volpe had decided to enter a guilty plea in the midst of his trial six months earlier. On Tuesday, June 8, 1999, a jury of five women and seven men, after 2 1/2 days of deliberation, convicted Charles Schwarz for his part in the incident, but acquitted three other police defendants.

In the early morning hours of August 9, 1997, Officer Volpe had responded with other officers to reports of a fight outside a club in Brooklyn. By the time the officers arrived, Abner Louima, apparently trying to break up the fight, had been drawn into it. In the melee, Volpe was sucker punched, and at trial, testimony indicated that he mistakenly believed Mr. Louima was the culprit. Louima was taken into custody. On the way to the 70th precinct station, prosecutors alleged, the patrol car was stopped twice, at which times officers Volpe, Thomas Bruder, Thomas Wiese, and Charles Schwarz beat Louima with their fists and a police radio. At the precinct station, Louima was handcuffed and taken by Volpe (and reportedly Schwarz) to a bathroom where Volpe rammed a two-to-three foot stick (variously reported as a toilet plunger or broken broom handle; the actual implement was never officially recovered) into Louima's rectum. Within an hour, an ambulance had been called. Louima was hospitalized and treated for rips in his lower intestine, punctures to his bladder, broken teeth, and other injuries consistent with a beating. A nurse gave a report of the incident to the Police Internal Affairs Bureau. Within hours of the report, the Louima case became a local and national media sensation. By August 19th the Internal Affairs Bureau investigation was well underway, the Brooklyn District Attorney's office had filed state charges, and the United States Justice Department had begun its investigation which was widened to include the issue of whether a pattern of tolerating brutality existed in the New York City Police Department. When the federal indictments came six months later, the Brooklyn District Attorney accepted the federal intervention, dropped the state charges, and allowed the case to proceed in Judge Nickerson's Federal District court where the charges carried heavier penalties and the rules of evidence were more friendly. Sergeant Michael Bellomo, a supervisor at the 70th precinct, was added to the list of defendants charged with trying to cover up the beatings of Louima in the car.

RODNEY KING CASE PARALLELS

The shadow of the Rodney King case falls across any consideration of the Louima case. All those involved directly in the Louima case, including police, lawyers, reporters, politicians, the victim, the defendants, and the judge, as well as to those hearing about it or trying to analyze it, had to compare and contrast it with the King case. King had a criminal history and, in fact, had failed to stop his speeding car. The beating that King was subjected to was a classic example of excessive force, while Volpe's assault on Louima was singular and bizarre, to the point that his codefendants' lawyers were referring to Volpe as a monster and his actions as defying humanity. There was a larger group involved in the King beating, but in both cases, multiple charges were brought against a group of people and some of the group were acquitted. In the King case, the police were tried on state charges, acquitted, and then tried on federal civil rights criminal charges concluding with the jury finding only Stacey Koon and Laurence Powell guilty. In the Louima case, the state prosecutors in Brooklyn were more willing to let the case go directly to federal court on federal criminal charges, but the federal jury, as in the King case, ultimately rendered a mixed verdict. Koon and Powell were sentenced to 30 months, much less than Volpe's 30 years. None of the defendants in the King case ever admitted guilt; Volpe did. The video tape of the King beating appeared to be powerful visual evidence supporting the charges; in the Louima case, it was the more typical brutality contest, the victim's word against the word of his attackers.

There was widespread rioting in Los Angeles after the nearly all-white jury in the state trial of the police charged in King's beating acquitted all of the defendants. The trial had been moved from Los Angeles to Simi Valley in Ventura County, a county predominantly inhabited by white residents and home to many police officers and firefighters. Louima's case saw periodic demonstrations in support of the victim and against police abuses in New York City as the incident was publicized and the case moved through the court system. But there was no rioting when the federal court jury of eight whites, three Hispanics, and one black acquitted three of the four defendants remaining after Volpe's guilty plea. There was no state trial of offenses against Louima, and no moving of the federal trial beyond New York City.

No cases involving two black men brutalized by white police officers can fail to raise questions of racism. In King's case, it has even been asked what drew initial attention to his car (the *DWB, Driving While Black,* offense). In the Louima case, a one side issue developed regarding the black fiancee of one of the indicted police officers. Louima testified that the beatings had been accompanied by racial slurs; a defense lawyer countered that his client's fiancee never would have had a child and moved in with a man who would use such slurs; a prosecutor chided that the officer was trying to hide behind the color of his girlfriend's skin; the officer's lawyers asked for a mistrial; the mistrial was denied.

Both Los Angeles and New York City police chiefs characterized the acts as aberrations and denied racism as being present in the police culture or a contributing factor to the incident. Critics of police cultures agreed that these cases were aberrations, but only in the sense that the excessive use of force by white police against minorities was widely publicized and punished. In both the King and Louima cases, there were misreports of the facts. King was characterized as high on PCP and a drug user even though no PCP showed up on tests at the hospital, and no drugs were found in his car. Later investigations conducted by the California Highway Patrol and the Christopher Commission inaccurately stated that King had been trying to elude police at speeds in excess of 100 miles per hour. Volpe's lawyer, in his opening argument at trial, continued to suggest that Louima's injuries had not been the result of a torturous assault but were caused by a consensual sex act with another man, presumably occurring before the police arrested Louima. By the end of the trial, lawyers for the other defendants sought to distance themselves from that statement by admitting it was despicable, insulting, and offensive to Mr. Louima.

THE STATE/FEDERAL COURT CHOICE

State prosecutors who routinely work with the police in the criminal courts often find themselves in a difficult position when they have to question police about police crime. Often, the defendants of a police case, such as the Louima case, will be tried in federal court rather than in the state courts. Major police brutality cases are usually brought by federal prosecutors under the civil rights criminal code provisions, Title 18, U.S.Code, section 242, detouring the state options. As with Rodney King, Abner Louima hired his own lawyer and has filed civil suits for damages, and there is the prospect of protracted legal battles relating to the incident in the criminal and civil, trial, and appellate courts for years to come.

The dual nature, i.e. federal/state, of our legal system has often been criticized as violating the spirit of the double jeopardy protections guaranteed criminal defendants. Federal and state law that criminalizes the same conduct seems to give the government two shots at a conviction. Many members of the public are similarly confused by the criminal/civil law relationship. Whatever the outcome in a criminal prosecution, the civil law may allow individual victims to seek special remedies (usually tort, personal injury suits) in trials where the rules governing the litigation, such as the burden of proof, are substantially different. These dualities, accepted as fundamental to the American legal system, have been harshly criticized in recent years as Congress substantially increases the number of federal crimes. However, police brutality cases, with good judgment and cooperation between state and federal authorities, demonstrate that positive outcomes are possible in the dual environment.

SWEARING CONTESTS AND POLICE WITNESSES FOR THE PROSECUTION

Louima's trial illustrated some of the problems for both sides in police brutality cases. One of the most serious problems for prosecutors is the *swearing contest* nature of the evidence (no video tape as evidence). In the King trial, the defense, given the tape, was more directed to justifying the police conduct; the defendants in Louima denied the assaults occurred. With Louima, the prosecutors had to find corroboration or circumstantial support for his account of the facts. Louima was not burdened with a criminal history as some victims might be, but at trial he admitted to two lies that had been widely reported initially as facts in the case. First, he admitted his assaulters had never said, "This isn't the Dinkens administration; this is Guiliani time." Second, he admitted it was probably a cousin that had scuffled with Volpe. These admissions, when coupled with minor inconsistencies in the many accounts of the incidents he had been called upon to make, created a huge credibility wall for the prosecution to scale on the central issues to which Louima would testify. They tried to meet that challenge by penetrating the proverbial blue wall of silence, and by convincing the jury that the acts against Louima could be expected within a police environment that condoned violence.

The key prosecution witness proved to be a rookie policeman in the 70th precinct who first gave Internal Affairs investigators his information six days after the incident. At trial, he testified that he saw Officer Schwarz leading Louima off (presumably to the restroom) and a few minutes later saw Volpe showing off a broken, feces-covered broomstick around the precinct. Three other officers gave damaging, corroborating testimony against Volpe, including how he had boasted of breaking a man. No direct testimony was provided by officers to back Louima's account of the car beatings.

To highlight the prosecution's broad attack on the police culture in the 70th precinct, the treatment of another Haitian immigrant, Patrick Antoine, was described. In summation, prosecutors alleged that Antoine was a totally innocent bystander in the vicinity of the Brooklyn Club on that August morning when he was attacked and arrested by Volpe during his search for the man who had allegedly hit him. Then, argued the prosecution, Volpe and Sergeant Bellomo conspired to file inaccurate reports to cover trumped-up charges rather than admit to making a mistake. This police culture, they said, was one in which street justice was rendered with impunity, false reports were routine, and evasions in the face of official investigations were the norm.

The defense tried to suggest the prosecution's police witnesses had career motives for their testimony, were misfits, or had been subjected to other pressures. But none of the witnesses claimed to be heroes for stepping forward, and on the stand they manifested their discomfort at having to give such evidence. A *New York Times* article based on anonymous interviews with other New York City police officers found few inclined to see the prosecution witnesses as rats or cheese eaters. Several noted that the usual practice for other officers would be to step in and stop a fellow officer before such payback got out of hand. Some saw the testimony as proof the proverbial code of silence was fading as the dominant police ethic. Most, however, made a distinction between petty incidents and the Louima attack.

An article in *New York* magazine based on similar interviews agreed that the heinous nature of the attack on Louima was extraordinary but urged administrators to look at the events surrounding it. In those events, argued the authors, many boundaries were crossed by these officers which raise issues on how the police are formally and informally trained and how they are managed on the job. An NYPD veteran gave his view:

> The cops who committed the act clearly believed they could tell some bogus story and get away with it . . . They weren't worried about the desk sergeant, who was the ranking officer on duty that night. Then the relief cops believed they could walk into the hospital and tell a bogus story. And it appears that reports were written to cover up what happened, which indicates that supervisors were involved. People want to say the act was an aberration, but everything about it seems to involve the abuse of authority as well as brutality. So clearly there is something going on here. It certainly looks like cowboy conditions existed at the seven-oh on the midnight-to-eight tour (Horowitz 1997, 33).

Another veteran expressed sympathetic concern for the prosecution's main witness:

> There's no way he could ever be a street cop again. No matter how right it was to come forward, he's still a rat. You gotta have trust. What should've happened is that someone in the precinct should've stopped it (Horowitz 1997, 35).

As the case against Volpe had mounted, he and his lawyers made the decision to plead guilty to all charges after two weeks of trial. The prosecutors claimed in their closing arguments that Volpe's admissions bolstered Louima's credibility on his charges of assaults while he was in the police car. However, not having him around at the end of the case against the others put the evidence in their cases in clearer relief. It could have been put to the jury in the following way: 1) Two officers say they saw Schwarz leading Louima to the restroom; Louima says he was held down by a second officer; Louima can't directly identify the officer but says he's the same officer who drove the car that took him to the police station; police records show Schwarz as the driver. 2) Louima says he was beaten by the two officers who took him by car to the police station; though, again, he can't directly identify them, records show Wiese and Schwarz to be the officers with the car; bloodstains in the car are a DNA match with Louima's. 3) Louima says while in the police car, Volpe and another officer he can't directly identify, came to the car and beat him; records show Bruder was partnered with Volpe that morning, and communications records put Bruder at the location. 4) Bellomo made statements to the F.B.I. and filed formal police reports containing statements the prosecution claims he knew were false; he made calls to officers and investigators to discourage at least one officer from giving evidence; a police friend says Bellomo acted frightened in the days immediately after Louima's arrest.

THE DEFENSE

Volpe's absence at the end of the case allowed the defense to more easily avoid being painted with the brush of revulsion the jury might have had towards Volpe's conduct. During his guilty plea, Volpe had admitted there was another officer in the bathroom but claimed that other officer hadn't participated. Volpe's lawyer later said the other man wasn't Schwarz and that they'd given the other name to the prosecution, but the prosecution told him, given the evidence they had, they didn't believe Volpe.

The only one of the four defendants to take the stand in his own defense was Bellomo. He denied any intentional mistakes and claimed he had to rely on information from the others. His lawyer in closing argument pictured Bellomo as a scapegoat, included as a management figure to bolster the prosecutorial climate theory. The other defendants relied on their lawyers, cross-examination of the prosecutors' case, and a few character witnesses. They claimed Louima made up the stories of the car beatings later, in anger for the primary assault by Volpe and that the blood in the car was from Louima's earlier injuries at the Brooklyn club fight. Prosecutors got Louima to admit that his "Guiliani time" lie was part of an effort simply to get people to pay attention to his assault charges. Other misstatements, they argued, could be expected from someone groggy from various medicines and still traumatized by the incident at the time he was being asked questions. But other contrasting explanations had to be resolved by the jury based simply on whom they believed while remembering that the prosecution had the burden of convincing them beyond a reasonable doubt.

The jury convicted Schwarz of two counts of violating Louima's civil rights in the bathroom attack (helping Volpe) but acquitted him, Wiese, and Bruder of the charges connected with the car beatings. Bellomo was acquitted of covering up the attacks on Louima and the false arrest of Antoine. While both sides claimed vindication for their positions (i.e. Volpe didn't act alone; Louima was not a victim of widespread misconduct), the jury verdict in fact left the argument about the police subculture unsettled. Perhaps it signaled again that one shouldn't expect the legal system to provide final answers to complex social problems.

VOLPE'S SENTENCE

Schwarz had appealed his conviction and had not been sentenced at the time this article was written. Volpe's sentence had, however, been rendered by Judge Nickerson and was determined in accordance with the federal sentencing guidelines that were created as part of the whole movement away from indeterminate sentencing to more determinate, fixed sentences. The federal government and about 20% of the states have abolished parole. The 30-year sentence actually given Volpe should remind us that the United States imprisons more people for longer terms than almost any other country in the world. There were times in the not-too-distant past in the United States when 30 years could have been considered a fair sentence for some aggravated murders.

Under these guidelines, the prosecutors and probation department (presentence report) had argued for a higher offense level. Judge Nickerson reached a lower level by eliminating the obstruction of justice element, concluding it had occurred contemporaneously with the incident.

He reduced it two more levels on the grounds that Volpe, as a police officer and coupled with the notoriety generated by the case, would be unusually susceptible to abuse during his incarceration. This last reduction is similar to that accorded Stacy Koon in the Rodney King case, and that decision had been upheld by the federal courts on appeal. Judge Nickerson rejected many other mitigating factors put forward by Volpe's lawyers. Nonetheless, the sentence raises questions of fairness, and some have suggested the sentence is a classic example of result-oriented judicial decision-making. Will Volpe really have a harder time in federal prison? Is the violent cop getting a better deal than nonviolent drug dealers? The courts have been very reluctant to allow departures for other types of vulnerability, the mentally or developmentally disabled for example. Yes, policeman are often targets in prison, but the prisons have ways of isolating and protecting targets, and the federal prisons have many classification options that might leave Volpe relatively comfortable. Should the policeman's violation of his public trust be more appropriately labeled as an aggravating rather than mitigating factor?

A review of the reactions to Volpe's sentence reveals an eerie Alice-in-Wonderland quality or role-reversal appearance to the case as hardliners argue for sufficient due process and sensitivity to the criminal, while civil libertarians focus on the need to make a societal statement and not to forget the victim. The police defendants were very critical of many of the prosecutorial decisions. Particularly singled out for criticism was the United States Attorney's decision to continue with the obstruction of justice cases against Schwarz, Wiese, and Bruder in a second trial still to come. The families of the defendants, too, were often quoted about the unfairness of it all. The prosecutor, two weeks after the trial verdict, signaled his seriousness about going after the police culture of silence (or was he irked at not winning convictions against Wiese, Bruder, and Bellomo?) by getting an indictment against two other officers for repeatedly lying to F.B.I. agents who questioned them. Is the prosecutor's decision to press on with an obstruction of justice case against Bruder, Schwarz, and Wiese and seek additional indictments an example of the overzealous, vindictive prosecutor or the dedicated public servant who knows offenses have been committed and is determined not to rest until the offenders are brought to justice?

Whatever one's answer, it is doubtful a prosecutor's patterns of behavior can be significantly changed over time. Ironically, like some police, a number of prosecutors believe in bullying and harassment on the theory that the ends achieved will justify the means used to get a conviction or plea. The sentencing guidelines are supposed to bring equity to the sentencing process and prevent disparities based on which judge happens to draw the case. Arguably, Judge Nickerson's sentence and opinion justifying it show how these guidelines can be used by any wise judge to reach a predetermined result. Elements of Volpe's offense—the fact Louima was handcuffed while attacked and Volpe's lukewarm acceptance of responsibility—lifted it to the level of a life sentence under the guidelines. Rather than simply applying the guidelines and letting the sentence take shape, perhaps Judge Nickerson felt a 30-year term was right, and then found the precedent supported variations that would allow him to get there.

ORDER MAINTENANCE POLICING

Some commentators feared the Louima case would disintegrate public support for what some have called the *broken windows* approach to policing in the community. This approach has also been labeled assertive policing or putting more emphasis on order maintenance. In the 1990s, New York City had come to represent to many the successful implementation of this policing strategy. In its most basic form, this strategy puts police on the streets vigilant for the smallest signs of disorder (broken windows, etc.). As symptoms of worse things to come, the small things are fixed before they get out of hand and lead to more seriously destructive criminal behavior. With the revelations about the attack on Louima, several editorials appeared cautioning the public and policy-makers against an overreaction. Others saw the Louima incident as revealing the worst dangers of "in-your-face" or zero tolerance police techniques. Interestingly, George L. Kelling, who, in a 1982 article written with James Q. Wilson, might be said to have instigated the modern consideration of these order maintenance techniques, spoke of the Louima case in a 1999 National Institute of Justice Research Report. The report was primarily devoted to providing a model for police to mentally process what they do while on the job. The bulk of the report concentrates on the themes Kelling developed over a period of years regarding the need for agency supervisors to welcome the pervasiveness of police discretion and depart from controlling police behavior simply with rules and regulations telling officers what not to do. In notes, he rejects equating order maintenance with zero tolerance, finds the zero tolerance phrase itself smacks of zealotry, and clearly resents efforts by some critics to equate order maintenance to a military model of policing.

Speaking directly to the Louima case and concerns about it, Kelling argues that it should not be seen as an inevitable consequence of a police mission to generally restore order in the community. Such a mission is not simply turning the police loose. In fact, Kelling's proposals for giving priority to common sense, values, and process in the exercise of police discretion lead, finally, to establishing real accountability. With other defenders of the current New York City police policies, Kelling points out corrupt and brutal acts by police are not new to the city, many having occurred during previous policing regimes.

WHY POLICE BRUTALITY?

Police actions of the type involved in the case of Abner Louima have long been studied by criminologists. Sutherland, in his 1940 article on white collar crime, discussed job-related criminal activity. Barker and Carter in their book on police deviance have suggested a two-point typology for police misconduct: 1) occupational deviance and 2) abuse of authority. Their first point focuses on the role of the police officer as an employee and subdivides into corruption and misconduct. Their second point focuses on the practice of policing and subdivides into physical, psychological, and legal abuse. In this framework, physical attacks on Louima were an abuse of authority while actions to coverup the abuse were considered misconduct. Numerous accounts of police brutality in newspapers and research papers confirm the fact that most police, to one degree or another, believe in the use of retaliatory force in specific situations in order to maintain control, ensure respect, or deter more dangerous violence. The Mollen Commission, created in 1992 to investigate corruption in the New York City Police Department, found widespread street justice practices and cover ups of brutality. The Christopher Commission created in the wake of the Rodney King case, found a significant number of Los Angeles police officers consistently ignoring department policies on the use of force. Explanations for such practices are discussed by Kappler, Sluder, and Alpert in their book, *Forces of Deviance: Understanding the Dark Side of Policing.* They also point out in their discussion of the King case that in most brutality cases, the state's characterizations of the victim divert attention from the officer's impropriety to the victim's impropriety. A 1999 research report of the National Institute of Justice, *Use of Force by Police,* reminds us that only a small percentage of police–public encounters involve force, that it is used infrequently by police, most typically at low levels (shoving, pushing, etc.), and, though more research is needed, "a small proportion of officers are disproportionately involved in use-of-force incidents" (9). Yet, because measures such as the incidence of lawsuits and/or citizen complaints are critically flawed, the real incidence of excessive or abusive uses of force by the police are not known with any research confidence.

The Louima case suggests that, from a legal perspective, conduct that is shocking to the conscience will be punished and generally not tolerated even in the insular police society. It gives no encouragement to notions that the line between the use of force and abusive use of traditional force can be easily drawn. In many ways, the Louima case, given the frequent equating of Volpe's actions to torture, appears as the exception that proves the rule in respect to the code of silence if one believes Louima was also roughed up during his transport to the police station; police witnesses were found on the issue of Volpe's actions, but none testified about the car beatings. Some have suggested that police are viewed as especially credible by juries because of the position of trust they hold and that juries are willing to give police latitude in their conduct. Alexa Freeman, in her 1996 study of police brutality cases, surmised that police may "comprise the only class of criminal defendants who are universally accorded the legally required presumption of innocence" (Freeman 1996, 726)

I think the prosecution's culture of violence argument, while not legally persuasive, is factually persuasive. No one stopped Volpe or reported him, even as he pranced around the precinct. Perhaps the extent of Louima's injuries were unknown, but his harassment was clear. It is hard to believe a person would violate Louima in the way Volpe did in a police precinct station, no matter how stressed or psychologically unique Volpe may have been without an expectation that street justice of almost any kind would be tolerated. Yet George Kelling is right, too. If street justice is a policeman engaging in the reasonable exercise of discretion in the exercise of his duties, it ought not to be discouraged. Honing the deterrence force of state and federal laws, internal investigation units, civilian review board procedures, and political responsibility will not end the phenomenon of police brutality as long as we live in a society that relies on police force to maintain domestic peace and order.

REFERENCES*

Barker, T. and Carter, D.L. (1994). *Police Deviance,* 3rd ed. Cincinnati, OH: Anderson Publishing Company.

Barstow, D. "The Code of Silence." *New York Times,* 3 June 1999: B6.

Barstow, D. "Even After Volpe's Guilty Plea, Jurors Doubted Louima's Word Alone." *New York Times,* 9 June 1999: B9.

Barstow, D. "112 Officers Accused of Lying to F.B.I. on Louima Inquiry." *New York Times,* 22 June 1999: B3.

Barstow, D. and Flynn, K. "Officer Who Broke the Code of Silence Defies Labels." *New York Times,* 15 May 1999: B1–2.

Conlon, E. (1997). "Men in Blue: Why Do Cops Go Berserk?" *The New Yorker,* 73 (September 29): 10–11.

Dunham, R.G. and Alpert, G.P. (1993). *Critical Issues in Policing: Contemporary Readings.* Prospect Heights, IL: Waveland Press.

Editor (1997). "Bad Cops, Good Cops." *The New Republic,* (September 8) 217: 10–11.

Flynn, K. and Roane, K.R. "No One Cries 'Rat' as Officers Take Stand in Louima Trial." *New York Times,* 23 May 1999: 29, 35.

Freeman, A.P., (1996) "Unscheduled Departures: The Circumvention of Just Sentencing for Police Brutality." *Hastings Law Journal,* 47: 677-727.

Fried, J.P. (1999). "Prosecution Rests in the Louima Case." *New York Times,* 28 May 1999: A1, B6.

Fried, J.P. (1999). "'Depraved' Night Detailed at Close of Louima Trial." *New York Times,* 3 June 1999: B1, 6.

Fried, J.P. "Defense in Louima Brutality Case Maintains Torturer Acted Alone." *New York Times,* 4 June 1999: B1, 6.

Fried, J.P. "Prosecutors Argue Against Dismissing Conspiracy Charge in Louima Case." *New York Times,* 4 September 1999: B3.

Hamblett, M. "Louima Jury Convicts One Officer, Acquits 3." *New York Law Journal* (9 June 1999): 1,4.

Horowitz, C. (1997). "Show of Force." *New York,* (September 22) 30: 28,30,31,33–37.

*David T. Stark, a SUNY-Brockport student, provided valuable bibliographic assistance to the author.

Kappeler, V.E., Sluder, R.D., and Alpert, G.P. (1994). *Forces of Deviance: Understanding the Dark Side of Policing.* Prospect Heights, IL: Waveland Press.

National Institute of Justice (1999). *"Broken Windows" and Police Discretion.* Washington, D.C.: U.S. Department of Justice.

(1999). *Use of Force By Police: Overview of National and Local Data.* Washington, D.C.: U.S. Department of Justice.

Sengupta, S. "Flatbush Immigrants Call Result Neither Outrage Nor Triumph." *New York Times,* 9 June 1999: A28.

Senkel, T.A., (1999). "Civilians Often Need Protection From the Police: Let's Handcuff Police Brutality." *New York Law School Journal of Human Rights,* XV, 385–420.

Smith, C. (1997). "The Police Police." *New York,* (September 22) 30: 32,33.

Staff (1997). "Only a Minority: Police Brutality." *The Economist(US),* (August 23), 344: 19.

Staff. "Chronology of Events in Brooklyn Torture Case." *Newsday,* 21 August 1997: A32.

Staff. "Juror's Views on the Police Department." *New York Times,* 4 June 1999: B6.

Wallance, G.J. (1999). "James Madison and Abner Louima." *New York Law Journal,* (June 19): 2.

White, J. (1999). "The White Wall of Silence: Fellow Cops Testified Against Justin Volpe, But Why Did It Take Them So Long?" *Time* (June 7) 153: 63.

ARTICLE 17

CRIMINAL LAW—THE RIGHT TO RUN: DEADLY FORCE AND THE FLEEING FELON. *TENNESSEE V. GARNER,* 105 S. CT. 1694 (1985).

Michael D. Greathouse

I. INTRODUCTION

The Supreme Court held in *Tennessee v. Garner*[1] that the use of deadly force on an unarmed fleeing felony suspect is unconstitutional. The case involved a burglary suspect who was killed by police as he fled. The district court held the shooting justifiable under Tennessee law, which allowed the use of deadly force on a suspected felon if there was no other means to prevent the suspect's escape.[2] The Court of Appeals for the Sixth Circuit reversed on grounds that the Tennessee statute violated the fourth and fourteenth amendments by authorizing the killing of an unarmed, nondangerous, fleeing felon to prevent his escape.[3] On appeal, the Supreme Court affirmed the decision, holding that the use of deadly force on an unarmed, nondangerous fleeing felon was an unconstitutional violation of the fourth amendment's protection against unreasonable seizures.[4]

Tennessee v. Garner established that the use of deadly force to stop a fleeing felony suspect must meet the fourth amendment's test of reasonableness, which requires a balancing of public interest and private rights.[5] The Court

---

[1] 105 S. Ct. 1694 (1985).

[2] *Id.* at 1698.

[3] Garner v. Memphis Police Dep't, 710 F.2d 240 (6th Cir. 1983).

[4] *Garner,* 105 S. Ct. at 1701.

[5] *Id.* at 1702; *see also* United States v. Place, 462 U.S. 696, 703 (1983) ("We must balance the nature and quality of the intrusion on the individual's Fourth Amendment interests against the importance of the governmental interests alleged to justify the intrusion.").

Michael D. Greathouse, "The Right to Run: Deadly Force and the Fleeing Felon, Tennesse v. Garner, 105 S. Ct. 1694 (1985) (as appeared in *Southern Illinois University Law Journal,* Vol. 11, 1986, pp. 171–184). Reprinted by permission from the *Southern Illinois University Law Journal,* Southern Illinois University School of Law, Carbondale, Illinois 62901-6804.

held that deadly force would be justified only if "it is necessary to prevent the escape and the officer has probable cause to believe that the suspect poses a significant threat of death or serious physical injury to the officer or others."[6] The constitutional standard set by the Court is much too restrictive and allows individual states little discretion or flexibility in determining what level of protection they wish to accord a fleeing felon within the boundaries of the fourth amendment. The Court has essentially made a public policy decision in the guise of constitutional adjudication. Further, the standard adopted by the Court is ambiguously defined. Only when the officer can determine, within the split second he has to fire, that the suspect poses a threat of death or serious harm to others can he use deadly force. Also, the Court did not outline what factors would indicate such "probable cause" that a suspect poses a significant threat of death or serious harm.[7] This narrowly drawn standard, combined with the ambiguity of when that standard will be met, effectively creates a right to run for many felony suspects.[8]

This case note analyzes the decision in *Tennessee v. Garner* and critically examines the standard the Court adopted for the use of deadly force. First, the background law on the use of deadly force is briefly reviewed, including the old common-law standard and how various constitutional challenges to this rule have been handled by the courts. Second, facts of the case are outlined and the specific holdings and reasonings of both the majority and the dissent are discussed. Finally, the applicability of the fourth amendment, the soundness of the standard adopted by the Court, and that standard's potential effects and ramifications are critically analyzed.

II. BACKGROUND

A. The Common Law Rule

The common-law rule allowed the use of whatever force was necessary to effect the arrest of a fleeing felony suspect,[9] including deadly force, but prohibited the use of deadly force on a misdemeanant.[10] The primary reason for this rule was that, at common law, all felonies[11] were punishable by death.[12] Additionally, felons were considered especially dangerous[13] and, given the lack of an organized police network at the time, if a felon escaped, he would most

---

[6]*Garner,* 105 S. Ct. at 1697.

[7]*Id.* at 1712 (O'Connor, J., dissenting).

[8]*Id.* at 1707.

[9]United States v. Clark, 31 F. 710, 713 (6th Cir. 1887).

[10]*Id.*

[11]The common-law felonies were murder, manslaughter, rape, arson, burglary, robbery, larceny, mayhem, sodomy, and escape when imprisoned for a felony. I R. Anderson, Wharton's Criminal Law and Procedure § 28 (1957).

[12]Comment, *Deadly Force to Arrest: Triggering Constitutional Review,* 11 Harv. C.R.-C.L. L. Rev. 361, 365 (1976) ("the use of deadly force was seen as merely accelerating the penal process").

[13]*Id.*

likely elude capture.[14] The common-law vein was that a felon had already forfeited his life when he committed the crime.[15]

B. Modern Acceptance of Common Law

At the time of the *Garner* decision, the common-law rule was still in acceptance in almost half the states. Nineteen states have codified the common-law rule and the courts of four other states have adopted it as well.[16] Two states have adopted the Model Penal Code approach[17] which authorizes the use of deadly force on a fleeing felony suspect only when the officer believes that: (1) the crime in question involved the use or the threatened use of deadly force, or (2) there is a substantial risk that the suspect will cause death or serious bodily harm to others if not apprehended.[18] Eighteen other states have adopted a rule that deadly force ran be used only if the suspect has committed

---

[14]*Id.*

[15]Petrie v. Cartwright, 114 Ky. 103, 70 S.W. 297, 299 (1902); Note, *Substantive Due Process and the Use of Deadly Force Against the Fleeing Felon:* Wiley v. Memphis Police Department *and* Mattis v. Schnarr, 7 CAP. U.L. REV. 497, 498 (1978).

[16]States enacting the common law by statute include: ALA. CODE § 13A-3-27 (1982); ARK. STAT. ANN. § 41-510 (1977); CAL. PENAL CODE ANN. § 196 (West 1970); CONN. GEN. STAT. § 53a-22 (1985); FLA. STAT. § 776.05 (1976); IDAHO CODE § 19-610 (Supp. 1986); IND. CODE § 35 41-3-3(b) (Supp. 1981); KAN. STAT. ANN. § 21-3215 (1981); MISS. CODE ANN. § 97-3-15(d) (Supp. 1985); MO. REV. STAT. § 563.046 (1979); NEV. REV. STAT. § 200.140 (1985); N.M. STAT. ANN. § 30-2-6 (1984); OKLA. STAT. tit. 21, § 732 (1983); ORE. REV. STAT. § 161.239 (1985); R.I. GEN. LAWS § 12-7-9 (1981); S.D. CODIFIED LAWS §§ 22-16-32, -33 (1979); TENN. CODE ANN. § 40-7 108 (Supp. 1985); WASH. REV. CODE § 9A.16.040 (1977). Wisconsin's statute is ambiguous, but should probably be added to this list. WIS. STAT. § 939.45(4) (1981–1982) (officer may use force necessary for "a reasonable accomplishment of a lawful arrest"). *But see* Clark v. Ziedonis, 368 F. Supp. 544 (Wis. 1973), *aff'd on other grounds,* 513 F.2d 79 (7th Cir. 1975).

States which have adopted the common law judicially include: Michigan, Ohio, Virginia, and West Virginia. Werner v. Hartfelder, 113 Mich. App. 747, 318 N.W.2d 825 (1982); State v. Foster, 60 Ohio Misc. 46, 59-66, 396 N.E.2d 246, 255-58 (1979) (citing cases); Berry v. Hamman, 203 Va. 596, 125 S.E.2d 851 (1962); Thompson v. Norfolk & W. Ry. Co., 116 W. Va. 705, 711-12, 182 S.E. 880, 883-84 (1935).

[17]HAWAII REV. STAT. § 703-307 (1976); NEB. REV. STAT. § 28-1412 (1985).

[18]MODEL PENAL CODE § 3.07(2)(b) (1962) states:

(b) The use of deadly force is not justifiable under this Section unless:

(i) the arrest is for a felony; and

(ii) the person effecting the arrest is authorized to act as a peace officer or is assisting a person whom he believes to be authorized to act as a peace officer; and

(iii) the actor believes that the force employed creates no substantial risk of injury to innocent persons; and

(iv) the actor believes that:

(1) the crime for which the arrest is made involved conduct including the use or threatened use of deadly force; or

(2) there is a substantial risk that the person to be arrested will cause death or serious bodily harm if his apprehension is delayed.

a felony involving deadly force or is likely to pose a threat of serious bodily harm if not apprehended.[19]

Many state courts have been reluctant to give a fleeing felon more protection than that under the common-law doctrine. This decision usually comes under the guise of "legislative deference." For instance, the Minnesota Supreme Court discussed at length the standard for using deadly force on a fleeing suspect in *Schumann v. McGinn*.[20] The plaintiff had stolen a car and taken flight after it had collided with another car. After repeated warnings to halt, the suspect was shot and seriously injured by police.[21] In rejecting plaintiff's argument that the Model Penal Code approach should be adopted, the court held that the determination of whether this policy should be adopted was a question for the state legislature and not the courts.[22]

The Supreme Judicial Court of Maine also bowed to the legislature in *Hilton v. State*.[23] A state trooper, while attempting to serve an arrest warrant on a suspect, shot and killed him when he attempted to escape and evade arrest. A panel of three justices, sitting without a jury, decided to follow the Model Penal Code approach in ruling for the plaintiff.[24] The Supreme Judicial Court of Maine reversed, holding that the common-law standard was the governing rule in Maine and that the adoption of any other standard should be left to the state legislature.[25]

C. The Common-Law Rule and the Constitution

Until *Garner,* the courts were split on whether the Constitution protected fleeing felons and, if so, under what standard that protection was afforded. The first standard, the "compelling interest" standard, was adopted in *Mattis v.*

---

[19]ALASKA STAT. § 11.81.370(a) (1983); ARIZ. REV. STAT. ANN. § 13-410 (1978); COLO. REV. STAT. § 18-1-707 (1978); DEL. CODE ANN. tit. 11, § 467 (1979) (felony involving physical force and a substantial risk that the suspect will cause death or serious bodily injury or will never be recaptured); GA. CODE ANN. § 26-901 (1983); ILL. REV. STAT. ch. 38, § 7-5 (1984); IOWA CODE § 804.8 (1979) (suspect has used or threatened deadly force in commission of a felony, or would use deadly force if not caught); KY. REV. STAT. § 503.090 (1985) (suspect committed felony involving use or threatened use of physical force likely to cause death or serious injury, and is likely to endanger life unless apprehended without delay); ME. REV. STAT. ANN. tit. 17-A, § 107 (1983) (commentary states that deadly force may be used only where an officer is defending himself or another against use of such force or "where the person to be arrested poses a threat to human life"); MINN. STAT. § 609.066 (1984); N.H. REV. STAT. ANN. § 627:5(II) (Supp. 1983); N.J. STAT. ANN. § 2C:3-7 (West 1982); N.Y. PENAL LAW § 35.30 (McKinney Supp. 1984-1985); N.C. GEN. STAT. § 15A-401(d)(2) (1983); N.D. CENT. CODE § 12.1-05-07(2Xd) (1985); PA. STAT. ANN. tit. 18, § 508 (Purdon 1983); TEX. PENAL CODE ANN. § 9.5 1(c) (Vernon 1974); UTAH CODE ANN. § 76-2-404 (Supp. 1986).

[20]307 Minn. 446, 240 N.W.2d 525 (1976).

[21]*Id.* at 448-49, 240 N.W.2d at 528.

[22]*Id.* at 467-68, 240 N.W.2d at 537.

[23]348 A.2d 242 (Me. 1975).

[24]*Id.* at 243.

[25]*Id.* at 247.

Schnarr.[26] *Mattis* involved the burglary of a golf driving range office. Fleeing the scene, the suspect was shot after he failed to heed a warning to Stop.[27]

The petitioner argued that the suspect had been deprived of his life without due process and denied equal protection under the law in violation of the fourteenth amendment.[28] The United States Court of Appeals for the Eighth Circuit held that the right to life was a fundamental right and therefore Missouri's fleeing felon statutes[29] could only be sustained if they could be shown to be protecting a compelling state interest.[30] Since the state could not demonstrate the existence of an interest equivalent to, or greater than, the fleeing felon's right to life, it could not justify the use of deadly force on all fleeing felons.[31] Based on this, the court of appeals held Missouri's fleeing felon statutes unconstitutional.[32] The court further held the statutes in violation of the equal protection clause since they incorrectly created a conclusive presumption that all fleeing felons posed a danger to the bodily security of the officers and the public.[33] The dissent in *Mattis* was highly critical of the majority for embarking on a new course which should have been left to the legislature,[34] holding that there is no constitutional right to flee from officers lawfully exercising their authority in apprehending fleeing felons.[35]

The *Mattis* "compelling interest" standard was expressly rejected by the Sixth Circuit in *Wiley v. Memphis Police Department,*[36] a Missouri case in which a youth was shot and killed when he fled the scene of a sporting goods store burglary.[37] After his repeated warnings to halt were ignored, the officer fired at and killed the suspect.[38] Plaintiff brought suit alleging violations of the suspect's fifth and fourteenth amendment rights.[39] The court declined to follow *Mattis* and stated that the *Mattis* rule "extends to the felon unwarranted protection, at the expense of the unprotected public."[40] The court in *Wiley* held

---

[26]547 F.2d 1007 (8th Cir. 1976), *vacated as moot per curiam sub nom.* Ashcroft v. Mattis, 431 U.S. 171 (1977).

[27]*Mattis,* 547 F.2d at 1009.

[28]*Id.*

[29]MO. ANN. STAT. § 559.040 and 544.190 (Vernon 1976).

[30]*Mattis,* 547 F.2d at 1019.

[31]*Id.*

[32]*Id.* at 1020.

[33]*Id.* at 1019.

[34]*Id.* at 1021-22 (Gibson, C.J., dissenting).

[35]*Id.* at 1023.

[36]548 F.2d 1247 (6th Cir. 1977).

[37]*Id.* at 1248-49.

[38]*Id.* at 1249.

[39]*Id.* at 1248.

[40]*Id.* at 1252.

that determining the proper use of deadly force was a matter for the state legislatures.[41]

Another standard was established in *Jenkins v. Averett*,[42] in which a fourth amendment analysis was used for the first time. A suspect took flight and was shot by police.[43] The suspect brought suit for damages under 42 U.S.C. section 1983. The United States Court of Appeals for the Fourth Circuit held that the fourth amendment's[44] protection against unreasonable searches and seizures included a person's physical integrity.[45] The court held that the plaintiffs constitutional rights had been violated since he had been subjected to excessive force unreasonable under the circumstances.[46]

Not all courts have agreed, however, that these constitutional grounds should be forced on the states. *Jones v. Marshall*[47] was a Connecticut case in which a suspect was killed by police as he fled the scene of an auto theft.[48] The United States Court of Appeals for the Second Circuit ruled that, while there was a discernible trend away from the common-law rule, and while a rule limiting the use of deadly force to situations where the crime involved threats of death or serious bodily harm would be preferable, such a rule should not be imposed on the states by federal Courts.[49]

III. EXPOSITION

A. Facts

On October 3, 1974, at approximately 11:00 p.m., two Memphis police officers answered a call about a possible burglary. Upon arriving at the scene, one of the officers, Elton Hymon, went around to the back of the house. As he did so, he heard a door slam and saw Edward Garner run away from the house through the back yard. Officer Hymon was unsure whether Garner was armed although he did testify that he "figured" Garner was armed. Hymon also did not know if there were any accomplices in the house.[50]

Officer Hymon identified himself and ordered the suspect to halt. Garner then sprang to the top of a fence at the rear of the yard to climb over it. Hymon, convinced that if Garner made it over the fence he would elude capture, and having no other means to prevent his escape, fired his pistol at him. Garner was mortally wounded and died on the operating table at the hospital.[51]

---

[41]*Id.* at 1253.

[42]424 F.2d 1228 (4th Cir. 1970).

[43]*Id.* at 1230-31.

[44]"The right of the people to be secure in their persons . . . against unreasonable searches and seizures, shall not be violated . . . ." U.S. CONST. amend. IV.

[45]*Jenkins,* 424 F.2d at 1232.

[46]*Id.*

[47]528 F.2d 132 (2d Cir. 1975).

[48]*Id.* at 134.

[49]*Id.* at 139-40.

[50]*Garner,* 105 S. Ct. at 1697.

[51]*Id.*

The deceased's father, the appellee, filed suit for alleged violations of Garner's constitutional rights.[52] The District Court for the Western District of Tennessee upheld the state statute which authorized Hymon, as an officer, to "use all necessary means to affect the arrest"[53] if a suspect resisted or fled.[54] As construed by Tennessee courts, the statute allowed the use of deadly force if the officer had probable cause to believe the person had committed a felony, warned the person that he intended to arrest him, and reasonably believed that no other means would have prevented escape.[55] The Court of Appeals for the Sixth Circuit reversed on grounds that the statute violated the fourth amendment's guarantee against unreasonable seizures.[56] The court reasoned that the killing of a suspect was a "seizure" under the fourth amendment[57] and was therefore constitutional only if it was reasonable.[58] The court held the Tennessee statute unconstitutional as applied to this case because it did not adequately distinguish between felonies of different magnitudes and that "the facts, as found, did not justify the use of deadly force under the Fourth Amendment."[59]

B. The Majority Opinion

The issue the Supreme Court faced was whether the Tennessee statute violated the fourth amendment's requirement that seizures must be reasonable. The Court held the statute unconstitutional insofar as it authorized the use of deadly force against an apparently unarmed, nondangerous fleeing felon.[60] The Court further held that "[deadly] force may not be used unless it is necessary to prevent the escape and the officer has probable cause to believe that

---

[52]The action was brought under 42 U.S.C. § 1983 which states:

Every person who, under color of any statute, ordinance, regulation, custom, or usage, of any State or Territory or the District of Columbia, subjects, or causes to be subjected, any citizen of the United States or other person within the jurisdiction thereof to the deprivation of any rights, privileges, or immunities secured by the Constitution and laws, shall be liable to the party injured in any action at law, suit in equity, or other proper proceeding for redress. For the purposes of this section, any Act of Congress applicable exclusively to the District of Columbia shall be considered to be a statute of the District of Columbia.

[53]TENN. CODE ANN. § 40-7-108 (1982) ("Resistance to officer.—If, after notice of the intention to arrest the defendant, he either flee or forcibly resist, the officer may use all the necessary means to effect the arrest.").

[54]*Garner,* 105 S. Ct. at 1698.

[55]*See* Johnson v. State, 173 Tenn. 134, 114 S.W.2d 819 (1938) (court held that such force could not be used against those suspected of committing a misdemeanor).

[56]Garner v. Memphis Police Dep't, 710 F.2d 240, 246 (6th Cir. 1983).

[57]*Id.* at 243.

[58]*Id.*

[59]*Id.* at 246.

[60]*Garner,* 105 S. Ct. at 1701.

the suspect poses a significant threat of death or serious physical injury to the officer or others."[61]

The majority reasoned that, while it is not clear what degree of police interference constitutes a seizure, the apprehension of a suspect by the use of deadly force clearly is a seizure.[62] The fourth amendment requires that seizures be "reasonable," and the Court has held that reasonableness depends not only on when a seizure is made, but also how it is carried out.[63] To determine whether a seizure is reasonable, the interests of the public must be balanced against the quality of intrusion on the rights of the individual.[64]

In balancing public versus private interests, the Court weighed society's interest in effective law enforcement and the importance of deadly force as an attribute of such enforcement against the individual's interest in his own life and society's interest in obtaining a judicial determination of guilt and punishment.[65] Because many police department policies forbid the use of deadly force against nonviolent suspects,[66] the Court concluded that there was substantial doubt that the use of such force was a necessary attribute of police arrest power.[67] Also, noting that "[t]he intrusiveness of a seizure by means of deadly force is unmatched,"[68] the Court concluded that the use of deadly force to stop all fleeing suspects was constitutionally unreasonable.[69] Similarly, the Court stated that "[w]here the suspect poses no immediate threat to the officer and no threat to others, the harm resulting from failing to apprehend him does not justify the use of deadly force to do so."[70]

One of the petitioner's arguments was that the fourth amendment had to be construed in light of the old common-law rule. The petitioners pointed out that the common-law rule was the prevailing rule when the fourth amendment was adopted and for sometime thereafter. Moreover, it was still the rule in many states. Therefore, the common-law rule had to be "reasonable."[71] The Court stated, however, that, while it was true that the common law was often looked to when evaluating reasonableness, it had not "simply frozen into constitutional law those law enforcement practices that existed at the time of the Fourth Amendment's passage."[72]

---

[61]*Id.* at 1697.

[62]*Id.* at 1699 (citing United States v. Mendenhall, 446 U.S. 544 (1980)).

[63]*Garner,* 105 S. Ct. at 1699 (citing United States v. Ortiz, 422 U.S. 891, 895 (1975)).

[64]*Garner,* 105 S. Ct. at 1699 (citing United States v. Place, 462 U.S. 696, 703 (1983)).

[65]*Garner,* 105 S. Ct. at 1700.

[66]*Id.* at 1701 ("The fact is that a majority of police departments in this country have forbidden the use of deadly force against nonviolent suspects.").

[67]*Id.*

[68]*Id.* at 1700.

[69]*Id.* at 1701.

[70]*Id.*

[71]*Id.* at 1701-02.

[72]*Id.* at 1702 (quoting Payton v. New York, 445 U.S. 573, 591 n.33 (1980)).

There are many felonies today that are no longer punishable by death, and numerous misdemeanors today involve conduct more dangerous than some felonies. Therefore, the Court concluded that "reliance on the common-law rule in this case would be a mistaken literalism that ignores the purposes of a historical inquiry."[73]

C. The Dissenting Opinion

Justice O'Connor, in dissent, framed the issue as whether the Constitution allows the use of deadly force as a last resort to apprehend a criminal suspect fleeing the scene of a nighttime residential burglary.[74] She criticized the majority for going beyond the specific circumstances of the case at hand and ruling on the constitutional validity of the Tennessee statute in general.[75] Justice O'Connor concluded that the use of deadly force under the given circumstances was not constitutionally unreasonable.[76]

Justice O'Connor agreed with the majority that shooting a suspect was a seizure subject to the reasonableness requirement of the fourth amendment. She disagreed, however, with the majority's outcome. The public has a substantial interest in apprehending burglary suspects because of the serious nature of the crime.[77] Further, there is a high potential for violence associated with burglaries which creates an unreasonable risk of death or serious bodily harm.[78] The public has a compelling interest in preventing burglary because it is such a dangerous felony, even if it necessitates using deadly force to apprehend a fleeing suspect.[79] Also, the majority's argument concerning police department policies forbidding the use of deadly force is not the test of constitutional validity.[80]

Justice O'Connor further argued that the suspect himself put his life at risk by perpetrating the crime and then disobeying a valid police order to halt.[81] Certainly, the suspect has a substantial interest in his life, but that interest does not include the right to flee unimpeded from the scene of a burglary.[82] Therefore, the Tennessee statute adequately protects the suspect's legitimate interest in his own life because all he need do to avoid losing it is obey a valid police order to halt.[83] Based on this reasoning, Justice O'Connor

---

[73] *Garner,* 105 S. Ct. at 1702.

[74] *Id.* at 1708-09 (O'Connor, J., dissenting).

[75] *Id.* at 1708.

[76] *Id.* at 1709-10.

[77] *Id.* at 1709.

[78] *Id.*

[79] *Id.* at 1709-10.

[80] *Id.* at 1710.

[81] *Id.*

[82] *Id.*

[83] *Id.* at 1710-11.

concluded that "[a] proper balancing of the interests involved suggests that use of deadly force as a last resort to apprehend a criminal suspect fleeing from the scene of a nighttime burglary is not unreasonable within the meaning of the Fourth Amendment."[84]

The majority's holding was additionally criticized because of the failure to offer any guidance as to what objects, used by a fleeing felon, would constitute a significant threat to others and would justify the use of deadly force.[85] Further, the majority failed to outline factors which would constitute probable cause that a suspect posed a significant threat of serious harm to others.[86]

IV. ANALYSIS

A. Introduction

The Supreme Court held in *Tennessee* v. *Garner* that the use of deadly force to apprehend a fleeing felony suspect is a "seizure" under the fourth amendment and, therefore, subject to the fourth amendment's test of reasonableness.[87] Determining whether a seizure is reasonable requires balancing "the nature and quality of the intrusion on the individual's Fourth Amendment interests against the importance of the governmental interests alleged to justify the intrusion."[88] The interests the Court considered in reaching its decision were the public's interest in effective law enforcement and the individual's interest in his own life.[89] The Court held that deadly force would be justified only if "it is necessary to prevent the escape and the officer has probable cause to believe that the suspect poses a significant threat of death or serious physical injury to the officer or others."[90]

The standard adopted by the Court for determining when deadly force would be justified to apprehend a fleeing felon is essentially the same as the Model Penal Code standard.[91] Both the Supreme Court's rule and the Model Penal Code rule embody the same principle: deadly force should only be used where there is reason to believe that the suspect will cause death or serious harm to others if not apprehended.

---

[84]*Id.* at 1711.

[85]*Id.* at 1712 ("Police are given no guidance for determining which objects, among an array of potentially lethal weapons ranging from guns to knives to baseball bats to rope, will justify the use of deadly force.").

[86]*Id.*

[87]*Garner,* 105 S. Ct. at 1699.

[88]*Place,* 402 U.S. at 703.

[89]*Garner,* 105 S. Ct. at 1700.

[90]*Id.* at 1697.

[91]*See supra* note 18 and accompanying text.

B. Arguments Against Application of Constitutional Limitations

The highest court in numerous states and several federal courts of appeals have held that the determination of when deadly force should be justified is a question more appropriately addressed by state legislatures than courts.[92] The question of when deadly force should be used on a fleeing suspect and the competing interests of effective law enforcement and the suspect's interest in his life have been hotly debated.[93] The nature of the debate reveals that one's view on when deadly force should be justified "is likely to be a highly ideological matter, turning upon one's philosophy of law enforcement."[94] Even among the Model Penal Code drafters there was a "strongly expressed controversy as to how the balance should be struck between the necessities of effective law enforcement and our society's dedication to the sanctity of human life."[95] This led the court in *Hinton* to conclude:

> modification of the common law principle . . . is an undertaking fraught with so high a degree of sensitivity and potential gravity of consequences that the evaluation of all the factors involved, theoretical and pragmatic, is appropriately the function not of the judiciary but of the Legislature as the most directly responsible representatives of the people best equipped to act with the minuteness or expansiveness, the rigidity or flexibility desirable to mesh current law with current needs.[96]

Courts faced with attacks on the common-law rule have consistently held that modification of that rule presents a policy question for the legislature, not the judiciary.[97] State legislatures are the appropriate forums to address issues of public policy and to arrive at a balance between the competing interests of effective law enforcement and a suspect's interest in his life. "It is clearly the prerogative of the state legislature to decide whether such restrictions on the use of [deadly] force are consonant with public policy."[98] The Tennessee statute reflects a determination that the use of deadly force in prescribed circumstances will generally serve to protect the public.[99] After considering the potential consequences and ramifications of the common-law

---

[92]*See Mattis,* 547 F.2d at 1021 (Gibson, C.J., dissenting).

[93]*Schumann,* 307 Minn. at 465, 240 N.W.2d at 536 (1976).

[94]*Id.*

[95]*Hinton,* 348 A.2d at 246 (Me. 1975).

[96]*Id.*

[97]Jones v. Marshall, 528 F.2d 132 (2d Cir. 1975); Cunningham v. Ellington, 323 F. Supp. 1072 (W.D. Tenn. 1971) (three-judge court); Hilton v. State, 348 A.2d 242 (Me. 1975); Schumann v. McGinn, 307 Minn. 446, 240 N.W.2d 525 (1976).

[98]Wiley v. Memphis Police Dep't, 548 F.2d 1247, 1253 (6th Cir.), *cert. denied,* 434 U.S. 822 (1977).

[99]*Garner,* 105 S. Ct. at 1710 (O'Connor, J., dissenting).

rule, the Tennessee legislature decided that the statute represented the desired balance between the interests of the public and the interests of the suspect.

Furthermore, as the Minnesota Supreme Court has pointed out: "While the court has the right and the duty to modify rules of the common law after they have become archaic, we readily concede that the flexibility of the legislative process—which is denied the judiciary—makes the latter avenue of approach more desirable."[100] State legislatures, according to this line of reasoning, are in a much better position to evaluate and investigate the issues involved in the use of deadly force on fleeing suspects and are the appropriate forum for deciding what the rule should be.[101]

C. The Constitutional Standard Adopted by the Supreme Court Is Too Restrictive

The Supreme Court has the responsibility of determining when the use of deadly force is permissible under the fourth amendment. The petitioner in *Garner* argued that, because the common-law rule prevailed at the time the fourth amendment was adopted, and for sometime thereafter, the use of deadly force must be reasonable.[102] The Court rejected this, pointing out that constitutional standards must change to meet society's changing needs.[103] When society's needs change, the courts have a responsibility to change the rules to reflect these needs. The majority, however, points out that it cannot be said that there is a major trend away from the common-law standard regarding the use of deadly force. This standard is still in force in almost half the United States and has been adopted in many of them fairly recently.[104] Thus, there is little justification for the Court's adoption of a more restrictive rule on the use of deadly force to stop a fleeing suspect.

If the fourth amendment is to apply to the use of deadly force, it should apply in a way which would allow state legislatures the widest possible discretion. The use of deadly force is a highly ideological issue[105] and involves strong public policy questions. While state legislatures cannot set federal constitutional standards, they are the ones most able to resolve the conflicting ideologies.[106] State legislatures are best able to evaluate all the information and public opinion and come to the proper balancing of public and private

---

[100]*Schumann,* 307 Minn. at 467, 240 N.W.2d at 537 (quoting Spanel v. Mounds View School Dist. No. 621, 264 Minn. 279, 292, 118 N.W.2d 795, 803 (1962)).

[101]*Schumann,* 307 Minn. at 467, 240 N.W.2d at 537.

[102]*Garner,* 105 S. Ct. at 1702.

[103]*Id.*

[104]*Garner,* 105 S. Ct. at 1705; *see also Id.* at n.21 (In adopting its current statute in 1979, Alabama expressly chose the common-law rule over more restrictive provisions. ALA. CODE § 13A-3-27 (1982) (commentary). Missouri likewise considered but rejected a proposal similar to the Model Penal Code approach in Mattis v. Schnarr, 547 F.2d 1007, 1022 (8th Cir. 1976) (Gibson, C.J.,dissenting), *vacated as moot sub nom.* Ashcroft v. Mattis, 431 U.S. 171 (1977). Idaho, whose current statute codifies the common-law rule, adopted the Model Penal Code in 1971, but abandoned it in 1972).

[105]*Schumann,* 307 Minn. at 466-67, 240 N.W.2d at 537 (1976).

[106]*Id.*

interests.[107] Therefore, the Supreme Court should adopt a standard that affords the fleeing felon essential constitutional protection, but allows the states as much discretion and flexibility as possible in determining the proper balance of public and private rights under that standard.

D. Failure of the Court to Provide Workable Standards

In drawing the standard for when deadly force is permissible, the Court has intruded into an area more appropriate for legislative action. The standard the Court has drawn has left only a very narrow area where the use of deadly force is justified and, as to the area itself, there is much room for ambiguity and second-guessing in determining when the use of such force is justified. For instance, "police are given no guidance for determining which objects, among an army of potentially lethal weapons ranging from guns to knives to baseball bats to rope, will justify the use of deadly force."[108] Furthermore, the Court fails to outline what additional factors will indicate probable cause so that the suspect poses a significant threat of death or serious harm to others, where the officer has probable cause to arrest, and the suspect refuses to obey an order to halt.[109] It is not always possible to determine whether the felon will use force against others if he is not immediately apprehended.

The Supreme Court has narrowly limited the use of deadly force and ambiguously defined the circumstances where it will be justified. A police officer usually has but a split second to determine whether a suspect poses a threat of serious harm to others, and such a determination is usually made under the most trying of circumstances. Under the Court's rule, if the police officer cannot, within the split second he has to decide, determine that the suspect poses a significant threat of serious harm to others, the suspect must be allowed to escape. The result of this is that a constitutional right to run has been effectively created for many felony suspects.

V. CONCLUSION

The Court in *Tennessee v. Garner* repudiated the common-law rule and established that deadly force is justified only where the officer has probable cause to believe the suspect poses a significant threat of death or serious bodily harm to the officer or others. The question of when deadly force is justified and the balancing of the conflicting interests of effective law enforcement and the sanctity of human life is, however, a matter of public policy still very much in debate. The legislatures of the respective states are the appropriate forums for striking the balance between public and private rights. Further, the standard adopted by the court allows deadly force to be used only under very limited circumstances and leaves a great deal of ambiguity as to what those circumstances are. In so doing, the Court has effectively created a constitutional right to run for many felony suspects.

---

[107]*Id.*

[108]*Garner,* 105 S. Ct. at 1712 (O'Connor, J., dissenting).

[109]*Id.*

ARTICLE 18

FACTORS RELATED TO KILLINGS OF FELONS BY POLICE OFFICERS: A TEST OF THE COMMUNITY VIOLENCE AND CONFLICT HYPOTHESES*

Jonathan R. Sorensen
University of Texas, Pan American

James W. Marquart
Sam Houston State University

Deon E. Brock
University of Texas, Pan American

This paper tests two perspectives on the use of deadly force by police officers: the "community violence" and the "conflict" hypotheses. From descriptive data on felons killed in the Supplemental Homicide Reports it appears that police-caused homicides are predictable responses to acts or threatened acts of violence. An examination of the largest U.S. cities revealed a strong relationship between levels of economic inequality and the rate of felon killing by police officers as well as a weaker, yet consistent relationship between percent black and felon killing, supporting the conflict hypothesis. A relationship exists between violent crime rates and felon killing, but violent crime most often plays an intervening role between other social factors and the rate of felon killing. Our findings suggest that economic inequality should be included in any macro-level explanation of police-caused homicide.

Currently, two perspectives offer seemingly contradictory explanations of the use of deadly force by police officers. According to one perspective, the "conflict" model, the use of deadly force by police officers is not distributed evenly among those policed. Proponents of this model argue that the use of deadly force is influenced by the social standing of the persons involved (Knoohuizen,

---

*Some of the data used in this study were supplied by Glen Pierce and William C. Bailey. The analysis was much improved by the efforts of Bob Wrinkle of the University of Texas-Pan American, three anonymous reviewers, a deputy editor, and the current and former editors of *JQ*.

Fahey, and Palmer 1972; Takagi 1974). Adherents of the conflict model suggest that police officers are more likely to use deadly force against persons who live outside the American mainstream, particularly members of minorities. Some of these observers also charge that police officers use deadly force on those volatile segments of the population which threaten the status quo (Harring et al. 1977). Rather than reacting to situational cues in violent communities, police officers, acting as agents of the ascendant classes, are likely to use deadly force in areas with a great degree of poverty or economic stratification in order to retain the tenuous balance of power existing in those areas (Jacobs and Britt 1979).

According to the other perspective, police officers use deadly force only when necessary. Proponents of this perspective argue that police use of deadly force is limited to situations in which the officer simply responds appropriately to a violent situation (Robins 1963). Closely aligned with this view is the "community violence" hypothesis, which asserts that the level of police violence in any community is a function of the level of violence in that community (Matulia 1985; Sherman and Langworthy 1979). From this perspective, the use of deadly force by police officers is a necessary response to violence typically encountered in the areas they police. Some authors add a subjective, cognitive component to the level of community violence, which takes into account "perceived dangerousness" based on officers' prior experiences or their "occupational personality" (Fyfe 1980, Kania and MacKey 1977; Meyer 1980).

After a review of empirical and theoretical studies on the use of deadly force by police officers, we use national data from the UCR Supplemental Homicide Reports to test the efficacy of these two models. In doing so, we analyze community-level social, economic, and cultural correlates of police-caused homicides in the largest U.S. cities during 1980-1984. This paper goes beyond earlier situational analyses by using data from a large geographical area and a long period of time. By incorporating the community-level variables into multivariate statistical models, we address the broader question of antecedent causes of homicides committed by police officers. Our main concern is which of the two hypotheses is more consistent with the empirical data, or whether the community violence and the conflict hypotheses possibly can be reconciled to offer a more complete explanation of police-caused homicides.

HOMICIDE BY POLICE OFFICERS

Before the 1970s, a widely varying amount of discretion was allowed to individual police officers in their use of deadly force. State statutes were grounded in the common-law doctrine that allowed deadly force in apprehending fleeing felons. Most departments lacked administrative regulations guiding deadly force. During the civil rights movement, the public position on this issue changed: questionable killings of minority-group members by (typically) white police officers often led to racial unrest, civil disorders and even riots. Findings from both the President's Commission in 1967 and The National Commission on Civil Disorders in 1968 supported this relationship. Civil rights activism brought the use of force by police officers into the public spotlight.

The Conflict Hypothesis

Against this backdrop of events, some early observers questioned the necessity of many of the killings. Some authors argued that in official reports, police officers often inflated the level of threat posed by the suspects to give the appearance of necessity to legitimize their shootings (Geller 1982:152). Police officers, they said, could state falsely that the victim threatened them with a weapon. Researchers who have examined police-caused deaths using alternative data sources often conclude that many such deaths are questionable and that some could even be classified as murder or manslaughter (Harding and Fahey 1973; Knoohuizen et al. 1972; Kobler 1975b). Until recently, police departments rarely sanctioned officers for shootings outside the realm of department policy. Furthermore, the coroner's inquest is often perfunctory, and the homicide usually is ruled justifiable. Prosecutors often are unwilling to charge police officers with crimes because of their symbiotic relationship with officers (Sherman and Langworthy 1979).

Because questionable killings often involve minorities, race has become the most controversial offender characteristic correlated with police use of deadly force. Most of the studies examining this characteristic have found the victims of police killings to be disproportionately black.[1] After finding that black men, on the basis of their representation in the population were killed during the 1960s at a rate nine to 10 times higher than that of whites, Takagi concluded that the "threshold of suspicion" for blacks was lower than that for whites when they were encountered by the police. He wrote that police have "one trigger finger for whites and another for blacks" (1974:30). Goldkamp (1976) refers to this as a "quasi-labeling view," which asserts that police single out members of minorities for more severe treatment. Such treatment results in both higher arrest rates and higher homicide rates at the hands of police officers. In a subsequent article Takagi and his colleagues argued that as the United States moves toward advanced stages of capitalism, the police must use more repressive measures to control volatile segments of the population. This situation accounts for the racial disproportionality in police killings (Harring et al. 1977).

The conflict hypothesis also predicts that more coercive measures are necessary to enforce middle-and upper-class norms when society becomes more stratified economically (e.g., Chambliss and Seidman 1971:33). This argument can be tested within a society by comparing the level of economic inequality with the repressive measures used. In order to test this assertion, Jacobs and Britt (1979) analyzed the rates of police-caused homicides per million residents in each state reported in the vital statistics from 1961 through 1970 (used previously in Kania and MacKey 1977). Economic inequality, as measured by the Gini index, was chosen as the preferred indicator of economic stratification to test conflict theory. As a measure of the level of community violence, Jacobs and Britt included an index based on the z-scores of the violent crime rate for

---

[1]An exception is the study by Jacobs and Britt (1979), who found a high zero-order correlation between percent black and police-caused homicides in the 49 states included in their analysis. This relationship, however, was no longer statistically significant when the authors controlled a number of other factors, using multiple regression.

1960 and 1962 and on the number of riots in cities between 1960 and 1969. Controlling for percentage black population, number of police per capita, percent change in population, percentage of residents living in large cities, and two regional variables, they showed through a multiple regression analysis that economic inequality was the most accurate predictor of police homicide rate, followed by the violence index and population change. Although Jacobs and Britt found support for the community violence thesis, they concluded that economic inequality was the most important factor contributing to the level of police-caused homicide.

The Community Violence Hypothesis

Although early studies often questioned the veracity of a number of police homicides, many also supported another perspective. These studies often concluded that in the majority of cases, the use of deadly force by police officers was necessary in response to threatening situations. Early studies found that two-thirds to three-fourths of the incidents involved the use or threatened use of weapons by those who were killed (Binder and Fridell 1984). Other studies noted that persons killed by police officers were almost exclusively male, with a median age of 24 or 25 (Fyfe 1978; Knoohuizen et al. 1972; Kobler 1975a; Robins 1963). These characteristics of offenders are consistent with the distribution of persons engaged in criminal conduct.

Disproportionate involvement in crime by a particular group of offenders obviously increases the group members' chances of being the victims of a police-caused homicide. Such disproportionate involvement is often used to explain the large number of police killings of blacks. Blacks' greater involvement in crimes of violence puts them at greater risk than whites because of a higher number of arrests and apprehensions. This leads, in turn, to a greater incidence of blacks resisting arrest, fleeing, and so on. It is not surprising that 59.6 percent of the victims of justifiable homicides in 57 cities during 1975-1979 were black when we consider that blacks constituted 73.1 percent of the victims of justifiable homicide by citizens; 66.1 percent of homicide arrestees, 71.0 percent of robbery arrestees, 63.7 percent of those arrested for violent crimes, and 57.9 percent of those arrested for weapons violations during the same period (Matulia 1985:34). Seventy percent of those killed by police officers in Chicago during 1974-1978 were black; in explanation of this fact, blacks constituted 72 percent of forcible felony arrests (Geller and Karales 1981:1846). Considering the level of danger (e.g., presence of a weapon, threatened use of a weapon, use of a weapon, other forms of assault), researchers have concluded that blacks are not fired upon disproportionately (Fyfe 1978). Further, studies have found that fatality rates for those fired upon by police officers are not higher for blacks than for whites (Blumberg 1981; Inn, Wheeler, and Sparling 1977).

Although some studies find that blacks are shot more often in elective shootings (e.g., fleeing felons) than in defense of life, these differences may result from the violent areas in which members of minorities live. In these areas, some authors contend, it is expected that police will shoot more unarmed suspects because of the greater level of subjective fear inherent in violent areas rather than because of overt discrimination (Meyer 1980). Findings that black officers are more likely than white officers to shoot a minority-group member

(Matulia 1985:40) are offered as further evidence that the racial disproportionality in shootings is due to the level of violence in the community, particularly because so many of these shootings involve off-duty minority police officers in their own communities (Fyfe 1981).

At the community level, many studies have noted that the level of violence in the community is the strongest predictor of police homicide rates. Fyfe found a correlation between total police shooting rates and arrest rates for violent felonies in the 20 command zones in New York City, which he stated had resulted from higher rates of stress on police officers in these areas (1980:107). He also found a strong correlation between general homicide rates and police shootings; this finding suggests that police shootings are related to public safety. Fyfe characterized some areas of the city as "sleepy hollows" and others as "free fire zones," where community violence, and consequently police violence, were common. He concluded that police shootings are a function of community characteristics: police officers respond to violent communities with violence.

In the 57 largest U.S. cities, Matulia (1985) found strong positive correlations between police-caused homicides and the following variables: general homicides, justifiable homicide by civilians, police officers murdered, robbery, UCR violent crimes, population, and number of officers. He concluded that the most important factor influencing the rate of justifiable homicides by police officers is the level of violence in the community itself, even when organizational characteristics and departmental policies are considered. Also at the city level, Sherman and Langworthy (1979) performed a correlation analysis incidental to studying the veracity of various measures of police-caused homicides. In addition to organizational and policy variables, they examined a number of community characteristic in selected cities during 1974-1976, using both the National Center for Health Statistics (NCHS) vital statistics and alternative data obtained from police departments. The variables related most strongly to the rate of police-caused homicide were the violent index crime rate and the homicide rate (both of which increase police perceptions of danger and thus make a violent response more likely in any given situation) as well as police per 1,000 population and violent arrest rates (both of which increase citizens' exposure to police use of deadly force). They also found that gun density was correlated positively with police homicides, whereas population density, unemployment rates, and suicide rates were not related significantly.

Kania and MacKey (1977) used a number of variables to test class conflict and occupational personality theories at the state level. One measure of class conflict, the size of the welfare recipient group in each state, was correlated positively with police homicides, whereas another indicator, number of riots, was not related. Rejecting the class conflict explanation, Kania and MacKey tested the theory of occupational personality: that is, "the policeman is thought to develop his occupational personality as a part of his learning process on the job, by exposure to various threats and stresses" (1977:35). Hence a greater degree of stress experienced by officers should be related to the rate at which officers respond with violence. Whereas the rates of police exposure to all reported offenses were correlated only modestly with justifiable homicides by police, the exposure of police to violent crimes was correlated highly with justifiable homicide rates. Kania and Mackey concluded that increased levels of stress lead to increased use of violence by the police. They also explored the relationship of justifiable homicides by police to the societal matrix as measured by the seven domains of human activity: nutrition, reproduction, quality of life, safety, recreation, mobility, and education. When stated in the negative, all of the various indices of the societal matrix (e.g., recreation = absence of television in occupied households) were found to be related positively to police homicides. Lack of safety, measured as public homicide rate and police exposure to violent crime, was correlated most highly with the police justifiable homicide rate. Kania and Mackey concluded that police officers react to the community in which they work, and essentially that communities receive the type of policing they deserve.

At the situational level of analysis, the conflict hypothesis predicts a disproportionate killing of minority members by police officers. At the community level of analysis, this hypothesis would be supported by the finding that killings are related to the level of economic inequality and absolute poverty in the community regardless of the level of violence in that community. A relationship between the proportion of blacks in communities and the rate of police killings also would support the conflict hypothesis if this relationship is independent of the level of violence in those communities. The community violence (or perceived dangerousness) hypothesis predicts that members of minorities will be killed by police at a rate commensurate with their risk of being killed by police.

At the situational level of analysis, the perceived dangerousness hypothesis would be supported if the bulk of police killings occurred out of necessity in nonelective shooting situations. At the community level, the community violence hypothesis would be supported by showing that the rate of police killings of felons is related most strongly to the level of violence in a community independent of the level of economic inequality. We test these hypotheses at both the situational level and the community level. This study adds to the literature by using 1) more recent data from 1980 through 1984; 2) the city as the unit of analysis—169 large U.S. cities; 3) UCR Supplemental Homicide Reports as the data source; 4) additional control variables; and 5) ordinary least squares (OLS) regression to predict the rate of felon killings by police.

DATA AND METHODS

Our main source of data is the Supplemental Homicide Reports (SHR) collected from local police departments by the FBI's UCR division. The SHR give details of killings nationwide not available from other sources. These data include individual characteristics of offenders and victims, relationships between victims and offenders, and situational variables such as the weapon used and the location. In the situational analysis we use all 4,419 "killings of felons" by police officers during 1976-1988; in the community-level analysis we use 1,231 cases occurring in large cities during 1980-1984.[2] Whereas many

---

[2]These data were supplied by Glen Pierce of the Social Science Research Center at Northeastern University. The data for 1978 are missing from the tape and therefore are not included here. Further, the coding of "killings of felons" by citizens and by police was transposed in the file, and therefore had to be revised.

of the previous studies on the use of deadly force by police officers included shootings and nonfatal woundings, the SHR data are limited to instances in which the use of deadly force by a police officer resulted in the death of a felon, a small subset of all deadly force episodes.

The reliability and validity of the SHR data have been questioned by Maxfield (1989). Differential reporting practices are one threat to reliability mentioned by Maxfield; coding procedures vary across cities. Some police departments guess at the type of homicide or relationship between offenders and victims in view of the circumstances; others code the "unknown" or "other" categories. Hence cities vary as to the percentage of cases with missing information.[3] It is possible that homicides by police are coded in different manners depending on the police department. A study by Sherman and Langworthy (1979) showed that the number of homicides by police officers in particular cities varied by the data source used. The authors found large differences between police department records and National Center for Health Statistics (NCHS) vital statistics in particular cities; the NCHS underreported by an average of 51 percent. Whereas intercity comparisons of magnitude would not be acceptable with either data source, a comparison of correlations between justifiable homicides and various factors showed substantial agreement between the two groups. Sherman and Langworthy concluded that either data source would be acceptable for correlation analysis. Because the SHR are collected from police departments, the data are more complete than the NCHS data on police-caused homicides. NCHS vital statistics do not include many of the individual and situational variables included in the SHR. For these reasons we chose to use the SHR data for analyzing the situations surrounding police-caused homicide and the rates of such homicide for various cities.

The first stage of analysis involves the use of the SHR data in aggregate form and describes the individual and situational characteristics of police-caused homicides. Unfortunately, an important situational variable considered in prior studies, the victim's conduct before death, is not available in the SHR data. Although this variable might have supplied some valuable insight, the veracity of such data, usually supplied by the assailant, would be open to question (Geller 1982), even if it were available. Also omitted from the SHR data are organizational, policy and legal variables. Organizational factors, policy directives, and local and state law restricting the use of deadly force by police officers have been found to affect significantly the number of questionable and elective shootings by police officers. Possibly these variables predict some of the variance in the use of deadly force by police officers,

---

[3]Studying 195,543 cases of homicide included in the SHR during 1976-1985, Maxfield (1989) noted a large number of cases in "unknown" and "other" categories concerning the type of homicide. He also noted the large number of unknowns in the offender-victim relationship category. Most often when the type of homicide was coded as unknown, the relationship between offender and victim also was unknown. Maxfield questioned the traditional wisdom that homicides overwhelmingly involve acquaintances in conflict situations, and argued instead that most of the cases in the "unknown" and "other" categories involve instrumental homicides in which the offender and the victim are strangers. Such criticism is less applicable to homicides by police officers, in which reporting of the occurrences and details of such offenses should be complete.

independent of the rates of inequality or violence in the communities. Nevertheless, community-level factors influence police policies regarding, and organizational support for, restrictions on the use of deadly force. Indeed, studies that concomitantly examine organizational variables and community variables find community-level variables to be stronger predictors of police use of deadly force (Matulia 1985).

In the second stage of analysis we attempt to find community-level correlates of killings of felons by police officers. States have been used as the unit of analysis in the past, but states are not really communities in any sense of the term. The use of standard metropolitan statistical areas (SMSAs) would introduce error into the analysis by including the suburbs and rural areas. Poverty and economic inequality are the measurements that could be affected most by this approach. When working- and middle-class suburban areas are added to the central city, the impact of poverty is decreased; the addition of wealthy suburban areas increases the impact of inequality (Parker 1989). The level of violence also is affected by including suburban areas. In SMSAs in which a smaller proportion of residents live in central cities than in the suburban areas, the rates of violence and killings of felons (mainly central-city phenomena) are underestimated. Further, many police departments are encompassed within an SMSA; they may have different policies regarding use of deadly force, as well as different recording practices. Therefore we chose the city as the unit of analysis. Although the city is not the most accurate measure of community, it is the smallest unit of analysis available for the dependent variables. Also, it is difficult to predict police use of deadly force; it occurs only infrequently, if at all, in certain areas. Therefore we chose only the largest United States cities over a five-year span. The sample includes all cities of more than 100,000 population at the time of the 1980 census (N = 169).[4] The community-level analysis is restricted to 1980-1984 because some of the measures are available only from the decennial census. The five-year interval also moderates the effect of yearly variation in rates of felon killing.

The dependent variable is the rate of police killings of felons (PkF) per million residents per year. In creating these rates we found it necessary to consider the possibility that some departments did not report data during particular periods. Failure of one of these large departments to report for an entire year is obvious, as in the case of Houston in 1982 and Chicago in 1984, but failure to report for any particular month is more difficult to ascertain. One means of estimating the total rate of PkF on the basis of the available months is to adjust for nonreporting; the UCR follows this practice in reporting rates of general homicide. As suggested by Williams and Flewelling (1987), we created a weighting factor by dividing the number of victims reported in the UCR by the number of victims reported in the SHR. Weights ranged from 1.0 to 1.47 (Houston); most were at or near 1.0. Then we multiplied these weights by the dependent variable (PkF) to achieve more accurate

---

[4]We excluded San Antonio from the sample because this city, with an average population of 837,997, reported no police killings during 1980-1984. After we discussed the problem with members of the San Antonio Police Force homicide and research divisions, the consensus was that an oversight had occurred. Attempts are being made to retrieve the data, but the figures are not readily available.

estimates of the number of such homicides. Next we calculated the yearly rates of police homicides, using the following formula:

$$\frac{PkF \times 1,000,000}{\text{Population of a city}} \Big/ 5 \text{ (years).}$$

We are concerned not with authorities' willingness to consider a homicide justifiable, but with the rates at which police officers are willing to kill those who engage in felonious or presumed felonious conduct. We realize that coding decisions influence the rates of justifiable homicide to some extent; however, killings of felons by police officers are the only homicides that the SHR data by definition are supposed to capture in "killings of felons." These homicides are less amenable to interpretation in coding than other types. Thus a number of variables theoretically can be predicted to cause higher rates of homicides by police officers.

The main independent variables of interest are those which test the conflict and the community violence hypotheses. We chose the Gini index to test the conflict hypothesis, as did Jacobs and Britt (1979).[5] The Gini index is a measure of income disparity based on the Lorenz curve; it is calculated by tabulating the share of the total income earned by residents of a given geographic location for available percentiles of the population (see Allison 1978). Perfect equality would be illustrated by a 45-degree angle, showing a direct linear relationship between cumulative percentage of the population and cumulative percentage of total income. That is, any 10 percent of the population would earn 10 percent of the population's total income, any 20 percent of the population would earn 20 percent of the total income, and so on. Perfect inequality would be depicted by a 90-degree angle, whereby the highest-paid percentile of the population would earn all of the income. The Gini index measures the curve that lies somewhere between these two hypothetical extremes; this curve ranges from 0, a straight line showing no income disparity, to 1, a right angle showing perfect income inequality. In addition to the Gini index, we employ a model including a measure of absolute poverty, percentage living below the poverty level, as in Kania and MacKey (1977), to determine whether either model has an effect on the rate of police killings of felons. In conjunction with this perspective, we also include the percentage black. If the conflict hypothesis is correct, a greater amount of force should be required in areas of economic inequality, poverty, and large minority populations, and should result in higher rates of PkF independent of the level of violence in the community.

We operationalize the community violence hypothesis as the rate of violent crimes, calculated from a yearly average per 100,000 residents during 1980-1984 from the UCR. The number of police per capita is included because more police "provide an increased risk or exposure of citizens to police use of deadly force" (Sherman and Langworthy 1979). Similarly, in densely populated areas, citizens are more likely to be killed when deadly force is used. Both of these variables also address the issue of perceived dangerousness. In

---

[5]The Gini index coefficients for the 169 cities were supplied by William C. Bailey of Cleveland State University.

densely populated areas with larger numbers of police officers, officers may be more likely to perceive certain situations as dangerous and thus as legitimating their use of deadly force. A positive correlation with the rate of PkF would support contentions that police use of deadly force is a justifiable reaction to actual or perceived levels of crime in the community.

We also include a regional control variable coded "southern versus other" according to the U.S. Bureau of the Census classification.[6] The south, for whatever reasons, has always had a higher rate of violence than other regions of the United States. Further, the use of violence by the state against criminals in the form of capital punishment is largely a southern phenomenon (Bowers 1984). Whatever factors operate to make capital punishment a widely used form of social control in the region should also lead to a higher rate of police killing of felons, which has been likened to an execution without a trial (Sherman 1978). Southern location is predicted to have a direct effect on the rate of police killings, as well as an indirect effect through the rate of violent crime.

RESULTS

Individual/Situational

At the individual/situational level of analysis, the national data refute the conflict hypothesis. As in the local studies discussed above, felons killed by police in the SHR during 1976-1988 tended to be young. The median age of victims of justifiable homicide by police officers was 26. In this group, 55.9 percent were under age 30. The felons were overwhelmingly male; females accounted for fewer than 2 percent of the total felons killed. These findings parallel those of earlier studies and also fit the profile of persons engaged in felonies.

Race is one variable of particular concern, which is available to test the hypotheses at the individual/situational level. The majority of PkF involved white felons (54%) and were intraracial: white police officers killed white felons in 51.8 percent of the instances and black felons in 34.6 percent, while black police officers killed black felons in 11 percent of the instances and white felons in 2.6 percent. As noted in previous studies, black police officers killed black felons at a rate twice that of white police officers; more than 80 percent of felons killed by black police officers were black, in contrast to 40 percent of those killed by white officers. A similar pattern exists when other ethnic combinations of police and felons are considered: non-Hispanic police officers killed non-Hispanic felons in 81 percent of the instances and Hispanics in 11.5 percent, whereas Hispanic officers killed Hispanic felons in 4.1 percent of the instances and non-Hispanics in 3.4 percent. This finding appears to support many experts' contention that the application of deadly force by officers is not racially motivated.

---

[6]According to the U.S. Census, the following jurisdictions are coded as southern: Alabama, Arkansas, Delaware, Florida, Georgia, Kentucky, Louisiana, Maryland, Mississippi, North Carolina, Oklahoma, South Carolina, Tennessee, Texas, Virginia, West Virginia, and the District of Columbia.

In order to assess accurately the issue of racial discrimination, however, more information is necessary. Many authors have noted that the situation must be taken into account in testing the discrimination hypothesis. Although few situational characteristics are available in the SHR, the precipitating event may be used to classify shootings as elective or nonelective. The precipitating event listed in the SHR includes the circumstances under which the killing took place (e.g., felon attacked officer, felon attacked fellow officer, felon attacked citizen, felon fled, felon shot in crime, felon resisted arrest). Those shootings which involved fleeing felons could best be termed elective. Police were most likely to use deadly force when being attacked (40.6%) or when a crime was in progress (30.8%). The percentages of black and white felons killed by police were nearly identical for these precipitating events. In view of the available national data, it does not appear that police officers at the situational level have "one trigger finger for blacks and another for whites."

Cities

After calculating the rates of felon killings per million population by police, we noticed that 38 of the 169 cities of more than 100,000 population had no PkF during 1980-1984.[7] We are attempting to predict a rare event. Because of the 38 cities with no felon killings, the distribution of the dependent variable here is not the normal bell-shaped curve. In using a variable that is not distributed normally, some form of adjustment typically must be made. We could run two separate equations, using logic to predict the presence, and OLS to predict the rate, of PkF. Predicting the presence of one PkF or more versus none over a five-year period, however, creates an indefensible distinction. Transformations such as taking the square root or adding logarithms do not change the measure of cities with no PkF, but merely change the magnitude of the measure for cities with PkF. The two cities with the highest rate of PkF could be termed outliers because they are beyond three standard deviations from the mean. Such measures, however, also assume a perfectly normal distribution. In looking at the rates of PkF across the cities, we see a progression in the data to the cities with the highest rates. Further, when the cities with no PkF are dropped, the standardized scores for the highest cities fall significantly. Thus, none of the cities truly could be termed outliers. Finally, in an effort to control for the influence of the cities with no PkF, we completed a second set of analyses limited to cities of more than 250,000 population (only one of the 56, St. Paul, Minnesota, had no PkF during 1980-1984). In the analysis of cities with populations greater than 250,000, the dependent variable is distributed more normally.

Regression diagnostics pointed to the need to transform some of the predictor variables, including population density, percent black, rate of violence, and number of sworn police personnel per capita. A logarithmic transformation of these variables to the base of 10 solved problems of outliers and nonlinearity when each was regressed against PkF. Table 1 presents the correlations

---

[7]For a list of total numbers and yearly rates of PkF per million residents for cities, contact the first author.

TABLE 1

CORRELATION MATRIX FOR PREDICTOR VARIABLES AND RATES OF
FELON KILLING BY POLICE OFFICERS (PKF) IN 169 U.S. CITIES
OVER 100,000 POPULATION, 1980-1984

	(1)	(2)	(3)	(4)	(5)	(6)	(7)	(8)
1. PkF	1.000							
2. Economic inequality	.460**	1.000						
3. Percent poor	.372*	.736**	1.000					
4. Percent black	.424**	.621**	.733**	1.000				
5. Police per capita	.293**	.526**	.614**	.600**	1.000			
6. Population density	.039	.179*	.306**	.065	.465**	1.000		
7. South	.289**	.334**	.218**	.364**	.031	−.384**	1.000	
8. Violent crime rate	.493**	.607**	.679**	.620**	.619**	.376**	.036	1.000
X	3.18	.375	14.39	19.34	202.9	4342	.355	921.1
S	2.96	.041	5.36	16.72	73.2	3384	.480	542.7

*p < .05
**p < .01

The following variables have been transformed by adding a logarithm to the base of 10: percent black, police per capita, population density, and violent crime rate. The mean and standard deviations reported are those of the variables before transformation.

among the independent variables and the dependent variable. The variable with the highest zero-order correlation with PkF is violent crime at .493, followed closely by the variables used to test the conflict hypothesis: economic inequality, .460; percent black, .424; and percent poor, .372.

The correlation matrix shows that the highest correlation occurs between percent poor economic inequality (Gini index) at .736. Violent crime rate has the highest zero-order correlations with the other predictor variables. The problem of collinearity observed in the correlation matrix was confirmed after each independent variable was regressed against the others. A commonly used measure of multicollinearity is the tolerance score, the equivalent of $1-R^2$ when all other independent variables are regressed against any one independent variable (see Wetherill et al. 1986). Although no standard correction for multicollinearity exists, more precise coefficients can be obtained from a subset of the full model (Weisburg 1980:176). Independent variables showing the lowest tolerance scores, however, thus indicating the highest level of multicollinearity, are also those of greatest theoretical import. Percentage of the population living below the poverty level had a tolerance score of .28, an indication that 72 percent of the variance in percentage in poverty could be explained by the other variables. This tolerance score is low mainly because of the positive correlation of this variable with the Gini index of income inequality. Collinearity between these two variables has plagued previous researchers, who attempted to incorporate both as predictor variables (see Land, McCall, and Cohen 1990). Because of the high correlation of .74 between these two variables, we decided to run two separate equations substituting these two variables.

Another variable with a low tolerance score (.41) was rate of violent crime, an indication that 59 percent of the variance in the violent crime rate is explained by the other independent variables. This outcome was expected because many of the other variables in the equation have been used in the past to predict rates of violent crime, especially the measures used in studies of homicide as indicators of stratification (Gini and percent poor) and subculture (percent black and south). Violent crime has the highest zero-order correlation with PkF at .49. In using various methods to enter variables into some of the initial regression equations, we found that violent crime was always the variable with the greatest influence on rates of felon killing. Together with the high zero-order correlation, this evidence supports what many researchers concluded in the past: that the rate of violence in the community is a very important influence on the rate of police-caused homicides. In an alternative explanation, which considers the level of collinearity between the predictor variables, this relationship is spurious.

Few researchers have tested the possibility that the correlation between violence and police-caused homicide is caused by some other factor (an exception is Langworthy 1986).[8] The possibility that violent crime may be only a proxy for economic inequality or percentage of the population which is black, thus suggesting a pattern of discriminatory policing, can be tested only when these other variables are controlled simultaneously. Yet again we encounter the major problem of collineartiy, which leads to inaccurate regression coefficients. The suggested correction—leaving this variable out of full model—is simply not feasible. Because the rate of violent crime has been linked theoretically and empirically to the other variables, we decided to regress all other variables against violent crime rate and to the residuals in the equation to predict rates of felon killing. The violent crime rate residuals incorporate into the model only that portion of the violent crime rate which is not explained by the other independent variables. In this way we are measuring the effect of violent crime rates on PkF totally independent of other variables.

Table 2 reports the results of the OLS regression analyses with the alternative measures of economic stratification and absolute poverty for the 169 largest U.S. cities with populations greater than 100,000. In the first model, we see that economic inequality is the strongest predictor of PkF; percent black and south also show significant positive coefficients. The residual violent crime rate is a significant predictor of rate of PkF, surpassed only by economic inequality. In the second model, poverty is not a significant predictor of rate of PkF, but the percent black and south coefficients become stronger because of their relationship to the excluded indicator of economic inequality. The strongest predictor in the second model is the residual of the violent crime rate not explained by the other independent variables in the equation. These findings suggest that economic inequality rather than absolute poverty, is related to the rate of felon killing, but also that the violent crime rate accounts for much of the variation in rates of felon killing by police officers.

In Table 3, the correlation matrix for the 56 cities greater than 250,000 presents a configuration similar to that for cities greater than 100,000 in Table 2. Violent crime, however, has a lower correlation (.447) than the conflict

---

[8]This possibility was acknowledged by Kania and MacKey (1977:43). In testing the temporal relationship between police shooting rates and criminal homicide from Fyfe's NYC data. Langworthy (1986) found it impossible to build an ARIMA model, a situation suggesting a spurious relationship.

TABLE 2

RATES OF FELON KILLING BY POLICE REGRESSED AGAINST PREDICTOR VARIABLES FOR 169 U.S. CITIES OVER 100,000 POPULATION, 1980-1984, INEQUALITY AND POVERTY MODELS

	Model 1: Inequality			*Model 2: Poverty*		
	b	*s.e.*	*Beta*	*b*	*s.e.*	*Beta*
Economic inequality	20.911***	(6.351)	.289			
Percent poor				.060	(.058)	.108
Percent black	.912*	(.477)	.183	1.159*	(.547)	.233
Police per capita	.418	(2.068)	.019	1.412	(2.070)	.066
Population density	.158	(.773)	.017	.315	(.803)	.034
South	.813*	(.490)	.132	1.181**	(.479)	.192
Violent crime (residual)	4.985***	(1.160)	.276	5.817***	(1.158)	.325
Constant	−7.390			−3.622		
	R^2	.332			.321	

*p < .05
**p < .01
***p < .001

TABLE 3

CORRELATION MATRIX FOR PREDICTOR VARIABLES AND RATES OF FELON KILLING BY POLICE OFFICERS (PkF) IN 56 U.S. CITIES OVER 250,000 POPULATION, 1980-1984

	(1)	*(2)*	*(3)*	*(4)*	*(5)*	*(6)*	*(7)*	*(8)*
1. PkF	1.000							
2. Economic inequality	.583**	1.000						
3. Percent poor	.490**	.710**	1.000					
4. Percent black	.534**	.502**	.667**	1.000				
5. Police per capita	.196	.447**	.545**	.602**	1.000			
6. Population density	−.007	.311*	.464**	.252	.653**	1.000		
7. South	.404**	.368**	.202	.301*	−.089	−.442**	1.000	
8. Violent crime rate	.447**	.601**	.670**	.606**	.545**	.477**	.002	1.000
X	5.15	.391	16.41	25.17	236.8	5375	.375	1222.2
S	3.09	.037	5.20	18.01	89.3	4297	.489	627.5

*p < .05
**p < .01

The following variables have been transformed by adding a logarithm to the base of 10: percent black, police per capita, population density, and violent crime rate. The mean and standard deviations reported are those of the variables before transformation.

variables. The indicators correlated most highly with PkF are economic inequality (.583), percent black (.534), and percent poor (.490), followed by south (.404). This more limited analysis, involving cities of more than 250,000 population, excludes many large suburbs and middle-sized cities with few or no police killings of felons. We are left with the largest urban areas in the nation. A comparison of Tables 1 and 3 reveals that the means of all the variables increase when the smaller cities are omitted. Only St. Paul, Minnesota lacks any PkF during 1980-1984. The distribution of the variables is similar to that in the larger sample, and percent black, police per capita, population density, and violent crime rate still need transformation by adding a logarithm to the base of 10. Again, the highest correlation among the independent variables is found between economic inequality and percent poor. A great deal of collinearity still exists between violent crime rate and the other predictor variables. For these reasons, the analyses of the 56 largest cities of more than 250,000 parallel those used for all 169 cities. Table 4 shows the separate regression models for both inequality and poverty.

In the regression equations using the sample cities greater than 250,000, inequality again is the strongest predictor of PkF, followed by percent black. The residual violent crime rate coefficient is not significant in the model with economic inequality but reaches significance in the model incorporating poverty. In the second model, percent black is a significant predictor of the rates of felon killing followed by percent poor. The residual violent crime rate became significant in this model because economic inequality was not included. The R^2 is higher in the model that includes economic inequality, as it was when all 169 cities were analyzed; this finding suggests a better fit to the data when economic inequality is included. This analysis refutes any explanation of police-caused homicides which excludes economic inequality.

All of the models show the importance of economic inequality and race, but diverge on violent crime. These inconsistencies can be removed by reducing the models to equations that include only the significant predictors. We do this for both samples of cities and depict them in a path model.[9] The model

---

TABLE 4

RATES OF FELON KILLING BY POLICE REGRESSED AGAINST PREDICTOR VARIABLES FOR 56 U.S. CITIES OVER 250,000 POPULATION, 1980-1984, INEQUALITY AND POVERTY MODELS

	Model 1: Inequality			Model 2: Poverty		
	b	s.e.	Beta	b	s.e.	Beta
Economic inequality	40.605***	(11.502)	.486			
Percent poor				.188*	(.099)	.317
Percent black	3.445**	(1.138)	.437	2.879*	(1.355)	.365
Police per capita	−4.299	(3.661)	−.197	−2.753	(3.868)	−.126
Population density	−1.216	(1.537)	−.131	−.767	(1.704)	−.083
South	.111	(.927)	.018	1.150	(.907)	.182
Violent crime (residual)	1.924	(2.092)	.093	3.570*	(2.130)	.180
Constant	−6.43			7.233		
	R^2		.495			.432

*p < .05
**p < .01
***p < .001

---

[9]The path model does not solve the problem of collinearity. This particular model is used for illustration and is grounded in the empirical research.

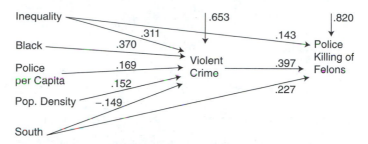

FIGURE 1.   Path Model for Predictors of Police Killing of Felons for 169 cities
over 100,000 Population, 1980-1984.

includes only the significant predictors rather than all possible predicted
causal links (Davis 1985). Economic inequality rather than absolute poverty is
used to test the conflict hypothesis because it has more theoretical import and
because empirically its coefficients explain more of the variance in the dependent variable.

Figure 1 shows the significant relationships between the independent variables and the dependent variables of violent crime and police killings of felons.
In this model all of the variables are related to violent crime. Because we are
concerned most with the magnitude of the relationships in our sample, the path
model includes standardized coefficients, or betas, which can be interpreted
in the same manner as in the earlier OLS regressions (see Asher 1983). The
strongest predictors are inequality and black, followed by police per capita and
population density. All of these variables had positive coefficients, but south
had an unexpected significant negative effect on violent crime. The residual
path coefficient, which represents the square root of the unexplained variance
in the dependent variable, is .653. Therefore the R^2 for violent crime is .573, an
indication that the predictor variables account for 57 percent of the variance in
violent crime in the 169 cities.

The only significant direct predictors of PkF are violent crime, south, and
inequality. Violent crime has by far the strongest direct effects on PkF; yet
many factors impinge on the rate of violent crime. Inequality has an indirect
effect on PkF of .123, which operates through the level of violent crime. This
value is obtained by multiplying the path coefficients between inequality and
violent crime and between violent crime and PkF (.311 × .397). The total effect of inequality, indirect and direct (.123 + .143), is .266, an indication that
an increase of one standard deviation in inequality leads to an increase of .266
standard deviation in PkF. South appears to have a large positive effect on the
rates of police killing of felons. The higher rates of police killings of felons in
the south, however, cannot be explained in terms of a higher rate of violent
crime because of the negative relationship of south with violent crime. The
net effect of south is (.397 × −.149) + .227 = .168, an overall effect lower
than inequality. The overall R^2 for the model is .327, an indication that nearly
33 percent of the variance in the rate of police killing of felons is explained by
the predictor variables.

Figure 2 shows an analysis of predictors of violent crime and PkF in the 56
cities with move than 250,000 population. The two significant predictors of

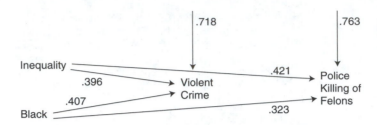

FIGURE 2.   Path Model for Predictors of Police Killing of Felons for 56 Cities over 250,000 Population, 1980-1984.

violent crime and PkF are black and inequality; these variables account for 49 percent of the variance in violent crime and 42 percent of the variance in PkF. Violent crime was not related directly to PkF in cities with more than 250,000 population. Because the standardized coefficients are used in the model, it is possible to say that each increase of one standard deviation in inequality is associated with an increase of .42 standard deviation in the rate of police killings of felons. Similarly, each standard deviation increase in percent black leads to a .33 standard deviation increase in the rate of police killing felons.

In the analyses of cities of more than 100,000 presented in Table 2 and Figure 1, violent crime exerts a strong influence on the rate of police killings of felons. Yet, in the analyses of cities greater than 250,000 presented in Table 4 and Figure 2, violent crime has no direct effect on PkF. The other measures of perceived dangerousness (police per capita and population density) only contributed to the rate of violent crime and did not influence PkF directly in any of the other models. The indicator of economic inequality, the Gini index, showed the strongest consistent relationship with PkF. From the analyses we see strong independent effects of inequality of PkF, as well as indirect effects operating through violent crime. Percent black also is related strongly to PkF in the models, although indirectly through violent crime in Figure 1. These findings suggest that the conflict model is supported more strongly by the data; the developmental model, however, would seem to offer the more complete explanation.

Although we have attempted to sort out, as far as possible, the relationships between economic inequality, violent crime, and the rate of police killing of felons, these findings must be interpreted cautiously. We suggest a developmental model because economic inequality and percent black influence not only PkF but also violent crime. Hence in areas with greater economic inequality and a larger proportion of minorities, the community shows higher rates of violence, which lead in turn to higher rates of police killing of felons. Yet the direct effects of economic inequality and percent black suggest that the police response in these areas is higher than is warranted by the levels of violent crime.

It is difficult to meet the stringent assumptions of causality. Some observers may suggest that PkF influences levels of violence, but, we argue that this is unlikely. Although police use of deadly force does lead to violent crime in a very few cases of collective violence, such cases represent only a small proportion of violent crime.[10] Ruling out spurious effects is very difficult in any casual analysis. Again, we believe that we include the strongest indicators of the two most commonly espoused explanations of the use of deadly force by police officers. Although organizational policies and procedures influence the use of deadly force, such policies are determined by many of the macro-level forces that we have included in our model.

DISCUSSION AND CONCLUSION

In this paper we tested two explanations of the use of deadly force by police officers: the conflict and the community violence hypotheses. At the situational level over the period 1976-1988, data from the SHR showed that most police killings of felons resulted from necessity when the officer either was being attacked or was attempting to stop a crime in progress. As in previous literature, these nonelective police shootings made up between 2/3 and 3/4 of all police shootings that resulted in the death of a felon. Most of the felons killed were black, but they were no more likely than whites to be killed in nonelective shootings. Further, black officers killed black felons at a much higher rate then did white officers. It is possible that suspect variables such as race and poverty make a difference in police response which is not detectable at the situational level when aggregate data from the SHR we used.

We performed a more reliable test of the hypotheses using data from the community level. We found support for the community violence thesis in the analysis of 169 U.S. cities with more than 100,000 population. The violent crime rate was highly predictive of the rate of felon killing by police officers across cities. After violent crime rates were regressed against other indicators, the residual violent crime rate still had a significant effect on PkF across cities in a regression analysis controlling for numerous alternative explanatory factors. In the path model including the 169 cities, the violent crime rate also had the largest direct influence on PkF. In the models including only the 56 U.S. cities of more than 250,000 population, the violent crime rate lost significance; therefore these findings offered little support for the community violence hypothesis in the nation's largest urban centers.

We found consistent support for the conflict hypothesis in all of the models. Economic inequality, as measured by the Gini index, was the most accurate predictor of the rate of felon killing in all of the models incorporating this measure. Absolute poverty, measured by the percentage living below the poverty level, was related to PkF only in cities of more than 250,000 population when economic inequality was not included in the model. Percent black also was a significant predictor of PkF in the models, even when we controlled for the level of violence in the community and other factors.

Our findings support the conflict hypothesis more strongly than the community violence hypothesis. Communities with greater economic inequality and a large percentage of minority residents experience a higher rate of PkF.

---

[10]We did not show time priority empirically (e.g., by lagging the data). To do so would require a much higher baseline of police killings. Casual order is implied in much of the previous literature, with the exception of Langworthy (1986), and also by logic.

Yet the rate of violence in a community tends to act as an intervening variable that can be seen most clearly in the developmental path model incorporating all cities of more than 100,000. Although violent crime exerts a significant influence on PkF, many other variables, particularly economic inequality, act as antecedent causes.

Previous studies overestimated the effect of violence on police-caused homicide rates because the authors typically considered only zero-order correlations. Our findings are consistent with the previous studies, which controlled simultaneously for many factors. Jacobs and Britt (1979) found level of economic inequality to be the most accurate predictor of the rates of police-caused homicide, although a slight relationship also existed between rates of community violence and police-caused homicide. Kania and MacKey (1977) found support for the community violence hypothesis and lack of support for the conflict perspective, but their study included only measures of absolute poverty, not of economic inequality.

Our analysis makes clear that economic inequality and the proportion of minorities in the population must be included in any future studies which attempt to explain the rate of police-caused homicide at the macro-level. Failure to consider the level of economic inequality will result in findings of a strong relationship between violent crime rate and the rate of felon killing. The violent crime rate, however, acts at best as a mediator between other social forces and the rate of felon killing by police officers.

REFERENCES

Allison, P.D. (1978) "Measures of Inequality." *American Sociological Review* 43:865-80.

Asher, H.B. (1983) *Causal Modeling.* 2nd ed. Beverly Hills: Sage.

Binder, A. and L.A. Fridell (1984) "Lethal Force as a Police Response." *Criminal Justice Abstracts* 16:250-80.

Blumberg, M. (1981) "Race and Police Shootings: An Analysis in Two Cities."
   In James J. Fyfe (ed.), *Contemporary Issues in Law Enforcement*, pp. 152-166. Beverly Hills: Sage.

Bowers, W.J. (1984) *Legal Homicide.* Boston: Northeastern University Press.

Chambliss, W. and R.B. Seidman (1971) *Law, Order, and Power.* Reading, MA: Addison-Wesley.

Davis. J.A. (1985) *Logic of Causal Order.* Beverly Hills: Sage.

Fyfe, J.J. (1978) "Shots Fired: An Examination of New York City Police Firearms Discharges." Doctoral dissertation, State University of New York, Albany.

—— (1980) "Geographic Correlates of Police Shooting: A Microanalysis." *Journal of Research in Crime and Delinquency* 17:101-13.

—— (1981) "Who Shoots? A Look at Officer Race and Police Shooting." *Journal of Police Science and Administration* 9:367-82.

Geller, W.A. (1982) "Deadly Force: What We Know." *Journal of Police Science and Administration* 10:151-77.

Geller, W.A. and K.J. Karales (1981) "Shooting of and by Chicago Police: Uncommon Crises—Part I, Shootings by Chicago Police." *Journal of Criminal Law and Criminology* 72:1813-66.

Goldkamp, J.S. (1976) "Minorities as Victims of Police Shootings: Interpretations of Racial Disproportionality and Police Use of Deadly Force." *Justice System Journal* 2:169-83.

Harding, R.W. and R.P. Fahey (1973) "Killings by Chicago Police, 1969-70: An Empirical Study." *Southern California Law Review* 46:284-315.

Harring, S., T. Platt, R. Speiglman, and P. Takagi (1977) "The Management of Police Killings." *Crime and Social Justice* 8:34-43.

Inn, A., A.C. Wheeler, and C.L. Sparling (1977) "The Effects of Suspect Race and Situation Hazard on Police Officer Shooting Behavior." *Journal of Applied Psychology* 1:27-37.

Jacobs, D. and D. Britt (1979) "Inequality and Police Use of Deadly Force: An Empirical Assessment of the Conflict Hypothesis." *Social Problems* 26:403-12.

Kania, R. and W. MacKey (1977) "Police Violence as a Function of Community Characteristics." *Criminology* 15:37-48.

Knoohuizen, R., R.P. Fahey, and D.J. Palmer (1972) *The Police and Their Use of Fatal Force in Chicago*. Chicago: Chicago Law Enforcement Study Group.

Kobler, A.L. (1975a) "Figures (and Perhaps Some Facts) on Police Killing of Civilians in the United States, 1965-1969." *Journal of Social Issues* 31:185-91.

Land, K.C., P.L. McCall, and L.E. Cohen (1990) "Structural Covariates of Homicide Rates: Are There Any Invariances across Time and Social Space?" *American Journal of Sociology* 95 (January): 922-63.

Langworthy, R.H. (1986) "Police Shooting and Criminal Homicide: The Temporal Relationship." *Journal of Quantitative Criminology* 2:377-88.

Matulia, K.J. (1985) *A Balance of Forces: Model Deadly Force Policies and Procedure* 2nd ed. Gaithersburg, MD: International Association of Chiefs of Police.

Maxfield, M.G. (1989) "Circumstances in Supplementary Homicide Reports: Variety and Validity." *Criminology* 27:671-95.

Meyer, M.W. (1980) "Police Shootings at Minorities: The Case of Los Angeles." *Annals of the American Academy of Political and Social Science* 452:98-110.

Parker, R.N. (1989) "Poverty, Subculture of Violence, and Type of Homicide." *Social Forces* 67:983-100.

Robins, G.R. (1963) "Justifiable Homicide by Police Officers." *Journal of Criminal Law and Criminology* 54:225-31.

Sherman, L.W. (1978) "Restricting the License to Kill: Recent Developments in Police Use of Deadly Force." *Criminal Law Bulletin* 14:577-83.

Sherman, L.W. and R. H. Langworthy (1979) "Measuring Homicide by Police Officers." *Journal of Criminal Law and Criminology* 70:546-60.

Takagi, P. (1974) "A Garrison State in a 'Democratic' Society." *Crime and Social Justice* 1:27-33.

Weisburg, S. (1980) *Applied Linear Regression*. New York: Wiley.

Wetherill, G.B., P. Duncombe, M. Kenward, J. Kollerstrom, S.R. Paul, and B.J. Vowden (1986) *Regression Analysis with Application*. New York: Chapman and Hall.

Williams, K.R. and R.L. Flewelling (1987) "Family, Acquaintance, and Stranger Homicide: Alternative Procedures for Rate Calculation." *Criminology* 25: 543-60.

TECHNOLOGICAL INNOVATION AND THE DEVELOPMENT OF LESS-THAN-LETHAL FORCE OPTIONS

Robert F. Scott, Ph.D
Ft. Hays State University

Michael P. Copeland, J.D.
Ft. Hays State University

. . . but a great need still exists to find simple, effective technologies and weapons that provide a safe alternative to deadly force . . .

—"Why Non-Lethal?" 1999, 27

In 1967, President Lyndon B. Johnson received the now-historic President's Commission on Law Enforcement and Administration of Justice, also referred to simply as the President's Crime Commission, a report on the state of law enforcement and the administration of justice in America. The 308-page report contained more than 200 recommendations, 11 of which dealt directly with police technology (President's Commission on Law Enforcement 1967). Specifically, the Crime Commission found that the nation's criminal justice system was suffering from a serious technology gap. In particular, the technological revolution which was alive and well in the American scientific community had had surprisingly little impact on the criminal justice system (President's Commission on Law Enforcement 1967), and the equipment of most police agencies had a level of technology consistent with that of three to four decades ago. To this day, the mainstay of most American law enforcement agencies is the use of the revolver and the baton, instruments whose use can be traced to the very genesis of organized policing in this country. A federal initiative followed the Crime Commission report, involving over half a billion dollars over the next fifteen years, in an effort to spur the growth, development and proliferation of the use of technology in law enforcement.

How this mandate manifested itself can be subdivided into several broad initiatives, including the proliferation of the use of computer technologies, the growth of information age technologies, the development of new-age control systems (including G.I.S. technologies and the like), as well as the creation and fostering of the use of a wide and growing range of what has come to be called *less-than-lethal* options. Early on, the clear focus of the initiative was computer-aided technology and information systems. However, the explosion of lawsuits which were being filed against the police and police agencies following the refinement of Section 1983 of the Civil Rights Act prompted the largest and best-funded agencies to begin to explore non-lethal and less-than-lethal alternatives.

CONCERN OVER CIVIL LIABILITY AS AN AGENT FOR CHANGE

The years 1967 to 1971 saw the number of suits filed against law enforcement and law enforcement agencies rise 124% (Kappeler 1997). A 1976 study (IACP 1976) found 13,400 suits filed annually, increasing to 26,000 in 1980 and a staggering 130,000 in 1991. Sadly, this exponential growth shows no sign of flattening out. In fact, indications are that the growth may be even more substantial than in the past.

While it is true that police agencies win the overwhelming number of suits filed against them (approximately 96% in state courts), the costs of losses, defending suits (won or lost), liability insurance, and the cost of out-of-court settlements have reached critical mass for many departments. Costs involved in a single large suit could cripple a small jurisdiction's budget. In fact, the cost of liability insurance once caused Essex County, New Jersey, to temporarily close the doors of its police academy and send 70 in-service cadets home because the county and the department could not afford the cost of liability insurance (Kappeler 1997). A National Institute of Municipal Law Enforcement Officers survey of 215 municipalities found $4.3 billion dollars in pending liability suits (Kappeler 1997). When Barrineau extrapolated these findings to all 39,000 municipal governments in the United States, the figure rose to a staggering $780 billion dollars worth of pending litigation (Barrineau 1994).

These fears of liability have also been driven, if in whole or in part, by several Supreme Court decisions which seriously altered the ways in which a law enforcement officer may carry out his or her profession. The cases of *Tennessee v. Garner* (1985) and *Graham v. Connor* (1989) both necessitated the development of a less aggressive policy with respect to suspect apprehension and care. The logical progression has been the move towards the battery of less-than-lethal tactics and technologies which are often times equally as efficient as more contemporary means and are frequently less of a liability with respect to their usage.

LESS-THAN-LETHAL TECHNOLOGIES

The following should by no means be considered an exhaustive list of less-than-lethal technologies presently in use or under development, but more so a list of some of the more popular and promising alternatives. This section will be divided into five sub-sections for organizational purposes: (1) ammunition; (2) aerosol spray; (3) gassing technology; (4) use of electricity, and; (5) miscellaneous less-than-lethal components.

AMMUNITION

5.56 Multi-Ball Ammunition

Made by MK Ballistic Systems of Hollister, California, the 5.56 mm X 45 mm NATO (.223 Remington) ammunition was made originally for military usage in the M–16, AR–15 and the Mini–14 where less-than-lethal force responses were called for. Crowd and riot control have been common usages. The round fires five .22 caliber lead balls at very low velocity (400 ft/s). The recommended firing range is 10-25 yards, and it is recommended that the target site be a clothed area. Although the round is not designed to penetrate the suspect, it is able to break the skin when fired at close range. The round has a very low sound signature, desirable for use in residential areas.

The 5.56 multiball has civilian law enforcement cross-over appeal from the military for a variety of reasons, beyond the less than lethal capability of the round. Potentially, the low velocity round and favorable dispersal pattern at ranges of 10 to 25 yards make it effective in quelling civil disturbances with little or no fear of fatal injury. Additionally, the round can be used for shooting out lights, breaking out windows as well as for animal control purposes.

RPL Mark II Rubber Bullets

The RPL Mark II rubber bullets are made and distributed by ALS Technologies of Bull Shoals, Arkansas. The riot projectile launcher launches .69 caliber rubber made projectiles at speeds up to 300 ft/s. Each hopper holds up to 140 individual shots. The CO_2 canister will support 400 shots before necessary recharging or replacement. Optimum range for firing is at a distance of 15–25 yards from the target or target area.

Created for riot control and presently included among the arsenal of less-than-lethal weaponry in the city of Los Angeles Police Department, the mechanics operate much like a paintball gun, operating via a CO_2 canister as a propellant. When used properly, the officer should aim either at the legs of the suspects (or unruly crowd), or at the ground directly in front of the individuals in question. The resulting force will cause the perpetrator to drop, allowing for ease of apprehension without the risk of lethal injury. This weapon/control device can also be equipped with a TASCO laser-dot aiming device for greater accuracy. Perhaps most important to law enforcement agencies, these bullets and their accompanying gun mechanism are relatively inexpensive.

Hornet's Nest

The Hornet's Nest, made and marketed by ALS Technologies, is essentially a small nylon bag filled with compressed rubber balls. These rounds are made for the shotgun, and are deployed at a very fast 470 ft/s. The Hornet's Nest gives law enforcement the same less than lethal benefits inherent to the RPL Mark II rubber bullets, with the added benefit of shotgun action. Each round contains 21 .30 caliber compressed rubber pellets. When deployed, they lay out a pattern similar to a shotgun blast, without the lethality of conventional bullets.

Bolo Round

ALS Technologies produce a snaring device known as a bolo round. This round, in terms of less than lethal technology, is an extraordinarily safe and efficient option. Fired from an optimal range of 20 to 40 yards from the suspect, the firing mechanism deploys three .27 caliber rubber balls connected by a 12 foot cord. When deployed at the legs, the whirling and twirling motion of the bolo wraps around the individual over and over until their legs are completely incapacitated. Apprehension then becomes a relatively safe and secure process. One hazard of this particular round is that, with three rubber balls projected in a relatively random shot pattern, the chance exists that a rogue ball could strike the head and cause injury if deployed at a range closer than the optimum firing distance.

UPCO Scorpion Launching System

For greater range than the RPL Mark II rubber bullets, the UPCO system launches *dead rubber* rounds via a compressed air cylinder at a speed of 300 to 500 ft/s. The dead rubber rounds come in two magazines, holding 10 pellets each. The mechanism which fires the dead rubber ammunition is especially preferable for night situations. The launcher comes with a low-light situation adapter, making it nightfire adaptable. Additionally, the mechanism comes equipped with a guidance/aiming system for increased accuracy.

Pepperball LTL

Jaycor Tactical Systems has developed a compressed gas pistol which fires rounds, either in the form of a liquid irritant or solid balls which burst on contact, containing pepper spray. Thus, unlike other types of alternative ammunition, the sheer force of the round itself is not the incapacitating agent. Incapacitating red pepper spray hits the body and spreads, paint ball style, about the individual. The perpetrator is effectively rendered harmless by the burning hot oleo capsicum peppers.

These rounds are considered very accurate at ranges up to 50 feet. Pepperball LTL rounds fire at a rate of 12 per second, and a firing cartridge holds up to 85 rounds. This type of ammunition is especially suitable for crowd control and as a restraint technique in situations which have not risen to the level where the use of lethal force would be justified.

Ring Airfoil Projectile (RAP)

The ring airfoil projectile is a two-decades-old development of military design. It is a nonlethal device used in a single-shot mode against individual targets. The device, a doughnut-shaped rubber projectile, produces a paralyzing stinging effect when it strikes the individual.

RAP is preferable to some law enforcement practitioners, because it tends to be less of an injury risk than rubber bullet and bean bag projectiles. RAP is fired by an adapted M–16 rifle, and has a long, effective firing range of 120 feet, extraordinary for a mechanism of this sort.

Additionally, Guilford Engineering, on a grant provided by the National Institute of Justice (NIJ), is studying the added less-than-lethal benefit of whether RAP can be adapted to deliver a cloud of pepper spray on impact.

PEPPER SPRAY

Oleo Capsicum Spray (OC Spray)

Oleo capsicum (OC) spray is a widely used control tool in law enforcement, corrections, and civilian circles. Oleo capsicum is, essentially, crushed red peppers in a liquid base, which is placed in a delivery canister in concentrations ranging from 1% upwards, although a 10% concentration is most common and utterly effective since its widespread introduction to the law enforcement community in 1982.

Contained most commonly in palm-sized, hand-held canisters, depressing the top shoots a stream of OC spray. Law enforcement is taught to aim for the eyes, ensuring a face shot which causes severe skin irritation and burning for 45 to 60 minutes. The instantaneous manifestation of the spray is an uncontrolled snapping shut of the eyes, and evacuation of the sinuses accompanied by an uncontrollable saliva gland reaction. For best results, the canister should be delivered 7 to 12 feet from the target area.

OC spray is unique to less than lethal developments in that it has evolved into an almost universally accepted tool of law enforcement due to its inexpense (a few dollars per canister), ease of use, efficiency and availability. Many departments actually have their officers wear a canister on their service belt as part of their equipment, while others stock it for use as situations dictate its need.

Another unique aspect of OC spray is the fact that it is adaptable to individual defense/control purposes or available in delivery methods for crowd/riot control situations. Beyond the previously described use by individual officers for control of individual offenders, OC can also be delivered via a fogging mechanism. This device, more along the line of a spray bottle gun than a palm-sized tube, deploys a fog to greater distances, encompassing more of a radial approach to the oleo capsicum delivery. Aside from its sheer effectiveness and irrespective of which situation or delivery method is in play, from a law enforcement perspective the beauty of OC spray is that it is a non-lethal control technique, as effective as lethal weapons for control purposes, but without the fear of civil liability and/or other forms of litigation.

Flameless Oleoresin Capsicum Expulsion Grenade

An extraordinarily advanced usage of the more conventional OC spray mechanism is the flameless oleoresin capsicum expulsion grenade, also known as a T–16. The grenade mechanism, for riot/crowd control, discharges micropulverized oleoresin capsicum chemical agents through two gas ports located on either side of the grenade. The grenade utilizes a CO_2 discharge mechanism which causes the device to move erratically following deployment. The primary purpose of this feature is that it makes it difficult to catch and throw back in the direction of law enforcement personnel.

These types of devices were recently, along with conventional smoke mechanisms, utilized at the Seattle disturbances which accompanied the World Trade Organization meetings. Typically local police were able to disperse and disband crowds numbering in the thousands. Four hundred suspects were neutralized and arrested at various times over a week-long period, through the use of non-lethal control techniques, without serious injury or death. Again, agency fears of civil liability were effectively eliminated. And the unit itself, as efficient as it is, sells for the relatively inexpensive cost of $35, affordable for all agencies, large and small.

GASSING TECHNOLOGY

CS Baton 9410

The CS Baton 9410 is a delivery method for various forms of incapacitating gas for use on crowds or small groups where control, rather than the repelling of an attack is the priority and a less-than-lethal response to the situation is justified. The instrument is a large-capacity, ultra-powerful, baton-style spray gun, originally made and marketed in Korea. The added benefit of this device is that it doubles as a more conventional defensive-use baton (nightstick) following discharge. The baton makes use of replaceable cartridges, both 270 mm and 330 mm cartridge size options, with an optimal firing range of 12 to 20 feet. The effective deployment time of the gas is 2 to 3 seconds. CS Baton 9410, although feasible as a tool of law enforcement, remains an unused option at this point in the United States.

CS Launcher 700

The CS Launcher 700 deploys gas canisters similar to that in the Baton 9410, with the exception that the cartridges are only 35 mm and rifle-deployed. The rifle can fire between 1 and 4 shells at once depending upon the style of the adapter mechanism. The deployment is flameless. Similar to the oleoresin capsicum grenade, a feature of this particular less-than-lethal response tool is the twisting and spinning pattern of the cartridge once deployed, making its retrieval during deployment by those it was intended for virtually impossible. An additional safety feature of this tool is a rubber canister, a significant factor in injury and civil liability avoidance.

A similar development in gas deployment is the American-made Defense Technology 37 mm gas gun. The DT 37 mm gun comes in both pistol and rifle form. In each case, the units can fire between one and eight gas canisters for medium- and long-range less-than-lethal deployments.

CS Multiple Shell 600 Gas Launcher

Made originally for Korean military and police usage, the CS Multiple Shell 600 Gas Launcher is used for the long-range and multiple deployment of gas canisters used in the 9410 and 700 models. Used for less-than-lethal control maneuvers in crowd and small group situations, this device deploys up to

64 shells before requiring re-loading. The mechanism's greatest safety feature is that the officer can deploy the canisters at effective ranges up to 500 feet at a relatively slow 90 ft/s. The officer is essentially out of harm's way when deployment takes place, and the scope of the deployment is so great that anywhere from a few to several hundred individuals can be incapacitated.

TP–1 Triple Phaser Canister Grenade

Very similar in form and function to the oleoresin capsicum grenade, the TP–1 is a military-style deployment tool. The device is made by Combined Tactical Systems, Inc. and sells for a very reasonable $30. The grenade delivers either CS gas or white smoke, and is launched either by hand or by a TL–1 37/38 mm launcher. Much like conventional hand grenades in military use, the TP–1 utilizes a pull-ring firing mechanism with a 1.5 second delay fuse. The TP–1 and the like are in use in several major American police departments, as well as standard equipment for National Guard units.

ELECTRICITY-BASED MECHANISMS

Air Tasers

Compressed nitrogen fires two air taser probes up to 15 feet at a speed of 135 ft/s. A 10,000- to 50,000-volt blast of electricity causes instantaneous loss of neuromuscular control. The device releases electric current in a pre-set sequence, including an initial 7-second blast, followed by several shorter blasts with a total shocking time of 30 seconds. The follow-up blasts were built into the system in order to ensure that there is no ability for the suspect to regain his or her equilibrium and present a safety issue for the officer or the public.

From the standpoint of liability avoidance, the air taser is preferred because it is not destructive to nerves or muscles, and no deaths have ever been directly attributed to its use. The device will not necessarily affect the operation of a pacemaker or other cardiac device. A January 1987 study in the Annals of Emergency Medicine found that tasers leave no long-term medical damage, compared to the 50% rate for gun-shot victims. It is also important to note that the device functions in all climate conditions and is not precipitation sensitive (AEM 1987).

When deployed at an optimal range of 7 to 10 feet, the taser, in addition to causing loss of neuromuscular control, will daze the suspect for several minutes afterwards and can actually render some briefly unconscious. Additionally, if the probes miss their target when fired, the unit can be used in a touch-stun mode. The net effect is that the air taser is a highly effective, highly safe control device that can be purchased for a very reasonable $250, or $400 with laser-sight targeting option.

Stun Taser

The stun taser is a small, hand-held touch version of the air taser mechanism. Stun tasers, such as the AT–9 model, can be purchased for as little as $100.

These control tools are in use in many law enforcement agencies in the United States and are most often used to subdue and control violent perpetrators, as well as those under the influence of drugs and/or alcohol.

Stun Baton

The stun baton can be procured through PureCyber.com in the United States for approximately $170. The device resembles a cattle prod, in that it is baton shaped, with two fixed metal prongs on the end to deliver a substantial 300,000 volt charge of electricity in a touch mode. Similar to other stun mechanisms, the stun baton can double as a conventional nightstick if necessary or if the situation dictates this to be an appropriate response. The use pattern is similar to that of the stun taser.

Stun Belt

The stun belt is better known under the trade name REACT, or Remote Electronically Activated Technology Stun Belt. The stun belt is exactly what the name indicates: a belt-type mechanism that is wired to deliver an electrical charge equalling 50,000 volts. More so than in police agencies, the stun belt has been gaining interest in correctional circles, including the Federal Bureau of Prison since 1994.

The stun belt is activated by means of a remote transmitter, incapacitating the offender in much the same fashion that other less-than-lethal control devices which utilize electricity do. The benefit of the stun belt is that, unlike other options, this device is fastened to the offender. There is no need for the officer to deploy the weapon and run the risk of missing the target. The officer, in fact, can activate the device from a range of up to 900 feet. Additionally, the mechanism will activate automatically if it is tampered with in an attempt to remove it.

When the belt is activated, the offender typically suffers a loss of neuromuscular control, resulting in immobilization, self-defecation, and self-urination. Needless to say, the offender becomes helpless to resist officers in their attempts to gain and maintain control of the individual and the situation. As far as control techniques are concerned, it has obvious benefits over other control techniques which involve the use of physical force and/or restraint.

MISCELLANY

There are many other alternatives in various forms, functions, which are in various stages of development and use in the American law enforcement community. Briefly, some of the more interesting mechanisms are:

1. *Immobilizing Sound Waves:* Acoustic weaponry, utilizing sound wave technology, allows for the incapacitation of an individual when struck by non-projectile sound waves. Sound waves are fired from a modified rifle.

2. *Microwave Neurological Disrupter and Immobilizing Radiation Beams:* Similar to immobilizing sound wave technology, modified rifles deliver non-projectile microwaves, or the like, causing an incapacitating effect similar to that created by the stun belt.
3. *Water Stream Technology:* The firing of a powerful stream of water incapacitates and controls either small or large groups, with little fear of serious injury or death. Can be discharged from a hand-held rifle for individual strikes, or from the more commonly known cannon design for crowd and riot control.
4. *Spiderman Snare:* The spiderman snare is essentially a net fired from a variety of guns or launchers. The snare surrounds the individual and quickly tangles, preventing escape. The snare comes with a weighted ball in each of the four corners of the net. Thus, there is a minimal risk of injury if the individual is struck in the head at close range by the corner weights.
5. *DiscoStrobe Light:* Incapacitatingly bright strobe effect utilizes the power of blinding light from a palm-held mechanism. It is effective on both individuals and small groups. The light effect disorients and makes for ease of apprehension and control.

ADVANCES IN LAW ENFORCEMENT PROTECTION MEASURES

1. *Back-Scatter Imaging System:* A hand-held device which serves as an electronic pat-down. The system tells the officer if the individual is carrying a weapon or weaponlike form with the use of x-rays, eliminating the need for actual physical contact.
2. *Heartbeat Detector:* In much the same way that back-scatter works, development is taking place on a heartbeat-detecting mechanism which can amplify sound through walls to articulate the number of individuals in a particular setting. This device has obvious officer safety ramifications, with little in the way of physical risk or liability concern.
3. *Through-the-Wall Surveillance:* Similar to the heartbeat detector, except this hand held infra-ray device tells the officer not only how many people are in a location, but where they are physically situated.
4. *Facial Recognition Technology:* Advanced imaging technology allows for the implantation of a photographic image into a computer database. Now, via car-bound computer terminals, a driver's license image can be loaded into the system, and the computer will search for a match, instantaneously telling an officer who he or she is actually dealing with and supplying the accompanying N.C.I.C. record match.

IMPEDIMENTS TO PROGRESS TOWARDS LTL DEVELOPMENT AND USAGE

Nature of Police Departments

LEMAS statistics indicate that, on many levels, the small department is the typical American law enforcement agency. This is true in that the typical agency is small size-wise, small budget-wise and small in terms of training and equipment funding (Reaves 1996). The demographic of the typical police department explains, in part, the lack of high tech equipment in many departments and resistance to this type of technically advanced wares.

It is reasonable to assume that the understanding of and willingness to use advanced technology are tied to a sufficient level of education and training. A Police Executive Research Forum study in 1996 indicated, in fact, this very point (PERF 1996).

Unfortunately, poorly educated officers and a relative lack of training coincide, generally, with department size. Since only a small fraction of the total number of agencies in this country could be considered large, possessing formal education requirements and advanced training of their officers, a technology gap forms. Essentially, the type of officers in many departments perpetuates a kind of have- versus have-not relationship between department types.

Funding Problems

Along the same lines as the education and training gap between large and small departments, the same situation often exists with respect to budgetary concerns. The National Institute of Justice statistics clearly show the nature of department size to overall budget (Seaskate, Inc. 1998), and it is clear that all these technological advances are only of benefit if agencies can afford them. LTL equipment, although quite effective, is also quite expensive, and beyond the budgetary capabilities of all but the largest and best-funded agencies. This point was confirmed by a 1996 study of the Police Executive Research Forum (PERF 1996). The study found that 83% of responding departments cited prohibitive cost as a barrier to procurement.

For many agencies, funding for high-tech equipment becomes a hit-or-miss function in the grant application world. Many state and federal agencies provide monetary grants to agencies for equipment and personnel needs. These monies are infrequent and unpredictable in their procurement and not part of a well-developed, long-term agency improvement plan.

The National Institute of Justice does note several viable options which should and could be explored to mitigate the funding dilemmas facing most agencies: (Seaskate, Inc. 1998, 87).

1. Achieve economies of scale by promoting buying consortiums;
2. Expanding the availability of technology-purchasing grants to smaller local agencies as a matter of course, not exception;
3. Establish a federal low interest loan program for purchasing police equipment;
4. Further loosening restrictions on Department of Defense surplus property.

Rural Versus Urban Setting

Ralph Weisheit (Weisheit et al. 1999) articulated an interesting feature in the difference between urban and rural settings, beyond department size and form. Weisheit found that levels of public expectation and acceptability relative to police tactics were often somewhat less liberal in rural settings. Many areas which would not be considered highly urbanized possess beliefs with respect to law enforcement centered on the premise that law enforcement tactics beyond a simple order maintenance or service model are undesirable, unneeded, and often unacceptable.

Thus, the resulting technology gap is often not only a function of a lack of funding or officer training, but is also the clearly articulated preference of the general public. Depending on one's perspective then, the technology gap between urban and rural settings, big vs. small departments, may be conversely viewed as a positive or a negative.

LESS-THAN-LETHAL ISSUES AND CONSTRAINTS

In 1987, the Report on the Attorney's General Conference on Less-Than-Lethal Weapons, a study on the development, effectiveness, necessity, and uses of less-than-lethal forms of weaponry and control provided a number of recommendations within its text. Among the most important findings were the following positives in favor of the development of less-than-lethal weapons, and related issues and constraints:

Reasons to Continue Development:

1. Avoid serious injury and death of fleeing felons
2. Decrease the number of law enforcement officers shot with their own weapons
3. Provide adequate force options
4. Respond more effectively to disturbed and/or violent perpetrators
5. Lessen the number of lawsuits involving police officers

Issues and Constraints:

1. Since any force that is used against an individual can be potentially lethal, acceptable limits of potential risk must be set.
2. The design of a new device should incorporate features to limit the potential for abuse.
3. The participation of biomedical experts is critical in order to clarify the physiological effects and consequences of new weapons.
4. Acceptance of the officers using the weapon is critical.
5. Administrative controls for actual use should be considered in development.
6. Devices must not be overly complex; they must be durable and simple for the officer to use, but potentially difficult for others to use.
7. The delivery system must be at least as accurate as a conventional handgun.

CONCLUDING THOUGHTS

What is the purpose of less-than-lethal technologies? Their development is clearly the next step in a long line of technological advances in the field of law enforcement. Many of the existing devices and much of the current research underway is of military origin, which then finds a "crossover" audience in the civilian police community. Expense, resistance to change, public expectations and department needs are all critical in the level of deployment of these mechanisms.

From the standpoint of policy and the agency, the potential reduction in civil liability has to be a primary concern and benefit. Only if these weapons do not sacrifice efficiency and officer and public safety for the sake of the offender's well-being can they be judged to be a success. A 1991 Los Angeles Police Department study of 502 use-of-force incidents judged the effectiveness of eight less-than-lethal devices versus norms expected from the use of conventional lethal weaponry (Meyer 1991). The study showed that the less-than-lethal devices were every bit as effective as the handgun and the like at diffusing and/or de-escalating situations.

In the end, factors dictate that the growth in the use of LTL technologies, as well as their continued development will be a slow, incremental process. We should not expect officers to soon give up their conventional sidearm or the baton, but the age of an increased arsenal of weapons at the disposal of the officer is clearly upon us.

APPENDIX 1
Police Technology Timeline*

1850: The first multishot pistol, introduced by Samuel Colt, goes into mass production.

1854–59: San Francisco is the site of one of the earliest uses of systematic photography for purposes of criminal identification.

1877: The use of the telegraph by police begins in Albany, New York.

1878: The telephone comes into use in police precinct houses in Washington, D.C.

1888: Chicago makes first use of the Bertillon system of human body classification for purposes of identification.

1901: Scotland Yard develops fingerprint classification scheme.

1910: First police crime laboratory opened in Lyon, France.

---

*Modified from *The Evolution and Development of Police Technology,* Seaskate, Inc., 1998. NIJ Grant 95-IJ-CX-Koo1 (S-3).

1923:   City of Los Angeles opens first American crime lab.

1923:   The use of the teletype is inaugurated by the Pennsylvania State Police.

1928:   Detroit police begin use of one-way radio.

1930:   The prototype of the modern-day polygraph is developed.

1934:   Boston police begin use of two-way radio.

1948:   Radar is inaugurated to traffic enforcement.

1955:   New Orleans police are the first to computerize, installing a punch card machine to store arrest and warrant records.

1958:   A former marine develops the conventional side-handled nightstick baton.

1960:   St. Louis police install the first computer-assisted dispatch system.

1966:   The National Law Enforcement Telecommunications System links all state police computers into a single network.

1967:   The President's Commission on Law Enforcement and the Administration of Justice concludes that the "police, with crime laboratories and radio networks, made early use of technology, but most police departments could have been equipped 30 or 40 years ago as well as they are today" (i)

1967:   The FBI inaugurates the National Crime Information Center (NCIC), the first national law enforcement computing center. NCIC is a computerized national filing system on wanted persons and stolen vehicles, weapons, and the like; and for many small departments was probably their first experience with computers.

1968:   AT&T establishes 911 emergency phone number system.

1960s: Early attempts at less than lethal (LTL) technology development and adoption.

1970s: The large-scale implementation of computers in police departments. Specifically, computer-assisted dispatch (CAD) and information storage and maintenance systems become widespread.

1972:   The development of Kevlar body armor.

1979:   The RCMP in Canada implements the first automatic fingerprint identification system (AFIS).

1982:   Pepper spray, widely used by police as a force alternative, is developed.

1990s: Development and adaptation of many military-developed projects to law enforcement use in the form of officer protection devices and less-than-lethal control mechanisms and weapons.

1990s: Departments in New York, Chicago, Houston, and elsewhere increasingly use sophisticated computer programs to map and analyze crime patterns.

1993:   More than 90% of U.S. police agencies serving a population of 50,000 or more are using computers. More are using them for such relatively sophisticated applications as criminal investigations, budgeting, dispatch, and manpower allocation.

1996:   The National Academy of Science announces that there is no longer any reason to question the reliability of DNA evidence.

1998:   The National Institute of Justice releases information and documentation advocating the increased use of less-than-lethal force technologies, computer technologies, and the like in police departments.

REFERENCES

Alpert, G. and R. Dunham (1996). *Policing Urban America,* 3d ed. Prospect Heights, IL: Waveland Press.

Barrineau, H. (1994). *Civil Liability in Criminal Justice,* 2d ed. Cincinnati, OH: Anderson.

Dunham, R. and G. Alpert (1997). *Critical Issues in Policing: Contemprary Readings,* 3d ed. Prospect Heights, IL: Waveland.

International Association of Chiefs of Police (1976). *Survey of Police Misconduct 1967–1976.* Dallas, TX: International Association of Chiefs of Police.

Kappeler, V. (1997). *Critical Issues in Police Civil Liability,* 2d ed. Prospect Heights, IL: Waveland.

Meyer, Greg (1991). "Non-lethal Weapons Versus Conventional Police Tactics: The Los Anlgeles Police Experience" in Seaskate, Inc. 1998.

"Why Non-lethal?" (1999). Paper presented at the Non-lethal Technology and Academic Research (NTAR) Symposium, Quantico, VA, May 3–5.

President's Commission on Law Enforcement and Administration of Justice (1967). *The Challenge of Crime in a Free Society.* Washington, D.C.: U.S. Government Printing Office.

Reaves, B.A. (1996). *Bureau of Justice Statistics Local Police Departments.* Washington, D.C.: U.S. Department of Justice.

Seaskate, Inc. (1998). *The Evolution and Development of Police Technology.* N.I.J. Grant #95-IJ-CX-Kool (S-3). Washington, D.C.: Office of Justice Programs, U.S. Department of Justice.

United States Office of Attorney General (1987). *Report on the Attorney General's Conference on Less Than Lethal Weapons.* Washington, D.C.: U.S. Department of Justice.

Weisheit, R., D. Falcone, and L. Wells (1999). *Crime and Policing in Rural and Small Town America.* Prospect Heights, IL: Waveland.

COURT CASES REFERENCED

Tennessee v. Garner, 53 U.S.L.W. 4410 (1985).

Graham v. Connor, 109 S. Ct. 1865 (1989).

WEBSITES CONSULTED

www.nlectc.org/techproj/nij
www.thespystore.com/physical.htm
www.nonlethal.com/catalog/lessleth/cat125i.htm
www.spie.org/web/abstracts
www.ornl.gov/orcmt/success/enclosed.htm
www.getec.com/nets/getec.net.launchers.oh18.html
www.saf.org/pub/rkba/general/hans220.html
www.nttc.edu/law/projects.html
www.surefire.com
www.laurin.com/content/jan99/techstop.html
www.berettausa.com/smartgun.htm
www.nraila.org/research
www.usnews.com
www.airtaser.com
www.store.securityplanet.com/ataser.htm
www.colt.com
www.igc.apc.org/deepdish/lockdown/ww3/react
www.safetytechnology.com
www.purecyber.com/stunguns
www.ozarkmtns.com/less-lethal/
www.bulldogdirect.com/armor_panels_.html

ARTICLE 20

POLICE PURSUITS AND THE USE OF FORCE: RECOGNIZING AND MANAGING "THE PUCKER FACTOR"—A RESEARCH NOTE*

Geoffrey P. Alpert
University of South Carolina

Dennis Jay Kenney
Police Executive Research Forum

Roger Dunham
University of Miami

Pursuit driving has become one of the most controversial and litigated topics in policing. One consistent theme in the research is that pursuits are adrenaline-driven and are highly stressful for the police officers involved. This study analyzes force used after a pursuit as part of the effort to take the suspect into custody. The data are part of a larger research project that includes four jurisdictions: the Metro-Dade Police Department in Miami (FL), the Omaha (NE) Police Department, the Mesa (AZ) Police Department, and the Aiken County (SC) Sheriffs Office. In addition, data were collected from jail inmates in three of these cities or the neighboring areas. We found that most officers act professionally, but some become anxious at the end of a pursuit and tend to "pull the suspect out of the vent window" to make an arrest. Suggestions to reduce this unprofessional behavior include enhanced training, supervision, and accountability systems. Further, if possible, an officer other than the primary pursuit driver should take physical custody of the suspect.

During the past decade, pursuit driving has become a hotly debated and controversial topic. Fortunately there is agreement on at least three aspects of pursuit: (1) pursuits are dangerous, (2) pursuits must be controlled, and

*Support for this research was provided in part by Grant 93-IJ-CS-0061 from the National Institute of Justice. Opinions stated in this paper are those of the authors and do not necessarily represent the official position of the National Institute of Justice.

Geoffrey P. Alpert, Dennis Jay Kenney, and Roger Dunham, "Police Pursuits and the Use of Force: Recognizing and Managing 'The Pucker Factor'—A Research Note" (as appeared in *Justice Quarterly*, Vol. 14, No. 2, 1997, pp. 371–385). Reprinted with permission from The Academy of Criminal Justice Sciences.

(3) involvement in a pursuit causes the participants' adrenaline and excitement to increase. Certainly, practitioners and researchers disagree about the degree of danger, of need for control, and of increase in excitement and adrenaline, but no one has disputed their presence. In fact, evidence suggests that these aspects vary: Some pursuits are more dangerous than others, some need more control than others, and some affect the participants more than others.

Researchers have demonstrated that organizational elements as well as individual differences contribute to the level of response and reaction to police pursuits (Alpert and Fridell 1992). On the organizational level, apprehending law violators is emphasized strongly; individual differences may explain how that emphasis is translated into action. In one study, Homant, Kennedy, and Howton warned that "[a]ny attempt . . . to regulate or rationalize police pursuit requires that attention be paid to individual-level personality variables, that may affect the patrol officer's decision making" (1993:293-94). Although these concerns span the spectrum of deviance, including use of excessive force (Geller and Toch 1995: Kappeler, Sluder, and Alpert 1994), we focus here on the vehicular pursuit.

The consequences of the presence of danger, need for control, and increased excitement have been the subjects of the debate on the reasonableness of pursuit and its management (Alpert 1995; Kappeler 1993; Urbonya 1991). The factors of danger or risk and need for control are central to the decision to continue or terminate a pursuit; the increase in excitement and adrenaline is important for the supervision of a pursuit. All three of these aspects are examined in the larger research project from which this study is derived.

The purpose of this study is to examine police officers' use of force after driving in a high-energy, adrenaline-driven pursuit. The research questions focus on the nature and frequency of physical force used by police to apprehend those who have been involved in a high-speed pursuit.

PURSUITS AND USE OF FORCE

According to the earliest study documenting force used after pursuits, approximately 30 percent of injuries suffered by suspects occurred after the vehicles had stopped and the suspect was being taken into custody (Alpert and Dunham 1990). These data were collected from several agencies in the Miami area between 1985 and 1987. Most of the injuries (87 percent) were minor and resulted in cuts, scrapes, and bruises. Unfortunately the data on use of force from voluntary terminations were not distinguished from data on force used after an accident.

As data collection has improved, a more thorough analysis of force used after a pursuit has become possible. The data for this study are part of a research project that includes four jurisdictions: the Metro-Dade Police Department in Miami (FL), the Omaha (NE) Police Department, the Mesa (AZ) Police Department, and the Aiken County (SC) Sheriffs Office. In addition, data were collected from jail inmates in three of these cities or neighboring areas. Because the Mesa Police Department was not part of the original research design, that agency's participation was limited to data from the officers and supervisors.

METHODS

At each site, police officers were sampled and asked to complete survey instruments about their attitudes and experiences concerning pursuit and the use of force. Further, suspects who ran from the police were interviewed in Omaha, Miami, and South Carolina. At all sites except Mesa, pursuit forms were collected and analyzed, and suspects were interviewed. Public opinion surveys were conducted in Omaha and Aiken.

In Aiken County, Omaha, and Metro-Dade, the police agencies provided pursuit forms that were completed each time a pursuit was conducted. The Aiken County data were collected in 1993 and 1994, the Metro-Dade information dated from 1990 to 1994, and the Omaha pursuits were conducted from 1992 to 1994. Although pursuit policies differed across agencies and even changed within the agencies during the study period, the standard for the reasonableness of force used to apprehend a suspect remained the same over time and across sites. The requirements for completing use-of-force or control-of-persons reports were similar: At each site an injury, a report of injury, or the use of any force beyond normal control and handcuffing without resistance necessitated a report.

Surveys of Police Officers

At the Metro-Dade Police Department, a 10 percent sample of the 2,732 sworn officers was administered a copy of the survey instrument during March, April, and May 1994. The questionnaires were administered during regularly scheduled training, which includes all officers, sergeants, and lieutenants. Officers were selected randomly from each station and specialized department to attend the two-day sessions, which run continuously. These sessions did not concern pursuit or any use-of-force application. Our sampling resulted in a slight overrepresentation of white males (54 percent versus 52 percent departmentwide).

The questionnaires were distributed in a classroom on the morning of the second day of training. Officers were assured that their responses were anonymous and were instructed not to write their names or identification numbers of the forms, once the informed consent page was removed. We collected information from 205 officers and 50 supervisors. Some information was incomplete and resulted in missing data.

In Omaha, officers and supervisors were also surveyed during training in February 1994. For a three-week period, all field personnel rotated through a one-day in-service training program. At the conclusion of this training, division trainers agreed to allow project staff members to administer the survey. Although officers were not required to complete the survey, almost all apparently considered it a part of their training and participated without comment. Only two officers refused to participate. Although efforts were made to reschedule those officers reporting sick, absent on injury leave, or on vacation or other leave, the division permitted most to forgo the training (and therefore the survey) altogether. In all, 491 of the department's 627 sworn personnel (80 percent) responded with completed survey instruments. The sample approximated the sworn force in age, gender, and ethnicity.

    In Aiken County, each of the 66 sworn officers (except the elected sheriff) was requested for a personal interview and asked to complete the survey instrument. Forty-three officers and nine supervisors (79 percent) completed usable surveys. These interviews were conducted during April and May 1994. The sample approximated the sworn force in age, gender, and ethnicity.

    In Mesa, during the spring of 1994, officers on the swing shift were asked to complete the survey instrument at roll call briefing at the beginning of the shift. Officers who were out sick, at training, or on vacation were not included in the sample. Seventy-seven of the 88 officers on duty (88 percent) completed the survey, as did the 14 on-duty supervisors. The sample approximated the sworn force in age, gender, and ethnicity.

Interviews with Suspects

Suspects who fled the police were also interviewed in South Carolina, Miami, and Omaha. To gain access to this sample of respondents, it was requested that interviewers from the Miami and Omaha Drug Use Forecasting (DUF) projects include a brief interview concerning suspects' experiences when fleeing from the police. In South Carolina, jail inmates in Lexington and Richland Counties were interviewed. The initial screening question was "Have you fled from the police in your vehicle during the past 12 months?" The interviews were held in 1994 and resulted in 51 successful surveys in Miami, 38 in Omaha, and 32 in South Carolina.

THE PRESENT STUDY

    The officially reported data from the Metro-Dade Police Department reveal a decline in the use of force to make an arrest after a pursuit. Although a downward trend is indicated, one must remember that these data are taken from only one agency. From 1990 to 1994, injury data from driving accidents were similar to data for earlier years (17 percent for the mid-1980s and 20 percent for the 1990s) but the proportion of suspects suffering injuries as a result of the arrest declined to 13 percent overall. The recent data are presented in Table 1: In 101 of the 784 arrests, force was used to arrest the suspect. In

TABLE 1

OFFICIALLY REPORTED USE OF FORCE AFTER A PURSUIT

Agency	Years	Pursuits	Total Arrests	Arrests with Accident	Arrests without Accident	Use of Force, Accident	Use of Force, No Accident	Death
Metro-Dade	1990-94	1,049	784	354	428	40	61	5
Aiken	1993-94	17	14	8	6	3	2	1
Omaha	1992-94	229	118	57	61	1	3	1
Total		1,295	916	419	495	44	66	7

TABLE 2

OFFICIALLY REPORTED USE OF FORCE IN FOOT CHASES AFTER A VEHICULAR PURSUIT

Agency	Years	Fleeing Suspects	Arrests	Escapes	Use of Force	Deaths
Metro-Dade	1990-94	479	357	115	45	1
Aiken	1993-94	6	5	0	3	1
Omaha	1992-94	71	45	26	3	0
Total		556	407	141	51	2

reviewing police use of force based on whether the suspect was involved in an accident, the recent data revealed that 428 arrests were made when no accident occurred (that is, the suspect stopped voluntarily). Sixty-one use-of-force reports (14 percent) were completed from these arrests. In pursuits where suspects were involved in an accident resulting from a pursuit N = 354), 40 control-of-persons reports (28 percent) were completed. In other words, police used force to make an arrest twice as often on suspects who were involved in an accident than on suspects who stopped voluntarily.

In many of these cases, suspects stopped the car voluntarily and fled from the police on foot. If involved in an accident, many suspects were not injured seriously or were able to recover from any injury sustained in the accident, and ran from the police. Table 2 shows when force was used to apprehend suspects who were involved in a foot chase after a vehicular pursuit. The Metro-Dade data reveal that 479 suspects were involved in a foot chase, 357 (76 percent) were arrested, and 115 (24 percent) successfully escaped immediate apprehension. Force was used in 45 confrontations that resulted in an apprehension (13 percent). One death resulted from the use of force. In the other 38 cases (85 percent), the injuries resulting from the use of force were minor.

In the Aiken County Sheriffs Office, only a small number of pursuits were reported; thus the data must be interpreted cautiously. The agency has 66 sworn officers who engaged in 17 pursuits during 1993 and 1994. Fourteen resulted in arrests, two involved accidents with injuries (16 percent), and one resulted in a death. These pursuits also generated five use-of-force reports. That is, in five of the 14 pursuits (36 percent) force was reported as used to make the arrest. Six suspects fled from the police on foot. Five were arrested, and three of those arrests involved the use of force. One suspect was killed; none escaped.

In Omaha 229 pursuits took place between 1992 and 1994; 118 resulted in arrests (52 percent), 26 involved accidents with injuries (11 percent), and one resulted in death. Fifty-seven arrests involved accidents, including the 26 that resulted in injuries. Sixty-one arrests were made when an accident did not occur. Use-of-force reports were filed in four arrests, one after an accident, and three when no accident occurred. Seventy-one suspects ran from the police; 45 were arrested, while 26 escaped. As a result of the 45 arrests, three use-of-force reports were filed. No deaths occurred as a result of apprehending a suspect who fled on foot.

Interviews with Officers

In each agency, officers and supervisors were asked a variety of questions about pursuit driving and the use of force. We asked, "What percent of arrests after a pursuit result in the use of force?" and "What percent of arrests after a pursuit result in excessive force?" The data from these questions are reported in Tables 3 and 4. This material reflects opinions that must be interpreted cautiously because each agency operated under different policies and procedures. In Mesa, for example, pursuits were permitted only for the most serious offenses and under very restrictive conditions. In Aiken County, no written policy existed until 1993. In Omaha, the policy changed from restrictive to an absolute ban to judgmental policy; in Metro-Dade, the policy became more restrictive. Although the type of policy in place is no excuse for the use of excessive force, it may help to explain some of the variance in the use of force if the offender is suspected of a violent offense and resists arrest with violence. In these cases, the use of force may reflect only the level of resistance by the suspect.

Most officers reported that the use of force occurs in approximately half of the arrests following a pursuit. The average proportion of arrests following pursuits in which officers reported using force ranged from 43 percent for Metro-Dade officers to 61 percent for Mesa officers. In Metro-Dade, only 14 percent of the officers reported that they believed force was used in 75 percent or more of the arrests, in contrast to 38 percent of the Mesa officers. Six (2 percent) of the Metro-Dade officers and five (1 percent) of the Omaha officers reported that no pursuit-related arrests involved the use of force. The Aiken deputies

TABLE 3

OFFICERS' PERCEPTIONS OF THE PERCENTAGE OF PURSUITS RESULTING IN THE USE OF FORCE

		Number and Percentage of Pursuits Believed to Result in Use of Force					
		0	1-25	26-50	51-75	76+	Mean
Metro-Dade	Officers	6	91	89	42	37	43
		(2%)	(34%)	(33%)	(16%)	(14%)	
	Supervisors	0	12	23	8	6	48
		0	(25%)	(46%)	(16%)	(12%)	
Omaha	Officers	5	89	118	63	103	53
		(1%)	(24%)	(31%)	(17%)	(27%)	
	Supervisors	0	28	32	24	15	48
		0	(28%)	(32%)	(24%)	(15%)	
Aiken	Officers	0	9	14	8	11	54
		0	(21%)	(33%)	(19%)	(26%)	
	Supervisors	0	2	6	1	0	39
		0	(22%)	(67%)	(11%)	0	
Mesa	Officers	0	12	28	7	29	61
		0	(16%)	(37%)	(9%)	(38%)	
	Supervisors	0	3	4	2	4	54
		0	(23%)	(31%)	(15%)	(31%)	
Total		11	246	314	155	205	50

TABLE 4

OFFICERS' PERCEPTIONS OF THE PERCENTAGE OF PURSUITS RESULTING IN THE USE OF EXCESSIVE FORCE

		Number and Percentage of Pursuits Believed to Result in Excessive Use of Force					
		0	*1-25*	*26-50*	*51-75*	*76+*	*Mean*
Metro-Dade	Officers	46	168	36	7	7	16
		(17%)	(64%)	(14%)	(3%)	(3%)	
	Supervisors	4	35	10	0	0	15
		(8%)	(71%)	(20%)	0	0	
Omaha	Officers	110	202	40	10	10	13
		(30%)	(54%)	(11%)	(3%)	(3%)	
	Supervisors	13	71	10	3	5	14
		(13%)	(70%)	(10%)	(3%)	(5%)	
Aiken	Officers	3	31	6	2	0	15
		(7%)	(74%)	(14%)	(5%)	0	
	Supervisors	1	7	1	0	0	12
		(11%)	(77%)	(11%)	0	0	
Mesa	Officers	36	34	3	1	0	7
		(49%)	(46%)	(4%)	(1%)	0	
	Supervisors	2	9	2	0	0	11
		(15%)	(70%)	(15%)	0	0	
Total		215	557	108	23	22	13

believed, as did the majority of officers in all four jurisdictions, that force is used in more than half (54 percent) of all arrests.

The supervisors presented a slightly different picture in some of the agencies. In their estimates, the average percentage of arrests in which force was used after pursuits ranged from 39 percent in Aiken to 54 percent in Mesa. In Metro-Dade, the supervisors reported figures that mirror their officers' reports. They differ only in the lower categories 1-25 percent and 26-50 percent): The supervisors reported slightly higher percentages of arrests resulting in the use of force after a pursuit than did their officers. In Mesa, the officers and the supervisors apparently have similar views of the use of force following a pursuit. The Omaha supervisors differed from their officers at the upper percentage categories (51-75 percent and over 76 percent): The supervisors reported lower proportions than did their officers. The Aiken County supervisors reported that force is used in fewer arrests than did their deputies. The use of force to make an arrest may be appropriate or even necessary. Such force is excessive, however, if it goes beyond what is reasonable or necessary (Alpert and Smith 1994; *Graham v. Conner* 1989; *Tennessee v. Garner* 1985).

The reported use of excessive force differs from the reported use of force in referring only to force beyond that which is necessary to make an arrest. Most officers reported that excessive force is used in some arrests after a pursuit, but many stated that no excessive force is ever used. The average percentage of arrests following pursuits that involve excessive force, as reported by the officers, ranged from 16 percent (Metro-Dade) to 7 percent (Mesa). Forty-six Metro-Dade officers (17 percent) reported that excessive force is never used. One hundred sixty-eight officers (64 percent) reported that excessive force is used in 1 to 25 percent of the arrests following a pursuit; 36 officers (14 percent) stated that excessive force is used in 26 to 50 percent of such arrests. In Omaha, 110 officers (30 percent) reported that excessive force is never used, but 202 (54 percent) reported that it is used in up to 25 percent of arrests involving pursuit. In Aiken, 31 deputies (74 percent) reported that excessive force is used in 1 to 25 percent of these arrests. In Mesa, almost half of the officers reported that no excessive force is used in arrests following a pursuit; most of the remaining officers stated that excessive force is used in 1 to 25 percent of such arrests.

In general, supervisors implied that they are aware of the use of excessive force in some arrests of suspects following a pursuit. The average proportion of arrests following pursuits that involved excessive force, as reported by supervisors, ranged from 15 percent (Metro-Dade) to 11 percent (Mesa). In Metro-Dade, 35 supervisors (71 percent) reported that excessive force is used in 1 to 25 percent of the arrests made after a pursuit. In Aiken, the supervisors reported the use of excessive force in approximately the same percentage of arrests as did their deputies. In Mesa, the majority of the supervisors reported that excessive force is used in 1 to 25 percent of the arrests.

The figures on the use of force are difficult to interpret, but the acknowledgment of excessive force by so many officers and supervisors can be viewed only as a serious problem for the agencies, especially because the officers' and supervisors' opinions reveal much more force and excessive force than do the figures entered on the official pursuit report forms. The suspects' experiences provide a picture more consistent with the officers' opinions than with the officers' official reports (Kappeler et al. 1994).

Interviews with Suspects

The suspects we interviewed had another perspective on use of force after a pursuit. Unfortunately, although these individuals acknowledged fleeing from the police, we do not know whether those pursuits involved officers from the agencies in our study. In other words, these suspects were jailed but could have been arrested or chased by officers from an agency other than those included in our study. For example, the inmates in the Dade County jail could have been referring to activities by an officer from any one of the 27 police agencies in the county. In fact, the suspect interviews in South Carolina were conducted in Richland and Lexington County jails, not in the Aiken County jail. In addition, many interviewees admitted running from the police on more than one occasion. Thus, we present these data merely as another way to understand the use of force by the police after a pursuit.

In Miami, 28 of the 51 suspects (55 percent) interviewed reported being beaten by the police. In South Carolina, 11 of the 32 inmates (34 percent) reported being beaten, as did 15 of the 35 subjects (43 percent) in Omaha. Fifty-seven percent of the subjects claimed that they had been beaten by the police after they were caught and while they were being apprehended. In addition, 10 percent of all suspects involved in pursuit reported that they suffered "serious" injuries. Twenty-four percent said they had filed excessive force complaints with the agency that chased, apprehended, and "beat" them. Clearly the officers and the suspects reported use of force at different rates (Alpert and

Smith 1994). Also, both officers and suspects reported that force is used significantly more often than was stated on the official pursuit reporting forms.

SUMMARY AND CONCLUSIONS

Although some observers claim that police deviance and excessive use of force can be explained by individual differences among officers, a more important inquiry examines the structural features of police work. Kappeler et al. comment:

> Police deviance is not the product of individual pathology residing in aberrant law enforcement officers. The suggestion that police deviance is primarily due to a few "rotten apples" is too simplistic and fails to consider the multitude of possible determinants of police deviance. The extent to which police deviance can be viewed as a pathology is limited to any pathology that exists in the structuring of society, the organizing of the police institution, and the opportunities inherent in the police role and function. (1994:87)

In other words, an analysis of police use of force must include an understanding of the police organization, the authority granted to officers to use force, and the management of police deviance.

There is a relatively rich literature on the use of force in nonpursuit arrests (Adams 1995; Geller and Toch 1995), there is precious little information on force used after a pursuit to arrest the suspect. The introduction of a pursuit, which is dangerous and exciting, adds adrenaline and fear as well as other factors caused by high speeds and the need to make quick decisions.

Once a vehicular chase has ended, the officers involved must attempt to take the suspect into custody. One consequence of an exciting, adrenaline-driven pursuit is the level of force used by the police to apprehend the suspect. Skolnick and Fyfe describe a possible response by the police to one who has exhibited serious defiance or disrespect toward the police and has engaged them in a pursuit:

> But regardless of how relatively minor the violations that lead to their flight, fleeing motorists commit a cardinal sin against the police: instead of submitting immediately, they challenge the police and attempt to escape their pursuer's authority. In doing so, in the eyes of the police officers accustomed to motorists and other citizens who do not only submit immediately to police authority but even check their speedometers in the mere presence of police cars, fleeing motorists become prime candidates for painful lessons at the ends of police nightsticks. (1993:111)

The nature and extent of that force and why it occurs depends on who is asked and under what circumstances. Certainly, not all suspects are beaten, but the discrepancies are quite extensive when use of force after a pursuit is examined.

Pursuit forms collected from each agency reveal one set of "facts." These forms document the officers' official actions but differ from officers' and supervisors' own statements about the use of force. In Metro-Dade, as in the other jurisdictions, no officer reported using excessive force, and only 13 percent of the arrests made after a pursuit involved force that was recorded on official forms. The Metro-Dade officers, however, stated that they believed force was used in 43 percent of the pursuit-related arrests and that force was excessive in nearly one-half of these cases (16 percent of the total). In Aiken County, 36 percent of the arrests involved officially reported force; officers, however, revealed that they believed 54 percent of the pursuit-related cases involved force, and that it was excessive in 15 percent of those cases. Omaha arresting officers reported the use of force in only 3 percent of their pursuit-related arrests, but estimated that force was used in 53 percent of the cases and that it was excessive 13 percent of the time.

The suspects provided another view of force used to make an arrest after a pursuit. Forty-six percent of the suspects claimed they had been beaten by the police as they were being arrested, and 24 percent said they had filed complaints of excessive force.

The data on use of force and what is perceived as excessive force revealed some important comparisons. As shown in Table 5, officers, supervisors, and suspects report similar perceptions: Officers acknowledged that force was used in 53 percent of the pursuit-related apprehensions, supervisors reported that it was used in 47 percent of the apprehensions, and suspects said they were beaten 57 percent of the times that they were apprehended. Similar comparisons emerge when the data on excessive force are reviewed. Officers reported that excessive force was used in 13 percent of the apprehensions following a pursuit, supervisors in 11 percent, and suspects in 24 percent. The official reports, however, indicate that force was used in only 17 percent of those apprehensions and that no excessive force was applied. The officers' interview data and the suspects' reports are closer to each other than is either to official reports. These differences raise some important organizational issues, concerns, and implications.

These differences may have several (and alternative) explanations. First, they may be a result of perspective: Some force may be perceived as reasonable by one officer but not by another or by a suspect. Certainly the terms *excessive* and *beating* may be interpreted in many ways, and the differences may be due to an error of measurement. Second, the differences may result from an officer's unwillingness to report force, especially force that might be

TABLE 5

PERCEPTIONS OF USE OF FORCE AND EXCESSIVE FORCE DURING APPREHENSION OF A SUSPECT AFTER A PURSUIT

| | *Perceptions of Officers, Supervisors, and Suspects, and Records on Official Forms* | | | |
| | Use of Force | | Use of Excessive Force | |
	N	%	N	%
Officers	715	53	93	13
Supervisors	174	47	19	11
Suspects	146	46	20	14
Official Forms	1,295	17	1,295	0

considered excessive. It is unlikely that officers will admit using unnecessary force, even if their actions were captured on videotape.

The differences in reported use of force may also be influenced by the excitement and danger of the pursuit. Adams (1995:71) made a comment to this effect after reviewing the available research on police use of force in general: "[O]bservational research suggests that police use force at least twice as often as suggested by official use-of-force reports. . . because they provide for a more generous definition of force than used by police to trigger the filing of a use-of-force report." In any case, the nature and extent of the force, and the differences in that force as recorded on the forms and reported by officers and suspects, raises management issues. The official version, which is described by the police, represents the lower boundary of the behavior and often omits critical information. Two highly visible examples of such an attempt to bias a report are the beating death of Arthur McDuffie and the beating of Rodney King (Alpert, Smith and Watters 1992).

The nature and extent of force used to take a suspect into custody after a pursuit suggests an immediate need for corrective measures. The targets of reform must be organizational elements including policies, training, supervision, and accountability systems. First, departments' pursuit policies should incorporate the requirement that, whenever possible, any officer other than the primary pursuit officer (i.e., a secondary officer) shall make the physical arrest of the suspect. This policy would permit an officer who has been less intensely involved in the chase to make physical contact with the suspect. A secondary officer is less likely to use unnecessary force than an officer who has been in an adrenaline-driven chase, and who is highly excited or extremely angry at the suspect.

Second, officers must be trained to understand the dynamics of pursuit and its effect on their state of mind. This training must include information about how to manage anger and frustration. Although an officer may have a natural desire to "teach the suspect a lesson" or provide a little "street justice," it is unprofessional and unacceptable to use more force than is necessary to take the suspect into custody (see Sykes 1986). In addition, Beach, Morris, and Smith (1993) and Homant et al. (1993) suggest that training should include the warning to officers and supervisors that personality factors may affect their decision making. Training officers must recognize that emotions cannot be eliminated but can be controlled (IADLEST 1989:3.2).

Supervisors hold another key to helping officers control their anger, their emotions, and the use of force and excessive force. Ineffective or incompetent supervision is translated into permission for officers to "do what comes naturally." Officers should receive serious direction, not supervision that winks at violations or circumvents policy. Supervisors also can establish a record of actions by interviewing officers and those arrested to determine the sequence and intensity of events. Car-mounted video cameras help greatly in determining what actually occurred during a pursuit and the apprehension of the driver. Proper supervision includes direction, training, investigation, and discipline; each element must be taken seriously and supported by the administration. This responsibility falls into the final category: departmental accountability systems.

A department's accountability system should hold its officers and supervisors responsible for their decisions and actions (Kappeler et al. 1994). In regard to pursuits, the formal reporting forms must be reviewed and the information provided must be investigated to assure accuracy. This is not to say that all pursuits must be subjected to a complete investigation. Yet if officers realize that a creative (though not necessarily accurate) report will relieve them of any further scrutiny or responsibility, it is likely that reports will become more and more inventive. It is important to learn from the participants' and witnesses' perspective what occurred during a pursuit and to know what level of force was used to apprehend a suspect. If this suggestion were taken seriously, investigators could randomly investigate pursuits, even those which resulted in no accident or significant injury. This practice would help to establish support from the public, which is concerned about pursuit driving, as well as influencing officers to provide accurate accounts. In addition, such investigations might keep officers from using excessive force.

Investigating and verifying the actions of police during and after pursuits may appear to be an unnecessary control tactic over an infrequent, often inconsequential event. After all, it is the suspect who has instigated a highly dangerous pursuit and who may be receiving "what he deserves." Does it really cause any harm to modify the report to justify the administration of street justice? The police, in turn, have the power to make official a particular version of an event. As Hunt and Manning inform us, many police agencies routinely engage in "normal" lies that are acceptable to some audiences, such as fellow officers (Hunt and Manning 1991:53). They report, "In the police academy, instructors encouraged recruits to lie in some situations, while strongly discouraging it in others" (1991:54).

In some departments "creative writing" may appear in pursuit reports. It may be known, approved, winked at, or not reviewed by supervisors who value protection of their officers over protection of the "guilty." If this is true, the effects on officers, supervisors, and the public may include multiple long-term consequences. Officers and supervisors may develop customs and practices that are not only bad police procedure but also violations of civil and criminal law. The most serious consequence, however, is the effect on the officers and the organization, who come to believe the lies they tell.

REFERENCES

Adams, K. 1995. "Measuring the Prevalence of Police Abuse of Force." Pp. 61–76 in *And Justice for All: Understanding and Controlling Police Abuse of Force*, edited by W. Geller and H. Toch. Washington, DC: Police Executive Research Forum.

Alpert, G. 1995. "The Management of Police Pursuit Driving." Pp. 599–609 in *The Encyclopedia of Police Science*, edited by W. Bailey, New York: Garland.

Alpert, G. and R. Dunham. 1990. *Police Pursuit Driving: Controlling Responses to Emergency Situations*. New York: Greenwood.

Alpert, G. and L. Fridell. 1992. *Police Vehicles and Firearms: Instruments of Deadly Force*. Prospect Heights, IL: Waveland.

Alpert, G. and W. Smith. 1994. "How Reasonable Is the Reasonable Man? Police and Excessive Force." *Journal of Criminal Law and Criminology* 85:481–501.

Alpert, G., W. Smith, and D. Watters. 1992. "Implications of the Rodney King Beating." *Criminal Law Bulletin* 28:469–79.

Beach, R., E. Morris, and W. Smith. 1993. *Emergency Vehicle Operations: A Line Officers' Guide*. Tulsa: Pecos Press.

Geller, W. and H. Toch, eds. 1995. *And Justice for All: Understanding and Controlling Police Abuse of Force*. Washington, DC: Police Executive Research Forum.

Homant, R., D. Kennedy, and J. Howton. 1993. "Sensation Seeking as a Factor in Police Pursuit." *Criminal Justice and Behavior* 20:293–305.

Hunt, J. and P. Manning. 1991. "The Social Context of Police Lying." *Symbolic Interaction* 14:51–70.

International Association of Directors of Law Enforcement Standards and Training (IADLEST). 1989. *Driver Training Reference Guide.* Washington, DC: IADLEST.

Kappeler, V. 1993. *Critical Issues in Police Civil Liability.* Prospect Heights, IL: Waveland.

Kappeler, V., R. Sluder, and G. Alpert. 1994. *Forces of Deviance: Understanding the Dark Side of Policing.* Prospect Heights, IL: Waveland.

Skolnick, J. and J. Fyfe. 1993. *Above the Law: Police and the Excessive Use of Force.* New York: Free Press.

Sykes, G. 1986. "Street Justice: A Moral Defense of Order Maintenance Policing." *Justice Quarterly* 3:497–512.

Urbonya, K. 1991. "The Constitutionality of High-Speed Pursuits under the Fourth and Fourteenth Amendments." *St. Louis Law Review* 35:205–88.

CASES CITED

Graham v. Conner 490 U.S 386 (1989)

Tennessee v. Garner 471 U.S. 1 (1985)

A R T I C L E   2 1

THE MOST DEADLY FORCE: POLICE PURSUITS

*Geoffrey P. Alpert**

*Patrick R. Anderson***

T he complexity of the current world forces us to live within the parameters of laws that were enacted for totally different reasons then those which would support laws today. It is the purpose of this paper to examine one such example of our drawing from history a mechanism by which to face a modern-day problem: police pursuits.

The Civil Rights Act, 42 U.S.C. Section 1983, has become the predominant vehicle for civil suits filed in federal court alleging police misconduct (Territo 1985). The number of such actions has sharply increased in recent years (Note 1976; Davis, et al. 1979), resulting in significant financial claims and decisions against municipalities and local government units. However, this Civil Rights Act was originally designed as a response to the activities of the Ku Klux Klan and the apathy of Southern states regarding those activities during Reconstruction. Congress granted direct access to the federal courts for plaintiffs who were unable to secure redress in state courts. As applied today, Section 1983 has become one means of controlling government misconduct through litigation (Schuck 1983; Note 1976).

The present day use of the Civil Rights Act as a way to seek redress for violation of constitutional rights is the result of interpretations and applications of the Act during the past two decades. In 1961 the Supreme Court in *Monroe v. Pape* addressed the plaintiff's claim that Chicago police officers had, "under color" of law, violated the constitutional guarantee against unreasonable

---

*Director, Center for the Study of Law and Society, University of Miami.

**Department of Criminal Justice, Louisiana State University.

Geoffrey P. Alpert and Patrick R. Anderson, "The Most Deadly Force: Police Pursuits" (as appeared in *Justice Quarterly,* Vol. 3, No. 1, 1986, pp. 1–14). Reprinted with permission from The Academy of Criminal Justice Sciences.

searches and seizures. The Court held that civil action was allowable under Section 1983 and that plaintiffs need not prove "specific intent" on the part of the defendants. Subsequent suits alleging police misconduct have been filed under Section 1983 despite the fact that the *Monroe* court held that units of local government were immune from liability under the statute.

However, the limitation on local government liability changed drastically in 1978 with the U.S. Supreme Court's decision in *Monell v. Department of Social Services* (436 U.S. 690), which stated in part:

> Local governing bodies, therefore, can be sued directly under Section 1983 for monetary, declaratory, or injunctive relief where as here, the action that is alleged to be unconstitutional implements or executes a policy statement, ordinance, regulation or decision officially adopted and promulgated by the body's officers. (436 U.S. 690).

The court further held that deprivations resulting from governments, "custom," even that which has not received official, formal approval, may be subject to suit. The "good faith" defense, though not addressed directly in *Monell*, was later held to be no defense at all in *Owen v. City of Independence* (445 U.S. 622) and *Main v. Thiboutot* (100 S. Ct. 2502).

Since *Monroe,* and more importantly *Monell,* suits brought against law enforcement agencies alleging wrongful police use of force, especially deadly force have resulted in defensive actions taken by police agencies to protect themselves as much as possible from litigation. These actions include: narrow policies regulating officers' use of deadly force, more and better training, and improved supervisory control, among others.

This article examines police use of the deadliest weapon in their arsenal, the motor vehicle. We will first review what we know about police pursuits, then turn to what we should know, how we can increase our knowledge, and finally, how social scientists can help interpret that information.

When a police officer engages in a high-speed chase in a high-powered police car, that vehicle becomes a potential deadly weapon. Although much has been written about police use of deadly force (Blumberg 1985), almost all of that literature focuses upon service revolvers. It is surprising that so little is known about police chases, the amount and type of danger which could result, or the type and adequacy of policies, training, and supervision[1]. The literature that does exist on the topic (cf. Schultz 1983; Beckman 1983; Territo 1982; Varenchik 1964) is non-scientific and contributes little to our knowledge regarding the phenomenon. This lack of information regarding police chases is discouraging—weapons are used in a very small percentage of police activity as compared to the use of the squad car, generally on inseparable extension of the police officer.

---

[1]Information which does exist and is disseminated through organizations such as the International Association of Chiefs of Police tends to be restatements of the obvious. See for instance Training Key #20, "Safe Driving Techniques," Training Key #92 "Pursuit Driving," and Training Key #113, "Emergency Calls"—all published by the IACP and each restating the other. Such incestuous "helps" tend not to be helps at all. Likewise, the IACP Legal Point (1982), "Liability From Vehicular Pursuits," adds little to an understanding of police pursuits. The absence of specificity in these publications reflects the lack of knowledge regarding this phenomenon.

POLICE AND POLICE CARS

Most information about police pursuits comes from the popular media. The Blues Brothers elude hundreds of police cars careening into one another on the streets of Chicago. Police officers drive at incredible speeds down beautiful boulevards in Miami Vice. In frequent, almost obligatory, scenes in *Hill Street Blues* and *Hunter*, television actors portray high-speed chases in carefully directed chorus lines of cars. Life may sometimes imitate art, but it is unfortunate when our "knowledge" of police pursuits derives from scriptwriters' inventions and stuntmen's antics instead of from real-life experiences. What we see on our screens are depiction's of police officers chasing the bad guys with reckless abandon. Rarely do we see what happens beyond the immediate chase; rarely do we see the final scene.

High-speed pursuits can end in one or more of the following situations:

a) the offender stops the car and surrenders;

b) the pursued vehicle crashes into a structure and the offenders are apprehended, escape or are injured or killed;

c) the pursued vehicle crashes into another vehicle without injuries to passengers or others;

d) the pursued vehicle crashes into another vehicle with injuries or death to passengers or others;

e) the pursued vehicle hits a pedestrian (with or without injuries or death);

f) the police use some level of force to stop the pursued vehicle, including firearms, roadblocks, ramming, bumping, boxing, etc.;

g) the police car crashes (with or without injuries to officers or civilians).

If the chase results in injury or death, there is a high probability that one party or another will bring legal action. This unintended consequence is virtually ignored by the entertainment media. Also ignored is the trauma of the injured victim in a high-speed pursuit. How often is the television police officer taken to court as a result of his or her negligence? Certainly not as frequently as it occurs in real life.

Police Pursuits

The police function includes protection of life as well as enforcement of the law and maintenance of an orderly community. Each of these functions must be performed within the limits of the law. In other words, police officers are themselves subject to the laws that they enforce. Most of the time, there is little question as to how an officer must act, and therefore how he must be trained. In situations requiring high-speed pursuits, however, it is by no means clear what constitutes reasonable or unreasonable behavior, sufficient or insufficient police training. To frame this issue properly, one might ask: under what circumstances is a police department or its officers responsible for injury to an innocent driver or passenger of a vehicle, or for the damages to property as a result of a high-speed pursuit? Generally, governmental agencies and agents may be held liable for injuries approximately caused by the reckless operation of a motor vehicle. In the majority of jurisdictions, however, police cars operating as emergency vehicles enjoy a special status and are exempt from certain traffic regulations. For example, emergency vehicles are usually exempt from laws relating to speed limitations, stop signs, traffic signals, and right-of-way, among others. The driver of an emergency vehicle cannot be found guilty of negligence as a matter of law solely because of his disregard of those traffic laws from which he or she is exempted. On the other hand, most of the statutes and ordinances require a police officer to drive with regard for the safety of all persons using the roadways. An officer acting in an emergency situation is not protected from the consequences of his reckless disregard for the safety of others. In fact, most laws and police procedures demand that a police officer operate his or her vehicle in a non-negligent manner.

We are faced with a need to balance vigorous law enforcement against the individual's right to be safe. In general terms, we can understand what factors fall an each side of the scale. On the side of law enforcement is the legal duty to apprehend criminals. On the side of citizens is the expectation of streets that are safe, not just from the bad guys, but from pursuing cops as well. The criteria for holding a police department or officer responsible for property damage or injuries to an innocent bystander are not easily determined.

The law is full of such difficult-to-draw lines. As social scientists we can provide information to guide police policy-makers and the courts in weighing the two horns of this dilemma. We will proceed by identifying the issues.

Consider the following definition of a police pursuit: *A high-speed pursuit can be defined as an active attempt by a law enforcement officer operating an emergency vehicle to apprehend alleged criminals in a moving motor vehicle, when the driver of the vehicle, in an attempt to avoid apprehension, significantly increases his or her speed or takes other evasive action.* This definition consists of several elements:

1) active attempt;
2) law enforcement officer;
3) emergency vehicle;
4) apprehend;
5) alleged criminal;
6) moving motor vehicle;
7) significantly increases speed; and
8) other evasive action.

One can determine relatively easily when a high-speed chase exists by examining the eight variables listed above. Most of these are self-explanatory or are defined legally. Perhaps the most problematic are 7) significantly increases speed, and 8) other evasive action. Since the word "increases" connotes advance, it is a relative term. What increment of speed in required to qualify as significant? The answer must be based on an analysis of the totality of the circumstances. Similarly, an intentional act to avoid capture must be analyzed in the context of the specific situation. Action which might be considered evasive in one situation may be reasonable in another.

Once it is agreed that a high-speed pursuit exists, we need to review the responsibilities of each actor in the event: the officer directly involved, other officers, the supervisors, and the departmental administrators. The levels of responsibilities are split into several categories: 1) the agency's policies, practices, and customs; 2) the required training; 3) the actions of the officer initiating the pursuit; 4) the actions of the back-up officers; 5) the actions of the supervisor; and 6) the actions of the administrator, who will compare the officers' actions with department policy.

The responsibilities of the agency include the kind of training provided for its officers, the policy under which they operate, and the practice and custom of the department. In other words, a strong, clearly-defined policy can be undermined if no one enforces it, or if those who violate it are not properly disciplined. The police officer who initiates the chase has his or her responsibilities, as does the back-up officer. Under what conditions should a chase be initiated? Under what conditions should it be terminated? What are the precise duties and limits of duty of the back-up officer? While many of these questions can be answered by a tightly-written policy, there are far too many split-second decisions which must be made in conditions unanticipated by policy. The duties and responsibilities of officers, supervisors, and administrators are dependent upon one another. As the situation changes, so should the action of the officers and the reaction of the supervisors. A closer look at existing departmental pursuit policies illustrates the problem. First, the question emerges as to the conditions under which a police officer should initiate a chase.

Why Pursue?

Many questions are posed by the Monday-morning quarterback. One question concerning police procedures that is repeatedly asked is "why get involved in high-speed pursuits at all?" As mentioned earlier, apprehension of a criminal is at the heart of the police mission. It can be argued that any law violator should be chased and arrested. It is also arguable that if a motorist initiates a chase, it is he or she who is responsible for any resulting damages. Even if an automobile has been identified in a chase, by the color, model, and license number it may be impossible to find and arrest the driver. It is one thing if the "crime" is a minor traffic violation; it is another if it is a rape or murder. If a police officer foregoes a chase, does this not violate his duty, affect his reputation, and perhaps encourage the next person to attempt to outrun the police? Moreover, since only a minority of all criminal offenders are identified and arrested, is it not likely that a police officer witnessing an offense or chasing an offender will want to make an arrest at all costs? Is a desire to do whatever is necessary to apprehend criminals simply unnecessary adrenaline, or rather energetic and responsible police work?

Finally, it may be argued that since too many offenders already escape the jaws of justice through a loophole, there is no reason to provide them with another. Failure to pursue an offender certainly reduces the chance of an accident, and virtually eliminates in many cases, the possibility of later capture. It may well encourage others to "jack-rabbit" if word is out that there will be no pursuit.

No data have been located on whether the incidence of police chases varies between jurisdictions with different policies. We do know, however, that the absence of a strong and convincing policy on police pursuits forces officers to react intuitively. This intuition is probably based on practice and custom. The consequences of aggressive police pursuits without established guidelines may include the unnecessary loss of property, personal injury, or death. Is occasional injury, death, or property damage the price one must pay to live in a democratic society? Although rhetorical, this question deserves attention in the creation of police policies.

HIGH-SPEED PURSUIT POLICIES

In 1981, Leonard Territo (1982) conducted a survey of police departments' policies on high-speed pursuits. Although not conclusive, it remains one of the few published studies on which an empirical model of police pursuits can be based. Territo summarized written policies he received from 45 police agencies from 37 states and reports:

> There were considerable variations in the quality and comprehensiveness of these policies. However, after reviewing each one, it has become clear that such a policy must impose strong controls upon the operation of police vehicles in emergency responses and high-speed pursuits if there is to be a reduction in the increasing number of injuries and deaths (Territo 1982:32).

With a method similar to that used by Territo, we have attempted to update his analysis. In January 1985, we collected 37 different policies from police departments in 25 states. In addition, we reviewed 35 court cases from 20 states in which police officers were being sued for negligence. Based upon the best available information, we can slightly adjust Territo's list and make some general comments in an attempt to establish a comprehensive policy.

Toward A Model Policy

Our model policy would include the following components:

A. *Officers' background and preparation.*
1. tactical preparation (training, experience, familiarity with the area including possible escape routes);
2. type of vehicle (condition, equipment, etc.); and
3. likelihood of successful apprehension (identification of offender, probability of apprehending offender at a later time, extent to which offender will go to avoid capture).

B. *Knowledge of incident, area and conditions.*
1. knowledge of the offense (nature and seriousness);
2. traffic conditions (density, speed etc.);
3. road conditions (width, lanes, fitness, surface);
4. geographic area (hills, side walks, curb-breaks);
5. weather (dry, rain, snow);
6. location of pursuit (school, residential, commercial);
7. time of day (light, dark, close to rush hour);
8. pedestrian traffic (light, heavy); and
9. visibility (fog, no lighting).

This list of variables is in no way complete. Moreover, each variable may be significant by itself, yet two or more may be taken together for a different effect. In other words, each variable must be taken into consideration for purposes of training, but the way in which each variable is to be evaluated or one variable's effects on other variables depends upon the total circumstances. In real-life situations these variables exist in some combination, having a joint as well as an individual effect. A decision to pursue must be made on an analysis of the combined effect, taking into account the incident, area, conditions, officers' background, and preparation, among other factors. If an officer responds to a call for a murder or other serious felony, he or she must weigh the need for immediate apprehension with the offenders' "need" to escape capture. In addition, policies and training must include guidelines on the use of emergency equipment, limitations of speed, closeness of pursuit, number and location of pursuit vehicles, non-police passengers, techniques of last resort and the supervisors' duties, among others.

Although policies and related training may include these variables, what values should be attached to them and how they should be interpreted is not clear. An officer's lack of experience may discourage him from initiating a chase, but his total familiarity with the area, including all dead-end streets and locations for the safest apprehension, may justify a limited pursuit. In the example cited above, an officer responding to a reported shooting would on face value be justified in pursuing a suspect at all costs.

In reality, however, the officer's zealous commitment to making an arrest should not necessarily justify a decision to engage in grossly reckless behavior that might endanger innocent motorists and pedestrians. The question of whether a pursuit should be initiated may depend an any combination of variables mentioned above (and perhaps ones which were not mentioned). Issues include whether an officer must employ emergency lights and sirens continuously; whether he or she may drive over 60, 70, or 100 miles per hour; whether an officer should engage in a chase if he has not checked out his equipment and has no back-up in sight. An analysis of actual high speed pursuits based on all the significant variables including policies and practices should shed light upon the answers.

PRIOR RESEARCH

We were able to locate five studies of pursuit driving which were based on empirical data. These included a one-month field study in 1970 commissioned by the United States Department of Transportation (DOT) in four police agencies, (Fennessy 1970), a one-week survey in 1968 of high-speed pursuits in which members of the North Carolina Highway Patrol were involved, a study prepared by Physicians for Automotive Safety (1968), and a study conducted in 1958–59 by the Michigan State Police. While these studies were all based upon empirical data, they must be considered only as theory-building contributions because each is so methodologically flawed that the data are not meaningful.[2] The fifth study was conducted by the California Highway Patrol

---

[2]For a review and analysis of these studies see Fennessey (1970).

in 1982 (California Highway Patrol 1983). The serious flaws of the other studies preclude a review of their findings, but the CHP study has important findings and conclusions.

The California Highway Patrol Study

Most of the 683 pursuits in this study involved California Highway Patrol officers. This means that most (95 percent) of the chases were initiated on highways or freeways, a fact which may well have affected the time and length of the speeds, the outcome, and other variables. Ten urban police departments joined the study in progress, but the results were published only in the aggregate. Unfortunately, we are not told how many chases involved city as well as highway driving. Therefore, we must view this study as a highway or freeway study, and cannot apply the findings to a city environment. Despite these limitations, the CHP study has the best available data. From those data we can create a profile of the typical pursuit and analyze more closely some of the specific variables, as follows:

The most likely pursuit:

1) will be initiated by an observed violation of the traffic code;
2) is at night;
3) travels one mile;
4) lasts one to two minutes;
5) involves two police patrol cars and no air support;
6) is terminated voluntarily by the offender; and
7) involves a male driver 20 years old.

Some of the more interesting findings of this study are:

1) 77 percent of the suspects were apprehended;
2) 70 percent of the pursuits ended without an accident; and
3) 68 percent of the pursuits lasted less than five miles.

Pursuits were coded into six types: 1) traffic code violations; 2) suspected intoxicated drivers; 3) suspected criminal activity other than traffic; 4) apprehending a known felon; 5) acting on a request from another agency; and 6) other.

The rate of apprehension is significantly affected by the event preceding the pursuit. The greatest number of pursuits followed an observed traffic code violation, and the rate of apprehension is significantly affected by the event preceding the pursuit. As the report notes "considering the training that peace officers received with regard to stopping known felon suspects, this result is not surprising. Generally, an officer will wait until he has sufficient back-up and can choose a favorable location for a stop before trying to apprehend a known felon" (California Highway Patrol 1983:42). Although the police may be more cautious in pursuit of known felons than traffic-law offenders, pursuits of felons end in a much higher rate of accidents than do other pursuits. Almost 50 percent of the pursuits which involve felons result in accidents, as compared to just over 30 percent of the non-felony pursuits.

THE ROLES OF THE SOCIAL SCIENTIST

Research

Although surveys of written policies regarding pursuit have been conducted, little is known about the effects of such policies. A prediction that police officers in a department with a restrictive policy on pursuits would be involved in fewer chases than would those in a department with a liberal policy would be consistent with research on police use of firearms (see Fyfe 1979 and Sherman 1983). Unlike the firearms situation, however, it is unknown whether a significantly greater number of drivers would attempt to elude police, or in what ways chases would differ between departments having restrictive versus liberal policies.

Only after careful analysis of police pursuits under a variety of conditions and with a variety of outcomes can any solutions or concrete suggestions be offered. It is in this area that the social scientist can contribute information to police planners or policy makers (see Galligher 1985). Pre-chase, in-chase, and post-chase conditions or situations—once identified as factors which define or explain the relative success of a police pursuit—can then be explicated.

Information concerning what actually happens during a pursuit, the kind and content of radio communications, supervisory or backup roles, and citizen or traffic interference, among other factors, could greatly benefit police administrators. Similarly, knowledge of the manner in which police pursuits are terminated and what occurs at that time could guide police trainers.

Police administrators, trainers, and scholars could directly benefit from research on police pursuit. Essential policies and training would be based upon empirical research data rather than on opinions, customs, or court decisions. In the final analysis the patrol officer could be given needed direction in the otherwise lonely and important discretion that must be exercised. Reactive judgments after the fact generally contribute little to our knowledge about events or to the creation of future solutions to problems engendered by police pursuits. In this case, a call for more research is an urgent plea rather than a mere face-saving device on the part of social scientists.

Applying the Research

The social scientist/criminologist can balance variables and can offer expert opinions an a variety of topics. It is appropriate that social research be utilized to assist the judiciary (Alpert 1984). Social science testimony in court is neither uncommon nor limited to police misconduct cases. In recent years social scientists have been engaged in cases involving school desegregation (Clark 1959; Kalmuss, et. al. 1982; Rossell 1980; Van den Haag 1960), capital punishment (Wolfgang 1974), prison conditions (Toch 1982; Merritt 1983; Leonard 1983), competency to stand trial (Louisell 1955; Lessen 1964; Cooke and Jackson 1971; Levine 1971), and a great deal more (Anderson 1984). Testimony from social science scholars, although sometimes based on empirical research such as survey or official data analysis (Wolfgang 1974; Loewen 1981), most frequently concerns standard practices and policies, as well as officer supervision and training, in police misconduct cases. Expert witnesses offering such testimony are qualified by the court based on education, training, and experience (Cleary, et. al. 1972).

Opinions on police pursuits by qualified criminologists can indicate whether a pursuit should have been initiated, when it should have been terminated, whether standard practice in the field was followed, whether proper policies or training existed, the type and quality of supervision, and more. This type of testimony, based an empirical research, would hopefully minimize the impact of those experts with testimony for sale.

Attorneys seeking either to assign or to deflect liability claims against local government units for losses incurred as a result of high speed police chases often must rely on expert opinions to educate the court. To date, these experts have presented testimony primarily derived from personal experiences and high-priced impressions. It has become standard practice to use expert witnesses in cases filed under 42 U.S.C. 1983 on police misconduct. Indeed, the testimony of expert witnesses is generally the determining factor in such cases, since physical evidence and factual testimony are typically not seriously disputed (see Alpert 1981). The expert can interpret events in the context of "generally accepted practices in the field."

Specifically, the expert can assist counsel in determining the critical elements of a case and in identifying additional theories for an attorney to explore. Also, the scholar-expert can synthesize the criminal justice literature. As stated earlier, there is a paucity of research literature on hot pursuit, but there exists a wealth of literature regarding police discretion, selection, training, supervision, and the establishment of written policies. An experienced expert, having worked with agencies in similar matters and having subjected various observations to vigorous scientific scrutiny, can determine those factors most favorable to each side and can assess whether or not a legitimate claim exists against a policeman or department.

POLICE PURSUITS: A LOOK TO THE FUTURE

The wail of a siren indicates an emergency vehicle traveling to assist or chase someone. It will more than likely be moving faster than the rest of the traffic and the driver will be taking risks. Hopefully, the driver is aware of the risks he or she is taking, knows how to calculate the necessary decisions, has training, and is monitored by a supervisor who is in-control of the situation. Before such conditions obtain, however, carefully guided research will have to be conducted and analyzed, and the knowledge thus gained will have to be implemented. If and when we achieve that level of performance, innocent bystanders will be safer, and 42 U.S.C. 1983 may be placed to rest as a means of litigating police liability due to improper high-speed pursuits.

COURT DECISIONS

Monroe v. Pape, 365 U.S. 167 (1961).
Monell v. Department of Social Sciences, 436 U.S. 690 (1978).
Main v. Thiboutot, 448 U.S. 165 (1980).
Owen v. City of Independence, 445 U.S. 622 (1980).
Tennessee v. Garner, 53 U.S. 441 (1985).

REFERENCES

Alpert, G.P. (1984) "The Needs of Judiciary and Misapplications of Social Research." *Criminology* 22:441-456.

—— (1981) "Criminal Defense Attorneys: A Typology of Defense Strategies." *Criminal Law Bulletin* 17:381-404.

Anderson, P.R. (1984) Scholarship in the Courtroom: The Criminologist as Expert Witness. *Criminal Law Bulletin* 20(5): 405-416.

Beckman, E. (1983) "High-speed Chases: In Pursuit of A Balanced Policy." *The Police Chief* (January) :34-57.

Blumberg, M. (1985) "Research on Police Use of Deadly Force: the State of the Art." A. Blumberg and E. Niderhoffer (eds.) *The Ambivalent Force.* New York: Holt, Rinehart and Winston.

California Highway Patrol (1983) *California Highway Patrol Pursuit Study.* Department of the California Highway Patrol, Sacramento, California.

Clark, K. (1959-60) "The Desegregation Cases: Criticisms of the Social Scientists Role." *Villanova Law Review* 5:224-240.

Cleary, E., V. Ball, R. Barnhart, K. Brown, G. Dix, E. Gellborn, R. Meisenholder, E. Roberts, and J. Strong (1972) *McCormick's Handbook on the Law of Evidence.* St. Paul, Minnesota: West Publishing Company.

Cooke, G. and N. Jackson (1971) "Competency to Stand Trial: Role of the Psychologist." *Professional Psychology* 5:373-376.

Davis, L. B., J.H. Small, and D.J. Wohlberg (1979) "Project: Suing the Police in Federal Court." *The Yale Law Journal* 88(4):780-825.

Fennessy, E.F. (1970) *A Study of the Problem of Hot Pursuit by the Police.* Harvard, Connecticut: The Center for the Environment and Man, Inc.

Fyfe, J.J. (1979) "Administrative Interventions on Police Shooting Discretion." *Journal of Criminal Justice* 7:309-324.

Galligher, G.P. (1985) "Lethal Force on Wheels, What Can Trainers Do?" *Training Aids Digest* 10 (Oct.): 1-7.

Kalmuss, D., M. Chesler, and J. Sanders (1982) "Political Conflict in Applied Scholarship: Expert Witnesses in School Desegregation Litigation." *Soc. Prob.* 30:167-178.

Kates, D.B. and J.A. Kouba (1972) "Liability of Public Entities Under Section 1983 of the Civil Rights Act." *Southern California Law Review* 45(131):131-167.

Leonard, E.B. (1983) "Judicial Decisions and Prison Reform: The Impact of Litigation on Women Prisoners." *Soc. Prob.,* 131(1):45-58.

Levine, F.J. (1971) "Psychologist as Expert Witness in "Psychiatric" Questions." *Cleveland State Law Review* 20:379-398.

Loewen, J.W. (1981) *Social Science in the Courtroom: Statistical Techniques and Research Methods for Winning Class Action Suits.* Lexington, Massachusetts: Lexington Books.

Louisell, D.W. (1955) "The Psychologist in Today's Legal World." *Minnesota Law Review* 39:235.

Note (1976) "Damage Remedies Against Municipalities for Constitutional Violations." Harvard Law Review 89(4):922-960.

Merritt, F.S. (1983) "Corrections Law Developments: Prisoner's Rights Litigation in the 1980's." *Criminal Law Bulletin* 19(2):157-161.

Newman, J.O. (1978)"Suing the Lawbreakers: Proposals to Strengthen the Section 1983 Damage Remedy for Law Enforcer's Misconduct." *The Yale Law Review,* 87(3): 447-457.

Physicians for Automotive Safety (1968) *Rapid Pursuit by the Police: Causes, Hazards, Consequences. A National Pattern is Evident.* Armonk, New York: Physicians for Automotive Safety.

Rossell, C.H. (1980) "Social Science Research in Educational Equity Cases: A Critical Review." *Review Research Education* 8:237-295.

Schultz, D.O. (1983) "High-Speed Chases: Vehicle Pursuit vs. the Law." *The Police Chief* (January) :32-36.

Sherman, L.W. (1983) "Reducing Police Gun Use: Critical Events, Administrative Policy and Organizational Change." M. Punch (ed.), *The Control of Police Organizations*. Cambridge, Mass: M.I.T. Press.

Territo, L. (1982) "Citizen Safety: Key Element in Police Pursuit Policy." *Trial* (August): 31-34.

——— (1985) *Police civil Liability*. Columbia, Maryland: Hanrow Press.

Toch, H. (1982) "The role of the Expert on Prison Conditions: The Battle of Footnotes in *Rhodes v. Chapman*." *Criminal Law Bulletin* 18(1):38-49.

Van den Haag, E. (1980) "Social Science Testimony in the Desegregation Cases—A Reply to Professor Kenneth Clark." *Villanova Law Review* 6(48):69-77.

Varenchik, R. (1984) "Officer in Pursuit." *Police Product News* (September) :54-67.

Wolfgang, M.E. (1974) "The Social Scientist in Court." *Journal of Criminal Law and Criminology* 65(2):238-247.

THE OTHER DEADLY FORCE: AN ANALYSIS OF ONE STATE'S HIGH-SPEED PURSUIT GUIDELINES*

Donald R. Liddick
University of Pittsburgh–Greensburg

T he use of deadly force by the police has long been an issue of great public concern. However, the instrument of deadly force most used by police officers is a patrol car, rather than a gun. According to statistics compiled by the National Highway Traffic Safety Administration, an average of 500 people are killed and 5,000 injured yearly due to high speed police chases (Eidemiller 1996). The problem is one which requires a delicate balance between two relevant issues: 1) the interest of the police in capturing criminals and 2) the safety of police officers and the general public.

ACADEMIC RESEARCH AND COURT DECISIONS

One of the earliest studies of high speed police pursuits was conducted by Edmund Fennessey in 1970. He discovered, among other things, that most pursuit, related fatalities are incurred by the fleeing driver, passengers, or uninvolved bystanders. Fennessey also found that in 90% of the cases examined, the event that triggered the pursuit by an officer was a traffic violation (Fennessey 1970). The Operational Planning Section of the California Highway Patrol published the results of a study in 1983 in which it was found that

*The author wishes to thank the University of Pittsburgh's Central Research and Development Fund for providing financial support toward this project. I also wish to thank Kristie Schickel, Josh Henderson, and Margie Vinkler for all of their help. Finally, a thanks is due to the Pennsylvania State Police Research Division for providing advice and assistance.

Donald R. Liddick, "The Other Deadly Force: An Analysis of One State's High-Speed Pursuit Guidelines" (unpublished paper presented at ACJS—March 1999). Reprinted by permission of the author.

29% of pursuits resulted in collisions and 1% resulted in deaths (California Highway Patrol 1983). In 1985, Erik Beckman looked at 424 pursuits conducted by 75 law enforcement agencies over a period of 6 months. His report found that the fleeing drivers were not usually dangerous felons and that fatalities occurred in about 3% of the pursuits examined (Beckman 1985). In 1992, legislation in California mandated that all California law enforcement agencies submit pursuit data to the California Highway Patrol. An analysis of that data for 1992 revealed that there were 7,323 reported police pursuits, of which 0.4% resulted in death and 17% in injury (Grimmond 1993). Other important studies of police pursuits have been conducted by Alpert (1987), Alpert and Anderson (1986), Alpert and Dunham (1988, 1989) and the Baltimore County Police Department (1985).[1] A review of all previous research indicates generally that between 1% and 3% of pursuits end in death, 5% to 24% end in injury, only 9% to 30% are initiated for felony crimes, and between 52% and 63% of pursuits are initiated because of traffic violations (Falcone 1994).

In recent years, a series of cases have set the stage for municipal liability for damages and injuries resulting from high speed police pursuits. In *Brower v. County of Inyo* (109 S.Ct. 1378), decided March 21, 1989, the Supreme Court said that setting up a roadblock and pursuing a fleeing driver into it causing his death constitutes a seizure within the meaning of the Fourth Amendment. Several years earlier in *Tennessee v. Garner* (471 U.S. 1, 105 S.Ct. 1694, 85 L.Ed.2d 1 [1985]), the Supreme Court said that deadly force to catch an unarmed fleeing suspect was an unreasonable seizure under the Fourth Amendment. Of course, in practice, a municipal government's liability is dependent on state law; if a state has waived sovereign immunity, then local governments may be liable. However, any municipality is potentially liable under 42 U.S.C. & 1983 for deprivation of civil rights. The civil rights protected under this federal statute include the right not to be deprived of life, liberty, or property without due process of law, provided by the Fourteenth Amendment, and the protection against unreasonable seizures, provided by the Fourth Amendment (Nugent, McEwen, Connors, and Mayo 1990). In *Monell v. New York City Department of Social Services*, the Supreme Court held that a municipality could be held liable for the actions of an employee if the municipality itself caused the Constitutional violation (Epstein 1994). Of course, the most frequent way that a municipality could be deemed liable for police pursuit damages is a claim of inadequate training, an issue addressed by the Supreme Court in *Canton v. Harris* (109 S.Ct. 1197). In that case, the Court said that a "deliberate and conscious" choice not to properly train officers in the use of deadly force could give rise to a claim of municipal liability (Epstein 1994). Some police agencies have responded to the potential for liability in high speed pursuit situations by implementing written pursuit guidelines.

THE PRESENT STUDY: GOAL, METHOD, AND DATA

In 1995, a Homerville[2] man successfully sued the city on behalf of his wife after she was killed by a vehicle chased by a police officer. Soon thereafter, the state issued a mandate requiring all Atlantic[3] municipalities to adopt written pursuit guidelines (Eidemiller 1996). The purpose of the present work was to assess the degree to which Atlantic municipalities complied with the mandate and to analyze the content of those written pursuit guidelines.

Because of a clause in the state law which requires municipalities to keep their pursuit guidelines confidential, the researcher constructed a cover letter which explained the purpose and scope of the project and assured the target audience complete anonymity. Instead of asking police departments to provide copies of actual pursuit guidelines, a non-intrusive questionnaire was developed for the purpose of assessing the content of guidelines without requiring the disclosure of specific rules or procedures. Issues addressed in the questionnaire were developed from a National Institute of Justice (NIJ) study which outlined a model pursuit guideline (Nugent, Connors, McEwen, and Mayo 1990).

The cover letter and questionnaire were mailed to all 2,582 Atlantic municipalities. Six hundred and eighty-nine municipalities responded (27%), of which 226 indicated that their municipality did not have their own police department. This left a remainder of 463 responses. Frequency distributions were calculated for each survey question.

RESULTS

The survey results, in Table 1, indicate that the vast majority of Atlantic municipalities complied with the state mandate by implementing written pursuit guidelines (99.15% of respondents). Further analysis suggests that the majority of municipalities have adopted written procedures which adequately address critical issues as outlined in the aforementioned model pursuit guideline published by the NIJ. For example, respondents indicated that their guidelines did contain decision-making criteria for the initiation (95.95%) and termination (96.58%) of pursuits. In addition, 90.81% reported that their guidelines provided for the termination of a pursuit if the suspect was identified to the point where later apprehension could be accomplished and the suspect was not a danger to the public. Almost three-fourths (74.68%) of responding police departments said that they prohibited high-speed pursuits for suspected minor violations such as traffic offenses. Similarly, 89.85% of respondents stated that their guidelines contained a component which outlined when or when not to pursue based on the level of potential danger posed by the suspect. Other responses indicate that the majority of Atlantic police departments have implemented guidelines that address important issues like traffic congestion, weather conditions, the use of roadblocks and ramming techniques, the use of unmarked police units, the use of firearms during pursuits, radio procedures, and the maintenance of pursuit episode records.

A few items were less positive. For example, only 53.02% of respondents indicated that they had an internal review process in place which analyzed pursuit episodes, and only 11.13% of responding departments made use of the stop stick (a device used by some state police that slowly and effectively deflates the tires of fleeing suspects).

When asked to describe their department's written pursuit guidelines, 3.5% stated that they were *discretionary* (allowing officers to make all major decisions relating to initiation, tactics, and termination; no formal written rules), 37% said *combination* (allowing officers to make many major pursuit decisions;

TABLE 1

DEPARTMENTAL RESPONSES TO SURVEY QUESTIONS

	yes	no
Does your department have written pursuit guidelines?	99.15	.85
Do your written pursuit guidelines contain decision-making criteria for the initiation of a pursuit?	95.95	4.05
Do your written guidelines contain decision-making criteria for the termination of a pursuit?	96.58	3.42
Do your written guidelines prohibit high speed pursuits for suspected crimes which might be considered minor?	74.68	25.32
Do your guidelines outline when to pursue based on the level of danger posed by the suspect?	89.85	10.15
Do your guidelines outline when to pursue based on current weather conditions?	76.02	23.98
Do your guidelines outline when to pursue based on traffic congestion?	79.66	20.34
Do your guidelines outline when to pursue based on type of road (rural, highway, etc.)?	57.30	42.70
Do your guidelines outline responsibilities for pursuing officers?	96.98	3.02
Do your guidelines outline responsibilities for the communications center?	60.78	39.22
Do your guidelines outline traffic regulations during pursuits (use of emergency equipment, etc.)?	97.44	2.56
Do your guidelines contain information related to roadblock usage?	83.98	16.02
Do your guidelines contain information related to pursuit tactics (ramming techniques, etc.)?	77.68	22.32
Do your guidelines outline communication and coordination pursuit protocol for interjurisdictional pursuits?	82.47	17.53
Does your department maintain records of pursuits?	95.93	4.07
Does your department make use of the "stop stick?"	11.13	88.87
Does your department permit unmarked units to participate in pursuits?	42.12	57.88
Do your written guidelines outline radio procedures to be used during pursuits?	84.30	15.70
Do your guidelines provide for termination of the pursuit if the suspect is identified and deemed to be a non-threat?	90.81	9.19
Do your guidelines provide for termination of the pursuit if the suspect is no longer in sight?	74.73	25.27
Does your department have a policy in place concerning the use of firearms in a pursuit?	84.98	15.02
Does your department have an internal review process in place which analyzes pursuit episodes?	53.02	46.98

*All responses recorded in percent.

some written guidelines), 46.9% said *restrictive* (placing numerous restrictions on officers' judgments and decisions; many specific written guidelines), and 12.6% said *discouraging* (severely cautioning against or discouraging any pursuit except in extreme circumstances).[4]

A major point of interest was whether the size of police departments was related to how the departments characterized their written pursuit guidelines. Respondents were asked to indicate the size of their department, the choices being small (1–24 officers), medium (25–100 officers), and large (more than 100 officers). With this in mind, the following contingency table was constructed.

A glance at the table reveals several things, the most obvious of which is that the vast majority of respondents (87%) were small police departments with 1–24 officers employed.[5]

Also, within each size category the greatest percentage of respondents characterized their written pursuit guidelines as restrictive, followed by combination. Although the number of respondents were small, it is also noteworthy that none of the medium or large police departments described their guidelines as discretionary.

Although one might conclude from a cursory examination of the contingency table, Table 2, that medium- and large-sized police departments tend to characterize their written pursuit guidelines as more restrictive than do small police departments, a more rigorous analysis is made possible by a hypothesis test for contingency tables called the chi-square test. The goal would be to determine whether there is indeed a relationship between the size of a police department and how written pursuit guidelines are characterized. Unfortunately, the chi-square test is inappropriate for the contingency table used here because some of the expected frequencies (a calculation used in determining the chi-square statistic) were less than five.[6]

DISCUSSION

The results of the survey indicate that not only have Atlantic police departments developed written pursuit guidelines, but that they have also included in those guidelines procedures which address relevant issues as outlined in the 1990 National Institute of Justice report previously cited (Nugent, Connors, McEwen, and Mayo 1990). However, the low response rate to the survey is a concern. Many non-respondents may have done so because they have failed to implement written pursuit guidelines. Likewise, the fact that the

TABLE 2

SELF-CHARACTERIZATION OF WRITTEN PURSUIT GUIDELINES BROKEN DOWN BY DEPARTMENT SIZE

	Small	Medium	Large	Total
Discretionary	16 (4.04%)	0 (0%)	0 (0%)	16 (3.5%)
Combination	154 (38.89%)	12 (23.53%)	2 (28.57%)	168 (37%)
Restrictive	178 (44.95%)	30 (58.82%)	5 (71.43%)	213 (46.9%)
Discouraging	48 (12.12%)	9 (17.65%)	0 (0%)	57 (12.6%)
Total	396	51	7	454

majority of respondents described their pursuit guidelines as either restrictive or discouraging could be because departments with those types of guidelines were predisposed to answer survey questions. Still, the available data indicate that many Atlantic police departments are implementing written pursuit guidelines which address important procedural issues and tend to place restrictions on the decision-making of police officers. Of course, whether written pursuit guidelines actually alter the behavior of police officers is a question that should be addressed in future research.[7]

CONCLUSION

Recent events underscore the importance of written pursuit guidelines. A 1998 Supreme Court decision in the case *County of Sacramento v. Lewis* may open the gates for unfettered police officer discretion when it comes to pursuing suspects. Justice Souter wrote: "high speed chases with no intent to harm suspects physically or to worsen their legal plight do not give rise to liability." Put another way, pursuing officers are liable only if their actions *shock the conscience.* The decision apparently leaves victims injured or killed in police pursuits no federal remedy against individual officers, law enforcement agencies, or municipal governments. While state legislatures may still provide rights to sue under state personal injury laws, the trend toward granting law enforcement agencies greater legal protection is evident in state courts as stated in the article "Police Pursuits Get Protection," in the *Pittsburgh Tribune Review,* May 22, 1998. In short, the prevailing legal climate is one in which incentives for restricting what might be unnecessary pursuits have been reduced. Consequently, the widespread adoption of written pursuit guidelines would be prudent.

According to an NIJ study (Nugent, et al. 1990), written pursuit guidelines should 1) give officers a clear understanding of when and how to conduct a pursuit, 2) help reduce injury and death associated with high speed pursuits, 3) maintain the basic police mission to enforce the law and protect life and property, and 4) minimize municipal liability in accidents that occur during pursuits. An analysis of the content of pursuit guidelines adopted by Atlantic municipalities suggests that police departments in that state are making efforts to achieve the aforementioned objectives.

The author concludes that the development and implementation of written pursuit guidelines should be required for every police agency in hope of maximizing the delicate balance between apprehending criminals and protecting life and property. The present research indicates that some Atlantic police department guidelines may serve as appropriate models.

REFERENCES

"1996 Annual Compilation and Analysis" (1996). *Pennsylvania Police Pursuit Report,* Pennsylvania State Police.

Alpert, Geoffrey (1987). "Questioning Police Pursuits in Urban Areas." *Journal of Police Science and Administration,* 15:298.

Alpert, Geoffrey, and Patrick R. Anderson (1986). "The Most Deadly Force: Police Pursuits." *Justice Quarterly,* Vol. 3, No. 1, March 1986.

Alpert, Geoffrey, and Roger Dunham (1988). "Research on Police Pursuits: Applications for Law Enforcement." *American Journal of Police,* Vol VII, No. 2.

Alpert, Geoffrey, and Roger Dunham (1989). "Policing Hot Pursuits: The Discovery of Aleatory Elements." *Journal of Criminal Law and Criminology,* Summer 1989.

Baltimore County Police Department, Planning and Research Unit (1985). *Motor Vehicle Pursuit Study.* December 1985.

Beckman, Eric (1985). *A Report to Law Enforcement on Factors in Police Pursuits.* School of Criminal Justice, Michigan State University. October 1985.

California Highway Patrol, Operational Planning Section (1983). *Pursuit Study,* July 1983.

Eidemiller, Maryann (1996). "When Should Police Pursue?" *The Pittsburgh Tribune Review,* August 25, 1996, Sec. B, pp.1-2.

Epstein, Jeffrey (1994). "Liability Under the Federal Civil Rights Act for Injuries Sustained During Police Pursuits." *Federal Bar News and Journal,* June 1994.

Falcone, David (1994). "A Study of Pursuits in Illinois." *The Police Chief,* July 1994.

Fennessy, Edmund (1970). "A Study of the Problem of Hot Pursuit by the Police." *The Center for Environment and Man, Inc.* July 1970.

Grimmond, Tim (1993). "Police Pursuits: Traveling a Collision Course." *The Police Chief,* July 1993.

Nugent, Hugh, Edward F. Connors III, J. Tomas McEwen, and Lou Mayo (1990). *Restrictive Policies for High Speed Pursuits.* U.S. Department of Justice, National Institute of Justice, Office of Communication and Research Utilization. Washington D.C.: U.S. Government Printing Office.

"Police Pursuits Get Protection." *The Pittsburgh Tribune Review,* 22 May, 1998.

CASES CITED

Brower v. County of Inyo, 109 S. Ct. 1378 (1989).

City of Canton v. Harris, 109 S.Ct. 1197 57 U.S.L.W. 4263 (1989).

County of Sacramento v. Lewis, 98 F.3d 434, 96 S.Ct. 1337 (1998).

Monell v. New York City Department of Social Services, 436 U.S. 658, 98 S. Ct. 2018, 56 L.Ed.2d. 611 (1978).

Tennessee v. Garner, 471 U.S. 1, 105 S.Ct. 1694, 85 L.Ed.2d 1 (1985).

ENDNOTES

1. Alpert's work is especially noteworthy; among other issues, he has examined the dynamics of police decision-making in relation to pursuit episodes.

2. A pseudonym for a large Atlantic coastal city.

3. A pseudonym for a state near the Atlantic coast.

4. The categories for describing departmental pursuit guidelines were taken from Nugent, Connors, McEwen, and Mayo's 1990 NIJ study. However, the NIJ study suggested only three categories. At the suggestion of Atlantic's chief research and statistics state police officer, a fourth category ("combination") was added for the purposes of the present study.

5. This was not unexpected. However, in retrospect it may have been better to divide the smallest category further, perhaps into a 1–5 officer category and a 6–24 officer category. A borough with a population of 350 with one full-time officer might certainly have different police/community dynamics than a first-class township with

three dozen officers and a population of 15,000. Also, the categories that were used were admittedly arbitrary. The author simply assumed that police departments with 24 or fewer officers would be policing "smaller" communities such as boroughs and townships, those with 25–100 officers would be representative of medium sized cities with populations up to 100,000 or so, and those with more than 100 officers would be characteristic of larger cities with hundreds of thousands of citizens or more.

6. Even when the medium and large columns were combined, the table contained expected frequencies of less than five. For what it's worth, the calculated chi-square statistic of 10.1175 did not exceed the chi-square sampling distribution figure of 10.645 with 6 degrees of freedom and a level of error set at .10. If the test had been appropriate in this case, the null hypothesis would have been accepted, meaning that there was no evident relationship between the size of the departments and the characterization of guidelines.

7. For example, a Pennsylvania state law requires that the state police not only develop written pursuit guidelines but also mandates that the state police compile an annual report detailing the incidence and nature of pursuit episodes in the preceding year. A review of information provided in the first annual report (1996) compiled under the law is important for contextual reasons and may provide a basis for future research. A review of the 1996 Pennsylvania State Pursuit Report reveals the following information:

1) 1,410 pursuits were reported in Northeast State in 1996.
2) The most common reason for the initiation of a pursuit was "other traffic" (meaning traffic violations other than DUI)—52.8%.
3) The second most prevalent reason for initiating a pursuit was for driving under the influence (17.7%), followed by stolen or suspected stolen vehicles (12%), felony criminal charges (7.7%), misdemeanor criminal charges (7.1%), and summary criminal charges (2.7%).
4) 73.1% of pursuits resulted in the arrest of the suspect.
5) 26.5% of pursuits were terminated by discontinuing the pursuit.
6) 21% of pursuits resulted in collisions (well below the national average of 34%), in which there were 243 injuries and eight fatalities. The vast majority of pursuit eposides did not involve injuries (82.8%).

An evaluation of subsequent annual reports as compiled by the Pennsylvania state police may serve as an indicator of the impact of written pursuit guidelines on the incidence and results of pursuit eposides.

PART 4

POLICE ACCOUNTABILITY

The first article in this section, "Morality in Law Enforcement: Chasing 'Bad Guys' with the Los Angeles Police Department" by Steve Herbert, discusses police work in terms of morality issues that arise from unique aspects of law enforcement's role in society. Herbert did field work with the patrol division of the Los Angeles police department to develop an explanation of the prevalence of police morality, the idea that the officer is always a defender of the good and is out to do battle with and defeat the forces of evil. Being an officer presents many intrapersonal difficulties (e.g. always falling short of the goal of crime prevention, facing situations that do not present cut-and-dried solutions, and being unable to please everyone in all circumstances), which can be soothed with police morality. This attitude, however, can be dangerous because it can lead to the acceptance of overly aggressive behavior. While he realizes the need to disambiguate, Herbert discourages the division of people and events into black-and-white categories.

In the article "Can Police Control Police Misconduct?", Michael J. Palmiotto strongly emphasizes the importance of recruiting police officers who will have creditable character that is free from prejudices and the need to control and abuse those over whom they have control. The effectiveness of police organizations depends upon the selection process. This article reviews traditional selection standards and makes recommendations to improve the quality of recruiting police personnel.

"Law Enforcement: Policing the Defective Centurion—Decertification and Beyond" by William Smith and Geoffrey Alpert, recommends that police officers lose their state certification when they are involved in police misconduct. The authors review defining misconduct, controlling the problem, the critical functions of the police, and police civil liability. The key component of this article is a model for decertification.

In "What's Wrong with Complaint Investigations?" Andrew J. Goldsmith evaluates the investigative process when citizens file complaints against police officers. During questioning and investigation, officers in charge of investigations are often found to be cold, distant, legalistic, and inclined not to see things from the perspective of the citizen. Goldsmith argues that investigators should be more aware and tolerant of differences in culture and show more appreciation for the individual complaints themselves. This article will help answer questions critics have about the handling of complaints.

The fifth article in this section written by Ronald Thrasher, "Internal Affairs: The Police Agencies' Approach to the Investigation of Police Misconduct," deals with how police departments handle citizen complaints and issues of police misconduct investigated by the departments' internal affairs unit. Thrasher outlines the legal guidelines that must be followed by the internal affairs investigator. This article illustrates the complexity and pitfalls of an internal investigation and explains how an internal administrative investigation differs from a criminal investigation. Also discussed are the future trends in police administration and how these can affect internal affairs investigations.

Ronald Fletcher, author of "Civilian Oversight of Police Behavior," outlines the initial responses of law enforcement to complaints of police misdonduct. He also indicates the pros and cons of civilian oversight of police behavior, especially as related to the public's right to know about the complaint, rights of police officers, conciliation between officer and complainant, who receives the complaint, and the inclusion of law enforcement officers on civilian oversight boards. One of the key solutions to this problem is trust between civilians and law enforcement.

William Bickel in his article "An Analysis of Section 1983 Litigation dealing with Police Misconduct," provides an excellent review of Section 1983 violent crimes committed by police officers. Bickel analyzes the litigation of three violent acts committed by police officers: sexual assault, robbery, and domestic violence. Not only are police officers held accountable for their criminal acts under the law, but police departments who employ them and cities where they work are held accountable for those criminal acts as well under Section 1983.

"Police Civil Liability: An Analysis of Section 1983 Actions in the Eastern and Southern Districts of New York" by David K. Chiabi examines the financial compensation claims of citizens who claimed that their Fourth Amendment rights were violated by police officers. In the cases considered, the most frequent allegations were assault and battery, false arrest, and false imprisonment. The increase in these kinds of cases has caused police departments to reevaluate their actions and policies pertaining to civil and constitutional rights.

The next article, "Preventing Excessive Force Litigation," by James F. Anderson, Laronistine Dyson, and Jerald Burns, considers the repercussions of excessive force cases in police departments and how to reduce the number of law suits. It first defines these cases and the legal resources available to guard the public from police abuse. The second section provides guidelines to help agencies reduce the number of excessive force cases brought against them. Some of these suggestions include better training and monitoring, higher standards, and civilian review boards.

The final article in this section, "Police Abuse: Can the Violence Be Contained?" by David Rudovsky, reviews the reactions of law enforcement agencies to officers' misconduct. He points out that blatantly unacceptable behavior is often overlooked. The author highlights several important cases dealing with specific types of police misconduct and compares them to the actions of fictitious officers in a fictitious city. According to Rudovsky, misconduct is difficult to prove, and he projects that this behavior will continue unnoticed and unpublished. In his opinion, the Supreme Court has failed to act because it recognizes neither the widespread nature of abuse nor its institutional causes.

MORALITY IN LAW ENFORCEMENT: CHASING "BAD GUYS" WITH THE LOS ANGELES POLICE DEPARTMENT

Steve Herbert

Police officers regularly construct their work in terms of a morality that is so pronounced that it must arise from unique aspects of their role in society. I draw on fieldwork conducted in a patrol division of the Los Angeles Police Department to develop an explanation for the prevalence of police morality. Three components of the police function create potent dilemmas that their morality helps ameliorate: the contradiction between the police's ostensible aim to prevent crime and their inability to do so; the imperative that they run roughshod over the ambiguity inherent in most situations they handle; and the fact that they invariably act against at least one citizen's interest, often with recourse to a coercive force that can maim or kill. Reliance on moralistic understandings for the police's mission provides a salve for these difficulties; however, it can also work to harm police-community relations. Paradoxically, the police's reliance on morality can encourage or condone overly aggressive actions that are, in fact, contradictory to the virtuous self-definition officers often construct.

Legality and morality are intimately connected. Most legal rules contain implicit or explicit normative messages; they point to proper behavior that ostensibly best serves social needs. It is not surprising, therefore, that the enforcement of law is often understood by police officers as a moral as well as a legalistic enterprise. As Silver (1967) pointed out, the growth of modern policing developed in tandem with a more pervasive sense of moral order created and protected by the state. Or, as Corrigan and Sayer (1985:4) have argued

My thanks to Katherine Beckett and two anonymous reviewers for helpful comments on earlier versions of this essay. Address correspondence to Steve Herbert, Department of Criminal Justice, Indiana University, Sycamore Hall 302, Bloomington, IN 47405-2601; e-mail Herbert@indiana.edu.

Steve Herbert, "Morality in Law Enforcement: Chasing the 'Bad Guys' with the Los Angeles Police Department" (as appeared in *Law & Society Review,* Volume 30, Number 4, 1996, pp. 799–818). Reprinted by permission of the Law and Society Association.

more generally: "Moral regulation is coextensive with state formation, and state forms are always animated and legitimated by a particular moral ethos."

The role of the state in creating a moral order, in part through creating a legal order, is a long-standing focus of major social theoretic work, including that of Durkheim (1986), Weber (1954), and Foucault (1990; see also Donzelot 1979; Polsky 1991). These works share an interest in the ways in which power marries with morality to imprint itself indelibly on the citizenry. The state's legal order is understood as part of an attempt to create a more peaceable populace that abides by a presumably morally justified set of rules and regulations. Without this sense of moral justification, state power would seem nakedly coercive and thus illegitimate; public assent would wither.

One of the moralistic ways that nation-states acquire public loyalty is through the construction of enemies. In the process of defining inferior others, nation-states simultaneously construct themselves as unique repositories of virtue, and thus compel compliance to their morally laudable aims (see Campbell 1992; Dalby 1990). Boundaries are constructed between pure and polluted (Douglas 1966, 1973), between good and evil, and the favored nation shines in the comparison. Internally, the state's moral aims work toward the construction of the model, normal citizen, who is well schooled, well behaved, and willing to sacrifice for the nation's welfare. This normality is, again, constructed in tandem with a contrasting pathology (Durkheim 1938), and those perceived as incorrigible are sanctioned and/or banished.

State rule thus requires and daily enacts morality, often through the construction and enforcement of its legal structure. It trains attention on those both within and without the state's boundaries, regularly trumpeting virtue by denigrating evil. This is certainly true of police officers, who serve as the state's principal internal cartographers in marking the boundaries between normal and pathological. Officers are preeminently focused on those who violate moral-cum-legal codes, and define their actions as part of an attempt to protect the good through expunging the evil.

A sense of moral fervor clearly attends much police behavior (Reiss & Bordua 1967; Skolnick & Fyfe 1993; Van Maanen 1978; Westley 1970); officers regularly draw on an abiding reservoir of virtue to sustain and justify their actions as part of a vital mission (Reiner 1992). Indeed, this sense of morality seems unusually pronounced in police subculture. This raises two provocative questions: What accounts for the regular and emphatic invocation of moralistic dictums to guide and justify police actions? And what influence does their morality have on police officers' practices?

Previous work on the police, as mentioned, has drawn attention to the extent of police moralism, particularly to the extent that it contributes to the development of an "us versus them" mentality (Niederhoffer 1967; Skolnick 1966; Westley 1970); only police officers, from this perspective, understand their particular mission, and hence they are isolated from the rest of the misguided populace. Van Maanen (1978) also points to one of the key advantages for the police of drawing sharp moral characterizations—it provides ample justification for whatever actions they choose to take, a point I develop further later in this article. However, none of the works that discuss police morality fully develop an explanation for its pronounced presence in officers' daily lives or fully discuss its implications for daily practice.

I draw below on field observations of officers in the Los Angeles Police Department (LAPD) to illustrate the centrality of morality to everyday understandings and justifications of police actions.[1] I follow with a three-pronged explanation of the prevalence of this fervent morality. More specifically, I focus on (1) the contradiction between stated police aims and the near impossibility of achieving those aims; (2) the inherent ambiguity in many situations that officers encounter, which must be ignored if the officers wish to effect speedy resolution; and (3) the inescapable demand that officers act against at least one person's interest in most situations, often with recourse to coercive and, ultimately, lethal force. All these fundamental constituents of the police's daily practice produce tensions, frustrations, and dilemmas that an overarching, trans-situational morality helps to ameliorate.

The final sections of the article consider the consequences of the prevalence of police morality, especially in terms of tensions between officers and minority communities, and also review the paradoxes that are central to that morality. Central here is the fundamental importance of coercive force to the police's function in society (Bittner 1970). On the one hand, the moral code regularly invoked by officers tends to sanitize or divert attention away from the tools of force they often wield. On the other hand, coercive force in a society that values peace is always difficult to justify unambiguously, and thus makes the police's omnipresent moralism ever uneasy.

I. MORALITY IN POLICING

It is early in the morning, and the attending officers seem a bit listless as the sergeant begins roll-call training. His topic for the day is traffic stops of passenger vans. He reminds the officers that traffic stops should never be considered routine in Los Angeles, because one could quite likely "have something more" than just a moving violation. He places great emphasis on how to approach a van safely, given its large number of doors and windows. Any of these portals, he cautions, could be conduits for an attack. Thus, officers should approach cautiously and vigilantly. Throughout his monologue, he makes repeated references to the "evil" that stalks the streets of Los Angeles, to the various people "who do not have a life" and therefore might just attack a police officer wantonly. In fact, some people might be heartless enough to indoctrinate young children into attacking the police; presumably this means that officers should not relax even if a van is full of kids.

---

[1]The fieldwork, in a single patrol division from August 1993 to March 1994, consisted primarily of 35 ride-alongs of an average length of six hours with sergeants, who served as supervisors of patrol officers in the field, and 20 ride-alongs of a average length of four hours with Senior Lead Officers, who are responsible for police-community relations and for monitoring locations of ongoing criminal activity. The ride-alongs stretched across different shifts, although they were primarily concentrated in the evening hours. In addition, I spent four evenings observing dispatch operations in the Communications Division, did single ride-alongs with specialized units focused on narcotics, vice, and street gangs, and rode in Air Support helicopters twice. I carried a small notebook while on the ride-alongs, which I used to jot down brief notations of events and conversations. These were later developed into fieldnotes which served as the data base for the analysis, and the sources of the vignettes described here (Herbert 1996). The vignettes are set off in italic type.

The sergeant's goal is to underline tactics to ensure officer safety, but he punctuates his remarks with repeated moralistic invectives against those the officers encounter daily on the streets. The sergeant simultaneously seeks to caution the officers and also to explain just why they need to be careful: there is evil out there, ready to overpower the unsuspecting. Indeed, evil can come disguised as a seemingly wholesome family enjoying a drive in their passenger van.

The discourse of evil is remarkably common in police discourse. The term "bad guy" is ubiquitous in police parlance, occasionally supplemented by such terms as "punk," "idiot," "knucklehead," or "terrorist." Another term commonly used, "predator," is quite evocative in displaying a sense of evil devouring good; like carnivores attacking prey, these dastardly fiends probe for vulnerable spots among the populace and attack for no logical reason. Observations of police in "Union City" provided Van Maanen (1978) insight into the ubiquitous usage of a similar term, "asshole," a category police reserved for any who refused to accede to officer prescriptions. This category, he argues, not only helps to justify a variety of police actions but also to increase an internal sense of police validity.

Recourse to "evil" as an explanation for the seeming chaos that Los Angeles officers encounter on the streets is long-standing. Note the following comments, one from William Parker, chief from 1949 to 1966, the other from one of his successors, Daryl Gates, who served from 1979 to 1992:

> There are wicked men with evil hearts who sustain themselves by preying upon society. There are men who lack control over their strong passions, and thus we have vicious assaults, many times amounting to the destruction of the life of a fellow man.
>
> To control and repress these evil forces, police forces have existed, in some form or another, throughout recorded history. (Wilson 1957:5)

> Society flinches from the truth; we do our very best to find psychological and sociological reasons to excuse behavior that our minds won't accept for what it is. You walk into court and you have all these attorneys explaining away all of the things that you can sum up in one simple word: Evil. (Gates 1992:165)[2]

As Douglas (1966) suggests, the construction of morality often rests on such stark distinctions between pure and impure. In this case, the distinction is between good and evil, between those who share a concern for their fellow citizens and those who are fundamentally, irrationally, and irrevocably opposed to common standards of behavior and decency. And it is the police's unique and valorous duty to intercede between these two groups, to protect

---

[2]The extent of this moralizing from the leadership suggests that perhaps the LAPD is unique in the extent to which it constructs the world in stark terms. However, as mentioned, police morality has been noted by numerous researchers as a pronounced aspect of the social world of a variety of police departments.

the one by detecting and banishing the other. It is perhaps easier, from this perspective, to understand officers' regular complaints about a lax judicial system that, in their view, enables evil to seep quickly back out of jail and to repollute otherwise peaceable neighborhoods. The power to banish some to jail allows officers to draw a boundary between pure and polluted and to nourish their morality with a sense of a clear victory over evil. If, however, suspects reappear quickly back onto the streets, the boundary erodes and with it the officers' sense of virtue.

Officers are particularly concerned about those they consider most vulnerable to "predators"—children and the elderly. An officer explains his concern about dice games in a fast-food outlet's parking lot; he wouldn't, he says, want his children to see that. Another officer makes the same complaint about alleged drug sales occurring across the street from an elementary school, and indicates that she will exert pressure on the dealers to convince them to relocate. A third officer keeps a similarly watchful eye on a group of young men who regularly gather in front of the home of an elderly woman. The woman has called the patrol station and complained that she is so afraid of the group that she will not leave her house. Enraged and protective, the officer informs the young men that unless they gather elsewhere, "Somehow, some way, you are going to jail."

Officers, in other words, act not just to enforce legal codes but to buttress wider notions of moral correctness (Banton 1964; Bittner 1967). Thus, the legal action of, say, arresting a spousal abuser is justified not just as a legal proscription but as a morally laudable act.

> *The sergeant is one of three officers who arrive simultaneously at a call about an alleged domestic incident. Their knock on the door is answered by the man of the house, who invites them into the living room. There they discover his wife with a fresh bruise above her eye. They also notice that the phone has been pulled from the wall. Their initial questions elicit little response, so they take the woman into a back bedroom, where she admits that she called the police and that her husband is the author of her injury. The officers inform her that California law requires that her husband be arrested. The woman protests. The sergeant explains that the law provides them no leeway. Further, he says that what her husband has done "simply isn't right" and that his time in jail will enable her "to sleep in peace."*

In this situation, the officers define their legally required act in larger moralistic terms and justify their actions as a prophylactic against unwanted violence that allows a woman to get some restful sleep. The police's sense of moral virtue in protecting good from harm rests most fundamentally in their acceptance of the unfortunate necessity that they may have to pay the "ultimate sacrifice" in enacting their responsibilities.

> *A sergeant is responsible for overseeing a "scenario" at a training event. In the scenario, a pair of officers is called to a home. When they arrive, they find a pair of officers, a man and a woman, play-acting a domestic dispute. The dispute quickly escalates when the man pulls a gun and points it at the woman. The officers are thus confronted with an important and sudden decision: whether to shoot the man. The decision is not simple, because the*

officers may fear the outcome should they not fire accurately. They could in-advertently wound the woman, or if they miss altogether, they could compel the man to shoot them instead. After witnessing several teams handle this scenario, the sergeant discusses the patterns he observed. Most striking to him was the generational difference between older officers, who usually chose to shoot, and younger ones, who typically demurred. He credits the fallout from the Rodney King beating as the key factor; younger officers, he reasons, are socialized into a different ethic that intensifies concern about inappropriate uses of force. For his part, the officer says simply, "I'm the police." It is his final comment.

The sergeant condenses a powerful sentiment in three simple words. He states, quite flatly, that it is his solemn duty not to fear potential damage to his personal safety or career advancement when a need for potentially lethal force is evident. For him, it is part of his sworn mandate to so endanger him-self if the welfare of a tormented citizen is at stake. It is a central component of his virtue as a police officer that he will sustain such risks to protect good from evil.

But note that police morality is not monolithic. It is not necessarily em-braced avidly by all officers, and may also be differentially employed across the varied populations of the city. Police officers do characterize various communities and social classes, and their moral characteristics, in markedly different terms (Alpert & Dunham 1988; Banton 1964; Bayley & Mendelsohn 1968; Bittner 1967; Brooks 1989; Manning 1993; Sacks 1972; Werthman & Piliavin 1967). Also, the high-minded moralism of an overtly self-sacrificing officer runs counter to another motivation commonly found in police organ-izations—the desire to lie low and avoid trouble. The "CYA [Cover Your Ass] syndrome" afflicts officers who live primarily in fear of administrative censure and thus avoid all situations that involve risks that might later be second guessed (Brown 1981; Kappeler, Sluder, & Alpert 1994; Reuss-Ianni 1983). This syndrome is also regularly displayed around the LAPD, as in other police organizations. If not monolithic, however, police morality is still robust in both its construction and consequences, and thus merits closer attention.

II. EXPLAINING POLICE MORALITY

Police officers, then, regularly nest discussions and justifications of their ac-tions within a discourse of morality that portrays them as proud and noble warriors protecting the peace from the chaotic and turbulent anarchy of evil. Why, however, is such an ardent moralism so prominent in police subculture? The answer, in short, is that the stated aims of police departments are gener-ally unattainable and that police work is inescapably ambiguous and ulti-mately coercive. These factors lead to tensions and dilemmas that officers can minimize through recourse to an overarching morality that provides a secure and even glorious rationale for their ever disputable and ultimately ineffective actions. Morality, in other words, works as a functional adaptation to the in-evitable uncertainties and failures that police officers daily must face.

A. The Problematic Rationale for Modern Policing

Advocates of modern, professionalized policing pitched their enterprise as one focused on crime prevention. The tools of this technologically sophisticated force—the radios, the patrol cars, the helicopters, the well-equipped crime labs—would combine to enable officers to easily capture and convict offenders. Such demonstrated success would convince would-be criminals to desist lest they ensure their own imprisonment (Walker 1977).

The effectiveness of modern police forces was clearly overdrawn; little evidence exists to substantiate its crime-fighting claims (Bayley 1994; Kelling 1983; Manning 1977).[3] Put simply, variations in policing have little impact on crime rates. Departments advertising themselves as primarily focused on reducing levels of criminal activity thus place themselves in a tenuous political position, because they cannot ultimately deliver the goods (Manning 1977).

The irony is not lost on some police officers, who from their daily practice become aware that their crime-fighting efforts are mostly ineffectual. Many wish to place regular surveillance on "problem areas" to "put the heat" on those who are engaged in, say, open drug sales. But such strict surveillance cannot be maintained forever, and thus the sales are difficult to snuff out fully. Further, many recognize that success in one area may only mean that the perpetrators will move to another area and become the problem of some other officer. And police officers can, of course, do little to address problems of poverty, poor education, and community disenfranchisement.

Police officers are thus put in a difficult position: They are given a task they cannot accomplish. Widely publicized as engaged in an important effort to rid society of the plague of crime and equipped handsomely to succeed in that mission, they are ultimately ineffectual, due to factors completely beyond their control. This startling contradiction between public image and actual practice can, however, be skirted with regular recourse to the discourse of an ardent morality. When "victories" do occur, when "predators" are in fact captured, officers perhaps overstate their significance with well-worn moralistic messages to help stave off a sense of incompetence that would accompany any more rational evaluation of their overall effectiveness. Caught between their image as crime fighters and the structural impediments to success, officers attempt to resurrect the nobility of their efforts by exaggerating the significance of their occasional triumphs. Their moralistic proclamations of good trumping evil provide a comforting refuge from the overall impotence of their crime-reduction capacities and allow them to ignore the vast chasm that divides their oft-stated goals and their actual success. Of course, the inability of the police to reduce crime rates to any significant extent does not necessarily lead to the construction of sharply defined categories of good and evil. However, understanding policing as ultimately concerned with the preservation of such grand values as liberty and peace through engaging the "enemy" who would destroy those values does have the effect of minimizing any sense of impotence that might result from a more sober assessment of the police's crime-fighting work.

---

[3]Sherman (1992) has attempted to make the case that police intervention can work to reduce crime. However, he is hard put to find examples of clear police successes or to find examples of strategies that would work in numerous locations.

B. Running Roughshod over Ambiguity

Police officers are regularly asked to resolve social situations that are chaotic and confused. They find themselves in the middle of disputes between spouses and partners, landlords and tenants, proprietors and customers, and countless others, and are subjected to loud and complicated claims and counterclaims. Faced with such situations, officers must not only attempt to untangle the web the disputants discursively create, but also must act quickly, decisively, and, it is hoped, fairly. In most cases, officers have other calls pending and cannot afford to burrow deep to the wellsprings of the dispute, even if they were inclined or skilled enough to do so. If complainants' stories differ, as they often do, then officers must make instant decisions about whose character is more worthy of respect, and thus which version to treat most seriously. As Bittner (1990:11) succinctly puts it: "The mission of the police is limited to imposing provisional solutions to uncontexted emergencies."

> *The sergeant accepts a call that is billed as a domestic dispute. Normally, he would not take such a call because he rides alone; domestic disputes are understood by officers to be often volatile and thus more than a single officer can handle. However, his reading of the information given him by the dispatcher is that this is actually a landlord-tenant dispute. This turns out to be not exactly accurate, although the key issue is indeed real estate.*
>
> *When he arrives, one woman emerges from the house in question and another from a car parked across the street. An elderly man remains seated in the parked car. A shouted exchange erupts between the women, during which they promise to alter each other's physical appearance. The sergeants impels the second woman to return to her car while he gets one side of the story.*
>
> *The current dispute began when a friend of the man seated in the car attempted to enter the guest quarters behind the house in question, apparently to retrieve some of the man's belongings. It turns out that the elderly man used to own the house but deeded it over to the woman who now resides there; she, in fact, is his niece. The niece claims that her uncle had remarried a few years ago and deeded the house to her so that his new wife would not simply divorce him and take over the house. The divorce did ultimately occur, and the woman seated in the car is a new romantic interest.*
>
> *The niece presents paperwork that appears to prove her rightful ownership of the property. The sergeant briefly inspects the documents and finds them legitimate, although he notes the presence of some white-out on one line. Still, he basically upholds the niece's position.*
>
> *The couple in the car have emerged by this point, and the man is muttering constantly if incomprehensibly, betraying a seeming senility. The sergeant encourages him to spend some time to retrieve his property from the premises and counsels him to challenge the niece in a more formal legal process if he feels his claim is warranted. The sergeant remains at the house during the 15 minutes the man uses to retrieve some clothing to ensure that the dispute does not become inflamed, but leaves when the man completes the retrieval.*

In a remarkably short time, the sergeant must attempt to calm the situation, gain an understanding of its significant dynamics, and make a decision.

This dispute is entangled in a confusing family history made more complicated by the questionable documents and the elderly man's incoherence. And
the stakes—ownership of a valuable piece of property—are quite high.

But the sergeant must act, and does so to the best of his ability. The niece
appears to have the more legitimate stake, but the sergeant is doubtful enough
to counsel the old man strongly to take the case to a higher authority. He then
grants the man the right to accomplish his short-term goal of retrieving his
goods, and ensures that this can occur peaceably.

> *The sergeant is called to the parking lot of a mini-mall by a patrol offi-
cer team. They are handling a complaint by a woman who maintains she was
harassed on the basis of sexual orientation. Another patron in the mall was
angered when he thought she cut him off in the tight maneuvering for parking spaces. In his tirade against her that followed, he referred to her as a "fat
dyke bitch." The woman now is displaying a pamphlet from a local gay and
lesbian resource center that discusses legal proscriptions against such harassment, and insisting that the officers arrest the man. They are reluctant to do
so, and seek the sergeant's imprimatur their decision.*
>
> *The sergeant agrees with the officers, and explains to the woman that the
man did not know her and thus did not know anything definitive about her
sexual orientation. Further, he notes that the dispute was really about a parking space, not sexual orientation. This contrasts, he maintains, to the sort of
acts the law was intended to address: groups willfully and consciously seeking
homosexuals for overt harassment.*
>
> *However, the officers do address her feelings by summoning the man
from inside the mall, explaining the situation to him, and persuading him to
apologize. After he does so, the officers leave the scene.*

In the span of only 10 minutes, the officers define the situation, establish
a course of action, and attempt to justify that action to the people involved.
This process involves quickly deciding for themselves the most important issues at stake, the best interpretation of those issues in terms of the law, and
the best means to bring some resolution. This is obviously a situation open to
varying interpretations, and their chosen course of action may betray an absence of sympathy for victims of harassment based on sexual orientation. Either way, however, the process is a decidedly speedy one in which a delicate
situation is resolved hastily and with minimal attention to the entire range of
issues at stake.

Regardless of the logic employed by the officers here, both situations illustrate the type of inchoate and complex situations they regularly face. Disputes are rarely simple, and evolve from a host of circumstances that officers
cannot fully decode. Further, these disputes can be inflamed by such larger
dynamics as homophobia, racism, or long-standing familial tensions. The situations officers face, in short, are inherently and irrevocably ambiguous.

But officers must ignore much of this ambiguity if they are to be effective in
restoring order and if they are to keep up with their call load. Effectiveness
often rests on decisiveness, so officers cannot hem and haw their way to a
half-hearted decision. And their increasing queue of yet-unanswered calls
places urgency on handling the dispute in the most parsimonious way possible.

The ambiguity inherent in the vast majority of police calls contrasts sharply with the clear-cut boundaries of good and evil that officers regularly construct in their moralistic discourse. Indeed, the contrast is probably not accidental. The overarching, trans-situational morality that officers construct seems a perfect antidote to any qualms that might arise from them running roughshod over the ambiguity in the disputes or other calls officers handle. Cast in terms of the broad and potent categories of good and evil, officers' actions take on a markedly less ambiguous character and provide a powerful justification for acts that may ultimately be open to question.

C. The Inevitable Harms of Policing

Regardless of the aims of police actions, many resolutions that officers accomplish come at the expense of one of the parties involved. Of course, many cases the police handle, particularly the more mundane order-maintenance tasks that occupy much of their attention, do not have a clear opposition of interests and/or a high level of tension. However, officers regularly encounter situations that are confused and highly charged. This is most likely when those involved tell diametrically opposed versions of events and desired outcomes. In some cases, officers do attempt to reach a resolution that can receive some minimal degree of communal consent, but time pressures often dictate a more brusque response. In many cases, of course, there is a clear victim and perpetrator, so swift restraint of the latter is not fundamentally in question; the harm caused by jailing is not something that would trouble officers. But given the ambiguity discussed above, actions that clearly favor one party over another are not always easy to justify.

The potential unease that might accompany acting against one party's interest is compounded for officers by the coercive means to which they often resort to eventuate their desired outcome. Resistance to police commands is inevitable, and officers possess a wide array of tactics and tools to ensure their ultimate authority. It is this coercive authority that distinguishes the police from other social agencies (Bittner 1970) and explains their importance in upholding the state's legal and moral rule. But coercive force is obviously harmful to the individual involved, and its use makes clear the extent to which the police can deleteriously affect members of the citizenry.

It is therefore not surprising that officers spend much time discussing whether and how to use force. During the fieldwork, I observed a number of roll-call discussions that focused on recent shootings within the department. Lieutenants and sergeants reviewed each situation, explaining how the officers acted and how those actions were or were not justified. This training is motivated both to ensure that officers prevail in any confrontations with armed and dangerous suspects and to prevent any unnecessary use of force. Supervisors would continually remind officers that in any postincident investigation, "every shot must be accounted for." In other words, officers would be expected to justify each shot they fired as a responsible and reasonable use of force that did not unnecessarily endanger the wrong people.

In many cases, however, the use of force is not seen in such wary terms but is a badge of distinction that officers wear proudly. Officers are referred to as "ghetto gunfighters" who have fallen victim to the "John Wayne Syndrome." For these hard-charging officers, occasional uses of force are necessary to fight evil and earn internal distinction. The majority of officers, however, do not fall into this category; indeed, many officers try to avoid working with their more aggressive counterparts because they fear the potential damage to their career that an out-of-control partner might cause.

Still, the enforcement of police authority often involves making some persons suffer by denying them pursuit of their preferred path of action and/or physically restraining them. This compounds the unease stemming from the ambiguity inherent in most situations officers encounter; not only must officers act decisively in confused situations, but they must also often act against one party's interest, sometimes with recourse to coercive and ultimately lethal force. Further, because police officers serve as a key mechanism of the state's coercive apparatus, they attract potentially lethal attention themselves from those who resist police authority. Officers are never unaware of the potential danger they face at a moment's notice. Given this unavoidable mandate—to ensure order via coercive force in often-inchoate settings at the risk of their own lives—it is perhaps understandable why officers take refuge in a moralistic discursive universe that avoids the irresolvable questions of whether this or that use of force is justified, and instead posit a more simplistic good/evil frame by which actions can be interpreted. This moralistic universe also defines a life lost in the line of duty as not a mere death but as a sacrifice for a large and worthy cause. An ardent morality provides officers a cushioned escape from the conundrums their social role foists on them, a retreat where they can wash away the difficult particularities of actual situations and thus helps them adapt to the reality of the potentially lethal risks they daily assume.

III. THE IMPLICATIONS AND PARADOXES OF POLICE MORALITY

Given the facts that police officers must quickly and coercively create order in ambiguous situations and that they are presumed to prevent crime when they cannot actually do so, it is easier to understand why simplistic moral frames might work to reduce their level of tension, why such moral frames might serve as an adaptive response to the inescapable and interminable anxieties of daily police practice. The difficult and easily questioned decisions they must constantly make are rendered less troublesome if they are nested in a broader and simpler discourse that bluntly describes behavior as either good or evil. The societal role of the police to create order coercively perhaps explains why their morality should be so singularly pronounced; the burden of their unique responsibility is alleviated by continually reinforcing the overall worth of their mission.

Police morality often yields laudable efforts. One can easily sympathize with an old woman who fears leaving her home and thus can endorse strong efforts on an officer's part to reduce her anxiety. In many cases, officers identify those who are most vulnerable—typically the elderly and children—and operate primarily to ensure their welfare. Given a strong desire to do good, many officers involve themselves deeply in their communities or work long hours. Indeed, many LAPD officers understood the recent inability of the officers' union to gain wide support for a "sickout" as a function of the inextinguishable desire of officers to serve; they simply could not condone leaving the citizenry unprotected. Similarly, officers worked many extra hours after the Northridge earthquake with little complaint.

But the dangers of excessive moralizing are equally clear. It is understandable why officers might regularly vilify those they define as their opponents. If the "bad guys" are defined as essentially evil, then officers' responses are more easily justified. Even if, say, the use of force was bit excessive, it was the perpetrator who initiated the encounter and who sought to harm the community. And whatever the officer did, he/she was ultimately motivated by the praiseworthy virtue of protecting the good from the depredations of evil. As Van Maanen (1978:234) put it, "In essence, the existence of an asshole demonstrates and confirms the police view of the importance and worth of themselves both as individuals and as members of a necessary occupation."[4]

The denial of ambiguity that excessive moralizing encourages is precisely the concern one must raise about it. Over time, officers' ability to discriminate between those who represent actual threats to public safety and those who do not may weaken, and thus all who reside in a given neighborhood may be too easily painted alike as evil. Given this understanding of people in these areas, officers may react brusquely and aggressively in situations where they do not face a clear danger. This will, of course, reverberate within the communities concerned, and tensions will develop. Relationships between the LAPD and the minority communities most liable to be labeled as incubators of evil have historically been tremendously strained (U.S. Commission on Civil Rights, California Advisory Committee 1963; Cray 1972; Raine 1967). As abhorrent as the tapes of Mark Fuhrman were on their own terms, the extent of their impact was a function of this historical mistrust. Indeed, it is easy to speculate that the ability of defense lawyers in the O.J. Simpson case to convince a largely black jury to cast doubt on the practices of the LAPD succeeded largely because of this historical backdrop.

It is misguided to lay the blame for police-minority tension in Los Angeles or other cities solely at the feet of police moralizing (see Skolnick & Fyfe 1993). However, it is clear that the crude frames of good and evil, no matter how comforting, encourage an erosion of officers' ability to discriminate with more sensitivity between residents in minority neighborhoods. Not all who dress, walk, and talk in an apparently threatening way are in fact a danger, but many moralistic officers are unable to appreciate that fact. Thus, they approach those they label as bad in a harsh and imperturbable fashion and needlessly antagonize many who merit a lighter hand.

The problem, of course, is that, as I have argued, police morality is as potent as it is precisely because it helps mitigate the inescapable dilemmas of the job; it serves as an adaptation to the uncertainties and ambiguities that daily policing generates. However, it is not necessarily the only adaptation available to police officers. As Muir (1977) has argued persuasively, the hallmark of a truly professional police officer is the maturity that enables a broad

---

[4]The value of this discourse was made obvious during the trials of the officers involved in the beating of Rodney King. The defense's strategy was to portray King as the true danger to social order and to justify the officers' violent response as a reasonable defense of that order (Herbert 1995).

perspective on human behavior, one that accepts ambiguity as an inherent component of human action and encounters. Police officers are perhaps unique in the extent to which they must regularly wrestle with the ambiguous nature of human reality. To the degree, however, that they use a structured morality to avoid the difficult task of discriminatingly interpreting social action, they are unable to police with the measured and delicate hand of a true professional. Officers pass the murkiness of the social world through the prism of their morality to reduce phenomena to a narrower spectrum of black-white/good-evil images. This is a comforting exercise but an ultimately troublesome one.

This discussion reveals the central paradox at the heart of police morality. In using their morality to render the social world in more sharply categorical terms, officers are led to enact or condone practices that are inconsistent with their virtuous self-definition. Their muscular morality enables them to justify various actions that are perpetually questionable and that almost unavoidably harm at least one citizen. They can therefore easily transform commendable actions into condonable ones by excusing police excesses as first and foremost acts to uphold the good. It was Rodney King, after all, who terrorized a suburban Los Angeles community with his reckless driving, and it was those officers' duty to restrain him in whatever way they could. By couching their actions as tactics in the monumental battle to stave off evil, officers can lose the capacity to read nuance in the social landscape or even to cast a critical eye on their own behavior. Police actions that are, in fact, inconsistent with the moral cast that molds their self-interpretation can be reinterpreted as excusable given the larger fight for virtue that defines their mission.

An integral part of the tension within police morality is the seeming incompatibility of coercive force, which can maim and kill, and the pursuit of peace, order, and the good. The difficulty of balancing the harm of lethal force against the larger social aims for which it is ostensibly employed is perhaps the most basic dilemma facing police officers (Muir 1977). On the one hand, officers wish to portray themselves as saviors for the troubled and the vulnerable, the "thin blue line" that protects the orderly from the chaotic. On the other hand, the police exist primarily as a repository of legitimate coercive force, which they stand ready to employ on extremely short notice. The tension between these two is usefully illustrated in the following incident.

> *A group of officers have followed a trail of clues from a shooting at a hamburger stand to a young woman's apartment. She is the girlfriend of the registered owner of a truck seen speeding from the scene. Because it is a fresh pursuit, the officers do not need a search warrant to enter the woman's house. She, however, is reluctant to open the door. The officers are polite and explain why they are there. They also attempt to compel her cooperation by discussing the general comfort the police bring her in times of trouble. "We are the police," one officer reminds her, "the people you call when you need help and protection."*
>
> *When this effort to create trust does not work, the officers inform her that the manager of the apartment building is on his way, and he will grant them legal access to her apartment. This is enough to convince her to open the door. Once inside, the officers search the apartment with aggressive thoroughness, overturning furniture and tossing items from closets. Two officers take the*

young woman into a back room where they press her for information about the suspect's whereabouts. One officer is overheard telling the woman that unless she tells them what they want to know, "We will thump you so hard it will hurt to sit down." The woman seems genuinely unable to provide them with any information, but she and the other three people in the apartment are taken to the station for further questioning.

The officers' early invocation of the cherished protective role of police in society was obviously motivated by a desire to talk their way into the woman's apartment. Still, the contrast between their advertised ability to comfort and the actual threat they pose to the woman's property and physical well-being is stark. Regardless of how much they may try to convince the woman to see the police as the ultimate source of community protection, the officers quickly reveal the coercive heart of their occupation by trashing the apartment and threatening physical harm. The facade of benevolence crumbles in the earthquake of strong-armed policing.

On the other hand, as I have suggested, the benevolent aspects of policing are often genuine, real, and commendable. To the extent, however, that officers' good/evil categories are inflexible, they undercut the very morality they attempt to claim for themselves. The pervasiveness of police morality is undoubtedly related to the coercive tasks society relegates to them, enabling officers to assuage their sense of responsibility or guilt when they must harm another. But the soil of the police's moral high ground is ever unstable, precisely because of their coercive function. The fact that the police can cause harm to others gives rise to the comforting refuge of their morality, but their capacity to maim and kill also threatens to undercut that morality. An uneasy tension is thus built into the core of the police's moral vision, as they try to obscure what they cannot escape. Whether police officers can be successfully trained to adopt the more nuanced and mature perspective that Muir sometimes observed is an open question. The track record of contemporary policing, especially in Los Angeles, suggests that it is a challenge worth addressing.

IV. CONCLUSION

The importance of morality for justifying and promoting state rule is obvious and is the focus of much scholarly attention. The legal order, for example, is not just a dry-as-dust set of stodgy regulations but an attempt to structure virtue into the populace. The precise mechanisms through which this morality is inculcated into the citizenry are certainly worthy of our attention, because to study them is to reveal the actual work that states must accomplish to sustain themselves. One can thus avoid reifying the state as some sort of coherent, transcendent unity, and instead focus on the actual practices by which state rule is created and maintained (Abrams 1988).

It is therefore important to investigate how the state, through its legal order, aims its focus on its subject population and attempts to mold a model citizenry through its various proscriptions, how it seeks to make a moral order more pervasive and binding. But it is useful not only to focus on the state's external relations but also to investigate the *internal* processes through which state legal actors justify their actions, often with recourse to moralistic dictums. Police officers, for example, drink regularly from the fount of morality and replenish their internal esprit de corps by invoking a larger virtue that their actions serve. Given its prevalence and seeming power, this morality deserves explanation.

My suggestion is that this morality flows from three fundamental constituents of modern policing: the gap between the stated goals of the police and their inability to achieve them; the inherent ambiguity in most police-citizen encounters that officers must ignore to affect order quickly; and the inevitable harm that police actions, coercive or otherwise, cause some citizens. Police officers are thus placed in a difficult position. They are asked to arrest crime when they cannot, they are required to enforce order when denied the time and tools to unearth the full range of disordering influences, and they are compelled to use coercive force in quickly developing and uncertain circumstances. The combination of these factors can create potent dilemmas, whose intricacies can be simplified and disquiet can be eased through an equally potent morality. Cast in terms not of ambiguity and contradiction but rather in the rigid categories of good and evil, police actions are more easily justified, even if they overstretch certain bounds. Thus, a use of force that perhaps was not fully necessary given a complete understanding of the event in question is more easily condoned if understood as ultimately motivated by a desire to expunge evil from otherwise peaceable streets. Individual excesses are the price one pays in the ongoing effort to clean the city of the polluting stains of the irrational and chaotic.

On the one hand, police morality can be both understood and, at times, applauded; officers who work long hours and are genuinely motivated to improve people's quality of life deserve our fullest appreciation. And their willingness to insert themselves in dangerous situations where our fundamental physical well-being is at stake is extremely laudable. On the other hand, police morality, to the extent that it too crudely categorizes individuals and their actions, threatens to condone needlessly aggressive or insensitive treatment of some members of the citizenry. It undoubtedly has contributed to the sort of police-minority tensions that rage in Los Angeles and other cities. The drive to reduce ambiguity is perhaps necessary given the dilemmas officers face, but in erasing gray areas from their world-views, officers are led to enforce order in ways that are, paradoxically, inimicable to their moral definition of themselves. Thus, the morality of officers is born from unique aspects of the police's role in society but also can exacerbate the intensity of the moral dilemmas they regularly confront.

Any efforts to reform the police must be attentive to their morally created world-view and to the ways it shapes their everyday practice. The challenge is to ratify the officers' understandable need to imbue their work with a sense of overarching purpose while encouraging an openness to ambiguity that would discourage too-simplistic categorizations of people and events. In a sense, officers need to be encouraged not to allow their fervent morality to contribute to actions that are inconsistent with that morality. Police morality needs to be saved from itself in order to actually allow the work it ostensibly encourages.

REFERENCES

Abrams, Philip (1988) "Notes on the Difficulty of Studying the State," 1 *J. of Historical Sociology* 58.

Alpert, Geoffrey, & Roger Dunham (1988) *Policing Multi-ethnic Neighborhoods*. New York: Greenwood Press.

Banton, Michael (1964) *The Policeman in the Community*. London: Tavistock.

Bayley, David (1994) *Police for the Future*. New York: Oxford Univ. Press.

Bayley, David, & Harold Mendelsohn (1968) *Minorities and the Police: Confrontation in America*. New York: Free Press.

Bittner, Egon (1967) "The Police in Skid-Row: A Study of Peacekeeping," 32 *American Sociological Rev.* 699.

———— (1970) *The Functions of Police in Modern Society: A Review of Background Factors, Current Practices and Possible Role Models*. Chevy Chase, MD: Center for Studies of Crime & Delinquency, National Institute of Mental Health.

———— (1990) *Aspects of Police Work*. Boston: Northeastern Univ. Press.

Bordua, David Joseph, ed. (1967) *The Police: Six Sociological Essays*. New York: John Wiley & Sons.

Brooks, Laurie (1989) "Police Discretionary Behavior: A Study of Style," in R. Dunham & G. Alpert, eds., *Critical Issues in Policing: Contemporary Readings*. Prospect Heights, IL: Waveland Press.

Brown, Michael (1981) *Working the Street: Police Discretion and the Dilemmas of Reform*. New York: Russell Sage Foundation.

Campbell, David (1992) *Writing Security: United States Foreign Policy and the Policies of Identity*. Minneapolis: Univ. of Minnesota Press.

Corrigan, Philip, & Derek Sayer (1985) *The Great Arch: English State Formation as Cultural Revolution*. Oxford: Basil Blackwell.

Cray, Ed (1972) *The Enemy in the Streets: Police Malpractice in America*. Garden City, NY: Anchor Books.

Dalby, Simon (1990) *Creating the Second Cold War: The Discourse of Politics*. London: Pinter.

Donzelot, Jacques (1979) *The Policing of Families*. New York: Pantheon.

Douglas, Mary (1966) *Purity and Danger: Analyses of Concepts of Pollution and Taboo*. London: Routledge & Kegan Paul.

———— (1973) *Natural Symbols: Explorations in Cosmology*. London: Barrie & Jenkins.

Durkheim, Emile (1938) *The Rules of Sociological Method*. Chicago: Univ. of Chicago Press.

———— (1986) *Durkheim on Politics and the State*. Stanford, CA: Stanford Univ. Press.

Foucault, Michel (1990) *The History of Sexuality*, vol. 1. New York: Vintage Books.

Gates, Daryl (1992) *Chief: My Life in the LAPD*. New York: Bantam Books.

Herbert, Steve (1995) "The Trials of Laurence Powell: Law, Space and a 'Big Time Use of Force,'" 13 *Environment & Planning D: Society & Space* 185.

———— (1996) *Policing Space: Territoriality and the Los Angeles Police Department*. Minneapolis: Univ. of Minnesota Press.

Kappeler, Victor E., Richard D. Sluder, & Geoffrey P. Alpert (1994) *Forces of Deviance: Understanding the Dark Side of Policing*. Prospect Heights, IL: Waveland Press.

Kelling, George (1983) "On the Accomplishments of the Police," in M. Punch, ed., *Control in the Police Organization*. Cambridge, MA: MIT Press.

Manning, Peter (1977) *Police Work: The Social Organization of Policing*. Cambridge, MA: MIT Press.

———— (1993) "Violence and Symbolic Violence," 3 *Police Forum* 1.

Muir, William (1977) *Police: Streetcorner Politicians*. Chicago: Univ. of Chicago Press.

Niederhoffer, Arthur (1967) *Behind the Shield: The Police in Urban Society*. Garden City, NY. Doubleday & Co.

Polsky, Andrew J. (1991) *The Rise of the Therapeutic State*. Princeton, NJ: Princeton Univ. Press.

Raine, Walter (1967) *The Perception of Police Brutality in South Central Los Angeles.* Los Angeles: Institute of Government and Public Affairs, Univ. of California.

Reiner, Robert (1992) *The Politics of the Police.* Toronto: Univ. of Toronto Press.

Reiss, Albert, & David Bordua (1967) "Environment and Organization: A Perspective on the Police," in Bordua 1967.

Reuss-Ianni, Elizabeth (1983) *Two Cultures of Policing. Street Cops and Management Officers.* New Brunswick, NJ: Transaction Books.

Sacks, Harvey (1972) "Notes on Police Assessment of Moral Character," in D. Sudnow, ed., *Studies in Social Interaction.* New York: Free Press.

Sherman, Lawrence (1992) "Attacking Crime: Police and Crime Control," in M. Tonry & N. Morris, eds., *Modern Policing.* Chicago: Univ. of Chicago Press.

Silver, Allan (1967) "The Demand for Order in Civil Society," in Bordua 1967.

Skolnick, Jerome (1966) *Justice Without Trial.* New York: John Wiley & Sons.

Skolnick, Jerome, & James Fyfe (1993) *Above the Law: Police and the Excessive Use of Force.* New York: Free Press.

U.S. Commission on Civil Rights, California Advisory Committee (1963) *Police Minority Relations in Los Angeles and the San Francisco Bay Area.* Washington: U.S. Commission on Civil Rights.

Van Maanen, John (1978) "The Asshole," in J. Van Maanen & P. Manning, eds., *Policing: A View from the Street.* Santa Monica, CA: Goodyear Publishing.

Walker, Samuel (1977) *A Critical History of Police Reform: The Emergence of Professionalism.* Lexington, MA: Lexington Books.

Weber, Max (1954) *Max Weber on Law in Economy and Society.* New York: Simon & Schuster.

Werthman, Carl, & Irving Piliavin (1967) "Gang Members and the Police," in Bordua 1967.

Westley, William (1970) *Violence and the Police: A Sociological Study of Law, Custom, and Morality.* Cambridge, MA: MIT Press.

Wilson, O. W. (1957) *Parker on Police.* Springfield, IL: Charles C. Thomas.

ARTICLE 24

CAN POLICE RECRUITING CONTROL POLICE MISCONDUCT?

Michael J. Palmiotto
Wichita State University

The police have a position of legal authority that requires them to engage the trust of the public. Reports of misconduct by police officers often result in citizens losing their confidence in the police. Even the appearance of wrongdoing can result in a loss of respect for the police. U.S. law enforcement officers must recognize the need to maintain the respect and trust of the community for whom they provide police service. Only through the help of witnesses and victims can offenders be identified, arrested, and prosecuted. The current strategy of community policing requires that the police cooperate and develop a partnership with the community. Without this trust, a successful relationship cannot be expected.

It is the premise of this paper to discuss how police misconduct can be minimized through employment procedures that rigidly examine the suitability of candidates to serve as police officers. This suitability would have an extremely important characteristic: the employment of police officers who potentially could be free from misconduct throughout their careers. Controlling police misconduct should begin during the early stages of recruitment. Ethical, moral, and intelligent police officers who bring no issues to their job, who are not overly aggressive, and who are capable of being open minded with the ability to control their prejudices are the most desireable type of police officers to have on the force.

SELECTION PRACTICES

The effectiveness of any police organization depends upon the selection of its officers. The employment of quality personnel would do much to improve police effectiveness and curtail episodes of misconduct which have plagued law enforcement agencies for decades. Since policing primarily involves working with people from all walks of life, the selection process needs to identify potential police officers who enjoy dealing with people and would refrain from misconduct.

Although the selection process of police officers will never completely eliminate misconduct, it can be used as a tool to curtail the number of police officers who engage in acts of misconduct. A large percentage of police misconduct can be contributed to police departments either not following through on their hiring standards or not having rigorous selection standards. Police departments such as Miami, Florida; Houston, Texas; New York City, New York; and Washington, D.C. often did not perform the necessary background checks when they were given a mandate by their city council to hire large numbers of police officers. The unfortunate part about this hiring practice was that criminals, drug dealers and users often joined the police force. After Miami relaxed its employment standards, it found that by 1987, eighty officers were either suspended or dismissed, a number which eventually reached one hundred. The offenses of these police officers included conspiracy and/or murder and the selling and use of cocaine (Sechrest and Bums 1992, 305).

In 1994 the New York City Police Department admitted that screening a police officer could take up to two years after an officer had already joined the force. The Mollen Commission, which investigated police corruption, concluded that the department's failure to complete background checks sooner posed a serious risk. "The department simply can't determine whether each of the thousands of new officers it places on the streets of New York each year is equipped with the moral values and psychological stamina necessary to meet the demands and temptations that police officers confront each day" (Sexton 1994, 11). The New York City Police Department's background investigation of recruits did not involve reviewing prior work history or conducting interviews with neighbors, and reference checks were not completed until after the candidate was hired. The New York City Police Department admitted that there could be unexplained gaps in employment or false information filed by the officer. How many police departments in the United States, similar to Miami and New York City, have relaxed their employment standards to quickly fill positions?

Standards

The traditional selection standards currently used by police departments should be reviewed before any recommendations can be made to improve the system. When a police officer vacancy is announced, the potential police recruit files a job application with the police department. The application requires the applicant to give his or her name, age, date of birth, current and past addresses, education, all employment positions, and references. The process generally includes the following:

- Written tests
- Polygraph test
- Fingerprints taken and submitted to FBI
- Records checks
- Background investigation
- Psychological testing

- Drug screening
- Physical/medical examination
- Physical agility test
- Assessment center
- Oral interview board

A candidate should successfully complete all components of the hiring standards, including a variety of written tests, before being offered a position with the police agency. Many of these tests measure reading comprehension and English usage and may require responding to an essay question to determine written communication skill level. Fyfe et al. (1997, 292) believe "it is usually impossible to demonstrate the job relevance of written examinations." Written tests are being used as qualifiers for placing candidates on employment eligibility lists.

Many police departments require a polygraph examination as a pre-employment test. The polygraph examination is utilized to determine an applicant's suitability for employment. Police agencies that require the polygraph as a condition for employment want to verify information contained in the application for the police position. Information of specific concern are theft tendencies, drug and/or alcohol problems, **or** any type of behavior that would mark the applicant as an at-risk officer (Nardini 1987). It is recommended that the polygraph be given as part of the background examination. The polygraph could obtain information that would eliminate a police candidate from being considered for a position prior to spending thousands of dollars on completing background investigations. The polygraph used to screen police applicants has other advantages as well. These include sending a message to the community that the police agency is making every effort to employ only the most suitable people while turning away applicants who believe that the polygraph will reveal questionable behavior (Swanson et al. 1998).

All candidates applying for a position as a police officer are fingerprinted, and the prints are then forwarded to the fingerprint division in their respective states as well as to the Federal Bureau of Investigation to determine if the candidate has a criminal record. Police agencies should also run a check of each candidate on the Automatic Fingerprint Identification System (AFIS), which matches fingerprints taken at crime scenes with a recorded fingerprint.

Police departments need to do records checks of all police candidates. These should include both state and local searches of police records in all areas where the candidate has lived. The National Crime Information Center (NCIC) should be searched to determine if the candidate is wanted for a crime. The need for a records check should be based upon the information provided by the candidate when disclosing their personal history. This should include arrest and criminal record information, traffic violations, medical history, names of friends and relatives, previous residence, previous employment, organizational affiliations, interests, hobbies, and so on (Wilson and McLaren 1977). This information is invaluable in the background investigation of the candidate.

The background investigation concentrates on the candidate's employment record, credit record, sociability, mental and emotional history, personal integrity, education, medical history, military records, civil court records, and criminal history. The investigation should be in-depth and accurate to allow for an honest appraisal of the suitability of the candidate for a police position. The background investigation should answer the following questions:

1. Does the applicant possess any racial or social prejudices?
2. Is he or she a good worker?
3. Does tardiness or absenteeism seem to be a problem?
4. Can the candidate work independently without close supervision?
5. Is the candidate dependable and, above all, honest?
6. Does the applicant have a healthy attitude toward work?
7. Has the applicant been arrested and/or convicted of a crime that has not been discovered up to this point?
8. Does the candidate have good moral habits?
9. Is the candidate emotionally stable based on reference interviews and discovered information?
10. Can the applicant handle the mature responsibilities of life, such as money management and so on? (Credit and indebtedness determine)
    A. A history of personal irresponsibility could indicate vulnerability to engage in activities of ill-repute and criminal activity.
    B. Clarify the cause of the financial irresponsibility-it may be unavoidable such as medical bills.
    C. Investigate any unexplained affluence. A lifestyle not commensurate with known income should indicate to the investigator that the investigation should be expanded to determine source of financial support.
    D. A suitable investigation should be initiated only if the candidate's affluence cannot be logically explained by documented sources of legitimate income.
11. Can the candidate hold a steady job or is he/she a job-hopper?
    A. Employment history stability can be considered a window to understanding the applicant's work habits and commitment to perform the job.
12. Is the candidate genuinely interested in a law enforcement career or will it be just another job?
13. Does the applicant have a poor or marginal educational record?
14. Has the applicant exhibited any unusual, bizarre, or undesirable behavior in the past?
15. Has the applicant falsified or been deceptive of anything during the application process? This should be well documented. Are there omissions of arrest, convictions, and incarceration?
16. Is the applicant an illegal narcotics user? This area has to be investigated thoroughly.
    A. The investigation should elicit information regarding an individual's use, transport, transfer, sale, cultivation, processing and manufacturing of hallucinogens, narcotics, drugs, other controlled substances and chemical compounds.
    B. A candidates involvement in these activities is of direct concern to determine the individual's capability to exercise the judgement required of a police officer. Involvement also presumes criminal activity (Birzer 1996, 7–8).

Nardini, in the annual report of the National Advisory Commission on Criminal Justice Standards and Goals, recommended that police applicants "be very carefully screened to preclude employment of those who are emotionally unstable, brutal, or who suffer any form of mental illness (1973, 338)." The purpose of the psychological examination is to weed out those unfit for police service. Generally, police work can be considered stressful and the police agency needs to employ police officers who are able to cope with the daily pressures of police work. Police departments need to eliminate candidates who are overly aggressive, abusive, and controlling of other human beings. A psychological examination of all candidates is usually the norm for police agencies, and often such examinations are conducted by clinical psychologists. The purpose of the psychological examination is to determine the emotional fitness of the candidate to perform police service and to determine if the candidate suffers from mental illness which would eliminate the candidate from further consideration. There are a wide variety of psychological tests that the psychologist can give the applicant. Psychological testing could include either an intellectual assessment, a personality assessment, or a clinical interview. The psychological test consists of either a questionnaire and/or a face-to-face interview in which the psychologist has an opportunity to observe the applicant's behavior. The psychologist's report can also eliminate the candidate from further consideration (Palmiotto 1997).

The police selection process includes drug testing of all police applicants. With the easy availability of drugs and a good percentage of Americans using drugs, police agencies can only eliminate drug users by drug testing. Police officers who are expected to enforce the laws of society cannot, themselves, violate the laws. This includes the use and/or selling of drugs as well as associating with known drug users. In our contemporary society, police officers will be exposed to and come into contact with illicit drugs, drug dealers and users. Police agencies cannot afford to employ officers who use or condone illicit drug use.

A medical or physical examination is required of all police applicants. Police agencies expect candidates to be healthy if they are to function as police officers. Generally, their weight has to be in proportion to their body structure. The medical examination should include a variety of sophisticated medical tests. All applicants should be required to submit to an eye examination as well.

Most police agencies require police applicants to successfully pass a physical agility test. The physical agility test differs for each police department, but the general purpose of the test is to determine the physical strength, endurance, and motor skills of the candidate.

Some police agencies use assessment centers to assist in the selection of police officers. The assessment center conducts performance exams in which the applicants are required to perform a variety of job-related tasks which are observed and graded by assessors. The performance dimensions include knowledge, skills, and abilities which are derived from job analysis.

An oral interview conducted by the police chief, police commanders, or a board is usually part of the screening process. The purpose of the oral interview is to provide the police administration with a way to assess a candidate's suitability for police service. During the interview process, the police interviewer should follow a structured interview that asks the same questions of all the candidates. Specific questions pertaining to sex, religion, race, age, and ethnic origin should not be asked. The police interviewer should be familiar with affirmative action and equal employment opportunity commission guidelines. All police interviews conducted by a police administrator should follow all state and federal laws and guidelines established for the pre-employment interview (Palmiotto 1997).

SUGGESTIONS FOR CONTROLLING POLICE MISCONDUCT

The selection standards reviewed in the previous section should be thoroughly followed. Only when the selection standards as outlined are completely followed can police agencies expect to curtail police misconduct. Police departments should not eliminate or take any shortcuts in the selection standards for any mass hiring of police officers as the Miami Police Department did in the early 1980s or as the District of Washington Police Department did in the early 1990s. No police officer should be employed unless a comprehensive background investigation has been completed. This failure has led to police departments such as New York City, Miami, and Washington, D.C. to hire police officers who had criminal and drug records or poor employment records. If these cities had followed the selection standards traditionally accepted by federal and state law enforcement agencies, they might have eliminated the police scandals that occurred in these police departments.

Background Investigation

The purpose of a background investigation is to develop a character profile of the police candidate. The more information obtained about a police candidate, the easier it is for an agency to determine if the candidate is suitable for police service. Once the decision has been made to initiate a background investigation, the police candidate should be informed that he or she is being considered for a position. At that time, the candidate should notify the department as to whether he or she is still interested in the position. It is unnecessary to perform a background investigation on a candidate who withdraws his or her application. A thorough background investigation centers on the following elements.

1. *Screening through criminal record sources,* such as the National Criminal Investigation Center and similar state systems. In many agencies, search results that include the discovery of conviction records for felons or some misdemeanors (usually involving violence, drugs, or evidence of dishonesty or sexual misconduct) are excluders, as are extremely bad traffic records. Arrests not resulting in conviction should be carefully scrutinized for evidence that outcomes favorable to candidates had nothing to do with whether candidates had committed the acts charged; a rapist who is acquitted because his victim ceases cooperation with prosecutors may not be a convict, but he is still a rapist and an inappropriate candidate for a police career.
2. *Checks with noncriminal sources of information,* such as job references, neighbors, and credit agencies, concerning candidates' reliability, discipline, and trustworthiness. Whenever possible, these checks should be done formally through the official mechanism prior employers have

put in place for this purpose, and such informal channels as former supervisors or coworkers who may be personally known to investigators
should be regarded as secondary, rather than primary, sources. These
checks should be as thoroughly documented as possible. (Fyfe et al.
1997, 297–298).

Examination of references should focus on obtaining information about the
character of the police candidate. This would include any negative tendencies
such as excessive use of alcohol, drugs, or gambling. The background investigator should solicit information about a police candidate's behavior. For example, is the candidate excessively aggressive or passive? Also, information
should be obtained about any organization that the police candidate is a member of or associated with, such as hate groups or anti-government militas.

Current and former employers should be interviewed. Information such
as consistent lateness, absenteeism, productivity level, and ability to get along
with fellow workers and supervisors needs to be obtained. The employment
check should indicate whether the police candidate is a job hopper. Does he
or she keep a job only a few months? Is he or she a productive worker? Does
the police candidate have ethics?

An area of investigation important to a police agency is the ability of
the police candidate to live within his or her economic means. An individual
who constantly lives beyond economic means may be prone to illegal activities to cover excessive lifestyle. Knowledge of the police candidate's driving
record is important if the department will be providing the candidate with a
police vehicle. Does the candidate have an excessive number of driving violations? Are there any citations for driving under the influence of alcohol? Are
there an excessive number of automobile accidents? A police candidate with
a poor driving record can be expected to continue these driving habits as a police officer.

The records of those candidates who served in the military should be obtained and reviewed. Unless a candidate was discharged from the military
with an honorable discharge or with a general discharge under honorable
conditions, he or she should not be employed as a police officer. A police candidate's military record should be taken very seriously. The military requires
discipline of its personnel, and if a candidate was unsuccessful in the military,
it can be anticipated that the candidate will, in all probability, have difficulty
functioning as a police officer.

The final area of investigation that should be completed is the police candidate's schooling and education level. Educators who are familiar with the
candidate should be interviewed including elementary and middle school
teachers, high school teachers, coaches, and university professors. If the police
candidate held a part-time position in a university setting, the former supervisors of that candidate should be interviewed.

College Education

The minimum qualification for employment as a police officer should be a
baccalaureate degree. Generally, the college graduate is better equipped intellectually to handle the demands of policing. For example

in a period of problem-oriented policing and community-oriented policing, there is a greater expectation of creativity and problem solving by police officers. If police organizations give more than lip service to community policing, then, for this philosophy to be successful, the rigidity of the police organization needs to decrease and disappear. An officer with a college education should be better able to cope with the changing philosophy of policing than a non-college educated police officer. (Palmiotto 1999, 85)

Recent policing strategies, which include problem-solving and community policing, are more readily accepted by college-educated officers who are able to recognize that crime-fighting image is more propaganda than reality. The college-educated officer usually performs better at public forums. Those police officers who have college degrees in criminal justice should be familiar with the various policing models and strategies and understand the various theories of crime. A college education offers several advantages for police officers:

- It develops a broad base of information for decision making.
- Course requirements and achievements inculcate responsibility in the individual.
- College education engenders the ability to flexibly handle difficult or ambiguous situations with greater creativity or innovation.
- Higher education develops a greater empathy for minorities and their discriminatory experiences through both coursework and interaction within the academic community.
- A greater understanding and tolerance for persons with different lifestyles and ideologies which can translate into more effective communications and community relations in the practice of policing.
- The college educated officer is assumed to be less rigid in decision-making . . .
- The college experience will help officers communicate and respond to crime and service needs of the public in a competent manner with civility and humanity.
- The educated officer is more innovative and flexible when dealing with complex policing programs and strategies such as problem-oriented policing, community policing, task force responses, etc.
- More "professional" demeanor and performance is exhibited by the college educated officer.
- The college experience tends to make the officer less authoritarian and less cynical with respect to the mileau of policing (Carter, Sapp, and Stephens 1988:16–18).

Age

The minimum age for all entry-level police officers should be 25. By making the minimum age 25, all candidates should have had at least three years of full-time work experience. This would allow for an evaluation of the work performance of a candidate. If a candidate is hired at the age of 21, right out of college, then he or she may not have had any full-time work experience. An additional benefit of hiring a 25-year-old is that, all things being equal, the 25-year-old should be more mature than the 21-year-old. It is also recommended that police departments consider recruiting police candidates who are in their late 30s and 40s. The older candidate has work experience, maturity, and usually will not challenge the policies and procedures of the police department. The 30- or 40-year-old is less likely to have the "John Wayne Syndrome." For example, it is more likely for the 21-year-old officer to drive to work speeding on his motorcycle than it is for the 40-year-old officer. Generally, when a candidate enters policing at age 30 or 40, he or she has tried a number of jobs and has come to the conclusion that policing is the field of career choice. There exists more of a tendency for the younger officer to be reprimanded, fired, or asked to resign because of misconduct, incompetence, or insubordination.

Ethics

Police service is a position of public trust. Only those police candidates with high moral character who function ethically in their public lives and in their private lives should be employed as police officers. Enforcers of society's standards should not only be held accountable for their actions but should also be held to a higher standard than that of the general public. Two points should be analyzed when reviewing the ethics of a police candidate: balanced perception and integrity. Balanced perception refers to "how an officer makes the best of circumstances" (DeLattre 1989, 12). For example, in an domestic dispute, an officer would need sound judgment and be able to recognize what is needed to settle the conflict. Qualities of good character are an integral part of both our public and private lives. A person of integerity behaves rightly, not just because he is concerned about being caught (DeLattre 1989, 12–13).

Ethics is an important issue to policing. The morals, the values, the attitude, and the work ethic of police officers is important to the reputation of any department. Police officers with ethics would probably not be involved in police misconduct. Therefore, determining the ethics of a police candidate should be integrated into the hiring process through background investigations, interviews, polygraph tests, psychological evaluations, and written exams. If police administrators want to gain control over police misconduct, then these steps must be included in the hiring process.

CRITERIA FOR DISQUALIFYING AN APPLICANT FOR A POLICE OFFICER POSITION

Not all candidates who apply for employment within the police department should be offered a position. There are a variety of reasons why an individual should not be employed by the police department. The following are reasons for disqualifying a candidate from a position as a law enforcement officer.

1. Not a citizen of the United States
2. Has not reached the minimum age
3. Does not meet the minimum educational requirements
4. Applicant who served in the military did not receive an honorable discharge or a discharge under honorable conditions
5. Has committed a felony crime

6. Has been placed on a diversion program by any state, the federal government, or the military for committing a felony crime
7. Has physical or mental conditions that would adversely affect the applicant's performance as a police officer
8. Has been convicted of morals, drugs, or weapons charges, e.g. prostitution, promoting prostitution and indecent exposure, sodomy, incest, commercial gambling, crimes against nature, and the illegal possession or sale of narcotics or drugs
9. Has had a conviction of violence and/or use of physical force
10. Has been convicted, placed on diversion, or entered a deferred judgement program for a misdemeanor of domestic violence
11. Has two or more convictions, diversions or expungement of driving while intoxicated
12. Has been convicted of theft/larceny or a property crime
13. Has been convicted of reckless driving, fleeing or attempting to elude a police officer, failing to stop at an accident scene, or is a habitual traffic violator
14. Has used or possessed marijuana illegally within the last three years or has distributed or sold marijuana (no time limit)
15. Discharged from employment as a result of poor behavior or inability to discipline
16. Repeated convictions of an offense which indicate disrespect for the law (Birzer, 1995, 10)

CONCLUSIONS

The employment process of the police agency in hiring officers can go a long way in controlling police misconduct. Police departments concerned with placing high quality police officers on their city streets will take steps to do all that is possible to employ the best candidates. Although there will never be a fool-proof system that will eliminate all types of misconduct by police officers, strategies exist that can keep misconduct by officers to a minimum. These strategies include selection processes that have been used by federal, state, and local law enforcement agencies for decades. We further believe that the recommendations made in this article will be an added stride in preventing misconduct by police officers.

REFERENCES

Birzer, Michael L. (1995). "Applicant Background Investigation Procedures: A Training Program for Detectives." Paper presented at a training session at the Wichita Fedgwick County Law Enforcement Training Center, October, 1995.

Carter, David L., Allan D. Sapp, and Darrell W. Stephens (1988). "Higher Education As a Bona Fide Occupational Qualification (BFOQ) For Police: A Blue Print." *American Journal of Police.* 7 (no. 2)

Delattre, Edwin J. (1989). *Character and Cops: Ethics in Policing.* Washington, DC: University Press of America.

Fyfe, James J., Jack R. Greene, William F. Walsh, O.W. Wilson and Roy Clinton McLaren. (1997). *Police Administration* (5th ed.). New York, NY: McGraw-Hill Publishers.

Nardini, William. (1987). "The Polygraph Technique: An Overview," *Journal of Police Science and Administration.* 15 (no. 3): 239–249.

National Advisory Commission on Criminal Justice Standards and Goals (1973) Police, Washington, DC: U.S. Government Printing Office.

Palmiotto, Michael J. (1999) "Should a College Degree Be Required for Law Enforcement Officers?" In *Controversial Issues in Policing,* ed. by James Sewell. Needham Heights, MA: Allyn and Bacon. 69–87.

Palmiotto, Michael J. (1997). *Policing: Concepts, Strategies and Current Issues in American Police Forces.* Durhan, NC: Carolina Academic Press.

Sechrest, Dale K. and Pamela Bums. (1992). "Police Corruption: The Miami Case," *Criminal Justice and Behavior.* 19 (no. 3): 294–313.

Sexton, Joe. (April 27, 1994) "Officers Put on Streets Before Screening Ends," *The New York Times,* 27 April 1994.

Swanson, Charles R., Leonard Territo, and Robert W. Taylor. (1998). *Police Administration: Structures, Processes, and Behavior* (4th ed.), Upper Saddle River, NJ: Prentice-Hall.

Wilson, O.W. and Roy Clinton McLaren. (1977). *Police Administration* (4th ed.) New York, NY: McGraw-Hill.

ARTICLE 25

LAW ENFORCEMENT: POLICING THE DEFECTIVE CENTURION—DECERTIFICATION AND BEYOND

William C. Smith*
Geoffrey P. Alpert**

Policing is perceived as a public service career, but recently that perception has come under critical scrutiny. Virtually every adult in the United States is familiar with the infamous videotape of the Rodney King beating, where Los Angeles police officers engaged in a "feeding frenzy."[1] The societal backlash against acquittal of the officers involved in the beating touched off a riot of proportions that should never be repeated. At the core of the Rodney King incident festers a question that, owing to its complex roots, may never be adequately answered: "How, in a system predicated upon the maxim of 'equal justice under law' could such police misconduct occur?"

The nature, extent, and costs of police misconduct and corruption are difficult to determine and impossible to justify. One commentator has observed that "as long as there have been police, there has been corruption."[2] One police historian has observed that police "corruption is one of the oldest and most persistent problems in American policing."[3] One of the most interesting and serious examples of police corruption is that of the so-called Miami River

William C. Smith and Geoffrey P. Alpert, "Law Enforcement: Policing the Defective Centurion—Decertification and Beyond" (as appeared in *Criminal Law Bulletin*, [March–April 1993], pp. 147–157). Reprinted by permission of West Group.

*Partner, Dennis & Smith, Columbia, S.C. Formerly Director, Legal Services, South Carolina Criminal Justice Academy, Columbia, S.C.

**Professor, College of Criminal Justice, Research Professor, Institute of Public Affairs, University of South Carolina, Columbia, S.C.

[1] Alpert, Smith & Watters, "Law Enforcement: Implications of the Rodney King Beating," 28 Criminal Law Bulletin 469, 470 (1992).

[2] L. Sherman (ed.), *Police Corruption: A Sociological Perspective* 1. (1974).

[3] S. Walker, *The Police in America* 262 (1992).

Cops, in which twelve Florida police officers were convicted of crimes ranging from drug dealing to murder.[4]

While there have been insightful studies of the extent and types of police corruption,[5] its direct and indirect costs have never been calculated. One hidden cost of police misconduct is its demoralizing effect on society in general and the police community.[6] This column will review the current concerns and discuss the decertification process as an ultimate method of accountability. In addition to decertification, police professionalism as a means of control will be considered.

Control and Misconduct

Every aspect of police behavior is subject to some type of control mechanism[7] since policing is perceived as a paramilitary function. This accounts for the belief that in a disciplined occupational group, the appropriate means of control is to allow very little discretion in the vast majority of tasks. From a clinical standpoint, the logic may be valid. However, reality dictates that officers must be prepared to make discretionary decisions in many of their activities and in these situations stringent control mechanisms are inappropriate.[8]

The behavioral repertoire of the average "street cop" includes a complex array of decisions, based on training and experience, that results in discretionary actions. Because members of society are so diverse, the police response to the multitude of social problems must be equally diverse.[9] Providing police training to address adequately all of these behaviors would be virtually impossible. The mediated response to this reality is a system in which training has come to address the critical "worst case scenario" and officers are forced to use limited, and frequently unguided, discretion in cases involving lesser evils. Were proper training available for handling the routine activities of police work, this approach would generate little controversy. However, the lack of proper training, i.e., minimal emphasis on ethical decision making coupled with the frequent refusal by management to relinquish tight control over virtually every aspect of officer behavior, may be a significant cause of the current allegations of police misconduct.[10]

---

[4]P. Eddy, H. Sabago, and S. Walden, *The Cocaine Wars* 194–198, 235–237 (1988).

[5]T. Barker and D. Carter (eds.), *Police Deviance* (1992); L. Sherman (ed.), Note 2 *supra*. H. Goldstein, *Police Corruption: A Perspective on its Nature and Control,* (1975); Knapp Commission, *Report of the New York City Commission to Investigate Allegations of Police Corruption and the City's Anti-Corruption Procedures* (1972). Murphy, "Corruptive Influences," in B. Garmire (ed.), *Local Government Police Management,* (1982); A. Simpson, *The Literature of Police Corruption: A Guide to Bibliography and Theory* (1977).

[6]P. Murphy and G. Kaplan, "Fostering Integrity," at 239–271, 255–257, in W. Geller (ed.) *Local Government Police Management* (1991).

[7]Smith and Alpert, "Police Policy: Is the Control Principle Out of Control?," Police and Security News, Sept./Oct. 1992, at 3,5.

[8]*Id.* at 32.

[9]M. Brown, *Working the Street: Police Discretion and the Dilemmas of Reform,* 244–245 (1981).

[10]S. Walker, *The Police in America* 269–270 (1992).

Police misconduct, however, can be organizational as well as individual. As an individual act, misconduct is the misuse of authority by an officer by which the officer or another benefits.[11] Such misconduct remains on an individual level until it is "condoned, supported or encouraged by the police organization."[12] If the misconduct is known or should have been known to the administrative staff and no disciplinary action is taken, the misconduct becomes organizational or institutional rather than individual. The key question in claims of organizational misconduct is whether the police agency took appropriate steps to control the actions of its individual officers once put on notice of their misconduct. Thus, the issue of control becomes critical in balancing officer and agency response to public need in an effort to maintain trust and confidence in the police.

Certainly, trust and confidence in the police is based on their interaction with citizens and the service and crimefighting functions that they perform.[13] When the police lose sight of their public service obligation, as they did during the beating of Rodney King, and in the incidents involving the Miami River Cops, there must be an accounting for the aberrance from their social contract to serve and protect.[14] Judicially, the accounting can range from findings of financial liability to criminal imprisonment. At the departmental level, firing or a lesser disciplinary sanction such as suspension may occur for individual officers. From a licensure perspective, however, decertification may be the only appropriate remedy where the individual officer's ability to police has become terminally compromised.[15]

The regulation of police misconduct has traditionally relied on the localities.[16] That is, once the individual officer becomes certified by the state regulatory agency, local agencies are free to hire, fire, or discipline an officer without oversight or state intervention. Because initial attempts to manage misconduct were limited to such internal control mechanisms, discipline frequently was subjectively imposed, with widely disparate punishments.[17] In many cases, this resulted in inconsequential disciplinary action taken against officers who had engaged in serious misconduct.[18]

Similarly, officers who committed serious offenses might be fired but find work subsequently in an agency that was unaware of the misconduct or simply indifferent to it.[19] Because of such discrepancies in treatment, many

---

[11]G. Alpert and R. Dunham, *Policing Urban America* at 103–119 (1992).

[12]*Id.* at 107.

[13]G. Alpert and R. Dunham, "Policing Multi-Ethnic Neighborhoods: The Miami Study and Findings for Law Enforcement in the United States 119–127 (1988).

[14]See notes 1 and 4 *supra*.

[15]Alpert, Smith and Watters, note 1 supra, at 475–478.

[16]Goldman and Puro, "Decertification of Police: An Alternative to Traditional Remedies for Police Misconduct," 15 Hastings Const. L. Q. 60 (1987).

[17]United States Civil Rights Commission, Who's Guarding the Guardians 128–149 (1981).

[18]R. Goldman and S. Puro, note 16 *supra*, at 60–65.

[19]Greenberg and Kaluhiokalani, "Policing Ourselves: The Decertification Process in Florida", 10 J. of Police Science and Admin. 473, 474 (1982).

states have enacted statutory or regulatory prerequisites for police service. In every state and the federal government, police officers must be licensed or certified.[20] Once an individual has earned the license and maintains it, he may continue in a career of law enforcement moving from one department to another. It is the license or certification that permits the individual to practice law enforcement in a particular jurisdiction. Unless the police officer's certification or license is withdrawn, the authority to exercise law enforcement powers continues. Other professions also regulate their members by granting and revoking licenses.[21] For example, an attorney or a medical doctor found guilty of immoral or illegal behavior may be professionally sanctioned.[22] As the practice of law enforcement entails the exercise of a significant number of critical functions, it is surprising that all states do not currently have mechanisms for decertifying officers who engage in serious police misconduct.[23]

Many states have a statutory or regulatory mandate that police officers cannot continue employment after being convicted of a felony or other such serious offense as one involving moral turpitude.[24] Additionally, some states have civil service systems with established continuing eligibility criteria for police.[25] However, these regulations affect only the most serious offenders and do not require that any action be taken against those who have violated the public trust in a less than criminal fashion. Thus, serious police misconduct within the penumbra of specific statutory or regulatory prohibitions may go unchecked unless accountability can be established for all police misconduct.

The need is clear: The state agency that certifies police officers must have the authority to remove the license to police where the licensee has proven unworthy. Like other professional groups, the police must keep their own house

---

[20]For example, in the state of South Carolina, Section 23-23-40 of the Code of Laws reads, in pertinent part:

> No law enforcement officer employed or appointed on or after July 1, 1989, by any public law enforcement agency in this state is authorized to enforce the laws or ordinances of this state or any political subdivision thereof unless he has been certified as qualified by the [Law Enforcement Training Council], except that any public law enforcement agency in this State may appoint or employ as a law enforcement officer, a person who is not certified if, within one year after the date of employment or appointment, the person secures certification from the council.

[21]For example, members of the legal and medical professions are closely regulated by professional licensure and are subject to censure and discipline for infractions of their regulatory guidelines. As an example, see ABA, Model Rules of Professional Conduct, American Bar Association (1992), governing the legal profession.

[22]For example, an attorney can be disbarred for acts that tend to bring the legal profession into disrepute or that involve dishonesty or moral turpitude. See the Model Code of Professional Conduct, n.21 *supra,* Rule 8.4: Misconduct.

[23]Puro and Goldman, "Police Decertification: A Remedy for Police Misconduct?" in 5 R. Homant and D. Kennedy (eds.), *Police and Law Enforcement* 118 (1988), who report that nineteen states had no authority to decertify police officers. Since the time of their report, at least Michigan and South Carolina have implemented decertification procedures.

[24]*Id.* at 116.

[25]*Id.* at 122.

in order.[26] Central to the implementation of any decertification procedure, however, is the need to define misconduct that would warrant what has been referred to as occupational capital punishment.[27]

Defining the Problem

Criminal acts committed by police officers are the most repugnant type of misconduct. Violations of the law committed by those sworn to uphold it shock the conscience of the community. Federal civil rights violations are often criminal as well as civil in nature.[28] In these instances of misconduct, police executives have little difficulty deciding to discipline police officers for errant behavior. But what of allegations of impropriety that fail to rise to the level of criminality? In these areas, administrators are without concrete guidance and are forced to walk a thin line, balancing between the obligation to serve the public with integrity and the need to maintain fair but firm treatment of officers without destroying morale. Even the most conscientious efforts at discipline at this level will vary significantly from department to department due to the lack of standardized guidance as to the seriousness of specific misconduct. A difficult first question then becomes, "What constitutes police misconduct for which officers should be decertified?"

Unlike many other "regulated" occupational fields, the police are not subject to uniform ethical principles or national standards. This results in regionalized and disparate judicial determinations of what precisely constitutes unacceptable conduct for the guardians of law and order. Such a balkanized approach explains the varying degrees of protection given to officers by different courts in ostensibly similar factual settings.[29] The lack of nationally binding ethical standards imposes an immense burden on the identification of behavior for which decertification is necessary or appropriate. Officers must be put on notice of expected behavior and given some degree of concrete guidance in its particulars or the process of insuring citizen rights will become mired in speculation.

While fundamental constitutional principles may preclude creation of an enforceable code of conduct at the federal level, altruistic principles of public service and economic concerns of risk and liability management should force every state to admit that deficient police officers must be subject to disciplinary action and delicensure if public trust is to be maintained. This conceptual aspect of decertification, however, is more easily explained than are its contours and limits defined.

---

[26]Savino and Brunung, "Decertification Strategies and Tactics: Management and Union Perspectives," 43 Lab. L. J. 210–210(1992).

[27]Johnson and Smith, "Blue Suits in Glass Houses: Can We Regulate Police Misconduct?" 2 S.C. Forum 6–11, (Summer 1992) at 8.

[28]Title 18 of the United States Code, Sections 241 and 242, specifically provide criminal sanctions for those persons who, under color of state law, conspire to violate federally secured rights of any citizen or actually violate federally secured rights of any inhabitant of the United States.

[29]For a useful discussion of the wide disparity in assessment of punitive damages against individual officers for their acts of misconduct see cases cited in I. Silver, *Police Civil Liability* 10-17-10-20 (2d ed. 1992).

As a practical matter, decertifiable misconduct is difficult to define. Frequently, the underlying behavior is linked by definition to the punishment or discipline meted out for it. It has been noted that the remedies for police misconduct take many forms, most notably, from a criminal standpoint, the application of the exclusionary rule.[30] An alternative remedy, the removal of the repeatedly deficient officer from the practice of law enforcement, has also been proposed.[31] Similarly, in an analysis of police misconduct in the Detroit Police Department, one author noted that:

> The police have developed an amazing resiliency against pressures to control their own abusive behavior. It seems that police will not alter conduct without outside compulsion; nor is altered conduct guaranteed even when outside compulsion is present.[32]

These authors have recognized a principle critical to definition: misconduct is that which warrants some sanction as a remedy for its occurrence. The seriousness of the sanction, or outside compulsion, is the proper domain of inquiry for discussions involving decertification. Certainly, inquiry must be made into the relationship of an officer's offensive conduct to the ability to provide police service. Where the behavior involves critical aspects of police duty and seriously compromises the officer's ability to provide protection to the public, decertification must be the appropriate sanction. To define the parameters of decertifiable conduct, however, requires analysis of those police functions that must be deemed critical and core to the providing of public service.

Core and Critical Functions

Certain behaviors may be said to be core functions of police work, i.e., fundamental to the performance of the police mission. On the one hand, core behaviors involve those activities, such as executing legal process, conducting traffic stops, and a host of others, that are the daily tasks of police work. On the other hand, critical functions are a small subset of core behaviors that have as their likely consequence great bodily injury or death if performed improperly. These would include such behaviors as discharge of a weapon or emergency response driving, including vehicular pursuit. One may conclude, from an analysis of the police mandate to serve the public, that decertification may be an appropriate remedy where willfull or wanton misfeasance[33] in a

---

[30]Goldman and Puro, note 16 *supra*, at 47–49.

[31]*Id.* at 63–65.

[32]Littlejohn, "Civil Liability and the Police Officer: The Need for New Deterrents to Police Misconduct", 58 U. Det., Journ. of Urban Law, 365, 366 (1981) (citations omitted).

[33]*Black's Law Dictionary* (5th ed. 1979) defines "misfeasance" as "[t]he improper performance of some act which a man may lawfully do" at 902. A "willful" act is "one done intentionally, knowingly and purposely, without justifiable excuse" and "done with evil intent, or with a bad motive or purpose, with indifference to the natural consequences" at 1434. "Wanton" conduct according to the same source, is that "characterized by extreme recklessness or foolhardiness [and] disregardful of the rights or safety of others or consequences, at 1418–1419."

critical function area is found after a full investigation is conducted. Where such misfeasance has occurred in a core function, the remedy should typically be less drastic, unless repeated or multiple occurrences are involved. This proposal is premised upon officers having been provided proper training in the delivery of police services in core and critical function areas. Typically, decertification would be inappropriate for misfeasance premised upon inadvertent or negligent behaviors that fall short of wanton or intentional conduct.

The importance of core behaviors can best be understood by evaluating a police department's frequency of critical public contacts. Exhibit 1 has been designed for risk management of police activities[34] and its author noted that the high-frequency, low-exposure functions can be discharged with minimal guidance and a strong system of shared values. The high-exposure activities, including the use of both lethal and nonlethal force and many other serious actions, including searches, seizures, and other activities significantly affecting the liberty interests of citizens, require explicit policies, training, and overall guidance. In this last respect, this classification would include all critical functions and many core functions. Of course, there exists a policy continuum along which the need for control increases proportionately with respect to the criticality of the police function.[35] While this continuum is addressed specifically to policy issues, it serves to identify those activities that are closely tied to the potential for serious injury or death, i.e., critical functions. Of necessity, the class of core behaviors must be broader than the class of critical functions. While the policy continuum identifies critical functions that *must* be tightly controlled because of the potential for serious injury or death, there also exists a body, or core, of police functions that are essential to public safety but that will not likely result in serious injury or death if improperly performed. These core and critical functions, once identified, should be the focus of a definition of decertifiable misconduct.

Therefore, to define decertifiable police misconduct one must isolate core and critical behaviors that have an impact upon significant rights of citizens, i.e., those guaranteed by the Bill of Rights and the Fourteenth Amendment and those created by state statutory and constitutional guarantees. An identification of actionable police conduct under such federal civil rights statutes as the 1871 Civil Rights Act would be the first step in this process.[36] Once this identification process has been completed, the second step is to establish qualitative guidelines for officers so that notice of permissible behavioral parameters is provided. Finally, notice must be given of possible punishment for transgressions. Linked to this last step is provision for due process protection for officers who are targets of misconduct allegations. Clarification of the

---

[34]D. LaBrec, "Risk Management: Preventive Law Practice and Practical Risk Management Methods for the 1980s," paper presented to the Annual Meeting of the National Institute of Municipal Law Officers, Miami, Fla. (1982).

[35]G. Alpert and W. Smith, "Developing Police Policy: Evaluating the Control Principle," 12 American Journal of Police (1993) (forthcoming).

[36]Codified at Title 42, U.S.C. § 1983. Such conduct would include wrongful arrests and detentions, malicious or retaliatory prosecutions, incidents involving use of excessive force and illegal searches and seizures to list a few. For a comprehensive review of actionable police misconduct, see *Police Misconduct, Law and Litigation,* M. Avery and D. Rudovsky, 2d ed. (1992).

impact of criminal indictment or information based upon core or critical functions must also be made.

Ultimately, the ability to decertify will serve both police and citizen interests by providing service with integrity. Additionally, elimination of officers who are no longer worthy of the public trust will reduce agency liability exposure. This threat of civil judgment may provide the final compulsion to alter or prevent abusive police behavior or prevent it.[37]

Police Civil Liability for Misconduct

The 1989 U.S. Supreme Court decision in *City of Canton v. Harris*[38] marked the beginning of an era of increased scrutiny of police training and operations. The case should be viewed as a harbinger of increased accountability for police conduct. A number of courts, both federal and state, have taken the *City of Canton* benchmark of "deliberate indifference" and applied it to a variety of incidents of police misconduct.[39] In *Davis v. Mason County*,[40] for example, the Ninth Circuit Court of Appeals recognized that the training afforded sheriff's deputies in the constitutional limits of the use of nonlethal force was so deficient as to amount to "deliberate indifference" to citizens' rights. The facts in the four *Davis* "incidents" provide sad commentary on the impact of deficient police training on the citizens the officers purportedly were required to "protect and serve."

City of Canton is of critical importance to police administrators and municipal risk managers, but it has brought no surprises to an occupational group already accustomed to repeated allegations of improper conduct. That case represents only part of the current concern over police misconduct, but it makes abundantly clear that where officer behavior can be seen as evidencing the policy, custom, or practice of the employing municipality and has resulted in constitutional injury to a plaintiff, municipal liability is virtually certain to

---

[37]Littlejohn, note 32 *supra*, at 365.

[38]109 S. Ct. 1197 (1989). *City of Canton* is frequently cited as holding that inadequacy of police training may serve as the basis for municipal liability under Title 42, U.S. C. § 1983 where the failure to train amounts to "deliberate indifference" to the rights of citizens with whom the police will likely have contact. The significance of the "deliberate indifference" standard is highlighted in footnote 10 of the case which posits that some police activities are so critical in terms of their potential for injury, if improperly discharged, that failure to provide training in their particulars is classifiable as deliberately indifferent. 109 S. Ct. at 1205 n. 10.

[39]G. Alpert, "Law Enforcement: *City of Canton v. Harris* and the Deliberate Indifference Standard," 25 Crim. L. B. 466–472(1989).

[40]927 F.2d 1473 (9th Cir. 1991). *Davis* involved four "incidents" in which Mason County, Washington, deputies engaged in a variety of arrest and detention tactics clearly disproportionate to the circumstances in which they were used. In holding Mason County and its sheriff liable under 42 U.S.C. § 1983, the Court of Appeals for the Ninth Circuit held that the county's failure to train its deputies on the constitutional limits of the use of force constituted "deliberate indifference" under *City of Canton v. Harris, supra* note 38 and that the sheriff was a "policymaker" for purposes of municipal liability.

follow.[41] Stated another way, failure to correct individual misconduct may result in a finding of organizational misconduct or corruption.

Twenty years ago, the National Advisory Commission on Criminal Justice Standards and Goals reported that when the most visible government agents, the police, flaunt the laws they are sworn to uphold, this has a significant demoralizing effect on members of the community. The Commission explained

> As long as official corruption exists, the war against crime will be perceived by many as a war of the powerful against the powerless; 'law and order' will be just a hypocritical rallying cry and 'equal justice under law' will be an empty phrase.[42]

Today, in 1993, the Commission's observations have a frighteningly contemporary ring in the realm of police misconduct studies and the problem is no closer to resolution than when the words were first written.

If, after *City of Canton v. Harris,*[43] departments have been placed on notice to identify so-called critical function areas for their officers and to provide appropriate training, why is there such a proliferation of "inadequate training" claims? If agencies have been put on notice that unchecked patterns of unconstitutional practices by their officers will likely result in a finding of deliberate indifference, why are claims of unconstitutional "custom" or "practice" rampant in civil rights litigation? An initial explanation might be that departments fail to understand the ramifications of deliberately indifferent training or discipline. A more considered response would probably reveal a lack of awareness of what steps may be taken to remove the bad actors who perpetuate patterns of defective policing. Many departments are without the means to rid the system of the renegade centurions who migrate from one department to another. There is also a tendency to protect fellow officers, even though such a practice undermines the police mission of public service and runs afoul of the *City of Canton* mandate.

It may at first appear that the relationship of *City of Canton* to police misconduct and decertification issues is tangential. However, it should become clear, under the now "famous" footnote 10,[44] that departments that continue to employ officers who, as a practice, violate the constitutional rights of citizens are at tremendous risk of liability. By raising the issue of "foreseeability" of

---

[41]R. Del Carmen, *Civil Liabilities in American Policing* 45 (1991).

[42]The National Advisory Commission on Criminal Justice Standards and Goals, Report on Police at 207 (1973).

[43]City of Canton v. Harris, 109 S. Ct. 1197 (1988).

[44]Footnote 10 states:

For example, city policymakers know to a moral certainty that their police officers will be required to arrest fleeing felons. The city has armed its officers with firearms, in part to allow them to accomplish this task. Thus, the need to train officers in the constitutional limitations on the use of deadly force . . . can be said to be 'so obvious' that failure to do so could properly be characterized as 'deliberate indifference' to constitutional rights.

It could also be that the police, in exercising their discretion, so often violate constitutional rights that the need for further training must have been plainly obvious to the city policymakers who, nevertheless, are 'deliberately indifferent' to the need. 109 S. Ct. at 1205 n. 10.

police behavior, *City of Canton* has invited departments to look at core and critical police functions that policymakers ought to know will impact citizens' rights. Certainly, the case sends out a strong message to manage officer behavior effectively by executive level guidance on the issue of departmental and societal expectations, and the imposition of a comprehensive system of discipline.

To eliminate the many regionalized approaches to police discipline, there must be a consistent approach to problems of decertifiable misconduct. Because of the need for such a standardized approach to retain public trust and confidence, solutions to the misconduct must come from a centralized state regulatory body, independent of regional or local variation. The process itself must provide a balance among the rights of officers, agencies, and citizens.

Mechanics of Decertification: A Generic Model

The first step in a decertification process is the identification of decertifiable misconduct. In an effort to address this definitional issue from a regulatory standpoint in South Carolina, two authors proposed that any definition of misconduct "must be constructed keeping in mind effectiveness, enforceability, and legal defensibility," taking into consideration the broad range of behaviors involved in law enforcement operations.[45]

Once these definitional concerns have been resolved, fundamental fairness and due process issues must be addressed.[46] Since accountability for misconduct is a part of law enforcement's "social contract"[47] with the public, citizen complaints must be solicited and investigated as efficiently as those internally generated. In our system of justice, officers accused of misconduct are entitled to a presumption of innocence. In order to comply with Administrative Procedures Acts[48] in most jurisdictions, it is suggested that officers be guaranteed a hearing before an administrative law judge or hearing officer in cases of contested allegations made in support of decertification. The outcome of the hearing must, additionally, be appealable to a court of competent jurisdiction if the findings at the initial hearing are contested.[49]

Once findings of misconduct are entered and finalized, appropriate sanctions must be considered. While some statutory and regulatory schemes allow

---

[45]Johnson and Smith, *supra* note 27, at 10.

[46]A number of state and federal protections may be available to officers under statute for their ostensibly job-related behaviors. Among these are state "whistleblower" statutes (i.e., S.C. Code of Laws as amended 58–27–20 (1976), Act H.354 effective March 19, 1988), the Americans with Disabilities Act, Pub. L. No. 101–336, 104 Stat. 327 (July 26, 1990), the Civil Rights Act of 1991, Pub. L. No. 102–166, 105 Stat. 1071, (Nov. 21, 1991), and others.

[47]H. Cohen and M. Feldberg, *Power and Restraint: The Moral Dimension of Police Work* 112 (1991).

[48]These acts typically prescribe the administrative recourse available to an individual affected by governmental action. Under the vast majority of such statutes, exhaustion of the administrative process is required before the filing of a lawsuit is permitted.

[49]For example, South Carolina's provisions are found generally at Code Sections 1-23-310–1-23-400, which allow judicial review of an administrative determination only after exhaustion of administrative remedies.

for no sanctions other than decertification where a finding of misconduct is substantiated,[50] another approach is preferable. Sanctions must be commensurate with the seriousness of the behavior. While it may be a foregone conclusion that willful misfeasance in performance of a critical function, such as discharge of a firearm at a fleeing misdemeanant, may warrant decertification, it does not logically follow that there should be no lesser punishment where the misconduct is considerably less severe. Finally, departmental discipline may be sufficient under a scheme allowing for lesser sanctions.

This much is clear: Every instance of misbehavior by an officer should not be considered "misconduct." Similarly, this proposal does not suggest that every instance of substantiated misconduct should warrant decertification. Every instance of substantiated misconduct, under any definition, however, should be reported for recordkeeping purposes, so that the state regulatory body is able to monitor patterns of individual officer misconduct. It is suggested that the issue of such appropriate lesser sanctions as temporary suspension of certification should be addressed under every state statutory or regulatory scheme.

Relationship to Departmental Discipline

The concept of decertification is analogous to occupational capital punishment. Once decertified, the officer loses the license to engage in a career in law enforcement. In many states, there is no procedure for reinstatement, even where a pardon may be granted for criminal conduct underlying the decision to decertify or where the officer has been rehabilitated with regard to underlying misconduct.[51] In situations involving wrongdoing that does not meet the definition of "misconduct" appropriate for decertification or lesser sanction, departmental discipline may be the sole means of accountability for officer misfeasance. Initiation of proceedings to decertify a deficient officer must not bar departmental disciplinary action. Departmental sanctions will in most cases be imposed long before the outcome of the decertification proceeding is finalized. Likewise, a department's decision to terminate an officer's employment cannot render moot the ultimate decision to decertify. Officers terminated for misconduct from one agency have frequently been accepted by sister agencies, with and without knowledge of the prior termination for misconduct. However, a decertified officer is not so marketable. Effectively, the decertification issue is one of moral and ethical fitness. While ineptitude may warrant sanction according to the terms of a department's disciplinary plan, it is unlikely that inept conduct would rise to the level of wanton or willful misfeasance warranting decertification.

---

[50]See South Carolina's Regulations of the Law Enforcement Training Council at R. 38-300 et. seq. (effective 1991).

[51]The issue of "irreversible" decertification is one over which police administrators are frequently at odds. Much of the debate is contingent upon the particular state statute or regulation involved. In some states, for example, decertification is terminal in that no reinstatement provision exists. See South Carolina's Regulations of the Law Enforcement Training Council at 38. South Carolina Regulations serve as an example of this approach.

Beyond Decertification

Certainly, the entire process of defining misconduct would be facilitated were all officers to operate under a uniform set of ethical principles. Thus, a logical first step is an enhanced effort to educate officers in ethical and moral decision-making.[52]

There is a dire need for national consensus on the ethical and moral parameters of police conduct. This concern is magnified when one considers that even where police misconduct is regulated by the state, sanctions may differ drastically for identical behaviors and there is no nationalized database for tracking decertified officers. Creation of a nationally accepted Code of Police Professional Responsibility would be a major step in guaranteeing equal treatment under law and in professionalizing the police. There must be a process of believing and accepting departmental policy, which itself must be premised upon service to the public with integrity.[53]

The hallmark of a profession is its ability to regulate itself internally by sanctioning members and tracking their continuing eligibility to practice professionally. Until the police keep their own house in an accountable fashion, true professionalism will remain an elusive goal.

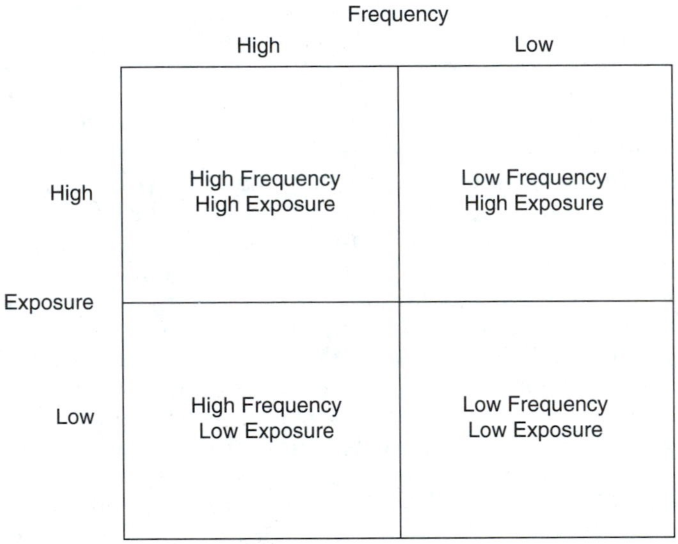

| | Frequency | |
	High	Low
Exposure High	High Frequency High Exposure	Low Frequency High Exposure
Exposure Low	High Frequency Low Exposure	Low Frequency Low Exposure

EXHIBIT 1   Categories of Risk

---

[52]Green, Alpert and Styles, "Values of Culture in Two American Police Departments: Lessons From King Arthur," 8 J. Contem. Crim. Just. 184–186 (1992).

[53]Alpert and Smith, note 35 *supra,* at 8.

WHAT'S WRONG WITH COMPLAINT INVESTIGATIONS? DEALING WITH DIFFERENCE DIFFERENTLY IN COMPLAINTS AGAINST POLICE

Andrew J. Goldsmith

The use of storytelling in the judgment process is based on the necessary assumption that experience and meaning are universal. In place of recognizing legitimate differences in the interpretation of social experience, jurors more often are compelled to regard unfamiliar story elements or dissonant interpretations as signs of guilt. When key elements in a case are anchored in different social worlds, defendants may be found guilty simply by reason of their social experiences and their communication styles. The important question arising from this state of affairs is whether anything can be done to correct biased judgment of trials.[1]

Securing access to justice means, at a minimum, recognition for the legitimacy—if not the validity—of one's grievances and aspirations.[2]

I INTRODUCTION

What is wrong with the way in which complaints against police officers are being investigated? Something is clearly amiss. Despite the proliferation of external oversight and civilian review agencies over the last fifteen years,[3] these additional accountability mechanisms have failed to placate the concerns of many complainants regarding their treatment by police. From outside the police there continues to be much criticism of the inadequate *accountability* of the police. For many aggrieved citizens, there seems little point in making a complaint since the investigations which ensue, when indeed they do ensue, often

Andrew J. Goldsmith, editor of *Complaints Against the Police* (1991), is Associate Professor of Law, Monash University, Melbourne, Australia.

Andrew J. Goldsmith, "What's Wrong with Complaint Investigations? Dealing with Difference Differently in Complaints Against Violence" (as appeared in *Criminal Justice Ethics,* Volume 15, Number 1, [Winter/Spring 1996], pp. 36–55). Reprinted by permission of the Institute for Criminal Justice Ethics, 555 West 57th Street, Suite 601, New York, NY, 10019-1029.

seem to achieve very little, if anything,[4] while within police forces, the investigation of citizen complaints against police officers is often taken to reflect a lack of public understanding of their difficult role or an excessive concern for vindictive criminal elements intent on paying back particular officers for just doing their job. Overall, changes to the investigation and handling of complaints seem to have contributed little, if anything, to the improvement of police-community relations.

These challenges exist across a number of common law countries. In the United Kingdom, for example, an evaluation by Maguire and Corbett of the Police Complaints Authority for England and Wales found high levels of complainant dissatisfaction with the process. What seems remarkable is the finding that "by far the greatest amount of dissatisfaction was . . . among complainants whose cases had been formally investigated."[5] Most striking of all, however, was that this continued to be true even of those cases in which complaints were upheld by the investigation. Overall, 70 percent of those complainants whose cases were formally investigated stated their views of the police had been changed for the worse as a consequence of having their complaint formally investigated. By contrast, those whose complaints were informally conciliated, and even those who withdrew their complaints, expressed significantly less disaffection with the complaints system .[6] In Canada, a recent study by the University of Toronto Centre of Criminology of complainants' perceptions of the Ontario Police Complaints Commission judged it to be seen as "either misunderstood or suspect due to its perceived passivity in individual complaints" and found complainants' greatest concern to be "the fact that the police investigate the police."[7] Observations of this kind are not new, nor are they confined to the United Kingdom and Canada.[8]

In this article, I want to focus upon the issue of the investigation of complaints against police by individual citizens.[9] The importance of the investigative stage to the subsequent career of police complaints cannot be taken too seriously. As Richard Terrill has observed, "the investigatory stage of any complaint procedure is central to reducing the criticism of the entire process, because it does influence both the integrity of the steps that precede it, and those that follow."[10] The context and justification for my inquiry is the continuing shortfall of public confidence in the institutions of public policing in many Western countries, in spite of developments such as external oversight and civilian review.[11] As indicated, particular criticism has focused upon the investigative stage of complaints handling. In the reports referred to here, as well as elsewhere, investigators have been seen to lack empathy, to be too legalistic in their approach, to be unresponsive to complainant concerns, and to see things too much the police officer's way. In general terms, investigators do not seem, or rather are not seen by complainants, to take complainants' concerns and points of view seriously. These failings, I shall suggest, reflect at least as much upon considerations of process as upon the particular outcomes of the investigations. The approach taken by many investigators towards complaint investigation, I want to argue, exhibits characteristics of an investigative and evidential philosophy and modus operandi that I call forensic realism. The breadth, flexibility and suitability of this investigative approach to the area of citizen complaints against police are issues that I shall consider.

Forensic realism refers to a strongly formalist and legalistic method of complaints investigation. As aspects of this method, particular cognitive and moral stances towards complainants and witnesses can be identified that influence the collection and analysis of information in relation to specific allegations. What is recognized as relevant evidence, and how complainant and witness credibility is assessed, are clearly vital factors in the conduct of any investigation. I wish to argue that the analytical and evaluative stages of complaints investigation are inhibited by an excessive adherence to the forensic realist approach.

In particular, this approach excludes and fails to reflect differences of perception, belief, value, and understanding among different sectors of the community. This degree of institutional closure, while explicable in large measure by the procedural and evidential requirements of disciplinary and, in some instances, criminal law processes, does not do adequate justice to the extent of cultural heterogeneity in our cities and communities and to the diversity of citizens' concerns about police conduct. It is not only coincidental that cultural disparities of these kinds are frequently present not just between the police and those groups that are highly policed, but also between the police and those individuals and groups whose experience and perception of complaints procedures is generally negative. Unless we are prepared to assume the absence of good faith of all persons from these groups who express criticism of police behavior (a clearly indefensible proposition), the implications of these cultural differences for police accountability ought to be recognized. Without some consideration of how and why citizen dissatisfaction may be connected to cultural differences, and of whether some possible alterations or modifications to present procedures for responding to complaints against police might be introduced, citizen dissatisfaction with current procedures and present levels of public antipathy towards the police seem unlikely to change.

Investigation of complaints is the focus of this article because of its primary and central significance in the evaluation of citizens' formal grievances regarding police conduct and because of the express criticisms made of this stage of complaint processing in a number of jurisdictions. Unfortunately, there are no systematic empirical studies of the investigation of police complaints, whether those investigations are undertaken by police officers or civilian investigators. In trying to understand and analyze the particular character of these investigations, we are limited in the forms of direct evidence available to complainant survey information. What is missing especially is observational data and, indeed, even survey and interview data with investigators. This state of affairs should not be surprising in view of the relative paucity of evidence of this kind in relation to police and indeed other forms of investigation. Under these circumstances, I propose to draw upon the available literature relating to police investigation of criminal matters because I believe that the analogy is the best available and, in those systems which rely extensively upon police officers to conduct complaint investigations (for example, Canada and Australia), is also empirically sustainable. Although civilian review systems in the United States, and indeed external oversight mechanisms elsewhere, do not depend exclusively (or indeed even substantially in some instances) upon investigators who are police officers or who have police backgrounds, many complaints investigators are currently serving or former police officers. This also needs to be seen in the context of the fact that the individuals whose confidence in complaint investigation is often lowest are also in many instances from those groups most heavily policed.[12] This tendency to "occupational alignment" makes it likely that on many occasions the perspective of the complaints investigator will reflect attitudes shaped by previous involvement in criminal investigation, or at least other forms of police work, that is, work which is frequently antagonistic in its relationship to persons from these groups.

Even where investigators come from non-police backgrounds, a survey of literature dealing with the conduct of investigations suggests a strong police emphasis, in particular in the priority accorded to interrogation and interview methods. Finally, the binary assessments required by formal procedures (guilty/not guilty, liable/not liable, and so on) and the limited number of organizational consequences which follow from these generally individually-focused assessments (for example, punishment, financial restitution, and expulsion) are inherent features of most formally conducted investigations. It is precisely this culturally and organizationally constrained, largely unitary approach towards investigations (and also formal determinations) that I argue gives rise to some fundamental problems of citizen dissatisfaction with the complaints process and the ends of the process. Although I recognize the place and legitimacy of investigative methods designed for the purposes of criminal and disciplinary proceedings (proceedings which can, of course, arise from a citizen's complaint), their limitations for the purposes of adjusting and reconciling relationships between police officers and members of the public need greater consideration.[13]

Before examining forensic realism in greater detail, I propose to sketch out some broader social features of contemporary life which make the kind of examination I am undertaking necessary as well as worthwhile. In particular, I will consider some of the implications of recent trends in cultural diversity for the mechanisms of public governance, and hence for the accountability of the police. With this background, I proceed to examine some of the limitations of current investigative methods. These limitations will be looked at in relation to the ways in which narrative diversity (between competing complainant or witness and police accounts) is managed and factual validity is established for official ends, and how the techniques of management are dominated by police or official perspectives to the exclusion or occlusion of the viewpoints and concerns of many complainants. In this way, considerations of communicative competence (and their cultural specificity) and hierarchies of values and outlook among investigators and complainants will be linked to the issue of cultural difference. In the concluding section I consider how current procedures might be modified on process grounds, and how the ends of the procedures might be extended or changed to take greater account of the consequences of cultural diversity for the effectiveness and legitimacy of our institutions of public governance. The argument, in effect, is for the greater democratization of our official dispute resolution and accountability mechanisms in the area of policing.

Finally, while the target for consideration here is forensic realism and its various implications for procedural application in the complaints setting, these implications should not be seen simply in procedural terms. I hope to show that what is of concern is partly a moral stance or ethical position with respect to the conduct of complaint investigations under conditions of cultural diversity. While conformity to current procedures explains part of the problem under consideration, it does not exhaust the empirical conditions or regulative ideals that influence how these investigations will be conducted. Tolerance of different viewpoints and empathy towards those whose complaints are being investigated, both of which I argue are needed in greater quantities, are qualities of being and acting which help constitute and define the moral capacity of the investigators. They thus affect the quality of the experience of complainants and witnesses, particularly their feelings of self-worth in relation to the legitimacy accorded their testimony. The context and subject of the inquiry here is not limited to considerations of procedural reform; indeed, it is precisely the limits of current procedures and their application which underlines this discussion.

II   THE ELUSIVENESS OF PUBLIC TRUST IN POLICE

In this section, I suggest that the climate for consideration of the adequacy of current investigative methods with respect to police complaints must take account of broader changes in attitudes to traditional authority, and in the polity generally, associated with new forms of information technology and political awareness. These factors point to the highly conditional character of public trust in institutions of governance, including the police, and to certain implications of process and attitude for those concerned by present levels of police accountability.

The Rodney King Factor

Public confidence in the police cannot be separated from the kinds of systems, general principles and procedures upon which we rely. In the words of Anthony Giddens, "the nature of modern institutions is deeply bound up with the mechanisms of trust in abstract systems."[14] However, this trust does not depend simply on such abstractions; it is ultimately a practical, intersubjective accomplishment. In other words, it depends upon the quality of interactions at the ground level. Problems of this kind affect other public institutions as well as the police. It is arguably part of a modern problem of declining faith in abstract systems. At a practical level, conceptions of knowledge and expertise about police work are linked reflexively to the experiences of participants at *access points,* defined by Giddens as "points of connection between lay individuals or collectivities and the representatives of abstract systems."[15] These are "places of vulnerability for abstract systems, but also junctions at which trust can be maintained or built up."[16] Giddens might argue then, in the case of police, that public trust in police in contemporary society is intimately related to heightened levels of self-awareness by participants in, and observers of, police work, which render the acceptance of police actions and explanations for their actions more problematic than before.[17]

It is in this environment, I wish to argue, that police complaints systems must operate, and in terms of which their significance must be appreciated and evaluated. The kind and magnitude of the challenge is illustrated by the Rodney King incident. Rodney King's fate, and that of the Los Angeles Police Department, owe a lot to the video camcorder and television. One of the defining characteristics of modernity is the impact of mass communication technology. Trust in abstract systems, Giddens observes, is affected by "updates of knowledge which, via the communications media and other sources, are provided for laypersons as well as for technical experts."[18] A consequence of these updates is a blurring of the lines between experts and laypersons, in turn affecting conventional perceptions of authority in particular fields. As traditional sources of authority are called into question, so does public trust in these authorities become much more contingent. We can in this way begin to appreciate why it was that public distrust towards police in the United States demonstrably increased in light of the Rodney King incident.[19]

In this single (but much repeated) televised incident, Rodney King's experiences at the hands of police officers became visible and accessible to millions of ordinary citizens. Unusually, rather than having to rely on less direct forms of evidence as to what transpired (for example, others' subsequent oral accounts), or upon official documentary reconstructions of events (for example, internal investigation reports), citizens in their capacity as viewers were able to see a contemporaneous visual record of dramatic events involving King and police officers. On this basis, they were able to draw their own conclusions about the propriety of the police actions *before* any official post hoc accounts of events could be constructed and publicly disseminated. As subsequent events showed, public disquiet arising from this incident was not effectively cordoned or defused by later attempts by the legal process to deal with the issues raised by the video recording. An amateur video operator thus managed to delegitimize the actions of police officers against King, by bringing to witness the event millions of television viewers. In a sense, this made them "home jurors," able to reach their own assessments of fact and responsibility outside the effective reach of police public relations departments and the usual channels of accountability in cases of this kind. The context for police accountability, including civilian review, therefore is changing dramatically. Factors of this kind contribute to what Giddens calls the "institutionalization of doubt"[20] in these modern times. It is in such an environment that police complaints systems as well as the police themselves must operate, and it is against this background that attempts to enhance public confidence in police must be crafted.

Things Are Different Now

Police responsiveness to changes in social composition and self-understandings within that social composition is a further dimension in understanding the elusiveness of public trust in contemporary society. While police institutions are commonly characterized as bureaucracies in terms of method of organization, planning, and service delivery, they are also socially situated entities. Therefore, they cannot remain unaffected by changes in the social field. In bureaucracies, Herzfeld points out, accountability must be understood in cultural terms:

> [A]ccountability is a socially produced, culturally saturated amalgam of ideas about person, presence and polity. Despite its claims to a universal rationality, its meanings are culturally specific, and its operation is constrained by the ways in which its operators and clients interpret its actions. Its management of personal or collective identity cannot break free of social experience.[21]

As an institution whose self-identity has been defined and understood largely in terms of professional authority and citizen deference towards it, it has been shaken by a growing awareness that the "the equation of knowledge with certitude has turned out to be misconceived."[22] This has occurred for a variety of reasons, in addition to the growth of new technologies. However, particularly significant in the post-World War II period has been the expansion of social diversity within our urban communities. In addition to the contribution of further immigration to the development of multiculturalism, other, new non-ethnically constituted social identities have emerged seeking recognition on social, political, and economic terms. Questions of "identity" and "recognition" have become central to modern social and political life. According to Charles Taylor, "[w]hat has come about with the modern age is not the need for recognition but the conditions in which the attempt to be recognized can fail."[23] Along with many other public institutions of governance, the police and police complaint systems have been caught in this mood of cultural contestation. I would argue that they have insufficiently recognized the degree of urgency of these challenges and that they have not adequately appreciated the implications for public trust in modem policing.

Among recent social movements of this kind, feminism has probably been the most influential in terms of calling into question epistemological as well as political and other conventions. It has suggested that fundamental mental constructs, including language, derive from a point of view or "standpoint" which is male, rather than common to both sexes. In turn, these constructs permeate and shape the allocation and interpretation of rights and resources. An example of its influence in the area of criminal justice has been in relation to victims of crime, in particular, women victims of sexual offences. In the United States, critical race theory has also made claims about the systematic conceptual and practical bias against persons of color in American public life, particularly in the administration of justice. Sexual identities have also become a rallying point for challenges to dominant conceptions of the family, and with respect to entitlements in the areas of health care, superannuation, and welfare support. Police have also been accused of institutionalized homophobia and mistreatment of gay persons.

Although new identities seem to be a constant feature of modern social life, often lying at the heart of problematic police-community relations, existing identities, categories, and social boundaries have been challenged, loosened, and even abandoned. As a result, the field of public debate on policing as on other issues has become punctuated by a disparate range of voices, as different interests, epistemologies, and political claims are aired and pursued. The languages of politics have proliferated; *difference* has become ubiquitous, clamorous, and unavoidable. Critically, in the words of Anna Yeatman, "[t]he acknowledgment of difference has brought about a loss of discursive innocence."[24] There is no possibility of restoring the old "master discourses" which promised certainty, universality, and uniformity of understandings and entitlements. We are compelled in these circumstances, says Yeatman, to adopt a "politics of representation":

> Central to this politics is the twofold strategic question: whose representations prevail? who has the authority to represent reality? To put the question

differently: who must be silenced in order that these representations prevail? whose voice is deprived of authority so that they may prevail?[25]

In these social fields of increasing cultural complexity, the implications of this loss of innocence must be acknowledged and given adequate response in our public institutions, including our police and police complaints systems; they cannot be wished away. This means, in turn, that we must reconsider the scope and limitations of present accountability mechanisms such as the procedures and conditions affecting the conduct of complaint investigations. In particular, we need to accept that it is possible to see and experience the social world very differently.

III THE LIMITS OF FORENSIC REALISM FOR COMPLAINT INVESTIGATIONS

> The horrible thing about all legal officials, even the best, about all judges, magistrates, barristers, detectives, and policemen, is not that they are wicked (some of them are good), not that they are stupid (several of them are quite intelligent), it is simply that they have got used to it. Strictly they do not see the prisoner in the dock; all they see is the usual man in the usual place. They do not see the awful court of judgment; they only see their own workshop.[26]

In this section, the argument is made that the complaints process is dominated by investigators who act as if we still have not lost our "discursive innocence." For the purposes of investigating complaints, they continue to act as if we all share the same fundamental attitudes, experiences, and values. This stance, applied to the investigation and handling of complaints, is forensic realism. "Forensic" refers to those official procedures used for the resolution or determination of formal allegations within the justice system. Collection of evidence for presentation before decision makers is "forensic" in this sense. The forensic character of complaint investigation is practically inescapable in view of the degree of formality and the legalistic nature of the ends associated with the system as presently organized. "Realism" however is an epistemological and, arguably, moral approach to the interpretation and assessment of factual material. In the mode of hard science, it rejects the contingent nature of knowledge and the relevance to the complaints process of plural yet genuinely held moral positions. Evidence is *real* rather than a matter of *representation*.

But the analogy between scientific and forensic practices cannot be pushed too far. For example, while science retains a commitment to the possibility of falsification of existing knowledge, the law's need for expediency and finality of process prohibits a process of revisable inquiry. Peter Manning has noted "the special social reality that the legal institution sustains,"[27] and proposes that the law "aims to counterfactually stabilize reality." While its milieu is often marked by conflicts and failures, it seeks to promote a particular vision of order and good government. There is a moral, persuasive aspect to legal or forensic work. As Manning observes, "[t]he sustaining nature of this belief in the singular reality produced and reproduced by legal decisions is such that it survives in spite of evidence of human character displayed in the work of legal institutions."[28]

There are clear costs to this investigative approach in terms of perceptions of injustice and the legitimacy of justice procedures. For example, as Chesterton laments, in the habitual rule-oriented practices of legal officials, the individuality of persons involved in legal procedures tends to disappear. The challenge of multiculturalism and other new social identities would conceivably magnify these problems. This Procrustean feature of legality will tread more roughly on "outsiders" than "insiders," whose cultural (including moral) attributes have already been more completely socialized to anticipate the implicit as well as explicit requirements of the justice system. If we view complaints (and conflicting related accounts) as narratives, forensic realism implies an acceptable range of narrative possibilities by which actions may be legitimately explained and understood, or, failing which, justifies the abandonment of the moral and factual content of the narrative(s) at issue, for example, in "unsubstantiated" complaints. My argument in essence is that the complaints process has not exhibited sufficient awareness of the kinds of social changes I have described earlier and has stuck excessively to forensic realism. In the process, much has been lost, as I will attempt to show. Something akin to what Johnson calls the Moral Law folk theory continues, at least subconsciously, to dominate the investigative and evaluative stages of the complaints process. This theory or perspective exhibits the following characteristics:

> (1) There must be one and only one correct conceptualization for any situation. Otherwise, we could never figure out which moral rule is supposed to apply to the situation. (2) There must exist literal concepts with univocal meanings, in terms of which the moral laws are stated and which also apply to the situation being considered. (3) Situations must be conceptualizable by a list of features that uniquely describe them (which is to say that concepts must be defined by sets of necessary and sufficient conditions for their application).[29]

Complaints investigators are caught in this epistemological and moral maelstrom but seem unaware of it. The decline of the law's institutional authority and the increasingly contested, rhetorical nature of public life make the position of justice agents invidious in many respects. Changes to operating procedures become not only desirable; they are inevitable.

"Just the Facts, Ma'am"

The police detective character in the old American television program Dragnet, Joe Friday, was presented as the quintessential forensic realist. His "just the facts" approach to the investigation of crime reflected a high degree of selectiveness in the collection of evidential material. Much was omitted or considered irrelevant—material which might be categorized (and dismissed from further consideration) as emotions, feelings, experiences, and instincts. Even in cases where investigators of this kind share a common cultural identity with the person they are investigating or interviewing, personal empathy has to be kept separate from the techniques and goals of forensic investigation.

The theoretical and pedagogical foundation for the realist approach to investigation and interrogation is not hard to find. The relevant literature points to the possibility and importance of "objectivity" in the investigative process.

The title of F.J. MacHovec's *Interview and Interrogation: A Scientific Approach*[30] is revealing in itself, confirming the strong reliance placed by police and other investigators upon questioning witnesses rather than upon other forms of evidence (direct observation, forensic evidence).[31] It also suggests the legitimating significance of "science" for investigative and other police or police-type practices.[32] This particular text instructs the reader that "the best questioners are scientific—impersonal, objective, organized, meticulous—like the great artists and craftsmen of all ages."[33] MacHovec also stresses the unproblematic status of facts: "Like scientists, expert interviewers and interrogators let the data take them where it will."[34] Inbau, Reid, and Buckley's *Criminal Interrogation and Confessions*[35] is another widely cited text in this field. Although less self-conscious about its scientific pretensions than the previous example, the book employs a definitive feature of the realist perspective, the truth/falsity distinction and, related to this, what Eglin has called the "appearances/reality dichotomy."[36] The book contains an exhaustive discussion of practical techniques for distinguishing the innocent from the guilty, counseling the student of investigative methods that "[p]sychologically, interrogation can be thought of as the undoing of deception."[37] The view that what is not truth must be deception reflects the strongly dichotomous form of practical reasoning found in forensic realism. Complexity of any kind (factual or normative) does not lie comfortably in this Procrustean environment.

There seems to be very little awareness of this, or even a dogged determination to ignore it; but, the warning signs are present. Though investigators must often be tempted to account for rejected evidence or narratives in terms of the dishonesty or mental problems of the interviewee,[38] the sense of genuineness noted by researchers in most complainants remains troubling.[39] Yet very often the investigative quest for facts and finality means that at least one story, and perhaps more than one, is disbelieved. The story is, in other words, granted no legitimate status by the complaints process. The ultimate unresponsiveness of this process to those persons who have gone to the extent of making a formal complaint ought to concern us.[40]

So how might we explain investigators' persistence in this regard? According to Bennett and Feldman, organizations develop particular "frames" or worldviews that provide them with interpretive tools and ideological justifications for carrying out work of an investigative and decision-making kind.[41] These frames are enabling for organizational workers in various sectors, by providing them with an integrated (and presumptively coherent) set of purposes and methods for the performance of their duties. In the instance of investigation of complaints against police, the difficulty suggested is that the scope and application of the investigators' frames means that factual and normative material is screened out from complainant accounts and dismissed from the complaint process in ways that leave high levels of complainant dissatisfaction.

From the perspective of narrative analysis, accounts generally reveal the components of scene, act, agent, agency, and purpose:[42]

> According to [Kenneth] Burke, we systematize information about social action in terms of the basic relations among these five elements. This social "frame" gives us a ready standard against which to identify quickly any connection that appears to deviate from the empirical, categorical, and other ratios ordinarily associated with the comparison frame. . . . Frames are thought to impose generic attributes on

specific data. . . .Frames make it unnecessary to reconstruct images that already have been assembled and stored in memory.[43]

Not everyone in a particular society, Bennett and Feldman suggest, possesses an equal capacity to utilize effectively these structural features of storytelling. One might anticipate difficulties of this kind arising between a complaint investigator and a complainant or witness from a culturally different background:

> To get interpreted properly, a story also requires that the teller and listener share knowledge about the world. . . .[B]ias can result when an adequate story is told, but the listener lacks the norms, knowledge, or assumptions to draw the inferences intended by the teller. The internal consistency and the significance of stories can be damaged if listeners and tellers live in different social worlds and hold different norms and beliefs about social behavior.[44]

There is arguably more to this process than solely the fit/lack of fit between the stock of knowledge and values of the story-teller complainant and those of the listener investigator. Bernard Jackson suggests that the pragmatics of narrative need also to be examined.[45] By this observation, he draws attention to the fact that different conclusions about stories derive as well from the ways in which stories are told or presented. Recent studies in anthropology, cognitive science,[46] and semiotics suggests that different cultures tend to possess their own "truth-certifying procedures."[47] The *credibility* of complainants and witnesses in interviews and in investigations generally is a key consideration in my argument. It is to this aspect of the complaint process that I now turn.

The Interrogation or Interview

In the absence of direct evidence, testimonial evidence in some narrative form becomes vital for forensic purposes. The typical interrogation resembles the courtroom production of narrative in its substantial reliance upon the question-and-answer format. Frequently, there is little narrative latitude in these situations and unacceptable digressions are sanctioned in various ways. As a consequence, the particular agenda of the investigative "listener" plays a major role in the production of the suspect's story. This investigative agenda will often involve a "theory of the case," or at least the elements of the initial suspicions that prompted contact with the "story-teller." Drawing upon the ethnomethodological work of D.R. Watson, Hester and Eglin have examined the police interrogation setting using Watson's distinction between "volunteered" and "invited" stories:

> [U]nlike [volunteered stories] invited stories allow the recipient of the story to take turns, and often quite long turns, throughout the course of the story. The invited story format for interrogations not only allocates to the suspect the turn type "telling a story," it also permits the recipient to ask questions and thereby collaboratively contribute to the build-up of the story. . . .By recurrently occupying first turn, so to speak, the police officer not only obliges the suspect to speak in next turn but also has some control over what the suspect talks about. The police

officer, within the limits of topical coherence imposed by the unfolding story, can introduce new materials for incorporation into the developing "confession."[48]

In a similar vein, McConville, Sanders, and Leng's recent research in the United Kingdom examined what they called the "construction of criminality" by police (and to a lesser extent, others) in the criminal justice system. They saw the nature of police interrogations as central to this process. In this context, facts emerged as socially produced, heavily influenced by police investigative agendas. The heavily pro-police bias of the co-produced interrogation outcome is powerfully captured in the following quotation, underlining the extreme difficulty many police interviewees face in being heard, let alone believed:

> [W]hereas suspects are generally keen to proclaim their innocence and endeavour to furnish evidence in support of their claim, these attempts are routinely rebuffed by the police. For the interviewing officer the suspect is presumptively guilty and the purpose of the interview is to produce a confession. Lines of defence raised by the suspect are irrelevant red herrings to be ignored or argued away. To show interest in the story which the suspect wishes to present is to demonstrate weakness of resolve in the battle of wills with the suspect. To permit material which contradicts guilt into the interview is to build weakness into the case and is the antithesis of constructing a case for the prosecution.[49]

In such uneven contests, the winner tends also to be the judge. Hence, McConville, Sanders, and Leng are able to conclude:

> The dramatic power imbalance between police and suspect enables the police to realign social relationships through words the suspect is induced to utter, thus maximising the legitimacy of the acts of low-level state officials. Interrogations are best understood therefore as social encounters fashioned to *confirm* and *legitimate* a police narrative.[50]

In the absence of reliable empirical data, one should be a little cautious about extrapolating from this research to the investigation of complaints. In the case of interviews with police officers, one might surmise that their occupational familiarity and experience of giving coherent and credible accounts of their actions will render them less vulnerable to the agendas of the interviewers. As "repeat players," most officers under investigation will thus offer less forensically vulnerable accounts than less experienced interviewees. While police-conducted interviews of police officers will continue to suffer the perception from outside that the "brotherhood" syndrome invariably works in favor of the officer under investigation, even civilian investigators must confront the allegation that their constant contact with police officers contributes to the development of a sympathetic attitude towards police officers, based to a substantial degree upon interpretations of police work provided by the police themselves. This scenario would hardly present the first example of "regulatory capture" in the area of law enforcement and regulation. In contrast, the adoption by complaint investigators of the "invited" story approach to complainant interviews conceivably would result in the interviewer's agenda being central to the account produced. A lack of familiarity by complainants with the format and its forensic implications is likely to disadvantage further the position of the complainant. For the purposes at least of the investigation, investigators are much more likely to share the same "frame" with police officers under investigation than with complainants. Even if we assume openly pro-police investigators do not investigate police officers in all or most instances, it seems unlikely that it is possible to dissociate the significant disparities of knowledge and experience, generally speaking, between police officers and many complainants and witnesses in the forensic setting from the issue of the relative plausibility of the accounts offered.[51]

Records of Interview

In the context of complaints against police, as for police investigations of crime, formal interview records play a vital role. How complaints get defined at an early stage in documentary form is highly influential to the future "career" of many complaints. The function of external review is very often highly dependent upon the records of interviews presented to them by police or civilian investigators. Where an external review agency undertakes no investigation of its own, or even in those cases in which there is a follow-up investigation by civilian investigators, the records taken from interviews with complainants, officers, and witnesses in the conduct of a primary investigation are foundational in determining how the complaint is subsequently perceived and handled. The opportunity presented by the initial investigation to determine who is interviewed, the lines of inquiry pursued, and how issues are reduced to documentary form make subsequent analysis and determination of complaints largely reactive to what is collected and how that material is presented at the primary stage. In many external review systems, limitations of resources, inter alia, mean that "on the papers" reviews of police-dominated investigation dossiers are the norm.

The first point to make in this regard is that any documentary record is a simplification or *reduction*. In typifying cases for organizational means, "particulars disappear."[52] So a crucial consideration in the assessment of investigative methods is who is in charge of the reduction process, as well as what are the criteria that influence the particulars presented and those excluded. Here, in particular, the concept of investigative "frames" is a useful analytical tool. In addition to the personal characteristics of the investigator, organizational imperatives and occupational experiences will combine to constitute these "frames." The accounts offered by McConville, Leng, and Sanders suggest that police investigative records are "particularly distortive, leaving out of account the critical social and environmental stimuli which influence the suspect's decision making."[53] As a result, they suggest, what emerges is a truly *police* narrative.[54] Where police officers themselves are the subjects of investigation, as in the case of complaints, it is even more likely that their "repeat player" experience in constructing coherent documentary accounts will contribute to the construction of a police narrative in a double sense!

The subsequent "career" of a complaint needs to be analyzed in terms of how and by whom it was reduced to writing. Any retrospective review must confront what Goffman called the "paper reality"[55] in deciding "what really happened." In order to challenge the investigative report, one must overcome the strong presumptive quality of the frame used in the production of the report and of the conclusions reached by the investigator. Studies of police-prosecutor relations indicate that this is frequently very difficult, and often practically impossible, to do.[56] In another bureaucratic setting, Zimmerman's study of the assessment of welfare eligibility shows the high level of reliance by welfare clerks and welfare organizations on "official" documentary confirmation. In Zimmerman's study we find an example of the *presumptive* quality of officially produced documentation. Welfare applicants not in possession of relevant documents were treated with routine skepticism, on occasions verging on open hostility. Throughout the welfare agency examined by Zimmerman, he found a *"suspension of belief* in the truth or accuracy of the applicant's statements" and a *"presumption of ineligibility,* i.e., a readiness to see in the applicant's (unverified) statements and actions a motivated project to 'manipulate' the agency for illegitimate ends."[57]

What studies of this kind point to is the powerful *defining* character of official records in influencing subsequent organizational behavior. Rather than indicating a conscious conspiracy against users of public services or even an absence of good faith by those working within these organizations, it points instead to certain structural features of bureaucratic life that influence how matters are processed by those organizations. Given the observation of these factors at work in police investigation of crime and welfare eligibility assessments, there seems little basis to suspect that they are not also present in police complaint procedures. If this is so, then the kind of investigative approach taken toward complaints, and the limits of that approach, will affect fundamentally the subsequent "career" of those complaints.

The Issue of Credibility

This issue, along with relevance, goes to the heart of the organizational significance of investigators and complainants occupying different social worlds.[58] I shall attempt here to demonstrate that the assessment of narrative accounts is not a culturally neutral occurrence. I propose to use the work of Binder and Bergman[59] to show how evidential material derived from different cultural settings can be disadvantaged in forensic determinations of credibility. Then, I plan to refer to the ethnomethodologically influenced work of Eglin,[60] Darrough,[61] and Dorothy Smith.[62] Specifically, I will focus upon the ways in which information surrounding allegations is managed semantically and rhetorically to affect determinations of credibility and hence to support particular interpretations as authoritative. The example used will relate to the Telegraph Avenue incident in Berkeley, California, in 1968.

Binder and Bergman identify a number of specific factors as relevant to findings of credibility with respect to accounts and account providers. From a practising lawyer's perspective, these factors must seem logical and at least implicit in good courtroom technique. However, their dependency upon circumstantial evidence leads us to recognize the ultimately *contingent* nature of determinations of this kind:

> As with other circumstantial evidence, the inference will rest on a generalization. It follows, then, that not all triers of fact will accept the same generalization. For example, from evidence that a witness made a prior inconsistent statement,

one trier of fact may infer that the witness is uncertain and thus not credible, while another may infer that the witness is thoughtful and flexible, and therefore more credible.[63]

They also point out that plausibility will depend in some measure upon the stock of common experiences that can be drawn upon. The more consistent a particular allegation is with our experience, the more plausibility we are likely to accord it. In situations of this kind, we have little or no difficulty empathizing with the person telling us the story. Our own experiences, values, and attitudes "fit" with those of the person making the allegation. In cases, however, where there is considerable cultural or experiential disparity, the absence of such a stock of shared experiences is likely to influence negatively a story's plausibility. The cultural resources for circumstantial corroboration of the allegation are just not present. Empathy and understanding under these conditions are much more difficult.

Other considerations affecting the credibility of stories, Binder and Bergman point out, include the consistency and coherence of the story, the availability of explanatory evidence to indicate *why* as well as *how* something occurred, the degree of detail provided, the emotional content, and the socio-political content of a story. These last two factors refer to elements in our decision making which are not *rationally based,* in the sense that they stem from emotions, feelings, and attitudes which are deeply seated and do not depend upon logic. A witness's credibility is explained in terms of the presumed competence of the person to comment (an expertise issue), consideration of motive, the status of the person in question (including the similarity or dissimilarity between the fact-finder and the witness), and the physical appearance and demeanour of the witness.

The degree of cultural dependence inherent in these factors going to credibility, and hence the socially constructed nature of credibility, ought to alarm us in terms of their potential significance for the operation and evaluation of complaint investigation procedures. It is far from clear that complaint investigators are aware of the impact of these cultural differences in the assessment of complainant credibility and the legitimacy of complaints generally. Indeed, the evidence referred to in the introductory section suggests quite the opposite. Consideration needs to be given to ways in which greater empathy can be fostered between complainants and investigators; procedures need to be put in place for handling complaints that reflect awareness of the potency of cultural difference to the fate of complaints and complainants. Forensic realism cannot be permitted to operate in a manner oblivious to the implications of this critique. This might be differently expressed, in terms of the need for greater *epistemological humility, openness, and tolerance* by those involved in handling citizens' complaints. This does not mean the abandonment of forensic realism, or the inappropriateness of disciplinary action or criminal prosecution in some complaints. I shall, however, leave my prescriptions for how this might be approached until the final section of the paper.

Lessons from Telegraph Avenue

In September 1968, on Telegraph Avenue, Berkeley, California, a violent confrontation occurred between police and citizens. How it was perceived and how official inquiries into "what happened" were managed are revealing in terms of providing an understanding of the ways in which complaint investigations approach and evaluate disparate factual material in order to arrive at a definitive account. In this particular case, the involvement of some "respectable" citizens as onlookers or participants meant that the events generated considerable controversy as well as differing accounts of what transpired in the confrontation. The documented accounts of events that emerged have provided the materials for Darrough's examination of the "colliding versions" of the events,[64] for Eglin's analysis of the "reality disjunctures on Telegraph Avenue,"[65] and for Dorothy Smith's account of "texts as constituents of social relations."[66] From each of these analyses, we gain some appreciation of the techniques of textual management and discursive authority which enable "official" accounts to triumph over the competing accounts of the same events. In this way, we come also to appreciate the nature of the relative disadvantages faced by "outsiders" in the production of official discourse.

Eglin's work is particularly instructive on this issue. His theoretical scheme addresses the techniques available for the management of "reality disjunctures" in official discourse. "Reality disjunctures" occur when complaint investigators are presented with two differing accounts of particular events. Eglin found four particular categorical or rhetorical devices being used by the local authorities to manage the divergent accounts of what transpired on Telegraph Avenue. The *evaluative* as well as *descriptive* significance of these devices needs to be appreciated. The four devices used were: (1) the appearances/reality dichotomy, (2) appeals to the physical conditions of observation, (3) the use of membership categorization devices,[67] such as professional/layperson, belief/fact and value/fact, and (4) the "special reasons" device.

The appearance/reality dichotomy reproduces a key aspect of the forensic realist approach: the belief that there is always an underlying, if not obvious reality, which rewards patient investigation. On this view, as Eglin points out, it is always possible to deal with divergent accounts by arguing that the non-official account is a misperception, perhaps one understandable from the particular point of view of the critic in the circumstances, but one that is at least incomplete if not wholly incorrect. In this way, the descriptive and interpretive adequacy of the observer's account is called into question; reality remains available, however, to the truly percipient. A second technique for casting doubt on an observer's perception is to comment critically upon the physical location of the observer. For instance, his or her presence in a crowded, chaotic situation may be taken to qualify the value of his or her remarks; after all, the *whole event* was not available to observation by the critic under those conditions. In this way, the "partial" nature of the account can both be explained and dismissed as not offering valid criticism.

Eglin's third device relates to ranked membership categories. The attribution of membership of particular status groups to witnesses of events in question permits certain inferences to be drawn regarding their competence to comment authoritatively on events. Thus, a "professional" is more credible than a "layperson." Presumably, in most aspects of police work, a police officer is more likely to be considered a professional witness than a layperson. According to Eglin, professionals are more closely associated with the ability to marshall facts dispassionately and to exercise logic in a given situation.

Laypersons on the other hand are seen as irremediably mired in the realm of mere beliefs and perceptions.[68]

The final device is "special reasons." In this instance, some feature of the critic's background or social characteristics is used to undermine the force of the complaint or criticism. In the Telegraph Avenue example, the professor whose letter provided the critical account in need of discursive management could be responded to by invoking his particular war time experiences and his presumed political affiliations (his letter was published initially in an "underground" newspaper) in order to cast doubt upon his objectivity. In the case of many complaints against police, the range of "special reasons" available to discredit complainants will be extensive. The membership category "complainant" or "suspect" does not provide an auspicious beginning to the provision of a credible account in many instances, especially when the setting, antagonistic nature, and implications of the events in question lend themselves to aspersions as to motive, character, competence, and credibility.

This is particularly so in cases in which a complainant has been charged by police, and especially if the police have been the subject of the complainant's complaint.[69] The disadvantages of social marginality in these circumstances are all too apparent, compounded as they are by the nature of the interaction in need of satisfactory accounting. It is possible to relate these observations to the problem of low substantiation rates in complaint cases. Low rates are commonly explained in terms of an "insufficiency of evidence" in particular cases. The "insufficiency" in individual cases may well reflect the outcome of the kinds of devices described by Eglin. Complainants from different cultural backgrounds will commonly exhibit a lack of social status (for example, by *not* being professional) or conversely a number of "special reasons" (for example, being from a heavily policed group, or being the subject of criminal charges) which will adversely affect their credibility for the purposes of providing an account of events.

IV WHAT IS TO BE DONE?

While it might sound trite, within the context of cultural differentiation, the real nature of the problem I have posed concerns communication competencies. The following comments by Bennett and Feldman, which relate to communication difficulties in court proceedings, apply with equal cogency to attempts at communication in the course of investigation of complaints:

> The victims of the trial justice process are people who cannot communicate in commonly accepted ways about their actions, and who, as a result of this communications gap, are also unable to explain convincingly the sense of frustration and injustice that results from their encounters with formal legal processes.[70]

Ways of overcoming the "communication gap" are crucial if there is to be any positive improvement in the present situation. The limits of forensic realism point to two kinds of response needed. The first is to modify existing complaint handling processes to minimize the impact of cultural and social differences on developing a substantial grasp of the complainant's reasons for making a complaint and on ensuring as far as possible that the complainant understands the objectives of the complaint system and has an opportunity to express a preference in terms of a desirable resolution to the complaint. But overarching these changes of procedure and investigative stance which would permit improvements of this kind, there is also a need to expand the range of functions served by police complaint systems, in other words, to escape the straightjacket of forensic realism. Though this does not mean the abandonment of criminal or disciplinary proceedings, it does put on the agenda the importance of linking the various motives for complaining to the range of capacities of the complaint system to respond to complaints. It is useful to begin this process by considering the different objectives attributed to complaint procedures. Maguire has suggested four objectives that would be met in an ideal complaints system:

1. Maintenance of discipline in the ranks;
2. Satisfaction of complainants;
3. Maintenance of public confidence in the police; and
4. Provision of feedback from "consumers" to police managers.[71]

Meeting all these objectives simultaneously in one complaints system does seem like a very tall order. The attempt to blend disciplinary with "consumer" and systemic objectives has been noted by some observers to be likely to induce role confusion or paralysis. There can be little doubt that the traditional *forensic* emphasis of complaint systems has not encouraged a very extensive consideration of systemic and consumer perspectives, either in terms of role definition or resource provision. Although the former concentrate upon determinations of culpability and individual responsibility, the latter place more weight upon the importance of user satisfaction, general public trust and systemic efficiency. My point is that there is no natural or obvious blueprint for linking these different objectives in one system. The dominance of the legalistic approach has meant that there has been little consideration of other methods that might exist in parallel with current methods. There are, however, some recent signs of directions that the reform of complaint investigations and complaint systems generally might take, which enable us to begin to consider what alternatives may be available.

Are We Already Becoming Less "Realistic"?

In the past five years or so, some attempt has been made to limit the extent to which forensic considerations dominate the complaint process. Recent interest in conciliation procedures to resolve particular kinds of police complaints[72] suggests that many consider existing procedures to be too legalistic and too cumbersome for some complaints. There would seem to be consensus between some complainants, police officers and those involved in complaint investigation and resolution on this question. Resource limitations have undoubtedly helped sharpen police management and external review agency thinking on how the number of complaints to receive a full investigation might be reduced. For example, in recent evidence to a New South Wales Parliamentary Committee examining the Ombudsman's role in police complaints, Dr. Greg Tillett described the existing process in that state as "unnecessarily cumbersome, adversarial and legalistic insofar as the majority of complaints are concerned."[73] In his evidence to the same committee, David Landa, NSW Ombudsman, expressed his concern at the over-investigation of minor complaints, and in so doing referred to the "rigid and formulaic approach taken to such investigations by police investigators."[74]

In response, the New South Wales Parliamentary Committee recommended as its first priority that "the conciliation of complaints against police be encouraged to ensure the most effective use of scarce resources in the areas of greatest need."[75] Conciliations should be considered integral to the handling of *every complaint,* and "independent police conciliators" should be used to assist conciliations.[76] Of particular interest in the Committee's reasoning was the view that resource savings effected by introducing conciliation could be directed to providing an "appropriate level of attention and resources to particular concerns of minority groups,"[77] who had tended to miss out under the existing system. According to David Landa, these were the "illiterate, juveniles, aborigines and the uneducated and ethnic, non-English speaking groups."[78] What specific forms this assistance to these socially and culturally disadvantaged groups might take were not outlined. However, the Committee's recognition that all groups were not being equally served by the existing complaints system, and that many complaints do not warrant full forensic treatment, illustrates both the need for, and possibility of, diversification in the ways complaints are investigated and resolved.

Like any other example of "informal justice,"[79] the development of conciliation of complaints will need to be monitored carefully to ensure that it does not become merely an informal means of achieving what forensic realism has tried to achieve more formally. Special training for conciliators, appointed from *outside* the ranks of police, is worth considering. Police-appointed conciliators are vulnerable to negative "special reasons" evaluations by complainants, which could undermine the credibility of such a move. But an expansion of conciliation is not enough. For one thing, the cultural sensitivity of conciliation would need to be shown. Other ways need to be found to modify the strong claims *discipline* has placed upon complaints systems: *compliance* of police behavior to a variety of democratically constituted norms and standards, rather than a singular or predominant focus upon individual responsibility and punishment, should become the fundamental goal of the modified system. As Goldstein reminds us:

> Both police and public become so preoccupied with identifying wrongdoing and taking disciplinary action against errant officers that they lose sight of the primary objective of control which is to achieve maximum conformity with legal requirements, established policies, and prevailing standards of propriety.[80]

Compliance however should not imply the absence of discretion in how it should be achieved or when it should be insisted upon, nor should its implementation assume the unchangeability or cultural invariability of its interpretation and application. Compliance in this sense presupposes a *dialogical, negotiated* approach to standards enforcement, one which is conspicuously empathetic in its methods and approach. It also suggests the possibility of achieving substantial organizational compliance over time through a variety of strategies. The kind of investigation called for in a complaint system in which a broader range of objectives is openly acknowledged, and which operates dialogically in a culturally sensitive manner, will clearly require a substantial degree of function redefinition and appropriate retraining in order to escape the traditional bonds of forensic realism.

Give Complainants (More of) What They Want

The substitution of compliance for discipline does not just refer to a preferred strategy for the efficient achievement of conformity among police officers. There is also the consideration that complainants frequently do not seek legalistic responses or solutions when making a complaint. As Maguire and Corbett found in their English study, complainants exhibit a range of motives for complaining. Against this background, a strongly forensic realist approach may not always be appropriate:

> They were incensed by what had happened, and expected some form of redress, if only an apology, a full explanation (at the very least, of why, precisely, their complaint was considered unjustified), or an assurance that steps would be taken to prevent a recurrence. The "black and white" nature of the outcome—the response to the complainant being totally dependent upon whether or not a breach of the disciplinary code could be proved against a named officer—meant that none of these wishes were met in the great majority of cases, and satisfaction was rare.[81]

These areas of complainant concern often come down, at least partly, to considerations which would seem almost trite except for their obvious influence on complainant perceptions of the process, and the relative ease with which they might be overcome. Something as simple as the provision of information about the rationale behind a particular police practice, or concerning the progress being made in a complaint investigation, are simple means whereby police and complaint investigators can provide accountability to persons who have brought a complaint. Some complaints systems are now endeavoring to meet informational objectives of this kind.[82]

But information provision, while important to the task of reassuring citizens with concerns about policing, is not enough by itself. The distinction between *information provision* and *communication* requires that we recognize the challenges of cultural difference and the need to foster methods of developing greater empathy between complainants and investigators (and indeed, between police and complainants). Police complaint systems must make institutional "space" for listening to the personal standpoint of those with whom they have contact (complainants, witnesses, police). Investigators, and indeed all police officers, need to practice the capacity to *imagine* what it is like for the citizen they are endeavoring to assist, a point emphasized by Maguire and Corbett:

> We would stress in particular the value of getting officers to understand the totally different perceptions of incidents which are held—in good faith—by many complainants: what appears to the officer a fairly trivial altercation can take on great significance for a member of the public.[83]

The failure of justice agents, in this case complaint investigators, to exhibit empathy towards complainants is arguably both a moral failure of recognition towards the integrity and worth of another person[84] as well as likely to result in serious misperceptions about what complainants are seeking from the system. Some concrete proposals for "softening" the stance of investigators towards complainants are necessary.

"Offensive" Language   A first step is to introduce greater sensitivity in the official language used to characterize different types of complaints. There is something inconsistent between an institutional commitment to the personal standpoint of complainants on the one hand and, on the other, the continued open use by civilian review agencies, police officers, and others of the word "trivial" to classify some of the less serious complaints on the other. The common use of this term and of the word "vexatious" by responsible officials to describe complaints is difficult to reconcile with a genuine commitment to greater openness to diversity. This is not to say that all complaints are of equal seriousness or that complaints are never vexatious.[85] But we need at the very least to employ this terminology sparingly and only very deliberately, so as to minimize the occasions upon which designations of these kinds are used to dismiss cases in which differences of perception and value would more validly explain the lack of seriousness or credibility attached by investigators to these cases.[86]

More "Volunteered" Stories   Another strategy investigators should consider is to making greater use of the volunteered story format where they are not already doing so. As we have seen, the volunteered story allows the person being interviewed far greater input and control in terms of story structure and content.[87] A frequent source of frustration for non-repeat players in adversarial forensic proceedings is the experience of not being able to put one's story across to the audience adequately. One example is the extreme frustration often felt by sexual assault victims interviewed by police or cross-examined by defense lawyers in court. Social psychologist Tom Tyler provides some insights into what participants involved in different justice processes seek from their participation. Rather than being simply preoccupied with securing particular outcomes, he noted:

> People are found to focus heavily on issues of process control, whether or not control over the procedure translates into control over outcomes. In other words, *people value the opportunity to state their case* to a third party, irrespective of whether what they say influences the decision made by the third party.[88]

Tyler observed a relationship between the opportunity to participate actively in the procedure and positive feelings of social status and recognition:

> [P]eople value their participation in organizations and the opportunities that it provides to affirm their status within the group. *Procedures that allow them to present evidence on their own behalf* affirm status, because they allow people to feel that they are taking part in their social group. Similarly, the willingness of the authority to listen to them and consider their arguments is a recognition of their social standing. If people are not allowed to express their views, they are being denied signs of their standing within the group, as well as opportunities for interaction with authorities that lead to positive beliefs about membership in the group.[89]

Victim impact statements, recently introduced in Australian criminal proceedings, might be viewed as responsive to these kinds of concerns. In the complaint investigation context, an analogous move might be to incorporate statements provided by witnesses and complainants in "volunteered story" format, that is, one using their own terminology, concepts and symbols. While statements of this kind need not form the exclusive basis for decision-making, they should accompany other evidential material collected. Special provision would need to be made to assist those unable or lacking confidence to prepare written statements of this kind. Getting an account from people "in their own words" or, at least, "in their own terms" would thus become a procedural task for investigators. If we sincerely attempt to put this into practice, Tyler seems to suggest, the rewards will be measured in terms of more positive public attitudes towards the procedures, agencies and personnel of the justice system.

Many Voices, Single System: Harmony or Cacophony?

Having assembled investigative materials in an empathetic manner, materials which include complainant and witness "volunteered" statements, the issue becomes one of how these materials might be employed and assessed in ways that lead to greater police compliance and citizen satisfaction. Of course, the desire to be "taken seriously" that Tyler describes is not completely exhausted by having one's say in one's own words. Some degree of responsiveness by the system to the problems raised by complainants will often be called for. The appropriate form of response will vary from case to case; it might be compensation in one case, a prosecution or disciplinary action in another, an apology or change of procedure in another. Often a case will call for more than one response. Police complaint systems need to think about ways of making coherent and balanced responses to the variety of needs raised by complainants. While it would be utopian to expect anything like consensus among a large number of the people involved on particular conclusions reached or policy changes recommended, it does seem sensible to maximize the potential for the various parties concerned to understand as much as possible about how particular decisions are reached and what they imply. There is a need overall for greater *transparency*.

Greater Information Sharing   De-emphasizing the weight attached to disciplinary considerations in complaint investigations should be accompanied by greater attention to the provision and use of knowledge about police work arising from complaints. Collection of evidence in individual complaints needs to be seen in part as facilitating "information feedback" about how police departments are operating and the state of police-community relations. Although external and civilian review agencies often produce annual reports which, in addition to statistical compilations, list organizational reforms and procedural changes recommended on the basis of complaint findings and patterns, more should be done to develop and publicize this aspect of their work. At present, in the case of many review agencies, this aspect receives little attention and certainly very little if any public profile. In addition, complainants should be accorded a higher priority in terms of being kept informed about progress in the investigation of their case and the significance attached to their complaint. In this latter respect, complainants who draw attention to a deficient police procedure which is consequently altered ought to receive recognition for their contribution. Clearly, information sharing of this kind will require different arrangements from those usually found in organizations dominated by forensic considerations.

More Diverse Offerings   The problem of low substantiation rates in some categories of complaint (typically, assault) requires that a broader range of response measures be available if complainants are not to feel constantly disappointed by the apparent pointlessness of making a complaint. In other words, Tyler would tell us, we need to find other ways of taking complaints seriously. There is a difference between being "listened to" and being "heard." Complainants need to know that they are being heard. Evidence of systemic change, as described in the previous section, would indicate to complainants that they had been "heard" and taken seriously. Conciliation in the appropriate form could operate for this purpose, especially where there is an apology or change of practice involved. The point is to find a variety of means for construing complaints not simply as individual grievances but also as redemptive opportunities for repairing police-community relations and improving police procedures.[90]

A Different Forensic Realism   Despite the expansion of objectives and responses for police complaints systems recommended in this article, one must inevitably confront the fact that there will be complaints for which a suitably amended forensic realist approach will remain appropriate. This will usually be so when serious disciplinary or criminal allegations are involved. But how should an investigator deal with, or make sense of, the potentially wider range of materials collected during the course of an investigation? Is the "clash of narratives" often associated with particular complaints (for example, the Telegraph Avenue incident) simply reproduced by this new method, except with a larger and more confusing range of evidential materials with which to work? Any legal system will require relatively prompt determinations and resolutions in respect of specific allegations and problems arising from complaints. This will mean that not all parties will emerge completely satisfied with the outcomes reached. Despite the best endeavors to take complainants seriously, this does not mean that the system in cases of this kind can accommodate taking all persons involved at their word, that is, in terms of what they allege. How might an optimal balance be reached in respect of processing complaints containing allegations of a disciplinary or criminal nature? What, if anything, can sensibly be prescribed?

In those cases defined as *serious* because of the gravity of the allegations against an officer, some ultimate factual finding or adjudicative determination will still be required. Here, clearly, investigators and complaint adjudicators cannot be allowed to wallow in some anomic sea of "facts" and irreconcilable perspectives, collected on the basis of the less skeptical, more empathetic investigative approaches I have advocated. However, a corollary of such approaches is a more inclusive process of deliberation and adjudication in terms of the factors expressly considered. Recognition of the complexity of particular situations that give rise to complaints, including the range of interests and motivations behind the participants in particular incidents, will require a different style of administrative or forensic judgment. It will be one that is deliberately aware in its investigations and determinations of differences of standpoint (worldview) and of the implications of these differences for the kinds of evidence considered relevant and of the kinds of responses sought from the complaint resolution procedure. In certain respects, those involved might imitate Martha Minow's feminist judge:

> By seeking pluralist understandings in these settings, I hope a judge would do more than nod blankly with the statement that my own viewpoint is partial. Instead, the judge should seek out an understanding of contrasting viewpoints, at least until glimpsing how incomprehensible her own view must be to some others. Knowing the partiality of her own knowledge, information and normative scheme may not change the outcome in some cases, but it should make the process of decision problematic. Further, by understanding the partiality of her own view, the judge may reach different conclusions some of the time.[91]

Police complaint investigators and review agencies occupy an analogous position to Minow's judge. They can reach decisions on the basis of narrowly construed information and criteria of relevance without recognition of the partiality of standpoint, or they can proceed with greater epistemological humility, consciously trying to make contact with the standpoints of those with respect to whom they must act. Let there be no mistake. In addition to my argument implying a wider range of evidence and relevant criteria, the processes of investigation and determination will also become more difficult and complex. Beside requiring more time and resources in many instances to collect evidence, the recognition of partiality and difference in standpoints will require a more painstaking process of decision making. Often, it seems likely, this complexity of deliberative process will not deliver substantially different decisions from those that might have been reached by a more forensic realist approach. But because of the greater sensitivity reflected in the investigative process to the complainants and their interests, the results should represent far more persuasive and democratically constituted accounts and resolutions of the event in question.

Not all parties will be satisfied by the outcomes, or by the kind of approach advocated here. Undoubtedly, absences of good faith will not disappear altogether. But it ought to follow from these proposals that the outcomes produced will more often stem from genuine dialogue and bureaucratically expanded forms of democratic participation than would be the case if a straightforward adoption of the forensic realist method was maintained. Although legal and quasi-legal procedures will always be blunt and unsatisfying in some ultimate *quasi-scientific* sense, because of their need for closure and finality in resolving matters of *practical* concern, the challenge, realistically, lies in ensuring that the procedures employed permit greater integration of the process values of the kind described by Tyler. Techniques of this kind promise to *universalize difference* through elaboration and discussion of personal viewpoints.[92] Though we may start from different world views, ordinary language philosophers (and commonsense) remind us that this does not mean that we occupy different worlds.[93] We need, however, procedures which expand and tap this dialogical potential and to find new points of convergence of interest or at least greater understanding of our differences on matters of public policing and peaceful coexistence generally.

V   CONCLUSION

> Legal decisions have authority to the extent that the stories judges tell resonate both in the world from which the disputes and conflicts come and in the specialized world of legal discourse. Without this dual appeal, legal judgments are cut adrift from the larger world or lay stories cannot find a legal connection.[94]

Because police complaint procedures form a very important part of the system of police accountability in many English-speaking countries and indeed elsewhere, I have argued that the procedures followed need to complement their realist orientation towards complaints investigations with broader methods of inquiry. These should be sensitive to cultural difference and more overtly geared to complainants articulating their concerns about police actions in their own words and according to what it is they are seeking. This is an argument with *moral* as well as practical and political implications. Investigations undertaken and judgments reached in the course of complaint processing should develop a greater tolerance for complexity of the situations and persons investigated which implies, in part, more empathy for the interests, values, and concerns of complainants from diverse social and cultural backgrounds. Processes need to display greater accommodation and reflection of the *individual worth* of complainants. Complaint investigators need to show evidence of greater *tolerance* for difference. Although conciliation, if properly structured and monitored, is arguably a step in the right direction toward meeting some of these needs, there is still a need for more pervasive changes that bring about significant behavioral, and eventually attitudinal, shifts toward complaint investigation and resolution. This article has sought to make the case for a reorientation of this nature, beginning with the evidence of significant public mistrust of current procedures, and then proceeding to sketch out some possible directions in which the investigation of police complaints might be developed.

What is proposed here should not be viewed simply as an attempt to pander to the divergent interests of the different ethnic and minority groups unhappy with some aspect of police behavior, although my argument advocates that the procedures need to be more openly responsive to these differences and concerns. It is rather, fundamentally, an effort to find ways to reduce hostility on both sides of the complaint process by improving the opportunities for communication and dialogue between the parties to complaints (police and citizens) who are often separated by significant social distance and who have

different priorities. It is important, I have argued, that the findings and determinations of complaint investigation procedures do not become "cut adrift
from the larger world," which is the danger presented by an unreflective pursuit of forensic realism under the kinds of social conditions I have described.
In the interests of greater police accountability, including more democratically
responsive police-community relations, we should insist that our methods of
investigating and resolving complaints against police officers contribute to,
rather than impede, the development of what James Fishkin calls a "self-
reflective political culture." This requires that we give "unimpeded and effective voice to the interests across every significant cleavage in society," with a
view to participants (complainants as well as police officers and complaint investigators) becoming "significantly self-critical as a result of unmanipulated
dialogue."[95] In terms of how the investigative process might best reflect these
goals, the admonition of Aristotle that "each person has something of his [or
her] own to contribute to the truth "[96] should not be forgotten. Any system for
dealing with complaints against police that fails to rise to the challenge indicated seems certain to face an even more difficult, and in all likelihood limited, future.

NOTES

Earlier versions of this paper have been given at the "Keeping the Peace" police
accountability conference, Sydney, May 1993 and the International Association of
Civilian Oversight of Law Enforcement Annual Meetings, Orlando, September 1994.
The author wishes to thank Richard Ericson for reading and commenting on an earlier
draft of this paper. He would also like to thank the two anonymous reviewers for their
comments, and the editors for their patience and constructive advice. The argument
and any errors remain the responsibility of the author.

1. BENNETT & FELDMAN, RECONSTRUCTING REALITY IN THE COURTROOM 179 (1981).
2. Sarat & Grossman *Access to Justice and the Limits of Law* 3 LAW & POL'Y Q. 125, 137
(1991).
3. This theme is behind the collection of essays in COMPLAINTS AGAINST THE POLICE:
THE TREND TO EXTERNAL REVIEW (A.J. Goldsmith ed. 1991) [hereinafter cited as
COMPLAINTS]
4. *See, eg.,* FEDERATION OF COMMUNITY LEGAL CENTRES (VICTORIA), REPORT INTO
MISTREATMENT BY POLICE 1991–92 (1992); COMPLAINTS, *supra* note 3
5. M. MAGUIRE & C. CORBETT, A STUDY OF THE POLICE COMPLAINTS SYSTEM 59 (1991).
6. Id.
7. T. LANDAU, PUBLIC COMPLAINTS AGAINST THE POLICE: A VIEW FROM COMPLAINANTS 77
(1994).
8. *See, eg.,* in relation to the situation in Toronto, *id.,* also Martin, *Organizing for Change:
A Community Law Response to Police Misconduct,* 4 HASTINGS WOMEN'S L.J. 131 (1993) and
McMahon, *Police Accountability: The Situation of Complaints in Toronto,* 12 CONTEMPORARY
CRISES 301 (1988); in Australia, there has been ongoing criticism of police
accountability mechanisms in respect of their responsiveness to indigenous peoples.
See REPORT OF THE ROYAL [AUSTRALIAN] COMMISSION OF INQUIRY INTO ABORIGINAL DEATHS
IN CUSTODY (1991).
9. While it can be argued that this distinction is artificial, in that a complaint can
lead to a criminal prosecution, it is not a meaningless distinction in the way in which
police forces and civilian review agencies institutionalize the investigation and
processing of complaints. The typical organizational separation of 'internal

investigation' from other areas of investigation in police departments, and the concern of review agencies at least initially to handle all citizens' complaints recognizes the fact that most complaints will not generate or justify criminal proceedings.

10. Terrill, *Complaints Against the Police in England,* 31 Am. J. Comp. L. 599, 620 (1983).

11. A note on terminology is necessary because of the breadth of my argument. I shall use both "external oversight" and "civilian review" in this article. "External oversight" is used to refer to external review mechanisms outside the U.S., where the term "civilian review" is less familiar and generally not used. The latter term tends to have a specific meaning in the U.S., referring to civilian oversight mechanisms. I suggest that the question I raise has implications beyond as well as within the U.S.

12. In Australia, these groups include working class youth, the homeless, and indigenous persons.

13. The question of police discipline falls uneasily between these distinctions. This is due to the enormous range of forms that discipline can take. In some cases, an informal apology can suffice whereas in other cases, formal disciplinary proceedings may occur, much along the lines of court proceedings.

14. A. Giddens, The Consequences of Modernity 83 (1990).

15. *Id.* at 88.

16. *Id.*

17. Robert Reiner has argued in the United Kingdom context that the 'Golden Age' of policing by consent was in the 1950s. *See* R. Reiner, The Politics of the Police (1985)

18. A. Giddens, *supra* note 14, at 91.

19. Lasley, *The Impact of the Rodney King Incident on Citizen Attitudes Toward Police,* 3 Policing & Soc'y 245 (1994)

20. A. Giddens, *supra* note 14, at 176.

21. R. Herzfeld, The Social Production of Indifference: Exploring the Symbolic Roots of Western Bureaucracy 47 (1992).

22. A. Giddens, *supra* note 14, at 39.

23. C. Taylor, Multiculturalism: Examining the Politics of Recognition 35 (1994).

24. A. Yeatman, Postmodern Revisionings of the Political 7 (1994).

25. *Id.* at 31.

26. Chesterton, *The Twelve Men,* quoted in R. Jack & D. Jack, Moral Vision and Professional Decisions: The Changing Values of Women and Men Lawyers 168 (1990).

27. Manning, *The Social Reality and Social Organization of Natural Decision-making,* 43 Wash. & Lee L. Rev. 1291, 1293–94 (1986).

28. *Id.*

29. M. Johnson, Moral Imagination: Implications of Cognitive Science for Ethics 8 (1993).

30. F. MacHovec, Interview and Interrogation: A Scientific Approach (1989).

31. *See, eg.,* M. McConville, A. Sanders & R. Leng, The Case for the Prosecution: Police, Suspects and the Construction of Criminality (1991); R. Ericson & P. Baranek, The Ordering of Justice (1982).

32. Ericson & Shearing, *The Scientification of Police Work,* in The Knowledge Society (G. Bohme & N. Stehr eds. 1986).

33. MacHovec, *supra* note 30, at viii.

34. *Id.* at 17.

35. F. Inbau, J. Reid & J. Buckley, Criminal Interrogation and Confessions (3rd ed. 1986) [hereinafer cited as Inbau].

36. Eglin, *Resolving Reality Disjunctures on Telegraph Avenue: A Study of Practical Reasoning,* 4 Canadian J. Soc. 359, 369 (1979).

37. Inbau, *supra* note 35, at 327.

38. Some complainants do exhibit psychiatric symptoms, of course. *See* Freckelton, *Querulent Paranoia and the Vexatious Complainant,* 11 Int'l J.L. & Psychiatry 127 (1988).

39. M. Maguire & C. Corbett, *supra* note 6.

40. The group of even greater concern is those who feel unable to complain. For the reasons why some citizens fail to complain, *see* Goldsmith, *External Review and Self-Regulation: Police Accountability and the Dialectic of Complaints Procedures* in COMPLAINTS, *supra* note 3, 20–21.

41. W. BENNETT & M. FELDMAN, *supra* note 1.

42. *Id.* at 62

43. *Id.*

44. *Id.* at 174–75.

45. B. JACKSON, LAW, FACT AND NARRATIVE COHERENCE (1988).

46. M. JOHNSON, MORAL IMAGINATION: IMPLICATIONS OF COGNITIVE SCIENCE FOR ETHICS (1993).

47. B. JACKSON, *supra* note 45.

48. S. HESTER & P. ELGIN, A SOCIOLOGY OF CRIME 138–39 (1992).

49. M. McConville, A. Sanders & R. Leng, *supra* note 31, at 76.

50. *Id.* at 79.

51. Credibility is explored further later in this paper. However, it ought be noted that the term "relative plausibility" is used deliberately here. "Absolute" plausibility of police accounts may not occur in many instances, but a police account may be sufficiently plausible in many cases in some respects at least to present the investigator with the compelling option that the complaint cannot be substantiated. In such cases, it might be argued, there is sufficient plausibility from a police officer's perspective in as much as no further action will be warranted, whereas (as this paper argues) a complainant is likely to feel empty-handed as well as disbelieved.

52. Manning, *supra* note 27, at 1298.

53. M. McConville, A. Sanders & R. Leng, *supra* note 31, at 76.

54. *Id.* at 79.

55. Manning, *supra* note 27, at 1298.

56. *See, eg.,* M. McConville, A. Sanders & R. Leng, *supra* note 31; R. Ericson & P. Baranek, *supra* note 31.

57. Zimmerman, *Tasks and Troubles: The Practical Bases of Work Activities in a Public Assistance Organization* in EXPLORATIONS IN SOCIOLOGY AND COUNSELING 256 (D. Hansen ed. 1969).

58. *See* W. BENNETT & M. FELDMAN, *supra* note 1.

59. D. BINDER & P. BERGMAN, FACT INVESTIGATION: FROM HYPOTHESIS TO PROOF (1984).

60. Eglin, *supra* note 36.

61. Darrough, *When Versions Collide: Police and the Dialectics of Accountability,* 7 Urban Life 379 (1978).

62. D. SMITH, TEXTS, FACTS AND FEMININITY (1990).

63. D. BINDER & P. BERGMAN, *supra* note 59, at 135.

64. Darrough, *supra* note 61.

65. Eglin, *supra* note 36.

66. D. SMITH, *supra* note 62.

67. This term was coined by ethnomethodologist Harvey Sacks.

68. Eglin, *supra* note 36, at 373.

69. Police critics of complaint procedures often raise questions about the motives of complainants where they are facing criminal charges arising from the same incident. In turn, one hears allegations by some complainants that they were only charged criminally after indicating to police that they intended to lodge a complaint.

70. W. BENNETT & M. FELDMAN, *supra* note 1, at 167–68.

71. Maguire, *Complaints Against the Police: The British Experience,* in COMPLAINTS, *supra* note 3, at 177, 186.

72. Corbett, *Complaints Against the Police: The New Procedure for Informal Resolution,* 2 POLICING & SOC'Y 47 (1991); REPORT OF THE [NEW SOUTH WALES,] JOINT COMMITTEE ON THE OFFICE OF OMBUDSMAN—INQUIRY UPON THE ROLE OF THE OFFICE OF THE OMBUDSMAN IN INVESTIGATING COMPLAINTS AGAINST POLICE (1992) [hereinafter cited as INQUIRY].

73. INQUIRY, *supra* note 72, at 14.

74. *Id.* at 82.

75. *Id.* at 142.

76. *Id.* at 142–43.

77. *Id.* at 75.

78. *Id.*

79. See The Politics of Informal Justice, (R. Abel ed. 1983)

80. H. Goldstein, Policing a Free Society 160 (1977).

81. M. Maguire & C. Corbett, *supra* note 5, at 196.

82. *See, eg.,* Clare Lewis's account of the Toronto scheme. Lewis, *Police Complaints in Metropolitan Toronto: Perspectives of the Public Complaints Commissioner,* in Complaints, *supra* note 3. But note the apparent failures of communication revealed by Landau's study. Landau, supra note 7.

83. M. Maguire & C. Corbett, *supra* note 5, at 200.

84. Zygmunt Bauman quotes Arne Johan Vetleson as noting that empathy is "the specific cognitive-emotional precondition of moral capacity." Bauman notes the tension between rulefollowing and the display of empathy when he writes: "Obedience to rules specifically excludes empathy; the crowd-style togetherness plays on emotional identification with the 'suprapersonal' intolerant of personal specificity'" Z. Bauman, Postmodern Ethics 143–44 (1993).

85. Freckelton, *supra* note 38.

86. *See* Manning, *supra* note 27, at 1298, where Manning refers to criminal justice organizational rules and practices that characterize cases as high or low yield cases for the purposes of further action, according to what is at stake, the state of the evidence, the freshness of allegations etc. Perceptions of complainants as "believable" or not appear similarly to influence organizational handling. *See* Zimmerman, *supra* note 57.

87. *Cf.* S. Hester & P. Eglin, *supra* note 48.

88. My emphasis. T. Tyler, Why People Obey the Law 133 (1990).

89. Id. at 175–76.

90. Complaints, *supra* note 3.

91. Minow, *Partial Justice: Law and Minorities,* The Fate of Law 170 (A. Sarat & T. Kearns eds. 1991)

92. Abrams, *Hearing the Call of Stories,* 79 Calif. L. Rev. 971 (1991).

93. The work of Donald Davidson provides an example of the philosophy of language I refer to here. *See* in relation to Davidson's position Literary Theory After Davidson (R.W. Dasenbrock ed. 1993).

94. Scheppele, *Facing Facts in Legal Interpretation in* Law and the Order of Culture 65 (R. Post ed. 1991).

95. J. Fishkin, The dialogue of Justice: Toward a Self-Reflective Society 134, 146 (1992).

96. Aristotle, Eudemian Ethics (quoted in C.D.C. Reeve, Practices of Reason; Aristotle's Nichomachean Ethics 46 (1992).

ARTICLE 27

INTERNAL AFFAIRS: THE POLICE AGENCIES' APPROACH TO THE INVESTIGATION OF POLICE MISCONDUCT

Ronald R. Thrasher
Stillwater Police Department

INTRODUCTION

People say that the greatest lie in any police department occurs when the internal affairs investigator tells the officer who is under investigation, "Trust me, I am here to help." The second greatest lie occurs when the officer responds, "I am glad that you are here." Although one of the oldest jokes in the police culture, these lines illustrate the depth of hatred and misunderstanding of the internal affairs function.

When a citizen rapes, murders, or steals, police conduct a criminal investigation. Following the investigation, police present the case to a prosecutor or state's attorney for criminal charges. When individuals feel that they have been wronged, a private investigator may be retained and the investigation presented to a private attorney for civil litigation seeking damages. But when a police officer stands accused of either criminal activity or simple misconduct, who investigates the police?

Stories of bad cops and police corruption sell newspapers, magazines, and movies. In reality, very few cases of police corruption occur compared to other professions. When corruption does occur, police misconduct draws massive public attention. Partly because we place so much power in our police and possibly because of media hype, we demand a higher standard and accountability for officer mistakes.

Internal affairs is that sometimes-feared, often-misunderstood police function that investigates police misconduct. Misconduct may be criminal (such as theft) or non-criminal (such as rudeness). Purpose and outcome distinguish the internal affairs investigation from the traditional criminal investigation.

Internal affairs as used in this article represents administrative investigations carried out for administrative purposes. In other words, internal affairs refers to investigations relative to employees within the police organization conducted as a means to develop evidence used to determine findings such as:

Findings/Classification

- **Unfounded**—The incident of misconduct did not occur;
- **Not Involved**—The employee was not present or not involved at the time the incident of misconduct occurred;
- **Exonerated**—The incident occurred, but actions taken by the employee were lawful and proper;
- **Not Sustained**—There is insufficient evidence to prove or disprove the allegation;
- **Sustained**—The allegation is supported by sufficient evidence.

Depending on the nature of the misconduct, those in administrative positions will set forth appropriate consequences, sanctions, or discipline. For example, a first-sustained complaint of rudeness may result in administrative discipline involving supervisory counseling or human relations training. A sustained complaint of theft may result in the administrative discipline of termination. Most agencies utilize a continuum of discipline depending on the nature of the incident, the officer's history of misconduct, and previous disciplinary actions. Termination represents the most severe consequence from an administrative internal affairs investigation.

This article begins with a story illustrating the complexity and pitfalls of an internal administrative investigation (IA) and why such an investigation differs from a criminal probe. Next, the development of laws and procedures that guide an internal affairs investigation will be described. Finally, the procedures of an IA investigation and the future trends in police administration will be discussed culminating in the prediction of future trends in internal affairs investigations.

THE STORY

Anytown represents a fictional, somewhat isolated, Midwestern community of about 50,000 people. Anytown supports a primarily farming, light industrial economy with the area community college being the single largest employer. The 75 men and women of the Anytown police department do a good job. Even though officers frequently investigate small thefts associated with the college, people generally feel safe and give little thought to crime.

Anytown police routinely collect transaction tickets from the local pawnshops. Investigators then enter the tickets into their computer, and compare the tickets to local stolen property. Frequently enough to continue the practice, investigators find that a college student pawned the stereo that was later reported stolen from the dorm room down the hall. Recently however, Anytown received a justice department grant that allows the downloading of pawn tickets into a state database to compare to stolen property statewide.

Fictional Officer Buzzard has five years service with the Anytown police. Buzzard works hoots (the night shift) and gets along well with the other hoot shift officers. Buzzard's supervisors describe him as an above-average officer. Buzzard gets his share of drunks, but his real interest is looking for burglars. Especially during school breaks, Buzzard leads the shift in finding open doors to businesses and structures, usually surrounding the local college.

Immediately after downloading Anytown's pawn transactions and stolen property data into the new statewide computer, the system reports a "hit." Apparently Officer Buzzard pawned a number of stolen items. The items were reported stolen in Anytown and later pawned at Capitol, a fictional metropolitan community about 60 miles away. Anytown investigators advised Buzzard of his Miranda rights and Buzzard admits to stealing the items and pawning them in Capitol. In a plea agreement with the district prosecutor, Buzzard pleas no-contest to one count of first degree burglary of the home of an elderly professor. In exchange for the no-contest plea, Buzzard receives a ten-year sentence to be served in the state penitentiary.

Immediately following the conviction, the Anytown chief of police fires Buzzard for committing the burglary and because state law prohibits a convicted felon from serving as a police officer and from possessing a firearm. Buzzard serves two of his ten-year sentence and appeals his conviction on the basis that his confession was forced and coerced by the threat of losing his job. Buzzard's case is remanded back to the local court for retrial. Because the physical evidence in the case was returned to the owner and now lost, and because the elderly professor victim has since died, the district prosecutor dismisses the case. Buzzard becomes a free man. As a routine matter, Buzzard petitions the court and receives an order expunging and sealing all records connected with his case. Now as far as the court records show, the incident never happened.

Next Buzzard sues the Anytown police department for two years back pay, reinstatement in his former job, and potential promotions. Buzzard contends that his original confession was coerced and according to Buzzard's personnel file, Buzzard was fired only because he was a convicted felon. With the charges dropped and the records sealed and expunged, Buzzard argues that he is no longer a convicted felon. Buzzard settles for an undisclosed amount of money and now works in another city department with the salary and benefits of an Anytown police sergeant.

Although these situations seem bizarre, professional internal affairs investigators must be aware of laws, policies, and procedures not only to protect themselves, but also the communities they serve. Generally, three considerations must be made before beginning any administrative investigation. They include the law, the labor contract, and departmental policy.

THE LAW

The United States Supreme Court decided one of the first cases to significantly impact current IA investigation procedures on January 16th, 1967.[1] This case began when the Supreme Court of New Jersey ordered the New Jersey attorney general to investigate the "fixing" of municipal traffic tickets in the New Jersey boroughs of Bellmawr and Barrington. Defendants in this case include Bellmawr Police Chief Garrity, Barrington Police Officers Holroyd, Elwell, and Murry, and Bellmawr Municipal Court Clerk Mrs. Naglee. Prior to reaching the United States Supreme Court, the Supreme Court of New Jersey affirmed convictions in two separate trials where the petitioners were convicted of conspiracy to obstruct the proper administration of the state motor traffic laws. Evidence indicated that separate conspiracies occurred in which court records had been falsified, traffic tickets altered, and monies from bail and fines diverted to unauthorized purposes.

Important to this discussion, a New Jersey deputy attorney general took statements from the petitioners in this investigation in August and November, 1961. The court records show no indication of duress on the part of the petitioners when statements were taken. Chief Garrity himself arranged the location for questioning at a nearby firehouse. Mrs. Naglee suffered from a heart condition but was assured that should she feel any physical discomfort, questioning would stop. None of the petitioners were either in custody nor had they been removed from office when questioned. Counsel represented three of the petitioners. Chief Garrity consulted counsel but told the assistant attorney general, as they strolled from the chief's office to the firehouse, that Garrity thought that counsel would not be needed at this stage of the proceedings. The state court later determined that the statements taken by the assistant attorney general were taken with a "high degree of civility and restraint."[2]

At the time of questioning, New Jersey law required that policemen could be discharged if they failed to provide information relevant to their public responsibilities.[3] With this in mind, the assistant attorney general advised each of the sworn officers of this law. The petitioners were also advised of their Miranda rights: availability of counsel and freedom from self-incrimination.[4] Although individual warnings vary slightly, the rights given Chief Garrity are typical of those given each sworn officer:

> *I want to advise you that anything you say must be said of your own free will and accord without any threats or promises or coercion, and anything you say may be, of course, used against you or any other person in any subsequent criminal proceedings in the courts of our State.*
>
> *You do have, under our law, as you probably know, a privilege to refuse to make any disclosure which may tend to incriminate you. If you make a disclosure with knowledge of this right or privilege, voluntarily, you thereby waive that right or privilege in relation to any other questions which I might put to you relevant to such disclosure in this investigation.*
>
> *This right or privilege which you have is somewhat limited to the extent that you, as a police officer under the laws of our State, may be subjected to a proceeding to have you removed from office if you refuse to answer a question put to you under oath pertaining to your office or your function within that office. It doesn't mean, however, you can't exercise that right. You do have the right.*

Mrs. Naglee received her Miranda warning, but she was not told that she could be removed from her position at the court if she refused to answer questions.

For the U.S. Supreme Court, the question in this case became whether a state, contrary to the requirement of the Fourteenth Amendment to the United States Constitution, can use the threat of discharge to secure incriminatory evidence against an employee. Are statements thus obtained "involuntary as a matter of law?"

The Court decided the question by acknowledging that statements obtained in this case were voluntarily given. The Court also said that the state is permitted to establish reasonable qualifications and standards for its employees. Further, it is not unreasonable for the state to insist that its employees furnish the appropriate authorities with information pertinent to their employment. As such, it does not minimize or endanger the employees' constitutional privilege against self-incrimination, again pertinent to their employment.

One of the next cases to significantly impact internal affairs investigations involves the issue of union representation.[5] In this case, the Weingarten Corporation operates a chain of retail stores, many of which contained lunch counters. Leura Collins worked at one of the Weingarten lunch counters. In June, 1972, a Weingarten security officer watched Leura for two days after receiving a tip that Leura stole from the cash register. Unable to find any evidence of theft, the security officer told the store manager of the surveillance. The manager responded to the security officer that another employee just reported Leura for obtaining a $2.98 box of chicken, but only putting $1.00 in the cash register.

The security officer and the store manager then questioned Leura about the chicken. During the questioning, Leura several times asked for and was denied an opportunity to call either the union shop steward or some other union representative.

As a result of the questioning, Leura admitted purchasing some chicken, a loaf of bread, and some cake to be donated to her church. Leura said that she bought four pieces of chicken for $1.00, but because the store was out of the small chicken boxes, Leura put the chicken in a larger size chicken box. The security officer confirmed that the company was out of the small size boxes and further that no one could say how many pieces of chicken Leura actually took. The security officer appologized for the incident. Leura then began to cry and said that the only thing that she had ever taken from the store was her free lunches. Questioning continued.

Leura again requested that the union shop steward be called to the interview. The store manager refused. The investigation revealed that the Weingarten store where Leura previously worked provided free lunches. The Weingarten store where Leura worked at the time of questioning did not provide free lunches. Most employees at both stores poorly understand the policy. The investigation also revealed that most if not all of the Weingarten employees, including the lunch department manager, take free lunches. Even the company headquarters told the security officer that the policy concerning free lunches was unclear at the store where Leura currently worked. Finally, the security officer prepared a written statement indicating that Leura owed the company $160.00 for lunches. The interview ended after Leura refused to sign the statement. As Leura left the interview, the store manager asked Leura not to discuss the incident because it was a private matter.

Leura immediately reported the incident to the union shop steward as an unfair labor practice. Later, the union filed an unfair labor practice charge with the National Labor Relations Board (NLRB). The NLRB issued a cease-and-desist order which the court of appeals subsequently refused to enforce. The US Supreme Court heard arguments November 18, 1974, and decided February 19, 1975, reversing the court of appeals. Several guidelines emerged from this decision:

1. Employees are guaranteed the right to act in concert for mutual aid and protection;
2. The right arises only in situations where employees request representation;

3. The right to representation as a condition to participate in an interview is limited to situations where the employee reasonably fears disciplinary action;
4. An employer can decide to forego an interview and continue the internal investigation;
5. The employer has no duty to bargain with any union representative within the interview.

THE LABOR CONTRACT

The labor contract consists of agreements between some bargaining unit for the individual police officers and the police department or governing entity. In the case of municipal policing, this may be an annual contract between the city and, for example, the Fraternal Order of Police or other union representation.

Labor contracts contain any number of agreements such as the accrual of sick and vacation time, salary ranges, grievance procedures, hours of work, and others. Another issue often addressed by labor contracts involves employee rights during IA investigations. The following *Police Officer Bill of Rights* is increasingly being included in many police labor contracts and as such impacts the way in which internal affairs investigations are conducted.

Police Officer Bill of Rights[6]

> *When an officer is under investigation by the police department for a complaint and is to be interviewed in respect to such complaint by other members of the department, when there is a logical possibility that any disciplinary action to include suspension, demotion, or dismissal may result, such interview shall be conducted as follows:*
> 1. *The officer shall be informed of the name of all complainants, if known;*
> 2. *Preliminary discussions with supervisory personnel with the police department, in relation to a complaint received, shall not be considered as an interrogation as used herein;*
> 3. *To the extent known at the time, the officer under investigation shall be informed of the nature of the investigation prior to any interrogation. If, during the course of the investigation, additional potential charges come to light, the officer under investigation shall be informed of the nature of those additional issues as soon as such information is identified;*
> 4. *The officer under investigation shall be informed of the rank, name of officer in charge of the investigation, the interrogating officer, and all persons present during the interrogation. All questions directed to the officer under interrogation shall be asked by and through one interrogator at a time;*
> 5. *Interrogation sessions shall be for reasonable periods and shall be timed to allow for such personal necessities and rest periods as are reasonably necessary;*
> 6. *The officer under interrogation shall not be subject to offensive language during the interrogation. No promise or reward shall be made as an inducement to obtain testimony or evidence;*
> 7. *The officer under investigation shall be completely informed of all his/her rights (to include Garrity Rights and the Weingarten Ruling), pursuant to this*

procedure prior to the commencement of the interrogation and his/her respon-
sibility to answer all questions;

8. *At the request of any officer under investigation, he/she shall have the right to be*
   represented by a union representative of his/her choice who shall be present at all
   phases of the interrogation. In addition, if the officer under investigation so
   chooses, he/she may have an attorney (or other such representative) present (at
   no additional expense to the government) during interrogation as long as this
   does not cause any delay in the proceedings. When so represented, this represen-
   tative shall be an observer only and shall not ask questions or enter into discus-
   sion with any party present during the official interrogation;

9. *Interrogation of officers under investigation may be taped or recorded in written*
   form at the discretion of the investigating officer. Officers under investigation may
   record the proceedings with his/her own equipment or provide written record at
   his/her own expense as long as such does not cause any delay in the proceedings.
   Records and tapes compiled by the department shall be exclusively retained by the
   department as confidential information, but may be used at the discretion of the
   city in administrative hearings or for other administrative purposes.

Other issues often addressed by labor contracts include how the department may receive a complaint on an officer and who within the department may receive and document the incident. Some labor contracts handle the case differently when the complainant refuses to give his/her name. Sometimes procedures vary between a citizen complaint and those complaints that originate from another officer or police employee. Sometimes contracts distinguish investigative procedures dependent upon the seriousness of the complaint. Most contracts, however, include the clause that no officer shall be discharged, disciplined, demoted, denied promotion, transferred, reassigned, or otherwise be discriminated against in regard to his/her employment, or be threatened with any such sanction, by reason of his/her exercise of his/her rights granted by the labor contract.

THE DEPARTMENT POLICY

The final issue to be addressed before beginning an administrative internal investigation is department policy. Like labor contracts, department policies vary. Increasingly, guidelines provided by the Commission on Accreditation for Law Enforcement Agencies, Inc. provide the standard for policy development.[7] The following guidelines are found in many department policies and generally conform to accreditation standards.

These policies often begin with a directive describing which complaints will be investigated. For example, "All complaints against the Anytown police department or any Anytown police employee will be investigated." Although not recommended, other policies state that only those complaints signed by the complaining party will be investigated. More acceptable are those policies that first designate categories of complaints and then require that all serious allegations be investigated and only those minor violations such as citizen rudeness require a signed complaint to receive an investigation. Policy also establishes how complaints are categorized.

Policies categorize complaints in a number of ways. Some agencies categorize complaints by the seriousness of the allegation. Other agencies categorize complaints by the seriousness of possible disciplinary action. Categories range from offenses that would likely result in routine discipline, to more serious categories such as corruption, brutality, civil rights violations, and criminal misconduct that would likely result in termination. Categories of complaints may also dictate how the complaint is routed and processed and who within the agency must be notified before starting an investigation.

Policy determines who investigates the complaint. A department may require that the employee's immediate supervisor investigate certain categories of complaints such as rudeness, tardiness, or laziness. More serious complaints and those complaints involving criminal behavior may be assigned to an IA investigator, a criminal investigator, a police administrator, or even the chief executive. Whoever investigates the complaint, policies frequently require that the investigating officer report directly to the chief of police during the course of the investigation.

Many departments insist that, when possible, involved employees are advised the nature of any complaint. Agencies handle this function in a number of ways. Some departments give a copy of the complaint to involved officers. Some departments provide written notice. Some agencies require a written receipt from the involved employee. Others simply note verbal notification in the investigative report. Policies also limit the duration of investigations and provide for extensions and investigative updates to the chief of police and the involved employees. Procedures dictate possible dispositions, notifications of final reports, which reports become personnel issues, and which may or may not become available as public records. Finally, many departments at the time of notification will also provide involved employees with a statement of employee rights and responsibilities.

Employee rights include those guarantees provided by *Garrity* and *Weingarten*, as well as other legal decisions, federal, state, and local laws. Rights and responsibilities also come from labor agreements and policy statements. Policies include those rights and responsibilities and mandate those conditions where an employee may be expected to provide written statements, submit to medical examinations, psychological evaluations, polygraph tests, participate in photo or actual line-ups, or disclose personal financial records or information. These issues must be considered in regards to legal requirements of local jurisdictions, case law, precedent, and consistency with other policy and administrative decisions.

Depending on the nature of a complaint, policy must include some provision for covert investigations. Investigators must be provided the opportunity to conduct lengthy covert investigations into allegations of embezzlement, extortion, drug trafficking, and protection rackets, for example. Policy should also establish the circumstances and authority to relieve an employee from duty. Many departments extend this authority to first-line supervisors. Supervisors may, in certain situations, immediately remove an officer's weapon, badge, and credentials and suspend an officer without loss of pay and benefits for certain serious allegations pending review from command authority.

Policy should address certain other administration functions. It must clearly state how officers and citizens will be notified of the conclusions and findings of administrative investigations. Policy should address how the public is informed and educated on the procedure for making an administrative complaint. The procedure for maintaining the confidentiality and security of non-public records must also be established and practiced. Finally, policy should address how investigative findings are classified and who makes recommendations and decisions for discipline when needed. With these things in mind, it is time to conduct an internal affairs investigation.

THE INVESTIGATIVE PROCESS

It is two o'clock in the morning when Jane Doe walks into the Anytown police department and asks for the supervisor. Jane cries. She shows the beginning of a bruise to her left eye. Her dress is soiled and torn as she sits down in the office of the Anytown police sergeant.

Jane tells Sergeant McNickle that for some time she has been dating Anytown Officer Smith. Earlier in the evening, Smith showed up at her apartment unannounced. Smith smelled slightly of beer, but was nowhere close to intoxication. Smith accused Jane of seeing another officer while Smith was on patrol. Smith became increasingly angry as he told Jane that he watched her apartment while he worked and had seen another officer's car parked in the neighborhood.

When Jane denied dating another officer, Smith hit Jane in the face with his collapsible department nightstick that he always carried in his back pocket. Jane fell to the floor crying for Smith to leave. Smith left when Jane asked if he was planning on raping her. Jane insisted that no sexual assault took place.

Hearing this, Sergeant McNickle took Jane to the local hospital for treatment and examination. McNickle completed a criminal police report with Jane as the victim and Smith as the alleged suspect. Next, McNickle completed an administrative citizen's complaint, again with Jane as the victim and Smith as the involved employee. Due to the seriousness of the allegations, Sergeant McNickle phoned the Anytown chief of police.

Since the Anytown police department does not have an internal affairs unit, Chief Dollar phoned the two Anytown police investigation supervisors. Chief Dollar assigned one of the supervisors to conduct a criminal investigation. The second supervisor was assigned the IA investigation. Chief Dollar instructed both supervisors not to discuss their cases between themselves and not to exchange reports during the course of their inquiries.

The criminal investigator interviewed Jane following the medical examination that night. By this time, Jane refused to talk to the criminal investigator saying only that she did not want to pursue criminal charges against Smith, but only wanted the Department to force him to get some help. Jane also refused to release her clothing and medical records to the criminal investigator and further refused to consent to a search of her apartment for physical evidence. Given the type of the offense and the wishes of the victim, the investigator did not seek a search warrant for either Jane's clothing nor for a search of her apartment.

Later, the criminal investigator interviewed Smith in reference to the criminal investigation. The investigator advised Smith of his Miranda warning stating:

Miranda Warning[8]

> *There is a chance that you will be charged with a crime, and since that is the case, there are certain Constitutional rights you have that must be protected.*
>
> 1. *You have the right to remain silent in the face of any questions that might be put to you.*
> 2. *You have the right to be represented by an attorney at all stages of the proceedings that will be had against you including this proceeding right now.*
> 3. *If you do not have funds to be represented by an attorney, one can be appointed by the court to represent you.*
> 4. *I must warn you that anything you say can and will be used against you in court if this case goes to court.*
> 5. *If you decide to answer questions or make a statement, and at any time you decide that you don't want to answer any further questions or make any further statements, you have the right to stop.*

Smith invoked his right to remain silent and refused to speak with the investigator. Based on this information, the state prosecutor declined to file criminal charges against Officer Smith in connection with the physical assault.

Unable to locate Smith that night, the IA investigator contacted Smith the following evening when Smith reported to work. According to policy, Smith received a copy of the complaint and was relieved from duty without loss of pay and benefits. Smith surrendered his badge, department weapon (including his baton), and identification card according to past department practice. The IA investigator ordered Smith to remain available by pager during those times when Smith would normally be on duty. The investigator also told Smith that he would be contacted the following day with an update on the investigation.

Next, the investigator contacted Jane and told her that he would be conducting an IA investigation separate from a criminal investigation that was also taking place. The IA investigator interviewed Jane and requested a release of her medical records concerning the assault. Jane cooperated.

Following the interview with Jane, the investigator contacted Smith and ordered Smith's presence at the police department for an administrative interview. The interview was audio taped according to policy and began with the warning:

Internal Affairs Investigation Warning[9]

> *I wish to advise you that you are being questioned as part of an official investigation by the Anytown police department. You, as a public employee, are entitled to representation in any investigatory interviews which you reasonably believe might lead to disciplinary action. You have the right to request representation or legal counsel. You do not have to make any statement until you have met with your representative. It should be noted that if you choose to have representation during the official investigation, your representative does not have the right to ask questions. Only you may invoke the right to have a representative. You cannot be disciplined or have any adverse action taken against you for exercising your right to representation. The City of Anytown as*

your employer may deny the representation request, but must discontinue the interview. You have the right not to be compelled to make any statement without first being informed of your Garrity Rights or given another appropriate administrative warning. You may only be compelled to answer questions specifically, directly, and narrowly related to your fitness for duty or otherwise related to the performance of your official duties. You cannot be compelled to speak with a criminal investigator, prosecutor, or testify before a grand jury under threat of an adverse employment action.

As a condition of employment, you will be asked questions specifically directed and narrowly related to the performance of your official duties or fitness for office.

You are entitled to all the rights and privileges guaranteed by the laws and the constitution of this state and the Constitution of the United States, including the right not to be compelled to incriminate yourself.

Your statements and any information provided by you or any evidence obtained by reason of such statements can not be used against you in any subsequent criminal proceeding. Your statements may only be used against you should a subsequent administrative action be commenced.

You may refuse to answer questions relating to the performance of your official duties or fitness for duty, however you may be subject to disciplinary action which could include job termination.

Smith declined the opportunity to have either an attorney or a union representative present during the interview. When questioned, Smith acknowledged that he drove to Jane's apartment after drinking a beer and that he became angry and struck Jane with his department-issued baton. Smith admitted that he refused to leave Jane's apartment when first asked and then became scared and left when Jane asked him if he planned on raping her. When questioned, Smith said that the only other person he had discussed the incident with was his best friend and hoot shift partner, Joe.

When interviewed by the IA investigator, Joe said that Smith must have called him right after the incident. Joe related the same sequence of events as both Jane and Smith. Joe admitted telling Smith to keep his mouth shut and to not answer the phone until the beer got out of his system and that maybe the department would not find out what happened.

The IA investigator submitted Jane's clothing to the department laboratory. The lab photographed and tested the clothing for body fluids such as blood and semen. The lab found that tears to the dress were consistent with a fall. Tests also showed no evidence of sexual assault. The chief's administrative assistant transcribed the interview tapes. Finally, the IA investigator compiled the information into a final report. The IA report contained:

Table of Contents

- The original complaint;
- An abstract or summary of the investigation and findings;
- Consent to search signed by Jane for her clothing;
- Release signed by Jane for her medical records;
- Signed IA warning acknowledgement from Smith;
- Signed IA warning acknowledgement from Joe;
- Written statement from Jane;

- Written statement from Smith;
- Written statement from Joe;
- Transcribed tape interview with Jane;
- Transcribed tape interview with Smith;
- Transcribed tape interview with Joe;
- Photographs of injury to Jane;
- Photographs of Jane's clothing;
- Jane's medical records;
- Property submission form for Jane's clothing;
- Laboratory examination report concerning Jane's clothing;
- Appendix containing actual interview tapes.

According to policy, the completed IA investigative report went to each of Smith's supervisors for review and recommendations. Next, according to policy and the labor contract, the report was submitted to an internal review committee for recommendation. The internal review committee had the opportunity to question witnesses, but chose to make recommendations based solely on the IA report. Finally, the Anytown chief reviewed the report and recommendations and made the final decision concerning discipline.

According to past practice and policy, Joe received supervisory counseling and a written reprimand. Joe failed to report Smith's behavior and further counseled Smith to not answer the phone in hopes that the alcohol would work out of his system and the department might not discover the incident. Smith received a written reprimand and one day of lost pay and benefits for the assault. The department also arranged for anger management training and a psychological assessment at the department's expense prior to Smith's returning to duty.

THE FUTURE

Traditionally, individual law enforcement agencies cherish their social isolation and their jurisdictional turf. In the past, police departments neither trusted nor talked to other area law enforcement agencies. Frequently, law enforcement agencies just a few miles apart or even within the same community remained uninformed of each other's cases. But, in a society of increasingly scarce resources with technological advances in transportation and communication, law enforcement faces new challenges.

Serial offenders travel the country committing the same crime in the same way in different jurisdictions. A stock market telephone fraud from New York generates victims around the country in a matter of hours. An Internet credit card scam generates millions of victims around the world in minutes. Law enforcement must adapt through communication, cooperation, and trust. This same cooperative need occurs in administrative investigations.

Today many police agencies augment the internal affairs function by combining internal affairs with other specialized activities such as public information, training, or crime prevention. Some agencies simply assign the occasional internal affairs investigation to the deputy chief or some other administrative individual. Problems emerge. In the small agency, the IA investigator becomes demonized among and apart from other officers. These ill feelings often generalize and affect other work done by the same individual. With only a few IA investigations to conduct each year, many times these individuals become ill equipped to handle the complexities of past practices, the law, the labor contract, department policy, community expectations, and modern investigative techniques.

In the future, police departments may enter into cooperative multijurisdictional agreements to share a single internal affairs investigator. Other agencies may contract out internal affairs investigations to a professional who specializes in this particular area. Just as policing agencies now employ chemists to examine DNA evidence, forensic odontologists to examine bite marks, or forensic entomologists to determine time of death by insect development on the corpse, in the future, specialists may emerge to investigate law enforcement misconduct.

Whether an in-house investigator, an administrator, or a contract professional, the internal affairs investigator must consider the law, the labor contract, the departmental policy, past practice, and mostly the community. When everything else is satisfied, the community sets the standard for police professionalism and conduct to which we must all conform.

NOTES

1. *Garrity v. New Jersey* 385 U.S. 493.
2. *Garrity v. New Jersey* 385 U.S. 493.
3. N.J. Stat. 2A :81–17.1.
4. *Miranda v. Arizona,* 384 U.S. 436, 461.
5. *NLRB v. Weingarten, Inc.,* 420 U.S. 251.
6. This Police Officer Bill of Rights represents an edited excerpt from the Police Services Agreement between the City of Stillwater, (Oklahoma) and the Fraternal Order of Police, Lodge #102, Inc. Contract Year 1998–1999 p. 13.
7. Commission on Accreditation for Law Enforcement Agencies, Inc. January, 1999. Internal Affairs, Fairfax, Virginia. p. 521-2.
8. *Miranda v. Arizona,* 384 U.S. 436, 461.
9. *NLRB v. Weingarten Inc.,* 420 U.S. 251 (1975) and *Garrity v. New Jersey,* 385 U.S. 493 (1967) and *Gardner v. Broderick,* 392 U.S. 273 (1976).

CIVILIAN OVERSIGHT OF POLICE BEHAVIOR

Ronald M. Fletcher
Human Relations Commission,
Hartford, Connecticut

T he issue of what role, if any, citizens should have in the review of allegations of police misbehavior is presently before many American cities, including Hartford, particularly in response to the media coverage of the Los Angeles incident involving Rodney King. Citizen oversight of police behavior gained significant attention as a result of the civil disorders which occurred in our cities in the mid-1960's and continues to be an issue to this day. As public servants, police officers have a special and unique role in providing public service related to "order maintenance" and safety in our communities. We vest police officers with the special responsibilities that give them the authority to arrest and/or detain people, to investigate and require answers or responses to their questions, to control free movement, to carry and to utilize weapons (a pistol and a nightstick), and so forth, all in the name of maintaining the "public good."

The disturbances of the 1960's called into question many policies and practices of police departments, particularly as they related to the treatment of minority citizens. The existing systems of internal checks and balances and the internal discipline procedures began to be questioned, particularly because in too many cases they functioned totally outside of the public view. The historical staffing patterns, wherein police departments were predominantly white

Ronald M. Fletcher is Executive Director of the Human Relations Commission, Hartford, Connecticut. This article was prepared as a position paper for the Human Relations Commission regarding the public policy implications of civilian oversight.

Ronald M. Fletcher, "Civilian Oversight of Police Behavior" (as appeared in *The Journal of Intergroup Relations,* Volume 19, Number 3, [Fall 1992], pp. 7–12). Reprinted with permission.

and policing predominantly minority neighborhoods and communities, further fueled the suspicion and mistrust of minority citizens in the ability and willingness of police departments to fairly review allegations of police misbehavior. Early studies of the patterns and results of police internal discipline mechanisms and various ad hoc incidents receiving public attention regarding police misbehavior continued to call into question the willingness and ability of police departments to oversee their own behavior.

The initial responses of police departments to respond to and resolve these concerns were:

1. to include minority citizens as police officers through affirmative action programming;
2. to emphasize professionalism of officers by raising employment and training standards; and
3. to establish codes of conduct and internal discipline mechanisms, such as internal affairs divisions.[1]

Hartford, as did other cities, actively instituted these actions in the 1970's. While the above steps were important, they were not sufficient to effectively negate the calls for civilian oversight mechanisms. The essential arguments being espoused both for and against civilian oversight have been as follows:

ARGUMENTS AGAINST:

1. Police voice opposition to civilian oversight because they believe it would decrease their effectiveness at fighting crime, demoralize police, lead to resignations, interfere with authority of the chief, and disrupt police operations through political interference.
2. Civilian boards would have legal problems. They would not have subpoena power and would create due process problems for officers required to appear before them.
3. Police misbehavior is an organizational problem, which is technical in nature and therefore can be solved by internal controls.
4. Citizens already have access to redress of their complaints through the court system.[2]

ARGUMENTS FOR:

1. Complaints of police behavior frequently have nothing to do with the law per se, but are more procedural or attitudinal, and best covered by internal policies, or rules of conduct and procedure, not the courts.
2. Internal review procedures enable police departments to ignore gravity and seriousness of abuse. The abuse may be a symptom of a larger organizational problem that needs to be addressed.[3]
3. The public needs a window on the process so that they know what occurs is fair and equitable and is responsive to the issue.

4. Civilian oversight helps police understand and know what the community values are related to policing, and will help police establish and maintain behavioral standards.

The process for, or implementation of, a civilian oversight mechanism can take any number of forms or meanings. The experience to date throughout the country has shown any number of variations for civilian oversight, such as:

1. Oversight agency receives, investigates, and adjudicates complaints, and recommends discipline to police executive.
2. Oversight agency only receives and adjudicates complaints, and recommends discipline to police executives. The actual complaint investigation, however, is done by the police department.
3. Oversight agency performs as either of the above: however, city's chief administrator (for example, mayor or city manager) acts as the arbitrator or mediator of disciplinary disputes between the oversight agency and the police executive.[4]

Inherent in any of these formats, however are the following issues, which must be addressed:

1. Public's right of access to information regarding the complaint and the process (how much or how little);
2. Conciliation: is it attempted between the complainant and the officer;
3. Who determines the discipline (the oversight agency or the police executive);
4. Rights of officers during the process;
5. Who receives complaints, and who investigates complaints:
6. Inclusion or exclusion of police officers on an oversight board.[5]

In the early 1980's, the issue of civilian oversight resurfaced as a major public issue in Hartford. The issue at that time was caused by vocal complaints by the local NAACP about police misbehavior and by the accidental shooting of a motorist stopped for a traffic check by a police officer. In 1982, as a result of political compromise, the City of Hartford established a police department Investigation Review Board (IRB), which for the first time included citizens in the process to review allegations of police misconduct. Significant points related to the IRB and how it continues to function are as follows:

1. IRB consists of: three ranking police officers, one of whom is chairperson, all appointed by the chief of police; three members of the City's Commission on Human Relations, appointed by the City Manager; one additional representative appointed by the City Manager; for a total of seven members.
2. IRB reviews citizen complaints which are filed against police officers, and which are investigated by the police department Internal Affairs Division (a unit of the police department). The Internal Affairs Division has the total responsibility to investigate the allegation and to prepare a report of their investigation, which is then submitted to the IRB. The IRB reviews and discusses the investigative report.

3. Until June 13, 1991, all IRB meetings were held in executive session, meaning the public, including the complainant, could not attend the meeting. A complainant could attend and reiterate the complaint, but could not stay to hear the discussion or receive copies of any material related to his complaint or its investigation.

4. Officers are not required to, nor do they, attend the hearing.

5. Based upon the I.A.D. investigative reports and the discussion of the issue, the board makes a finding (exonerated, unfounded, not sustained, partially sustained, sustained), which is then sent to the chief of police as a recommendation.

6. The chief of police makes the final decision. If a complaint requires further disciplinary action, that is accomplished through another internal disciplinary hearing, in which no civilians participate.

7. The only information provided to the civilian members of the board and the complainant is the final decision of the chief regarding the finding. Information as to what, if any, discipline is taken is not made available, nor is any information provided as to how or why the conclusion was reached.

The significant issues which we continue to face in Hartford regarding the IRB relates to what I believe is the public perception, particularly in the minority community, that:

1. Issues related to police misbehavior are not sufficiently addressed through internal controls; and

2. The internal review and discipline procedures are not fair or equitable.

Opponents of civilian review point out that the number of complaints being filed against the police department are not excessive, given the number of calls for service, and therefore this is not a real issue. The problem I note, however, is that many people will not file a complaint, because they don't believe anything will happen. As presently structured, I don't foresee—no matter how fair or equitable the internal process is—that the perception of unfairness which many have related to the above will be changed, using the IRB process as now constituted. Whatever the format or representation used regarding civilian oversight, the following issues must be addressed if we wish to assure a credible process in which the public can have faith and confidence:

1. **Public right to know.** The hearing and decision-making process regarding citizen complaints needs to be done in a format open to the public view.

2. **Representation of police and citizens.** Inclusion of both police personnel and civilian personnel will be important to establish confidence of all affected parties that their perspective and views will be included and considered.

3. **Discipline and training.** The board must see its role beyond that of finding fault or no fault, but also address the issues of policy and

training, to support more effective community policing, which may evolve from their review of complaints.

4. **Authority of the Chief.** The authority of the chief of police to administer and impose discipline should not be compromised. The board, however, should be empowered to recommend the kind of discipline, which may be training, and be advised of final decisions.

5. **Investigation.** In special circumstances, the board should be empowered to initiate its own investigation and fact-finding of citizen complaints.

6. **Receipt of complaints.** Procedures for other than police personnel to receive citizen complaints in a non-intimidating and non-hostile environment must be established and continually publicized.

7. **Rights of officers.** The review process and access of the public to information must be established in a way that protects the rights of officers and their families.

The establishment of civilian oversight is in all too many cases being projected as anti-police, at a time when the role of policing is becoming much more critical, particularly in our urban inner city neighborhoods. This in part is caused by the media attention to gross police misconduct, which is then followed by calls for civilian oversight as an answer related to discipline and control. Police departments must recognize that their roles must expand beyond the traditional law enforcement/order maintenance functions. The Hartford Police Department now defines a more comprehensive role for itself in its newly established mission statement which reads:

> The mission of the Hartford Police Department is to enhance the quality of life in the City of Hartford by developing partnerships within the community and the other entities of government, in a manner that promotes preservation of life and property, maintains public order, reduces fear, and provides a safe environment by the enforcement of law with respect for human dignity.[6]

Inherent in this changing role is establishing and building trust and confidence within and between the department and the community which it serves. Properly instituted and implemented, civilian oversight can effectively establish the means to dispel the mistrust that has occurred regarding internal control of discipline and provide to the community and the police department a means to establish a moral consensus for policing within the community.

ENDNOTES

1. George Kelling, Robert Wasserman, Hubert Williams, "Police Accountability and Community Policing." National Institute of Justice, November 1988, p. 2.
2. Richard J. Terrill, "Alternative Perception of Independence in Civilian Oversight." *Journal of Police Science and Administration,* 1990, Volume 17, No. 2., page 78–79.
3. Terrill, page 79.
4. Werner E. Petterson, "Civilian Oversight of Policing—United States of America," (unpublished) p. 22.
5. Petterson, pages 27–30.
6. City of Hartford Fiscal Year 1991/1992 Adopted Budget, p. C-65.

REFERENCES

Bittner, Egon, Ph.D. "Functions of Police in Modern Society," National Institute of Mental Health, November 1970.

City of Hartford Fiscal Year 1991/1992 Adopted Budget.

Kelling, George; Wasserman, Robert; and Williams, Hubert, "Police Accountability and Community Policing." National Institute of Justice, November 1988.

Petterson, Werner E. "Civilian Oversight of Policing—United States of America," (Unpublished).

Terrill, Richard J. "Alternative Perception of Independence in Civilian Oversight." *Journal of Police Science and Administration,* 1990, Volume 17, No. 2.

ARTICLE 29

AN ANALYSIS OF SECTION 1983 LITIGATION DEALING WITH POLICE MISCONDUCT

William Bickel
Baltimore County State's Attorney Office

pproximately 650,000 police officers serve to protect law and order throughout the United States (Wilson 1996, 54). Police officers have legal authority to enforce societal norms that have been codified into laws, either by statute or custom, that govern individual and collective behavior. Police officers are placed in a position of trust. When an officer breaches that trust, it can significantly affect the overall performance of the justice system.

In any given year, a percentage of our police force will be sanctioned for minor infractions of departmental procedures; an even smaller percentage of police officers will be convicted of serious felony crimes. However, any impropriety, whether actual or merely perceived, no matter how slight, can have an adverse impact upon public confidence in the police that can lead to public distrust and lack of cooperation and support in investigations, which ultimately will have an adverse effect on the prosecution of criminals. This article examines police officer misconduct in three sections: case analysis, methods of handling misconduct, and the ramifications of police officer misconduct on society.

CASE ANALYSIS

Police officer misconduct is defined as "any wrongdoing committed by a police officer, whether the wrong doing is a criminal violation or a violation of departmental rules" (Palmiotto 1997). For the purpose of this article, police officer "misconduct" will be limited to severe departures from the law including rape, murder, domestic violence, and robbery.

Sexual Assault

On July 23, 1988, North Little Rock Police Officer William Kovach approached a parked car that had been reported stolen. Police Officers Donnell Luckie and David Dallas responded as backups to the call. Kovach, the lead officer, determined that the female passenger, later identified as Eddie Parrish, should not be arrested. Officer Luckie, however, laughed and told Parrish, "Ho, Ho, Ho! You could go to jail, too." Officer Luckie then told the other officers that he was going to scare Parrish by telling her that the driver of the car told him that drugs found in the car belonged to her. Officer Luckie informed Parrish of her Miranda rights, put her in the rear of his police cruiser, and secured her purse in the front seat. He then drove Parrish to an isolated portion of North Little Rock and forced her to perform fellatio on him. He then took her to the precinct, where she was processed and subsequently released. [*Parrish v. Luckie,* 963 F.2d 201 (8th Cir. 1992)]

After being released, Parrish went to a relative's house and called the police. Officer Dallas, who responded to the call, was one of the officers who responded to the scene of the initial arrest. Officer Dallas refused to take Parrish's statement, claiming she would have to complain personally to Dallas' supervisor. Officer Dallas immediately informed Officer Luckie of the complaint. Officer Luckie told Dallas not to report the incident to his supervisor because he knew that the department would not investigate the incident without a written complaint. Parrish filed a written complaint with the police department. Ultimately, Officer Luckie was charged with rape and pleaded guilty to first-degree assault. [*Parrish v. Luckie,* 963 F.2d 201 (8th Cir. 1992)]

Murder

On September 29, 1990, Officer Jerry Knick, who was an eight-year veteran of the Lexington police department in Lexington, Virginia, brutally shot and killed his wife. Prior to the murder, Officer Knick and his wife had been experiencing marital problems. On the day of the murder, Officer Knick, while on duty and in uniform, stopped by his house, where he discovered his wife, Lisa, talking to a fellow police officer. The officer was a friend of both parties. Lisa Knick had been discussing her marital problems with the officer and had told him that she was prepared to leave her husband. Officer Knick became angry at the presence of the other officer but left his house without incident. A short time later, Officer Knick, still on duty, returned to the location. At that time, the other officer left the Knicks' residence and, moments later, Officer Knick shot and killed his wife with his service revolver. The fellow officer, who consoled Lisa Knick prior to her murder, responded to the scene, and Officer Knick admitted that he had assaulted his wife and then shot her. Officer Knick was subsequently convicted of second-degree murder and received a 10-year sentence. (Taylor May/June 1994, 102).

Domestic Violence

In June of 1988, Chicago Police Officer Ruben Garza, while on patrol with his partner, received permission from his supervisor to go outside his jurisdiction.

They drove to a neighboring area, where Officer Garza found his estranged wife, Mary Czajkowski traveling in a vehicle with their six-year-old son. Officer Garza activated his emergency lights and sirens and pulled Mrs. Czajkowski over for an alleged traffic offense. He also stated that he wanted to recover some keys from her. After the stop, and in the presence of his partner, Officer Garza grabbed her around the neck, pulled the keys from her ignition, gouged her in the chest with them, and tried to take custody of their son. At the time of this incident, Mrs. Czajkowski had a protective order issued by a court prohibiting Officer Garza from having any contact with her. Officer Garza did not charge her with any criminal or traffic violations (Taylor March/April 1994, 91).

Immediately following this confrontation, Mrs. Czajkowski reported the incident to authorities. Charges were filed against Officer Garza and an internal affairs investigation was commenced. Ultimately, Officer Garza pleaded guilty to battery. He received probation. The internal affairs investigation resulted in Officer Garza being suspended for thirty days without pay (Taylor March/April 1994, 91).

Robbery

On July 3, 1991, Deputy Michael Stanewich, a 10-year veteran of the San Diego sheriff's department, was killed by a fellow deputy who responded to the scene of a robbery in progress. Deputy Stanewich was working as a detective in the narcotics street team. In May of 1991, he was part of a team that executed a narcotics search warrant on the residence of Donald and Helen Van Ort. The search turned up negative for narcotics but detectives found a safe in the Van Ort's home containing around $60,000 in cash, jewelry, and coins (Jones 1994, B-1).

On July 3, 1991, Deputy Stanewich donned a ski mask, dark glasses, and a gun and went to the Van Orts' residence. Helen Van Ort, Donald's 80-year-old grandmother, answered the door. Deputy Stanewich said, "[I]t's a robbery, grandma." He then proceeded to attack and torture 35-year-old Donald Van Ort. Donald's girlfriend managed to escape the melee and called 911. Deputy Gary Steadman responded to the call. When Deputy Steadman arrived at the residence, he heard Helen Van Ort screaming for help. He entered the house through a back door and saw a man with a nylon stocking over his face pouring lighter fluid on a hog-tied Donald Van Ort, threatening to set him on fire, and demanding access to their safe. On two occasions, Deputy Steadman ordered the masked subject to freeze. When the subject refused, Deputy Steadman shot him. He then unmasked the subject and immediately exclaimed, "Mike!" Stanewich responded, "[Y]es, it's me, I'm wrong," and died ("Off-Duty Officer" 1996, 2).

Subsequent investigation of Deputy Stanewich's personnel file and his criminal record revealed a number of civilian complaints, some of which were substantiated, and a prior arrest for impersonating a police officer. Despite this assortment of disciplinary problems, Deputy Steadman was promoted through the ranks of the San Diego County sheriff's department from traffic duty to a position on the prestigious narcotics street team. This last promotion enabled him to operate with only minimal supervision (Jones 1994, B-1).

METHODS OF HANDLING MISCONDUCT

Historically, police departments have been responsible for the policing of the police. It has been accomplished through an internal police department hierarchy or chain of command. The police commissioner or chief is at the top of the chain of command and is responsible for the actions of the police force. The command structure is very similar to that found in the nation's military organizations. Essentially, the chain of command is the line officer to his or her supervisors, the supervisors to the administrators, administrators to the police chief, the chief to elected officials, and elected officials to the community. Ultimately, the police are accountable to the citizens of the city (Palmiotto 1997).

Police officers who break the law are subject to possible criminal prosecution as well as departmental sanctions by the chief. Officers who violate departmental procedures are subject to punishment by the chief. In determining the appropriate punishment, the controlling authority usually will take into account the nature of the offense, the victim, and the officer's service record. Possible sanctions may include a written reprimand that is placed in the officer's personnel file, loss of vacation, suspension without pay, or any combination thereof, or the ultimate sanction: termination from the police force. Officers subjected to administrative punishment have the right to a hearing where they can be represented by counsel and can appeal the findings and punishment to a court of competent jurisdiction (Palmiotto 1997).

In the 1990s the nation's police departments came under increased scrutiny concerning accountability for officer misconduct, especially police brutality and excessive use of force. From the Rodney King case in 1991 to the Mark Fuhrman tapes in 1995 and the Louima and Diallo beating cases of 1997 and 1998 respectively, civic associations and minority groups increasingly have been outspoken in their demand for stronger measures to hold officers accountable.

One method that has gained considerable support is the Civilian Review Board (CRB). In 1980, only thirteen U.S. cities had some form of civilian review of police. By the mid 1990s, there were almost 70 civilian review boards in place (Wilson 1996). CRBs are enacted by city government through legislation or by the mayor via executive order. Their design and structure varies from city to city. Some CRBs consist of citizens who are elected by the public, while others are controlled by members who are appointed by city government.

A recent trend has been to increase the powers allocated to the boards to make them more effective. These powers include subpoena power to compel witnesses and the authority to obtain police disciplinary records. CRBs generally function like an administrative hearing, where the members review complaints filed against police officers. Ultimately though, a CRB only makes findings and recommendations regarding disciplinary action that can be accepted or rejected by the police commissioner or chief. The CRB does not have the ability to enforce them (Wilson 1996).

Do CRBs work? A recent study of 17 CRBs nationwide provides evidence that review boards sustain more complaints and receive five times as many excessive force allegations than do internal affairs departments (Wilson 1996). As CRBs increase in numbers, power, and effectiveness, they have come under more stringent attack by police unions using ever-more sophisticated legal arguments to undermine them. Police unions have challenged the legal authority of CRBs in both state and federal courts. In particular, they have challenged the grant of subpoena powers as well as the power to compel police disciplinary records. Additionally, police unions have challenged a review board's existence before state public employees relations commissions as an unfair labor practice based on the local government's refusal to submit to mandatory bargaining negotiations. Most of these challenges have proven unsuccessful (Wilson 1996).

Another alternative to combat department-wide deficiencies in handling police misconduct is federal intervention. In 1994, with the passage of 42 U.S.C. Sec. 14141, the U.S Department of Justice (DOJ) received broadened enforcement powers to investigate department-wide patterns or practices of misconduct in local police departments and to collect statistics on police abuse. An example of the use of this statute can be found in Pittsburgh, PA (Curriden 1996).

In 1997, DOJ filed a lawsuit for declaratory and injunctive relief against the Pittsburgh Bureau of Police (PBP). The lawsuit was settled before trial by consent order. Under the terms of the order, the PBP agreed to implement sweeping remedial measures specifically designed to address systemic problems within the department. "These problems included racism, gender bias, and other basic police attitudes which lead to the excessive use of force and other related police misconduct, the police code of silence, failure of supervision, monitoring and discipline, and the lack of proper reporting procedures" (Taylor 1997, 115). This case should prove helpful to police misconduct reform advocates in developing a standard for establishing proper police procedures and monitoring (Taylor 1997).

RAMIFICATIONS OF POLICE OFFICER MISCONDUCT ON SOCIETY

In 1871, Congress enacted Title 42 of the United States Code. Section 1983 of that act provides redress to individual citizens for violations of federal constitutional rights, as provided for in the Bill of Rights, as well as specific rights guaranteed by federal statutes. In recent times, this statute has been used to combat police misconduct. Since the 1970s, the U.S. Supreme Court has carved out a body of law, which has brought financial liability to municipalities based on the misconduct of its police officers (Palmiotto 1997).

This section will set forth a legal analysis of municipal liability for police officer misconduct and a review of the cases that were discussed previously as they relate to municipal liability. In the end, the reader should be able to answer two basic questions: (1) What are the legal standards relating to municipal liability for police officer misconduct? and (2) When will a municipal government be responsible financially for the misconduct of its police officers?

To understand the legal issues involved in this section, a cursory examination of 42 U.S.C. Sec. 1983, is necessary. That section provides in relevant part:

> Every person who, under the color of any statute, ordinance, regulation, custom, or usage, of any State or Territory or the District of Columbia, subjects, or causes to be subjected, any citizen of the United States or other person within the jurisdiction thereof to the deprivation of any rights, privileges, or immunities secured by the Constitution and laws, shall be liable to the party injured in an action at law, suit in equity, or other proper proceeding for redress. (42 U.S.C. Sec. 1983)

The leading case dealing with municipal liability is *Monell v. Department of Social Services,* 436 U.S. 658, 663 (1978), which established the premise that municipalities could be "persons" under Section 1983, thereby giving rise to liability. After *Monell,* a municipal government could be liable for the actions of its employees providing that a plaintiff could prove that a municipal policy or custom was the moving force behind a constitutional violation perpetrated by a person acting under color of law (*Monell* 1978).

We can break this ruling into three distinct requirements. First, there must be a showing of a municipal policy or custom. Secondly, there must be a constitutional violation. Lastly, the actor must commit the constitutional violation based on a municipal policy or custom while under color of law. All three requirements must be satisfied before liability can be established. A large body of law has developed in each area with some of the federal courts adopting different interpretations for each requirement (Kean 1999).

POLICY OR CUSTOM

The definition of what conduct or action constitutes a municipal policy or custom has taken many years to develop. It began to take shape in *City of Oklahoma v. Tuttle,* 471 U.S. 808 (1985). According to court records, the *Tuttle* case involved a police officer who shot and killed a fleeing felon. The officer responded to a robbery in progress. Upon arriving at the scene, he came in contact with Tuttle and attempted to detain him. A struggle ensued whereby Tuttle broke free and fled. The police officer gave chase and as Tuttle cleared the outside door of the establishment, the officer saw him crouch down in an apparent attempt to reach inside his boot. Believing that his life was in danger, the officer shot and killed Tuttle. A toy gun was found in Tuttle's boot.

The ruling held that "proof of a single incident of unconstitutional activity is not sufficient to impose liability under *Monell,* unless proof of the incident includes proof that it was caused by an existing, unconstitutional municipal policy itself attributed to a municipal policymaker" (*Tuttle* 1985 823-824). The essence of this holding was that a plaintiff cannot establish a municipal policy or custom of inadequate training based solely on a showing of a single bad act; he or she must uncover the specifics of police department policies to demonstrate the requisite fault and causation.

Shortly after the *Tuttle* decision, the Supreme Court once again addressed this issue. In *Pembaur v. City of Cincinnati,* 475 U.S. 469 (1986), the court ruled that a municipal government could be held liable for a constitutional deprivation for a single decision, provided that the decision-maker possessed final authority to establish municipal policy with respect to the action ordered. The court took great pain to distinguish between the exercise of delegated policymaking authority, i.e., final authority, and the exercise of mere discretion. In the case of the latter, no liability would follow. The court stressed that final authority requires that the official have ultimate responsibility for the policy that causes the deprivation of constitutional rights.

In 1989, the Court ruled that the policy or custom prong of municipal liability could be established by a showing of deliberate indifference to the constitutional rights of individuals the police serve (*City of Canton v. Harris,* 489 U.S. 378 (1989). In *Harris,* the plaintiff alleged that the police violated her

Fourteenth Amendment due process rights while in police custody because she did not receive medical aid for an emotional ailment. The plaintiff asserted that the municipal policy in question delegated sole authority for determining the medical needs of prisoners to shift commanders but failed to adequately train them beyond basic first aid. However, the Court required plaintiffs to show that the deliberate indifference caused the injury. This causation element proved to be very important to the development of future case law (Kean 1999).

For the purpose Section 1983 litigation, a plaintiff can establish a municipal policy or custom by proving: (1) a policy directly established and documented by the municipality; or (2) a decision by a policy-maker possessing the final authority to establish municipal policy with respect to the action ordered; or (3) a deliberate indifference to the training of police officers (Kean 1999). "The latter is the most prevalent avenue of approach in police misconduct lawsuits, taking the form of allegations of inadequate training, inadequate police officer supervision, and inadequate disciplinary practices and procedures" (Kean 1999).

CONSTITUTIONAL VIOLATION

Once a litigant establishes that a municipal policy or custom was in effect, he or she must prove a constitutional injury. This involves proof that the injury was caused by a violation of a constitutional right. These rights include all individual rights conferred by the Bill of Rights as well as those established by federal statutes. However, not all federal statutes are covered: statutes that were not intended to create enforceable rights and those explicitly excluded by Congress do not provide actionable rights under Section 1983. Police misconduct cases, brought pursuant to alleged violations of Section 1983, generally involve illegal search and seizure violations of the Fourth and Fourteenth Amendments, and allegations of the use of excessive force in violation of the Fourteenth Amendment's due process and equal protection clauses (Kean 1999).

The standard of proof requirement for a constitutional injury was addressed by the Supreme Court in *Collins v. City of Harker Heights,* 530 U.S. 115 (1992). *Collins* involved a claim from a former sanitation worker that the city failed to train and warn its employees of hazardous working conditions. The plaintiff sufficiently proved a deliberately indifferent training policy. However, the court held that there was no constitutional injury because there was no Fourteenth Amendment due process right to minimum levels of workplace safety and the city's conduct was not arbitrary or conscience shocking.

In *County of Sacramento v. Lewis,* 118 S.Ct. 1708 (1998), the Supreme Court addressed the issue of constitutional injury in the context of police officer misconduct. *Lewis* involved an accident resulting from a high-speed police chase. The Court ruled that in order to show a constitutional injury in this context, the petitioner must show that the police officer intended to cause harm. This holding made the constitutional injury requirement in high-speed police chases even tougher to prove than under the *Collins* standard. The Court reasoned that a higher standard of proof was necessary because police officers facing a potential high-speed chase scenario are subjected to similar demands for fast action and evaluation, and the Court determined that a similar standard should govern their conduct. In the context of Section 1983 cases, it is unlikely that courts will define the arbitrary and conscience-shocking standards to always require intent to harm as in the case at hand (Kean 1999).

UNDER COLOR OF LAW

The last prong of the analysis involves a showing that the municipal employee was acting under color of law, while pursuing a municipal policy at the time of the constitutional injury. In *United States v. Classic*, 313 U.S. 2999 (1941), the Supreme Court stated that "misuse of power, possessed by virtue of state law and made possible only because the wrongdoer is clothed with the authority of state law, is the action taken 'under color of law.'" One of the early Supreme Court cases addressing this requirement in the context of police officer misconduct is *Screws v. United States*, 325 U.S. 91 (1945). *Screws* involved an African-American who was arrested and ultimately beaten to death by three police officers. The Court ruled that the officers acted under color of law because the requirement includes action under the pretense of law. It stated that while "acts of officers in the ambit of their personal pursuits are plainly excluded . . . acts of officers who undertake to perform official duties are included whether they hew to the line of their authority or over step it" (*Screws* 1945, 111).

In evaluating the under color of law requirement, courts employ a totality of the circumstances approach (Kean 1999). As the sixth Circuit Court wrote in *Stengel v. Belcher*, 522 F.2d 438 (6th Cir. 1975), "the fact that a police officer is on or off duty, or in or out of uniform is not controlling. It is the nature of the act performed, not the clothing of the actor or even the status of being on duty or off duty, which determines whether the officer has acted under color of law." Additionally, courts pay particular attention to the officer's motivation at the time of the action because privately motivated misconduct may fall outside of the color of law requirement (*Screws* 1945).

RESULTS FROM THE CASE ANALYSIS

Returning to the cases set forth in the section titled Case Analysis, this section will explore how some courts have applied these standards. The first case concerned the sexual assault of Eddie Parrish. Ms. Parrish filed suit in federal court pursuant to Section 1983 against Officer Luckie, both in his individual and official capacity, and the police chief. She alleged a deprivation of her constitutional rights in that she was falsely arrested and raped. Further, she urged that the "police chief had acted with deliberate indifference in implementing a policy of avoiding, ignoring, and covering up complaints of physical and sexual abuse by Luckie and others" (*Parrish* 1992, 204).

The case was tried before a jury. Ultimately, the jury determined that both Officer Luckie and the police chief were liable for the misconduct in their official capacities. It awarded damages in the amount of $150,00 against Officer Luckie and $50,000 against the police chief. The city appealed (*Parrish* 1992).

On appeal, the city argued that the evidence was insufficient to show a city policy or custom of failing to accept, act on, or investigate complaints of violence by police officers. The court applied the standard enunciated in *Harris v. City of Pagedale,* 821 F.2d 499, 504 (8th Cir.) *cert. denied,* 484 U.S. 986, 108 S.Ct. 504, 98 L.Ed.2d 502 (1987). In *Harris,* the court held that "to establish a city's liability based on its failure to prevent misconduct by employees, the plaintiff must show that city officials had knowledge of prior incidents of police misconduct and deliberately failed to take remedial actions" (*Parrish* 1992, 203).

In applying the above standard, the court found the record to be replete with evidence supporting the plaintiff's case. It highlighted the evidence presented at trial regarding Officer Luckie's disciplinary record as well as a number of citizen complaints filed against him. Also, the department had procedures in place that required a citizen to follow through in writing any complaints against officers. If they did not do so, the complaints would be "unsubstantiated" without further inquiry. In sum, the court stated that "overwhelming evidence supported the jury's finding that North Little Rock police offices operated a system where reports of physical or sexual assault by officers were discouraged, ignored, or covered up" (*Parrish* 1992, 205).

The next case concerned the murder of Lisa Knick. Mrs. Knick was murdered by her husband, Officer Jerry Knick, while he was on duty with the Lexington Police Department. Mrs. Knick's estate filed suit under Section 1983 against the City of Lexington and the police chief. The estate alleged that Mrs. Knick's murder resulted from municipal policies and practices which included the department's failure to train and discipline Officer Knick and its retention of him on the force despite a history of abusive behavior. At trial, evidence was presented that showed Officer Knick had a troubled past which included prior complaints of abusive behavior and domestic violence (Taylor 1997).

In an unpublished opinion, the court dismissed the case. It held that, "Officer Knick's murder of his wife was in no way connected to his duties or responsibilities as a police officer. Officer Knick was not arresting his wife, serving papers, or performing any other police duty. Officer Knick was not acting under the pretense of the law." According to the court, case law indicates that if a police officer misuses the power he or she possesses, Section 1983 liability may follow. However, it found that "Knick did not misuse any power he possessed as a policeman while he was in his home arguing with his wife. Knick was not clothed in indicia of state authority even though he was on duty, was in uniform, and was using his service revolver when he shot and killed his wife. This was a garden-style domestic dispute which had a tragic ending." *Vincent v. City of Lexington,* No. 91-0048-L (W.D.Va.Aug 28, 1992) The court went to great lengths to analyze Officer Knick's motives behind the killing and determined that his actions were privately motivated by his problematic marriage.

The Czajkowski case also culminated with litigation pursuant to Section 1983. Recall that court records revealed that Officer Garza, while on duty, assaulted his wife in the presence of his partner, Officer Hrebanek. The main issue in this case was whether Czajkowski's injury, which involved expert evidence that she suffered from post-traumatic stress disorder stemming from the assault, resulted from municipal policies or practices of the Chicago police department. In establishing this requirement, court records show that Czajkowski presented evidence that the Chicago police department failed to respond to Officer Garza's acts of domestic violence, failed to respond to domestic violence on a department-wide level, and generally failed to adequately respond to excessive force, including domestic violence (Taylor 1997).

There was extensive discovery in this case that ultimately revealed substantial testimonial evidence supporting the plaintiff's claims. "The evidence came from five major sources: women who worked in the battered women's network, the director of the Office of Professional Standards, the deputy superintendent in charge of internal disciplinary investigations, the superintendent of police, and the supervisory police personnel, including those who ran the problem employee division" (Taylor 1997, 92). Court records indicated that 10 percent of excessive force complaints involved reports of domestic violence allegations committed by police officers. Police officers accused of domestic violence rarely were arrested or prosecuted. Moreover, a former deputy superintendent testified that "on at least two occasions he raised these shortcomings with successive superintendents and proposed a change in policy but each time his proposal was rejected because he could not 'break through the police culture'"(Taylor 1997, 92–93).

At the close of discovery, the parties litigated several motions and held numerous pretrial conferences dealing with documents and witness testimony. For the most part, the rulings favored the plaintiff although the court did attempt to narrow the focus of the case to evidence involving the domestic violence aspect of the claim. However, on the eve of trial, the case was settled (Taylor 1997).

Another case discussed previously involved Deputy Michael Stanewich of the San Diego County Sheriff's Department who attempted to rob the Van Orts in their home shortly after his department had executed a search warrant and found a safe containing cash, jewelry, and coins. Like the other cases previously reviewed, the Van Orts filed suit pursuant to Section 1983 against Stanewich's estate, San Diego County, and the sheriff, alleging various violations of their constitutional rights ("Off-Duty Officer" 1996).

At trial, the plaintiffs tried to show that Deputy Stanewich was a time bomb waiting to explode. In particular, they highlighted his disciplinary record, which contained eleven citizen complaints, six of which were sustained by investigators. They emphasized that, in spite of his disciplinary problems, Deputy Stanewich was promoted through the ranks of the department. Countering this argument, the defendants presented expert testimony suggesting that Deputy Stanewich's superiors were unable to properly evaluate his character because under state law, largely resulting from the lobbying efforts of police unions, disciplinary records of deputies could not be considered during yearly employee evaluations unless the misconduct occurred in the past twelve months (Jones 1994, B-1).

The only issue before the jury was whether the sheriff's department was deliberately indifferent to the public safety by failing to have an early warning system for officers with repetitive patterns of misconduct. In this regard, the evidence established that no other police department in California had an early warning system in place at the time of the incident. However, the jury found for the plaintiff and awarded $850,000 to the Van Orts. It apportioned eighty percent of the verdict to the county because the sheriff's department should have realized that Stanewich was an accident waiting to happen (Jones 1994, B-1).

After the jury rendered its decision, the district judge set aside the verdict. Judge Gonzalez ruled that, "[T]he primary evidence before the jury on causation was Deputy Stanewich's disciplinary record. On the basis of that record, it was foreseeable to the County that he might occasionally use excessive force toward citizens in the course of his duties. However, it is difficult to see how that record makes the violent and malicious acts Stanewich committed toward the Van Orts foreseeable to the county. Deputy Stanewich's disciplinary record cannot support a finding that he would use information gained in the course of his employment to commit wholly independent crimes . . . no other sheriff's deputy in history had ever committed any crime similar to his" (Jones, 1994 B-1).

This case illustrates another aspect of Section 1983 litigation, that a municipality will not be held liable for the actions of its employees where the proximate cause of the injury is not foreseeable. In essence, it appears that the court applied ordinary personal injury standards of causation analysis to reach its conclusion. Can the same result be reached by applying the "under color of law" analysis in *Screws*?

It is evident that the interplay of the legal requirements of Section 1983 is very complicated. So much so that there is a split of authority in United States Circuit Courts as to its application (Kean 1999). Nonetheless, Section 1983 continues to provide an effective redress for citizens who experience misconduct at the hands of those police officers entrusted with their protection.

However, Section 1983 has come under attack recently by national police organizations and California legislators who maintain that reform is needed to prevent the skyrocketing expense of litigation and punitive damage awards. These groups lobbied for the enactment of the Law Enforcement Officer's Civil Liability Act of 1995 (H.R. 1446). Advocates in favor of the bill suggest that our tax dollars are better spent putting additional police officers on the streets rather than litigating frivolous lawsuits. These groups maintain that the only persons benefiting from Section 1983 litigation are the lawyers who file the suits. If this bill were passed, it would have effected the following changes to Section 1983 litigation:

1. Raised the standard of proof for punitive damages to clear and convincing evidence of conduct "specifically intended unlawfully to cause serious personal injury" or conduct "engaged in with flagrant indifference to the rights of the injured party and with an awareness that such conduct is likely to result in serious personal injury and is unlawful,
2. Limited the amount of punitive damages to $10,000, and
3. Limited the recovery of attorney's fees to one-third of the monetary damage award (Taylor and Zimmerman 1996, 1).

Opponents of the bill have labeled it the "Rogue Officer's Bill of Rights" (Taylor and Zimmerman 1996, 1). They claim that the bill seeks "to protect officers who engage in the most serious forms of misconduct from any serious civil penalties because it would eliminate civil rights lawsuits against police departments except under circumstances where the compensatory damages are obvious and dramatic" (Taylor and Zimmerman 1996, 6–7).

Opponents further stress that limiting attorney's fees and punitive damages would effectively end litigation in this area. They regard Section 1983 as an important tool in deterring and punishing police departments who are either unwilling or unable to effectively control and police their own. Opponents contend that most of the victims in these cases are viewed by juries as unsympathetic because they have been convicted of crimes, sometimes very onerous ones, and usually the same crimes for which the officer and the municipality are being sued. Given this perception of victims, juries rarely award large sums of money for compensatory damages. Opponents also contend that because these cases often involve complex, time-intensive preparation and litigation, awards based solely on compensatory damages and contingency fees would result in attorneys receiving less-than minimum wage for their work. As a result, less than meritorious cases would not be brought into the court system and out-of-control police departments would continue unrestricted (Taylor and Zimmerman 1996, 6–10).

In sum, it is apparent that the controversy surrounding Section 1983 litigation is not easily resolved. Both sides have valid arguments in support of their positions. Only time will tell as to how we as a society ultimately settle this most important issue. But no matter which side you support, you must accept the premise that something must be done to deter and punish officers who violate citizens' constitutional rights.

CONCLUSION

Throughout the course of this article, several important issues regarding police misconduct were explored. Specifically, actual incidents of violent police misconduct as well as some of the case laws illustrating various judicial approaches designed to handle them were examined. While you may agree or disagree with the outcome of some or all of the cases, hopefully, you have a gained a better understanding of how the end result was reached and what standards were applied to get there.

Ultimately, the entire legal system is based on accountability, deterrence, and punishment. We, as citizens of the United States, have influenced the enactment of laws either through custom or statute that control our conduct. Should police officers be treated differently? Should we trust police departments to police themselves? Do we allow ordinary citizens or corporations for that matter to police themselves? Do we turn a blind eye to our legacy of police brutality, excessive use of force, and corruption?

Indeed, the United States is governed by a Constitution, which by its design is premised on a variety of checks and balances to ensure that the various entities are kept under control. It seems only fitting that police departments, which are entrusted with controlling individual and collective conduct, should be subjected to similar review. While the particular means necessary to accomplish that end are debatable, we must strive to hold overzealous and/or unfit police officers accountable for their actions. Otherwise, we are likely to lose much of the freedom that our founding fathers fought so hard to achieve.

REFERENCES

City of Canton v. Harris, 489 U.S. 378 (1989).
City of Oklahoma v. Tuttle, 471 U.S. 808 (1985).
Collins v. City of Harker Heights, 530 U.S. 115 (1992).

County of Sacramento v. Lewis, 118 S.Ct. 1708 (1998).

Curriden, Mark, "When Good Cops Go Bad," *American Bar Association Journal,* Vol. 82, May 1996, 62–65.

Jones, J. Harry, "County 'Not Liable' for Rogue Cop/Judge Sets Aside $680,000 Judgment in Stanewich Case," *The San Diego Union-Tribune,* (November 24, 1994), B-1.

Kean, Seth M., "Municipal Liability for Off-Duty Police Misconduct under Section 1983: the 'Under Color of Law' Requirement," *Boston University Law Review,* Vol. 79, February 1999, 195–230.

Monell v. Department of Social Services, 436 U.S. 658, 663 (1978).

"Off-Duty Officer Terrorizes Man and Grandmother," *National Bulletin on Police Misconduct,* Vol. 5, (Nov. 1996), 2.

Palmiotto, Michael J., *Policing Concepts, Strategies, and Current Issues in American Police Forces,* (North Carolina: Carolina Academic Press, 1997).

Parrish v. Luckie, 963 F.2d 201 (8th Cir. 1992).

Pembaur v. City of Cincinnati, 475 U.S. 469 (1986).

Screws v. United States, 325 U.S. 91 (1945).

Stengel v. Belcher, 522 F.2d 438 (6th Cir. 1975).

Taylor, G. Flint, "Case Studies of Police Domestic Violence," *Police Misconduct and Civil Rights Law Report,* Vol.4, No. 8, March/April 1994, 91–95.

Taylor, G. Flint, "Case Studies of Police Domestic Violence," *Police Misconduct and Civil Rights Law Report,* Vol.4, No.9, May/June 1994, 102–104.

Taylor, G. Flint, "U.S. Government Obtains Pittsburgh Consent Decree," *Police Misconduct and Civil Rights Law Report,* Vol. 5, No. 10, July/August 1997, 114–116.

Taylor, G. Flint and Clifford S. Zimmerman, "Sections 1983 and 1988 Under Congressional Attack: The Testimony For and Against H.R. 1446," *Police Misconduct and Civil Rights Law Report,* Vol. 5, No. 1, Jan/Feb 1996, 1–10.

United States v. Classic, 313 U.S. 2999 (1941).

Van Ort v. Estate of Stanewich, 92 F.3d 831 (California, 1996).

Vincent v. City of Lexington, No. 91-0048-L (W.D.Va. Aug 28, 1992).

Wilson, Lynn, "Democracy vs. Collective Bargaining: Countering Police Union Attacks on Citizen Review," *Police Misconduct and Civil Rights' Law Report,* Vol. 5, No. 5, Sept/Oct 1996, 49–58.

ARTICLE 30

POLICE CIVIL LIABILITY: AN ANALYSIS OF SECTION 1983 ACTIONS IN THE EASTERN AND SOUTHERN DISTRICTS OF NEW YORK

*David K. Chiabi**
Jersey City State College

ABSTRACT: *This article examines the Section 1983 civil damage remedy and the Bivens-type action—the direct claim of the victim of official wrongdoing to obtain compensation for the denial of his or her Fourth Amendment rights. Using court records of cases filed under this statute from 1983 to 1987 in the Eastern and Southern districts of New York, the study determined: (1) the nature and volume of damages awarded by the courts in Section 1983/Bivens actions, (2) the differences in the amount of damages recovered from bench trials, jury trials, and settlements, (3) the parties involved in Section 1983 suits, (4) the trials and settlements, and (5) the time and resources spent by the parties and the courts on these cases. The analysis of the data was used to gauge the impact of these suits on individual police and police administrators.*

This article examines the claims of victims of official (usually police) wrongdoing who seek to obtain compensation for the denial of their Fourth Amendment rights. Police functions, which sometimes require the use of force, often place the police at loggerheads with members of the public and occasionally result in suits against police for alleged violations of citizens' constitutional and civil rights. Although other remedies (e.g., state tort actions) are available to individuals whose constitutional rights have been violated, plaintiffs' lawyers generally consider Section 1983 suits and *Bivens* actions the most effective means of obtaining relief (Kappeler, 1993; McCoy, 1986, 1987).

The study examines the Section 1983/*Bivens* damage remedy in the Eastern and Southern districts of New York. It analyzes Section 1983/*Bivens* actions filed in these districts from 1983 to 1987. The study focuses on plaintiffs'

*Direct all correspondence to: David K. Chiabi, Jersey City State College, 2039 Kennedy Blvd., Jersey City, NJ 07305-1597.

David K. Chiabi, "Police Civil Liability: An Analysis of Section 1983 Actions in the Eastern and Southern Districts of New York" (as appeared in the *American Journal of Criminal Justice*, Volume 21, Number 1, 1996, pp. 85–104). Reprinted with permission.

efforts and their difficulties encountered in pursuing civil damages. It further identifies the types of defendants (individual police officers, police chiefs, departments, cities, and state) and ascertains their liability.

In order to develop a profile of Section 1983 and *Bivens* actions, and to uncover the range of damages recovered from the actions, this article poses a number of research questions: (1) What types of constitutional violations are police officers alleged to have committed under Section 1983/*Bivens*? (2) Who are the parties involved in Section 1983/*Bivens* suits? (3) What are the chances (and degree) of success in prosecuting Section 1983/*Bivens* actions? (4) What methods are used to dispose of Section 1983/*Bivens* actions? (5) How much court time is taken up by Section 1983/*Bivens* actions? (6) What are the nature and volume of money damages gained in Section 1983/*Bivens* actions? (7) How does the amount of damages vary by nature of violation, manner of disposition, and amount of damages asked in the complaint? (8) What factors predict successful prosecution of Section 1983/*Bivens* action and the award of damages?

RESEARCH DESIGN AND DATA COLLECTION

Data were collected from the Federal Southern and Eastern District Courts of New York. The jurisdiction of these two courts covers both large and small police departments of suburban towns, cities, and counties. Because some have questioned the use of federal courts to vindicate the wide array of rights asserted in Section 1983 actions (Eisenberg, 1982), an additional reason to focus on the federal court experience was to determine the extent to which these actions fill the federal dockets. These two districts were selected because their jurisdictions cover both large and very small police departments in the New York City metropolitan area and are also characterized by a high volume of these types of cases in recent years (Adams, 1991).

The cases in the study covered a five-year period between January 1983 and December 1987. Of the 465 cases examined, 270 (58%) were from the Eastern district and 195 (42%) from the Southern district. More cases from the Eastern district are included because it had a better coding system, which made it easier to identify Section 1983/*Bivens* type cases. Moreover, more cases would be expected from the because of its greater population, even though the arrest rate is higher in the Southern district. (From 1993 to 1997 the Eastern district had a population of approximately 7,240,451, while the Southern district had a population of 4,551,933. The arrest rate per 100,000 was 4,559 and 7,522 for the Eastern and Southern districts, respectively.) For reasons not ascertainable from this study, the crime rate is similar in the two districts, but the number of Section 1983/*Bivens* actions per 100,000 arrests is higher in the Eastern district.

Data collection focused on lawsuits filed against law enforcement personnel. In addition, all civil rights cases filed during this period were searched to identify those Section 1983 cases that alleged civil rights and constitutional violations by police officers, police departments, the state, and/or any federal agency. Information from the court files provided a profile of the nature of civil and constitutional violations, characteristics of the different parties, and the manner of disposition of the suits and the outcomes. Every identified Section 1983/*Bivens* action was included in the study.

Once a case file was located, it was reviewed to collect information on the parties involved, causes of action, police involvement, means of disposition of the case, case identification number, and the information needed to track cases to their final disposition. This information was recorded on a data collection form.

Cases were not included in the study if the case file failed to state explicitly that it was a Section 1983 or a *Bivens*-type action, or that the violation alleged involved the Fourth Amendment. All cases were also checked individually for police involvement. Cases were included in the study only if they involved an allegation of police misconduct.

To complement the case record analyses, a few interviews were conducted with individuals who had dealt with Section 1983 cases. These included police department personnel, lawyers for the office of corporation counsel, and plaintiffs' attorneys. These general information interviews were used to identify factors and considerations that affect settlements, the range of damages, and police policy decisions. They also allowed for a contrast of the perspective of plaintiffs' attorneys with that of corporation counsels representing the different police agencies.

Other data used for the study were drawn from reports of civil trials, annual reports of the Director of the Administrative Office of the United States Courts, reports of the New York City Civilian Complaint Review Board, police records, and reports of the New York City Comptroller's Office. The court records and the annual reports of the Director of the Administrative Office of the United States Courts provided data on the administering and processing of civil cases and in particular on the time of disposition of other civil cases. Data on the number of police complaints alleged against the New York City police departments and amounts of civil damages paid by New York City were obtained in the reports from the New York City Comptroller's Office, the police department, and the Civilian Review Board. These data were used to gauge the effect of Section 1983/*Bivens* actions on the New York City metropolitan area.

A number of limitations were encountered during data collection. A fundamental source of information was the actual complaint, which typically originated from an account of the events of police misconduct as related by the plaintiff. Neither the complaint nor most other case information, however, provided the defendant's version of the incident in question. Causes of action were recorded as they were alleged without consideration for plaintiff's accuracy or whether such causes of action were ever fully proved. Because in general a good number of cases are settled out of court, documentation of the terms of such settlements, particularly the amount of the awards, was sometimes impossible to obtain or too difficult to attempt.

Determining which cases are Section 1983/*Bivens* cases presented another problem, Most civil suits include multiple claims, of which Section 1983 and *Bivens* claims are but two of the categories. It is possible that some cases filed under other claims might have been omitted if they could not be identified as Section 1983/*Bivens* actions. In summary, although the study had a number of limitations, these limitations may not significantly affect the findings. The limitations may not appear to introduce any biases, although it cannot be completely assumed that the missing data will have no effect on the findings.

This exploratory study considers the impact of several independent variables on the processing and award of damages under Section 1983/*Bivens* lawsuits. Independent variables in the study were the causes of action, malice, amount of damages asked, type of defendant, manner of disposition, type of representation, district, and time of disposition. Two dependent variables were measured: (1) the successful prosecution of an action, and (2) the amount of damages awarded.

To obtain descriptive statistics on all the variables in the study, frequency analyses were run. To study the relationship between the categorical variables addressed by research questions, a series of crosstabulation analyses were conducted. Correlational analyses and bivariate scatterplot analyses were used to study the relationship between the variables when the data were measured on interval scales. In the case of such complex data such as causes of action and defendant type, factor analysis was used as a data reduction technique. Following the classification of the factors derived from these analysis, indices were constructed that were be used in subsequent analyses involving these variables. Finally, two logistic regression analyses were used to test which of the variables in the study have an impact on the successful prosecution of cases in Section 1983/*Bivens* actions and whether damages were awarded in Section 1983/*Bivens* actions.

ANALYSIS AND PRESENTATION OF FINDINGS

The study found that assault and battery, false arrest, and false imprisonment were the causes of action most often alleged by plaintiffs. Another finding was that causes of action tended to occur in three clusters: (1) violations involving individual liberties (false arrest, false imprisonment, and malicious prosecution); (2) those involving property rights (trespass, invasion of privacy, and search and seizure); and (3) those involving the use of violence (assault and battery and other violations). Approximately 82% of the cases had multiple defendants. More of the cases (32%) were disposed of by settlement than by any other means. The median time of disposition for all cases was about 25 months. Approximately 41% of the actions were not successfully prosecuted. Overwhelmingly, *pro se* actions were not successful (77% of the 115 *pro se* cases were not successfully prosecuted, in contrast to 41% of the 250 counseled cases). Nineteen percent of the cases resulted in recorded damages; the mean award was $15,000, and the majority of cases resulting in damages were settled. The districts studied did not differ in terms of the violations alleged, but did differ in number of plaintiffs and the frequency of representation by counsel. Eighty-two percent of plaintiffs in the Eastern district were represented by council, as opposed to 67% in the Southern district.

Violations

Most plaintiffs alleged multiple causes of action. The top three complaints were assault and battery (59%), false arrests (57%), and false imprisonment (47%). Among the charges that were made less frequently, malicious prosecution was alleged in 28% of actions. Illegal searches and seizures were alleged in 17% of the cases. Invasion of privacy was alleged in 10% of the cases and 5% of the actions alleged trespass. There were numerous other actions, including actions for abuse of due process, conspiracy, harassment, and false testimony.

A factor analysis of the cluster of violations suggested a way to classify Section 1983/*Bivens* cases. A principal component analysis using a varimax solution resulted in three factors. Factor one is comprised of false arrest, false imprisonment, and malicious prosecution (titled "liberty violations" for the purpose of this study). Factor two is comprised of trespass, invasion of privacy, and search and seizure (titled "property/privacy violations"). Factor three is comprised of assault and battery, officer's malice, and fifth Amendment violations regarding confessions and interrogations (called "violent violations").

In order to classify cases into groups for use in subsequent analyses, indices were computed following the classifications obtained from the factor analysis results. Items on each scale were given an equal weight. Three categories of just "liberty," "property," or "violence" cases were obtained. Liberty refers to all violations that affected individual's freedom, property refers to all violations that affected property, and violence refers to all violations with an element of violence. The mixed category, therefore, included cases with a combination of types of violations. Cases in the "mixed" category were further subdivided into "liberty and violence," "property and violence," and "liberty and property." Table 1 shows the final result of the classification process.

Parties to Section 1983 and Bivens Actions

Plaintiffs were classified as either single or multiple and whether they were represented by counsel or filed their cases *pro se*. Unfortunately, limited and

TABLE 1

NATURE OF VIOLATION

Type of violation	Number of cases	Percent
Just liberty	74	16
Just property/privacy	12	2
Just violence	92	20
(Mixed *n* = 287		
Liberty and violence	149	32
Property and violence	20	4
Liberty and property	17	4
All 3 indices	58	12
Unknown	43	9
Total	465	100
Any liberty violation	298	64
Any property violation	107	23
Any violence violation	319	69

inconsistent data in the court files made it impossible to ascertain any other specific characteristics of the plaintiffs. Most cases (72%) were brought by single plaintiffs and with counsel. The study examined the *pro se* plaintiff and the importance of legal representation in Section 1983/*Bivens* actions. One hundred and fifteen cases were brought by *pro se* plaintiffs. The vast majority (92%) of *pro se* cases and the majority of counsel cases (72%) had a single plaintiff.

There were two major classifications of defendants: individual defendants (i.e., individual police officers and police chiefs) and governmental defendants (i.e., department, city/county, state, and federal government). The individual police officer was a defendant in 91% of the cases. The police chief was named as defendant in 28% of the suits, while the department was a defendant in 44%. Cities and other counties were named as defendants in 61% of the cases. In only 3% of the cases the state was a defendant, and the federal government was named as a defendant in only 2%. In 82% of the cases, multiple defendants were named. A cross-tabulation analysis (see Table 2) indicated that there was a relationship between the type of plaintiff and the type of representation. A majority of cases with counsel named had the municipality as defendant, while *pro se* plaintiffs were twice as likely to name individuals as defendants and almost three times as likely to name departments as defendants.

Case Disposition

Cases were primarily disposed of by settlement or dismissal. Only 11% of Section 1983/*Bivens* suits went to trial, with 5% tried on the bench and 6% by jury. Approximately 23% of the total number of the cases studied were

TABLE 2

CROSS-TABULATION OF TYPE OF REPRESENTATION BY DEFENDANT

Type of defendant	Counsel	Type of Representation Pro se	Total
Officer	15	30	15
Chief	4	10	6
Dept.	10	27	14
City	51	21	4
County	18	7	16
State	3	5	3
Fed.	3	1	2

Defendant groups reclassified into individual and government representation.

Individual	19	39	21
Government	81	61	79
	100% (349)	100% (112)	100% (461)

dismissed. Most of the dismissed cases were *pro se* complaints. Only 2 cases (0.4%) were resolved by an uncontested default for the plaintiff. About 12% of the actions were disposed by summary judgment. Table 3 presents the manner of case dispositions in the two districts.

Dispositions listed as "other" (9%) consisted of actions resolved by none of the methods listed above. These included actions that were withdrawn by the complainant, discontinued, or consolidated with other actions in the same court. Open cases (those civil suits still pending), mostly actions brought in 1986 and 1987, accounted for 21% of the cases. Twenty-one cases with unknown manner of disposition may have been open cases. Sometimes actions were marked closed without stating any specific method of disposition.

Time of Disposition

Cases in which violence was alleged were disposed in a slightly longer time than cases alleging liberty and property violations. Table 4 shows the time of disposition by type of action. Mixed cases were further analyzed to see if any differences could be found (property/violence and liberty/violence had similar medians of 28 months, while liberty/property had 25 months). Both the mean and median time of *pro se* actions are lower than that of cases presented by counsel. The median time of disposition for all cases studied is 25 months. The average time of disposition for trials in this study is 26 months. The median time of trial for bench and jury trials for the study was 27 and 39 months, respectively.

Damages

Of the 465 cases analyzed, 90 (19%) resulted in total monetary relief of $4,536,702 to the plaintiffs. The amounts awarded ranged from $400 to $950,000. The average amount of damages awarded was $50,408 for suits that produced damages, but the median award was $15,000. This mean was disproportionately increased by three cases that involved the use of excessive force and accounted for almost half of the total damages. These three actions cases accounted for $2,070,500 of the total recovery of $4,536,702 for the 90 cases that resulted in damages. For the other 87 cases, the average award was $28,295.

Although the data show that approximately 20% of the cases had damages awarded, there are other indications that more cases resulted in damages. According to the court records, 148 (32%) were settled, and the court records indicated that 70 settled cases resulted in some form of damages. However, the interviews showed that settlement of these cases usually resulted in damages for the plaintiff. It is therefore probable that damages were awarded in the remaining 78 (17%) cases settled. Thus, damage award cases could have been as high as 37%.

Only one *pro se* complaint resulted in recorded damages. The majority of actions resulting in recorded damages were settled. This accounted for approximately 47% of the total number (148) cases resolved by settlements. Of the 21 cases that were tried at the bench, only 2 resulted in damages and only

9 of the 30 jury trials resulted in damages. Cases with legal representation were more likely to produce recorded damages from settlements.

The amount asked for in the complaints ranged from $100,000 to $500 million. For all cases, the median amount demanded in the complaints was $2 million. The average amount of damages, therefore, represents approximately 7% of the relief demanded in the complaint, while the average award demanded in the actions resulting in damages was $2 million. The average damage award was $15,000. A weak relation existed between the amount of damages asked and the amount awarded.

In order to obtain a more comprehensive picture of how the characteristics of the complaint impact on the successful prosecution of Section 1983/*Bivens* actions and the award of damages, a logistic regression analysis was used to look at two dependent variables: success and damages. The first dependent variable tested successful prosecution of cases. A case was considered successfully prosecuted if all the necessary steps toward prosecution were undertaken by the plaintiff, regardless of the outcome.

The second dependent variable, damages, took into account whether or not damages were awarded. This variable indicates whether or not a case resulted in damages or was settled (i.e., either a case was settled or damages awarded or neither of the two held). Settled cases were included, because from the results of the interviews and from the literature on Section 1983/*Bivens* actions, there is general agreement among the corporation and plaintiffs' counsels that settled cases produce damages although the amounts may not be indicated in the court files.

The independent variables used in the logistic regression analyses are elements that are introduced by plaintiffs when the case is filed. These included causes of action (i.e., the liberty, property, and violence indices), defendant type (government or not), presence of malice, type of representation (counsel v. *pro se*), district (Eastern vs. Southern), and amount of damages asked.

Table 3 presents the result of the logistic regression analysis using success as the dependent variable. The classification table of success predictors shows that the prediction rate is a fair one. Some 73% of the cases were correctly classified according to whether or not they were successfully prosecuted, successfully. However, there was a higher success rate for successful prosecution compared to unsuccessful prosecution (88% v. 52%).

Type of representation, violence, and the presence of malice were found to predict successful prosecution of cases. Again, the regression reflects what was suggested throughout the earlier analyses of the data—that representation by an attorney made a difference in the outcome while holding other elements constant. The model suggests as well that violence as a cause of action is a significant predictor of successful prosecution, along with a less convincing effect of the element of malice in the complaint.

Prior elements that predict the award of damages were determined by using a multivariate model with the same set of independent variables. The results of the second logistic regression analysis are presented in Table 4. The classification table indicates that 68% of the cases were classified correctly. As with success, type of representation and violence are found to predict the amount of damages awarded holding other elements constant. Inclusion of a government agency as a defendant in the suit is found to be a significant predictor of damage award as well.

TABLE 3

REGRESSION: SUCCESSFUL PROSECUTION OF COMPLAINT

-2 Log Likelihood	544.6371		
	Chi-square	df	Significance
-2 Log Likelihood	439.311	394	.0571
Model chi-square	105.327	8	.0000
Improvement	105.327	8	.0000
Goodness of fit	397.635	394	.4393

Classification table for success

	Predicted		
Observed	Unsuccessful	Successful	Percent correct
Unsuccessful	86	78	52.44%
Successful	29	210	87.87%
		Overall	73.46%

Significant Predictors

Variable	Wald	df	Sign.
Pro se	42.9200	1	.0000
Violence	9.7768	1	.0018
Malice	3.6975	1	.0545
(Constant	.1440	1	.7044)

TABLE 4

REGRESSION: DAMAGES

-2 Log Likelihood	535.07216		
	Chi-square	df	Significance
-2 Log Likelihood	452.612	392	.0185
Model chi-square	82.460	8	.0000
Improvement	82.460	8	.0000
Goodness of fit	421.854	392	.1437

Classification table for success

	Predicted		
	No		
Observed	Damages	Damages	Percent correct
No damages	181	65	73.58%
Damages	63	92	59.35%
		Overall	68.08%

Significant Predictors

Variable	Wald	df	Sign.
Pro se	24.5635	1	.0000
Government	6.0021	1	.0143
Violence	5.8981	1	.0152
(Constant	30.7951	1	.0000)

DISCUSSION AND CONCLUSIONS

Violations

The findings that most of the plaintiffs alleged assault and battery, false arrest, and false imprisonment are consistent with findings of other studies (Eisenberg & Schwab, 1987). Fisher et al. (1989) noted that this pattern existed in both federal and state suits. These are expected results because the Section 1983 remedy was created to redress exactly these kinds of deprivations of the individual rights (Vaughn & Coomes, 1995). Moreover, use of force has been the traditional complaint of plaintiffs in Section 1983 suits (Barrineau, 1987; Beyer, 1994; Kappeler, 1993).

Parties to Section 1983/Bivens Actions

Most encounters with police involve individuals and, occasionally, citizens as a group (Avery & Rudovsky, 1992). The finding that almost 25% of the cases were *pro se* complaints is significant. Records indicated that most *pro se* actions were brought by detainees or convicts. Often *pro se* cases were not prosecuted successfully. It is reasonable to speculate that at least some of these plaintiffs were in jail or prison, which made prosecution difficult because of such problems as traveling from the cell to court, and seeking permission to go to court, being moved from one prison to another. When forced by circumstances to wait until they are released to prosecute the suit, *pro se* plaintiffs often are faced with the reality that the statute of limitations has expired or that the cause of action has been dismissed for lack of prosecution.

Individual officers were usually named as defendants on the complaint, except in the few cases alleging the abuse of due process and/or conspiracy by the police chief and department. Even when the city or county was not directly named as a co-defendant in the complaint, the municipality was almost always involved in the defense and subsequent payment of damages.

The relationship between the type of plaintiff and type of representation was demonstrated by the fact that a majority of the cases with counsel have a city as the defendant. *Pro se* plaintiffs were twice as likely to name an individual defendant, and almost three times as likely to name the department as defendant as plaintiffs with counsel. Having multiple defendants in most cases was expected, given the obvious legal strategy in joining defendants and similar findings reported by previous studies (Fisher et al., 1989). While almost 90% of the cases with counsel had multiple defendants, only about two thirds of the *pro se* cases had multiple defendants. *Pro se* plaintiffs often are not aware of the advantages of including governmental agencies as defendants in their complaints.

The impact of *Monell v. Department of Social Services* (1978), which permitted plaintiffs to include municipalities as defendants in Section 1983/*Bivens* suits, was demonstrated by the inclusion of municipalities as defendants by a majority of plaintiffs, a finding supported by earlier research (Eisenberg & Schwab, 1987; Fisher et al., 1989). The administrator of the police organization often is not mentioned as the defendant because he or she is rarely involved with civilians. However, departments are likely to be defendants because they are capable of paying large monetary awards to defendants (del Carmen, 1991).

Since most of the violations that trigger civil liability suits stem from activities of police officers employed by municipalities, federal agencies are rarely included as co-defendants. Also, the low number of actions brought against the federal government (10) was expected because the federal government is immune from liability under Section 1983. Although federal officials are subject to *Bivens* action suits, the federal government is only subject to suit under the Federal Tort Claims Act of 1946. *Bivens* actions against a federal official and tort actions under this Act can be joined in the same suit.

Case Disposition

The percentage of Section 1983/*Bivens* cases reaching bench trial in this study was roughly comparable to the number of other civil cases reaching trial in the two courts during this period (Annual Reports USDC/SDNY and USDC/EDNY, 1989). The manner of disposition also reflected the pattern reported in other studies, in particular those disposed by trial (Eisenberg, 1982; Eisenberg & Schwab, 1987). For example, Fisher et al. (1989) found that 57% of the cases in their study were settled while only 5% were tried.

The higher percentage of settlements as opposed to trials can be seen in light of the trend for active judicial roles. Although it appears that there is encouragement to settle cases as a result of FRCP, Rule 16, and perhaps some other factors, it should be noted that case files often do not reveal the terms of settlement. Most cities that are unwilling to gamble with whether juries will find in favor of their officer or award judgments of large sums against them prefer to settle out of court (Kappeler, 1993).

From the records and interviews, there was no indication of specific guidelines used when making case settlements. Such factors as time spent on the case, nature of injury, type of crime, the receptiveness of the jury, and the general atmosphere created by the presiding judge were identified as being important in settlement decisions by a number of plaintiffs' attorneys and corporation counsels. Most important, the kind of change and policy the plaintiff is attempting to effect is also considered prior to the assessment of a possible settlement.

Time of Disposition

The median time of disposition for the cases studied was higher than the median time of disposition of other civil cases during the same period of the study (Table 5). The average time of disposition for trials of 26 months is far greater than the average of trials of other civil cases tried in the two district courts during this period. The median time of disposition for general civil trials in the Eastern district at this time ranged between 20 to 22 months and 13 to 17 months in the Southern district. The national median time for civil trials stayed constant at 14 months.

Similarly, the median time for bench and jury trials—27 and 39 months, respectively—is far greater than the median time of bench and jury trials of other civil cases in these courts during this period. Though the median time

TABLE 5

MEAN AND MEDIAN TIMES (IN MONTHS) OF DISPOSITION BY DISTRICT

District	Number of cases	Mean time (1983 and Bivens)	(SD)	Median time (1983 and Bivens)	Median time all civil (1983-87)
EDNY	215	27	16.03	26	9
SDNY	187	26	16.85	24	8
Total	402	26	16.40	25	

Average Median Time for the Five-Year Period

	EDNY	SDNY
All civil (1983–1987)		
Bench trials	20	15
Jury trials	23	15
All	22	15
1983/*Bivens* actions		
Bench trials	25	28
Jury trials	30	41
All	28	34

of disposition for the failed actions suits (considered not properly prosecuted) was slightly lower than the average time of disposition for cases in the study, the median for the failed cases was still higher than the average time of disposition of the other civil cases decided during this period.

One finding that is particularly illustrative of the nature of Section 1983/*Bivens* is the longer time it takes to dispose of these actions than it takes for processing other civil cases. Although the study did not measure the cost of processing these actions, it can be inferred from the time spent on the processing of these actions (as confirmed by plaintiffs' lawyers) that considerable resources are spent on them. Other plaintiffs' attorneys indicated in interviews that they spent from $1,000 to $25,000 in the preparation of these suits.

As Eisenberg (1982) notes, the extent to which courts conduct hearings is an important measure of the burden of Section 1983/*Bivens* actions. This is more evident when the court costs and other costs of civil case management are considered in the disposition of these cases. As indicated by the median time of disposition (25 months for all cases), the results of the study indicate that these actions may require a significant amount of judicial attention, even though most cases did not reach trial. Considering only the actual cases tried, the study found that Section 1983 civil suits do not seem to pose any burden on the system. Only 11% of the cases were tried. However, considerable judicial time may be spent on the cases that never make it to trial. This accounts for the long time it takes to dispose of the cases. Thus, tried cases, by themselves, do not measure the amount of judicial attention and time devoted to these cases because many of them are often settled just before trial (Eisenberg, 1982; Kappeler, 1993).

Damages

In some cases, the settlement agreement did not indicate whether damages were awarded. However, according to the corporation counsel for New York City, nearly all settled cases usually resulted in damages even if not recorded. Others interviewed for this study supported this claim. It must be noted that, because many damage awards come from settlements (some negotiated out-of-court). it is difficult to determine the precise number of cases that produced punitive damages.

Moreover, when only cases with counsel are considered, the rate of recorded damage recovery rises from 20% to approximately 26%. Damages are meant to compensate the plaintiff financially for injuries caused by the violation of his or her civil or constitutional rights. Therefore, damages were assumed to be compensatory except in the cases that the courts specified they were punitive, in which case punitive damages may be awarded for malice (Silver, 1986).

Malice was alleged in 29% of the cases that resulted in damages. However, the Supreme Court in *Smith v. Wade* (1983) held that the plaintiff need not prove actual malice to obtain punitive damages. It is enough that the police officer acted with reckless or callous indifference to constitutional rights of the defendant (Silver, 1986; *Smith v. Wade,* 1983).

The mean damages ($28,295) recovered by the plaintiffs in this study are similar to those reported by plaintiffs in other studies of Section 1983 actions conducted in other parts of the country. For example, in their California study, Eisenberg & Schwab (1987) realized a total recovery of $379,000 for 18 cases and additional attorneys' fees of $112,500 for an average of $21,055, without attorneys' fees. In a New Jersey study, Fisher et al. (1989) found $2.7 million total damages but a smaller average amount of $6,000. Their study, however, included state court actions. Lloyd's (1983) survey of these kinds of suits listed the average award against police as $565,000 in excessive force cases only, a finding that is generally not consistent with other studies.

These studies (including the present one) confirm that the dollar amounts recovered in these cases usually are not very large. Occasionally, and particularly in assault and battery (excessive force) cases, the courts do grant large damage awards that may amount to hundreds of thousands of dollars, such as in the three large awards in this study. However, Kappeler and Kappeler (1992) found that, in federal cases where a judgment against police or a jury award was reported, the awards and attorney fees averaged $87,669.

Although it is difficult to make definite statements about the amount of damages awarded in the trial cases because of the small number of cases, settled cases seem to have resulted in lower amounts of damages as compared to bench and jury trials. The low average for settlements may result in part from the nominal or low amounts obtained from settlements of nuisance suits (Kappeler, 1993). These are cases that either fail to state a claim upon which relief can be granted or simply concern trifling matters (Maahs & del Carmen, 1995). Though these cases lack merit, they often present an issue of fact making dismissal before trial difficult. They often are settled for nominal amounts to avoid trial expenses. The lower average of damage awards derived from settlements also suggests that the more serious cases may make it to trial and/or that jurors at times grant higher awards than the plaintiffs' attorneys are able to obtain from settlements.

As noted above, because of out-of-court settlements, court records often indicated fewer damage awards than were actually accorded. Thus, the financial burden of Section 1983/*Bivens* actions is probably greater than the court records indicate. This may also be an indication that the financial burden of Section 1983/*Bivens* presents a problem for those municipalities that have to pay damages—in particular, large cities such as New York. Generally, police liability is a burden on all parties defending the suits (Kappeler, 1993).

Of all the cases filed *pro se*, only one resulted in damages. This is an indication that representation by counsel played an important factor in plaintiffs' success. Although the study did not examine specific characteristics of *pro se* plaintiffs, a reading of the court files indicated that the cause of action/claim was better stated by counsel, as opposed to the *pro se* claims that were often so inarticulately presented that they tended to preclude serious consideration. The transience of many *pro se* plaintiffs may make it difficult to follow up their actions successfully. Thus, many of the *pro se* actions were dismissed as frivolous or for failure to state a cause of action or prosecute. This manner of processing *pro se* actions is supported by another study conducted in the Southern district, one of the courts in which data was collected for this study (Annual Report of the USDC/SDNY, 1989).

In general, the results reflect, theoretically and from a legal standpoint, that the nature of the violation affects the volume of damages in civil actions. Thus, violence was found to be the cause of action most often alleged by the plaintiffs—and the most productive. Two independent variables (representation and violent violations) held as predictors of damages in two regressions indicate that Section 1983/*Bivens* actions caused by police physical abuse are most likely to result in successful prosecution and damages for the plaintiff if they are well prosecuted.

CONCLUSION

Past studies indicate that increased use of Section 1983/*Bivens* suits has led to pressure on police departments and their employing municipalities to adjust their policies and general approach to civil rights and constitutional violations. The failure of other available remedies to protect the public from police violations of their Fourth Amendment rights means the momentum behind Section 1983/*Bivens* actions will continue to increase. Moreover, the additional incentive of monetary damages in Section 1983 actions likely will continue to make the statute appealing to victims of police abuses in the future. As more and more members of the public become aware of their rights, they will react to police abuses by seeking justice and compensation in the courts.

This article approached the damage question from a different angle than previous studies of Section 1983 have done (Eisenberg, 1982; Eisenberg & Schwab, 1987; Fisher et al., 1989). Unlike previous research on civil liability that focused on the requirement of deprivation of constitutional or statutory rights (Barrineau, 1994; del Carmen, 1993) and on the growing number of suits brought against police (Kappeler & Kappeler, 1992; Kappeler, Kappeler & del Carmen, 1993), it looked at damages from the amounts indicated in the court files, but also included settlements because court records and interview data indicated that most settlements resulted in damages. This study showed that there were probably more cases resulting in damages than previously had been supposed.

Earlier studies, as well as the conclusions of this study, show that the objective of Section 1983 is being fulfilled. If the public accepts that there are police abuses of civil and constitutional rights that cannot be fully protected by alternative available remedies, then Section 1983 and its federal counterpart, *Bivens,* are serving an important function. Therefore, attention should be focused on what Section 1983/*Bivens* are seeking to achieve, as well as how to implement the remedy without negatively affecting the police function.

Because police activities are essential and affect so much of the public, and because the public values both the functions of police and their civil and constitutional rights, any threat that affects the relationship between the police functions and the public's cherished rights deserves the kind of examination this research provides. The issues examined here come at an opportune time for both the police and members of the public. An understanding of both the relationship between police and the public and the need to respect the public's civil and constitutional rights is beneficial to all parties. Further research is necessary on a number of issues—specifically, on careful training and internal discipline, the payment of judgment awards, Section 1983/*Bivens* damage awards against police at the state level, and the differences in the amounts obtained from jury trials and settlements—to aid administrators and municipalities in decisionmaking, and, particularly, to improve understanding between police and the public.

REFERENCES

Adams, E, A. (1991). Brutality claims, payments at record highs. *New York Law Journal,* 1.
Avery, M., & Rudovsky, D. (1981). *Police misconduct: Law and litigation.* New York: Clark Boardman.
Barrineau, H. E. (1994). *Civil liability in criminal justice.* Cincinnati, OH: Anderson Publishing.
Barrineau, H. E. (1987). *Civil liability in criminal justice.* Cincinnati, OH: Anderson Publishing.
Beyer, W. C. (1994). Strategies for excessive force claims. 42 U.S.C. Section 1983. *Trial, 30,* 24–27.
Champion, D. J. (1988). Some recent trends in civil litigation by federal and state prison inmates. *Federal Probation, 52*(30), 43–47.
Civil Rights Act of 1971, § 1, 42 U.S.C. § 1983 (1874).
Congressional Globe, 42d Cong., (1871) 1st Session, 334.
del Carmen, R. V. (1991). *Civil liabilities in American policing: A text for law enforcement personnel.* Englewood Cliffs, NJ: Prentice Hall.
del Carmen, R. V. (1993). Civil liabilities in law enforcement: Where are we and where should we go from here? *American Journal of Police, 12*(4), 87–99.
del Carmen, R. V., & Kappeler, V. E. (1991). Municipalities and police agencies as defendants: Liability for official policy. *American Journal of Police, 10*(1), 1–17.
Eisenberg, T. (1982). Section 1983: Doctrinal foundations and an empirical study. *Cornell Law Review, 67,* 482–556.
Eisenberg, T., & Schwab, S. (1987). The reality of constitutional tort litigation. *Cornell Law Review, 72,* 641–695.

Fabrizio, L. E. (1990). *FBI National Academy: A study of the change in attitude of those who attend.* Chicago: Office of International Criminal Justice, University of Illinois at Chicago.

Fisher, W. S., Kutner, S., & Wheat, J. (1989). Civil liability of New Jersey police officers: An overview. *Criminal Justice Quarterly, 10,* 45–78.

Gallagher, P. G. (1990). Special focus: High risk liability issues. *Police Chief, 57*(6), 18–44.

Kappeler, S. F., & Kappeler, V. E. (1992). A research note on Section 1983 claims against the police: Cases before federal district courts in 1990. *American Journal of Police, 11*(1), 65–73.

Kappeler, V. E. (1993). *Critical issues in police civil liability.* Prospect Heights, IL: Waveland Press.

Kappeler, V. E., Kappeler, S. F., & del Carmen, R. V. (1993). A content analysis of police civil liability cases: Decisions of the Federal District Courts, 1978–1990. *Journal of Criminal Justice, 21,* 325–337.

Lloyd, A. (1983). *Money damages in police misconduct cases. A compilation of jury awards and settlements.* New York: Clark Boardman.

Maahs, J. F., & del Carmen, R. V. (1995). Curtailing frivolous Section 1983 inmate litigation: Laws, practice and proposals. *Federal Probation, 9,* 53–61.

McCoy, C. (1984). Lawsuits against police—What impact do they really have? *Criminal Law Bulletin, 20,* 49–56.

McCoy, C. (1986). Civil liability for Fourth Amendment violations: Rhetoric and reality. *Criminal Law Bulletin, 22,* 461.

McCoy, C. (1987). Police legal liability is "not a crisis" 99 chiefs say. *Crime Control Digest, 21,* 1.

Nahmod, S. H. (1982, October). Constitutional accountability in Section 1983 litigation. *Iowa Law Review, 68,* 1–33.

Nahmod, S. H. (1984, Spring). Damages and injunctive relief under Section 1983. *Urban Law, 16,* 201–216.

Nahmod, S. H. (1991). *Civil rights and civil liberties litigation: The law of Section 1983.* New York: McGraw-Hill.

Reynolds, C. D. (1988). Unjust civil litigation—A constant threat. *Police Chief, 7,* 1.

Rudovsky, D. (1992). Police Abuse: Can the violence be contained? *Harvard Civil Rights Liberties Law Review, 27*(2), 465–501.

Silver, I. (1986). *Police civil liability.* New York: Matthew Bender.

Titus, A. (1992). The federal due process limitations on the termination of state and municipal law enforcement. *American Journal of Police, 11*(1), 53–64.

United States District Court. (1989). *Annual Report of the USDC/SDNY.*

Vaughn, M. S., & Coomes, L. F. (1995). Police civil liability under Section 1983: When do police officers act under color of law? *Journal of Criminal Justice, 23*(5), 395–415.

Wunsch, E. J. (1995). Fourth Amendment and Fourteenth Amendment—malicious prosecution and Section 1983: Is there a constitutional violation remediable under Section 1983? Albright v. Oliver, 114 S. Ct. 807 (1994). *Journal of Criminal Law and Criminology, 85,* 878–908.

CASES CITED

Bivens v. Six Unknown Named Agents of the Federal Bureau of Narcotics, 403 U.S. 388 (1971).

Bivens v. Six Unknown Named Agents of the Federal Bureau of Narcotics, 456 F. 2d 1339 (2d Cir. 1972).

Malley v. Briggs, 475 U.S. 344 (1986).

Monell v. Department of Social Services, 436 U.S. 658 (1978).

Smith v. Wade, 461 U.S. (1983).

ARTICLE 31

PREVENTING EXCESSIVE FORCE LITIGATION

James F. Anderson,[a,]* *Laronistine Dyson*[b] *and Jerald Burns*[c]
[a]*Department of Sociology, Criminal Justice and Criminology, University of Missouri at Kansas City, Haag Hall, 5100 Rockhill Road, Kansas City, Missouri 64110;* [b]*Kentucky State University;* [c]*Alabama State University*

Despite the widespread use of *Section 1983* litigation to prevent police excessive force, civil rights violation cases continue to increase. Police agencies could reduce these cases with improved training and monitoring, empowering civilian review boards and seeking accreditation. These efforts would demonstrate to judges and juries that agencies are not *deliberately indifferent* to the public they are sworn to serve and protect.

Keywords: Force; safeguards; deadly force; review boards

INTRODUCTION

While depicting police practices, *Hollywood* has created the *"Super Cop"* image in the minds of the American public. The stereotype portrays police officers as super humans with heroic characteristics that enable them to approach and quickly resolve dangerous situations with little effort (Fyfe 1985). These images have been popularized in movies such as *Dirty Harry, Die Hard, Serpico,* and *Beverly Hills Cop.* However, what the media has failed to present in realistic terms are the increasing liability cases filed against police officers and departments each year. Del Carmen (1995) reports that an estimated 30,000 civil suits are filed annually against police. What is more alarming is that one in every thirty officers is sued each year. Despite the uncertainty of each monetary award, studies show the average awards are between $187,000 and $1.75 million per case, not to mention the millions spent on legal fees. This grim reality has created concerns for police officials and the public.

---

*Corresponding author.

James F. Anderson, Laronistine Dyson, Jerald Burns, "Preventing Excessive Force Litigation" (as appeared in *The Justice Professional,* Volume 12, Number 1, 1999, pp. 83–93). Reprinted with permission.

When police officers perform their duty (order maintenance; enforce criminal laws; provide community services: and enforce convenience norms) for a considerable amount of time, one sad reality is that the negative experiences that they encounter do adversely affect some officers. As a result, these officers engage in behavior that is dangerous to the public, and potentially expensive and damaging to the image of the police. Unfortunately, during this time, some officers use excessive force against suspects which violates their constitutionally protected rights. When this occurs, civil litigation lawsuits could be imminent.

This article examines the impact that excessive force cases have on police agencies and the public. It suggests strategies that police can use to prevent excessive force. The discussion is divided into two parts: Part I provides a definition of excessive force and legal remedies. Further, it addresses how excessive force violates constitutional protections and *Section 1983* leading to legal liability. Part II offers strategies police can use to reduce lawsuits. The authors conclude that with improved training and monitoring, empowering civilian review boards and acquiring accreditation, excessive force litigations could be reduced.

PART I: EXCESSIVE FORCE AND LEGAL REMEDIES

Though the police are charged with dispensing justice and fairness, there are limitations placed on their behavior by federal and state constitutions, statutes, and departmental policies (Mayhall, Barker, and Hunter 1995). These safeguards are designed to protect individuals from arbitrary abuse. Because civil liberties and constitutional freedoms are essential to the American way, civil and criminal remedies exist to protect the public from police abuse. For example, officers engage in excessive force when their behavior violates proper law enforcement procedures (Mayhall *et al.* 1995; Peak and Glensor 1996). When officers act in an excessive manner and the circumstances do not justify such behavior, they exceed their authority and open the door for civil litigation.

del Carmen (1995) argues that there are two types of force cases: *nondeadly* and *deadly* force. *Nondeadly force* occurs when police are accused of brutality or using "excessive force." Departmental policies allow officers to engage in nondeadly force if the amount of force used is reasonable under the circumstances. *Graham v. Conner* (1989) established reasonable force as the amount of force that a prudent officer would use given similar circumstances. It is the amount of force used to achieve legally acceptable results. The amount of force needed is dictated by the circumstances of each case. The officers must be sure that the circumstances justify the level of force used. del Carmen (1995) further contends that force is sometimes determined by the conduct of the person being arrested or subdued.

The use of *deadly force,* as seen by a reasonable officer, would indicate that the final outcome has a high risk of death or serious bodily injury. Firearms, fists, and night sticks are instruments of death depending on how they are used. Rules on the use of deadly force vary from state to state and department to department. For example, in most states, the use of deadly force is based on the proportionality of the crime committed (del Carmen 1995; Kappeler 1997).

In cases where misdemeanor suspects are fleeing capture, officers are instructed not to use deadly force to apprehend them. However, in felony cases, *Tennessee v. Garner* (1985) established an officer may resort to deadly force if his life or the life of another is in jeopardy and the use of force will prevent imminent death. Where no departmental policy on deadly force exists, state law must prevail.

Officers may justify using "excessive force" if they can show their actions were reasonable under the circumstances. Again in *Graham,* the Court stated the reasonableness requirement must be based on how a reasonable officer on the scene would perceive the situation. The Court also put forth a reasonableness test. The Court asked, "Are the officers' actions objectively reasonable in light of the facts and circumstances confronting them, without regard to their underlying intent or motivation?" Thus, any motive the officer may have had for using force is irrelevant.

EXCESSIVE FORCE VIOLATES *SECTION 1983* AND LEADS TO LIABILITY: SEVERAL CASES OF POLICE MISCONDUCT

Liability under federal law is based on deprivation of rights. These cases come under *Title 42 of the U.S. Code of Section 1983.* According to *Section 1983,* any person acting under color of law cannot cause other individuals to suffer a deprivation of rights, privileges, or immunities secured by laws and the Constitution. Anyone responsible for such actions shall be liable to the injured party. Since in federal court the discovery procedures are liberal and plaintiffs are able to recover attorney fees and monetary awards, civil rights actions are the most commonly used remedy by plaintiffs. The actions of police officers are considered civil rights violations if they deny constitutionally-or federally-guaranteed rights to plaintiffs. The basic elements of *Section 1983* lawsuits are that defendant must be acting under color of law (as a police officer) and a constitutionally-or federally-protected right was violated.

In excessive force cases, plaintiffs file lawsuits alleging infringements on their Fourth and Fourteenth Amendment rights. The Fourth Amendment prohibits unreasonable searches and seizures of persons, houses, papers, and other areas without a valid warrant or probable cause. The Fourteenth Amendment protects against the deprivation of life, liberty, or property without due process of law and ensures equal protection. These suits affect the officer, supervisor, police organizations and community. When civil rights violations (brutality or wrongful death) occur, lawsuits can be expensive and the aftermath can have far-reaching impact on police-community relations (Kappeler 1997; Peak and Glensor 1996). Police excessive force cases sometimes lead to distrust and tensions between police agencies and the people they are sworn to serve and protect (Mayball *et al.* 1995).

Several Cases of Police Misconduct

Section 1983 cases where plaintiffs have successfully sued police are common. In *Wilks v. Reyes (1993),* the Ninth Circuit Court ruled that a citizen pursuing excessive force claims does not have to show significant bodily injuries. In *Yang v. Hardin (1994)* the *Seventh Circuit Court* ruled that supervisory or nonsupervisory police officers are civilly liable when they are present and fail to intervene where fellow officers become "out of control" and engage in excessive force to subdue offenders. In *Yang,* the court determined the plaintiff was unjustifiably arrested and beaten. In *Mick v. Brewer (1996),* the *Eleventh Circuit Court* ruled that the district court did not err in its denial of qualified immunity for the officers' use of excessive force. Officers alleged there was no established guideline on excessive force during a *Terry* stop. The *Eleventh Circuit Court* sighted *Graham.*

In *Hale v. Townley (1981),* the *Eighth Circuit Court* ruled that police misconduct was sufficient for a civil rights claim after an officer slammed the suspect against a car, rammed his fist into the suspect's testicles, and beat his head against a table. The *Sixth Circuit Court,* in *Russo v. City of Cincinnati (1982),* reasoned that police are liable if they engage in force that goes beyond their authority. Similarly, in *Thomas v. Fredrick (1991),* the *Western District Court* in Louisiana found police liable after an officer threw a black woman against a car shortly after she protested the arrest of her husband for writing a bad check. During this violent episode, the victim sustained back injuries. The court discovered that the victim had not threatened the officer, had no weapon, and did not act aggressively. In *Lewis v. Downs (1985),* the police were ordered to pay $10,000 to a family that was physically assaulted by police officers. The *Sixth Circuit Court* discovered that when police were dispatched to resolve a family dispute, the police engaged in excessive force by kicking a father in his groin and beating him on the head with a night stick. In addition, the officer kicked the mother in the buttocks as she lay handcuffed, face down in mud. The officer also injured the son. Neither the father nor any other family member posed a threat to police.

In *Young v. City of Killeen (1985),* police lost a wrongful death action and were ordered to pay a surviving family $202,295.80. In *Young,* police shot and killed a suspect who was allegedly making a drug buy. The officer argued he shot in self-defense, but the judge, relying on expert testimony ruled that the officer used excessive force rather than following proper procedure. In *Malloy v. Monahan (1996),* the *Tenth Circuit Court* upheld a $232,433 award when officers beat the victim with a baton and sprayed mace in his face while he was handcuffed. In *Davis v. Mason County (1991),* a plaintiff was awarded $1,171,600 where a pattern of unchecked physical abuse was established, including choking, punching, and unlawfully using an electric stun gun.

In *Marchese v. Lucas (1985),* the *Sixth Circuit Court* awarded the plaintiff $125,000 because police failed to properly train and discipline officers. In this case, the plaintiff was severely beaten twice while in custody. Similarly, in *Zuchel v. City and County of Denver, Colo. (1993),* a judgment of $330,000 was awarded to the plaintiff when officers used deadly force by shooting and killing an unarmed suspect. In *Wilson v. Beebe (1985),* $2,569,638 was paid to a plaintiff after an officer's revolver discharged and shot a handcuffed suspect. Further, in *Frazell v. Flanigan (1996),* the plaintiff was awarded $158,500 when officers sat on him and beat his back, head and feet, causing him to bleed profusely. Similarly, in *Herrera v. Valentine (1981),* a pregnant woman was awarded $300,000 when an officer kicked her in the stomach causing the death of her unborn child. Finally, in *Bieros v. Marino (1995),* the *Eastern District Court of* Pennsylvania ruled civil rights violations occur even if police use minor force on subjects in custody. While these cases highlight police misconduct, they are not meant to be an exhaustive list of police abuse of power. Because many lawsuits are filed against police each year, strategies must be implemented to protect the public from excessive force as well as to preserve the integrity of policing.

PART II: STRATEGIES TO REDUCE EXCESSIVE FORCE LITIGATIONS

Training and Monitoring

Properly trained officers could reduce excessive force litigation. They know departmental and state policies governing excessive force, hence, they do not make as many mistakes as untrained officers. They know the scope of their authority. Training prepares officers on when not to engage in unnecessary force. They learn when their actions border on criminal behavior. Failure to properly train or take a proactive role could mean that officers will not act in a legally responsible manner and the outcome of their actions might serve as the basis for civil litigation (Alpert and Smith 1990; Barrineau 1987). In *Sager v. City of Woodlawn Park (1982)*, the court ruled that improper training resulted in a prisoner's death at the hands of police. *Popow v. City of Margate (1979)* is also instructive here. In Popow, an innocent bystander was killed in a police hot pursuit chase. The court held the city negligent because the officer had not been properly trained to fire at night, at a moving target, or how to use a firearm in a residential area. In *Beverly v. Morris (1972)*, a police chief was held liable for improperly training and supervising his officers following the blackjack beating of a citizen by a subordinate officer.

Canton v. Harris (1989) is considered a leading case highlighting the Courts position on a failure to train. In *Harris,* the Court ruled that if it can be shown that police acted with *"deliberate indifference,"* plaintiffs will prevail. *Deliberate indifference* refers to a complete disregard for the welfare of the suspect in police custody where assistance is needed. In *Harris,* liability ensued after police failed to provide medical assistance to a woman in custody who had fallen on the floor at the police station. Instead of officers seeking medical help for *Harris,* they allowed her to remain on the station floor. After her release, she was taken to a hospital by family members and was diagnosed as suffering from emotional ailments. She was hospitalized for a week and received outpatient treatment. *Harris* filed a *Section 1983* action claiming that police officers violated her constitutional rights and that officers had not been properly trained to assist suspects with medical ailments, thereby, showing deliberate indifference. As such, the jury felt that when police walked around and over *Harris,* this was a show of deliberate indifference to the needs of someone in police custody who had taken ill. The implication of *Harris* is that if officers are not properly trained to assist those in custody, this might signal to juries (with the power to grant monetary awards) that police agencies are deliberately indifferent to those in custody. Therefore, documentation of training could be essential for reducing litigation. While *Harris* is significant, the burden of proof is on complainants to show that deliberate indifference occurred.

After training, officers should be monitored to determine whether training has had a positive impact on their behavior. Peak (1998) argues that because of existing complexities and constant changes in the legal system, training should be ongoing for neophytes and veteran officers. Superiors can monitor officers by examining the number of complaints filed before and after training. By engaging in this practice, police demonstrate a proactive role in their commitment of ensuring that officers are trained to handle any existing situation within the framework of procedural and legal safeguards.

Standards and Accreditation

Another strategy that goes along with training that can help reduce civil liability lawsuits is to increase police accountability. One way to achieve this objective is to encourage police to strive for nationally recognized standards. The Commission on Accreditation for Law Enforcement Agencies (CALEA) supports police departments accepting a proactive role in accountability. Since police accreditation is voluntary, departments expressing an interest must contact CALEA. CALEA then evaluates a department to determine if it has effective policies. By observing, they see if existing standards are satisfactory to meet daily operations. If CALEA is not satisfied with a department's existing arrangements, it introduces proper standards and policies and offers training to officers. CALEA awards certification after standards are met.

While certification and standards do not guarantee officers will not engage in excessive force, accredited departments provide officers with proper training and guidelines that discourage misconduct. Goldman and Puro (1988) report that decertification could serve as an effective alternative to traditional remedies for police misconduct. Departments that require officer certification could punish violators by decertifying them as officers. Because many state boards require officer certification, those who are decertified will be unable to retain their position. This, they contend, ensures conformity to rules governing legitimate police behavior. Accreditation demonstrates to the public that a department is committed to professionally training officers to execute their duties in an ethical manner. Perhaps accreditation and certification should be required of all departments. When police departments have on record that they are professionally certified after extensive training, this negates any issue of deliberate indifference that might surface if excessive force cases are filed. Therefore, departments would do well to strive to achieve standards and accreditation.

Civilian Review Boards

Civilian review boards function with objectivity because they are free from police influence. These boards examine grievances filed against police misconduct. They examine how police departments handle citizen complaints. Those who compose these boards are not sworn police officers. Despite this remedy to review complaints of police misconduct, Walker and Bumphus (1991) report that these boards lack the power to demand a formal investigation or that an officer be disciplined. These boards only make recommendations that an officer receive remedial action. Though over 16,000 police agencies exist in the US, a 1994 survey revealed that only 66 agencies had some form of civilian review. Walker and Wright (1995) report that of the 50 largest cities in the US, 36 now have civilian review boards, as do 13 of the next 50 largest cities. Despite the small number, police departments regard civilian review with contempt and have lobbied to reduce its limited influence (Cole and Smith 1998).

The mistrust that police have of review boards is unjustifiable. For example, police protest having civilians review complaints on the grounds that they have little knowledge of policing. This view is undeserved since these boards consistently show leniency towards the police. Kerstetter (1985) reports that civilian boards are, by far, more lenient than police internal review boards. While their effectiveness is yet to be proven, some scholars report that their presence could improve police-citizen relations. These boards could prove to be assets to police departments. Moreover, if more boards existed, some citizen might take comfort in knowing that the "bad" officers will receive disciplinary action or punishment for their misdeeds. However, if this mechanism does not exist, victims might regard civil courts as their only option for justice. Therefore, police departments might do well to have civilian review boards in place. This might demonstrate to juries that police are not deliberately indifferent to victims of excessive force and departments are not trying to hide police misconduct. Furthermore, if officers are aware that recommendations from review boards will be taken seriously, they would commit themselves to working within the scope of law. This begins with empowering civilian review boards.

CONCLUSION

The number of civil lawsuits filed against police departments alleging the use of excessive force is alarming. Del Carmen reports that the number exceeds 30,000 and the average award is between $187,000 and $1.75 million. Though the actual number of these cases is known, many cases are settled before a judgement is made. Furthermore, sometimes when defendants prevail, police agencies may appeal the decision. In the final analysis, legal maneuvering may hide the truth about the outcome of these cases. Despite this, the issue of excessive force is a grave one with consequences that have national implications. Such implications may place an added economic strain on already limited departmental resources or continued use of excessive force against citizens by some officers. The authors believe that these cases could be prevented if departments would engage in proactive practices, such as proper training and monitoring, empowering civilian review boards, and seeking accreditation. While these recommendations may not shield all departments from litigation, the results might mean better trained, responsible, and professional officers. These efforts will signal to judges and juries that departments are not operating with deliberate indifference towards citizens they are sworn to serve and protect. A failure to heed these recommendations might mean paying expensive lawsuits coupled with distrust and tensions that could frustrate police and community relations.

REFERENCES

Alpert, G. and Smith, W. (1990). *Defensibly of law enforcement training.* Criminal Law Bulletin, **26**(5): 452–58.

Barrineau, H. (1987). *Civil liability in criminal justice.* Cincinnati, OH: Anderson Publishing Company.

Cole, G.F. and Smith, C.E. (1998). *The American System of Criminal Justice System* (5th ed.). Belmont, CA: West/Wadsworth.

del Carmen, R.V. (1995). *Criminal procedures: Law and practice* (3rd ed.). Pacific Grove, CA: Brooks/Cole.

Fyfe, J.J. (1985). *Police management today: Issues and case studies.* New York: International City Management Association.

Goldman, R. and Puro, S. (1988). Decertification of police: An alternative to traditional remedies for police misconduct. *Hastings Constitutional Law Quarterly,* **15**: 45–80.

Kappeler, V.E. (1997). *Critical issues in police liability* (2 ed.). Prospect Heights, IL: Waveland.

Kerstetter, W.A. (1985). Who disciplines the police? Who should? Police leadership in America. ed. W.A. Geller. New York: Praegar, 141–181.

Mayhall, P.D. Barker, T. and Hunter, R.D. (1995). *Police–community relations and the administration of justice* (4 ed.). Englewood Cliffs, NJ: Prentice-Hall.

Peak, K. (1998). *Justice administration: Police, courts, and corrections management.* Upper Saddle River, NJ: Prentice-Hall.

Peak. K.J. and Glensor, R.W. (1996). *Community policing & problem solving: Strategies & practices.* Englewood Cliffs, NJ: Prentice-Hall.

Walker, S. and Bumphus, V.W. (1992). The effectiveness of civilian review: Observations on recent trends and new issues regarding the civilian review of the police. *American Journal of Police* **21**(4): 1–26.

Walker, S. and Wright, B. (1995). Citizens review of the police, 1994: A national survey. *Fresh Perspectives.* Washington, D.C.: Police Executive Research Forum.

CASES CITED

Beverly v. Morris, 470 F.2d 1356 (5th Cir. 1972)
Bieros v. Marino, 70 F.3d 1254 (E.D. Pa. 1995)
Canton v. Harris, 489 U.S. 378 (1989)
Davis v. Mason County, 927 F.2d 1473 (9th Cir. 1991)
Frazell v. Flanigan, 102 F.3d 877 (7th Cir. 1996)
Graham v. Conner, 109 S.Ct. 1865 (1989)
Hale v. Townley, 45 F.3d 914 (8th Cir. 1981)
Herrera v. Valentine, 653 F.2d 1220 (8th Cir. 1981)
Lewis v. Downs, 774 F.2d 711 (6th Cir. 1985)
Malloy v. Monahan, 73 F.3d 1012 (10th Cir. 1996)
Marchese v. Lucas, 758 F.2d 181 (6th Cir. 1985)
Mick v. Brewer, 76 F.3d 1127 (10th Cir. 1996)
Popow v. City of Margate, 476 F. Supp. 1237 (1979)
Russo v. City of Cincinnati, 953 F.2d 1036 (6th Cir. 1982)
Sager v. City of Woodlawn Park, 543 F. Supp. 282 (D.Colo., 1982)
Tennessee v. Garner. 471 U.S. 1 (1985)
Thomas v. Fredrick, 113 F.3d 1245 (W.D. LA. 1991)
Wilks v. Reyes, 5 F.3d 412 (9th Cir. 1993)
Wilson v. Beebe, 770 F.2d 578 (6th Cir. 1985)
Yang v. Hardin, 37 F.3d 282 (7th Cir. 1994)
Young v. City of Killeen, 775 F.2d 1349 (5th Cir. 1985)
Zuchel v. City and County of Denver, Colo., 997 F.2d 730 (10th Cir. 1993)

A R T I C L E   3 2

POLICE ABUSE:
CAN THE VIOLENCE BE CONTAINED?

*David Rudovsky**
University of Pennsylvania School of Law

I. INTRODUCTION

Thirty years ago, in *Monroe v. Pape*,[1] the United States Supreme Court first addressed the question of whether or not abuses committed by state police officers were subject to suit under the Ku Klux Klan Act of 1871, popularly known as Section 1983.[2] *Monroe* presented allegations of police abuse in a quintessential form: several heavily armed police officers broke into the plaintiffs' home without a judicial warrant, ransacked the house and terrorized the occupants, making racial and other derogatory slurs as they proceeded in their search. No contraband was found and no arrests were made.[3]

The Supreme Court ruled that these allegations stated a cause of action under Section 1983 for the violation of the plaintiffs' Fourth Amendment rights. The Court held that the phrase "under color of state law" in Section 1983 was intended to include actions undertaken by government officials without state approval or authorization.[4] Most incidents of police abuse involve the actions of officers who act contrary to state law, and, in determining

David Rudovsky, "Police Abuse: Can the Violence be Contained?" (as appeared in *Harvard Civil Rights—Civil Liberties Law Review*, Volume 27, Number 2, 1992, pp. 465–503). Reprinted with permission.

*Partner, Kairys & Rudovsky; Senior Fellow, University of Pennsylvania School of Law; B.A. Queens College (CUNY); LL.B. 1967, New York University School of Law. I am proud to contribute to an issue of the *Harvard Civil Rights-Civil Liberties Law Review* honoring Norman Dorsen, whose contributions to civil liberties over the past three decades are legion. Starting with my fellowship in the Arthur Garfield Hays Civil Liberties Program at NYU in 1966–67, I, like many of my colleagues, have greatly benefited from Norman Dorsen's unmatched skills as a teacher, lawyer and civil libertarian.

[1]365 U.S. 167 (1961), *overruled in part.* Monell v. New York Dep't of Social Servs., 436 U.S. 658 (1978).

[2]42 U.S.C. § 1983 (1988), originally enacted as § 1 of the Ku Klux Klan Act of 1871, ch. 22, § 1, 17 Stat. 13.

[3]365 U.S. at 169.

[4]*Id.* at 183–85.

that Section 1983 was intended to counter these violations, the Court held out the promise of an effective federal remedy for police abuse.

Unfortunately, the expectations engendered by *Monroe* have not been fully realized. After three decades and much constitutional litigation,[5] the abuses continue, in many ways unabated. The beating of Rodney King by Los Angeles police in 1991 and the highly controversial acquittal of the officers involved focused attention once again on the problem of police abuse and demonstrated the continuing existence of the practices and policies that cause it.

Almost everyone who viewed the tape of the King beating was appalled by the display of senseless brutality. While some attempted to explain or defend the police actions, the evidence of brutality and abuse was so strong that a defense was rendered implausible.[6] The incident had the earmarks of classic police abuse: extremely excessive force used by white officers against a black suspect, an event infused with racism, and carried out with an attitude of impunity.[4] For some, the event echoed numerous similar events in the past. Responding to the King incident, New York City Police Commissioner Lee P. Brown declared that "the problem of excessive force in American policing is real."[7] For many others, it was a first-time eyeopener, a window into a world of official violence that could not be squared with our cultural and political norms.[8]

The bookends of *Monroe v. Pape* and Rodney King embrace volumes of law and politics. An essential question that emerges from this thirty-year period is whether the institutions, programs and principles we have developed to empower the police are also adequate to the task of controlling the police. We must also ask whether in our society, which relies substantially on the courts to regulate and control governmental behavior, the legal response to police abuse is sufficiently sensitive to the institutional nature of the problem.

Enforcing the proper restraints on police power is a difficult problem in any society. In the United States there is both a fear of governmental abuse

---

[5]*See, e.g.,* Estelle v. Gamble, 429 U.S. 97 (1976) (Eighth Amendment); Graham v. Connor, 490 U.S. 386 (1989) (Fourth Amendment); Katz v. United States. 389 U.S. 347 (1967) (Fourth Amendment); Tennessee v. Garner, 471 U.S. 1 (1985) (Fourth Amendment). *See also* Harry A. Blackmun, *Section 1983 and Federal Protection of Individual Rights—Will the Statute Remain Alive or Fade Away?,* 60 N.Y.U. L. REV. 1. 19–20 (1985).

[6]*See generally* Report of the Independent Commission on the Los Angeles Police Department (1991) (on file with the *Harvard Civil Rights-Civil Liberties Law Review*) [hereinafter LAIC].

[7]George James, *Police Chiefs Call for U.S. to Study Use of Force,* N.Y. TIMES, Apr. 17,1991, at B3.

[8]Judge Alex Kozinski of the United States Court of Appeals for the Ninth Circuit has stated:

[F]or a lot of naive people, including me, [the King case] puts a real doubt on the posture of prosecutors that police are disinterested civil servants just "telling it as it is."

We should have known all along what this incident points out: that police get involved in what they do and that they are participants in the process just like anyone else. They are subject to bias and they do have a stake in the outcome.

Darlene Ricker, *Behind the Silence,* 77 A.B.A. § 45, 48 (1991). This observation was foreshadowed by Justice Jackson's important insight, made over forty years earlier, that, in considering Fourth Amendment claims, we should be fully aware that the police are involved in the "often competitive enterprise of ferreting out crime." Johnson v. United States, 333 U.S. 10,14 (1948).

and a tolerance of repressive measures, the latter reflecting a belief that police excesses are necessary to combat crime.[9] The pervasiveness of violence, the lack of social cohesiveness, racial and ethnic discrimination, and sharp disparities in privilege, wealth and power supply a fertile ground for crime and social unrest. Frustration with disorder and crime in turn leads to a public acceptance of extra-constitutional police practices. Because police abuse is most often directed against those without political power or social status, their complaints are often dismissed or ignored.

Acceptance of a certain level of police abuse is a predictable majoritarian response to crime, upheaval and threats to the status quo. The true test of our society's commitment to constitutional constraints is how government and the courts respond to these systemic deviations from constitutional norms. If we examine current police conduct in light of this test, it is clear the response of government and the courts has been insufficient. We have manifested an indifference to documented abuses, and we have fostered official violence through social, political and legal structures that reinforce patterns of unlawfulness. We know much about the principles of accountability and organizational control, yet we often fail to apply these basic precepts to law enforcement officials.[10]

In order to explore the sharply differing perceptions of the nature of police abuse and analyze the contemporary legal and political disputes over this profoundly difficult problem, it is helpful to consider an updated version of *Monroe v. Pape.*

II. METROPOLIS, U.S.A., 1992

Metropolis, a large urban area, like many of its sister cities across the country, has over the past fifteen years experienced an increase in crime and has suffered the pernicious effects of drugs, unemployment and poverty. The police department is structured and operated along the lines of most large city departments. It has devoted an increasing amount of resources to training and supervision, and has recruited and hired additional minority members. The

---

[9]While most commentators condemn proven cases of police abuse, excuses are still made. For example, in the aftermath of the highly publicized beating of Rodney King, syndicated columnist Patrick Buchanan wrote:

> In our polarized and violent society, most Americans have come to look upon the cops as "us," and upon King, a convicted felon, as "them." He is the enemy in a war we are losing, badly; and we have come to believe the cops are our last line of defense.

Patrick J. Buchanan, *The Police Are the Last Line of Defense,* L.A. TIMES, Mar. 10, 1991, at M5.

Also writing after the King beating, another commentator wrote: "[T]he tape of some Los Angeles-area cops giving the what-for to an ex-con . . . is not a pleasant sight, of course; neither is cancer surgery. Did they hit him too may times? Sure, but that's not the issue: it's safe streets versus urban terror." Llewellyn H. Rockwell, *It's Safe Streets Versus Urban Terror,* L.A. TIMES, Mar. 10, 1991, at M5.

[10]*See. e.g.,* JEROME H SKOLNICK & JAMES J. FYFE, ABOVE THE LAW: POLICE AND EXCESSIVE USE OF FORCE (forthcoming from Free Press 1992) (on file with the author); KENNETH CULP DAVIS, POLICE DISCRETION (1975). *See also* Susan Sturm. *Resolving the Remedial Dilemma: Strategies of Judicial Intervention in Prisons,* 138 U. PA. L. REV. 805 (1990).

training program is well in line with professional standards, setting forth the appropriate constitutional standards for the use of police powers.[11]

The police are under substantial pressure to control and deter violent crime and illicit drug transactions. A special narcotics squad with city-wide jurisdiction has been established to combat drug activity. Members of this squad report only to the Unit Commander. The squad is responsible for building intelligence with respect to drug activity, conducting raids of suspected drug locations, recruiting informants and targeting areas that have significant drug and drug-related problems.

The nation is involved in a "war on drugs."[12] Congress and state legislatures have given the police and prosecution a powerful array of new law enforcement measures.[13] At the same time, the Supreme Court has drastically limited the substantive protections of the Fourth Amendment[14] and has significantly narrowed the exclusionary rule,[15] thus authorizing increasingly invasive police searches, seizures and other investigative practices.

Enormous sums of money have been expended on the drug war, primarily on the law enforcement side of the equation.[16] Between 1975 and 1990, there

---

[11]There are no binding national standards for police officer training. Each jurisdiction sets its own requirements, but all require a course of instruction in constitutional law. Metropolitan police forces typically exceed their state's minimum requirements. For example, the Boston Police Academy, while required to offer 420 training hours to recruits, provides over 800 hours of training, which includes approximately thirty hours of constitutional law. Instruction primarily consists of lectures conducted by the Constitutional Law Instructor, who is both a lawyer and a police officer. Police officers also receive annual updates. Telephone Interview with Lt. James Moore, Constitutional Law Instructor, Boston Police Academy (Apr. 17, 1992).

[12]The "war on drugs" was officially declared by President Ronald Reagan on October 14, 1982 in a speech to the United States Department of Justice. Leslie Maitland, *President Gives Plan to Combat Drug Networks,* N.Y. TIMES, Oct. 15, 1982, at A1. *See also* THE WHITE HOUSE, NATIONAL DRUG CONTROL STRATEGY (1989).

[13]*See generally* MARC MAUER, THE SENTENCING PROJECT, AMERICANS BEHIND BARS: A COMPARISON OF INTERNATIONAL RATES OF INCARCERATION 7–11 (1991); Paul Finkelman, *The War on Defense Lawyers, in* NEW FRONTIERS IN DRUG POLICY 113 (A.S. Trebach & K.B. Zeese eds., 1991); Max D. Stern & David Hoffman, *Privileged Informers: The Attorney Subpoena Problem and a Proposal for Reform,* 136 U. PA. L. REV. 1783 (1988); David Rudovsky, *The Right to Counsel Under Attack,* 136 U. PA. L. REV. 1965 (1988); United States v. Monsanto, 491 U.S. 600 (1989).

[14]*See, e.g.,* Florida v. Bostick, 111 S. Ct. 2382 (1991) (holding that searches of consenting bus passenger's luggage without articulable suspicion not per se unconstitutional); California v. Hodari D., 111 S. Ct. 1547 (1991); Michigan Dep't of State Police v. Sitz, 110 S. Ct. 2481 (1990); National Treasury Employees Union v. Von Raab, 489 U.S. 656 (1989).

[15]*See, e.g.,* United States v. Leon, 468 U.S. 897 (1984) (holding that exclusionary rule should not apply to evidence obtained by officers reasonably relying on a search warrant ultimately found to be invalid); Stone v. Powell, 428 U.S. 465 (1976); United States v. Calandra, 414 U.S. 338 (1974).

[16]At the federal level, total funding for drug enforcement was $4.6 billion in 1985, $6.6 billion in 1989 and $8.2 billion in 1992. The proposed budget for 1993 has earmarked $8.6 billion for drug enforcement efforts. OFFICE OF MANAGEMENT AND BUDGET, BUDGET OF THE UNITED STATES GOVERNMENT FISCAL YEAR 1993, 190 (1992). There are substantial additional costs for the courts, prosecutors, appointed counsel and the prisons. On the state and local level, a 1987 study by Wharton Econometric Forecasting Associates estimated state and local police expenditures (not including outlays for courts and prisons) at $5 billion for 1985. Ethan A. Nadelmann, *Drug Prohibition in the*

has been a three-fold increase in the number of prisoners in the United States; in 1992 we hold well over a million people behind bars, the largest prison population per capita of any industrialized country.[17] The war on drugs is largely accountable for this development, due to greater numbers of arrests and significantly increased sentences caused by mandatory minimum sentences and guideline sentencing schemes.[18] Whatever the merits of this heavy-on-enforcement approach (and the results certainly justify acute skepticism),[19] the directives to police forces around the country have been unambiguous: it is a war, and virtually any means will be tolerated on the battlefield.

The Metropolis narcotics squad has for the past six months investigated drug selling the Circle Park section, a predominantly African-American, lower-income neighborhood. Complaints by community residents and articles in the city newspaper have led to heightened concern over the drug problem in this area. Rumors have associated Charles and Linda Raft with known drug sellers. To secure further information about these individuals, the police decide to arrest Robert Castle, a convicted drug abuser, who they believe is a friend of the Rafts. The police arrest Castle on false charges and tell him that things will go much better for him if he cooperates in the investigation of the Rafts. Castle agrees to cooperate and tells the police that cocaine is stored in the Raft residence and that he has seen them sell the drug as recently as two weeks before. Based on these assertions, the police obtain a warrant to search the Rafts' home.[20]

United States: Costs, Consequences, and Alternatives, 245 SCIENCE 939, 940 (1989). State spending on prisons today is twelve times what it was just twenty years ago. Neal Pierce, *Filling Our Prisons Isn't Deterring Crimes,* PHILA. INQUIRER, Jan. 13, 1992, at 7A. Far less money is spent on drug rehabilitation and education programs. *See* Larry Gostin, *The Interconnected Epidemics of Drug Dependency and AIDS,* 26 HARV. C.R.-C.L. L. REV. 113 (1991); MAUER, *supra* note 11, at 13; MARC MAUER, THE SENTENCING PROJECT, AMERICANS BEHIND BARS: ONE YEAR LATER 9 (Feb. 1992) [hereinafter MAUER 1992 UPDATE]. *See also* BUDGET OF THE UNITED STATES GOVERNMENT FISCAL YEAR 1993, *supra,* at 190.

[17]MAUER, *supra* note 11, at 4, 6; Pierce, *supra* note 16, at 7A.

[18]*See* Marc Mauer, *Americans Behind Bars,* 6 CRIMINAL JUSTICE 12, 16–17, 38 (1992); MAUER 1992 UPDATE, *supra* note 16, at 7–9.

[19]*See generally* Michael Levine, *The Drug "War": Fight It At Home,* N.Y. TIMES, Feb. 16, 1992, at E15; Nadelmann, *supra* note 16: John Kaplan, *Taking Drugs Seriously,* THE PUBLIC INTEREST, Summer 1988, at 32; Milton Friedman, *A War We're Losing,* WALL ST. J., Mar. 7, 1991, at A14; STEVEN WISOTSKY, BEYOND THE WAR ON DRUGS (Prometheus Books 1990) (1986). *See also* Gostin, *supra* note 16 (arguing that this "penal" approach to controlling drug abuse has greatly contributed to other social ills, such as the needle-borne spread of AIDS).

[20]The affidavit of probable cause in the search warrant application states:

The undersigned affiant is a member of the Narcotics Unit of the Metropolis Police Department and has been involved in the investigation of drug and drug-related crime for the past three years. On [date] a confidential informant told the affiant that cocaine is stored in the residence of Charles and Linda Raft (address). The informant has provided reliable information in the past. On three occasions, information provided by the informant resulted in the arrest of drug suspects or in the seizure of controlled substances. The confidential informant saw drugs in the Rafts' house two weeks ago. The Rafts sell the drug from their home to other persons. Based on the informant's contacts and sources, he believes that the Rafts will have a large amount of cocaine in their house on this date, in preparation for a large sale tomorrow.

At 7:30 p.m., ten heavily armed officers arrive to execute the warrant. They sledgehammer the front door and gain entry to the living room. To immobilize the occupants of the house, they order the Rafts and their twelve-year-old son to lie on the floor, guns trained at their heads; they are warned that if they move they will be shot. Police fan out through the house searching for drugs. They do not find any cocaine, but in the process of the search they do discover a small amount of marijuana. During the search, the police empty closets, over-turn tables, take apart household equipment and tools and dismantle several pieces of furniture. Two of the officers direct racial epithets at the family; Mr. Raft is called a "black-ass drug dealer."

Frustrated by their lack of success, the police take Mr. Raft into the base-ment and threaten him with arrest for possession of marijuana unless he sup-plies them with information about drug dealers in the neighborhood. Raft tells the police that he knows nothing about drug transactions, and that the marijuana is left over from a party they gave several months before. The po-lice inform Raft that their informant had been in the house and had observed narcotics transactions; Raft again states that he has no information and that he does not deal in drugs. Raft does add that he had recently been involved in a dispute with a person in the neighborhood who is known to be involved in drugs, Robert Castle. Raft asks the police if Castle was the informant, but the police decline to answer.

Believing that Raft is lying about his involvement in drug activity, the po-lice decide to arrest him for possession of marijuana, even though they know that the amount involved is below the level established by the District Attor-ney as a minimum threshold for criminal charges. At the narcotics division, Raft is again questioned about drug activity; upon his denials, he is struck several times by one of the officers. He suffers injuries to the face and arms. He is then charged with assaulting a police officer and resisting arrest.

At the preliminary hearing on the charges, an assistant district attorney of-fers to drop the criminal charges against Raft if he will agree to waive his right to sue the police. Raft agrees to these conditions, and the criminal charges are dismissed.

This version of *Monroe v. Pape,* updated to the 1990s, provides a point of de-parture for examining the key elements and dynamics of police misconduct.[21] The next section analyzes the hypothetical in terms of the legal response the institutional causes of the conduct and the culture of police abuse. In the con-cluding section of this Article, I explore a possible agenda for reform.

III. JUDICIAL AND ADMINISTRATIVE REMEDIES FOR POLICE MISCONDUCT: THE FAILURE OF THE COURTS AND THE POLITICAL PROCESS

As a matter of public policy and constitutional law, one would expect that the conduct of the police in our hypothetical would be subject to strong

---

[21]The facts in this hypothetical present events that occur on a far too regular basis. *See* HOUSE COMM. ON THE JUDICIARY, REPORT ON THE OMNIBUS CRIME CONTROL ACT of 1991, H.R. REP. No 242, 102d Cong., 1st Sess., pt. 1, at 135–39 (1991).

condemnation. Indeed, a video portrayal of these events would probably inspire reactions similar to those generated by the Rodney King video. Yet, in the real world of civil rights litigation and police administration, we can expect to find just the opposite: a good deal of the misconduct will not be remediable in the courts and, as an internal administrative matter, little if any evaluative or disciplinary action would be taken against the officers. In fact, as we will see, their actions were a predictable result of police policies and legal doctrine that subordinate individual rights to police power.

The hypothetical raises distinct issues of legal and administrative process, as well as social policy. To elucidate these systemic problems, it is helpful to examine each aspect of the Metropolis police officers' conduct.

A. The Search Warrant

The process by which the police obtained the warrant is highly problematic. The officers used an illegal arrest to put pressure on an informant, withheld this information from the judge who issued the warrant, and submitted an affidavit that arguably fell short of probable cause. In a civil suit, the warrant could be attacked for its failure to provide a sufficient factual basis for believing the informer's tip.[22] However, even if a reviewing court found there was no probable cause to justify the warrant, the doctrine of qualified immunity would preclude a damage awarded against the officer who secured it unless no reasonably well-trained officer would have believed that probable cause existed.[23] Thus, even if a constitutional violation could be proven, the officer would be protected from liability in damages.[24]

The facts suggest that the informant acted out of a personal grudge against the Rafts and may have provided false information. However, unless this fact was known to the police, it would not provide an adequate basis for challenging the warrant.[25] Indeed, the warrant could still be upheld even if the police deliberately withheld the fact that they had illegally arrested Castle

---

[22]See Illinois v. Gates, 462 U.S. 213, 239 (1983); Aguilar v. Texas, 378 U.S. 108 (1964).

[23]Malley v. Briggs, 475 U.S. 335. 345 (1986). In *United States v. Leon,* 468 U.S. 897, 922 n.23 (1984), the Supreme Court adopted the same standard for a "good-faith" exception to the exclusionary rule. *Leon* has been the subject of extensive discussion. *See* Abraham Goldstein, *The Search Warrant, the Magistrate, and Judicial Review,* 62 N.Y.U. L. REV. 1173 (1987); Craig Uchida et al., *Acting in Good Faith: The Effects of* United States v. Leon *on the Police and Courts,* 30 ARIZ. L. REV. 467 (1988); Donald Dripps, *Living with* Leon, 95 YALE L.J. 906 (1986); Steven D. Duke. *Making* Leon *Worse,* 95 YALE L.J. 1405 (1986).

[24]The doctrine of qualified immunity shields government officials from damage awards in civil rights cases where their conduct "does not violate clearly established statutory or constitutional rights of which a reasonable person would have known." Harlow v. Fitzgerald, 457 U.S. 800, 818 (1982). For further discussion of this doctrine, *see infra* notes 35–37, 42–43 and accompanying text.

[25]Where an officer has a reasonable basis to credit the assertions of an informant, the fact that the informant knowingly provided false information is a not basis for attacking the warrant. Franks v. Delaware, 438 U.S. 154 (1978). *See also* Commonwealth v. Bradshaw, 434 A.2d 181 (Pa. Super. 1981).

and pressured him to talk.[26] Suing Castle would not be a real option for the Rafts either, given the informant's privilege and the difficulty of establishing the level of state action necessary to bring his conduct within the purview of Section 1983.[27]

Finally, the Rafts could not assert a violation of their own Fourth Amendment rights based on Castle's unlawful pretext arrest. Even if the police deliberately violated Castle's rights to enable them to obtain information to be used against the Rafts, the Rafts would lack standing to challenge such unconstitutional conduct.[28]

There is a direct link between the legal standards regarding the search warrant process and the tactics used by the Metropolis police. Warrants can issue on little more than hearsay allegations of informants,[29] and the Court has erected virtually insurmountable barriers to requiring further judicial inquiry into the informant's credibility, motives or even her very existence.[30] Thus, the police have been told that barring the most unusual circumstances there will be no inquiry into the truthfulness of what the informant alleged or the truthfulness of the officer's assertions.

If Metropolis is true to contemporary police administration, it will have no standards for informant control.[31] Each detective or officer is relatively free to develop her own network of informants, and there is little overall supervision of individual informants' credibility, reliability or usefulness.[32] Moreover, in

[26]In *Franks,* 438 U.S. 154, the Court ruled that a search warrant will be deemed invalid for reasons of an affiant's misrepresentations only where the false information was given deliberately or in reckless disregard of the truth, and where probable cause would not have existed without that information. *See also* Leon, 468 U.S. at 923.

[27]On the informant's privilege, see McCray v. Illinois, 386 U.S. 300 (1967) (as a general rule, government need not reveal identity of informant at suppression hearing; disclosure only required where defendant makes a substantial showing that informant may not exist or that affiant has deliberately misstated information received). *See also* Franks, 438 U.S. at 167. In civil suits, the courts generally have not found informants to be acting "under color of state law" and therefore not subject to suit under § 1983. *See e.g.,* Ghandi v. Police Dep't of City of Detroit, 823 F. 2d 959 (6th Cir. 1987).

[28]Wong Sun v. United States, 371 U.S. 471 (1963). Indeed, even where the police commit a criminal act to obtain information about a third-party suspect, the Supreme Court has denied the third party standing to challenge the illegality, ruling that the federal courts should not invoke their supervisory powers to exclude the evidence obtained. *See* United States v. Payner, 447 U.S. 727 (1980).

[29]*See, e.g.,* Illinois v. Gates, 462 U.S. 213 (1983); *McCray,* 386 U.S. 300 (1967).

[30]Absent extraordinary circumstances, the identity of the informant will not be disclosed. *See Franks,* 438 U.S. 154; *McCray,* 386 U.S. 300. *See also* Irving Younger, *The Perjury Routine,* THE NATION, May 8, 1967, at 596.

[31]The general practice among police departments is that informants are treated as the "property" of individual investigators; interactions between informants and investigators are most often informal and go undocumented. However, a more centralized and professionalized system has recently been proposed by groups such as the International Association of Chiefs of Police National Law Enforcement Policy Center. *See* INTERNATIONAL ASSOC. OF CHIEFS OF POLICE NATIONAL LAW ENFORCEMENT POLICY CENTER, MODEL POLICY: CONFIDENTIAL INFORMANTS—CONCEPTS AND ISSUES PAPER (June 1990). These standards have yet to be adopted on a national scale.

[32]*See* Selwyn Raab, *Chief Warns of Corruption in Drug* Unit, N.Y. TIMES, Jan. 9, 1992, at B1 (revelations that NYC narcotics investigators lied to strengthen cases and obtain arrest warrants demonstrates need for tighter internal controls and supervision).

cases where a court actually strikes down a warrant and suppresses evidence in a criminal case, or awards a plaintiff damages in a civil matter, the adjudication is not likely to be reported to the department.[33]

The police and prosecutor also know that under the "good faith exception" to the exclusionary rule, even if the warrant does not state probable cause, it will be upheld if a reasonable officer would have believed that it did, a standard that has sustained the most questionable of warrants.[34] The qualified immunity doctrine would then preclude recovery against the Metropolis officers where the conduct, though adjudged unconstitutional, had not been previously clearly proscribed.[35] The defense would be available even where the officers acted with malice or with an intent to violate the citizen's rights.[36] The policy considerations supporting some form of immunity—such as the desire to protect officials from suit where they were not reasonably on notice of the legal standards governing their conduct—could be satisfied with a far narrower defense.[37]

Whatever the theoretical and policy merits of qualified immunity, we must recognize that broader immunity creates greater incentives to cut constitutional corners. Where more surveillance or investigation might be indicated prior to seeking a warrant, an officer could decide to forego this work, knowing that she only has to approximate probable cause. Furthermore, an officer might be tempted to falsely assert than an informant has a strong record of reliability. Even worse. an officer could entirely fabricate an informant with minimal fear of negative repercussions. In the Rafts' case, there was a distinct possibility that the informant acted out of personal malice in providing the information, yet the officers had no incentive to examine his truthfulness.

B.   Execution of the Search Warrant

Similar incentives to cut constitutional corners exist in executing the warrant. The officers' entry into the Raft house appears to have been a violation of the Fourth Amendment, as there was no "knock and announce" before the police used a sledgehammer to invade the premises.[38] Of course, the police might

---

[33]Response of Defendant City of Philadelphia to Interrogatories in Campbell v. City of Philadelphia, C.A. No. 91–4512 (E.D. Pa. 1991) (copy on file with author).

[34]*See* United States v. Leon, 468 U.S. 897, 920 (1984); United States v. Bishop, 890 F.2d 212, 216–18 (10th Cir. 1989).

[35]Anderson v. Creighton, 483 U.S. 635 (1987); Harlow v. Fitzgerald, 457 U.S. 800, 818 (1982).

[36]*Harlow,* 457 U.S. at 815–19.

[37]*See* David Rudovsky, *The Qualified Immunity Doctrine in the Supreme Court Judicial Activism and the Restriction of Constitutional Rights,* 138 U. Pa. L. Rev. 23 (1989); Richard H. Fallon, Jr. & Daniel J. Meltzer, *New Law, Non-Retroactivity, and Constitutional Remedies,* 104 Harv. L. Rev. 1731, 1822–23 (1991).

[38]State and federal statutes typically require the police to " knock and announce their purpose unless there are exigent circumstances that justify immediate entry. *See. e.g.,* Cal. Penal Code § 844 (West 1982); 18 U.S.C. § 3109 (1988). The Fourth Amendment also appears to require the "knock and announce," absent exigent circumstances. *See* Ker v. California, 374 U.S. 23 (1963).

dispute whether or not there was any prior announcement of purpose, presenting a factual issue at trial.

Moreover, it is possible that the officers would testify that they dispensed with the knock and announce procedure based on their belief that violence or destruction of the drugs would have resulted if they had identified themselves. While it seems to be settled law that an announcement of purpose is generally not forgiven in these circumstances, and that permission to dispense with these requirements must by granted by the judge who issues the warrant,[39] the police could still raise a qualified immunity defense to this claim.[40]

Several institutional factors also encourage police entry without announcement. The Metropolis police know that if drugs are found during the search, their testimony that they did in fact knock and announce—or that some exigent circumstances justified their entry without identification—would almost always be credited. The police also know that if nothing is found, legal action will be, highly unlikely, and therefore the illegality of their entry will be rendered purely academic.

The manner in which the police searched the Raft house raises serious problems under the Fourth and Fourteenth Amendments. The occupants were terrorized; the police pointed guns at them and forced them to lie on the floor during the search. The destruction of personal property during the search may have constituted a Fourth Amendment violation.[41] The police would likely respond with a potent defense: in narcotics raids they often face violent opposition, and their tactic is to scare and immobilize the occupants to prevent anyone from getting hurt. The destruction of property would be justified by asserting that drugs are often hidden in these areas and that a close and intrusive search is permissible under the circumstances.

While a good case could be made that the search techniques were excessive, it is not at all clear that the Rafts would prevail as to all aspects of the search. Again, under the qualified immunity doctrine, there could be no recovery in damages against the officers unless the law was previously clearly established that the challenged conduct was unconstitutional.[42] Moreover, because a court can decide the immunity question without reaching the merits of the issue, it is possible that no clearly established principles would ever be articulated in this area, thus leaving the police free to engage in similar conduct in the future.[43]

---

[39]*See, e.g.,* Commonwealth v. Grubb. 595 A.2d 133 (Pa. Super. 1991); State v. Cleveland. 348 N.W.2d 512, 519 (Wis. 1984).

[40]The issue under the qualified immunity doctrine would be whether it was clearly established that an unannounced entry based on the generalized exigencies inherent in a drug search must be reviewed by the judge or magistrate reviewing the search warrant and not by the police officer. *See e.g.,* Mitchell v. Forsyth, 472 U.S. 511 (1985).

[41]*See* Tarpley v. Greene, 684 F.2d 1, 9 (D.C. Cir. 1982) ("[D]estruction of property that is not reasonably necessary to effectively execute a search warrant may violate the Fourth Amendment.").

[42]*See supra* notes 24, 35–37 and accompanying text.

[43]*See* Rudovsky, *supra* note 37, at 53–55. *See also* Borucki v. Ryan, 827 F.2d 836 (1st Cir. 1987); Ramirez v. Webb, 835 F.2d 1153 (6th Cir. 1987); Walentas v. Lipper, 862 F. 2d 414 (2d Cir. 1988), *cert. denied,* 490 U.S. 1021 (1989).

It is unlikely that Metropolis police command officials would critically review these search practices.[44] It is also unlikely that the department would take remedial action. The failure to evaluate practices such as the "use of intimidation" during drug raids undermines individual officer accountability by providing implicit departmental approval of these questionable practices.

Even if a court found the officers' conduct to be unconstitutional, supervising officials would rightly consider it unfair to discipline them since the officers involved were not responsible for the adoption of the search techniques employed at the Raft house. It would be appropriate for the department to reconsider its search policy at this point, but unless the courts seem inclined to suppress evidence or to assess damages, the department's belief that these practices are essential to drug enforcement would almost certainly preempt any reform.

Municipal liability would be a potential source for relief. Qualified immunity would not be a defense here.[45] However, under the remedial scheme of Section 1983, municipalities are liable for unconstitutional police conduct only where a municipal policy, law or custom demonstrably caused it.[46] Because these search practices are unlikely to be "official" departmental policy, the Rafts would have the heavy burden of demonstrating a pattern of such excessive searches sufficient to prove a settled practice or custom.[47] The failure of the department to train or properly supervise its officers in this area is a basis for liability, but only where the plaintiff can show that policy makers were "deliberately indifferent" to the rights of the public.[48]

Given the problematic nature of a remedy in damages, the Rafts would probably seek equitable relief. But the Supreme Court has imposed substantial obstacles to such an action. In *City of Los Angeles v. Lyons*,[49] the court refused

---

[44]Even if the unit command had reviewed plans for the search, since no command officials were present during its execution, review would be unlikely unless the Rafts initiated court proceedings. The average metropolitan police department has so device in place to evaluate the performance of officers and teams. *See* Raab *supra* note 32.

[45]*See* Owen v. City of Independence, 445 U.S. 622 (1980).

[46]In *Monell v. New York Dep't of Social Servs.*, 436 U.S. 658 (1978), the Court ruled that a municipality was liable under § 1983 only where "the action that is alleged to be unconstitutional implements or executes a policy statement, ordinance, regulation, or decision officially adopted and promulgated by [the municipality]." *Id.* at 690–91. The *Monell* doctrine has been further refined in more recent case law. *See, e.g.*, City of Canton v. Harris, 489 U.S. 378, 388–89 (1989) (holding that unsatisfactory training of police officers constitutes insufficient grounds for holding city liable unless city exhibited deliberate indifference); City of St. Louis v. Praprotnik, 485 U.S. 112, 122 (1988) (stating that a municipality is liable only if the challenged action was pursuant to official policy); Pembaur v. City of Cincinnati, 475 U.S. 469, 483–84 (1986) (recovery from a municipality can be based upon acts sanctioned by officials responsible for establishing municipal policy).

[47]*See* cases cited *supra* note 46. *See also* City of Oklahoma City v. Tuttle, 471 U.S. 808, 820–22 (1985); Languirand v. Hayden, 717 F.2d 220, 227–30 (5th Cir. 1983).

[48]*City of Canton*, 489 U.S. at 389. For application of this standard in the lower federal courts, *see, e.g.*, Davis v. Mason County, 927 F.2d 1473, 1481–82 (9th Cir. 1991); Gentile v. County of Suffolk, 926 F.2d 142, 152–53 (2d Cir. 1991); Kerr v. City of West Palm Beach, 875 F.2d 1546, 1555–57 (11th Cir. 1989).

[49]461 U.S. 95 (1983).

to grant injunctive relief to a plaintiff who had suffered permanent physical injuries when a police officer administered a "chokehold" in effecting an arrest. Relief was denied even though the record demonstrated that this police practice was commonly used in circumstances not justifying such force and had resulted in sixteen deaths in recent years."[50] The Court determined that the past injury had no continuing effects sufficient to provide standing for prospective relief and that the plaintiff was unable to show that he, as opposed to any other citizen, would again be subject to the same unconstitutional conduct.[51] The Court has been disinclined to enjoin most local police procedures,[52] and it is highly unlikely that the Rafts would be granted equitable relief.

C. Pretextual Arrests

The Metropolis police executed two pretextual arrests to accomplish their goals. They arrested Castle without probable cause; then they arrested Mr. Raft on charges for which they knew he would not be prosecuted. But Castle's arrest, regardless of its illegality, would not provide the Rafts with a constitutional claim.[53] Mr. Raft's own arrest for drug possession was constitutionally permissible since it was supported by objective probable cause.[54] Accordingly, unless the police department restricts the power of its officers to make pretext arrests or searches, this conduct is likely to be repeated.

The Raft case demonstrates how the Court's jurisprudence on pretext arrests provides incentives to the police to violate or avoid basic constitutional guarantees. The police knew in advance that their illegal arrest of Castle would be a moot legal issue in any resulting investigation or arrest of the Rafts. Castle was unlikely to complain since he was the beneficiary of a deal to drop all charges against him. Raft's arrest on drug charges would never have been made in the normal course of events, but the police used it in this

---

[50]*Id.* at 100, 110–13.

[51]*Id.* at 101–05.

[52]*See, e.g.,* Rizzo v. Goode, 423 U.S. 362 (1976).

[53]*See* United States v. Payner, 447 U.S. 727 (1980); Rakas v. Illinois, 439 U.S. 128 (1978). *See also supra* note 28 and accompanying text.

[54]Most federal courts have ruled that where a reasonable police officer could have taken the action in question consistent with the Fourth Amendment, the fact that she did it for improper purposes is irrelevant. *See, e.g.,* United States v. Causey, 834 F.2d 1179, 1184-85 (5th Cir. 1987) (en banc); United States v. Hawkins, 811 F.2d 210, 213–15 (3d Cir. 1987). Other courts have ruled that where no reasonable officer would have made the pretextual stop, even though technically allowed under the Fourth Amendment, the evidence should be suppressed. *See, e.g.,* United States v. Guzman. 864 F.2d 1512, 1515—18 (10th Cir. 1988); United States v. Smith, 799 F.2d 704, 708 (11th Cir. 1986). The Supreme Court recently denied certiorari, over Justice White's dissent, in three cases that presented this issue: Cummins V. United States, 90–1628, 60 U.S.L.W. 3358 (Nov. 12, 1991); Trigg v. United States, 91–5013, 60 U.S.L.W. 3358 (Nov. 12, 1991); Enriquez-Nevarez v. United States, 91–5087, 60 U.S.L.W. 3358 (Nov. 12, 1991).

See generally Daniel S. Jones, *Pretext Searches and the Fourth Amendment: Unconstitutional Abuses of Power,* 137 U, PA. L. REV. 1791 (1989); John M. Burkoff, *The Pretext Search Doctrine Returns After Never Leaving,* 66 U. DET. L. REV. 363 (1989).

case to gain leverage against Raft. This leverage was used both in the investigation and later to obtain the release of the officers from civil liability in exchange for the dismissal of the criminal charges. Surely, if deterring police misconduct is a principal purpose of the Court's Fourth Amendment doctrine, the pretextual arrests made in Metropolis should be classic candidates for strong remedial action.

There is substantial evidence that police are quite sophisticated in exploiting the many loopholes created by the Court's constitutional remedies jurisprudence. For example, in *Cooper v. Dupnik*,[55] the police deliberately refused to honor the suspect's request for counsel during interrogation. The police knew that any statement given by the defendant would be suppressed at trial, but they also knew that the Supreme Court had ruled that such statements could be used to impeach the defendant if he testified at trial.[56] The defendant was in fact innocent and was exonerated of all charges. In an ensuing lawsuit under Section 1983, the police admitted that they had hoped their illegal questioning would result in a statement that would deter the defendant from testifying. The court nonetheless ruled that *Miranda* is not a constitutionally mandated rule, and that the plaintiff was not harmed by lack of counsel since no fruits of the questioning were introduced against him.[57] Cooper reveals a troubling judicial complacency and rigidity in the face of a police practice that consciously manipulated and ignored basic constitutional guarantees. If the courts do not address deliberate misconduct, it is unrealistic to believe that other institutions will respond.

In a world where most police officers and administrators continue to believe that ends justify means, few departments will forego pretextual police practices in the absence of judicial pressures to reform. This is particularly true of a narcotics unit operating under few, if any, meaningful constraints with respect to policies involving informants and undercover activity.

D. Excessive Force

The Metropolis officers' conduct back at the Narcotics Division probably violated the Fourth and Fourteenth Amendments.[58] Raft would argue that the

---

[55]924 F.2d 1520 (9th Cir. 1991). *reh's granted en banc.* 933 F.2d 798 (1991).

[56]*See* Harris v. New York, 401 U.S. 222 (1971).

[57]*Cooper,* 924 F.2d at 1528.

[58]In *Graham v. Connor,* 490 U.S. 386 (1989), the Court ruled that the use of excessive force by the police during an arrest or other seizure of a person violates the reasonableness standard of the Fourth Amendment. The Court rejected the state's assertion that such claim should be decided under a substantive due process test. Two issues have been contested in the wake of *Graham.* The first is the issue of what standard applies after the suspect has been arrested and taken to the police district. The Court has ruled that the Eighth Amendment applies to post-conviction claims of excessive force. *See* Hudson V. McMillian, 112 S. Ct. 995 (1992) (use of excessive physical force against a prisoner may violate Eight Amendment although no serious injury resulted); Whitley v. Albers. 475 U.S. 312 (1986). The lower federal courts have divided on the question of how to evaluate claims by persons held between arrest and detention. *See* Wilkins v. May, 872 F.2d 190, 192–93 (7th Cir. 1989), *cert. denied.* 493 U.S. 1026 (1990) (applying substantive due process test); Titran v. Ackman, 893 F.2d 145, 147 (7th Cir. 1990) (applying due process standard which court describes as similar to the Fourth Amendment test); Austin v. Hamilton, 945 F.2d 1155 (10th Cir. 1991) (applying Fourth Amendment test).

police used excessive force by striking him while they were questioning him, and that his arrest for the false cover charges constituted malicious prosecution and false imprisonment.[59] However, proving these allegations would not be easy. The police would undoubtedly testify that Raft became unruly and assaulted an officer, and that reasonable force was used to subdue him. Because of the police code of silence,[60] the officers who witnessed the assault would testify either that they did not observe the incident or, if they did, that the police acted properly in self-defense. The incident, unlike the Rodney King beating, would not have been videotaped.

Excessive force is a product of a police culture that rationalizes physical abuse as appropriate punishment for persons who are viewed as troublemakers or deviants. Studies of excessive use of force point out that a predictable catalyst to abuse is the officers' perception that their authority is being questioned or defied.[61] Even verbal questioning of authority leads many police officers to believe that their power and position have been threatened. In these situations, the police will demand immediate compliance and acquiescence. If obedience is not forthcoming, the incident escalates and an arrest and use of force is likely to follow.[62]

Physical abuse is a constant threat and will occur most frequently in departments that do not take this conduct seriously.[63] The potential for illegal use of force is so great that the experienced administrator knows that without a meaningful system of accountability, officers will act illegally more frequently.

The second question that has arisen is whether the plaintiff must demonstrate a certain level of injury to establish an excessive force claim. *Compare* Johnson v. Morel, 876 F.2d 477, 479–80 (5th Cir. 1989) (per curiam) *with* Gray v. Spillman, 925 F.2d 90, 93–94 (4th Cir. 1991). The Court's recent ruling in *Hudson*, 112 S. Ct. 995, makes clear that the nature of the physical injury suffered is not a controlling factor for Eighth Amendment purposes.

[59]A police defendant accused of using excessive force should not be able to prevail using the qualified immunity doctrine. Assuming the use of force was unjustified, the defendant cannot claim that a reasonable officer would have believed his actions to be lawful simply because it was not clear to him what legal standard applied. *See* Dixon v. Richer, 922 F.2d 1456, 1460–62 (10th Cir. 1991) (rejecting qualified immunity defense because legal standard for unreasonable force during seizure was clearly established at time of incident).

[60]The "police code of silence" is an unwritten rule and custom that police will not testify against a fellow officer and that police are expected to help in any cover-up of illegal actions. The code of silence has been recognized and documented in litigation and studies of police culture. *See, e.g.,* Brandon v. Holt, 469 U.S. 464, 467 n.6 (1985) (quoting Brandon v. Allen, 516 F. Supp. 1355, 1361 (W.D. Tenn. 1981)); Bonsignore v. City of New York, 521 F. Supp.394, 398–99 (S.D.N.Y. 1981), *aff'd*, 683 F.2d 635 (2d Cir. 1982); ALBERT J. REISS, THE POLICE AND THE PUBLIC 213–14 (1971); JEROME H. SKOLNICK, JUSTICE WITHOUT TRIAL: LAW ENFORCEMENT IN DEMOCRATIC SOCIETY 58, 249 (2d ed. 1975). The code of silence is discussed in greater detail below. *See infra* notes 83–89 and accompanying text.

[61]*See* PAUL CHEVIGNY, POLICE POWER: POLICE ABUSES IN NEW YORK 51–83 (1969); SKOLNICK, *supra* note 60.

[62]*See* CHEVIGNY, *supra* note 61, at 51–83, 88–98.

[63]LAIC *supra* note 6, at 151–79; Recommendations of the Task Force on the Use of Force by the Kansas City, Missouri Police Department 45–49 (January 1991) (on file with the author) [hereinafter Kansas City Task Force]; Report of the Boston Police Department Management Review Committee 99–136 (January 1992) (on file with the *Harvard Civil Right-Civil Liberties Law Review*) [hereinafter Boston Police Report].

Even those officers who normally would not use illegal force will be more likely to do so if they know it will be tolerated.[64]

The Rodney King incident is a paradigmatic event demonstrating the serious consequences of the failure to impose accountability. Rodney King underwent a beating that was both protracted and public. The officers involved had to be fully confident of their colleagues' silence and of their department's dismissal of any complaints made by the numerous witnesses to this incident. Indeed, so sure were these officers of their immunity from punishment that they bragged about their abuses on the official police computer system and to medical personnel at the hospital where King was belatedly taken for treatment. Only officers assured by prior experience and knowledge of departmental attitudes that the department would not investigate or punish this type of abuse (regardless of the credibility of the witnesses or of their own incriminating statements) could have rationally taken the risk of engaging in this type of behavior.[65]

---

[64]*See supra* notes 61 and 63. *See also* SKOLNICK & FYFE, *supra* note 10.

[65]The LAIC described the radio transmissions as follows:

Computer and radio messages transmitted among officers immediately after the beating raised additional concerns that the King beating was part of a larger pattern of police abuse. Shortly before the King beating. Powell's and Wind's patrol unit transmitted the computer message that an earlier domestic dispute between an African-American couple was "right out of 'Gorillas in the Mist'", a reference to a motion picture about the study of gorillas in Africa.

The initial report of the beating came at 12:56 a.m., when Koon's unit reported to the Watch Commander's desk at Foothill station. "You just had a big time use of force . . . tased and beat the suspect of CHP pursuit, Big Time." The station responded at 12:57 a.m., "Oh well . . . I'm sure the lizard didn't deserve it . . . ."

. . . . In response to a request from the scene for assistance for a "victim of a beating," the LAPD dispatcher called the Los Angeles Fire Department for a rescue ambulance:

P.D.: . . . Foothill & Osborne. In the valley dude (Fire Department dispatcher laughs) and like he got beat up.

F.D.: (laugh) wait (laugh).

P.D.: We are on scene.

F.D.: Hold, hold on, give me the address again.

P.D.: Foothill & Osborne, he pissed us off, so I guess he needs an ambulance now.

F.D.: Oh, Osborne. Little attitude adjustment?

P.D.: Yeah, we had to chase him.

F.D.: OH!

P.D.: CHP and us, I think that kind of irritated us a little.

F.D.: Why would you want to do that for?

P.D.: (laughter) should know better than run, they are going to pay a price when they do that.

F.D.: What type of incident would you say this is?

P.D.: It's a . . . it's a . . . battery, he go beat up.

At Pacifica Hospital, where King was taken for initial treatment, nurses reported the officers who accompanied King (who included Wind) openly joked and bragged about the number of times King had been hit.

LAIC, *supra* note 6, at 14–15. *See also* Paul L. Hoffman, Legal Director, ACLU Foundation of Southern California, Prepared Remarks Submitted to the House Subcommittee on Civil and Constitutional Rights of the House Committee on the Judiciary, Mar. 20, 1991, 3–6 (on file with the author) [hereinafter Hoffman].

Examples from adjudicated cases and from independent investigations provide hard documentation of the systemic flaws in the complaint processes in many police departments.[66] It is not uncommon to find that officers who have been the subject of numerous citizen complaints of brutality are rarely disciplined and continue to serve on the force.[67] In Los Angeles, for example, the Independent Commission investigating the Rodney King incident determined that several officers who had been found responsible for the illegal use of force on civilians had at the same time received performance reviews that made no mention of these findings and which praised the officers' attitude toward civilians.[68]

It is quite likely that our hypothetical Metropolis has similar infirmities in its review and adjudication of civilian complaints. Not so hypothetically, assume that a study of the civilian complaints lodged against members of the Metropolis police department discloses that for a two-year period preceding this incident "a total of 756 individual officers were named as subjects of civilian complaints . . . . The names of 29 officers appeared collectively 303 times, each being named nine or more times . . ."[69] If the officer who assaulted Raft was one of the officers with nine or more complaints, his conduct on this occasion should not be surprising.

The department's failure to investigate allegations of abuse, or to impose appropriate punishment, would lead the reasonable police officer to assume that even repeated violations of citizens' rights would be condoned within the department.[70] The failure to hold these officers accountable for their prior misconduct is a direct link to the abuse of Raft. The deleterious consequences of the department's failure to monitor and discipline these officers run far wider than the encouragement it might give them to continue to abuse civilians. The message that violence and abusive conduct will be ignored is also sent to every other officer on the force.[71]

For its part, the Supreme Court either does not grasp the institutional causes of abuse or, as a matter of ideology, is using the doctrines of federalism and judicial restraint to allow these conditions to persist. There is a striking disjunction between the widely recognized causes of abuse and the Court's response. The Supreme Court's rulings reflect a belief that abuse occurs in isolated instances and is caused by an occasional aberrant abusive officer. Faced

---

[66]*See, e.g.,* Gutierrez-Rodriguez v. Cartagena, 882 F.2d 553, 562–66 (1st Cir. 1989); Spell v. McDaniel, 824 F.2d 1380, 1391–95 (4th Cir. 1987), *cert. denied,* 484 U.S. 1027 (1988); Harris v. City of Pagedale, 821 F.2d 499, 508 (8th Cir. 1987). For commentary on this issue, see LAIC, *supra* note 6, at 151–79; Kansas City Task Force, *supra* note 63, at 45–49; Boston Police Report, *supra* note 63, at 99–119 (The Boston Police Department, rather than responding to citizen complaints of abuse, "tries to outlast the [complaining] victim, to continue it and continue it until the victim gets fed up and no longer comes to the hearings.").

[67]*See* LAIC, *supra* note 6, at 37–48; Kansas City Task Force, *supra* note 63, at 45–46; Boston Police Report, *supra* note 63, at 113–14.

[68]LAIC, *supra* note 6, at 137–48.

[69]Kansas City Task Force, *supra* note 63, at 45.

[70]LAIC, *supra* note 6, at 153–79. *See also* Boston Police Report, *supra* note 63, at 113–20.

[71]*See* LAIC, *supra* note 6, at 153–79; Boston Police Report, *supra,* note 63, at 113–20; Kansas City Task Force, *supra* note 63, at 45–49.

with records that reflect institutional causes, the Court recoils at the argument that the Constitution requires intervention on that level.

In several key cases the Court has deliberately passed up the opportunity to craft an approach that would take into account systemic patterns of abuse. In *Rizzo v. Goode*,[72] a federal district court had ruled that there was a pattern of police abuse in Philadelphia. In response, the court ordered the implementation of an internal police department mechanism for the review and adjudication of civilian complaints against officers. The district court made the fairly obvious and well-supported finding that the failure of the police department to investigate these complaints and to discipline officers led to the high level of abuse. The district court's order was focused and limited. It did not, for example, create a civilian review or oversight board.[73]

The Supreme Court reversed, stating that principles of federalism and comity prohibited this kind of relief as an impermissible intervention in the affairs of local government.[74] As a matter of local governmental policy and police administration, the fact that the nation's fourth largest city (one with a well-earned reputation for police abuse) did not have a functioning internal review system is a cause for serious concern. The refusal of the Supreme Court to permit such a remedy demonstrates a studied ignorance of the political and social realities of police misconduct. In addressing the tension between the protection of constitutional rights and local governmental prerogatives, the Court adopted a judicial calculus that reinforces the systemic aspects of police abuse by abdicating any judicial responsibility for the proven structural causes of misconduct.

The Court followed a familiar doctrinal approach in *City of Los Angeles v. Lyons*,[75] in which it refused to enjoin the Los Angeles Police Department's use of the deadly "chokehold." The Court found, *inter alia*, that the improper and illegal application of the chokehold was not a routine City policy, and therefore had been unauthorized.[76] Equitable relief was justified only if "the City ordered or authorized police officers to act [illegally]."[77]

The formalism of *Lyons* is disturbing both as a matter of constitutional adjudication and as a matter of social policy. *Lyons* sent a chilling message to the Los Angeles Police Department: as long as abuses like the chokehold do not become city "policy," the Court would not interfere. It should come as no

---

[72]357 F. Supp. 1289 (E.D. Pa. 1973), *rev'd,* 423 U.S. 362 (1976).

[73]423 U.S. at 366–70.

[74]*Id.* at 377–78.

[75]461 U.S. 95 (1983). *See also supra* notes 49–51 and accompanying text.

[76]*Lyons,* 461 U.S. at 107–08.

[77]*Id.* at 106, *Lyons* has been the subject of severe criticism. *See, e.g.,* David Cole, *Obtaining Standing to Seek Equitable Relief: Taming* Lyons, *in* CIVIL RIGHTS LITIGATION AND ATTORNEY FEES ANNUAL HANDBOOK 101,102 (J. Lobel ed., 1980) (arguing that *Lyons* should be construed narrowly to limit its potentially illegitimate reach); Richard H. Fallon, Jr., *Of Justiciability, Remedies, and Public Law Litigation: Notes on the Jurisprudence of* Lyons, 59 N.Y.U. L. REV. 1 (1984) (arguing that the Court's use of the doctrines of standing and equitable restraint to restrict public law litigation is flawed). The doctrinal flaws discussed in these articles are not the only problems with *Lyons*; the opinion reflects a startling lack of sensitivity to the fatal consequences of the police practice.

surprise that the Rodney King incident occurred in Los Angelos. There is a direct line from *Lyons* to Rodney King, and the Supreme Court bears some responsibility for the pattern of brutality in the Los Angeles Police Department that claimed King as one of its victims.

In a more recent case, the Court did finally understand the link between internal police policies and abuse. In *City of Canton v. Harris,*[78] the Court ruled that in some circumstances the failure of a police department to properly train or discipline its officers may give rise to municipal liability under Section 1983.[79] The causal connection between training and discipline and the incidence of abuse are well established and the Court's ruling should prompt further moves toward increased accountability. In this regard, *City of Canton* represents a short step towards correcting the ostrich-like approach in *Rizzo v. Goode.*[80] It is only a short step, however, because the Court limited the potential reach of its decision by insisting that the failure to train or discipline be the result of "deliberate indifference" of city officials. This is a level of culpability that approaches intentionality and that poses significant problems of proof.[81] The decision is further limited by the fact that the remedy for the failure to train is simply to extract damages from the municipality. This is significant in ensuring compensation for the victim, but unless the damages are substantial, they will probably have little or no affect on policymakers. Whether the judgment will be considered a cost of doing business or will operate as an incentive to reform is an open question in most jurisdictions.[82]

Investigation and adjudication of claims of excessive force (as well as other forms of police abuse) are often frustrated by the police "code of silence."[83] In our hypothetical, several officers witnessed the attack on Mr. Raft. It is a virtual certainty that none of these officers would provide any evidence in an internal proceeding or court case against the offending officers. A former United States Attorney for the Eastern District of Pennsylvania, in recommending leniency for a police officer who testified in a police corruption trial, stated:

> [T]here is a custom that has developed within the Philadelphia Police Department that Philadelphia police officers will acquiesce in the illegal and improper conduct

---

[78]489 U.S. 378 (1989).

[79]*Id.* at 388.

[80]*See* discussion *supra* at notes 72–74 and accompanying text.

[81]*City of Canton,* 489 U.S. at 388–92. Decisions in the lower federal courts demonstrate the difficulties involved in satisfying this burden of proof. *See, e.g.,* Colburn v. Upper Darby Township, 946 F.2d 1017 (3d Cir. 1991); Santiago v. Fenton, 891 F.2d 373 (1st Cir. 1989).

[82]See LAIC, *supra* note 6, at 55–61. *See also* SKOLNICK & FYFE, *supra* note 10.

[83]The "code of silence" has been openly recognized by law enforcement officials. *See, e.g.,* Selwyn Raab, *Five Police Officers Indicted by Jury in Torture Case,* N.Y. TIMES, MAY 3, 1985, at A1 (Police Commissioner urges prison sentences for police officers to help shatter "the blue wall of silence"); Athelia Knight & Benjamin Weiser, *D.C. Police Chief Praises Officer Who Broke Police Code of Silence,* WASH. POST, Dec. 16, 1983, at B1; LAIC, *supra* note 6, at 168–71; Boston Police Report, *supra* note 63, at 59, 116, 124. *See also supra* note 60.

of their fellow officers and that when called to tell the truth, as is the duty of every other citizen in this nation when called before a grand jury or questioned by lawful authorities, that the Philadelphia police officer will remain silent.[84]

The code of silence does more than prevent testimony. It mandates that no officer report another for misconduct, that supervisors not discipline officers for abuse, that wrongdoing be covered up, and that any investigation or legal action into police misconduct be deflected and discouraged.[85] In Boston, for example, experienced investigators will not volunteer for the Internal Affairs Division unless they are promised the ability to choose their next assignment "because they fear retribution once they [go back on the street]."[86] Officers shun temporary promotions to "acting sergeant," despite higher pay and prestige, because they do not want to have to be in the position of disciplining a fellow officer when they "might be back riding with that officer sometime in the future."[87]

Other participants in the criminal justice system abet this policy: prosecutors are highly reluctant to indict police for their illegal acts, judges rarely disbelieve even incredible police testimony, and allegations of police abuse often lead to more severe treatment of the accuser.[88]

There are ways in which the pernicious effects of the code of silence can be mitigated. First, the department must make clear that officers who fail to report and provide information regarding unlawful actions of fellow officers will be subject to serious discipline. To be effective, these sanctions should be directed at supervisory officials who abet the code by uncritical acceptance of reports that demonstrate a pattern of silence. Particular attention should be paid to cases in which the allegations of the complainant are sustained either in internal proceedings or in court, and where officers who observed the incident have either not come forward or have supported the false testimony of the offending officer.

Second, the courts should recognize liability both for officers who fail to file truthful police reports or who remain silent concerning abuses that they have witnessed and for municipalities on a theory that a department's failure to take steps to deal with the code of silence constitutes a municipal policy under *Monell*.[89]

E.   Racially Motivated Conduct

The use of racially derogatory language towards the Rafts is strong evidence that at least some of the officers' misconduct was racially motivated. Such

---

[84]Tim Weiner, *Ex-Officer Who Broke Code of Silence Given Probation,* Phila. Inquirer, Feb. 13, 1985, at 1 (Statement of U.S. Attorney Edward S.G. Dennis, Jr.).

[85]*See supra* notes 60, 83.

[86]Boston Police Report, *supra* note 63, at 124.

[87]*Id.* at 59.

[88]Anthony G. Amsterdam, *The Supreme Court and The Rights of Suspects in Criminal Cases,* 45 N.Y.U. L. Rev. 785, 787–89 (1970).

[89]*See supra* note 46.

conduct is actionable under Section 1983 (and other civil rights acts),[90] although once again the burden of proof is significant. No independent witnesses could confirm the remarks; the police would maintain that they were firm but polite during the search of the house; and most jurors would be disinclined to believe that the police acted out of racial motivation.[91]

The racism reflected in the derogatory remarks made to the Raft family is a legacy of our Nation's history of racial discrimination. Racially motivated conduct is hurtful in any form, but where it infects police practices the risks to the victim are particularly great. Historically, police abuse against minorities has been the single most cited cause for the deep distrust and suspicion that inhere in virtually all police-minority community contacts and that have led on several occasions to rebellions and riots.[92]

Even today, police tactics that would not be countenanced in middle-class suburban communities are the norm in poorer urban areas where minorities make up the majority of the residents. It is not uncommon for the police to conduct sweeps of certain neighborhoods, to stop or arrest persons without individual suspicion, and to conduct searches like the one conducted at the Raft home.[93] The LAIC's report of virulent racism in the Los Angeles Police Department should give pause to those who believe that we have eliminated overt racial prejudice from the criminal justice system.[94] The police justify their differential treatment of minority communities by exploiting the universally shared fear of crime. But people whose lives are threatened daily by criminal activity should not be subjected to police abuse as a price of police protection.

---

[90]*See, e.g.,* Johnson v. Morel, 876 F.2d 477, 479 (5th Cir. 1989) (en banc). Racially motivated police misconduct is also actionable under 42 U.S.C. §§ 1981 and 1982.

[91]Of course, if the police are as openly racist as they were in Los Angeles in the Rodney King incident, police radio transmissions or other recorded statements may provide additional proof of racially motivated abuse.

[92]*See, e.g.,* NATIONAL ADVISORY COMMISSION ON CIVIL DISORDERS, REPORT 157–68 (Government Printing Office 1968) [hereinafter KERNER COMMISSION REPORT].

[93]*See, e.g.,* City of Los Angeles v. Lyons, 461 U.S. 95 (1983); Hall v. Ochs, 817 F.2d 920 (1st Cir. 1987); Spring Garden United Neighbors v. City of Philadelphia, 614 F. Supp. 1350 (E.D. Pa. 1985); Sheri Lynn Johnson, *Race and the Decision to Detain A Suspect,* 93 YALE L.J. 214, 225–37 (1983).

[94]The LAIC reviewed police transmissions and found "an appreciable number of . . . racial remarks," including:

> "Well . . I'm back over here in the projects, pissing off the natives."
> "I would love to drive down Slauson with a flame thrower . . . we would have a barbeque."
> "Sounds like monkey-slapping time."
> "Oh always dear . . . what's happening . . . we're huntin wabbits."
> "Actually, muslim wabbits."
> "Just over here on this arson/homicide . . . be careful one of those rabbits don't bit you."
> "Yeah I know. . . . Huntin wabbits is dangerous."

LAIC, *supra* note 6, at 72.

As long as racial discrimination exists in our culture, it will necessarily impact the criminal justice system.[95] However, we have the capacity to reduce the incidence of racially motivated misconduct. First, police departments must impose serious disciplinary sanctions for racist conduct. Second, departments must continue to integrate their forces both racially and sexually. Third, significant changes must be made in the training of officers with a view toward broadening their respect for persons of different races, sexual orientations, national origins and cultures.[96] Finally, police departments must address their failure to assure minorities quality assignments and equal opportunities for promotions.[97] It is remarkable that *all* of the officers involved in the Rodney King beating were white. While no one would suggest that minority officers do not commit abuses, their presence would assuredly provide some deterrence to overt racism.

F. Institutional Obstacles

There are other significant barriers to judicial vindication of the rights of victims of police misconduct. First, victims are not assured access to counsel. There is probably a very small civil rights bar in Metropolis; most lawyers would not be interested in a contingent fee case against the police or the city, even with the possibility of court-awarded attorney's fees if the suit is successfull.[98] Second, many civil rights plaintiffs are burdened by characteristics that may prejudice juries against them. They are often poor, or members of racial minorities, or uneducated or inarticulate; some have criminal records. Jurors tend to dismiss their allegations, often awarding them less than a full measure of compensation.[99]

Third, release agreements can be insidious obstacles to the vindication of civil rights in police abuse cases: if they are validated by the courts, they will add to the arsenal of those interested in covering up police misconduct. In the Metropolis hypothetical, Raft agreed not to sue the police or the city in return for the dismissal of the criminal charges against him. There is a distinct possibility that this agreement would bar Raft's claims. In *Town of Newton v. Rumery,*[100] the Supreme Court ruled that a release agreement is valid if it is

---

[95]*See* McCleskey v. Kemp, 481 U.S. 279, 286–87 (1987) (discussing racial bias in death penalty prosecutions in Georgia); MAUER, *supra* note 11, at 10; MAUER 1992 UPDATE, *supra* note 16, at 11–12. The drug war has had a highly disproportionate effect on racial minorities, particularly Blacks and Latinos. *See, e.g.,* Lisa Belkin, *Airport Drug Efforts Snaring Innocents Who Fit 'Profiles',* N.Y. TIMES, Mar. 20, 1990, at A1; E.J. Michell, Jr., *Has Drug War Become a War Against Blacks?* DETROIT NEWS, Apr. 26, 1990, at A1; Rose Marie Arce, *Crimes, Drugs and Stereotypes,* NEWSDAY, Dec. 2, 1991, at 5; Minnesota v. Russell, 60, U.S.L.W. 2425 (Dec. 13, 1991).

[96]*See, e.g.,* LAIC, *supra* note 6, at 91–92, 136.

[97]*See, e.g.,* KERNER COMMISSION REPORT, *supra* note 92, at 166; LAIC, *supra* note 6, at 78–91.

[98]*See* Amsterdam, *supra* note 88, at 787; Caleb Foote, *Tort Remedies for Police Violations of Individual Rights,* 39 MINN. L. REV. 493, 500 (1955).

[99]Foote, *supra* note 98, at 500–08.

[100]480 U.S. 386 (1987).

"the product of an informed and voluntary decision,"[101] and if "enforcement of [the] agreement would not adversely affect the relevant public interests."[102] Where a prosecutor played a role in the release negotiations, he must have "an independent and legitimate reason to make this agreement directly related to his prosecutorial responsibilities."[103] The burden of "establish[ing] that the agreement was neither involuntary nor the product of an abuse of criminal process" rests upon civil defendants.[104] If the prosecutor's motivation was simply to protect the police from a civil damages action, the public policy prong of *Rumery* would probably be violated.[105]

Fourth, it is very possible that the individual officers would be judgment proof.[106] If they are, and if there is no provision for indemnification, recovery must be sought directly from the municipality. But under Section 1983, municipal liability can be established only where a city policy, practice or custom has caused the constitutional violation; there is no respondent superior liability.[107]

---

[101]*Id.* at 393.

[102]*Id.* at 398

[103]*Id.*

[104]*Id.* at 399 (O'Connor, J., concurring in part and concurring in the judgment of the plurality).

[105]*See id.* at 400. *See also* Lynch v. City of Alhambra, 880 F.2d 1122, 1127 (9th Cir. 1989); Seth F. Kreimer, *Releases, Redress, and Police Misconduct: Reflections on Agreements to Waive Civil Rights Actions in Exchange for Dismissal of Criminal Charges,* 136 U. PA. L. REV. 851, 934 (1988).

[106]Local and state governmental units differ significantly in their provisions for the defense and indemnification of officers in civil rights suits. Some municipalities provide counsel, subject to case-by-case determinations regarding possible conflicts of interest with the municipality itself. *See, e.g.,* Dunton v. County of Suffolk, 729 F.2d 903 (2d Cir. 1984), *vacated in part on other grounds,* 748 F.2d 69 (2d Cir. 1984); Kevlik v. Goldstein, 724 F.2d 844 (1st Cir. 1984). In some jurisdictions, insurance carriers will provide counsel, while in others, the department may retain outside counsel to represent the officer or provide funds for the officer to do so.

Practices also differ with respect to payment of settlements or judgments. The municipality may pay such awards or provide indemnification to the officer. Insurance may cover the settlement or judgment. In some jurisdictions, recovery may be limited to the pocket of the individual defendant, who may be judgment proof.

These varying practices serve different interests. Where the municipality pays the costs of litigation (including counsel) and any monetary awards, the plaintiff is assured of payment, but there is virtually no deterrent value with respect to the officer (particularly where the city does not otherwise discipline or retrain the officer). Where the officer is responsible for payment, deterrence is better served, but at the possible cost of depriving the plaintiff of compensation. For extended discussions of these important competing interests, see PETER H. SCHUCK, SUING GOVERNMENT: CITIZEN REMEDIES FOR OFFICIAL WRONGS (1983); Ronald A. Cass, *Damage Suits Against Public Officers,* 129 U. PA. L. REV. 1110 (1981); and Daniel J. Meltzer, *Deterring Constitutional Violations By Law Enforcement Officials: Plaintiffs and Defendants As Private Attorneys General,* 88 COLUM. L. REV. 247, 283–86. (1988).

[107]*See* Monell v. New York Dep't of Social Servs., 436 U.S. 658, 658–59 (1978).

IV. AN AGENDA FOR REFORM

If the analysis I have made of the judicial and administrative responses to the misconduct involved in the Metropolis hypothetical is correct, the measures necessary for reform are fairly obvious. In the judicial arena, the Supreme Court must make significant doctrinal adjustments with respect to constitutional litigation. These changes should be tailored to the political and administrative realities of policing, and must take explicit account of the systemic nature of most forms of police abuse.

The Court consistently considers operational exigencies of governmental law enforcement in its adjudication of Fourth and Fifth Amendment claims. In those cases, in the balancing of interests, weight has always been given to the "realities" and dangers of policing.[108] Recognizing the realities only on the governmental side has created a jurisprudence of consistent deference to law enforcement officials and an array of procedural obstacles to the vindication of personal liberties.[109] It is the politics of the Court, and not immutable legal doctrine, that will foreclose appreciable change in the Court's approach to police misconduct in the foreseeable future.[110]

Individual damage suits may continue to generate incremental changes in policy, particularly where the aggregate amounts in any particular locale become so large as to create a political issue concerning the public fisc. Similarly, if the courts develop the doctrinal kernel of *City of Canton* and require municipalities to adequately train, supervise and discipline police, we are likely to see at least some police departmental response to seriously flawed procedures.

However, it is unrealistic to rely on judicial intervention as a source of fundamental change. Regardless of the judiciary's response, we must focus attention on other alternatives. The most important factor in the control and reduction of abuse is organizational accountability. All other remedies will ultimately fail if not accompanied by a system of training, supervision and discipline that is structured to ensure that departmental policies relative to use of force and other restrictions on the arbitrary use of power are implemented and enforced. The numerous commissions and studies which have examined the problems of police abuse are unanimous in their recommendations: only a dramatic change in the enforcement of new norms of behavior by the police will dislodge the deeply entrenched culture that currently prevails.[111]

There are several possible ways in which the culture can be modified and in which practices that are more respectful of the normative limitations on

---

[108]*See, e.g.,* Maryland v. Buie, 494 U.S. 325 (1990); New York v. Quarles, 467 U.S. 649 (1984); Michigan v. Summers, 452 U.S. 692 (1981); Terry v. Ohio, 392 U.S. 1 (1968).

[109]*See supra* notes 72–81.

[110]*Cf.* Payne v. Tennessee, 111 S. Ct. 2597, 2619 (1991) (Marshall, J., dissenting: "Power, not reason, is the new currency of this Court's decisionmaking.").

[111]*See* LAIC, *supra* note 6, at 151–81; Kansas City Task Force, *supra* note 63, at 45–49; Boston Police Report, *supra* note 63.

police power can be created. The processes of reform involve different institutions in our society; to be successful, they must be mutually reinforcing.

A. Police Administration and the Politics of Change

Despite the formidable obstacles, there is some hope for internally generated police reform. There have been significant advances in recent years in the scope and quality of police training and in the development of official policies and practices. Most departments are managed by professionals who understand the harm to policing that is inflicted when communities are alienated from the police because of patterns of abuse. In part in response to court-imposed sanctions for the violation of rights—including exclusion of evidence from criminal prosecutions and monetary damages against police and municipalities—police departments have developed extensive training programs on the constitutional limits on critical police practices in the arrest, search, interrogation and other investigation areas. However, reliance on judicial intervention as a source of basic change is unrealistic.[112] Of course, as the Supreme Court continues to restrict constitutional rights of suspects, these important incentives for training and supervision will be reduced accordingly.

Further, in some areas the police have taken the responsibility for changing abusive practices. For example, in the 1970s and 1980s public concern over the unjustified use of deadly force led several departments to reconsider their regulations on this practice.[113] Years before the Supreme Court ruled that deadly force could be used to stop a fleeing felon only where the suspect posed an imminent threat of serious physical harm, many police departments had limited deadly force to such situations. As a result, the number of shootings decreased dramatically without any increase in harm to the police.[114]

The reasons for the police initiative on this issue were several, not the least of which was the political pressure of community groups and others

---

[112]Imposition of municipal liability under *Owen* and *Monell* has prompted some changes in police practices. A study conducted pre-*Monell* found that suits against individual officers had little impact on institutional policies. *See* Lant B. Davis, John H. Small & David J. Wohlberg, Project, *Suing the Police in Federal Court,* 88 YALE L.J. 781, 809–18 (1979). More recent studies credit the threat of municipal liability as an incentive to police departments to better train, supervise and discipline officers. *See* Candace McCoy, *Enforcement Workshop: Lawsuits Against Police—What Impact Do They Really Have?,* 20 CRIM. L. BULL. 49, 50–53 (1984); Wayne W. Schmidt, *Section 1983 and the Changing Face of Police Management, in* POLICE LEADERSHIP IN AMERICA 226, 235 (William Geller ed., 1985). *See also Report Says Tighter Policies Reduce Killings by the Police,* N.Y. TIMES, Oct. 20, 1986, at A20 (attributing police leadership in new restrictive shooting policies, in part, to the financial influence of civil litigation). The deterrent effect of civil damage payments by municipalities on the conduct of individual officers, however, remains highly questionable. *See* Meltzer, *supra* note 106, at 285–86. *See also* discussion *infra* note 141 and accompanying text.

[113]*See* James J. Fyfe. *Police Use of Deadly Force: Research and Reform,* 5 JUST. Q. 165 (1988) [hereinafter *Deadly Force*]; James J. Fyfe, *Garner Plus Five Years: An Examination of Supreme Court Intervention into Police Discretion and Legislative Prerogatives,* 14 AM. J. CRIM JUST. 167 (1990); Albert J. Reiss, Jr., *Controlling Police Use of Deadly Force,* 452 ANNALS AM. ACAD. POL. & SOC. SCI. 122 (1980). *See also* Tennessee v. Garner, 471 U.S. 1 (1985).

[114]Fyfe, *Deadly Force, supra* note 113, at 181, 186–88. *See also Justice Department Battle Against Conflicts Between Police and Minorities,* N.Y. TIMES, Nov. 13, 1983, at A30.

concerned with the illegitimate use of such force.[115] Not only did the official rules change,[116] but so did the, police culture. Violations of the policy resulted in discipline and retraining (and in some cases prosecution).[117] Police officers soon understood that their departments were serious about these new policies and adjusted their conduct accordingly.[118] That the new rules were imposed internally on a "voluntary" basis no doubt played a part in their overall acceptance. Indeed, the change in policy was so successful that, when the Court ultimately was faced with the constitutional issue, professional police organizations urged the Court to discard the broad and easily-abused fleeing felon rule.[119]

Other areas of police duties are equally amenable to significant internal change in norms and conduct. There is no reason why specific practices, for example, the use of police dogs,[120] nondeadly weapons,[121] and the control of public demonstrations[122] cannot be subjected to careful study and control in a

---

[115]*See, e.g.,* Richard Higgins, *Debate Over Deadly Force,* BOSTON GLOBE, Sept. 8, 1983, at A1; Judith Miller, *New Questions Arise on Policing Police,* N.Y. TIMES, Apr. 3, 1983, at 4.

[116]*See, e.g.,* Joel J. Smith, *Gun Use—A Dilemma for Police,* DETROIT NEWS, Oct. 22, 1981, at A1 (describing policy changes in Detroit, Beverly Hills and Dearborn, Michigan); Arnold Markowitz, *Chiefs Revise Deadly Force Rules in Dade,* MIAMI HERALD, Dec. 15, 1983, at D1.

[117]*See Justice Department Battles Against Conflict Between Police and Minorities, supra* note 114, at A30.

[118]For example, in 1980 in Philadelphia, after a mayoral campaign that focused in large part on the brutality of the city's police force, the new administration adopted strict limitations on the use of deadly force, and made it known that it was serious about enforcement. *See* SKOLNICK & FYFE, *supra* note 10. An officer told this author at the time that word had gone out in the department that "if you shoot, you had be right."

[119]Fyfe, *Deadly Force, supra* note 113, at 200 (brief of *amici curiae* against Tennessee and Memphis Police Department in *Garner* was filed by the Police Foundation and joined by nine associations of police and criminal justice professionals, the chiefs of police associations of two states, and 31 law enforcement chief executives).

[120]The City of West Palm Beach, Fla., has been held liable for its failure to adequately train and supervise its canine police unit. Kerr v. City of West Palm Beach, 875 F.2d 1546 (11th Cir. 1989). The LAIC reported citizen complaints that Los Angeles police officers ordered their dogs to attack minority suspects who were already in police custody or under control. LAIC, *supra* note 6, at 77–78.

[121]Attention was focused on the use of electric stun guns in 1985 when three New York City police officers were accused and convicted of using the devices to torture confessions from four men arrested on minor drug charges and other minor offenses. Joseph P. Fried, *Ex-Sergeant's Release Ordered in Stun-Gun Case,* N.Y. TIMES, Sept. 16, 1990, at 35; Robert D. McFadden, *Youth's Charges of Torture By an Officer Spur Inquiry,* N.Y. TIMES, Apr. 22,1985, at B3. Electric stun guns deliver 40,000-volt charge without inflicting permanent injury and leave only a pair of small burn marks on the skin. *New York City Police Officers Convicted In 'Stun Gun' Case,* CRIM. JUST. NEWSL., May 15, 1986 at 7, 8. At the time of the incident, many police departments across the country regularly used electric stun guns. *Alleged Torture Brings Focus on Police Use of Stun Guns,* CRIM. JUST. NEWSL., May 15, 1985, at 3.

[122]On the night of August 6, 1988, a demonstration of 150 to 200 people protesting the closing of Tompkins Square Park in Manhattan degenerated into four hours of fighting between the crowd and the officers policing the event. Todd S. Purdum, *Melee in Tompkins Square Park: Violence and Its Provocation,* N.Y. TIMES, Aug. 14, 1988, at A1. There were almost 100 complaints of police

manner that limits possibilities for the abuse of power. As evidenced by the dramatic results achieved across the country in the difficult field of hostage takings,[123] training of special units that incorporate as a basic tenet the use of all means to save human life can produce remarkable improvements in police work. Over the years, the professionalization of this aspect of policing has substantially reduced the number of persons killed or injured in these volatile situations.[124]

Not all potentially abusive practices are as amenable to administrative efforts at reform. The patterns of harassment, indignities and violence that attend the everyday work of investigation, searches and arrests are far more resistant strains of misconduct, which emanate from a strong police subculture reinforced by political demands such as the "war on crime." If part of the community is seen as a deadly enemy, law enforcement tactics are bound to reflect that conception. If the resulting abuses are to be contained, more fundamental structural change will be required.

One promising development is the practice of community-oriented policing. This model is built on the premise that there are mutual community and police interests and that reciprocal respect for these concerns and interests will provide a more effective and progressive means of policing. Community policing relies less upon the practices of the past three decades which emphasized proactive, aggressive policing aimed at apprehension and prosecution; rather, it stresses the principle of police-community cooperation by increasing foot patrols, supporting community citizen patrols, and developing mutually acceptable goals for particular communities.[125]

Of course, the case for community-oriented policing can be overstated, and there should be no expectation that it alone will generate progressive change. If the police view this concept merely as a matter of labeling, as opposed to one of substantive change in which they have a voice and a stake, the program will not succeed.[126] A necessary corollary to police understanding and acceptance of community policing as a new philosophy is the willingness of community leaders to support effective and fair policing, while at the same time condemning excesses and abuses. The community should not be held hostage to a pattern of abuse as a quid pro quo for police protection.

---

brutality; 44 civilians and police officers were injured. *Id.* The police violence was attributed to poor planning, tactical errors, the youth and inexperience of the officers and a shortage of sergeants and lieutenants. David E. Pitt, *Roots of Tompkins Sq. Clash Seen in Young and Inexperienced Officer Corps*, N.Y. TIMES, Aug. 25, 1988, at B7; Purdum, *supra*, at A1. As a result of the police riot, the N.Y.C. Police Department instituted "sweeping improvements in training, command structure and equipment." Pitt, *supra*, at B7.

[123]*See* SKOLNICK & FYFE, *supra* note 10; Robert W. Taylor, *Hostage and Crisis Negotiation Procedures: Assessing Police Liability*, TRIAL, March 1983, at 64.

[124]SKOLNICK & FYFE, *supra* note 10.

[125]LAIC, *supra* note 6, at 95–106; Boston Police Report, *supra* note 63, at 29–53.

[126]Indeed, the Boston Police Department tried to implement a community policing program in March 1991. It has been widely recognized as a failure because the Department merely added community policing onto existing policies, rather than radically rethinking its philosophy of protection as a whole. Boston Police Report, *supra* note 63, at 39, 44–51.

Civilian review of the police is a necessary component of a system of accountability.[127] There has been bitter debate about the concept of civilian review of police, but it is now firmly established in varying forms in thirty of our fifty largest cities.[128] The success of civilian review will depend in large part on the proper allocation of power between police and civilians. It is essential that the civilian oversight include the full power to investigate complaints, conduct hearings, subpoena witnesses, including police officers, and issue reports or findings on the complaints. If the civilian review board does not have authority to impose sanctions, its recommendations for discipline should be given careful consideration by the police commissioner. Civilian review procedures should also include the authority to make policy recommendations and to gather statistical data relevant to patterns of abuse.

The early intervention initiative utilized by an increasing number of police departments provides a related means of breaking the cycle of abuse. Statistical studies within various departments show a disturbingly disproportionate number of complaints regarding excessive force against relatively few officers.[129] The fact that these numbers are as high as they are points to significant deficiencies in the monitoring and disciplining process. But even if internal discipline is effective, many officers reject findings made against them in adversary administrative or judicial proceedings as the illegitimate products of a system that fails to understand the pressures and dangers facing the officer on the street. The officers may moderate their conduct for fear of sanctions, but their own standards and world view remain unchanged.

For some officers who repeatedly engage in abusive conduct, an early intervention program based on principles of non-punitive retraining may be a more effective means of reducing unnecessary violence in police confrontations with citizens. These programs include a mix of retraining on rules governing use of force, role playing, psychological interviews and improving oral communication skills. In an experiment in Oakland, California, a police violence prevention unit used a peer review approach on street officers who, on average, had engaged in physical confrontations with citizens at a rate nearly four times that of non-participation officers. Over time, the officers who participated in this program reduced their violent incident records by more than fifty percent.[130]

B.   Federal Intervention

In light of the nationwide scope of the problem, consideration should be given to federal intervention. The power of the federal government in enforcing the

---

[127]*See id.* at 128–33.

[128]Samuel Walker & Vic. W. Bumphus, *Civilian Review of the Police: A National Survey of the 50 Largest Cities, 1991, in* Focus: Criminal Justice Policy 1, No. 91–3 (Dept. of Criminal Justice, Univ. of Neb., 1991).

[129]*See, e.g.*, LAIC, *supra* note 6, at 31–65; George Jones, *Police to Track Brutality Charges Against Officers*, N.Y. Times, Nov. 7, 1991, at B2; Don Terry, *Kansas City Police Force Go After Own 'Bad Boys,'* N.Y. Times, Sept. 10, 1991, at A1.

[130]See Hans Toch & J. Douglas Grant, Police as Problem Solvers 242–43 (1991).

constitutional rights of citizens against local police officials has been bitterly disputed.[131] Historically, the Department of Justice has generally refrained from investigation and prosecution of local police abuse. The limits on federal authority are largely self-imposed, although a narrow statutory authority is also a contributing factor. The magnitude of the abuse problem calls for a substantial change of direction.

The federal government has authority to bring criminal prosecutions against state officers who violate or conspire to violate the civil rights of citizens.[132] These criminal statutes require the government to prove that the defendant specifically intended to deprive the victim of a constitutional right,[133] a factor that is often cited by the Justice Department as the reason why there are so few police abuse prosecutions.[134] It is unlikely that the failure of the federal government to prosecute police can be so easily explained. It is far more likely that the reasons behind the lack of federal prosecutions are the same as those explaining the paucity of state prosecutions: prosecutors do not like prosecuting fellow law enforcement officers (with whom they work on a day to day basis); evidence of such misconduct is often shielded by the code of silence; victims are more readily subject to impeachment (prior records, life styles, etc.); and juries are inclined to give the benefit of the doubt to the police.[135]

On the civil side, the Justice Department lacks authority to bring injunctive actions even where police abuse is alleged to be widespread.[136] Congress

---

[131]The traditional argument against intervention is deeply ingrained. For example, John Dunne, Assistant Attorney General in charge of the Civil Rights Division of the Justice Department, stated during Congressional hearing on police brutality in the wake of the Rodney King incident: "We are not the 'front-line' troops in combatting instances of police abuse. That role properly lies with the internal affairs bureaus of law enforcement agencies and with state and local prosecutors. The federal enforcement program is more like a 'back-stop' to these other resources." John Dunne, Statement to the House Subcommittee on Civil and Constitutional Rights of the House Judiciary Committee (March 20, 1991) [hereinafter Dunne Statement], *quoted in* HUMAN RIGHTS WATCH, POLICE BRUTALITY IN THE UNITED STATES 4–5 (July 1991).

[132]18 U.S.C. §§ 241, 242 (1988).

[133]*See, e.g.,* United States v. Guest, 383 U.S. 745, 760 (1966).

[134]The FBI investigates approximately 2500 complaints of police abuse per year. Dunne Statement, *supra* note 131, at 5. However, very few of these result in prosecution. Mr. Dunne has stated that in the three years preceding the Rodney King incident, there were 98 prosecutions in this area. *Id.* Yet, in the City of Los Angeles, despite documented cases of serious abuse, no prosecutions had been initiated in several years. Hoffman, *supra* note 65, at 4–5. The jurisdictional confines of the federal law have provided a rationalization for not doing so.

[135]*See supra* notes 60, 83–85, 88, 91, 99 and accompanying text.

[136]In *United States v. City of Philadelphia,* 644 F.2d 187 (3d Cir. 1980), the Justice Department sought an injunction against the police department of the City of Philadelphia to end the department's "practice of violating the rights of persons they encounter on the streets and elsewhere in the city," a departmental policy "implemented with the intent and the effect of inflicting abuse disproportionately on black and Hispanic persons." *Id.* at 190. The Court of Appeals for the Third Circuit refused to recognize an implied power in the federal government to bring an action to enjoin violations of constitutional rights. *Id.* at 192–201.

can give the Attorney General the power to bring litigation to protect against widespread violations of constitutional rights. Congress has authorized injunctions in cases of employment discrimination,[137] discrimination in public accommodations,[138] deprivation of voting rights[139] and, for persons in prisons, mental institutions and nursing homes, where "egregious or flagrant conditions which deprive . . . persons of any rights, privileges or immunities secured or protected by the Constitution or laws of the United States."[140]

Without the availability of private or public enforcement of constitutional rights in this area, local governments are free simply to pay as they go for the violation of the rights of their people without any possibility of judicial intervention to prevent abuses before they occur. In Los Angeles, even the payment of more than $10 million in police abuse judgments in 1990 alone (more than $1,000 per sworn officer in the LAPD) has had no perceptible, impact on these problems.[141]

Legislation introduced in Congress in the wake of the Rodney King incident would allow greater federal intervention. The Attorney General and aggrieved individuals would be authorized to bring pattern or practice suits.[142] In recommending these provisions, the House-Senate conference proposed the use of injunctions to meaningfully address patterns of police abuse.[143]

The bill would also require the Department of Justice to compile and publish data on the use of excessive force by police officers.[144] The lack of information on the incidence of excessive force and other forms of police abuse is a significant barrier to both political and legal reform.[145] Without credible information on the scope and pervasiveness of the problem, the public is left

---

[137]42 U.S.C. § 2000e-6 (1988).

[138]42 U.S.C. § 2000a-3 (1988).

[139]42 U.S.C. §1971 (1988).

[140]42 U.S.C. §1997a (1988).

[141]John L Mitchell, *$11.3 Million Paid in 1990 to Resolve Abuse Cases*, L.A. TIMES, Mar. 29, 1991, at Al. In other cities, payment of similarly high figures as compensation for police abuse does not seem to deter such activity. *See, e.g.,* Sean Murphy, *City Paid $3.4 Million in Civil Suit Settlements in '88*, BOSTON GLOBE, May 14, 1989, at 29 (police misconduct cases cost city $1.1 million out of total $3.4 million paid). Part of the reason stems from the fact that, in most cases the police officer faces no financial risk or other disciplinary sanctions if his conduct leads to a civil suit. *See* discussion *supra* note 106. Even being sued repeatedly does not necessarily hinder promotion or assignment to elite training or narcotics units. Bill Wallace, *San Francisco Pays in Many Suits Against Cops*, S.F. CHRON., May 30, 1990, at Al. Provisions for municipal payment of settlements and judgments may suffice to compensate victim of police abuse, but unless taxpayers are offended by the amounts paid or police departments consider such judgments in disciplining their officers, there will be little deterrence of individual officers' behavior from these payments.

[142]See H.R. 2972, 102d Cong., 1st Sess. (1991). This proposal has been incorporated in part by the Senate-House conferees on the "Violent Crime Control and Law Enforcement Act of 1991." H.R. CONF. REP. NO. 405, 102d Cong., 1st Sess. 97 (1991).

[143]H.R. CONF. REP. NO. 405. 102d Cong., 1st Sess. 97.

[144]*Id.*

[145]HUMAN RIGHTS WATCH, *supra* note 131, at 8.

with the impression that the abuses are more aberrational than systemic. Significant changes on the national level will not occur unless there is detailed evidence that the abuse is not isolated or local in nature.

The federal government has a large program of assistance to local law enforcement agencies under the Office of Justice Programs.[146] It is appropriate for the federal government to establish standards for the use of force, including the proper use of weapons, and for internal review of police performance. Further, meaningful and institutionalized respect for constitutional rights should be a condition of the receipt of federal funds for law enforcement.[147]

V. CONCLUSION

On April 29, 1992, as this Article was about to go to press, a jury without any African-Americans (drawn from a conservative suburban community) returned a verdict of not guilty as to all the officers charged with beating Rodney King. This shocking verdict touched off widespread protests and rioting in Los Angeles and other cities around the country. While the reasons behind the jury's conclusion are not yet clear, the verdict unfortunately confirms the thesis of this Article: the law and order mentality that has pervaded the consciousness of America, coupled with strong elements of racism, lead many to believe that the police should retain a free hand in order to protect "us" from "them."

The Rodney King incident demonstrates once again the tragic consequences of our failure as a society to respond to the systemic and institutional aspects of police abuse. Official misconduct endures in large part because we respond to its many manifestations in an episodic manner. As long as the courts and both federal and state government treat police abuse as a series of isolated incidents, or as a regrettable by-product of the war on crime, the Monroes, Rafts and Rodney Kings will continue to pay an unconscionable price for our misguided policies. Police violence will be contained only if we challenge fundamental aspects of police culture and hold the police politically and legally accountable. Experience teaches that structural problems require structural remedies. We ignore that lesson at the peril of individual victims of abuse, the core values and institutions of constitutional government and the very integrity of our society.

---

[146]For example, the Bureau of Justice Assistance Grant Programs can make direct grants to local law enforcement agencies for the acquisition of equipment and other programs dedicated improving the criminal justice system, 42 U.S.C. § 3751 (1988).

[147]It is a common device under federal law to condition a grant upon compliance with some other provision of federal law, and it is already used in the federal law enforcement assistance programs. Under 42 U.S.C. § 3789(d) (1988), for example, a federal grant for local law enforcement may be suspended if it is found that the local body has discriminated in employment on the basis of race, religion, nationality or gender.

INDEX